D1090828

The Wisdom Background and Parabolic Implications of Isaiah 6:9–10 in the Synoptics

Studies in Biblical Literature

Hemchand Gossai
General Editor

Vol. 100

PETER LANG
New York • Washington, D.C./Baltimore • Bern
Frankfurt am Main • Berlin • Brussels • Vienna • Oxford

Donald E. Hartley

The Wisdom Background and Parabolic Implications of Isaiah 6:9–10 in the Synoptics

PETER LANG
New York • Washington, D.C./Baltimore • Bern
Frankfurt am Main • Berlin • Brussels • Vienna • Oxford

Library of Congress Cataloging-in-Publication Data

Hartley, Donald E.
The wisdom background and parabolic implications
of Isaiah 6:9–10 in the synoptics / Donald E. Hartley.
p. cm. — (Studies in biblical literature; v. 100)
Includes bibliographical references and index.
1. Bible. O.T. Isaiah—Relation to the Gospels. 2. Bible. N.T. Gospels—Relation
to Isaiah. 3. Bible. O.T. Isaiah VI, 9–10—Criticism, interpretation, etc.
4. Bible. N.T. Gospels—Criticism, interpretation, etc. I. Title. II. Series.
BS2387.H34   226'.06—dc22   2006013152
ISBN 0-8204-8665-5
ISSN 1089-0645

Bibliographic information published by **Die Deutsche Bibliothek**.
Die Deutsche Bibliothek lists this publication in the "Deutsche
Nationalbibliografie"; detailed bibliographic data is available
on the Internet at http://dnb.ddb.de/.

The paper in this book meets the guidelines for permanence and durability
of the Committee on Production Guidelines for Book Longevity
of the Council of Library Resources.

© 2006 Peter Lang Publishing, Inc., New York
29 Broadway, New York, NY 10006
www.peterlang.com

All rights reserved.
Reprint or reproduction, even partially, in all forms such as microfilm,
xerography, microfiche, microcard, and offset strictly prohibited.

Printed in Germany

Dedication

To Melissa, whose wisdom has in many ways been my salvation.

Contents

Editor's Preface

More than ever the horizons in biblical literature are being expanded beyond that which is immediately imagined; important new methodological, theological, and hermeneutical directions are being explored, often resulting in significant contributions to the world of biblical scholarship. It is an exciting time for the academy as engagement in biblical studies continues to be heightened.

This series seeks to make available to scholars and institutions, scholarship of a high order, and which will make a significant contribution to the ongoing biblical discourse. This series includes established and innovative directions, covering general and particular areas in biblical study. For every volume considered for this series, we explore the question as to whether the study will push the horizons of biblical scholarship. The answer must be *yes* for inclusion.

In this volume Donald Hartley examines Isaiah 6:9–10 in the manner in which this text is interpreted and used in the New Testament. The author proceeds with an understanding that this text is significant for an understanding of the entire Isaiah prophecy. In particular, Hartley examines the six times in which this text is used in the New Testament with the fattening/hardening perspective. The principal focus of this study is on the congenital nature of the fatness of the heart. The argument is compelling and scholars which are interested in this area of biblical scholarship will find in this volume a mine of information to be reckoned with.

The horizon has been expanded.

Hemchand Gossai
Series Editor

Acknowledgments

This monograph first appeared as a dissertation under the direction of Drs. Darrell L. Bock, Harold W. Hoehner, and Gordon H. Johnston of Dallas Theological Seminary. Each member contributed significantly to the overall form and development of this work and to each one I owe a debt of gratitude not just to their expertise but for their patience and endurance. Despite his demanding schedule, Dr. Bock made himself available and offered encouragment at various junctures. Dr. Hoehner dried up the ink wells by correcting my form and sending me back to the sources. Dr. Johnston provided valuable insights and pointed me to sundry materials. This acknowledgment in no way implies a complete endorsement of the views espoused here by the author.

I would also wish to acknowledge the advice I received on many occasions from my twin brother Douglas especially in the area of philosophical prolegomena. In addition, I would like to thank my friend Steve LeBlanc for his encouragement and support as well as my dear pastor Matthew St. John for his prayers, gentle wisdom, and indestructable confidence. My appreciation also goes to Dr. Bruce W. Waltke for permission to cite from a private correspondance. I especially wish to thank my wife, Melissa, for her unbending belief in her husband as well as reading through the tome and giving helpful advice. And Joshua...who loves to stay up late and talk about the things of God with his dad. Other close friends including Rev. Glenn Monro and Dr. Michael J. Svigel walked with and prayed for me during the process. Likewise, I include 'flock group' members in the Discipleship class of Scofield Memorial Church especially John Blank. Finally, I extend a thanks to my dear but late father-in-law, the Rev. David L. Deck, who never ceased to inspire, encourage, and pray for his favorite son-in-law.

Abbreviations

Primary Literature

Ancient Greek, Jewish, and Early Christian Literature

Ach.	Acharnenses
An.	*De anima*
A.J.	*Antiquitates judaicae*
Autol.	*Ad Autolycum*
b.	Babylonian
Bar	Baruch
Barn.	*Barnabas*
B. Bat.	*Baba Batra*
Ber.	*Berakot*
B.J.	*Bellum judaicum*
Cat.	*Categoriae*
Cels.	*Contra Celsum*
Cim.	*Cimon*
Civ.	*De civitate Dei*
1 Clem.	*1 Clement*
2 Clem.	*2 Clement*
Comm. Luc	*Commentarii in Lucam*
Comm. Matt.	*Commentariorum in Mattheum*
Conf.	*Confessionum libri XIII (Confessions)*
Conf.	*De confusione linguarum (Philo)*
Congr.	*De congressu eruditionis gratia*
Consol.	*Consolatione Philosophiae*
Corrept.	*De correptione et gratia*
Dem.	*Epistula ad sacram Christi virginem Demetriadem*
Det.	*Quod deterius poriori insidari*

Deus	*Quod Deus sit immutabilis*
Dial.	*Diologus cum Heraclide*
Diogn.	*Diognetus*
Ebr.	*De ebrietate*
Enchir.	*Enchiridion de fide, spe, et caritate*
Epist.	*Epistulae*
Eq.	*De equitande ratione*
1 Esd	1 Esdras
Fug.	*De fuga et inventione*
Gen. Rab.	*Rabbah Genesis*
Georg.	*Georgias*
Gest. Pelag.	*De gestis Pelagii*
Gos. Thom.	*Gospel of Thomas*
Grat.	*De gratia et libero arbitrio*
Grat. Chr.	*De gratia Christi, et de peccato originali*
Haer.	*Adversus haereses*
Hag.	*Hagigah*
Her.	*Quis rerum divinarum heres sit*
Hom. Act.	*Homiliae in Acta apostolorum*
Hom. 2 Cor.	*Homiliae in epistumum ii ad Corinthios*
Hom. Matt.	*Homiliae in Matthaeum*
Hist.	*Historiae*
Hul.	*Hullin*
Il.	*Ilias*
Institution	*Institution de la religion chrestienne*
Jdt	Judith
Lev. Rab.	*Rabbah Leviticus*
[*Lib. ed.*]	*De liberis educandi*
LXX	Septuagint
m.	Mishnah
1 Macc	1 Maccabees
2 Macc	2 Maccabees
3 Macc	3 Maccabees
4 Macc	4 Maccabees
Marc.	*Adversus Marcionem*
Meg.	*Megillah*
Metaph.	*Metaphysica*
Migr.	*De migratione Abrahami*
Mos.	*De vita Mosis I, II*
Mut.	*De mutatione nominum*

Od.	Odyssea
Odes Sol.	Odes of Solomon
Oed. col.	Oedipus coloneus
Op.	Opera et dies
Opif.	De opificio mundi
Paenit.	De paenitentia
Pelag.	Adversus Pelagianos dialogi III
Persev.	De dono perseverantiae
Pesiq. Rab.	Pesiqta Rabbati
Phaedr.	Phaedrus
Post.	De posteritate Caini
Praem.	De praemiis et poenis
Phys.	Physica (Physics)
Plant.	De plantatione
Pol.	Politicus
Praed.	De praedestinatione sanctorum
Praescr.	De praescriptione haereticorum
Pr Azar	Prayer of Azariah
Princ.	De principiis (Peri archon)
Prom.	Prometheus vinctus
Ps.-Clem.	Pseudo-Clementines
Pss. Sol.	Psalms of Solomon
Q	Quelle
Qoh. Rab.	Rabbah Qoheleth
Ran.	Ranae
Res.	De resurrectione carnis
Resp.	Respublica
Retract.	Retractationum libri II
Rhet.	Rhetorica
Ros Has.	Ros Hassanah
Sabb.	Sabbat
Sac.	De sacerdotio
Sacr.	De sacrificiis Abelis et Caini
Sanh.	Sanhedrin
[Scut.]	Scutum (Shield)
Sept.	Septem contra Thebas
Serv.	De servo arbitrio
Herm. Mand.	Shepherd of Hermas, Mandates
Herm. Sim.	Shepherd of Hermas, Similitudes
Herm. Vis.	Shepherd of Hermas, Visions

Sir	Sirach
Sol	Solomon
Sol.	*Solon*
Somn.	*De somniis I, II*
Spec.	*De specialibus legibus I, II, III, IV*
Strom.	*Stromata*
Sum. C. Gen.	*Summa contra Gentiles*
Sum. Theol.	*Summa theologica*
Suppl.	*Supplices*
Sus	Susanna
Symp.	*Symposium*
Theod.	Theodotion
Tob	Tobit
Tract. Ev. Jo.	*In Evangelium Johannis tractatus*
Trin.	*De Trinitate*
Virginit.	*De virginitate*
y.	Jerusalem
Wis	Wisdom

The Dead Sea Scrolls

1Q22	(1QDM) 1Q Words of Moses [DM (apocr Moses^a)]
1Q26	1Q Instruction [Wisdom Apocryphon =Instruction]
1Q27	(1QMyst) 1Q Mysteries
1Q35	(1QH^b) 1Q Hodayot^b
1QHa	(1QH^a) 1Q Hodayot^a
1QM	(1QM) 1Q War Scroll
1QpHab	1Q Pesher to Habakkuk
1QS	1QS title
1QSb	(1QSb) 1Q Rule of Benedictions
2Q28	2Q Unidentified text
4Q156	(4QtgLev) 4Q Targum of Leviticus
4Q157	(4QtgJob) 4Q Targum of Job
4Q162	(4QpIsa^b) 4Q Isaiah Pesher^b
4Q171	(4QpPs^a) 4Q Psalms Pesher^a
4Q174	(4QFlor) 4Q Florilegium [4Q Midr Eschat$^{a?}$]
4Q175	(4QTest) 4Q Testimonia
4Q183	4Q Historical Work [4QMidr Eschat^e?]
4Q184	4Q Wiles of the Wicked Woman
4Q185	4Q Sapiential Work
4Q201	(4QEn^a ar) 4Q Enoch^a [(recto of 4Q338)]

4Q204	(4QEn^c ar) 4Q Enoch^c
4Q223–24	[4Q223–4Q224] (4QpapJub^h) 4Q papJubilees^h
4Q256	(4QS^b) 4Q Rule of the Community^b
4Q257	(4QpapS^c) 4Q Rule of the Community^c
4Q258	(4QS^d) 4Q Rule of the Community^d
4Q259	+ 4Q319 (4QOtot) 4Q Rule of the Community^e + 4QOtot
4Q265	4Q Miscellaneous Rules
4Q266	(4QD^a) 4Q Damascus Document^a
4Q267	(4QD^b) 4Q Damascus Document^b
4Q268	(4QD^c) 4Q Damascus Document^c
4Q269	(4QD^d) 4Q Damascus Document^d
4Q270	(4QD^e) 4Q Damascus Document^e
4Q271	(4QD^f) 4Q Damascus Document^f
4Q275	4Q Communal Ceremony
4Q298	4Q cryptA Words of the Maskil to All Sons of Dawn
4Q299	(4QMyst^a) 4Q Mysteries^a
4Q300	(4QMyst^b) 4Q Mysteries^b
4Q301	(4QMyst^c?) 4Q Mysteries^c?
4Q306	4Q Men of People who Err
4Q308	4Q Sapiential Fragments
4Q364	(4QRP^b) 4Q Reworked Pentateuch^b
4Q365	(4QRP^c) 4Q Reworked Pentateuch^c
4Q370	4Q Exhortation Based on the Flood
4Q372	(4QapocrJoseph^b) 4Q Apocryphon of Joseph^b
4Q380	4Q Non-Canonical Psalms A
4Q381	4Q Non-Canonical Psalms B
4Q382	4Q Paraphrase of Kings
4Q385	(4QpsEzek^a) 4Q Pseudo-Ezekiel^a
4Q387a	(4QpsMoses^b) 4Q Pseudo-Moses^b
4Q390	(4QpsMoses^e) 4Q PseudoMoses^e
4Q392	4Q Works of God
4Q393	4Q Communal Confession
4Q397	(4QMMT^d) 4Q Halakhic Letter^d
4Q398	(4QMMT^e) 4Q Halakhic Letter^e
4Q400	(4QShirShabb^a) 4Q Songs of the Sabbath Sacrifice^a
4Q401	(4QShirShabb^b) 4Q Songs of the Sabbath Sacrifice^b
4Q403	(4QMasShirot {Olat HaShabbat^d) 4Q Songs of the Sabbath Sacrifice^d
4Q405	(4QShirShabb^f) 4Q Songs of the Sabbath Sacrifice^f

4Q406	(4QShirShabb^g) 4Q Songs of the Sabbath Sacrifice^g
4Q410	4Q Vision and Its Interpretation
4Q411	4Q Sapiential Hymn
4Q412	4Q Sapiential-Didactic Work A
4Q413	4Q Composition concerning Divine Providence
4Q414	(4QRitPur A) 4Q Ritual of Purification A
4Q415	4Q Instruction^a
4Q416	4Q Instruction^b
4Q417	4Q Instruction^c
4Q418	4Q Instruction^d
4Q418a	4Q Instruction^e 4Q Sapiential Work A
4Q418c	4Q Instruction^f 4Q Sapiential Work A
4Q421	4Q Ways of Righteousness^b
4Q422	4Q Paraphrase of Genesis and Exodus
4Q423	4Q Instruction^g
4Q424	4Q Instruction-like Composition B
4Q425	4Q Sapiential-Didactic Work B
4Q426	4Q Sapiential-Hymnic Work A
4Q427	(4QH^a) 4Q Hodayot^a
4Q428	(4QH^b) 4Q Hodayot^b
4Q432	(4QH^f) 4Q Hodayot^f
4Q433	4Q Hodayot-like text A
4Q434	(4QBarki Napshi^a) 4Q Bless Oh mySoul^a
4Q435	(4QBarki Napshi^b) 4Q Bless, Oh my Soul^b
4Q436	(4QBarki Napshi^c) 4Q Bless. Oh my Soul^c
4Q437	(4QBarki Napshi^d) 4Q Bless, Oh my Soul^d
4Q365	(4QRP^c) 4Q Reworked Pentateuch^c
4Q384	(4QapocrJer^b) 4Q Apocryphon of Jeremiah^b?
4Q417	4Q Instruction^c
4Q418	4Q Instruction^d
4Q429	(4QH^c) 4Q Hodayot^c
4Q455	4Q Didactic Work C
4Q461	4Q Narrative B
4Q468a	4Q468b, 4Q468c, 4Q Unidentified Fragments C
4Q486	(4QpapSap A?) 4Q Sapiential Work A?
4Q487	(4QpapSap B?) 4Q Sapiential Work B?
4Q491	(4QMa) 4Q War Scroll^a
4Q497	4Q War Scroll-like Text A
4Q498	(papSaplHymn) 4Q Hymnic or Sapiential Fragments
4Q504	(4QDibHam^a) 4Q Words of the Luminaries^a

4Q510	(4QShir³) 4Q Songs of the Sageᵃ
4Q511	(4QShirᵇ) 4Q Songs of the Sageᵇ
4Q525	(4QBeat) 4Q Beatitudes
4Q528	4Q Hymnic or Sapiential Work B
4Q541	(4QapocrLeviᵇ? ar) 4Q Apocryphon of Leviᵇ?
5Q13	5QRule
11Q5	(11QPsᵃ) 11Q Psalmsᵃ
11Q10	(11QtgJob) 11Q Targum of Job
11Q17	(11QShirShabb) 11Q Songs of the Sabbath Sacrifice
11Q29	11Q Fragment Related to Serekh ha-Yahad
11QT	(11QTᵃ) 11Q Templeᵃ
CD	A Damascus Documentᵃ

Secondary Literature

AB	Anchor Bible
ABRL	Anchor Bible Reference Library
ACCS	Ancient Christian Commentary on Scripture
AfO	*Archiv für Orientforschung*
AGJU	Arbeiten zur Geschichte des antiken Judentums und des Urchristentums
AJSL	*American Journal of Semitic Languages and Literature*
ASV	American Standard Version
AUSS	Andrews University Seminary Studies
AUSS	*Andrews University Seminary Studies*
BDAG	Bauer, Walter, Frederick William Danker, W. F. Arndt, and F. W. Gingrich. *A Greek-English Lexicon of the New Testament and Other Early Christian Literature*. 3d ed. Chicago: University of Chicago Press, 2000.
BDB	Brown, Francis, S. R. Driver, and Charles A. Briggs. *A Hebrew and English Lexicon of the Old Testament*. Translated by Edward Robinson. Oxford: Clarendon, 1907.
BDF	Blass, F., A. Debrunner, and Robert W. Funk. *A Greek Grammar of the New Testament and Other Early Christian Literature*. Translated by Robert W. Funk. Chicago: Chicago University Press, 1961.
BECNT	Baker Exegetical Commentary on the New Testament
BHS	Elliger, Karl, and W. Rudolph., eds. *Biblia Hebraica Stuttgartensia*. Stuttgart: Deutsche Bibelstiftung, 1977.
Bib	*Biblica*

BJRL	*Bulletin of the John Rylands University Library of Manchester*
BKAT	Biblischer Kommentar, Altes Testament
BM	*Bet Mikra*
BSac	*Bibliotheca sacra*
BT	*The Bible Translator*
BTB	*Biblical Theological Bulletin*
BZ	*Biblische Zeitschrift*
BZAW	Beihefte zur Zeitschrift für die alttestamentliche Wissenschaft
CBQ	*Catholic Biblical Quarterly*
CBQMS	Catholic Biblical Quarterly Monograph Series
CGTC	Cambridge Greek Testament Commentary
CJT	*Canadian Journal of Theology*
CQR	*Church Quarterly Review*
CSR	*Christian Scholar's Review*
CRBR	*Critical Review of Books in Religion*
CSJH	Chicago Studies in the History of Judaism
DELG	*Dictionaire étymologique de la language greque: Histoire des mots.* Edited by Pierre Chantraine. 3 vols. Paris: Klincksieck, 1968.
DSS	Dead Sea Scrolls
ETL	*Ephemerides theologicae lovanienses*
EvQ	*Evangelical Quarterly*
ExpTim	*Expository Times*
FBBS	Facet Books, Biblical Series
FP	*Faith and Philosophy*
FPS	Foundation of Philosophy Series
GBS	Guides to Biblical Scholarship
GNS	Good News Studies
GNTE	Guides to New Testament Exegesis
GTJ	*Grace Theological Journal*
HALOT	*The Hebrew and Aramaic Lexicon of the Old Testament.* Edited by Ludwig Koehler, Walter Baumgartner, and Johann Jakob Stamm. Translated by M. E. J. Richardson. Rev. ed. 6 vols. Leiden: Brill, 1994–2001.
HKNT	Handkommentar zum Neuen Testament
HSM	Harvard Semitic Monographs
HTR	*Harvard Theological Review*
HUCA	*Hebrew Union College Annual*

IBC	Interpretation: A Bible Commentary for Teaching and Preaching
ICC	International Critical Commentary
IJT	*Indian Journal of Theology*
Int	*Interpretation*
JB	Jerusalem Bible
JBL	*Journal of Biblical Literature*
JBR	*Journal of Bible and Religion*
JETS	*Journal of the Evangelical Theological Society*
JNES	*Journal of Near Eastern Studies*
JNSL	*Journal of Northwest Semitic Languages*
JSJ	*Journal for the Study of Judaism in the Persian, Hellenistic, and Roman Periods*
JSNT	*Journal for the Study of the New Testament*
JSNTSup	Journal for the Study of the New Testament: Supplement Series
JSOT	*Journal for the Study of the Old Testament*
JSOTSup	Journal for the Study of the Old Testament: Supplement Series
JSPSup	Journal for the Study of the Pseudepigrapha: Supplement Series
JSS	*Journal of Semitic Studies*
JTS	*Journal of Theological Studies*
KEK	Kritisch-exegetischer Kommentar über das Neue Testament
LCL	Loeb Classical Library
LD	Lectio divina
LEC	Library of Early Christianity
LEH	*A Greek-English Lexicon of the Septuagint*. Edited by J. Lust, E. Eynikel, and K. Hauspie. 2 vols. Stuttgart: Deutsche Bibelgesellschaft, 1992–96.
L&N	Louw, Johannes P., and Eugene A. Nida. *Greek-English Lexicon of the New Testament Based on Semantic Domains*, 2 vols. New York: United Bible Societies, 1988.
MHT 1	Moulton, James Hope. *Prolegomena*. Vol. 1, *A Grammar of New Testament Greek*, ed. James Hope Moulton, 3d ed. Edinburgh: Clark, 1908.
MHT 2	Moulton, James Hope, and Wilbert Francis Howard. *Accidence and Word-Formation*. Vol. 2, *A Grammar of*

	New Testament Greek, ed. James Hope Moulton. Edinburgh: Clark, 1929.
MHT 3	Turner, Nigel. *Syntax.* Vol. 3, *A Grammar of New Testament Greek,* ed. James Hope Moulton. Edinburgh: Clark, 1963.
MHT 4	Turner, Nigel. *Style.* Vol. 4, *A Grammar of New Testament Greek,* ed. James Hope Moulton. Edinburgh: Clark, 1976.
MM	Moulton, J. H. and G. Milligan. *The Vocabulary of the Greek Testament: Illustrated from the Papyri and Other Non-Literary Sources.* London: Hodder & Stoughton, 1930. Reprint, Grand Rapids: Eerdmans, 1997.
MS/MSS	Manuscript/Manuscripts
MT	Masoretic Text
NA^{25}	*Novum Testamentum Graece,* 25th ed. Edited by Erwin Nestle and Kurt Aland. Stuttgart: Württembergische Bibelanstalt, 1963.
NA^{26}	*Novum Testamentum Graece,* 26th ed. Edited by Kurt Aland, Matthew Black, Carlo M. Martini, Bruce M. Metzger, and Allen Wikgren. Stuttgart: Württembergische Bibelanstalt, 1979.
NA^{27}	*Novum Testamentum Graece,* 27th ed. Edited by Barbara and Kurt Aland, Johannes Karavidopoulos, Carlo M. Martini, and Bruce M. Metzger. Stuttgart: Deutsche Bibelgesellschaft, 1993.
NAC	New American Commentary
NAS	New American Standard
NCB	New Century Bible
NDH	Neukirchener theologische Dissertationen und Habilitationen
NEB	New English Bible
NET	New English Translation
NewDocs	*New Documents Illustrating Early Christianity.* Edited by G. H. R. Horsley and S. R. Llewelyn. 8 vols. Sydney: Macquarie University Press, 1981–98.
NIBCNT	New International Biblical Commentary on the New Testament
NIDNTT	*The New International Dictionary of New Testament Theology.* Edited by Colin Brown. 4 vols. Grand Rapids: Zondervan, 1975–86.

NIDOTTE	*New International Dictionary of Old Testament Theology and Exegesis.* Edited by Willem A. VanGemeren. 5 vols. Grand Rapids: Zondervan, 1997.
NIGTC	New International Greek Testament Commentary
NIV	New International Version
NovT	*Novum Testamentum*
NRSV	New Revised Standard Version
NT	New Testament
NTAbh	Neutestamentliche Abhandlungen
NICNT	New International Commentary on the New Testament
NICOT	New International Commentary on the Old Testament
NRTh	*La nouvelle revue théologique*
NTS	*New Testament Studies*
OBO	Orbis biblicus et orientalis
OBT	Overtures to Biblical Theology
OT	Old Testament
OTC	Old Testament Commentaries
OTL	Old Testament Library
OTM	Oxford Theological Monographs
PG	*Patrologia graeca* [= *Patrologiae cursus completus: Series graeca*]. Edited by J. -P. Migne, 161 vols. Paris: Seu Petit-Montrogue, 1857–66.
RB	*Revue biblique*
RevQ	*Revue de Qumran*
RHPR	*Revue d'histoire et de philosophie religieuses*
RSV	Revised Standard Version
RevTL	*Review of Theological Literature*
SANT	Studien zum Alten und Neuen Testaments
SBLDS	Society of Biblical Literature Dissertation Series
SBLMS	Society of Biblical Literature Monograph Series
SBLSP	Society of Biblical Literature Seminar Papers
SBT	Studies in Biblical Theology
SC	Sources chrétiennes (Paris: Cerf, 1943–).
ScC	*La scuola cattolica*
SE	*Studia evangelica*
SECT	Sources of Early Christian Thought
SELMP	Synthese Library: Studies in Epistemology, Logic, Methodology, and Philosophy of Science
SFEG	Schriften der finnischen exegetischen Gesellschaft

SJFWJ	Studia Judaica: Forschungen zur Wissenschaft des Judentums
SJT	*Scottish Journal of Theology*
SNTMS	Society for New Testament Studies Monograph Series
SP	Sacra pagina
Str-B	Strack, Hermann Leberecht, and Paul Billerbeck. *Kommentar zum Neuen Testament aus Talmud und Midrasch*, 6 vols. Munich: Beck, 1922–61.
SVTQ	*St. Vladimir's Theological Quarterly*
SwJT	*Southwestern Journal of Theology*
TANZ	Texte und Arbeiten zum neutestamentlichen Zeitlalter
TB	*Tyndale Bulletin*
TDNT	*Theological Dictionary of the New Testament*. Edited by Gerhard Kittel and Gerhard Friedrich. Translated by Geoffrey W. Bromiley. 10 vols. Grand Rapids: Eerdmans, 1964–76.
TDOT	*Theological Dictionary of the Old Testament*. Edited by G. Johannes Botterweck and Helmer Ringgren. Translated by J. T Willis, G. W. Bromiley, and D. E. Green. 12 vols. Grand Rapids: Eerdmans, 1974–2003.
THKNT	Theologischer Handkommentar zum Neuen Testament
ThWAT	*Theologisches Wöterbuch zum Alten Testamen*. Edited by G. Johannes Botterweck and Helmer Ringgren. 8 vols. Stuttgart: Kohlhammer, 1970–95.
Tischendorf[8]	*Novum Testamentum Graece*, 8th ed. Edited by Constantine von Tischendorf, 2 vols. Leipzig: Giesecke & Devrient, 1869–72.
TJ	*Trinity Journal*
TLNT	*Theological Lexicon of the New Testament*. Ceslas Spicq. Translated and edited by James D. Ernst. 3 vols. Peabody, MA: Hendrickson, 1994.
TLOT	*Theological Lexicon of the Old Testament*. Edited by Ernst Jenni and Claus Westermann. Translated by Mark E. Biddle. 3 vols. Peabody, MA: Hendrickson, 1997.
TLZ	*Theologische Literaturzeitung*
TOTC	Tyndale Old Testament Commentaries
TS	*Theological Studies*

TWOT	*Theological Wordbook of the Old Testament*. Edited by R. Laird Harris, Gleason L. Archer Jr., and Bruce K. Waltke. 2 vols. Chicago: Moody, 1980.
TZ	*Theologische Zeitschrift*
VT	*Vetus Testamentum*
WBC	Word Biblical Commentary
WH	Westcott, Brook Foss, and Fenton John Anthony Hort. *The New Testament in the Original Greek: Text.* Cambridge and London: Macmillan, 1881.
WUNT	Wissenschaftliche Untersuchungen zum Neuen Testament
ZAW	*Zeitschrift für die alttestamentliche Wissenschaft*
ZNW	*Zeitschrift für die neutestamentliche Wissenschaft*
ZRGG	*Zeitschrift für Religions- und Geistesgeschichte*
ZTK	*Zeitschrift für Theologie und Kirche*

Need, Method, and Accomplishments of Inquiry

Statement of the Need

Isaiah 6:9–10, by any definition or estimation, is a difficult text to understand. It reads, [9]And he said, "Go and say to this people, 'Hear indeed but do not perceive and see indeed but do not know.' [10]Cause [or 'permit'] the heart of this people to be [remain] fat and their ears to be [remain] heavy, and their eyes to be [remain] blind lest ['otherwise'] they see with their eyes and hear with their ears and perceive with their heart and return and be healed." On the face of it, the passage seems to affirm that God intends to fatten hearts in order to prevent perception, understanding, knowledge, and therefore to prevent repentance and forgiveness from occurring. The precise meaning of this intention is therefore a key concern.

Since this text, which is part of the commissioning of Isaiah, is most likely programmatic for the entire prophecy, understanding it takes on paramount importance. In addition, the passage appears a half-dozen times in the NT at critical junctures in varied forms suggesting multiple understandings or perspectives of fattening/hardening itself. The importance of the text to both Isaiah and NT authors, therefore, can hardly be overestimated.

This text is responsible for varied traditions also found in the NT. On the one hand it stresses divine *intent* to fatten/harden the heart (Mark 4:12; Luke 8:10; John 12:40; Rom 11:8) while on the other hand it focuses on the present *state* of man as fat/hard-hearted (Matt 13:14–15; Acts 28:26–27). Does this divergence suggest disagreement among the traditions? If so, which one is more representative of Isaiah's theology? If not, is there a way to harmonize these traditions? Is there an historical, hermeneutical, or theological construct that can serve to unify these traditions in a way that does not view them as mitigating the other? Or is one left with conflicting views?

The subject of the fat/hard–heart is not a new field of investigation.[1] Indeed, the focus of fat/hard-heartedness in conjunction with the use of Isa 6:9–10 is not unique either.[2] In spite of this, monographs and dissertations continue to be written producing a vast array of views. Several major works either focus on one or another specific use of Isa 6:9–10 in the New Testament or attempt a comprehensive treatment.[3] No study, however, focuses on *congenital*

---

[1] See the following monumental works on hardening. Martin Luther, *The Bondage of the Will: The Masterwork of the Great Reformer*, trans. J. I. Packer and O. R. Johnston (Old Tappan, NJ: Revell, 1957); Karl Ludwig Schmidt, "Die Verstockung des Menschen durch Gott," *TZ* 1 (1945): 1–17; Frederik Henrik von Meyenfeldt, *Het hard (leb, lebab) in het Oude Testament*, Academic proefschrift (Leiden: Brill, 1950); Franz Hesse, *Das Verstockungsproblem im alten Testament: Eine frömmigkeits geschichtliche Untersuchung*, BZAW, vol. 74 (Berlin: Töpelmann, 1955); M. Erb, *Porosis und Ate. Begriffsgeschichtliche Untersuchungen zur neutestamentlichen Verstockungstheologie und ihren Beziehungen zur hellenischen Religiosität* (Tübingen: Huth, 1964); Heikki Räisänen, *The Idea of Divine Hardening: A Comparative Study of the Notion of Divine Hardening, Leading Astray and Inciting to Evil in the Bible and the Qur'an*, Publications of the Finnish Exegetical Society, vol. 25 (Helsinki: Finnish Exegetical Society, 1976); Robert B. Chisholm, "Divine Hardening in The Old Testament," *BSac* 153 (1996): 410–34; idem, *Handbook on the Prophets* (Grand Rapids: Baker, 2002), 24–28.

[2] Joachim Gnilka, *Die Verstockung Israels: Isaias 6:9–10 in der Theologie der Synoptiker*, SANT, ed. Vinzenz Hamp and Josef Schmid, vol. 3 (Munich: Kösel, 1961); Leo P. Stanford, "Interpretation, Motive and Procedure in the Ante-Nicene Use of Isaiah 6:9–10: A Comparative Study" (Ph.D. diss., Marquette University, 1975); Craig A. Evans, *To See and Not Perceive: Isaiah 6:9–10 in Early Jewish and Christian Interpretation*, JSOTSup, ed. David J. A. Clines and Philip R. Davies, vol. 64 (Sheffield: JSOT, 1989).

[3] Philip Bailey, *The Blindness of the Jews in Matthew 13:13–15, Mark 4:12 and Luke 8:10* (Rome: Typis Scholae Tipographicae Missionariae Dominicanae, 1956); William Robert Myers, "Disciples, Outsiders, and the Secret of the Kingdom: Interpreting Mark 4:10–13" (Th.M. thesis, McGill University, 1960); Heikki Räisänen, *Die Parabeltheorie im Markusevangelium*, Schriften der finnischen exegetischen Gesellschaft (Helsinki: Finish Exegetical Society, 1973); Charles Allen Woodward, "The Place of Mark 4:10–12 in the Second Gospel" (Th.D. diss., New Orleans Baptist Theological Seminary, 1979); Charles B. Puskas, "The Conclusion of Luke-Acts: An Investigation of the Literary Function and Theological Significance of Acts 28:16–31" (Ph.D. diss., Saint Louis University, 1980); Roman Kühschelm, *Verstockung, Gericht und Heil: exegetische und bibeltheologische Untersuchung zum sogenannten Dualismus und Determinismus in Joh 12, 35–50* (Frankfurt am Main: Hain, 1990); Johann Rauscher, *Vom Messiasgeheimnis zur Lehre der Kirche: die Entwicklung der sogenannten Parabeltheorie in der synoptischen Tradition (Mk 4, 10–12 par Mt 13, 10–17 par Lk 8, 9–10)* (Desselbrunn, Austria: Rauscher, 1990); Günter Röhser, *Prädestination und*

(innate, natural, inborn)[4] fatness of the heart as the key to understanding *how* God fattens nor do any connect the effects of this motif, namely, the failure to *perceive, understand,* and *know,* to the wisdom tradition which defines this condition as the absence of wisdom. No study begins with the conceptual link between Isaiah's fatness of heart and the lack of wisdom.[5] In addition, no study

---

Verstockung: Untersuchungen zur frühjüdischen, paulinischen und johanneischen Theologie, TANZ, ed. Klaus Berger et al., vol. 14 (Tübingen: Francke, 1994); Barry M. Foster, "The Contribution of the Conclusion of Acts to the Understanding of Lucan Theology and the Determination of Lucan Purpose" (Ph.D. diss., Trinity International University, 1997); Timothy J. Scannell, "Fulfillment of Johannine Signs: A Study of John 12:37–50" (Ph.D. diss., Fordham University, 1998); Volker A. Lehnert, *Die Provakation Israels: die paradoxe Funktion von Jes 6,9–10 bei Markus und Lukas: ein textpragmatischer Versuch im Kontext gegenwartiger Rezeptionsasthetik und Lesetheorie,* NDH, vol. 25 (Neukirchen-Vluyn: Neikirchener, 1999).

[4] The concept that will be derived from Isaiah and developed in later chapters is the proposition that all people are born with a fat-heart. This is the sense of 'congenital' in this study. Later, the fat-heart will be specifically defined as a heart that lacks *salvific wisdom* that, if possessed, would inevitably produce repentance bringing forgiveness/healing. That people are not born forgiven/healed and that salvific wisdom inevitably leads to repentance and forgiveness/healing provides one reason for holding that man is currently and congenitally without this wisdom. This view of the *fat-heart* will impact how one understands the nature of divine *fattening.* How God 'causes' an already fat-heart to be fat as well as defining the exact nature of the divine act from both a divine and human perspective will be a primary concern throughout this Study.

[5] A possible exception is Luther's *De Servo arbitrio,* originally published in 1525. Even though Luther appears plain in his view of the bondage of the will, a phrase he borrowed from Augustine, his position is still misunderstood by many writers including Watson (Philip S. Watson, "Review of *Bondage of the Will,* by Martin Luther," *ExpTim* 69 [1958–59]: 267), who assigns to the reformer (as does Erasmus) the doctrine of 'psychological compulsion' and views Luther's entire exegetical task as speculation. Luther, however, stands in the tradition of Augustine who indicates that "we do by our free will whatsoever we know and feel to be done by us...but it does not follow that, though there is for God a certain order of all causes, there must therefore be nothing depending on the free exercise of our own wills ...." (Augustine *Civ.* 5.9–11). To accuse Luther of advancing 'psychological compulsion' is a straw man. Other reviewers are more sympathetic with and accurately reflect Luther's belief in 'free psychological choice' and that "unredeemed man has no power and knows no way to effect his own redemption" (James Atkinson, "Review of *Bondage of the Will,* by Martin Luther," *CBQ* 159 [1958]: 450). For another complimentary review, with some reservations on the introductory material see James L. Garrett, "Review of *Bondage of the Will,* by Martin Luther," *SwJT* 4 (1961): 118–19.

attempts to unify the divergent traditions of Isa 6:9–10 under a sapiential world-view. All studies, as this one, share the common goal of both accounting for the purposive language and attempting to harmonize this with its simultaneous usage stressing the present condition. How does divine purpose to fatten harmonize with the human condition of fat-heartedness? This study attempts to equally stress both streams by appealing to the wisdom tradition and offering another paradigm for divine fattening.

The General Method of Inquiry

The first chapter will comprise two major sections. Part one surveys both general and specific works on the fat/hard-heart noting the strengths and weaknesses of non-sapiential approaches. Part two will highlight various paradigms for understanding these texts. These paradigms, in turn, are intended to provide some way of comprehending the texts in a unified fashion. The chapter intends, then, to be a survey of the treatment of Isa 6:9–10 and how texts like it are approached. This will be merely prefatory for the study that follows.

Chapter 2 will address philosophical issues of God, time, causality, and human freedom. The purpose of this chapter is to show how philosophical issues effect and in some ways determine how texts, like Isa 6:9–10, are handled not so much by historical inquiry as by a priori. This study will oppose a libertarian approach to freedom in favor of a compatibilist perspective.

Chapter 3 sets forth a new paradigm for treating Isa 6:9–10. This paradigm is triggered by the text itself, namely, the use of wisdom terms like perception, knowledge, and understanding. A later chapter (chapter 4) will develop Isaiah's use of this tradition and his unique definition of the heart without wisdom, namely, as *fat*. The former terms and concepts go back to the wisdom tradition and are part and parcel of wisdom itself whereas the latter term appears in wisdom texts only after Isaiah. This chapter examines the relationship of these terms to wisdom itself beginning with the MT and progressing through various other Jewish sources. The point is to show that wisdom produces perception, knowledge, and understanding. This will lead to showing that salvific wisdom in Isaiah inevitably produces these effects that secure repentance and forgiveness.

Chapter 4 focuses exclusively on Isaiah. It develops along several lines. First, it will be argued that Isaiah uses wisdom as a metanarrative. This background is crucial for his understanding of the fat-heart and thus divine fattening. Second, an examination of Isa 6:9–10 in the Hebrew text and its reuses in that book are compatible with a purposive strain in terms of strong as opposed to weak divine causality.[6] Third, the so-called mitigating texts in the Septuagint (and Greek versions), Qumran, Targum, and later Jewish sources furnish two additional streams of tradition; one which emphasizes the congenital fat-hearted condition of man and the other which appears to mitigate both strong divine causality and congenital fat-heartedness. By proceeding in this fashion, it will be demonstrated that these beneficial prerequisites, as part and parcel of Isa 6:9–10, are gratuitously imparted by God and so guarantee the exercise or absence of repentance. On the other hand, the heart will be so defined as one that lacks these requisites, and since it naturally lacks them, it is therefore best to view the heart as naturally or congenitally fat.

---

[6] These two views of divine causation need further clarification. Throughout this dissertation, *strong divine causality* will refer to the idea that God is the cause of an action or state unprecipitated by other conditions (contributory or necessary). This is to say that his action is unprovoked by human behavior and independent of preemptive necessity. God is the ultimate cause of an act where the cause of his causes are unstated, unknown, or known not to be necessary. The second view will be labeled *weak divine causality* which will refer to God as the cause of an action or state of being but where this act finds its provocation in previous actions of others providing the necessary impetus. In this view God is the ultimate cause but he is dependent on other necessary causes in order to act as ultimate cause. Both *strong* and *weak* divine causality are biblical concepts and the designation 'weak' is thus not intended to be pejorative. There are acts that God does that do not require other conditions in order to perform them like creation or monergistic regeneration (both strong divine causality), and acts God does where he requires human acts in order to act himself like justification *by faith*. The question here, then, is deciding whether one or the other applies to divine hardening *in Isaiah*. On the difficulty of hardening texts in general and God as the cause of 'evil' in particular a certain amount of animosity exists. For example, Gibson notes, "People today are unable to stomach this notion [God hardening Pharaoh's heart] and doctor the story in accordance with their own view of how God should behave" (J. C. L. Gibson, *Language and Imagery in the Old Testament* [Peabody, MA: Hendrickson, 1998], 24). Von Rad has similar sentiments and says, "There is no tolerably uniform, consistent pre-history of the concept of hardening the heart" (Gerhard von Rad, *The Message of the Prophets*, trans. D. M. G. Stalker [New York: Harper & Row, 1965], 123–24). He then points to precursors of hardening in the OT and concludes that "They offer no escape from the theological dilemma; indeed, in a sense they enhance it, for they show that Yahwism had little difficulty in accepting even such obscure acts from the hand of Yahweh" (ibid., 124).

Chapter 5 will then develop the use of Isaiah 6:9–10 in the Gospel of Mark especially in terms of noetic obtuseness rather than linguistic obscurity of parables. Chapter 6 will round out the Synoptic Gospels of Matthew and Luke as they contrast and compare with Mark. A final chapter will provide a summation of the study.

Intended Accomplishments

The goal of this Study is threefold: (1) To demonstrate that man congenitally lacks salvific wisdom and is dependent upon God for its bestowal. (2) To harmonize two divergent traditions in relation to fattening in texts involving Isa 6:9–10 by appealing to the wisdom tradition. (3) To demonstrate that Isaianic fattening is best understood as an act of divine deprivation, that is, a purposive *withholding* of wisdom thereby preventing one from salvifically repenting and receiving forgiveness. In the NT this lack of wisdom is associated with the inability to understand parables, interpret signs, and receive the gospel. That this deprivation is non-punitive and non-transformational in nature is so precisely because man is congenitally fat-hearted.

Review and Assessment
of Current Literature

Major Treatments of Isa 6:9–10 and NT Passages

The following is an examination and evaluation of major treatments of Isa 6:9–10 and its parallels in the NT including general and specialized works. The purpose is to demonstrate the inattention to the wisdom tradition and the sapiential matrix from which Isaiah's terminology and world-view seem to point. This will prepare for the justification of this emphasis in the following chapters.

General Works on Hardening

Karl Ludwig Schmidt.[1] Schmidt treats terms used for hardening, the hardening of Pharaoh and how it applies to the heart, unbelievers, enemies of Israel, and God's chosen people (in both OT and NT). He teaches that hardening is a combination of self-hardening and retribution but a tension remains between predestination and human responsibility in relation to God's justice—a tension Paul addresses (Rom 9). Hardening is set in terms of *Heilsgeschichte* and predestination.[2] But it is the hardening of God's people (Jews) that sparks consternation (Rom 9–11).[3] Jewish hardening (esp. Rom 9–11) serves as a warning to Christians who can harden themselves and suffer the same fate (Heb 3:8, 13, 15; 4:7).

---

[1] Karl Ludwig Schmidt, "Die Verstockung des Menschen durch Gott," *TZ* 1 (1945): 1–17.

[2] Ibid., 3–4.

[3] Matt 13:15; Mark 3:5; John 12:40; Acts 19:9; 28:27; Rom 2:5, 9, 18; 11:7; 2 Cor 3:14; Heb 3:8, 13, 15; 4:7.

The hardening of Isa 6:9–10 serves the same purpose for believers in the NT (Acts 28). It is directed towards the 'senses' of unbelievers (2 Cor 3:14) and occurs because God is both just and merciful. Schmidt says, "Gott selbst verstockt; aber der Mensch wird gemahnt, eben doch auch nicht sich selbst zu verstocken."[4] The key for Schmidt is this bracketing of the behavior of men within epochs of salvation.[5]

He examines NT terms (πωρόω/πώρωσις) and texts in order to arrive at the total concept of hardening. Mark applies hardening to the disciples (6:52; 8:17) but "wie es sonst nur den Juden als den Repräsentanten der pharaonischen Verstockung eignet, die Uebersetzer zu nennen vermeiden."[6] However, Mark avoids directly calling the disciples 'hard-hearted.' Pharaoh is an example of one who becomes reprobate through obstinacy. The point is to not follow his example.

The 'fattening' of the heart is examined from varying renditions including the LXX, Matt 13:15, and Acts 28:27 that "hat der LXX-Text das gemildert" to John 12:40. The latter alters the Hebrew imperatives to indicatives but "läßt jedenfalls ausdrücklich Gott als den Urheber der Verstockung erscheinen."[7] Various effects like blindness are discussed (Rom 11:25; Eph 4:18), with Greek variants (πηρόω/πήρωσις for πωρόω/πώρωσις) and their causal links (John 12:40, τυφλόω). He provides a plethora of hardening terms,[8] concedes that the relationship of guilt and responsibility to God's judgment is complex, but holds that there is both a human and divine strain of causality throughout and that hardening is a judicial act of retribution.

A few issues asserted may require further qualification. First, although the complications of hardening are acknowledged, there remains no distinction between Pharaonic *hardening* and Isaianic *fattening*. Second, a retribution sense to hardening is adopted. Third, hardening appears to be self-caused but it is unclear what type of

---

[4] Schmidt, "Die Verstockung des Menschen durch Gott," 7.

[5] Ibid., 7–8.

[6] Ibid., 10.

[7] Ibid., 12.

[8] These include the following: πλάνω, ἀποπλήνησις, σκολιότης, ἐπιτηδεύματα, ἐπιθυμήματα, ἀρεστά, κατάνυξις, καμμύω, βαρύνω, παχύνω, σκοτίζω, σκοτόω, νεκρόω, νέκρωσις, and πώρωσις.

hardening is in view. Fourth, the natural condition of the heart is omitted as its relationship to hardening. Finally, there is the absence of a metanarrative[9] that may be useful in sorting out the differences that (as Schmidt concedes) are present in the various hardening texts.

Franz Hesse.[10] Hesse's monograph is designed to set forth OT hardening as the basis, preliminary background, and *sine qua non* for approaching NT hardening passages.[11] It is comprehensive (covering all forms of hardening), sensitive to a world-view that construes these texts, descriptive, employs the language of systematic theology within a framework of the history-of-religions approach, and is confessedly preliminary.

Hesse provides several significant observations in forming a definition.[12] He begins with a NT vocabulary (without specifying the type of hardening),[13] identifies the object of hardening as the heart—the seat of religious life and moral attitude—and notes the inabilities of the hardened-heart in both moral functions and belief.[14] He rightly identifies the problem of the hard-heart as the inability ("gestört oder gar zerstort ist"[15]) to perceive or understand[16] and

---

[9] One way of defining a *metanarrative* is to examine the term itself. The prefix *meta-* refers to "analysis not on the ordinary level, but at a deeper level that views the adequacy or inadequacy of concepts at the ordinary level" (Gregory Pence, *A Dictionary of Common Philosophical Terms* [New York: McGraw-Hill, 2000], 34). It is an essential construct that provides the key by which particulars are organized, recognized, and understood.

[10] Franz Hesse, *Das Verstockungsproblem im alten Testament: Eine frömmigkeits geschichtliche Untersuchung*, BZAW, vol. 74 (Berlin: Töpelmann, 1955).

[11] Ibid., 1, 2, 3.

[12] Ibid., 3–6.

[13] He lists the following terms: πωρόω, σκληρύνω, παχύνω, πώρωσις, σκληρότης, and σκληροτράχηλος.

[14] Hesse, *Das Verstockungsproblem*, 4.

[15] Ibid.

[16] He points out the verbs συνίημι, νοέω, γινώσκω and nouns νόημα, διάνοια, ἄγνοια, in emphasizing this aspect of hardening (ibid, 5 fn. 1). He says that "Dem Verstockten is das Erkennen und Verstehen unmöglichgeworden" (Hesse, *Das Verstockungsproblem*, 4).

distinguishes this from the disciples' lapses (Mark 8:16–18).[17] Spiritual perception and understanding are the obedient and grateful acknowledgments of God's works.[18] Perception is the moral component absent from the hard-heart, hardening is permanent, and conversion (Isa 6:9–10) is impossible. Although obstinacy is the effect (Acts 7:51) and (for some Jews) continues to the present time (Rom 11:8), it is divinely caused and renders men *non posse non peccare*.[19]

---

[17] On this passage he says, "Wenn die Jünger die Worte Jesu falsch verstehen, so ist das ein Zeichen, daß sie eine καρδία πωπωρωμένη haben; ihre Sinesorgant tun nicht den Dienst, zu dem sie gegeben sind" (Hesse, *Das Verstockungsproblem*, 5). He distinguishes this idea from the spiritual sense quoted by Bultmann.

[18] Ibid. Cf. Rudolf Bultmann, "γινώσκω," *TDNT* 1:707.

[19] This is an Augustinian phrase. Augustine's view of humanity at present is *massa peccati* 'mass of sin' (Augustine *Enchir*. 1.673). The will is truly free when it is not a slave of sin (*Civ*. 14.11). Although Adam's sin flowed from his evil will or pride (*Civ*. 14.13), this does not explain how evil sprang from the heart in the first place (*Civ*. 7.3–5). This sin effects all Adam's posterity (contra Pelagius) because all mankind is corporately connected to Adam by being 'in Adam' and therefore participating in his fall (*Civ*. 13.14; 14.15). This sin of Adam took him from *posse pecare* (able to sin) to *non posse non pecare* (not able not to sin). The fall brought with it a loss of true freedom (*Conf*. 1.7; 7:3, 16; 8:5, 9, 10), a noetic downgrade in powers of reasoning with a positive proclivity toward sinful biases, an absence of grace (*adjutorium*), a loss of paradise, the presence of concupiscence (predilection for the sensuous), physical death, and hereditary guilt (a condition or *habitus* of the human nature [either traduced or created]). It is the issue surrounding original sin that sparks the controversy with Augustine and Pelagius because the latter saw no need to baptize infants for sin they had not committed. Augustine saw baptism of infants as taking away guilt (*reatus*) but not sin itself (*concupiscentia*). It is Augustine's understanding of the fall that dictates how he construes grace and free will whereas it is Pelagius' view of creation that dictate how he understands human nature.

Pelagius was a moralist (ascetic) who understood the commands of God as implying human capability (and culpability) while arguing that God would not command the impossible (*ought-implies-can* is his overriding axiom). Therefore, Pelagius was offended at Augustine's prayer, "Command what you will and grant what you command" (*Conf*. 10.29.40) referring to the gift of obedience. Pelagius reasoned that God gave man freedom, the *bonum naturae*, that has both *the possibilitas boni et mali* (Augustine *Grat. Chr*. responding to Pelagius *Defense of the Freedom of the Will*) and that this is part of man's indestructible nature. Man's will is inconvertibly good and a perpetual *tabula rasa* without inclination, predisposition, or predilection to sin. Thus he rejected both inherited sin, *tradux peccati*, and original sin, *peccatum originis*, and attempted to link, albeit unsuccessfully, Augustine's views to Manichaeism (Pelagius *Marius Com*. 2.10). The prevalence of sin is due to habit that collectively forms societiel norms that in turn influence the person to sin (Pelagius *Dem*. 8). Society is evil not the person. Grace simply facilitates doing righteousness

Isaiah 6:9–10 exercises considerable influence on subsequent passages of the OT and his own prophecy. His influence is seen in Jer 5:21, Ezek 12:2, and Deut 29:3 which is post-exilic and conveys a type of deprivation underway "so sind ihm nach dieser Stelle sogar (Herz), Augen und Ohren vorenthalten."[20] Israel exists in a privation of God's knowledge and God is the author of these conditions.[21] Zechariah 7:11 'heavy ears' shows dependence. This divine initiative leads Hesse to ponder, "wieso ein Mensch dann noch für seine Sünde verantwortlich gemacht werden kann, wenn Gott ihm gar die einschlägigen Sinnesorgane Vorenthalten hat."[22] Intratextually, Isaiah repeats his own theme throughout his prophecy (42:20; 43:8; 44:18). The early versions, including the LXX, Greek versions (Aquila and Symmachus), the Vulgate, the Peshitta, and the Syriac are viewed in terms of their dependence or departure from the Hebrew text.[23]

The NT lists eight passages that are directly linked to Isa 6:9–10.[24] He mentions the crux of Mark 4:12 and issues surrounding the ἵνα and μήποτε clauses, the freer (Matt 13:13) and explicit (Matt 13:14–15) citation in Matthew, its less severity than Mark and its stress on human culpability, the similarity (retaining of ἵνα) and dissimilarity

---

but it is not necessary (Augustine *Gest. Pelag.* 22.46; *Grat. Chr.* 35.38; *Retract.* 2.68; *Corrept.* 10.26–12.38). God's grace is external and consists of instruction whether in the Law or Christ's teachings (Pelagius *Dem.* 8; Augustine *Grat. Chr.* 7.8). Several condemnations of Pelagianism include the following: (1) Trial and condemnation of Caelestius, a disciple of Pelagius, in Carthage (A.D. 411). (2) African Synods (A.D. 416) condemn Pelagius' views. The following year Pelagius and Caelestius appeal to Zozimus who calls the council of Carthage. (3) Council of Carthage (A.D. 418) condemns Pelagius and Coelestius and affirms Augustine's views. (4) Council of Ephesus (A.D. 431) condemns Pelagianism. (5) Synod of Orange (A.D. 529) moderately reaffirms Augustinianism but condemns Pelagianism. For a popular summary see R. C. Sproul, *Willing to Believe: The Controversy over Free Will* (Grand Rapids: Baker, 1997), 33–66; J. Patout Burns, ed., *Theological Anthropology*, trans. J. Patout Burns, Sources of Early Christian Thought, ed. William G. Rusch (Philadelphia: Fortress, 1981), 1–22; B. R. Rees, *The Letters of Pelagius and His followers* (Rochester, NY: Boydell, 1991).

[20] Hesse, *Das Verstockungsproblem*, 61.

[21] Ibid.

[22] Ibid., 62.

[23] Ibid., 63–64.

[24] Mark 4:12; Matt 13:13–15; Luke 8:10; John 12:40; Acts 28:26–27; Mark 8:18; John 9:39; Rom 11:8.

(omission of μήποτε) of Mark to Luke 8:10, and the impossibility of faith in John 12:40. He notes tensions between the MT/John and the LXX/Synoptics as well as between John 12:40. Acts 28:26–27 is a divinely orchestrated failure, hardening is a consequence of unbelief but the disciples (Mark 8:18) are a different matter. John 9:39 is rhetorically linked to John 12:40 and Rom 11:8 is a free reproduction of two texts (Isa 29:10 and Deut 29:3) where God is the author because he has not given them eyes to see and ears to hear.

Hesse recognizes that Isaianic 'hardening' is different than that of Pharaoh, entails an incapacity of wisdom, renders man unable to believe, and remains permanent. Some inconsistencies still remain. The hard-heart causes unbelief but in John it is the result of unbelief during a time when faith is possible. While there is the recognition of man's inherent inability to believe, it is placed alongside the act of hardening that renders one unable to believe—the superfluity is undetected and unresolved. There is the articulation and defense of a retributional basis of hardening and a lingering ambiguity to the identity of the hardener based on texts emphasizing either God (MT, Mark, Luke, John, Rom) or man (LXX, Matt, Acts).[25]

Heikki Räisänen.[26] Räisänen provides a history of religion approach to hardening in the Qur'an, Old Testament, intertestamental literature, and the New Testament. His goal is to do away with what appears to be arbitrary predestination while preserving human freedom.[27]

This is a philosophical treatise from the perspective of libertarian freedom. Because individuals are responsible and appeals are made to their will (*ought-implies-can*), these do away with arbitrary

---

[25] Hesse, *Das Verstockungsproblem*, 65. The harshness must be that God responds in such a way as to deplete them of the ability to believe and renders this as a permanent condition.

[26] Heikki Räisänen, *The Idea of Divine Hardening: A Comparative Study of the Notion of Divine Hardening, Leading Astray and Inciting to Evil in the Bible and the Qur'an*, Publications of the Finnish Exegetical Society, vol. 25 (Helsinki: Finnish Exegetical Society, 1976).

[27] Very early on he points out that his study is about *liberum arbitrium* and against *praedestinatio ad malum* (ibid., 8–9, 12). Malina points this out as a weakness of his study (Bruce J. Malina, review of *The Idea of Divine Hardening*, by Heikki Räisänen, *CBQ* 36 [1974]: 136).

predestination (or double predestination).[28] Predestination and free will are "logical contradictions"[29] because the ancient Hebrews did not distinguish between primary and secondary causes.[30] That people deserve perdition, under a predestinarian perspective, is arbitrary. Religious texts on divine hardening are not metaphysical but polemical statements (why not both?) with the pragmatic purpose of fostering repentance and belief.[31] While the demonic character of God is granted for 1 Sam 26:19, other texts emphasize God's justice (retribution) in response to offenses.[32] Hardening is therefore retributional, transformational, non-permanent, and reversible through man's 'free-will.' The libertarian approach carefully guides the reader towards these ends.

Specialized Treatments

Philip Bailey.[33] Bailey proposes to ascertain the meaning of the phrase 'to see and not see' and "whether as a matter of fact this expression really signifies spiritual blindness as is commonly taught."[34] Although he takes it as a Hebrew idiom derived from Isa 6:9–10, he regards the MT as harsh and the LXX less so. Of the Synoptics, Matthew agrees with the LXX, Mark with the LXX except for the ἵνα clause with an ending (μήποτε) agreeing with the Targum, while Luke quotes only Isa 6:9 and inverts the order of clauses.

He focuses on the expressions 'hearing you shall hear' and 'seeing you shall see' in Isa 6:9–10 and other parts of the OT. The phrases involve a Hebrew or Semitic idiom that serve to *intensify* a *repeated*

---

[28] Räisänen, *The Idea of Divine Hardening*, 12.

[29] Ibid., 15.

[30] Ibid., 47.

[31] See Udo Tworuschka, review of The Idea of Divine Hardening, by Heikki Räisänen, *ZRGG* 26 (1974): 174–75 and Günther Bröker, review of *The Idea of Divine Hardening*, by by Heikki Räisänen, *TLZ* 99 (1974): 338–42.

[32] Tworuschka, review of The Idea of Divine Hardening, by Heikki Räisänen, 175 notes this.

[33] Philip Bailey, *The Blindness of the Jews in Matthew 13:13–15, Mark 4:12 and Luke 8:10* (Rome: Typis Scholae Tipographicae Missionariae Dominicanae, 1956).

[34] Ibid., 2.

action (hearing and seeing) that is strictly physical.[35] He notes that 'perceiving' (בִּין) is in reference to the heart, the seat of intelligence and alludes to the wisdom tradition by comparing Isa 6:9–10 to a proverb which conveys brevity, sense, piquancy, and popularity—in keeping with the Hebrew and Greek terms (מָשָׁל, παραβολή and παροιμία). It is a term employed for prophetic oracles, songs, and poems dominated by irony and derision.[36] Bailey believes Jesus may have used Isa 6:9–10 as a loose quotation or much like the English proverb and that it should be interpreted in this light.[37]

On his treatment of Mark 4:12 (and pars.) he addresses the 'to see and not see' clause, the nuances involving ἵνα, that only Matthew quotes the LXX and is induced to do so by 13:13, and the verbs βλέπω, ὁράω, ἀκούω, συνίημι (which he distinguishes from νοέω), and γινώσκω in arguing for a distinction between ocular/acoustic versus noetic phenomena.[38] He identifies the ἵνα clause (of Mark and Luke) as relevant to identifying the cause of blindness. *Purpose* is the most common usage that he accepts.[39] He also mentions *causal* but cautions that each NT usage may be explained otherwise.[40] He dismisses the Synoptics as parallel passages, Lagrange's quotation formula for ἵνα as a "specious meaning of the particle,"[41] but nevertheless accepts this very view based on Matt 13:14–15. The ἵνα clause is therefore both purposive and preemptory.[42]

Bailey appreciates the importance of the idiom 'to see and not see,' posits a proverbial (wisdom?) nature of Matt 13:13, and sees a double function of the ἵνα clause. Less convincing ideas include the use of ἵνα in Mark as fulfillment and that Matthew's causal ὅτι is irreconcilable to Mark and Luke's purposeful ἵνα clause. There also appears to be a breakdown in the argument. If the ἵνα clause functions in the fashion he advocates, then how does it resolve the

---

[35] Ibid., 29, 32.

[36] Ibid., 43.

[37] Ibid., 51.

[38] Ibid., 56.

[39] Ibid., 58.

[40] Ibid., 60.

[41] Ibid., 62.

[42] Ibid., 65–66.

initial problem of contradiction between purpose and cause and why is it necessary to dismiss them as parallel passages?

William Robert Myers.[43] This work is divided into two parts, a historical survey (pp. 1–93) and then an exegetical examination of Mark 4:10–13 (pp. 94–176). Part one covers early interpreters of the ancient church through Augustine,[44] reformation and post-reformation times,[45] and since the beginning of modern critical scholarship including ten European, fourteen British, and eight American scholars up to 1960.[46] This historical survey is a positive feature of the work as it shows how the early fathers through modernity interpret the sayings. Problematic is crediting Augustine with circular reasoning[47] and Luther of inconsistencies,[48]

---

[43] William Robert Myers, "Disciples, Outsiders, and the Secret of the Kingdom: Interpreting Mark 4:10–13" (Th.M. thesis, McGill University, 1960).

[44] These includes Herm. *Sim.* 5.4.3; *Gos. Thom.* 62; Irenaeus *Haer.* 1.25.5; 2.27.3; Tertullian *Praescr.* 22; *Res.* 33; Clement of Alexandria *Strom.* 1:1; 5.7, 10; 12; *Ps.-Clem.* 19:20; Origen *Comm. Matt.* 10.4, 16; 11.4; *Princ.* 3.1.16–17; *Dial.*; *Cels.* 3; Cyril of Jerusalem *Catechetical Lectures* 6.23–29; Chrysostom *Hom. Matt.* 45.26; *Hom. 2 Cor.* 8:2; Jerome *Epist.* 48; 58; John Cassian *Conf.* 13.12; 23.6; and Augustine *Praed.* 40; *Persev.* 35; *Tract. Ev. Jo.* 63.3.

[45] This includes Desiderius Erasmus, Martin Luther, Ulrich Zwingli, John Calvin, Theodore Beza, John Knox, and Johann Albrecht Bengel.

[46] Scholarship is restricted, obviously, to works pre-1960. *European*: Bruno Bauer, Adolf Jülicher, H. H. Wendt, Wilhelm Bousset, Wilhelm Wrede, Albert Schweitzer, Johannes Weiss, E. Klostermann, Rudolf Bultmann, Rudolf Otto, and Joachim Jeremias. *Great Britian*: Alexander Balmain Bruce, W. O. E. Oesterly, Henry Barclay Swete, A. E. J. Rawlinson, T. W. Manson, R. H. Lightfoot, C. H. Dodd, B. T. D. Smith, A. T. Cadoux, William Manson, Matthew Black, Austin Farrer, Vincent Taylor, and C. E. B. Cranfield. *America*: Benjamin W. Bacon, Ezra P. Gould, George Arthur Buttrick, Charles Cutler Torrey, B. Harvie Branscomb, Frederick C. Grant, Otto A. Piper, and C. W. F. Smith.

[47] Augustine asserts God's predestination, ascribes the beginning of faith to God (*Praed.* 40, commenting on Col 4:2 and citing John 6:66; Matt 13:11), and insists that obedience is also necessary for those predestined-to-believe. Myers accuses him of circular reasoning (Myers, "Disciples, Outsiders, and the Secret of the Kingdom," 21). But Augustine simply links ears to hear with the gift to obey. This is not circular. Augustine is also faulted for not explaining how some things can be spoken of openly and not openly at the same time (*Tract. Ev. Jo.* 63.3 on John 18:19–20). It may be explained in terms of *linguistic* versus *noetic* obscurity.

[48] Ibid., 27.

misconstruing Calvin's notion of 'accidents' in hardening,[49] and imbuing Knox with views that go beyond Calvin.[50] He positions the apostolic fathers against Bengel [51] who in the end does not really differ from earlier views except he believes "that divinely-sent judicial blindness is added to their voluntary blindness."[52]

In the exegetical portion of the work he maintains that parables are not intended to conceal meaning from anyone although they might not understand it.[53] Reasons for incomprehension might include the lack of understanding, training, a hearing ear, or an understanding heart and at other times rebellion is the cause. His primary disagreement may be seen in his link of knowing and knowledge to the mysteries; but gratuitous impartation of wisdom is omitted.[54] Later he says, "It is God's prerogative to give the kingdom...*to whom he will*,"[55] where the 'giving' is solely external and predicated on man's response. Myers omits both the pre-temporal divine action of election and internal working of regeneration that

---

[49] Calvin explains that the parables are not unclear but rather the darkness resides in the human heart (John Calvin, *Commentary on a Harmony of the Evangelists Matthew, Mark, and Luke*, trans. William Pringle [Edinburgh: Calvin Translation Society, 1845–46; reprint, Grand Rapids: Baker, 1999], 108). In this way hardening is *accidental*, because the parables are not designed *by nature* to harden. The use of 'accidental' comes from Aristotle's distinction between an object's substance, or what is essential to its nature, and its *accidens*. Peter Kreeft defines *accidens* as "that mode of being which can exist only in another being, as a modification or attribute of a substance (thing); e.g. the redness of the nose" (Peter Kreeft, ed., *A Summa of the Summa: The Essential Philosophical Passages of St. Thomas Aquinas' Summa Theologica Edited and Explained for Beginners* [San Francisco: Ignatius, 1990], 23; cf. Aquinas *Sum. Theol.* 1.3.7; 1.75.6; Aristotle *Cat.* 5; *Metaph.* 5.4, 11; 9.8). The nature of the accident here is best described as a 'proper accident' involving the *property* of the man not the parable (ibid., 28). Myers says, "So the word of God 'accidentally' hardens the reprobate because of their own depravity" (Myers, "Disciples, Outsiders, and the Secret of the Kingdom," 33). The real contention Myers has with Calvin (as with Augustine and Luther) is that the latter place obtuseness in man rather than the parables.

[50] Myers, "Disciples, Outsiders, and the Secret of the Kingdom," 34–35.

[51] Ibid., 35–36.

[52] Ibid., 36–37.

[53] Ibid., 159.

[54] Ibid., 159–60. See also his discussion on the verb δίδωμι and whether the phrase 'to give a mystery' is equated to mean 'to reveal a mystery' (ibid., 172–74).

[55] Ibid., 124.

initiates one's entrance into the kingdom. He relates the unbelief of those outside Qumran with their lack of access to the *mode* of revelation and those outside Jesus simply to their preference. That they lack some prerequisite that renders them *unable* to positively respond is not mentioned.[56]

On the ἵνα/μήποτε construction in Mark, Myers accepts the reading as given but, along with Matthew Black, regards the final clause as inauthentic[57]—a conjectural mistranslation of the Aramaic ד.[58] On the seeing/hearing motif he notes that the 'seeing eye' and the 'hearing ear' are granted by God (Prov 20:2), that they are described by Jesus as 'discerning' and 'perceptive,' but does not indicate the basis of this bestowal.[59] Those who exercise these qualities are 'blessed' while 'hearing' and 'repenting' are parallel. He argues that because Jesus requires repentance, that he "evidently felt they could do it."[60]

Like Räisänen, Myers subscribes to libertarian freedom. He therefore credits the acceptance of Jesus to 'free-will' and identifies the opposing view as God play-acting or that "Jesus was a deluded, misguided product of a meaningless heritage."[61] Even Judas was 'free' to accept or reject Jesus.[62] Hearers "were able, if not always

---

[56] Later Myers astutely likens 'understanding the parable' to 'getting a joke' (ibid., 161).

[57] Ibid., 163. Later he says when this μήποτε clause is removed, it then frees one to lean in the direction of adopting the relative clause for ἵνα as the original saying of Jesus (ibid., 167). Myers then sets forth his idiosyncratic view and somewhat fallacious argument for setting aside the final line of the saying. He reasons that the passage places repentance before forgiveness that violates Jesus' own modus operandi (ibid., 167–68, 178). Myers confuses the modus operandi of Jesus' ministry (the offer of forgiveness that is followed by repentance) with individual experience to that message (repenting in order to be forgiven). He faults the redactor for appending this Targumic ending unwittingly reversing Jesus' teachings (ibid., 170). But the passages on teachings (Mark 1:15; 2:5; Luke 7:47; Matt 11:21; Luke 10:13; Matt 18:22; Luke 19:9), parables (Matt 20:1–16; Luke 14:16–35; 15:4, 8, 11) and his deeds (Mark 2:16; Matt 11:19; Luke 7:34, 39; 19:7) do not support his view.

[58] Ibid., 174–76.

[59] Ibid., 189–90.

[60] Ibid., 195, 197.

[61] Ibid., 205.

[62] Ibid., 206.

willing, to exercise their own judgment about his words and actions."[63] The deeper issue, which he does not address, is why some were *positively* willing and others were not so inclined.[64] He denies Jesus held a theology of divine hardening and that some are predestined to hear while others are not.[65] A merit-based theology is the result.

Myers seems right that the *linguistic* message may not be obscure but this alone does not account for the concealing role of the Father in some other (*noetic*) sense (Matt 11:25–27; Luke 10:21–22). Straightforward appeal may necessitate *natural* ability without implying *moral* ability to respond.[66] It may not be required to construe the mode of communication as necessitating a *moral* ability (ought-implies-*moral*-can) but only a *natural* ability (ought-implies-*natural*-can).[67] Natural ability to respond may make one accountable because man is responsible for the absence of moral ability lost in the fall.

---

[63] Ibid.

[64] He says, "Denying predestination simply eliminates one possible answer to the question" (ibid., 211).

[65] Ibid., 207.

[66] Ibid.

[67] This is the Pelagian axiom that derives from his view of creation driven by merit theology. Pelagius says, "I usually begin by showing the strength and characteristics of human nature. By explaining what it can accomplish, I encourage the soul of my hearers to the different virtues. To call a person something he considers impossible does him no good" (*Dem.* 2). Not recognizing this ability leads to low morals (ibid.). Since God is good and God created man's nature, man must be good, intractably so (ibid.). He follows up with a *libertarian* view of freedom. "The glory of the reasonable soul is located precisely in its having to face a parting of the ways, in its freedom to follow either path. I contend that the dignity of our nature consists entirely in this: this is the source of honor, of reward, of the praise merited by the best people. If a person could not go over to evil, he would not practice virtue in holding to the good. God decided to give rational creatures the gift of good will and the power of free choice. By making a person naturally capable of good and evil, so that he could do both and would direct his own will to either, God arranged that what an individual actually chose would be properly his own. The good could be done voluntarily only by a creature which was also capable of evil. Therefore the most excellent creator decided to make us capable of both" (ibid., 3). "Our ability to do evil is, therefore, itself a good…. It removes the bonds of necessity and makes the person free do decide, makes the will voluntary in its own right. Thus we have freedom to choose or oppose, to accept or reject" (ibid.). Examples in the OT serve to reinforce this inherent ability (ibid., 6). "Where we see willing and refusing, choosing and rejecting, we

Joachim Gnilka.[68] This study's interest lies in the relationship between hardening and the use of Isa 6:9–10.[69] It is divided into three main parts dealing with Mark (pp. 23–86), Matthew (pp. 89–115), and Luke-Acts (pp. 119–54). It is preceded by a treatment of Isa 6:9–10 (pp. 13–19) and followed by both an excursus on Qumran (pp. 155–85) and a summary of the work (187–205). One reviewer calls it a 'Summa Exegetica.'[70] Methodologically, it is guided by the redactionary seams, order of the pericopes, and redactionary modifications of the logia of Jesus. His focus is each Gospel's accentuated aspects regarding the heart.[71] He seeks to establish not only the *Sitz im Leben Ecclesiae* of each Gospel, but also the *Sitz im Leben Jesu* of Mark's logion (4:11–12).

Modifications of the MT on Isa 6:9–10 are of special concern. The LXX changes the imperatives with the result that "daß das Volk vollends verstockt werde."[72] The Targum is changed in a number of places as well (the relative particle –דְּ, substitution of דלמא for פֶּן and שבק for רָפָא).[73] The NT cites the LXX precisely (Matt 13:14–15; Acts

understand the functioning of freedom of the will, not the forces of nature" (ibid.). "We do…refute the charge that nature's inadequacy forces us to do evil. We do either good or evil only by our own will; since we always remain capable of both, we are always free to do either" (ibid., 8). "Unless each could have done both, neither would the former have deserved to be punished nor the latter to be chosen by a just God" (ibid.). "Doing good has become difficult for us only because of the long custom of sinning, which begins to infect us even in our childhood" (ibid.). "Christ's grace has taught us and regenerated us as better persons" (ibid.). "'That is too hard, too difficult! We cannot do that! We are only human; our flesh is weak!' What insane stupidity! What impious arrogance!…. We imply that the creator of humanity has forgotten its weakness and imposes precepts which a human being cannot bear…. First we complain that he commands the impossible; then we assume that he condemns people for things they cannot avoid. We portray God as working to condemn rather than save us, something it is sacrilegious even to suggest" (ibid., 16).

[68] Joachim Gnilka, *Die Verstockung Israels: Isaias 6:9–10 in der Theologie der Synoptiker*, SANT, ed. Vinzenz Hamp and Josef Schmid, vol. 3 (Munich: Kösel, 1961).

[69] John L. McKenzie, review of *Die Verstockung Israels, Isaias 6, 9–10 in der Theologie der Synoptiker*, by Joachim Gnilka, *TS* 23 (1962): 459–61; Gnilka, *Die Verstockung Israels*, 9.

[70] Jean Carmignac, review of *Die Verstockung Israels, Isaias 6, 9–10 in der Theologie der Synoptiker*, by Joachim Gnilka, *RevQ* 3 (1962): 585–87.

[71] J. Coppens, review of *Die Verstockung Israels, Isaias 6, 9–10 in der Theologie der Synoptiker*, by Joachim Gnilka, *ETL* 38 (1962): 117–19.

[72] Gnilka, *Die Verstockung Israels*, 16.

[73] Ibid., 48–50.

28:26–27) with the exception of αὐτῶν and καὶ τοῖς ὠσίν in 6:10 and adopts the interpretation of the LXX. Mark 4:12 quotes partially from Isa 6:9 and partially from Isa 6:10 with minor changes but adds a Targumic phrase (replaces ἰάσομαι αὐτούς with ἀφεθῇ αὐτοῖς), and has ἵνα serving both as a "Finalpartikel" and "einleitende Partikel."[74] He also notes a few word order changes and their significance.

He devotes an appendix to the Qumran literature and notes similarities with the Gospels. The emphasis is on election, viewing outsiders as hard-hearted, mode of revelation, divine secrets, divine illumination, and a doctrine of the remnant. He even lists wisdom vocabulary including בִּין, יָדַע, and שָׂכַל (along with their nominals).[75]

Gnilka perceives obduracy in terms of punishment for the willfully blind in their refusal to accept divine revelation rather than as a congenital condition[76] and in terms of degree.[77] It is unclear whether this is solely conditioned by some previous action (self-imposed, divinely conferred, or both) or is congenital. He distinguishes the hard-heart of the disciples in terms of a gradual enlightenment rather than degrees of hardness.[78] He also rejects the linguistic obscurity of parables, expands it to the deeds of Jesus, and credits the rejection to God's providence and concealment.[79] He regards the words as authentic but denies that Jesus ascribed to parables the role of hardening.[80] The Targumic addition shows a Palestinian provenience but it follows the spirit of the MT in having a

<hr/>

[74] Ibid., 47–48, 50.

[75] Ibid., 95–102, 75–83.

[76] McKenzie, review of *Die Verstockung Israels*, 459; Thomas W. Leahy, review of *Die Verstockung Israels, Isaias 6, 9–10 in der Theologie der Synoptiker*, by Joachim Gnilka, *JBL* 81 (1962): 88–89; cf. Gnilka, *Die Verstockung Israels*, 82.

[77] "Das Volk ist verstockt, wie der Prophet voraussah" (Gnilka, *Die Verstockung Israels*, 89).

[78] Leahy, review of *Die Verstockung Israels*, 88. He also distinguishes between the disciples incomprehension as "intellectual blindness" and others as "bad will" (Gnilka, *Die Verstockung Israels*, 32–33). But this distinction hardly explains the similarity of texts applied to each (Isa 6:9 and Jer 5:21). Cf. Schuyler Brown, "The Secret of the Kingdom of God (Mark 4, 11)," *JBL* 92 (1973): 62.

[79] Gnilka, *Die Verstockung Israels*, 193, 96.

[80] Leahy, review of *Die Verstockung Israels*, 89.

divine purpose.[81] Matthew, on the other hand, softens the Hebrew by following the LXX and adopting the ὅτι clause.[82] His treatment of Qumran lacks reference to 4Q424 f3:6–8 where the 'fat-heart' is defined as absence of wisdom.

Heikki Räisänen.[83] This is a second study by Räisänen. Here he argues that the parable of Mark 4 develops (redaction critically) in four separate stages; alone (4:1, 3–8), then with an interpretation (4:13a, 14–20), a repeated theme (4:33), and the call to hear (4:9). The effect is that the parable is transformed into a linguistically opaque mode of speech that requires interpretation given only to insiders.[84] He argues that although the original purpose of parables was didactic and not designed to conceal truth (Messianic secret), at present, Mark 4:12 contradicts the rest of Mark along with this original intent.

This treatment contains some beneficial aspects.[85] He argues persuasively that the original intent of parables was not to conceal and that the text (at present) seems to suggest the opposite. His precise point is that *original* linguistic perspicuity of parables in Jesus' preaching has given way to *present* linguistic obscurity in the text. The crucial point, however, is whether his exegesis of Mark 4:10–12—that parables are designed to be obscure requiring explanation—is sufficiently justified. Although his argument may be seen as opposing an obscurity limited to a *linguistic* phenomenon, he does not propose the alternative notion that obscurity may rest entirely in the *noetic* realm ('in riddles'). This latter construal comports well with Mark and aspects of authenticity.

---

[81] He also takes the μήποτε clause in the sense of 'lest' in the context of the Hebrew OT that has the salvation of the remnant in mind.

[82] Thus he anticipates the later study of Evans in seeing some type of mitigation of the Hebrew text, but leaves ambiguous the nature and cause of hardening.

[83] Heikki Räisänen, *Die Parabeltheorie im Markusevangelium*, Schriften der finnischen exegetischen Gesellschaft (Helsinki: Finnish Exegetical Society, 1973).

[84] For a summary of these stages see Jack Dean Kingsbury, review of *Die Parabeltheorie im Markusevangelium*, by Heikki Räisänen, *TZ* 32 (1976): 108–09; Philip Sellew, "Oral and Written Sources in Mark 4.1–34," *NTS* 36 (1990): 253–55.

[85] For these and other shortcomings see Hans-Wolfgang Kuhn, review of *Die Parabeltheorie im Markusevangelium*, by Heikki Räisänen, *TLZ* 101 (1976): 121–23.

Charles Alan Woodward.[86] Woodward posits that the words ascribed to Jesus in Mark 4:10–12 are too harsh yet indicates that intentional divine hardening is a conclusion reached only by a superficial reading of Isaiah.[87] Secondary causality is the culprit behind the deterministic language, a mediated causality barely acknowledged by the Hebrew mind,[88] where ultimate causality or purposiveness is a circumlocution for secondary human causality. Isaiah 6:9–10 forecasts a judgment by hardening motivated by love but brought about due to their persistence in sin. The stress in Mark is on the 'givenness' of the mystery not its exclusivity and that it must be 'received' by individuals.[89] The latter clause of Mark 4:12 (ἵνα) is *result* not *purpose.*[90] Hardening is really self-imposed and not prior to the rejection of Jesus' message.

This work gives evidence of keen insight[91] but is guided by the precepts of libertarian freedom. This perspective may lead to misidentifying the divine initiative in the revealing process both externally *and* internally.[92] His perspective of how one acquires

---

[86] Charles Allen Woodward, "The Place of Mark 4:10–12 in the Second Gospel" (Th.D. diss., New Orleans Baptist Theological Seminary, 1979).

[87] Ibid., 26–29.

[88] Ibid., 26.

[89] Ibid., 47. Later he defines this 'givenness' as *further explanation* to the disciples (ibid., 65). For a similar view of 'giving' = 'giving further explanation' see C. F. D. Moule, "Mark v, 1–20 Yet Once More," in *Neotestamentica et Semitica: Studies in Honour of Matthew Black*, ed. E. Earl Ellis and Max Wilcox (Edinburgh: Clark, 1969), 95–113.

[90] Woodward, "The Place of Mark 4:10–12 in the Second Gospel," 64, 77, 17–23.

[91] Like Hesse above he argues that the disciples hardness of heart refers to lack of perception rather than rebellion (ibid., 95–96). The Pharisees and disciples are 'hardened' in different ways (ibid., 107).

[92] An example of this confusion is his discussion on the acquisition of 'perception.' He says, "Perception was a gift that God granted through revelation. This gift was available *to those who were willing to have faith in Jesus*" (ibid., 60, emphasis added). This appears to be a case of getting the *fiduciary* cart before the *epistemological* horse. Woodward follows up by saying, "Everyone stands under the judgment of being an 'outsider,' but the miracle of comprehension is promised to all" (ibid., 63). But where is this promise? "An unlikely assertion is that he had a negative goal of obscuring the truth in 4:10–12. He came not to obscure but to communicate the truth" (ibid., 77). Three assumptions appear to contribute to his reasoning. First, he *equates* the

perception (συνίημι) is less than coherent.[93] He makes repentance the condition for perception, a view that finds its source in rabbinic literature,[94] and regeneration a prerequisite for the very effects he earlier indicates are prior to it.[95] Regeneration becomes unnecessary and equated with 'healing' that comes in response to repentance. But 'healing' is equal to 'forgiveness' not regeneration. Also, his view depends on a coordinate syntactic arrangement of ἵνα/μήποτε where the latter conjunction serves as the logical condition for the former. Neither point receives ample validation.

Some of his conclusions are puzzling. Jesus reportedly fails in his mission, namely, to bring everyone on the inside;[96] the unfruitful soils are not examples of outsider responses, but rather struggles in faith; and the reference to 'the many' (Mark 10:45) represent not only those who would accept him, but everyone else, including those who would never accept him.[97]

---

communication of truth to a select few with the purpose of obscuring it to others in such a way that the former obliterates the latter. Second, he views *intent* to communicate to some and the *intent* to harden others as incompatible notions. But these two notions work side by side when varying groups are among the audience. Third, he equates proving Jesus' words linguistically understandable to being noetically understood. Lack of clarity or obscurity is not the issue. The issue is *where* obscurity lies, in man (noetic) or in the parables (linguistic).

[93] Woodward says 'understanding' "is not native to man but is a gift of God" (ibid., 61). This seems reasonable until he notes that this 'understanding' actually comes by means of faith (ibid.). He espouses a 'blind' faith (pun intended) where one exercises faith in a message or person he does not yet perceive or understand. This understanding arises from a coordinate understanding of the syntax of ἵνα and μήποτε which may support the view that a full comprehension of Jesus' ministry is not possible until one repents (ibid., 73). For a similar opinion see J. R. Kirkland, "The Earliest Understanding of Jesus' Use of Parables: Mark IV 10–12 in Context," *NovT* 19 (1977): 7.

[94] Woodward, "The Place of Mark 4:10–12 in the Second Gospel," 90.

[95] Later he addresses the verb ἐπιστρέφω in terms of the ability of mankind (ibid., 63).

[96] Ibid., 101.

[97] Ibid., 84. Reference to 'the many' abounds in Qumran where the number is limited not unlimited (1QS 6:17–23, et al.).

Craig A. Evans.[98] Evans represents a watershed work on obduracy and the use of Isa 6:9–10.[99] He appreciates the employment of Jewish midrash, takes at face value the strong causality of the MT,[100] accepts the differences presented by subsequent tradition (Qumran, the LXX,

---

[98] Craig A. Evans, *To See and Not Perceive: Isaiah 6:9–10 in Early Jewish and Christian Interpretation*, JSOTSup, ed. David J. A. Clines and Philip R. Davies, vol. 64 (Sheffield: JSOT, 1989). This is an updated and revised edition of his earlier dissertation, "Isaiah 6:9–10 in Early Jewish and Christian Interpretation" (Ph.D. diss., Claremont Graduate School, 1983). This dissertation is preceded by a number of articles dealing with the same subject. Craig A. Evans, "A Note on the Function of Isaiah vi, 9–10 in Mark iv," *RB* 88 (1981): 234–35; idem, "The Function of Isaiah 6:9–10 in Mark and John," *NovT* 24 (1982): 124–28; idem, "The Text of Isaiah 6:9–10," *ZAW* 94 (1982): 415–18. After his dissertation and before his monograph, he continued to publish on the passage. See Craig A. Evans, "On the Isaianic Background of the Sower Parable," *CBQ* 47 (1985): 464–68; idem, "An Interpretation of Isa. 8:11–15 Unamended," *ZAW* 97 (1985): 112–13; idem, "On Isaiah's Use of Israel's Sacred Tradition," *BZ* 30 (1986): 92–99; idem, "Obduracy and the Lord's Servant: Some Observations on the Use of the Old Testament in the Fourth Gospel," in *Early Jewish and Christian Exegesis: Studies in Memory of William Hugh Brownlee*, ed. Craig A. Evans and William F. Stinespring, vol. 10 (Atlanta: Scholars Press, 1987), 221–36. Subsequent to the publication of his monograph in 1989, he wrote a dictionary article on hardening (Craig A. Evans, "Hardness of Heart," in *Dictionary of Jesus and the Gospels*, ed. Joel B. Green, Scot McKnight, and I. Howard Marshall [Downers Grove, IL: InterVarsity, 1992], 298–99). He continues to publish significantly not only in regard to Isaiah in particular, but NT hermeneutical issues and its use of the OT in general.

[99] The reviews of Evans' monograph are very positive overall with only minor dissension. Unmitigated praise of his monograph come from the following critics: Anthony T. Hanson, review of *To See and Not Perceive: Isaiah 6.9–10 in Early Jewish and Christian Interpretation*, by Craig A. Evans, *ExpTim* 101 (1989–90): 212; Mary Ann Beavis, review of *To See and Not Perceive: Isaiah 6.9–10 in Early Jewish and Christian Interpretation*, by Craig A. Evans, *JTS* 42 (1991): 264–66; Dan G. Johnson, review of *To See and Not Perceive: Isaiah 6.9–10 in Early Jewish and Christian Interpretation*, by Craig A. Evans, *CBQ* 53 (1991): 413–14.

[100] Some reviewers question the *causative* (Hiphil) element of the verbs that Evans sees in the MT. Heflin simply questions Evans' overall interpretation not its specifics (Boo Heflin, review of *To See and Not Perceive: Isaiah 6.9–10 in Early Jewish and Christian Interpretation*, by Craig A. Evans, *SJT* 34 [1992]: 37). Brower raises questions on whether God deliberately hardens the heart to accomplish his purposes (K. E. Brower, review of *To See and Not Perceive: Isaiah 6.9–10 in Early Jewish and Christian Interpretation*, by Craig A. Evans, *EvQ* 63 [1991]: 265). Foster proposes that the Hiphils in Isa 6:10 can be *permissive* rather than *causal* and therefore subsequent tradition merely brings out the true meaning (Barry M. Foster, "The Contribution of the Conclusion of Acts to the Understanding of Lucan Theology and the Determination of Lucan Purpose" [Ph.D. diss., Trinity International University, 1997], 229–30).

Targum, and Peshitta), attempts to reconcile these traditions, gives a comprehensive treatment of texts, and accomplishes this feat under the guiding principle that obduracy is the expression of God's sovereignty reinforced by strict monotheism in the midst of Israel's rebellion. He takes a decidedly non-libertarian view of freedom.

One weakness of Evans' work may be his insistence that the term 'mitigation' describes subsequent texts that are not as explicit as the MT. He sees them as threatening sovereignty and monotheism by denying divine ultimacy.[101] But this interpretation requires more than just differing texts with alternative renderings. It requires knowledge of the intent of the authors, proof that the resultant understanding of a particular text is reworked in order to deny that tenet of theism, and after other alternatives that seek to harmonize them are shown to be inadequate. Although he acknowledges that withholding the receptive heart is 'deprivation,'[102] he nevertheless does not treat or develop this insight any further.[103] This dissertation is indebted to his treatment and takes it the next step.

Mary Ann Beavis.[104] Beavis is not concerned with hardening, per se, but rather in establishing that the motifs in Mark 4:11–12 are not alien to the gospel but rather programmatic of various themes including perception, comprehension, and private teaching. She does this

---

[101] See H. G. M. Williamson, review of *To See and Not Perceive: Isaiah 6.9–10 in Early Jewish and Christian Interpretation*, by Craig A. Evans, *VT* 40 (1990): 509; Bruce Chilton, review of *To See and Not Perceive: Isaiah 6.9–10 in Early Jewish and Christian Interpretation*, by Craig A. Evans, *CRBR* (1991): 82.

[102] He says: "Ultimately such understanding could be had only if the Lord provided a mind (or 'heart') of understanding (compare 30.6). Without such a disposition, wonders and signs cannot be perceived correctly, as in the case of Pharaoh and, unfortunately, as in the subsequent history of Israel. Isa. 6.9–10 represents the other side of the same coin in that obduracy may also be explained as that which the Lord himself produces. *Thus, the deprivation of the receptive heart and the production of an obdurate heart can be thought of as one and the same process.* In either way of expressing this concept, the Lord is regarded as the ultimate agent or cause, either of receptivity or obduracy" (Evans, *To See and Not Perceive*, 51 emphasis added).

[103] To be fair to Evans, he alerts the reader as to the purpose of his study stating, "This book is interested in a particular text and the hermeneutic to which it gives expression. But it is not intended to be a study of the motif of obduracy" (ibid., 16).

[104] Mary Ann Beavis, *Mark's Audience: The Literary and Social Setting of Mark 4, 11–12*, JSOTSup, ed. David Hill and David E. Orton, vol. 33 (Sheffield: JSOT, 1989).

through reader-response criticism, or a literary and social-historical perspective, through the insights gleaned from literary criticism, rhetorical study, and sociological analysis.[105] Mark 4:11–12 is central to the evangelist's thought and the entire work is interpreted from a Graeco-Roman rhetorical perspective designed for public reading. The oral performances of such works have a sociological purpose of propaganda.[106] The χρία of 4:11–12 serves "like an oracle in a Greek play or novel" and "foretells how the narrative will develop; true understanding will dawn on the insiders, while to 'those outside' everything will remain in parables."[107] Thus the pattern established by Mark is not *sui generis*, teaching and preaching are synonymous, Jesus is an esoteric teacher, and Mark is not intended exclusively for Christians, but is propaganda for non-Christians.[108]

Although the similarity of Mark to ancient Greek tragedies is not entirely convincing, the anchoring of 4:11–12 to the Gospel by way of thematic connection in a programmatic way serves to counter arguments that this passage, taken in a purposive fashion, is alien or is somehow contrary to the rest of the Gospel.

Günter Röhser.[109] Röhser presents a revised thesis under the direction of K. Berger of the University of Heidelberg.[110] The work is divided

---

[105] Referred to as a 'literary and social-historical perspective' (Leslie Houlden, review of *Mark's Audience: The Literary and Social Setting of Mark 4.11–12*, by Mary Ann Beavis, *Theology* 93 [1990]: 481–82), a 'reader-response criticism' (Eugene V. Gallagher, review of *Mark's Audience: The Literary and Social Setting of Mark 4.11–12*, by Mary Ann Beavis, *CBQ* 53 [1991]: 692–93) and gleaned from insights from literary criticism, rhetorical study and sociological analysis (Hugh Anderson, review of *Mark's Audience: The Literary and Social Setting of Mark 4.11–12*, by Mary Ann Beavis, *JTS* 42 [1991]: 657–58). Cf. Jens-W. Taeger, review of *Mark's Audience: The Literary and Social Setting of Mark 4.11–12*, by Mary Ann Beavis, *TLZ* 116 (1991): 272–74.

[106] John Muddiman, review of *Mark's Audience: The Literary and Social Setting of Mark 4.11–12*, by Mary Ann Beavis, *ExpTim* 102 (1990–91): 278.

[107] Gallagher, review of *Mark's Audience*, 693.

[108] As summarized by Anderson, review of *Mark's Audience*, 658.

[109] Günter Röhser, *Prädestination und Verstockung: Untersuchungen zur frühjüdischen, paulinischen und johanneischen Theologie*, TANZ, ed. Klaus Berger et al., vol. 14 (Tübingen: Francke, 1994).

[110] Charles Grappe, review of *Prädestination und Verstockung*, by Günter Röhser, *RHPR* 77 (1997): 206.

into three parts. The first part addresses the debate in terms of the history of religions, including an examination of OT texts (Exod, Isa) and intertestamental literature (*Jub., 1–3 En., 1QH*).[111] He employs a spatial model (*Raum Modell*) in presenting the divine human working by depicting man in a play-ground (*Spielraum*) where the dominant conception is the intervention of God (*In-Wirken*). This *Spielraum* circumscribes a boundary to human freedom but maintains man's free-agency within it (*In-Wirken*).[112] The second part turns to a discussion of Pauline terminology where he subjects his 'spatial model' to passages like Phil 2:12b–13 and Rom 8:28–30.[113] He concludes (from Rom 9–11) that in Pauline theology, God actively carries some to faith, but negatively hardens others. Only some Israelites are predestined to be saved but the hardening of most of ethnic Israel includes a final salvific purpose. Finally, part three deals with John whom he conceives as concerned with the process of faith or non-faith and hardening that shows itself through one's works.[114] The priority involves both the divine initiative and revelation of God that is now represented by Jesus Christ. John and Paul, however, do not have identical views but represent two divergent streams from the same fount.

There are several distinctive features to this work. First, it's exegetical precision is noticeable. Second, there is not a great distinction made between divine hardening (*Verstockung*) and self-hardening (*Selbstverstockung*) or the sinfulness of man that resists God's goodness.[115] Although the implications are open to ambiguity, this does leave room to consider deprivation as a means of

---

[111] Röhser, *Prädestination und Verstockung*, 9–92. The intertestamental literature is especially supportive of a double-predestinarian point of view.

[112] The phrase 'In-Wirken' is used to "describe the idea of an arena enclosed by God's will, within which human action can still be described as free; here, human actors improvise on stage within the framework of a screen-play, written and directed by God" (James C. Hanges, review of *Prädestination und Verstockung*, by Günter Röhser, *CRBR* 9 [1996]: 262). "According to Röhser, Exod 3:8, 17–22 presents both perspectives with no indication of conscious paradox or redactional negligence" (ibid.).

[113] Röhser, *Prädestination und Verstockung*, 93–178.

[114] Ibid., 193–243.

[115] See David Flusser, review of *Prädestination und Verstockung*, by Günter Röhser, *JSJ* 26 (1995): 372–73.

hardening.[116] Third, he insists on a compatibilism[117] between God's determinism and human free-will, namely, that efficient causation or determinism is in no way incompatible with human freedom (of a non-libertarian sort).[118] Under this scheme he views man as acting without compulsion and at the same time holds to limitations of this freedom. Thus predestination and divine-hardening are viewed as compatible concepts with human responsibility and self-hardening.

Barry M. Foster.[119] Foster's dissertation is the most recent and extensive treatment of the use of Isa 6:9–10 in Acts 28:23–28. Positive features include thoughtful exegesis, special attention to the finer issues of verbal aspect, and taking μήποτε as 'lest' in the sense of 'otherwise' where it serves to explicate γάρ.[120] Criticisms of Foster's work arise from two factors: over emphasis on the corporate solidarity of Israel and his view (albeit unstated) of human *libertarian* freedom that rules out intentional hardening by God.

A major hermeneutical shift occurs in Acts 28 because he attributes to each a generic hardening even to those who salvifically believe in Paul's message.[121] While attempting to discover the constituency of the audience, the nature of their division, who leaves and why, and the relation to Paul's speech, he arrives at some

---

[116] Hanges, review of *Prädestination und Verstockung*, 26.

[117] Compatibilism "claims that determinism and free will can both be true. In other words, every event may have a cause and I am still free to make my own choices" (Pence, *A Dictionary of Common Philosophical Terms*, 10). The doctrine of compatibilism, therefore, is diametrically opposed to the doctrine of *libertarian* free-will or *contra-causal* freedom (see below). By definition the concepts of libertarian free-will and compatibilism are mutually exclusive.

[118] Hanges, review of *Prädestination und Verstockung*, 262.

[119] Foster, "The Contribution of the Conclusion of Acts."

[120] This is a legitimate view and one that will be support below with respect to the Synoptic usages (BDAG 648–49).

[121] Ibid., 168. He argues quite rightly that those who were persuaded by Paul were believers (ibid., 181–82). He bases this on four factors: (1) The οἱ μὲν... οἱ δέ construction makes an antithetical contrast between the two groups; (2) The verb πείθω stresses the outcome or result and is equivalent to 'belief' (cf. ἀπιστέω); (3) The imperfect tense of the verb is *customary* or *iterative*; and (4) The mixed responses (belief vs. unbelief) reaffirms a well established pattern in Acts (Foster, "The Contribution of the Conclusion of Acts," 181–85).

unlikely conclusions.[122] He argues that Paul quotes the Isaian passage to all the leaders because of unbelief, but it is clear that not all who leave are unbelievers as he himself acknowledges.[123] The result is that even *believing* Jews hear but do not understand, see but do not perceive, leaving a "portrait of a *corporate* figure representing Israel's *general* condition."[124] But how can believing Jews be *generally* without understanding or perception especially if salvific understanding is in view? There is little to suggest that believing Jews bear the brunt of Paul's rebuke.

The author argues that hardening is self-caused based on *prior action* rather than congenital and perpetual. He does this by rejecting ἐπαχύνθη as a divine passive in Acts 28:27.[125] Hardening is brought on *by one's own rebellion* resulting in a permanent (or not) removal (depletion) of one's sensitivities. Only in the case of rebellion is the heart "consequently been rendered insensitive, so that it is unresponsive."[126] He follows this up by labeling and linking the subordinate conjunction (γάρ) as the grounds to 28:26:c–d not 28:26b.[127] In other words, the γάρ ('for their heart is hardened') introduces the ground for the directive to the prophet to *quote* the passage (28:26a–b) not the reason accounting for *why* they do not understand or perceive (28:26c–d).[128] This is parallel to taking the

---

[122] Ibid., 186.

[123] Ibid., 193.

[124] Ibid., 211.

[125] Ibid. U. Becker, "Hard, Hardened," *NIDNTT* 2:153–56.

[126] Foster, "The Contribution of the Conclusion of Acts," 212.

[127] Ibid., 208–09.

[128] In Foster's view, γάρ modifies 'go' and 'say' rather than 'understand' and 'perceive.' He argues that both the initial command and the explanation represent words to the prophet alone and lie outside of the reported speech to the people. Even if Foster's syntactic argument is granted, it does not necessarily break the linkage between the hard-heart and lack of perception and understanding. Foster insists on *the text saying too little*, for in saying 'x' it is a given that he includes all that is said in 'x' for the following reason contained in the γάρ clause is given as the explanation for 'going' and 'saying' *what* he says. To maintain that γάρ modifies these previous verbs (or just the 'say' verb) while not including the *content* of direct speech, viz., the latter two verbs of the saying clause, is overly reductionistic. Thus it is virtually irrelevant whether the γάρ modifies one or the other pair of verbs here. But that Foster thinks his construal voids the relationship between the hard-heart as the cause of

ἵνα/μήποτε construction as coordinate rather than hypotactic. The purpose is to expand the recipients beyond a few.

Having reversed the hardening from causal (or *purpose*) to self-caused ('hardened as a *result*...') on the one end, he proceeds to disconnect the causal connection between the hard-heart and its effects on the other end. Grammatically, he seeks to sever the relation between the *effect* (lack of understanding or perception) and the *cause* (hard-heart). However, the clause may not be the ground for God ordering Isaiah *to say* what he says, but necessarily include and indicate *why* he says what he says assuring a causal relationship between hardening and incomprehension. God may not command Isaiah to inform the people as to the cause of their inability to comprehend but he does explain to Isaiah why they have an incomprehension problem, namely, *because* they have a fat-heart. Foster denies the causal linkage between the hard-heart and its effects, insists that that the message refers to all of Israel rather than just the rebellious, and maintains that hardening is reversible by human means.

Other less than persuasive views include arguing that 'difficulty in hearing' refers to hearing loss rather than deafness;[129] that closing of the eyes causes deliberate mental blindness rather than the reverse; insisting that both hearing/seeing difficulties are a result of previous action taken;[130] relating the verbs harden, hear, and close, in such a way as to deny a causal link and describing their relationship in terms of a "poetic description of Israel's unresponsiveness";[131] the idea that hardening is self-caused and takes place in stages;[132] and caricaturing an opposing view that 'repentance' is a turning away from being hardened rather than a turning away from unbelief.[133]

The original commission of Isaiah is also reevaluated. He argues that the Hiphils are really permissive rather than causal,[134] that

---

incomprehension is an example of *him saying too much*. The following μήποτε clause also seems to argue against his view.

[129] Foster, "The Contribution of the Conclusion of Acts," 212.

[130] Ibid., 212, 13.

[131] Ibid., 214, 22–24, 33 fn. 74.

[132] Ibid., 223 fn. 75.

[133] Ibid., 226.

[134] He cites Evans, *To See and Not Perceive*, 19 where Evans entertains the possibility

Isaiah's message of repentance is incompatible with an intent to harden,[135] that the presence of a non-hardened remnant refutes it,[136] and that the message does not command hardening to occur but merely predicts and confirms it.[137] Its function in Acts 28 shows "it is unlikely that he is here pronouncing the cessation of any efforts to win the Jews to the gospel" and "Luke is not making a theological judgment that all Jews henceforth are hardened and incapable of understanding the Gospel."[138] Belief is possible even to the hard-hearted and future reversal shows hardening is not permanent. But neither of these points are really in contention.

He also treats the issues of predestination and reprobation. Based on the view that the audience of hardening is everyone without distinction, he thereby denies its severity to individuals. He holds that extrapolating an individual emphasis is illegitimate because the passage addresses the entire nation and does not warrant a universal principle.[139] His guiding hermeneutic is that Paul has the entire nation, everyone in that nation, and only that nation in view.[140] But the counter-example in Rom 11 leans in the other direction—there

---

(albeit improbability) that the Hiphils may be permissive rather than causative according to Cohen (Abraham Cohen, "עשח, הכבר, השמן," *Bet Mikra* 50 (1972): 360–61). On the *permissive* Hiphil see Bruce K. Waltke and M. O'Connor, *An Introduction to Biblical Hebrew Syntax* (Winona Lake, IN: Eisenbrauns, 1990), §27.5.b. Three reasons might be given for rejecting the *permissive* Hiphil. First, the semantic situation dictates that the permission is not given by the object(s) to the causative agent but rather from the causative agent to the object(s). Thus it is difficult to see how the *permissive* Hiphil helps in any way the case for self-hardening. Second, the act is supposed to be (but not necessarily so) *agreeable* to the object but that seems even more unlikely. Third, it is more likely that these are *toleration* Hiphils where "the caused activity is welcome to the undersubject [Isaiah] but unacceptable or disagreeable to a third party ['this people']" (ibid., §27.5.c).

[135] Foster, "The Contribution of the Conclusion of Acts," 230.

[136] Ibid., 230–31.

[137] Ibid., 231.

[138] Ibid., 232.

[139] Ibid., 233.

[140] Even granting Foster's view that it only applies to the nation is illegitimate. According to Paul in Rom 9, election and reprobation precede the founding of the nation in the persons of Abraham and Isaac.

some ethnic Jews at the present time are not hardened.[141] Contra Foster, since election/reprobation does not apply universally to every Israelite, there is no reason why it must be restricted to that nation either. Thus his view of national election operates in such a way as to rule out individual election.

Because the message is to everyone, he argues, it necessarily follows that no one would be rendered capable of responding to a message intended to harden. Since some do respond, hardening is therefore neither an intent of God nor irresistible.[142] But did he not earlier insist that all of Israel (including believers) is hardened? How can the same individuals be hardened and not hardened at the same time? Romans 11 (esp. 11:25) teaches that Paul regards only a part of Israel as hardened while another part (remnant) as certainly not.[143] And this is ascertained by faith versus unbelief not ethnic consanguinity. He must either equivocate on hardening or have Paul contradict himself.

Foster operates from a libertarian perspective. He points to culpability verses to sustain his view that it is incompatible with intentional hardening and that genuine responsibility necessarily rules out any strong divine causality view.[144] But Foster makes Acts say too much and ignores other strong divine causality texts that include notions of culpability arguing *prima facie* for their compatibilism.[145] Compatibilism is the opposite of *libertarian* or *contra-causal* freedom.[146] He dismisses reprobation as unlikely.[147]

---

[141] Rom 11:1–10 is a passage that indirectly derives from Isa 6:9–10 via Isa 29:10.

[142] Foster, "The Contribution of the Conclusion of Acts," 234.

[143] The debate is how to syntactically construe the phrase ἀπὸ μέρους…γέγονεν in Rom 11:25 as either modifying πώρωσις ('partial hardening' on all of Israel including the remnant) or τῷ Ἰσραήλ ('part of Israel' excluding the remnant). For a discussion see Charles H. Cosgrove, *Elusive Israel: The Puzzle of Election in Romans* (Louisville, KY: Westminster, 1997), 16–17.

[144] Foster, "The Contribution of the Conclusion of Acts," 234–35. For various views on the supposed incompatibility of these issues see James K. Beilby and Paul R. Eddy, *Divine Foreknowledge: Four Views* (Downers Grove, IL: InterVarsity, 2001).

[145] See Evans, *To See and Not Perceive*, 120–23 for a helpful summary of this idea.

[146] Compatibilism means human choices are always (1) made in conformity to what one *wants* to do (free and unforced) but (2) in *accordance* with the will's strongest inclination at the moment of choice (causal determinism). See chapter 2.

[147] Foster, "The Contribution of the Conclusion of Acts," 234.

Foster's dissertation bears signs of a careful exegesis. However he relies too heavily on an incompatibilist view of freedom and a strictly corporate understanding of Israel to the exclusion of individual election/reprobation.

Timothy J. Scannell.[148] Scannell defends a tripartite division (signs/glory) of John's gospel that undermines the view that signs refer only to the first part of the book.[149] He argues that a detailed examination of 12:37–50 shows a two-fold function as a link between two types of signs and as a conclusion to Jesus' public teaching.[150] He adds that a major link between Jesus' signs and the sign he became is a thematic one.[151] His tripartite division does not greatly affect the nature of his exegesis.[152]

Signs fail in their purpose (faith in Jesus) due to some fault in man not the sign.[153] That signs are intended to garner faith is doubtful as Scannell concedes.[154] He omits any reference to the divine initiative like the certainty of Scripture fulfillment in terms of reprobation (13:18) or election (18:9), the 'arm of the Lord' quotation in reference to the external signs performed rather than the internal working of the Spirit, and the apparent *fait accompli* aspect of the revealing process. He acknowledges that God's hardening makes them incapable of repentance and this in fulfillment of Scripture.[155] But

---

[148] Timothy J. Scannell, "Fulfillment of Johannine Signs: A Study of John 12:37–50" (Ph.D. diss., Fordham University, 1998).

[149] Ibid., 63.

[150] Ibid., 52.

[151] Ibid., 64.

[152] It should not be overlooked that the word 'sign' appears seventeen times in this Gospel (2:11, 18, 23; 3:2; 4:48, 54; 6:2, 14, 26, 30; 7:31; 9:16; 10:41; 11:47; 12:18, 37; 20:30) and only once outside chaps. 1–12. Ladd says, "That this is a deliberate selection from the many miracles is clear from the fact that John asserts that Jesus did many other signs (20:30; 2:23; 11:47; 12:37)" (George Eldon Ladd, *A Theology of the New Testament*, ed. Donald A. Hagner, rev. ed. (Grand Rapids: Eerdmans, 1993), 309).

[153] Scannell, "Fulfillment of Johannine Signs," 72.

[154] Ladd, *A Theology of the New Testament*, 310; Scannell, "Fulfillment of Johannine Signs," 54–55.

[155] Scannell, "Fulfillment of Johannine Signs," 78. Earlier he says, "John concludes, in light of these two Isaian texts, that people did not believe in Jesus as a consequent of

Scannell's appraisal treats the inability theme as an altogether *new* phenomenon in 12:37–40 rather than a consistent theme throughout John.

In place of the human inability theme, Scannell substitutes three other culprits including the devil, a lack of the vision of God's glory, and a desire for human glory.[156] Although he concedes God as the ultimate cause of hardening, he prefers to place the devil as its proximate cause.[157] The problem here is that nowhere is this stated and it is much more likely (as with most commentators) that it is the Father. Tension between the Father and Son is not counterevidence.[158] Second, passages he adduces to show Satan is the hardener (6:64, 70, 71; 12:31–33; 13:2, 27; 14:30; 16:11; 18:2; 19:11; 1 John 2:11; 2 Cor 4:4) may only indicate his control of those who are already hard-hearted, not that he aids in bringing it about.[159] Third, his analysis skips over John 9:35–41 that links human blindness to a *congenital* condition not Satanic influence. Fourth, he argues for a transformative view of hardening and necessitates it by interjecting an intermediate agency.[160] Various themes throughout John (darkness) serve to reinforce a congenital defect of mankind.[161] For these reasons it seems

---

his signs because they could not, in fact, believe" (ibid., 69).

[156] Ibid., 94–108, 108–22, and 122–28.

[157] Ibid., 104.

[158] He dismisses the tension that hardening and healing introduce in the Godhead and thus interjects the Devil in its place (ibid., 96).

[159] With respect to 2 Cor 4:4, it is unclear whether the reference is God rather than the devil. It is one of the passages that alludes to Isa 6:9–10 and as such argues in favor of God as the agent.

[160] Scannell, "Fulfillment of Johannine Signs," 108.

[161] Night (νύξ) is used six times in John's gospel, four of which have spiritual implications (3:2; 11:10; 13:30; 19:39). Darkness (σκότος) occurs once (3:19) and another word for darkness (σκοτία) occurs six times, of which four are certainly linked to a spiritual reality (1:5; 8:12; 12:35, 46). Other concepts related to seeing (βλέπω, εἶδον, θεωρέω, ὁράω) occur frequently as well such as the *inability* to see/understand (1:18; 3:3; 5:37; 6:46; 9:1, 21, 41; 12:40; 14:17), *futility* in what is merely physically seen/understood (2:23; 4:48; 6:2, 26, 30, 36; 7:3, 52; 9:8, 15, 19, 21, 25, 39; 10:12; 12:9; 14:19; 15:24; 16:10, 17, 19; 20:5, 6, 12, 14, 18, 25, 29), and *salvific* seeing/understanding or something greater than mere physical sight (1:34, 50, 51; 3:11, 32, 36; 4:23, 45; 6:40, 62; 8:38, 51, 56, 57; 9:7, 15, 19, 21, 25, 37; 11:9, 40; 12:21, 41, 45; 14:7, 9; 16:16, 17, 19, 22; 17:24; 19:35, 37; 20:8, 20; 25, 27, 29; 21:20). This is without consideration of other verbs that are close synonyms such as νοέω or γινώσκω. John

less feasible to lay blame for man's hard-heartedness at the hoofs of the Devil.

His second substitute for the inability theme is the lack of the vision of God's glory. The identity of this defect as 'the insight of faith' and its linkage to regeneration in John 3, which points to the inability of man to 'see the kingdom of God,' is helpful.[162] But Scannell (a Roman Catholic) finds the solution in the sacraments of baptism (John 3) and the Eucharist (John 6). These are the dual means whereby 'insight' is bestowed and blindness is overcome. Whether these defects are innate (congenital) or a product of retribution he does not say.

His final substitute for the inability theme is the desire for human glory. "This preference for the 'glory of men' made them incapable of believing."[163] This is the closest he gets to the Johannine inability theme. He notes that man has no love for God in him (5:42), prefers darkness (3:19), and therefore argues that God's role in shutting the eyes (9:29–33) is a just *punishment* for those who love darkness rather than the light (9:39). But are not these descriptions better depicted as a work of *deprivation* on God's part that harmonize with a congenital blindness and hard-heartedness? An alternative is to view God's act of 'blinding' as a further deprivation of seeing eyes. In John, God deprives by *not regenerating*, an act that would take away the stony heart, enlighten the eyes, enable the recipient to see the kingdom of God, and impart affection for God's glory.

Other assertions made by Scannell indicate that he does not quite capture the full essence of the Isaian allusion. He argues, for example, that the explanation of 12:40 is meant to account for their unbelief rather than the inability to believe.[164] Moreover, he reads into the omission of 'deaf ears' in 12:40 an ability of man to still hear.[165] The

---

uses darkness and synonyms both in an *ethical* (they walk in darkness) and *ontological* sense (as unregenerate). Function *necessarily* follows ontology.

[162] Scannell, "Fulfillment of Johannine Signs," 111.

[163] Ibid., 123.

[164] Ibid., 66–67.

[165] Ibid. But this is reading too much into the account. First, it weakens the connection between the mutual and concurrent effects of the hard-heart, viz., blindness and deafness. Second, the reference to 'hearing' has already been alluded to in 12:38 (Isa 53:1) and is associated with the internal activity of God revealing to particular recipients. Thus the implicit Isaian theme of 'hearing they hear not and seeing they

exact nature of the hard-heart, namely, whether this state is congenital or a result of judgment is never fully explored. Scannell does have some movement in the direction of the former.

Volker A. Lehnert.[166] Lehnert defends a pragmatic approach to the use of Isa 6:9–10 in the NT, specifically in regard to Mark (4:10–13) and Luke (Luke 8:9–10; Acts 28:25–27). He attempts to answer three questions. "Wieso lässt Markus Jesus seine Gleichnisse mit dem Ziel der Unverständlichkeit verkünden? Warum positioniert Lukas dieses Wort ans Ende seines Doppelwerkes und überlässt dann ganz plötzlich den Leser sich selbst? Welche Absicht verfolgt er damit?"[167] A pragmatic purpose lies behind the paradoxical strategy of the difficult texts where the paradox itself is not only designed to provoke and persuade Israel to repentance but also a reader response.[168]

Lehnert's work can be grouped into four parts.[169] The first part reviews major works on hardening.[170] The second part examines the

---

see not' permeates the passage. Third, the numerous occurrences of ἀκούω (fifty-nine times) in John, and the explicit claim that only the sheep hear his voice (10:3, 8, 16, 20, 27) hardly lends credence to Scannell's assumption that its absence here argues for the latent ability to still hear. Finally, the omission of 'ears' is probably because 'eyes' serve a literary purpose that 'ears' would not in pointing back to the story of the blind man (John 9). It is unlikely, then, that the omission is designed to engender hope for man's potential in hearing the words of Jesus. Scannell admits this much, but makes unwarranted use of the argument from silence (ibid., 89).

[166] Volker A. Lehnert, *Die Provakation Israels: die paradoxe Funktion von Jes 6,9–10 bei Markus und Lukas: ein textpragmatischer Versuch im Kontext gegenwartiger Rezeptionsasthetik und Lesetheorie*, NDH, vol. 25 (Neukirchen-Vluyn: Neikirchener, 1999).

[167] Ibid., iv.

[168] Ibid., 1–3. In this regard he focuses on four dimensions of inquiry including the *actual*, the *methodological*, the *theological*, and the *homiletical*. He asks, "Deinen sie der Ankündigung des Gerichtes Gottes oder zur Warnung und damit potentiel zur Verhinderung seines Vollzuges" (ibid., 2)?

[169] His monograph consists of seven major chapters not including the introduction and conclusion. The division here is based on his content and method of approach to the passages at hand.

[170] He reviews the following: K. L. Schmidt, Franz Hesse, Joachim Gnilka, Heikki Räisänen, Craig A. Evans, Roman Kühschelm, Günter Röhser, and Robert B. Chisholm Jr. (Lehnert, *Die Provakation Israels*, 4–10).

exegetical problems associated with Isa 6:9–10 and NT usage along with their history of interpretation.[171] The third part sets forth his major contribution (two chapters) articulating his method for re-examining these texts.[172] The fourth and final part is the application of this approach to these texts.[173] The strength of this study lies in the pragmatic purpose whether the texts serve literally to harden (Westermann), judge (Kilian), are final, retrospective, consecutive, serve to prevent conversion (Evans), signify the end to Jewish election (Gnilka), or address anti-Judaistic tendencies (Haacker). However they are understood exegetically, their pragmatic purpose is to inspire repentance, especially among Jews.

This study is an example of taking the purposive speech of Isaiah and its reuses literally while adding a pragmatic design without mitigating the former and in this regard is unique.

Summary of Works

Two studies do not distinguish between Exod 4–14 and Isaianic hardening (e.g., Schmidt, Hesse). Many (if not all) regard hardening as judicial in some respect (e.g., Schmidt, Hesse, Myers, Gnilka, Foster) and as transformative in a *depletive* sense (e.g., Hesse, Foster) but different when the disciples are in view (e.g., Schmidt, Gnilka). Only one author hints that hardening is an act of divine deprivation (Evans). The hard-heart is either incapable of repentance (e.g., Hesse, Scannell) and perception (Hesse) or still capable of repentance (e.g., Räisänen, Foster). Much of the latter is driven by a *libertarian* view of freedom (e.g., Räisänen, Myers, Woodward, Foster). Several authors accept the purposive sense to the passages (e.g., Evans, Beavis, Röhser, Lehnert) while recognizing that subsequent texts depart from the Hebrew of Isa 6:9–10 (e.g., Hesse, Gnilka, Evans). Most think parables are meant to be understood (e.g., Myers, Gnilka, Räisänen) although the text as it stands in Mark seems to teach the opposite according to some (e.g., Räisänen, Woodward). Lack of understanding is due either to the absence of revelation or explanation (e.g., Myers, Gnilka) and implies that obscurity lies in the mode of communication rather than in man himself. Although most

---

[171] Ibid., 11–48.

[172] Ibid., 49–84, 85–101.

[173] Ibid., 102–272.

allude to the wisdom tradition (e.g., Schmidt, Hesse, Bailey, Myers, Gnilka, Woodward, Beavis, Scannell), none make much of the connection.

Major Alternative Schemes of Isa 6:9–10 and NT Passages

In distinction to the major *works* are several *ways* of approaching Isa 6:9–10 and its parallels. Here alternative views that take this passage as less than literal will be considered. Because the 'softer' texts are deemed better representatives of the true intent of Isaiah's 'harder' texts, the issue centers on how and to what degree the weaker texts modify the harder texts. Major alternatives include irony, effect-purpose idiom, psychological, higher critical, and a combination of alternatives. This is not to suggest that all purposive views are uniform.

The Irony View

Irony is meant to convey the opposite of its surface structure.[174] The two main reasons for invoking irony include the absurdity of the reading and the so-called 'mitigating' texts. The latter (non-ironic texts) reportedly preserve the deep structure meaning of the ironic (hard) passages.

Bruce Hollenbach.[175] Hollenbach takes the phrase in Isa 6:10, "lest they should turn and be healed" (and pars.) as ironic. He uses three

---

[174] Irony is defined as, "1. a figure of speech in which the literal meaning of a locution is the opposite of that intended, esp., as in the Greek sense when the locution understates the effect intended. 2. an utterance or the use of words to express a meaning which is different from, and often the direct opposite of, the literal meaning. 3. *Lit.* a. a technique of indicating, as through character or plot development, and intention or attitude opposite to that which is actually or ostensibly stated. b. (esp. in contemporary writing) a manner of organizing a work so as to give full expression to contradictory or complementary impulses, attitudes, etc., esp. as a means of indicating detachment from a subject, theme, or emotion. 4. See Socratic irony. 5. See dramatic irony. 6. an outcome of events contrary to what was, or might have been, expected. 7. the incongruity of this. 8. an objectively sardonic style of speech or writing. 9. an objectively or humorously sardonic utterance, disposition, quality, etc." (*Webster's Encyclopedic Unabridged Dictionary of the English Language*, [New York: Portland House, 1989], 752–53).

[175] Bruce Hollenbach, "Lest They Should Turn and Be Forgiven: Irony," *BT* 34 (1983): 312–21.

criteria ("conditions") for detecting and inferring irony when explicit literary features are absent.[176] First, the statement is contrary to the speaker's point of view. Second, its aim is ridiculing an audience. Finally, the surface structure represents the audience's view. In Isa 6:9–10, God really desires the people of Judah to see, hear, and understand, although they do not want to, and they are scorned because of this attitude.[177] The LXX, Matt 13:15, and Acts 28:27 support this interpretation overturning the ironic passages preserved by the MT (and Mark). Though less colorful, these non-purposive texts present what the original ironical meaning of the Hebrew text picturesquely obscures.[178] Passages like Matt 13:15 and Acts 28:27 are non-ironic because they emphasize man's condition not God's intention while Mark 4:12 and John 12:40 are ironic.

Because there is a subjectivity involved in the process of detecting irony, irony itself should not therefore serve as a guiding hermeneutic. The proposed grid is useful only for *depicting* irony when it is known to be there but not effective as criteria for *determining* the presence of irony.[179] Applying his criteria regarding reported speech does not fit here. Underlying this view is an implied disjunction that prevents a resolution of both types of text. The view is not arrived at or tested exegetically (re-uses of Isaiah) but merely assumed from the start along with a particular view of hardening (self-hardening). He also argues for a retributive and transformative

---

[176] The desire to appeal to irony, he says, is because "the notion that God purposes that they not see, hear, understand, turn, and be healed approaches absurdity...*Such absurdity is the only clue to the presence of the figure of speech called irony*" (ibid., 313 emphasis added).

[177] Ibid., 316.

[178] The view is held by Alexander and Gould (Joseph A. Alexander, *The Gospel according to Matthew Explained* [London: Nisbet, 1861; reprint, Lynchburg, VA: James, 1979], 358; Ezra P. Gould, *Critical and Exegetical Commentary on the Gospel according to Mark* [Edinburgh: Clark, 1896; reprint, New York: Scribner's, 1913], 73).

[179] On Mark 4:12 and John 12:40 he says, "The biggest problem is that the translator must either leave the irony implicit, running a high risk that it will go unperceived, or else spell it out precisely what it is saying in non-figurative fashion, which will yield a strong divergence between the form of the source text and the form of the translation" (Hollenbach, "Lest They Should Turn and Be Forgiven: Irony," 319). He notes that even commentators have stumbled here and that no commentary he examined perceives the irony he regards as self-evident (ibid., 319 fn. 8).

hardening in the sense of *depletion* (of comprehension).[180] Subtraction of wisdom runs counter to the prior inability to comprehend. The evidence suggests favoring the notion that unbelievers are naturally without saving comprehension rather than possessed and then disinherited of it.

Robert B. Chisholm Jr.[181] Chisholm deals primarily with the hardening of Pharaoh but the last five pages turn to Isa 6:9–10 and 63:17. Only slight distinctions are made between Pharaonic hardening and Isaianic fattening. Its ingenuity lies in its attention to the grammar, sensitivity to rhetoric, detection of the hardening cycles of Pharaoh, and assessment of Isaianic fattening as "militant irony."[182] Several reservations, however, may be identified.

First, *direct* versus *indirect* hardening seems overly restrictive. 'Direct' hardening is where God supernaturally *overrides* the human will while 'indirect' utilizes intermediate causes to 'harden' the object.[183] Both presume a *transformation* is involved. But could hardening be indirect and non-transformational? The statement that Yahweh's hardening *"forced* Pharaoh to act in accord with his deep-seated nature"[184] implies coercion. "An initial act of refusal precluded repentance later on. Any move toward repentance was aborted by God."[185] But this seems to further complicate issues about God's fairness.

Second, he argues that hardening is only non-arbitrary if retributive. Direct hardening is not *arbitrary* because it is "in response to rejection of God's authoritative word or standards."[186] He says, "As

---

[180] Ibid., 318.

[181] Robert B. Chisholm, "Divine Hardening in The Old Testament," *BSac* 153 (1996): 410–34.

[182] Ibid., 430.

[183] Ibid., 411. In a footnote against Kaiser's (and Driver's) view that God only hardened in response to Pharaoh's self-hardening, he notes that Kaiser "overlooks the important fact that the narrative suggests that Pharaoh would have relented *against his basic nature*, if God had not hardened him" (ibid., 413 fn. 5 emphasis added).

[184] Ibid., 429 emphasis added.

[185] Ibid., 429.

[186] Ibid., 434.

in the case of Pharaoh, Yahweh's hardening was not arbitrarily imposed on a righteous or even morally neutral object. Rather, His hardening was an element of His righteous judgment on recalcitrant sinners."[187] But is not everyone a recalcitrant sinner to some degree? However, he may be speaking only in functional categories. Again, "Yahweh's hardening of Israel through Isaiah came in *response* to their covenantal rebellion" and it "comes in *response* to rejection of God's authoritative word or standards."[188] But does not the OT reverse this cause and effect pattern? Is it not the hard-heart that produces covenant rebellion rather than covenant rebellion the hard-heart (Deut 5:29; 29:3)?[189] Yahweh, he argues, *inaugurates* hardening not Pharaoh but Pharaoh *initiates* it by his rejection of the divine commands. Does this mean that Yahweh makes him *more* rebellious because he *continues* to act rebellious?

Third, the threefold categorizing of those as recalcitrant, righteous, and neutral where only the recalcitrant are hardened seems to go beyond the textual data. "As in 5:2, the author stated that Yahweh was not dealing with a morally righteous or neutral individual, but a proud enemy who thought nothing of trifling with the sovereign God."[190] Does this mean that Pharaoh did not have a hard-heart prior to hardening? Who is it that qualifies as 'neutral'? How can a neutral heart (or person) act, become recalcitrant, be subject to hardening, or be righteous? The categories seem artificial and optimistic of mankind, though he may have in mind only a functional appraisal.[191] Hardening in general seems to fall under the rubric of transformation and retribution rather than deprivation.

Fourth, he adopts an oscillation view of hardening. Pharaoh progresses from non-hard-hearted to hard-hearted, reverts back to non-hard-hearted, and must be re-hardened.[192] "If hardening were like a switch turned on and left on, this repetition of the transitive

---

[187] Ibid., 432.

[188] Ibid., 433–34 emphasis added.

[189] For comments on the meaning of Deut 5:29, especially the phrase מִי־יִתֵּן see chapter 3.

[190] Chisholm, "Divine Hardening in The Old Testament," 423.

[191] Gen 6:5 and 8:21 show the root of the problem (see chapter 3).

[192] Chisholm, "Divine Hardening in The Old Testament," 416.

verb would be unnecessary and confusing. It is better to conclude that Pharaoh returned to a 'neutral' or autonomous position at the beginning of each new plague pericope, with the possible exception of the passages noted above."[193] But does *transitive* necessarily entail an act of *transformation*, or to avoid redundancy, *oscillation*? Indeed, what is the mechanism of oscillation? Oscillation requires Pharaoh to be non-hard prior to 'hardening' and non-hard in-between statements of divine hardening.[194] Hardening is thus by *transformation* (direct or indirect).

Fifth, libertarian freedom is assumed.[195] In arguing against Fretheim's open theism but in favor of libertarianism, Chisholm indicates, "Yahweh's offer was legitimate because Pharaoh was autonomous at those points."[196] When divine hardening is not mentioned, Chisholm reasons, "Pharaoh was acting autonomously (as in 5:2)."[197] In another footnote he agrees with Fretheim's libertarianism because an ultimatum assumes the possibility of fulfillment for it to be a genuine choice. If hardening is continuous, he argues, then "the ultimatum here and in later verses are

---

[193] Ibid., 420 fn 31.

[194] For a similar view see Pelagius *Dem.* Cf. Philip Schaff, *History of the Christian Church*, vol. 3 (New York: Scribner, 1867; reprint, Grand Rapids: Eerdmans, 1952–53), 803–04; Cornelis Augustijn, *Erasmus: His Life, Works, and Influence*, trans. J. C. Grayson (Toronto: University of Toronto Press, 1995), 141. Openness theologians also hold that God can override libertarian free-will in the case of hardening the heart (Gregory A. Boyd, *The God of the Possible: A Biblical Introduction to the Open View of God* [Grand Rapids: Baker, 2000], 38). This is one of those strange inconsistencies of libertarian freedom.

[195] An accepted definition of libertarian freedom is provided by Thomas P. Flint, "Two Accounts of Providence," in *Divine and Human Action: Essays in the Metaphysics of Theism*, ed. Thomas V. Morris (Ithica, NY: Cornell University Press, 1988), 175. "Necessarily, for any human agent S, action A and time *t*, if S performs A freely at *t*, then the history of the world prior to *t*, the laws of nature, and the actions of any other agent (including God) prior to and at *t* are jointly compatible with S's refraining from performing A freely." It is usually summarized in quips like 'freedom-to-the-contrary,' 'power to the contrary choice,' 'the liberty of indifference,' or 'contra-causal freedom.' See the statement of Chrysostom *Hom. Matt.* 45. See John Martin Fischer, *The Metaphysics of Free Will: An Essay on Control*, Aristotelian Society Series, ed. Martin Davies, vol. 14 (Cambridge, MA: Blackwell, 1994).

[196] Chisholm, "Divine Hardening in The Old Testament," 413 fn. 11.

[197] Ibid., 420.

disingenuous."[198] But must genuine responsibility be predicated on the ability to perform what is required?[199]

Sixth, Isaianic fattening is said to be indirect and retributional. Chisholm says these verses are "militant irony."[200] "The imperatives and jussives are employed rhetorically in anticipation of the response Isaiah would receive."[201] He also acknowledges that the insensitivity of "the people are bent on that anyway."[202] Indeed, "the people were hardly ready or willing to repent. Therefore, Isaiah's preaching was not needed to prevent repentance!"[203] But does this not imply that they were fat-hearted before fattening? No attempt is made to reconcile this already state to the command to fatten. Instead the ability to repent is taken away.

Chisholm links Isaianic hardening as a response by Yahweh to covenant rebellion.[204] But where is this view articulated in the Mosaic covenant? Hardening (or fattening) in Isa 63:17 is nevertheless an "idiom of lament" that is "sometimes ironic and hyperbolically deterministic."[205] Even though it is more explicitly divinely caused, it

---

[198] Ibid., 420 fn. 31. Although Chisholm does not technically promote libertarian freedom, he does assume it.

[199] For an assessment of libertarian freedom from a compatibilist perspective see John M. Frame, *No Other God: A Response to Open Theism* (Philipsburg, NJ: Presbyterian & Reformed, 2001), 119–42; Stephen Varvis, *The "Consolation" of Boethius: An Analytical Inquiry into His Intellectual Processes and Goals*, vol. 16, Distinguished Dissertation Series (San Francisco: Mellen, 1991), 3.

[200] Chisholm, "Divine Hardening in The Old Testament," 430–31. Chisholm uses a plethora of terms to drive this home. He calls verse 9 "clearly ironic" (ibid., 431), "ironic words" (ibid.), verse 10 as "clearly sarcastic" (ibid.), a "sarcastic statement" (ibid.), "sarcastic statement" (ibid., 432), an "emphatic way" of making something clear (ibid.), verses 9–10 as a "sarcastic framework" (ibid.) and verse 10 as "ironic" (ibid.), verse 9 as "rhetorical" (ibid.), verses 9–10 together as an "indirect act of divine hardening" (ibid.), "not arbitrarily imposed" (ibid.), "ironically" (ibid.), and "ironically" (ibid., 433). Isa 63:17 is a lament that is "ironic and hyperbolically deterministic" (ibid.), really "more indirect" than even 6:9–10 where "the speaker saw it as one of the effects of rebellion against Yahweh" (ibid.).

[201] Ibid., 431.

[202] Ibid.

[203] Ibid.

[204] Ibid., 433.

[205] Ibid.

is still *"more* indirect" (than Isa 6:9–10), if it refers to the effects of captivity, where the "speaker saw it as one of the effects of rebellion against Yahweh."[206] It seems more likely that rebellion and captivity are better construed as effects of rather than the cause for the fat-heart.

The Effect-Purpose Idiom View

This view appeals to Hebrew thinking especially as it relates to causality and intentionality.[207] The effect-purpose idiom refers to an effect written as if it were an intended purpose when the effect actually precedes purpose.[208] There is a move from ultimate causality to self-hardening.

Edmund F. Sutcliffe.[209] The effect-purpose idiom expresses an effect caused by the human agent but foreseen by divine foreknowledge and therefore written as purpose.[210] Purpose logically follows result (conduct) rather than result (conduct) is caused by purpose.[211]

---

[206] Ibid., 433 emphasis added.

[207] Others holding this view (or a very similar one) include Räisänen, *The Idea of Divine Hardening*, 47; Woodward, "The Place of Mark 4:10–12 in the Second Gospel," 26; Foster, "The Contribution of the Conclusion of Acts," 229–30, who earlier calls the strong causal language a *"poetic* description of Israel's unresponsiveness" (ibid., 214 emphasis added); Bastiaan van Elderen, "The Purpose of the Parables according to Matthew," in *New Dimensions in New Testament Study*, ed. Richard N. Longenecker and Merrell C. Tenney (Grand Rapids: Zondervan, 1974), 189–90 calls the parallelism of Matthew, Mark, and Luke, a Semitism, where Matthew's ὅτι clause preserves the words of Jesus describing a present state contrary to a purpose statement in Mark; Krister Stendahl, "The Called and the Chosen. An Essay on Election," in *The Root of the Vine: Essays in Biblical Theology*, ed. Anton Fridrischson (New York: Philosophical Library, 1953), 65 indicates that "the frame of New Testament ideas in a philosophy of finality, not one of causality." Cf. Scannell, "Fulfillment of Johannine Signs," 76.

[208] François Bovon, *Luke 1: A Commentary on the Gospel of Luke 1:1–9:50*, ed. Helmut Koester, trans. Christine M. Thomas, Hermeneia—A Critical and Historical Commentary on the Bible, ed. Helmut Koester et al. (Minneapolis: Fortress, 2002), 312.

[209] Edmund F. Sutcliffe, "Effect as Purpose: A Study in Hebrew Thought Patterns," *Bib* 35 (1954): 320–27.

[210] Ibid., 320. Cf. Gnilka, *Die Verstockung Israels*, 46.

[211] Sutcliffe, "Effect as Purpose," 320.

Applied to the hardening of Pharaoh, it means that Pharaoh hardened himself even when divine hardening is the *prima facie* reading. Appeals to Pharaoh illustrate that "man is a free agent, responsible for his own actions" and the "supreme gift of free will."[212] Responsibility is thereby maintained. Isaiah 6:9–10 means that "the failure of the mission was foreseen, and the outcome to which it would lead is spoken of as its purpose."[213] With Pharaoh the "attribution to God…did not mislead the ancient Hebrews as they understood clearly that Pharaoh hardened his own heart and was himself responsible."[214]

Determinism does not erode responsibility as this view indicates. In addition, this view depends on a view of foreknowledge that is wholly contingent on human acts. God *(fore)knowingly determines* (foreknowledge view) rather than *determinately (fore)knows* (Augustine-Calvinist view).[215] On the contrary, in a theistic worldview, God knows all contingencies (what will happen) and counterfactuals (what could happen), but knows nothing contingently. The effect-purpose idiom is partly driven by a particular view of human freedom (libertarian) rather than fidelity to Hebrew thinking. The problem with this argument is that it may equally go the opposite way.

C. F. D. Moule.[216] Moule says Mark 4:12 involves a purpose clause but only non-literally as a "vigorous and hyperbolic description of its

---

[212] Ibid., 321–22.

[213] Ibid., 322. He adds other texts supporting this idiom including OT (Pss 33:10–11; 16–17; 127:1; Prov 16:1; 19:21) and NT texts (Matt 13:13; Mark 4:12; Luke 8:10; Rom 9:18).

[214] Ibid., 326.

[215] Norman L. Geisler employs the Boethian view of time with a vengeance. "God *determinately* knows and *knowingly* determines what we are freely deciding" (Norman Geisler, "God Knows All Things," in *Predestination & Free Will*, ed. David Basinger and Randall Basinger [Downers Grove, IL: InterVarsity, 1986], 73). This view is in keeping with God's simplicity. Contra Geisler, simplicity (non-composedness) refers to the indivisibility of God's *being* not his *acts* (including the *logical* ordering of his decree). So his alternative is a category mistake and an evasion of the question (ibid., 85–8; cf. Aquinas *Sum. Theol.* 1.3).

[216] Moule, "Mark v, 1–20 Yet Once More," 95–113.

conditions."[217] While the saying explains the functional status of outsiders not the purpose of parables, its harshness is a product of the Hebrew mentality.[218] The text is not prescriptive or determinative, but descriptive of what frequently accompanies the preaching of Jesus. The parables are not enigmatic, do not "positively harden,"[219] and are not related to predestination. The phrase "in parables" is shorthand for "in parables *without interpretation*."[220] 'Insiders' and 'outsiders' are *functional* depictions of the individual in regard to further inquiry not *ontological* status. Proof, says Moule, is that 'hardening' is applied to Jesus' own disciples in Mark 8:17, 21.[221] The 'giving' is more information to inquiring minds.[222] Transformational hardening "[is] a pitifully literal reading of Isaiah 6."[223] Parables do not obscure truth but rather illuminate it while functioning on the level of a political cartoon.[224] Parables, as an obscuring agent, find no precedent in Jewish literature. Failure is due to the soil not the seed.[225]

There is much that is agreeable to Moule's study but some statements require comment. First, describing the purposive grammar as a vigorous and hyperbolic description of its conditions is

---

[217] Ibid., 100. Marshall follows Moule labeling ἵνα in Luke 8:10 "a vigorous way of stating the inevitable" but adds that it is shorthand for a Scripture fulfillment formula (I. Howard Marshall, *The Gospel of Luke: A Commentary on the Greek Text*, NIGTC, ed. I. Howard Marshall [Grand Rapids: Eerdmans, 1978], 323; cf. Joseph A. Fitzmyer, "The Use of the Old Testament in Luke-Acts," in *Society of Biblical Literature Seminar Papers 1992*, ed. Eugene H. Lovering Jr., vol. 31 [Atlanta: Scholars Press, 1992], 527 who says it is also a formula for Scripture quotation).

[218] C. F. D. Moule, *An Idiom Book of New Testament Greek*, 2d ed. (Cambridge: Cambridge University Press, 1959), 142.

[219] Moule, "Mark v, 1–20 Yet Once More," 105.

[220] Ibid., 104.

[221] Ibid., 99.

[222] Ibid., 105.

[223] Ibid. Earlier he stated Mark 4:12 should be read "in a reasonable and intelligent way not in pitiful literalism" (ibid., 99). But his "pitifully literal reading of Isaiah 6" is the *transformative* view of hardening, or what he calls 'positive' hardening.

[224] Ibid., 96.

[225] Ibid., 108.

questionable.[226] Second, appeal to Hebrew thinking suffers from assuming a particular mind-set (legitimate or not) necessarily flows from language.[227] Third, denying parables *positively* harden is not the same as denying that God purposes a *negative* (or deprivational) hardening. Moule opposes a transformative view of hardening but does not entertain any other type. Fourth, to equate 'parables' (= riddles) to 'parables *without interpretation*' assumes a *linguistic* obscurity rather than *noetic* obtuseness.[228] It also assumes (contrary to Moule's whole thesis) that parables alone are incomprehensible.[229]

---

[226] Moule evades the grammar by invoking theological criteria (Stanley E. Porter, *Verbal Aspect in the Greek of the New Testament, with Reference to Tense and Mood,* Studies in Biblical Greek, ed. D. A. Carson, vol. 1 [New York: Lang, 1989], 325; idem, *Idioms of the Greek New Testament,* 2d ed., Biblical Languages, vol. 2 [Sheffield: Sheffield Academic Press, 1994], 236; BDF §369(2)).

[227] For an extreme example see Thorleif Boman, *Hebrew Thought Compared with Greek,* trans. Jules L. Moreau (New York: SCM, 1960). For the classic refutation see James Barr, *Semantics of Biblical Language* (Oxford: Oxford University Press, 1961).

[228] A student of Moule subsequently published a paper attempting to answer a similar critique offered by J. Drury (John W. Bowker, "Mystery and Parable: Mark iv. 1–20," *JTS* 25 [1974]: 300–17).

[229] See David Daube, "Public Pronouncement and Private Explanation in the Gospels," *ExpTim* 57 (1945–46): 175–77 where he cites three rabbis (rabbis Johannan ben Zaccai, Joshua ben Karha, and Simlai) and gives examples where they are questioned by outsiders who receive one answer, then are questioned by their disciples who receive a different answer. For Johannan ben Zaccai (*y. Sanh.* 19b; *Pesiq. Rab.* 40a–b; *b. Hul.* 27b), Joshua ben Karha (*Lev. Rab.* 4) and Simlai (*y. Ber.* 12d, 13a). The pattern: (1) pronouncement in public, (2) departure of outsider and question by disciples, and (3) a deeper explanation. Given these parallels, Daube cautions against toning down the ἵνα clause in Mark 4:12 and affirms that some are "pushed away with a fragile reed" (ibid., 177). Cf. David Daube, *The New Testament and Rabbinic Judaism* (London: Athlone, 1965; reprint, Peabody, MA: Hendrickson, 1998), 141–50; Bowker, "Mystery and Parable," 304–11. Baird (J. Arthur Baird, "A Pragmatic Approach to Parable Exegesis: Some New Evidence on Mark 4:11, 33–34," *JBL* 76 [1957]: 201–7) has also shown that of the sixty-three parables of Jesus, forty-one were explained while twenty-two are unexplained. To the disciples, twenty-eight were explained, thirteen unexplained to non-disciples. Seven parables are unexplained to the disciples but fifteen to non-disciples. Lemcio borrows from Dodd (C. H. Dodd, "The Dialogue Form in the Gospels," *BJRL* 37 [1954–55]: 54–67) a four-fold dialogue scheme to show that the Evangelist used traditional materials, traditional arrangements of those materials, and traditional theology in describing and dealing with a traditional problem. The Dodd scheme is (1) ambiguity (oracular utterance), (2) incomprehension (blank incomprehension or crude misunderstanding by an interlocutor), (3) surprised/critical rejoinder (reproachful retort), and (4) and

Proving the near perspicuity of parables does not address or disprove the noetic issue.[230] Other issues of a less important nature are insufficiently addressed.[231]

The Psychological View: Frank E. Eakin

This view insists that hardening is self-caused (like above) but in the sense that the psychological resilience of *will not* crystallizes into *cannot*.[232] God is either altogether or partly removed from the process as a permitting spectator.

---

explanation (explanation or extension of the enigmatic saying) which he links to Hellenism (Eugene E. Lemcio, "External Evidence for the Structure and Function of Mark iv. 1–20, vii. 14–23 and viii. 14–21," *JTS* 29 [1978]: 323). Lemcio shows that Mark 4 follows a pattern found in the OT (Ezek 17:1–24; Zech 4:2–14), non-canonical literature (*1 [Ethiopic] Enoch* 24; *2 [Syriac] Baruch* 13:1–15:8), and other NT texts (Mark 8:14–21; Matt 16:5–12; John 3:1–21; 14:1–11). He lists three types of patterns (Type 1: OT; Type 2: OT & non-canonical texts; Type 3: rabbinic traditions) with six possible elements (diatribe, ambiguity, privacy, incomprehension, surprised/critical rejoinder, and explanation). Type 1 has all the elements except surprised/critical rejoinder. Type 2 has all elements except diatribe and privacy. Type 3 has all elements except diatribe and surprised/critical rejoinder. His conclusion is that the pattern in Mark 4:12–20; 7:14–23, and 8:18–21 (and 6:33–34), each of which has all six elements, is at home in OT and Jewish tradition rather than Hellenism (ibid., 330–31). Each of these studies argue against Moule's assumption that deliberate ambiguity or leaving some in the dark is non-Jewish and hence out of the question for Jesus to employ, even in the case of parables. If his purpose is to deny deliberate *linguistic* ambiguity of Jesus in contrast to Jewish parallels, then the point is well taken.

[230] See Raymond E. Brown, "The Pre-Christian Semitic Concept of 'Mystery'," *CBQ* 20 (1958): 428–229; idem, "The Semitic Background of the New Testament *mustērion* (I)," *Bib* 39 (1958): 426–48; and idem, "The Semitic Background of the NT *mustērion* (II)," *Bib* 40 (1959): 70–87. Brown says what is added is not further explanation or revelation but "added perception gained through faith, so that the hearers may comprehend what they have already heard" (Brown, "The Semitic Background of the New Testament *mustērion* (I)," 431). See Sirach 39:2–7.

[231] Moule, "Mark v, 1–20 Yet Once More," 110. He points to a study by Birger Gerhardsson, "The Parable of the Sower and Its Interpretation," *NTS* 14 (1967–68): 165–93 where a connection is made between the *Shema* and the parable. See his more recent Birger Gerhardsson, *The Shema in the New Testament* (Lund: Novapress, 1996); Madeleine I. Boucher, *The Mysterious Parable: A Literary Study*, CBQMS, ed. Bruce Vawter et al., vol. 6 (Washington DC: Catholic Biblical Association, 1977), 47.

[232] Räisänen can be placed here but differs in the 'cannot' designation. He rejects the notion that will not crystallizes into cannot (Räisänen, *The Idea of Divine Hardening*, 38). Frank E. Eakin, "Spiritual Obduracy and Parable Purpose," in *The Use of the Old*

Eakin, along with Walther Eichrodt, argues that only this view preserves human responsibility.[233] God may or may not be involved in the final stages. In advancing the notion that hardening (= stubbornness) is retribution for unwillingness to heed the message, Eakin criticizes Key for dismissing the possibility of retribution based on past experiences and for holding that hardening is a product of divine fiat.[234] Eakin regards hardening as a divine judgment arising from an unwillingness to heed a message either prior to or after Isaiah's commission.[235] Hearers, then, digress from possessing the ability but unwillingness to heed a message to a divine judgment resulting in inability and unwillingness to heed it at all. This involves a transformation from non-hard to hard-hearted by either self-depletion (of wisdom) through bad habits, or divinely aided self-depletion (of wisdom) through bad habits and retribution.

Von Rad disputes the notion that 'will not' is punished by 'cannot.' This form of the *lex talionis* is not consistent with statements made in the OT where the act is by God and not a result of the human nature.[236] Tsevat adds two other objections to this view. First, if consistently applied, psychologism drains the humanities of their essence. As a system, this scheme is recurrent in Greek philosophy, but it has little relevance to OT study where it surfaces only in special cases when the going is rough and an exegetical answer is unavailable. "In the process, philology is surrendered; moreover, psychologism is itself, abused since it is employed only as a mere convenience."[237] Second, as a natural process the psychologistic solution itself is unfulfilling.

Testament in the New and Other Essays: Studies in Honor of William Franklin Stinespring, ed. James M. Efird (Durham, NC: Duke University Press, 1972), 87–107.

[233] Walther Eichrodt, *Theology of the Old Testament*, trans. J. A. Baker, vol. 2, OTL, ed. G. Ernest Wright et al. (London: SCM, 1961), 380. Eakin, "Spiritual Obduracy and Parable Purpose," 94.

[234] Eakin, "Spiritual Obduracy and Parable Purpose," 92–93. See Andrew F. Key, "The Magical Background of Isaiah 6:9–13," *JBL* 86 (1967): 198–204.

[235] Eakin, "Spiritual Obduracy and Parable Purpose," 94.

[236] Gerhard von Rad, *The Message of the Prophets*, trans. D. M. G. Stalker (New York: Harper & Row, 1965), 122–23. Cf. Matitiahu Tsevat, "The Throne Vision of Isaiah," in *The Meaning of the Book of Job and Other Biblical Studies: Essays on the Literature and Religion of the Hebrew Bible* (New York: KTAV, 1980), 155–76.

[237] Tsevat, "The Throne Vision of Isaiah," 161.

Now a natural, inexorable process does not need a prophetic intervention. And should one argue that Isaiah's function is merely to work with the natural process, to strengthen and accelerate it, then the supposed philological aporia, which has given rise to the proposed solution, remains and the proposition has solved nothing: supportive prophetic occluding of the mind is occluding of the mind, and the concern of the reader is not lessened when he is told that the prophet only accelerated what was happening anyway. What disturbs him is the principle that occluding of the mind is a legitimate device of a prophet.[238]

The Higher Critical Views

The inauthentic view is confined mostly to the NT reuse of Isa 6:9–10. Montefiore indicates that Mark 4:10–12 is outright inauthentic.[239] Guelich points to shifts of audience in Mark 4 that show 4:11–12 are inserted.[240] Anderson holds that both 4:11–12 and its interpretation are additions.[241] These additions are early church formulations going back to the Jewish-Christian, Aramaic-speaking church in Palestine.[242] Jeremias and Dodd, in an effort to mitigate allegorical interpretation, regard 'mystery/mysteries' as a stumbling block imposed by the redactor and therefore exclude Mark 4:11–12 entirely.[243]

The authenticity issue will crop up in chapter 5 but a rigorous defense will not follow. The reason is that 'authentic' may suffer from equivocation depending on the person using it. Here authentic applies to the *ipsissima verba* (the very words), the *ipsissima verbis* (in

---

[238] Ibid.

[239] C. G. Montefiore, *The Synoptic Gospels*, vol. 1 (London: Allen & Unwin, 1909), 123–24.

[240] Robert A. Guelich, *Mark 1–8:26*, WBC, ed. Ralph P. Martin, vol. 34A (Dallas: Word, 1989), 203. The same problem of audience shift is earlier noted by Fred D. Gealy, "The Composition of Mark 4," *ExpTim* 48 (1936–37): 41 who explained the sudden shift in terms of Mark having "left the world of space-time for the world of ideas" (ibid.). Of Luke he says, "He succeeds…in relating Mark's v. 10 to the Parable of the Sower only to destroy its connexion with vv. 11–12 (Lk 8:10). The answer of Jesus then becomes a *non sequitur*" (ibid.).

[241] Hugh Anderson, *The Gospel of Mark*, NCB, ed. Ronald E. Clements and Matthew Black (London: Marshall, Morgan, and Scott, 1976), 129–30.

[242] Ibid., 130–31.

[243] Robert M. Arida, "Hearing, Receiving and Entering ΤΟ ΜΥΣΤΗΡΙΟΝ/ΤΑ ΜΥΣΤΗΡΙΑ: Patristic Insights Unveiling the *Crux Interpretum* (Isaiah 6:9–10) of the Sower Parable," *SVTQ* 38 (1994): 212.

the very words), or the *ipsissima vox* (the very voice) of Jesus. To be inauthentic one must show that it can be none of these options. The ancient view of speeches may be helpful here while the modern memorex view should be seen as clearly anachronistic.[244] Determining the boundaries remains a promising field for NT researchers. Two points may be helpful here. First, the use of inauthentic may be loosely applied on the grounds that Jesus *would* never say such a thing. This criterion is always tangential at best. Second, signs of redaction may rule out one avenue of authenticity but not all means of establishing such.

A Combination of Views[245]

Larry W. Hurtado.[246] Hurtado suggests that the quotation of Isa 6:9–10 in Mark 4:12 is prophetic irony because it gives the result as though it was intended, but it is not.[247] Thus he combines the irony view with the purpose-effect idiom or rather *defines* prophetic irony as the effect-purpose idiom.

F. F. Bruce.[248] Bruce says of Mark 4:12 that "if the saying means what it seems to mean, then Jesus tells his disciples that the purpose of his use of parables is that his hearers in general (those that are not his followers) may hear him but not understand him; and it is difficult to believe this was so."[249] He credits Hebrew thinking for this harsh language.

> Should this commission [of Isaiah] be pressed to mean that Isaiah was ordered to go and tell the people to pay no heed to what they heard him say? Was it his prescribed duty to prevent them from hearing and

---

[244] See the insightful article by A. W. Mosley, "Historical Reporting in the Ancient World," *NTS* 12 (1965): 10–26; Joseph A. Fitzmyer, "The Language of Palestine in the First Century," *CBQ* 32 (1970): 501–31.

[245] See Foster, "The Contribution of the Conclusion of Acts," 214, 29–30.

[246] Larry W. Hurtado, *Mark*, NIBC, ed. W. Ward Gasque, vol. 2 (Peabody, MA: Hendrickson, 1989).

[247] Ibid., 73–74.

[248] F. F. Bruce, *Hard Sayings of Jesus*, The Jesus Library, ed. Michael Green, vol. 1 (Downers Grove, IL: InterVarsity, 1983).

[249] Ibid., 99.

understanding his message, and thus make it impossible for them to repent and so escape the destruction that would otherwise overtake them? No indeed; *if that impression is given, it is simply due to the Hebrew tendency to express a consequent as though it were a purpose*…If we remember that in the idiom of Jesus and his contemporaries a result might be expressed as though it were a purpose, the saying [of Mark 4:12] remains hard, but not intolerably hard.[250]

Isaiah's (and Jesus') audience would refuse to accept Isaiah's (or Jesus') words "to the point where they will have rendered themselves incapable of accepting it."[251] Bruce thus combines the purpose-effect idiom with the psychological view (*will not* becomes *can not*).

Eugene E. Lemcio.[252] Lemcio holds that in Mark 4:12 "all things happen in parables to prevent repentance by obscuring the truth."[253] However, he also cites Eakin in favor of the psychological view.[254] Thus Lemcio combines a purposive and a psychological view.

Summary of Schemes

These views arise because of the unacceptability of the plain reading. The purposive hardening that prevents wisdom and forgiveness may happen only if due to retribution.[255] Moreover, a non-retributional hardening is deemed as *arbitrary* and *unfair*. However, these views do not substantiate the assertions exegetically or provide evidence for a contingent, retributional, or transformational basis of hardening. To insist there is a fault that solicits retribution falls under the legitimate criticism of Walther Eichrodt.[256]

---

[250] Ibid., 100, 102 emphasis added.

[251] Ibid., 100.

[252] Lemcio, "External Evidence for the Structure and Function of Mark iv. 1–20, vii. 14–23 and viii. 14–21," 323–38.

[253] Ibid., 333.

[254] Ibid., 334.

[255] Although not discussed above, this applies to Rom 11:7 as well. See E. C. Blackman, "Divine Sovereignty and Missionary Strategy in Romans 9–11," *CJT* 11 (1965): 130.

[256] Walther Eichrodt uses the phrase 'unbiased exegesis' in pointing out assumptions of exegetes on such passages (Eichrodt, *Theology of the Old Testament*, 179). On the issue of retribution (after discussing the case of Pharaoh and Isaiah) he says, "But it is

Commenting on John 12:38, Gerald L. Borchert states, "The implications of the telic sense have generally been avoided by contemporary writers unless they espouse a Calvinistic point of view."[257] So merely to assume purpose-idiom, irony, or any other scheme that may find its impetus in the offended affections rather than the evidence, is no solution. This does not imply that all who do propose these views do so because of assumptions, prejudice, or absence of objective criteria. Nor does this imply that these views do not demand an evidential hearing on their own merits. But to avoid circularity, one must not only develop an alternative to a purposive intent by credibly excluding it, but also examine without a priori what Isaiah (Mark, Matthew, Luke, John, and Paul) seems to be saying within a credible and unifying reconstruction. To do less is to short-circuit biblical theology. Although no reconstruction endowed by its creator as valid is faultless, neither are all reconstructions thereby created equal.

Conclusion

This chapter examined major works on hardening as well as specific paradigms that are used as metanarratives in order to understand Isa 6:9–10 (and pars.). These constructs are designed to make sense of the difficult text, account for differences among its subsequent occurrences, unify them with a single meaning, and in the process make the meaning palatable to the modern ear. As pointed out earlier, however, many exegetical works neglect the wisdom tradition altogether or treat it only superficially while others proceed upon (or combine this with) fundamental a priori assumptions that predetermine the perimeters of the meaning at the outset. These assumptions are never fully (if at all) either stated or defended.

Given these obstacles, an exegetical examination of Isa 6:9–10 (chapter 4) will be postponed until two conditions are met. First, there needs to be an excursion into the philosophical arena to partially account for why Isa 6:9–10 and passages like it are subjected to such

---

not always possible to manage with this explanation. More than once an unbiased exegesis is unable to discover any fault on the part of men which could have decided Yahweh on his action (cf. especially 1 Sam. 16.14ff; 26:19; 2 Sam 24.1)" (ibid.).

[257] Gerald L. Borchert, *John 12–21*, NAC, ed. David S. Dockery et al. (Nashville: Broadman & Holman, 2002), 64.

an array of views (chapter 2). Second, an appraisal of the sapiential tradition itself needs to be undertaken in order to provide what is deemed the biblical metanarrative from which the Isaian passage should be construed (chapter 3).

Philosophical Prolegomena
and Presuppositions

Introduction

If the putative purpose statement of Isa 6:9–10 is taken at face value, resulting from 'unbiased exegesis,' that is, *unwarrantedly reading into the text a retributive sense without justification*,[1] then one is left to face how, who, when, and why the divine act of (Isaianic) fattening occurs.[2] As the previous chapter illustrates, many studies are rife with controversial presuppositions over how and why God acts and the extent of man's involvement in those acts. These

---

[1] In a broad sense there is no such thing as unbiased exegesis. One must not either pretend he has no presuppositions nor hold up presuppositions as reason for complete skepticism. Instead truth is reached by submission to the biblical data and being presuppositionally self-critical (Dan McCartney and Charles Clayton, *Let the Reader Understand: A Guide to Interpreting and Applying the Bible*, 2d. ed. [Philipsburg, NJ: Presbyterian & Reformed, 2002], 9). But this is not what 'unbiased' in '*unbiased* exegesis' refers to here.

[2] Walther Eichrodt uses this phrase in arguing against any sense of retribution to some types of divine action. He says, "This state of affairs may, nevertheless, become somewhat easier to understand if we scrutinize more closely the precise instances in which a divine causality is especially emphasized. If we do, we find first of all that it frequently implies no more than *the power of evil to grow and spread*, whereby it becomes ripe for judgment" (Walther Eichrodt, *Theology of the Old Testament*, trans. J. A. Baker, vol. 2, OTL, ed. G. Ernest Wright et al. [London: SCM, 1961], 179). On the issue of retribution (after discussing the case of Pharaoh and Isaiah) he says, "But it is not always possible to manage with this explanation. More than once an *unbiased exegesis* is unable to discover any fault on the part of men which could have decided Yahweh on his action (cf. especially 1 Sam. 16.14–23; 26:19; 2 Sam 24.1)" (ibid. emphasis added).

underlying views are too often employed to determine (or override) the data at difficult junctures.

When human contingency is introduced in the human-divine situation, a plethora of alternate and unorthodox explanations seem to emerge.[3] If man is imbued with contra-causal freedom, then God becomes in some way a contingent time-bound being. Although it is possible for one to argue that since God is a time bound being that therefore man has libertarian freedom, the argument has instead proceeded on the assumption that man possesses this freedom. Proponents of libertarian freedom recognize a departure from historic orthodoxy.[4] It is from this one fount that time and contingency issues emerge along with a reappraisal of God's immutability, eternality, simplicity, unity, and infinity. If the peg (libertarian freedom) upon which other non-orthodox philosophical issues logically depend (simple, limited, foreknowledge views, God in time, etc.) is dismantled, then not only does the whole structure collapse against the historic orthodox view of theism, but the parts are recognized as red herrings. If the thesis here is that man is congenitally fat-hearted, that is, unable to salvifically perceive, know, and understand then this strikes at the very heart of libertarian freedom.

The discussion below begins in reverse order dealing first with God and time, then causation, and finally with human freedom, or God, God and man, then man. Differing views provide the occasion for the multivalency of purposive speech as in some way dependent or not on the human will. Each of these matters are much more complex than this treatment suggests. Philosophers and systematicians alike might view it as either sufficient but not necessary or necessary but not sufficient. The purpose is not to provide a rigorous philosophical treatise but to account for the general critique of previous works, show the weakness of libertarianism, and provide a compatibilist background for the exegetical task that follows. Reliance is made on recent treatments and standard expressions of orthodoxy including Augustine, Aquinas, Calvin, Luther, and Edwards.

---

[3] For example see John Sanders, *The God Who Risks: A Theology of Providence* (Downers Grove, IL: InterVarsity, 1998), 194–207.

[4] Clark Pinnock is an Openness theologian who admits he departs from historic orthodoxy (Clark Pinnock, *The Most Moved Mover: A Theology of God's Openness* [Grand Rapids: Baker, 2001]).

God and Time

Introduction

Variety of Views. Discussions about time are not only philosophically complex as they relate to definition,[5] sequence, and eternity, but also scientifically so because they invoke the latest in the complex discipline of physics.[6] "There was a time (in a space universe) when

---

[5] See Robert Jastrow, *God and the Astronomers* (New York: Norton, 1978); David Wilkinson, *God, the Big Bang and Stephen Hawking* (Grand Rapids: Monarch, 1993), 149–59; William Lane Craig, *The Existence of God and the Beginning of the Universe* (San Bernardino, CA: Here's Life, 1979); William Lane Craig and Quentin Smith, *Theism, Atheism, and Big Bang Cosmology* (Oxford: Clarendon, 1993); Richard Taylor, *Metaphysics*, 3d ed., FPS, ed. Elizabeth Beardsley, Monroe Beardsley, and Tom L. Beauchamp, vol. 18 (Englewood Cliffs, NJ: Prentice-Hall, 1983), 63–70 (Space and Time), 71–79 (Time and Eternity), and 80–89 (Causation); Paul Davies, *God and the New Physics* (New York: Simon & Schuster, 1983), 119–34; Paul Davies and John Gribbin, *The Matter Myth: Dramatic Discoveries that Challenge our Understanding of Physical Reality* (New York: Simon & Schuster, 1992), 63–98; Gregory E. Ganssle, ed., *God & Time: Four Views* (Downers Grove, IL: InterVarsity, 2001); John M. Frame, *No Other God: A Response to Open Theism* (Philipsburg, NJ: Presbyterian & Reformed, 2001), 119–42; Douglas Wilson, ed., *Bound Only Once: The Failure of Open Theism* (Moscow, ID: Canon, 2001), 123–34; John Piper, Justin Taylor, and Paul Kjoss Helseth, eds., *Beyond the Bounds: Open Theism and the Undermining of Biblical Christianity* (Wheaton, IL: Crossway, 2003), 77–110; D. A. Carson, *Divine Sovereignty and Human Responsibility: Biblical Perspectives in Tension*, 2d ed. (Grand Rapids: Baker, 1994; reprint, Eugene, OR: Wipf & Stock, 2002), 209–10. "Charles Lamb in 1810 probably summed up most people's thoughts when he stated, 'Nothing troubles me more than time and space; and yet nothing troubles me less, as I never think about them'" (David Wilkinson, *God, Time and Stephen Hawking* [Grand Rapids: Monarch, 2001], 115).

[6] If time is coterminous with the creation of the world, then statements referring prior to this event must be speaking ontologically not chronologically. If time, space, and matter were created simultaneously, then it follows that time has an ontological beginning and is not everlasting. The issue centers on God's relationship to time and if one is possible without entailing succession and change. On the concurrency of time and space Davies writes, "God cannot be omnipotent if he is subject to the physics of time, nor can he be considered the creator of the universe if he did not create time. In fact, because time and space are inseparable, a God who did not create time, created space neither" (Davies, *God and the New Physics*, 133). Hawking believes opposite, viz., that the universe existed apart from time where there was a time (imaginary) when time was not (Stephen W. Hawking, *A Brief History of Time: From the Big Bang to Black Holes* [New York: Bantam, 1988], 15–34; cf. Craig and Smith, *Theism, Atheism, and Big Bang Cosmology*, 279–300 where Craig criticizes Hawking's view of an uncaused and eternal cosmos). Hawking refers to the two together as spacetime. This is the problem with the 'everlasting' view. The problem with the

time was not" (Hawking)[7] is equally as confusing as "There never was a God when time was not" (Padgett, Wolterstorff)[8] or "Time is not real" (Berkeley, Einstein, Kant, McTaggart).[9] The complexity of the subject is equaled by the diversity of opinions. The classic position (e.g., Augustine, Aquinas, Luther, Calvin, Edwards) that time's *terminus a quo* is coterminous with creation is no longer part of these assured results but on the other hand it finds substantiation in modern physics (the Standard Model). One's view of time impacts difficult passages in the Scriptures especially in light of God's knowledge (causative or passive), causality itself (necessary [deist or pantheist], necessary and contingent [theist], or contingent [non-determinist]), knowledge as it relates to causality (as causative or cognitive), and human freedom (determined and free or free from determinism). Isaiah 6:9–10 is indirectly impacted by such views as will be discussed below.

'eternalist' view is that it is difficult (but not impossible) to view God as personal and interactive (Davies, *God and the New Physics*, 133–34). Choosing which presupposition is easier to accept determines both the problem and how one approaches the solution—this is the modern debate (on God and time) in a nutshell. Elsewhere Craig states, "The beginning predicted by the Standard Model involves an initial cosmological singularity, which constitutes an edge or boundary to physical space and time" (William Lane Craig and Walter Sinnott-Armstrong, *God? A Debate between a Christian and an Atheist*, Point/Counterpoint Series, ed. James P. Sterba, vol. 2 [Oxford: Oxford University Press, 2004], 60). Barow and Tipler say, "At this singularity, space and time came into existence; literally nothing existed before the singularity, so, if the Universe originated at such a singularity, we would truly have a creation *ex nihilo*" (John Barrow and Frank Tipler, *The Anthropic Cosmologial Principle* [Oxford: Clarendon, 1986], 442).

[7] Hawking, *A Brief History of Time*, 21–34.

[8] The view that time is everlasting is also logically problematic. Aquinas viewed God as the metaphysical first cause of *creatio continuans* as logically possible without implying *creatio originans* (Aquinas *Sum. Theol.* 1.2.3; 1.7.2; 10.1–4; *Sum. C. Gent.* 2.16, 32–38; *De Aeternitate Mundi contra Murmurantes*). He left Scripture to determine the former. But it is difficult if not impossible to arrive at a point in an infinite tensed-facts continuum. The same problem that applies to 'points' in eternity would apply here, viz., an infinite regress. Point demands a beginning at the very least. It also begs questions like, Why did God wait so long before he created?

[9] "The reason for this is that, according to relativity theory, time does not 'happen' bit by bit, or moment by moment: it is stretched out, like space, in its entirety. Time is simply 'there'" (Davies and Gribbin, *The Matter Myth*, 82). Those who advocate this view see the future as fixed since past, present, and future share equal status.

Time-Talk and God. How does one refer to the creation of time without using time as a marker? One solution is to use 'when' in "when time began" in an ontological sense in distinction to eternity. The classic view understands God as existing 'in eternity' (as opposed to simply everlasting) because he *is* eternal.[10] By definition, being eternal means not subject to time or change.[11] But even here the language is imprecise. 'Exist' literally means 'to stand out of' [being] and applied to non-time assumes a contingent ontological beingness on some necessary Being which does not *exist* as *act-potency* but rather *pure-act* or *being* (using Aquinas' terminology borrowed from Aristotle).[12] But, presumably, what ontologically exists prior to the creation of time, namely, non-time, has no *beingness* and therefore cannot *exist* at all. In addition, since God is *pure-act*, he does not *exist* ('stand out of being') either.[13] But he *is* there. But *where* is there? Or is spatial language even appropriate at all especially when referring to time (*in* or *above* time)? Before spacetime exists, is it appropriate to speak of *where* or *when*? Metaphysical singularity breeds linguistic imprecision. Discussions of creation *ex nihilo* likewise beg the ontological status of 'nothing'[14] because nothing by definition has no

---

[10] Aquinas *Sum. Theol.* 1.10.

[11] Ames writes that "the quality which is called passive is not in him: He is therefore immutable. Ps. 1–2:26, 27, *Thou remainest…thou art the same*; Rom. 1:23, *The glory of the incorruptible God*; Jas. 1:17, *With whom there is no variableness or shadow of turning*" (Ames *Medulla theologica* 1.4.17; Calvin *Institution* 1.17.13).

[12] Aquinas *Sum. Theol.* 1.3–25; Aristotle *Phys.* 3.1–3; *Metaph.* 1.6–7; 5.8; 7.3, 7–17; 8.4–6; 9.6–9; 12.2–5.

[13] Heb 11:6 should read, "Without faith it is impossible to please him, for the one who comes to God must believe that he is *faithful* and that he is a rewarder of those who diligently seek him." There is little to support the translation, "that he *exists*."

[14] This statement was originally designed to avoid two errors, *dualism* and *pantheism*. The first error is that something outside of God is coeternal and thus uncreated material that is simply fashioned by him into the known world (*ex materia*). The second error avoids the notion that God creates out of his own essence so that what is created is an extension of it (Amos 5:19). Creation *ex nihilo* views the divine act in contrast to either a mere fashioning or conserving of being that is there (Theophilus *Autol.* 1.4; 2.4, 10, 13; Irenaeus *Haer.* 3.10.3; Fourth Lateran Council [1215]). The doctrine is not simply concerned with ontological origin but temporal beginning. A minority report among theologians is *creatio ex Deo*. The strength of this view is that it avoids pantheism, precisely because creation is seen as a modification of Being in some way, and avoids the formal absurdity of *ex nihilo*. Creation *ex nihilo* would align itself with the A-series of time while creation *ex Deo* would tend towards the B-series.

beingness and nothing cannot be used by something (however great) to create something. Time, knowledge, causation, and liberty are all complex individually, but together, their complexity is greater than the sum of their parts.

The Biblical Precedent. Biblical revelation seems to teach that both space and time have a *terminus a quo* although (if so) it does not explicitly relate either how this occurs, how it is to be reconciled with the attributes of God, or how precisely God relates to this space-time world.[15] Of the two, time is more complex an issue than space (and

---

For a defense of creation *ex nihilo* in constrast to a B-theory of time see William Lane Craig, *The Tenseless Theory of Time: A Critical Examination*, SELMP, ed. Jaakko Hintikka et al., vol. 294 (Boston: Kluwer, 2000), 218–21.

[15] Although there is evidence of a continuing or sustaining aspect of God's action in regard to creation (Heb 1:2; Col 1:17), a variety of Greek phrases seem to presuppose that time had a beginning, viz., in that creation. In this regard there are two lines of biblical data. First, those that presuppose *time* has a beginning include the following: (1) πρὸ τοῦ αἰῶνος 'before time' (Prov 8:22–23; Ps 54:20 [LXX 55:19]; Sir 24:9; 42:21; Theod. Tob 6:17; 1 Cor 2:7). (2) πρὸ παντὸς τοῦ αἰῶνος 'before all time' (Jude 25). (3) πρὸ χρόνων αἰωνίων 'before eternal times' or 'before times of eternity' (Titus 1:2–3; 2 Tim 1:9). Second, those that presuppose a beginning to the world of *space and matter* which include the following: (1) πρὸ καταβολῆς κόσμου 'before the foundation of the world' (John 17:24; Eph 1:4; 1 Pet 1:20). (2) ἀπὸ καταβολῆς κόσμου 'from the foundation of the world' (Matt 13:35; 25:34; Luke 11:50; Heb 4:3; 9:26; Rev 13:8; 17:8). Cf. L&N §§67.1–68.82 on the semantic domains of time and aspect. Hawking argues that space-time (or spacetime) is a four-dimensional continuum a phrase used to refer to events that happen in a space at a particular time (Hawking, *A Brief History of Time*, 23–24; Davies and Gribbin, *The Matter Myth*, 63, 77–86). The general theory of relativity reveals how intricately space and time work together and support the idea that both have the same beginning (Hawking, *A Brief History of Time*, 33–34; Ames *Medulla theologica* 1.8.5, 23–26). Hawking's confusion of time and space (space-time), equation of imaginary time with ontological time, and reference to time as the fourth dimension of space (spatializing time) is critiqued successfully by William Lane Craig (Craig and Smith, *Theism, Atheism, and Big Bang Cosmology*, 288–300). "Since Hawking reduces empirical time in the very early history of the universe to a spatial dimension and conflates empirical time with ontological time, his model requires a tenselessly existing spacetime which he wishes to pass off as reality. Added to these errors the fact that the time involved is imaginary in its early stages, and the metaphysical absurdity of Hawking's vision of the world seems starkly apparent" (ibid., 299). On the biblical issue, however, a number of questions still surface including whether time and space-matter have the same beginning or whether there is such a thing as time before time or different types of time. See Craig, *The Tenseless Theory of Time*, 220; idem, *God, Time, and Eternity: The Coherence of Theism II: Eternity* (Boston: Kluwer,

space is infinitely complex). Is time simply indexical (past, present, future) or is it measured *and* metaphysical? Is there such thing as metaphysical time as distinguished from indexical time? Does the absence or presence of time demand that God's thoughts or acts are/are not sequential? The purpose here is not to plumb the depth of the conundrums and complexities of God and time but to question the influence of any particular philosophical view of time and its impact on the *prima facie* or putative purposive statements like that in Isa 6:9–10.

Four views of time in relation to Scripture have risen to prominence, namely, *divine timeless eternity* (Paul Helm), *eternity as relative timelessness* (Alan G. Padgett), *timelessness and omnitemporality* (William Lane Craig), and *unqualified divine temporality* (Nicholas Wolterstorff).[16] Each position can be seen in light of two perspectives of time; the A-theory known as *process* or *tensed* theory, and the B-theory alternatively called the *stasis* or *tenseless* theory.[17] The A-series

---

2001), 143–284. Nearly everyone in the scientific community now holds that the universe and time had a beginning (Craig and Sinnott-Armstrong, *God?* 8).

[16] This summary is derived from reading Ganssle, ed., *God & Time: Four Views.*

[17] The A- and B-series of time come from John McTaggart Ellis McTaggart, *The Nature of Existence,* Cambridge Paperback Library, ed. C. D. Broad, vol. 2 (Cambridge: Cambridge University Press, 1927), §§303–51. He says both A- and B-series are unreal but that a still third C-series is real (ibid., §347). McTaggart, like Einstein and Kant, believes that all distinctions between past, present, and future are only illusions. B-theorists hold events in relation to each other as important while A-theorists hold the most important thing is that some events are past, present, and future. B-theorists use *before, simultaneous with,* and *after* while the A-theorist argue for a real 'now.' B-theorists hold all events exist in the same way as all events do while the A-theorist emphasize the 'now' in a way the past and future is not. In the end, if the A-theory is valid, then God's relationship to time might be temporal. The B-theory denies God is temporally related and therefore precludes the possibility of change in God. The classic view sees the B-theory of time when related to God but viewed as the A-theory by man (Boethius *Consol.* 5.6; Augustine *Trin.* 15.7, 22; *Conf.* 1.7.20; 8.5–10; 11.11–27; 13.29.44; Anselm *Monologion* 21; Calvin *Institution* 1.17.13; Ames *The Medulla theologica* 1.7.41–54). Cf. Davies, *God and the New Physics,* 133. For an appraisal and critique of McTaggart's paradox see William Lane Craig, *The Tensed Theory of Time: A Critical Examination,* SELMP, ed. Jaakko Hintikka et al., vol. 293 (Boston: Kluwer, 2000), 169–217. Craig says that McTaggart denies change occurs within the B-series. "First, events in a B-series can neither cease to be nor begin to be events.... Secondly, neither can moments in absolute time cease or begin to be.... Finally, can events change their characteristics? McTaggart responds that there is only one class of characteristics with respect to which events can change, and that this is the

refers to position as 'past, present, and future' while the B-series refers to position as 'earlier, simultaneous, and later.' The former is in flux while the latter is static. Although change occurs only in the A- not the B-series, there can be no B- without the A-series.[18] Views range from the A-series alone, a combination of the A- and B-series, or B-series alone.[19] The divide over 'time' might be said to stand between Heraclitus (change) and Parmenides (stasis).

Divine Timeless Eternity

Paul Helm holds to *divine timeless eternity*. This is the classic view of Augustine, Boethius, Anselm, Aquinas, and Calvin which insists that God is not in time but is eternal, impassible, and without change or the possibility of change.[20] God sees all of time as a whole whereas eternity is not in time nor does it have its own metaphysical time. The *beginning* of time, especially views of creation *ex nihilo* (or *ex Deo*) is troublesome but not incoherent. Creation is metaphysically contingent on God but there can be no chronology (indexicals) *before* creation. Creation is either eternally contingent on God and thus has no beginning (Aquinas argued that an efficient cause does not necessarily precede its effect in time) or is eternally decreed *ex nihilo*. Being eternal, God does not know tensed-facts, that is, he cannot

---

determination of the events by the terms of the A-series" (ibid., 171, the determinations are past, present, and future). McTaggarts two-fold argument is (1) that the A-theoretic determinations are essential to the temporality of events and (2) that these determinations are self-contradictory (*argumentum ad absurdum*) and do not exist (ibid. 169). Since nothing that exists can be temporal, time is unreal (McTaggart, *The Nature of Existence*, §304).

[18] McTaggart, *The Nature of Existence*, §312.

[19] For a critical (but Molinist) examination of both the A- and B-series see Craig and Smith, *Theism, Atheism, and Big Bang Cosmology*, 295–300; Craig, *The Tensed Theory of Time*; idem, *The Tenseless Theory of Time*; idem, *Time and Eternity: Exploring God's Relationship to Time* (Wheaton, IL: Crossway, 2001), 115–65; idem, *God, Time, and Eternity*, 3–139.

[20] See Augustine *Conf.* 11.1–13.53; Boethius *Consol.* 5.6.25–31; Anselm *Monologion* 21; Aquinas *Sum. Theol.* 1.3, 7, 9, 10, 14, 19, 23; *De Veritate* 4.5; Calvin *Institution* 1.17.13. Boethius' famous words are "*Aeternitas igitur est interminabilis vitae tota simul et perfecta possesio*" ("Eternity, then, is the whole, simultaneous and perfect possession of boundless life.").

know the *nowness* of events without becoming temporal.[21] On the other hand, if he knows all things including tensed-facts, then he would be temporal.[22] Certainly an eternal God would not have indexical knowledge but a non-eternal God would not know propositions that express knowledge of the universe from the perspective of a timeless eternity. Biblical *language* that makes predications of God or implies change in God is metaphorical (Aquinas)[23] or a result of divine accommodation (Calvin).[24] God's actions in the world of time are effects of one eternal act of his will uncaused by anything but himself (Aquinas).[25] Although God's perspective is B-series, man only experiences the A-series of time. These two series are incompatible.

A consistent application of this view would theoretically have no problem with taking the statements of Isa 6:9–10 as *purposive* (or any other view). Since God is not contingent to time or anything in it, issues of predestination are not difficult to address. God works all things according to the counsel of his will. Who can resist God's will? No one. The pre- in *pre*destination and fore- in *fore*know or *fore*ordain are not problematic in this scheme either; although a strict Boethian view might reduce them to *destine, know,* and *ordain* but only if the ordering of the decree is understood temporally or if God's simplicity is confused with his acts or decree. But these prefixes are not meaningless *temporal* indicators but rather *logical* orderings of the decree of God in timeless eternity as they eternally relate to time. They indicate a non-contingency.[26] Logical ordering of thoughts, like cause and effect, do not demand temporal sequence. God *fore*knows because he has *fore*ordained, he does not *fore*ordain because he *fore*knows (contra Molinism). Furthermore, exhaustive divine

---

[21] For an explanation of how God genuinely interacts with his creation, on the one hand, yet knows everything from a classical (albeit slightly modified) perspective see Bruce A. Ware, *God's Lesser Glory: The Diminished God of Open Theism* (Wheaton, IL: Crossway, 2000), 73–74.

[22] Objections of this kind are most often driven by the thought of injury of what an infallible knowledge of the future would do for human (libertarian) freedom.

[23] Aquinas *Sum. Theol.* 1.13.2; 1.19.7, 11.

[24] Calvin *Institution* 1.17.13. Cf. Ames *Medulla theologica* 1.4.1–7, 22; 1.7.5; 1.4.62.

[25] Aquinas *Sum. Theol.* 1.14.1, 8, 9, 11, 13; 1.19.4, 5.

[26] Ames *Medulla theologica* 1.25.4.

foreknowledge is detrimental to *libertarian* freedom. The search for contingent features that solicit God's fattening are less likely to be drawn into the passage(s).

This view is not without its problems. First, biblical language seems to present God as genuinely interacting with humans. Does this not require both knowledge of tensed-facts and a sequence of acts in time not just an atemporal decree to act eternally within time? Is it a given that a changeless God is really superior to one who genuinely succumbs to change? Does not a more literal or natural interpretation of Scripture, the incarnation, and a personal God require it? Second, if God is omniscient, how can he be absent of knowledge of tensed-facts? Sure, a time bound God might not know propositions that express knowledge of the universe from the perspective of timeless eternity, but is this a reasonable trade off? And does this not demand a modification of omniscience? Third, since creation and time have a beginning, does not this view threaten a meaningful doctrine of creation? Does anything ever really come to be? Is metaphysical contingency alone sufficient to account for a putative temporal universe? Does not this require that one treat time (A-series) as unreal and stretch the bounds of human credulity? Fourth, why can not God be meaningfully conceived as temporal where time is contingent on him rather than the reverse? Why not a metaphysical time? Fifth, if all time-bound acts of God are an effect of a decree in timeless eternity, then how can this view escape the charge of deism? Does not God's transcendence come at the expense of his immanence? Although these charges are not new nor the responses scarce, their persistence reveals something of the angst over the solutions given.

Eternity as Relative Timelessness

The three remaining views are all in agreement against the timeless eternity position in viewing God as effected either by time or agents in time. In turn, each view espouses *libertarian* freedom. Alan G. Padgett champions *eternity as relative timelessness*. Padgett views the *everlasting eternity* view (Wolterstorff) as problematic because it seems counter intuitive to both the beginning of time and threatens God's transcendence while *timeless eternity* (Helm) especially threatens libertarian freedom and ignores tensed facts.[27] *Relative timelessness*

---

[27] This is the crux issue. Padgett says, "The doctrine that God determines every event 'from eternity' is incoherent with a libertarian understanding of human free will. For

accounts for two types of time, one uncreated (*pure duration*) and the other created by God (*measured time*). In this way God is both independent of created time (transcendent) but not completely unattached to time (*pure duration*) itself. "God's Being is *conceptually prior* (in terms of ontological dependence) to eternity, even though God's life is not temporally prior to God's time."[28] God's relationship to pure duration is like the sun's relationship to light. He advocates the A-series of time and views *pure duration* as measured but not by means of *created* time.

Besides the incoherency of two types of time, its cumbersome nature, and its necessity in the first place, the implications of this view are detrimental to purposive statements like Isa 6:9–10. All purposive statements would be turned into ecbatic statements. First, God is purely contingent on future activities of man which he may or may not (more likely) know in advance (openness view) what their decisions might be. Only a retributive notion could be entertained if at all. Second, God himself is subject to the *libertarian* free-will choices of humans which makes his purpose to withhold wisdom, if done at all, *depletive* at best and impossible at worst (for God would presumably never deplete one of libertarian freedom). Third, since the idea of God as sole determiner of every event from eternity is rejected and God becomes contingent, he cannot by divine fiat determine whether man will or will not believe. He is not in absolute control of man's salvation. Finally, any view that suggests man is congenitally without the ability to salvifically perceive, know, or

---

this reason many have rejected (rightly in my view) the notion that God determines every event" (Alan G. Padgett, "Eternity as Relative Timelessness," in *God & Time: Four Views*, ed. Gregory E. Ganssle [Downers Grove, IL: InterVarsity, 2001], 94). In regard to timelessness and omniscience he says, "The Boethian way of the dilemma of divine omniscience and human freedom may not be the only road available to us" (ibid., 109–10). On this score and related to the whole notion of human freedom, openness of the future, and tensed logic, Helm says, "The fact that Authur Prior's strongly held views about human freedom and the openness of the future (expressed, for example in idem, *Papers on Time and Tense* [Oxford: Clarendon, 1968]) led him to pioneer the development of tensed logic (as found, for example, in Authur Prior, *Past, Present and Future* [Oxford: Clarendon, 1968]) is one piece of evidence to suggest that it is not the logic that drives the metaphysics but the other way around" (Paul Helm, "Response to Alan G. Padgett," in *God and Time: Four Views*, ed. Gregory E. Ganssle [Downers Grove, IL: InterVarsity, 2001], 113).

[28] Padgett, "Eternity as Relative Timelessness," 107.

understand God must be rejected (like *timeless eternity*) because it represents a frontal assault on *libertarian* freedom. Texts that seem to imply God's absolute control must be reinterpreted in this light.

Timelessness and Omnitemporality

William Lane Craig advocates the *timelessness and omnitemporality* view which holds that God is both timeless before creation and temporal post-creation. He does not hold that this pre-creation metaphysical status is in any way a type of time (contra Padgett), nor that God is simply timeless (contra Helm), nor that God is purely temporal (contra Wolterstorff).[29] In this way Craig is able to hold that time is a created thing, that God existed prior to time and is thus eternal, but that God knows tensed facts and has undergone a form of change in order to become temporally related to his creation.[30] God is *causally* rather than *temporally* prior to creation. Time itself is not a necessary property of God. He thus combines the A- and B-theories of time into one. But if one denies tensed facts and adopts a static or tenseless theory of time (Helm), Craig acknowledges, then all the arguments for God's temporality evaporate.

This view is not abjectly opposed to purposive statements in passages like Isa 6:9–10. God knows the future exhaustively but also all possible worlds. In furtherance of this view of time is Craig's

---

[29] While the timeless eternity view follows Boethius et al., other views stressing God's temporalness (Padgett, Craig, Wolterstorff) follow John Duns Scotus (ca. 1266–1308) who reacted against Boethius. "Eternity will not, by reason of its infinity, be present to any non-existent time.... If (assuming the impossible) the whole of time were simultaneously existent, the whole would be simultaneously present to eternity.... For the 'now' of eternity is formally infinite and therefore formally exceeds the 'now' of time. Nevertheless it does not co-exist with another now" (*Ordinatio* 1.38–39.9–10).

[30] He does indicate, because he views time as having a beginning, that God has not *existed* for infinite time—this involves more a play on 'time' than on 'existence.' But a problem is his insistence that God *exists* prior to creation. But the very notion of existence, as noted earlier, assumes God is an *act-potency* being rather than *pure actuality*. The problem is that Craig holds this prior to God becoming temporally related to his creation, before he undergoes change, when he is supposed to be eternal. But according to Craig's view, God is indeed never *pure actuality* for he indeed is a being that does eventually undergo change. Helm says that this view of *creatio ex nihilo*, if it requires a change in God, contradicts Craig's earlier assertions that God is fully timeless prior to this event (Paul Helm, "Response to William Lane Craig," in *God & Time: Four Views*, ed. Gregory E. Ganssle [Downers Grove, IL: InterVarsity, 2001], 164).

advocacy of *middle* knowledge (*scientia media*), the notion that God envisioned all possible worlds and chose among them the one that would produce the best results for the most people *before* he decreed which world he would make.[31] The future is settled but in light of what man would do with his *libertarian* freedom—a post hoc decree. Those who are either unevangelized or remain unsaved in this world are those who would never be saved in any possible world anyway. God is not to blame for he does the best he can with the world he has chosen. Craig and middle-knowledge proponents refer to these individuals as having "trans-world depravity," a depravity that ensures that no matter what world envisioned, they would not

---

[31] This view goes back to the Jesuit Luis de Molina (1535–1600) who argued against the Dominicans (Luis de Molina *Concordia liberi arbitrii cum gratiae donis* 5.1.11; 14.13.12, 40; 23.4; 47.9; 49.9). Molina taught that 'middle-knowledge' preceded the decree. Middle-knowledge is not strictly knowledge of counter-factuals but rather a particular view of counter-factual knowledge that follows God's *natural knowledge* (what could be) but precedes his *free knowledge* (what will be). The Augustinian-Calvinist (and Dominican) order is the following: Natural knowledge, decree, free knowledge, knowledge of counter-factuals (Augustine *Trin.* 10.6; 13.24; 14.13; 15.22, 25; Aquinas *Sum. Theol.* 1.9.1–2; 1.14.1–15; 1.19.1–11; 22.1; 1.23.1–8; 1.25.4; 1.103.1–7; Ames *Medulla theologica* 1.7.10, 13, 15, 23–31; 1.25.4, 14; 1.4.53–56). Under this latter scheme, middle-knowledge is a misnomer and non-existent. This concept arose from the Jesuits attempt "to defend the semi-Pelagian heresy of foreseen faith and good works in election, and to support the figment of free will in order the more easily to free themselves from the arguments of the Dominicans who rejected such a foresight" (Francis Turretin *Institutes of Elentic Theology* 213). "From this one foundation all errors of merit and foreseen faith can be sufficiently refuted. For if a particular decree of God depended upon any foresight then an idea of God would have come to him from somewhere else, which hardly agrees with his nature" (Ames *Medulla theologica* 1.7.18). For a summary of Molina and his context see William C. Placher, *The Domestication of Transcendence: How Modern Thinking about God Went Wrong* (Louisville, KY: Westminster, 1996), 148–52. Cf. David P. Hunt, "Divine Providence and Simple Foreknowledge," *FP* 10 (1993): 396; William Lane Craig, "The Middle-Knowledge View," in *Divine Foreknowledge: Four Views*, ed. James K. Beilby and Paul R. Eddy (Downers Grove, IL: InterVarsity, 2001), 119–43; Gregory A. Boyd, "An Open-Theism Response (to Middle-Knowledge)," in *Divine Foreknowledge: Four Views*, ed. James K. Beilby and Paul R. Eddy (Downers Grove, IL: InterVarsity, 2001), 144–48; David P. Hunt, "A Simple-Foreknowledge Response (to Middle-Knowledge)," in *Divine Foreknowledge: Four Views*, ed. James K. Beilby and Paul R. Eddy (Downers Grove, IL: InterVarsity, 2001), 149–54; Paul Helm, "An Augustinian-Calvinist Response (to Middle-Knowledge)," in *Divine Foreknowledge: Four Views*, ed. James K. Beilby and Paul R. Eddy (Downers Grove, IL: InterVarsity, 2001), 155–59.

believe.[32] Against this, however, is that Scripture indicates that all men, not some, have this type of depravity, a depravity that mitigates and militates against the very notion of *libertarian* freedom.[33] Only a contingent fattening or a purposive notion in light of foreseen human

---

[32] For a discussion see Paul Copan, *"True for You, But Not for Me": Deflating the Slogans that Leave Christians Speechless* (Minneapolis: Bethany, 1998), 125–53. He says, "God has arranged this world in such a way that those who never hear the Gospel would not have responded to it even if they had heard it. Those who are beyond the reaches of the Gospel in the actual world could be those who would never have responded to the Gospel in any possible world" (ibid., 128). Later he says, "In the middle-knowledge perspective, some persons possess 'transworld depravity' or 'transworld damnation' and would have been lost in any world in which they were placed" (ibid., 130; cf. William Lane Craig, "Politically Correct Salvation," in *Christian Apologetics in the Postmodern World*, ed. Timothy R. Phillips and Dennis L. Ockholm [Downers Grove, IL: InterVarsity, 1995], 86–97). The problem here is that the Bible describes the natural state of *all* men, not just some, as having transworld depravity. That is why without the efficacious grace of regeneration, no man would be saved. Moreover, it does not solve the problem. How can a God bring these types of people into existence in any world and still be a loving God? Admittedly, Calvinism teaches the same thing. But isn't Molinism designed to counter this claim and posit a more gentler and kinder God? See R. Todd Mangum, "Is There a Reformed Way to Get the Benefits of the Atonement to Those Who Have Never Heard?'" *JETS* 47 (2004): 121–36.

[33] It is the *concept* behind what middle-knowledge proponents call 'transworld depravity' rather than the term itself that occurs in Scripture. To insist that the phrase 'transworld depravity' must be found in Scripture is to commit the word-idea fallacy. The word 'Trinity,' for example, does not occur in the Bible as Jehovah's Witnesses readily point out to Christians. The assumption lying behind the limitation of this concept to certain people is that all possess libertarian freedom. It attempts to account for why God fails to convert everyone and why some never hear the Gospel. This is not surprising because Molinism began with that very purpose in mind. The whole Molinist enterprise is circular. First, middle-knowledge is invented to make room for libertarian freedom then middle knowledge is used to prove that man has libertarian freedom. Several verses clearly demonstrate that no one possess the ability to believe apart from the divine initiative and thus all men possess 'transworld depravity,' i.e., they would be lost in any world they were placed. Jesus said, "No man can come to me unless the one who sent me draws him" (John 6:44). Since in John "come to me" refers to belief in Jesus, and the statement is given as a universal negative (no one in this world is excepted) concerning this ability, it means that no man (in this or any conceivable world) has the ability to believe in Jesus apart from this effect. The exception clause refers to the *necessary* condition for this reversal to occur. It is called 'dragging' (= regeneration in John). Jesus says, "And I will raise *him* on the last day." Because the same 'him' that is dragged is the 'him' that is raised on the last day, the 'dragging' is both a *necessary* and *sufficient* condition for faith in Jesus. This one verse alone (in multiple ways) unambiguously refutes libertarian freedom.

decisions could be reached with this view of time and/or middle-knowledge. That man either lacks the very conditions itself for salvation (perception, knowledge, understanding), thus evidencing a *trans-world universal congenital depravity*, or has as his only remedy the divine initiative, is rejected.

Unqualified Divine Temporality

The final view, *unqualified divine temporality*, is represented by Nicholas Wolterstorff which states that God is in time, always has been, is, and will be in time, that time itself has no *terminus a quo*, and that time is a necessary part of his Being. God has a history and is necessarily *everlasting* but not *eternal*. Scripture seems to teach that God genuinely enters into human affairs and does so ultimately in the incarnation. He subscribes to the A-series of time. Indexical systems relate everything to the present whereas a nonindexical system (*timeless eternity*) is not sufficient. The key issue for Wolterstorff is "whether there's a history of God's actions and responses, and of *the knowledge that lies behind those.*"[34] God's responsiveness proves he has knowledge of tensed facts and this change in knowledge disputes the notion of aseity, simplicity, and immutability classically understood. To affirm divine timeless eternity, says Wolterstorff, is to embrace deism[35] and to deny either human freedom for counterfactuals of

---

[34] Nicholas Wolterstorff, "Unqualified Divine Temporality," in *God & Time: Four Views*, ed. Gregory E. Ganssle (Downers Grove, IL: InterVarsity, 2001), 203 (emphasis added). God makes decisions, as a tensed-fact being, based on relevant counterfactuals (sounds like middle knowledge view here). "But human beings are central to God's decisions; and if we are capable of free action, then there must be facts of the matter as to what we would do in various situations, and God must know those facts. There must be 'counterfactuals of freedom'.... Then would simply have to take a risk. Hence it is that those who hold to God's eternity either deny human freedom or embrace the thesis that there are counterfactuals of freedom" (ibid., 208). He seems to be advancing middle knowledge, a view which says God knows the future including all counter-factuals, but he also advances the notion that future events are not facts (ibid., 197), and if not facts, then not knowable, a view that denies middle knowledge (of counter-factuals) and supports an open future. The same criticism is mentioned by Helm (Paul Helm, "Response to Nicholas Wolterstorff," in *God & Time: Four Views*, ed. Gregory E. Ganssle [Downers Grove, IL: InterVarsity, 2001], 217).

[35] Wolterstorff, "Unqualified Divine Temporality," 205. Against the charge of deism Helm says, "The eternalist position is not deistic because of course on Aquinas's scheme (the general outlines of which an eternalist will endorse) God eternally

freedom. In other words, *libertarian* freedom is the main concern for insisting God is in time. Anselm's arguments of God's simplicity, aseity, and excellence are thus rejected (*Monologium* chaps 17–25). According to Wolterstorff, God's knowledge of the future is only general because it is contingent on man's libertarian freedom.

This view encounters a plethora of problems. First, it denies God knows the future because God, as a temporal being, can only know known tensed facts, namely, the present and the past. This is favorable to an open view of God though Wolterstorff mentions the incompatible (to his own view) idea of God's knowledge of future counter-factuals as essential.[36] Thus he seems to believe as an openness theologian but argues, on occasion, as a middle-knowledge proponent. In this scenario, even a simple foreknowledge view of God is impossible. But if this knowledge is impossible, then neither an irony, effect-purpose idiom, nor a purposive interpretation of Isa 6:9–10 are possible options. For all these views may ascribe to the idea that the future is settled and known by God. Second, he endorses *libertarian* freedom, a view that supports his rejection of the eternity, aseity, and simplicity of God. Here, man's freedom implies that all his decisions are necessarily uncaused either internally or externally. Man possesses *freedom-to-the-contrary* that rejects any form of determinism including internal inclination. Man must be able to choose for no reason (a Pelagian doctrine of free-will) or possibly against his strongest inclination at the moment of choice. That man is

---

upholds the entire cosmos and intervenes miraculously, and (the Christian eternalist will say) he intervenes in the incarnation. But he does not intervene by forming the will to do so in time" (Helm, "Response to Nicholas Wolterstorff," 216). He adds, "While it is true that there is a kind of responsiveness that requires tensed knowledge, an eternal God could eternally decree a response to what he knows will happen at a given time" (ibid.). "When, in time, Moses asks God for his name, God timelessly knows when (in the temporal series) that is, and timelessly responds…he responds by timelessly willing to act in time…and the meaning of response in such a situation may for that reason be said to be like, but not precisely the same, as its meaning in cases of human responsiveness" (ibid., 217).

[36] He gives a human illustration but labels counterfactual knowledge "relevant counterfactuals" in regard to human freedom (Wolterstorff, "Unqualified Divine Temporality," 207). Helm also questions him on this point. "If the future is general and so cannot be referred to, how can it be that in the counterfactuals of freedom, which Nick appears to endorse, there are facts of the matter known to God as to what we would do in various situations" (Helm, "Response to Nicholas Wolterstorff," 217)?

congenitally fat-hearted (as Isaiah seems to define it) is impossible. On the contrary, fattening must be self-imposed and alleviated only by the utilization of free-will, a will that has available to it either a congenital wisdom or the latent ability to acquire it.

Summary on Time

Divine timeless eternity is the orthodox position held by Augustine, Boethius, Aquinas, Luther, Calvin, Edwards, and countless others. Moreover, it is the only view of the four presented that does not arise because of the attempt to make room for libertarian freedom. Given its Christian antiquity, the final three views carry the burden of proof.[37] But even so, this does not imply that significant insights

---

[37] The Synod of Orange (A.D. 529) did not fully embrace Augustinianism's double predestination but it was far from endorsing libertarian freedom. Insightful is the preface written by Pope Boniface II to Caesarius of Arles. He roundly condemns Pelagianism and the ability of man to exercise faith apart from grace. Included is the canons (25 of them), a section on the definition of faith, and selections from the early Fathers. The canons of the Synod are worth noting: (1) Canons 1–2 assert, contra Pelagius, that Adam's sin effects/affects the whole of every person and therefore the whole person is corrupt. Quotations come from Ezek 18:20; Rom 6:16; 2 Pet 2:19; Rom 5:12. (2) Canon 3–4 say that man appeals to God because of grace and is unable to do so apart from it. It is by the Holy Spirit who works in them to will and do of his good pleasure. Quotations come from Isa 65:1; Rom 10:20; Prov 8:35[LXX]; Phil 2:13. (3) Canon 5 rejects any notion that faith can be present apart from regeneration. Quotations come from Phil 1:6, 29; Eph 2:8. (4) Canon 6 denies man can reach out to God apart from God's gift of faith or gift of humility and obedience. Quotations come from 1 Cor 4:7; 15:10. (5) Canon 7 denies that consent in salvation is necessary and a part of human nature apart from the Holy Spirit. Quotations come from John 15:5 and 2 Cor 3:5. (6) Canon 8 contrasts the mercy of baptism (regeneration) with free will reportedly inherent in all men. Quotations come from John 6:44; 1 Cor 12:3. (7) Canons 9–11 refer to the necessity of good works flowing from this grace. Quotation is from 1 Chr 29:14. (8) Canon 12 says that God loves the elect complacently because of what they will by grace not merit. (9) Canon 13 says that baptism (regeneration) alone restores free choice and Canon 14 says without God's intervention man is in bondage. Quotations come from John 8:36 and Ps 79:8. (10) Canons 15–16 refer to the permanent change in Adam for the worse and permanent change in the elect for the better by grace. Quotations come from Ps 77:10; Eph 4:8. (11) Canon 17 says that the Christian has courage from the indwelling Spirit and quotes Rom 5:5. (12) Canons 18–19 say no merit precedes grace but rather grace produces good works. Moreover, no one can remain saved without grace. (13) Canon 20 insists that no person can do good without God. (14) Canon 21 says that if the human nature can attain salvation, then Christ died in vain. It quotes Gal 2:21; Matt 5:17; Luke 19:10. (15) Canon 22 says that man only lies and sins. (16) Canon 23 says that the divine and human will, when good, is done freely even though God prepares and commands what they will (Prov

might not be gained from interacting with these positions. However, it cannot be ignored that orthodoxy has never endorsed but rather rejected libertarian freedom as even proponents of it acknowledge. Although divine timeless eternity does not *completely* satisfy nor answer *every* issue to the satisfaction of *everyone*, for reasons indicated above, it does convince this writer more sufficiently than the other views—although the other views are not equally unpersuasive. God remains eternal.

God and Causation

Hardening/fattening presumably involves at least one or two agents; he who is hardened/fattened and the one who hardens/fattens (unless agents are identical). The act of hardening/fattening demands an answer in regard to the *role* of the agents involved. In addition comes the question as to the *basis* of hardening/fattening. The following discussion explores several alternatives for addressing the problem regarding the interaction of human and divine causation, specifically those offered by Mavrodes and Feinberg. Each view will then be applied to Isa 6:9–10.[38] Mavrodes begins with Pharaoh. An

---

8:35). (17) Canon 24 states that life comes from the vine so that the vine gives life to the branches not vise versa. (18) Canon 25 says the love that a Christian has for God is a gift from God and quotes Rom 5:5. The canon is not completely Augustinian in that it denies double-predestination. However, on the nature of the inability of man to do good apart from grace, it quotes from Augustine, Ambrose, and Jerome all against Pelagius in order to show that this belief is not limited to Augustine. The point is that if one disagrees with Augustine, he also disagrees with Jerome and Ambrose. Jerome relates this to the attainment of wisdom: "In order that we may realize that every good we do is from God [he then quotes Jer 24:6–7 which makes reference to the bestowal of perception and judgment then concludes that].... If perception and judgment are given by God, if knowledge of the Lord springs from the root of the one we are to know, then where is the proud boasting of free choice" (*Gest. Pelag.* 2.27)? Having re-read the Synod, I can find no hint whatsoever of an endorsement of libertarian freedom.

[38] The views below are derived from the interchange between Mavrodes, Feinberg, and Pinnock. See George Mavrodes, "Is There Anything Which God Does Not Do?" *CSR* 16 (1987): 384–91; Clark H. Pinnock, "A Comment on 'Is There Anything Which God Does Not Do?' by George Mavrodes," *CSR* 16 (1987): 392–93; John Feinberg, "Divine Causality and Evil: Is There Anything Which God Does Not Do?" *CSR* 16 (1987): 394–402; George Mavrodes, "A Reply to Professors Feinberg and Pinnock," *CSR* 16 (1987): 403–04.

alternative scheme of acting agents will be added to these for construing the subject-object of fattening in Isa 6:9–10.

George Mavrodes's Four Schemes[39]

Mavrodes is disturbed by the pancausality implied in Amos 3:6 where it asks, "Shall evil befall a city, and Yahweh has not *done* it?"[40] The focus is on Yahweh's *doing* evil.[41] This seems to him incredible. He likens the doing of evil to the hardening of Pharaoh and the teachings of Paul in Rom 9–11. At times God hardens or will harden (Exod 4:21; 7:3; 9:12; 10:1, 20, 27; 11:10, 14:4, 8, 17), Pharaoh is in a hardened state (7:13, 14, 22; 8:15[19], 9:7, 35), or Pharaoh hardens himself (Exod 8:11[15], 28[32]; 9:34). His proposed solution is guided by the questions, "*Who* hardened Pharaoh's heart?" and "*How* can this be done without implicating God in evil?" There is every reason to suppose that Mavrodes would apply the exact causative paradigm to Isa 6:9–10 and its parallels in the NT. However, Isa 6:9–10 and its reuse in Isaiah as well as NT texts do not mention self-hardening (probably because 'self-hardening' is *functionally* oriented).[42] He

---

[39] Pinnock says on the issue that God is certainly not the doer of everything that is done. He is in favor of a "plausible non-determinist model" that "can do justice to certain biblical expressions and relieve us of the Calvinist model which wreaks such havoc upon both the character of God and human moral responsibility.... The key notion is that of God's voluntary self-limitation" (Pinnock, "A Comment," 393). He encourages people like Mavrodes to "keep pushing away the narrow walls of the determinist theology until they collapse" (ibid., 393). For similar sentiments towards Calvinists see Pinnock, *The Most Moved Mover*, 10–18.

[40] His purpose is "to explore the idea of God's sovereignty which might be expressed in statements like that of Amos, and in the more general principle.... I am not even primarily concerned with the full generality of the principle that God is the doer of everything that is done.... I will focus instead on the special case of claims to the effect that God is the doer of certain deeds which we are inclined to think are bad deeds" (Mavrodes, "Is There Anything Which God Does Not Do?" 385).

[41] The term for 'evil' is the adjective רָעָה which occurs 255 times in the MT (274 if alternate Hebrew texts are included). The nominal form is given in BDB as *evil, misery, distress, injury*. The three definitions include (1) *evil, misery, distress*, (2) *evil, injury, wrong*, and (3) ethical *evil* (948–49). The LXX uses a number of terms to translate the adjectival form.

[42] The NT passages like Matt 13:15 and Acts 28:27 indicate that the heart is already fat. Likewise, in the story of Pharaoh, there are passages that focus on the fact that Pharaoh's heart is hard (Exod 7:13, 14, 22; 8:15[19]; 9:7, 35). Thus three types of passages must be fit into the causative scheme, viz., passages where *God* hardens,

proposes four models to account for how God and human agents are both involved in hardening.

Alternating Agents. This view insists that over a period of several weeks, at times Pharaoh hardened his own heart while at other times God did. This view avoids dual agency altogether. Who hardens Pharaoh's heart? "The answer would be that it happened several times, and some times it was God who did it and at other times it was Pharaoh himself."[43] Each agent is the sole hardener at different times. There is no *explicit* logical connector between the agents, that is, God does not harden *because* Pharaoh hardens himself and vice versa. Mavrodes is not convinced by this scheme, however, because one side involves God as either a direct or ultimate cause behind hardening. Feinberg agrees with Mavrodes in rejecting this model echoing Piper that "the hardening of Pharaoh's heart on each occasion comes after a prediction that God will harden Pharaoh's heart."[44] Thus a causative connection is made with the divine operating in the ultimate role. The remaining models involve some form of dual agency.

Joint-Agency. Joint-agency involves more than one agent in order for the task to be complete. It is best described as a form of synergism involving a symbiotic relationship. Who hardened Pharaoh's heart? "The full answer would be that the two of them did it together, and each one of them would figure in partial answers to the question. The moral questions would remain to be dealt with, but we would have a ready way of fitting together the two answers about who did the hardening."[45] Mavrodes rejects this option as well for not being quite commensurate with the text as it stands. Feinberg agrees that this

---

where *Pharaoh* hardens, and where Pharaoh is described in a *state* of hard-heartedness. There is also linguistic evidence that two different issues are involved, namely, rebellion (with Pharaoh) and lack of wisdom (with Isaiah). Moreover, Mavrodes assumes that self-hardening and divine hardening of Pharaoh are the same act. But this is unlikely. Divine hardening is deprivational, non-transformational, and ontological whereas self-hardening is functional.

[43] Mavrodes, "Is There Anything Which God Does Not Do?" 386.

[44] Feinberg, "Divine Causality and Evil," 395. Cf. John Piper, *The Justification of God: An Exegetical & Theological Study of Romans 9:1–23*, 2d ed. (Grand Rapids: Baker, 1993), 159–81.

[45] Mavrodes, "Is There Anything Which God Does Not Do?" 386.

model gives the impression that neither God nor Pharaoh could accomplish the hardening alone.

Proximate and Remote Agency. This model "allows us to assign two (or more) causes for a single effect, without thinking of them as joint causes."[46] Each can be said to be the sole cause of hardening but a distinction is made between proximate and remote cause. He has in mind a series of causes, for example, a gunshot wound to the chest causes internal bleeding, bleeding causes death. The pattern is x is the cause of y, and y is the cause of z, therefore, x is the cause of z. Problems emerge here. First, Mavrodes sees this as morally troublesome not because God is the ultimate (or remote) cause, but that it both makes blameworthiness difficult and presents God doing evil (hardening) which seems to violate his goodness.[47] Second, how can man be held responsible if God is the remote cause? His underlying premise is, *"Remote agents and causes drain moral responsibility away from proximate agents and causes."*[48] In Rom 9:18–19, says Mavrodes, the interlocutor presents Pharaoh as faultless yet unable to resist God's will. Although the passage presents a version of the second problem above, the reply given by Paul answers the first question. Since a retribution sense seems not to be the case, he rejects this view.[49]

On this score Feinberg disagrees with Mavrodes. Mavrodes argues that no one can be held morally responsible for actions that are not free. Feinberg responds, "But, is it true that all cases for which an action is attributed to a remote and proximate cause are cases where the proximate acts unfreely and without responsibility?"[50] He goes on

---

[46] Ibid.

[47] Mavrodes says that if God hardened Pharaoh's heart, then God is bad (ibid., 387). The assumption here is that hardening is evil, that man does not deserve hardening, or if God does harden he owes an explanation for why he does so. But there is a more fundamental assumption underlying this one, viz., hardening is transformative. For those who hold to a transformative view, a solution would be that the idea of retribution is the cause. God did not arbitrarily harden but did so on the basis of bad behavior. Theoretically, either view (non-transformative or retributional-transformative) provides an answer to this objection.

[48] Ibid., 388.

[49] Ibid., 390.

[50] Feinberg, "Divine Causality and Evil," 396.

to explain that the definition of 'free' needs to be understood as not apart from causal determinism but rather without internal coercion. He says, "So long as all agents involved act freely (in some legitimate sense of 'free'), then regardless of how many remote causes there are, moral responsibility is not drained away from the proximate cause."[51] All depends on the meaning of 'freedom' here and the indeterminist does not have a monopoly on that definition.

Overdetermining Agents. Here is Mavrodes' unique view in solving the problem. This model "depends on the idea of the over-determination of an effect or event."[52] Mavrodes explains: "Imagine two assassins, acting independently, stalk the same victim. By chance, they shoot him simultaneously, and the two bullets meet in the victim's heart. The autopsy shows that each shot would have been fatal by itself—the victim would have died in the same way at the same time. There thus seems to be two causes for that death, and two agents would have acted in ways that were sufficient to bring it about. The death would be overdetermined."[53] Each gunman is the killer of the victim. It is not a joint-act (for each does something sufficient for the effect and without complicity) nor remote/proximate (for it is not an ordered hierarchy) dual agency but rather "dual agency" of over-determination—neither one *causes* the action of the other.[54] The attempt to avoid responsibility by claiming the other one would have killed the victim is negated by the fact that either shot would have produced the same effect. Instead both are responsible for the death of the victim. "Overdetermination, unlike remote agency, does not seem to drain moral responsibility away."[55]

---

[51] Ibid.

[52] Mavrodes, "Is There Anything Which God Does Not Do?" 390.

[53] Ibid.

[54] This is similar to views of *pre-established harmony* or *occasionalism* as it applies to mind/body interactionism (Taylor, *Metaphysics*, 8–16; R. C. Sproul, *Not a Chance: The Myth of Chance in Modern Science & Cosmology* [Grand Rapids: Baker, 2000], 196–98; Gregory Pence, *A Dictionary of Common Philosophical Terms* [New York: McGraw-Hill, 2000], 39; Norman L. Geisler and Paul D. Feinberg, *Introduction to Philosophy: A Christian Perspective* [Grand Rapids: Baker, 1980], 179–92).

[55] Mavrodes, "Is There Anything Which God Does Not Do?" 390.

Although this model does not drain moral responsibility, it does, he admits, make divine hardening superfluous, pointless, and meaningless. His conclusion is that there are things God does not do, although he is not even convinced of this admitting, "perhaps there is some sense, after all, in which God *is* the doer of every act."[56] Feinberg agrees with the redundancy that this view generates for "each agent works independently of the other to accomplish the same effect, and that whatever each does is sufficient without the action of the other to accomplish the act...the action of one or the other becomes superfluous."[57]

John Feinberg's Solution[58]

Feinberg seeks to present a form of the proximate and remote agency view that resolves the tension felt by Mavrodes and others. First, he focuses on the issue of sovereignty as *whatever is done is done by God.*[59]

---

[56] Ibid., 391.

[57] Feinberg, "Divine Causality and Evil," 396–97.

[58] Feinberg says (1) Mavrodes' article raises three major issues and one minor issue that underlie the whole discussion of the hardening of Pharaoh's heart. "The foundational issue is how it is that God does everything, i.e., in what sense is it true that God does everything" (ibid., 395)? (2) The compatibility of causal determinism and human freedom. (3) The compatibility of causal determinism and moral responsibility. (4) The accuracy of Scripture. He sets "ground rules" for the discussion. (1) The model he proposes (in response to the three major issues) is relevant to both morally good and evil actions. (2) The sufficient condition or cause of an action or event may be either simple or complex. "Prima facie, therefore, there is no impossibility or absurdity about two agents being responsible in (or even as) the sufficient condition for accomplishing one and the same action" (ibid.). (3) What is actually asserted when one claims that there is a contradiction. The complaint is that there is no possible resolution to the difficulty. He presents a possible way to remove the contradiction. Although there may be more than one possible solution, he offers one.

[59] Augustine says, "It is true of all his creatures, both spiritual and corporeal, that he does not know them because they are, but that they are because he knows them" (*Trin.* 15.22). The sentence before this states, "To know this [needs revealed in prayer] he did not get to know it at a certain time, but without beginning he foreknew beforehand all future temporal things, and among them what we were going to ask him for and when, and whom he was going to listen to or not listen to, and about what things" (ibid.). Aquinas adds, "The knowledge of God is the cause of all things. For the knowledge of God is to all creatures what the knowledge of the artificer is to things made by his art. Now the knowledge of the artificer is the cause of the things

He critiques Mavrodes' models and proposes his own. His model, first of all, distinguishes between *mediate* and *immediate* actions. Mediate action is subdivided into two areas: first, cases where God is involved as a *remote cause* and the creature is a *proximate cause,* and second, instances when God is the *remote cause* but is involved along with his creature as a *proximate cause* (cf. 2 Pet 1:20–21). God is doing (either *immediately* or *mediately* [*remote* or *proximate* cause]) the act in all cases (Eph 1:11).[60]

Second, he focuses on *how God does everything but man is free.* Here he discusses and dismisses *indeterminism* (*libertarian* free-will) as not the only 'freedom' there can be. Indeterminism is defined as "the notion that regardless of what causal influences play upon the will, nothing decisively inclines the will in one direction or another, so the

---

make by his art,…[but] the intelligible form does not denote a principle of action in so far as it resides in the one who understands unless there is added to it the inclination to an effect, which inclination is through the will…. (*Sum. Theol.* 1.14.9; Augustine *Civ.* 5.5, 9; *Grat.* 32; Martin Luther *Serv.* 720–22, Jonathan Edwards, *Freedom of the Will,* ed. Paul Ramsey, The Works of Jonathan Edwards, ed. Perry Miller, vol. 1 [New Haven, CT: Yale University Press, 1957], 239–69; Ames *Medulla theologica* 1.25.7–11, 13–14; John Locke, "An Essay Concerning Human Understanding," in *Lock, Berkeley, Hume,* Great Books of the Western World, ed. Robert Maynard Hutchins, Mortimer J. Adler, and Wallace Brockway, vol. 35 [Chicago: Encyclopedia Britannica, 1952], 83–395). "For there is properly only one act of will in God because in him all things are simultaneous and there is nothing before or after. So there is only one decree about the end and means, but for our manner of understanding we say that, so far as intention is concerned, God wills the end before the means" (Ames *Medulla theologica* 1.25.14). God's knowledge does not *discover* form (Kantian epistemology) but *imposes* form (and matter too). With this in mind a foreknowledge view (Arminian view) of determinism becomes impossible. How can God see to a form that he has not imposed? To say that another imposed a form is to posit another God. It is in this sense that both Augustine and Aquinas held that God's knowledge is the cause of all things. For a judicious summary of Aquinas see Norman L. Geisler, *Thomas Aquinas: An Evangelical Appraisal* (Grand Rapids: Baker, 1991), 103–35; Peter Kreeft, ed., *A Summa of the Summa: The Essential Philosophical Passages of St. Thomas Aquinas' Summa Theologica Edited and Explained for Beginners* (San Francisco: Ignatius, 1990), 53–85.

[60] "Given verses like Ephesians 1:11 that claim God wills and does all things, and given the obvious empirical point that God's creatures are involved in many of the actions and events that occur in our world, it is safe to say that God has chosen to do most things that he does in our world mediately, not immediately" (Feinberg, "Divine Causality and Evil," 397). Thus when the Bible says God did something, it can refer to either *immediate* or *mediate* agency (*remote* or *proximate* cause). Cf. Ames *Medulla theologica* 1.6.

agent could always have done otherwise than he did."[61] To this Feinberg insists that "freedom is eliminated only if one thinks that indeterministic freedom is the only kind of freedom there could be."[62] He proposes instead 'soft determinism' or 'compatibilism' where actions are *causally determined* but freedom of the creature is maintained because no one is *constrained* to act against his will or desires.[63] He acts in accord with causes and reasons without being forced to act contrary to his wishes and thus acts freely.

Third, he focuses on *how God does all things and yet man is responsible*. It is two-pronged, manward and Godward. Man is responsible because he acts freely of his own free will, irrespective of the ultimate agency of God. Significantly he notes that, "the hardening of Pharaoh's heart is parallel to the choice of Jacob over Esau…. Likewise, God's decision to harden Pharaoh did not come in *response* to Pharaoh, but was based solely on God's will."[64] Although the objector's points are both intellectual and attitudinal, Paul is answering only an attitudinal issue in Rom 9:20, not a question about God's moral responsibility (Mavrodes).[65] Feinberg ends with defense (an apologetic) against evil.

Mavrodes's Rebuttal

Mavrodes objects to dual agency because in cases of unspeakable evil, like the rape of a child, one would have to say, since God is the doer

---

[61] Feinberg, "Divine Causality and Evil," 399.

[62] Ibid.

[63] He defines soft determinism or compatibilism as that freedom where "actions are causally determined (the will is decisively inclined toward one option as opposed to another) and yet free so long as the causes do not constrain the agent to act against his will or desires. If the agent acts in accord with causes and reasons that serve as the sufficient condition for his doing the act, and if the causes do not force him to act contrary to his wishes, then a soft determinist would say he acts freely" (ibid., 399–400).

[64] Ibid., 401.

[65] "I cannot completely agree with the conclusions he [Mavrodes] does derive [from Rom 9:19–20]. Mavrodes claims that the objection is raised as a question about human responsibility, whereas the answer about the potter and the clay responds to the objection about God's moral responsibility. I agree that the objector focuses on man's responsibility, but I am dubious that Paul's reply is meant to answer the question of God's guilt" (ibid.). Cf. Piper, *The Justification of God*, 185–204.

of all things, that God raped the child.[66] "Why might God not *allow* that act to be done, without being the doer of it, immediately or mediately or in any other way?"[67] What Mavrodes finds objectionable is what is commonly referred to as the doctrine of *concurrence*, namely, the working of two wills, the divine and human, in the same act (cf. Gen 50:20). If God is shown to be clearly the author of the most horrific of evils, then rape, incest, perjury, murder, etc., cannot be used to argue that God is not the doer in a remote sense. Case in point *a maximis ad minima* is the crucifixion of Jesus.

No sin imaginable is more horrific than the crucifixion of Jesus Christ. Yet, Scripture indicates that this was *done* by God the Father to God the Son (mediately) through the immediate agency of sinful human beings in the crucifixion (Isa 52:13–53:12; Acts 2:23; 4:28).[68] If this is the worst possible evil that can be imagined,[69] and God is clearly the ultimate cause behind it, then why be repulsed by divine

---

[66] Pinnock mentions rape as well (Pinnock, *The Most Moved Mover*, 16). He says, "God's sovereign authorship of every rape and murder, his closing down the future to any meaningful creaturely contribution, and his holding people accountable for deeds he predestined them to do they could not but do."

[67] Mavrodes, "A Reply to Professors Feinberg and Pinnock," 404.

[68] These two verses are absolutely detrimental to a variety of non-determinist points of view. Acts 2:23 indicates that logically foreordination precedes foreknowledge (τοῦτον τῇ ω ρισμένῃ βουλῇ καὶ προγνώσει τοῦ θεοῦ ἔκδοτον διὰ χειρὸς ἀνόμων προσπήξαντες ἀνείλατε). In other words, God foreknows because he has foreordained rather than foreordains because he foreknows (based on the future free acts of human *libertarian* freedom). For a justification of the logical rendering of two singular impersonal nouns in the G-Sharp *construction* see Daniel B. Wallace, *Greek Grammar beyond the Basics: An Exegetical Syntax of the New Testament* (Grand Rapids: Zondervan, 1996), 288. This verse teaches (1) God is the doer of all things, (2) God knows future free acts of men (sinful or otherwise), (3) God is behind the most heinous act of all history, (4) evil men are used to perform the act, (5) these individuals do what they do freely, (6) and they are held accountable for their evil deed.

[69] That Christ willingly died does not make murder less evil than involuntary rape (although not all rape is involuntary—some cases of statutory rape). The final cause of God, salvific or otherwise, no more alleviates the guilt of the murderers of Christ than it does the brothers of Joseph. It is infinitely more evil to murder God incarnate than any other sin of any other kind imaginable. Jesus said to Pilate, "He [Judas] that delivered me unto you has committed greater sin" (John 19:11). Admittedly, the final cause of Christ's death is the salvation of many whereas with the rape of a child it is unknown or otherwise unknowable.

pancausality when it comes to rape of a child as if this is a greater evil? If God is the ultimate agent behind the worst of all possible evils, then there is no justification for denying he is the ultimate agent behind lesser evils irrespective of its final cause from the divine perspective. It is difficult to imagine a psychological refuge in a God who simply *allows* these acts to occur but does not or cannot stop them as opposed to a God who remotely but ultimately causes all things. At least with the latter one can hope, if not presently understand it, that a greater purpose is served.

Another problem is that Mavrodes views things in terms of good versus evil when it is more complicated than that. Gerstner (as well as Aquinas)[70] argues that everything done is good because everything that happens is according to God's good pleasure (Eph 1:11). There are, however, degrees of goodness such as the good/good and evil/good. The first category (*good*/good vs. *evil*/good) is what is normally meant by good versus evil. It is inconceivable for Mavrodes and others to see that the rape of a child is *good* in the decretal sense.[71] No one wants to hear that the rape of his child (or any other unspeakable evil/good) is ultimately or in any way good. It is without question *prescriptively* evil.

Two things in conclusion should be stated. First, the problem of evil is called a mystery precisely because God is the doer of all things (including sinful acts mediately performed) yet he is without sin (2 Thess 2:7). To deny God is the ultimate cause and doer of all things is to replace theism with another world-view—and this is Mavrodes's difficulty, namely, the implications of theism. Second, whatever respite from the consequences of sin man enjoys is to be thought of as undeserved mercy instead of as an inherent right. Why God did *not* choose Esau but Jacob is not the question. Why he *did* choose Jacob or anybody else for that matter is. This thinking requires a change in perspectives.

A New Proposal

The above discussion assumes two actors in the act of hardening (Pharaoh and God) and discusses within that confine how God can be

---

[70] Aquinas *Sum. Theol.* 1.19.4, 7, 9.

[71] John H. Gerstner, *Primitive Theology: The Collected Primers of John H. Gerstner* (Morgan, PA: Soli Deo Gloria, 1996), 42.

the doer of not only all things but also of what is normally understood as 'evil' acts. Attempts are made in formulating *how* God can or cannot be the doer of these acts, how this can be so without violating man's 'freedom' or implicating God as evil, and how man is still held responsible. These constructs, however, do not directly apply either to Exod 4–14 or Isa 6:9–10. Why? First, 'hardening' in Exodus is ontological and deprivational when God does it and functional when Pharaoh does it. Second, because Isaianic fattening involves only one actor not two. This is in contrast to the hardening of Pharaoh. Third, the 'hardening' of Pharaoh addresses volition not cognition as in Isaiah and is not identical to Isaianic 'fattening.' Fourth, no instance in Isaiah endorses self-fattening and the clear actor is God. One clear similarity of the two, however, is that both operate from a non-retributional *basis* and a divine deprivational *mode*. Indeed, they might (and perhaps always) include a retributional *purpose*, but this is a separate issue.

However, these passages do not explicitly indicate *how* either occurs or if the acts effect a change in state at all. The Hebrew stem (Hiphil) in the verbs of Isa 6:9–10 indicate that God is the *cause* of fattening but his role can be construed logically as causally *creative* or *continuative* or grammatically as *ingressive* or *constative*. The former demands a *transformative* view whereas the latter a *deprivational* undertaking. It will be argued below that God is the *continuative* cause of Isaianic fattening by the deprivation of the new (or wise) heart. Thus God is the *cause* of continual fattening without *doing* the act of transformational fattening. This implies that man is naturally without salvific perception, knowledge, and understanding, that is, he is *congenitally* fat-hearted. This invariably leads to the issue of freedom below.

God and Freedom[72]

The discussion above on both time and causality invariably elicit comments on free-will and in particular the widely accepted notion of *libertarian* free-will. This view of freedom received popularity when represented by a British monk by the name of Pelagius (which can be traced back to Greek philosophy through Tertullian[73] by means of

---

[72] For an interesting discussion on how modern physics impacts views of freedom and God see Davies, *God and the New Physics*, 135–43.

[73] Tertullian *An.* 21.5–7; 22.1–2; 24.4.

Theophilus of Antioch) who ran afoul of the western theologian Augustine of Hippo.[74] It is not necessary to recast the debate but rather to highlight what Augustine means when he argues that man possesses *free-will* but no *liberty*.[75] His discussion is important because church history sides with him against Pelagius (and semi-Pelagianism) and later writers such as Aquinas, Luther, Calvin, and Edwards (to mention a few) advance his views. In this Study, therefore, further comment on man's ability will be treated in later chapters.

Augustine and the Will

Augustine taught that every man possesses *liberum arbitrium* (free-will) in the sense of possessing the ability to choose what he wants without external constraint.[76] He understood man to be free in this

---

[74] Pelagius's main treatises include *De natura* and *Demetrius*. Augustine has several works including *Contra duas epistulas Pelagianorum ad Bonifatium* (*Against the Two Letters of the Pelagians*), *De gratia Christi, et de peccato originali* (*The Grace of Christ and Original Sin*), *De gratia et libero arbitrio* (*Grace and Free Will*), *De correptione et gratia* (*Admonition and Grace*), *De gestis Pelagii* (*Proceedings of Pelagius*), *De libero arbitrio* (*Free Will*), *De natura et gratia* (*Nature and Grace*), and *De praedestinatione sanctorum* (*The Predestination of the Saints*). For a popular and concise discussion on the history of free-will and the church see R. C. Sproul, *Willing to Believe: The Controversy over Free Will* (Grand Rapids: Baker, 1997). On the early controversies see J. Patout Burns, ed., *Theological Anthropology*, trans. J. Patout Burns, SECT, ed. William G. Rusch (Philadelphia: Fortress, 1981). For a contemporary Calvinist perspective see Thomas R. Schreiner and Bruce A. Ware, eds., *Still Sovereign: Contemporary Perspectives on Election, Foreknowledge, and Grace* (Grand Rapids: Baker, 2000). For the Arminian perspective see Clark H. Pinnock, ed., *The Grace of God and the Will of Man: A Case for Arminianism* (Minneapolis: Bethany, 1995).

[75] The debate *redivivus* occurs later between Luther and Erasmus. It must be viewed in terms of the literary history. First, Luther publishes his *Assertio* in 1521. This is followed by Erasmus' *De libero arbitrio* in 1524. Luther then responds with his *De servo arbitrio* in 1526 which is followed by Erasmus's two rejoinders, *Hyperaspistes* (part one) in 1526 and *Hyperaspistes* (part two) in 1527. For background and summary see Cornelis Augustijn, *Erasmus: His Life, Works, and Influence*, trans. J. C. Grayson (Toronto: University of Toronto Press, 1995), 119–60 and the introduction by J. I. Packer to Martin Luther, *The Bondage of the Will: The Masterwork of the Great Reformer*, trans. J. I. Packer and O. R. Johnston (Old Tappan, NJ: Revell, 1957), 13–61.

[76] Adler says this phrase refers to "a free judgment of the mind" (Mortimer J. Adler, *How to Think about the Great Ideas: From the Great Books of Western Civilization*, ed. M. Weismann [Chicago: Open Court, 2000], 36).

sense before salvation (*non posse non peccare*), during salvation (*posse non peccare*), and in the eternal state when one is *non posse peccare*. Man, God, angels, and every rational being, always does what he *wants* to do. The second aspect is what Augustine called *libertas* (liberty) that he says man does not presently possess. This liberty in turn is controlled by *libido* (pleasure or desire). The *libido* is that which determines what is pleasurable to a person, the inclinations that form the basis of all free-will decisions. True *libertas* is having *libido* in the righteous deed, a holy bondage according to Augustine. Since the fall of Adam, man lacks this righteous *libido* and thus genuine *libertas*. Therefore, man is unable to want the truly good or to take pleasure in the righteous deed. This is in contrast to Pelagius who believed in *possibilitas utriusque partis*, 'possibility of either side'—exactly the doctrine of *libertarian* freedom. So Augustine taught a paradox that man is both free (free-will) and not free at the same time. These intractable inclinations are inherent and a result of the fall of Adam.

The distinction between the two views of freedom are crucial. Essentially all views of free-will, including up to the present time, side with either one or the other perspective in part or in whole.[77] Pelagius taught that commands imply the ability to obey, that is, *ought-implies-can*, else the injunctions are disingenuous and a mockery. The impact of this assumption is that man by nature possesses the ability to do good or evil (*possibilitas boni et mali*) if he so chooses. This view ignores clear biblical passages that teach man is unable to will the good because he is in bondage to sin. Man is spiritually dead in the sense that he cannot will to will the good or that which pleases God. Edwards argued that although man has the *natural* ability to believe, repent, obey, etc., he lacks the *moral* ability to do so since the fall. It is in this sense that man is dead. True *libertas* is partially restored in regeneration, a regeneration that gives spiritual and moral life to those for whom Christ died and restores a *libido* that seeks God's righteousness. Then and only then does man exercise his *liberum arbitrium* in faith and repentance.

---

[77] Other crucial works in agreement with Augustine on freedom are Aquinas *Sum. Theol.* 1.82.1–4; 83.1–4; 1–2.6.4; 1–2.8–9, 13, 18–20; Luther *Serv.* and Edwards, *Freedom of the Will.* Luther emphasized *libertas* while Edwards the *liberium arbitrium* of Augustine's doctrine. Despite the apparent disparity of the titles, they both teach essentially the same thing.

Edwards and Freedom

Jonathan Edwards' *A Careful and Strict Inquiry into the Modern Prevailing Notions of the Freedom of the Will*, is his greatest literary achievement.[78] It examines every conceivable alternative to the Augustinian view of freedom and provides the most thoroughgoing refutation of the Pelagian and semi-Pelagian doctrine of the will. The book has four major sections: The first (pp. 137–67) explains the terminology and proper boundaries of the subject; the second (pp. 171–273) considers whether there can be any such thing as libertarian freedom both logically or actually; the third (pp. 277–333) covers whether libertarian freedom is a necessity in order for moral agents to be blame or praiseworthy; and the fourth (pp. 337–429) addresses the reasoning of Arminians in support of this freedom and provides a refutation of each point. A conclusion (pp. 430–39) catalogues the treatment of the issue by non-Calvinists especially as it relates to the doctrines of grace.[79] Ramsey writes, "For Edwards as a theologian the issue is a simple one: either contingency and the liberty of self-determination must run out of this world, or God will be shut out."[80] A few noteworthy issues derived from Edward's treatment should be briefly mentioned.[81]

---

[78] Paul Ramsey writes in the introduction the following: "Into the writing of it he poured all his intellectual acumen...Edwards sent forth to combat contingency and self-determination...and in which he delivered the most thoroughgoing and absolutely destructive criticism that liberty of indifference, without necessity, has ever received.... This book alone is sufficient to establish its author as the greatest philosopher-theologian yet to grace the American scene" (Edwards, *Freedom of the Will*, 1–2). Edwards is one of those rare theologians that command the attention of friend and foe alike. But if Edwards himself is enough to *command* one's attention on any subject, then this book above all others of his ought to *capture* it. A thoroughgoing acquaintance with this inquiry alone might help to squelch the modern resurgence of libertarian freedom under the guise of Openness theology.

[79] The book is prefaced by an excellent introduction by Paul Ramsey (ibid., 1–128) and contains an appendix consisting of two letters written by Jonathan Edwards to the Reverend John Erskine (ibid., 443–52).

[80] Ibid., 9.

[81] Much of what follows is dependent on the groupings of Paul Ramsay in the introduction (ibid., 1–133).

First, according to Edwards, freedom is defined as man being free to do what he wills but not what he does not will.[82] Ramsey notes the following:

> A brief summary of the agreement between Edwards' opinions and those of many present-day philosophers needs to note at least the following crucial points: (1) Since ordinary language is notoriously inexact, 'freedom' and all other terms to be used in this discussion must be carefully defined. Freedom means the ability to do what we will, or according to our pleasure. (2) That men indubitably have such freedom, and only such freedom, can be demonstrated by an exhaustive analysis of an act of volition. In defining freedom and analyzing the nature of an act of volition, questions about what *goes before* and act of willing should not be raised. By *placing brackets around* all such questions and removing them from consideration, we can be sure of sticking close to the actual *experience* of freedom and not be tempted to import into the discussion notions of freedom that are the product of confused metaphysical speculation. (3) Not only is the determination of action by will, motive, or pleasure of the agent consistent with morality, but morality actually requires determinism, since law and commandment, praise and blame apply to the motive or inclination inherent in the willing agent. (4) There can be no event without a cause. (Here, consciously or unconsciously, the brackets are removed and both Edwards and contemporary determinists introduce consideration of events before the act of willing.) There are no grounds for supposing a 'pure ego' intervening from without to influence the course of voluntary action. (5) In speaking of causation, however, it is the *connection* or *correlation* between antecedent and consequent rather than efficient causation that we should have in mind. (6) Moreover, *moral* necessity needs to be distinguished from natural necessity, and *determinism* from *compulsion*. Determinism and moral necessity are consistent with praiseworthiness and blameworthiness (indeed, they require it), while compulsion and natural necessity are not.[83]

This note implies that Edwards regards the cause of the inclinations and thus the determinations (or indeterminations) of the choices as a separate issue and inconsequential (either way) as to how freedom is defined. The same applies to the concept of volition.[84] However, the act of willing itself is such that acts necessarily follow in accordance with the inclinations so that it cannot be otherwise. These

---

[82] Edwards, *Freedom of the Will*, 164.

[83] Ibid., 11–12.

[84] Ibid., 347. See also Mortimer J. Adler, *The Idea of Freedom: A Dialectical Examination of the Conceptions of Freedom* (Garden City, NY: Doubleday, 1958), 400–583.

inclinations are not a result of chosen or self-determined inclinations (infinite regression follows) but are determined and determinant of the acts that follow.[85] One cannot be inclined to change an inclination without an inclination to do so as antecedent cause. This inclination is opposed to the notion of 'indifference' for this presupposes an effect without a cause. If one is not inclined to a particular action then no action can result. The will is the mind choosing according to the last agreeable dictate of the understanding or the strongest inclination at the moment of choice.[86]

Second, according to Edwards, to deny man possesses the *will-to-the-contrary* does not absolve him of moral responsibility nor is its possession necessary for this to occur. Because man lacks the moral ability to believe, repent, or please God does not imply that he is not morally responsible to believe, repent, and please God. Responsibility is based on *natural* not *moral* ability. The latter was lost in the fall. The retort that man must not be blamed for what he is morally unable to do is as baseless as the notion that God must not be praised for doing what he is unable not to do. Both propositions stand or fall together.[87]

Libertarian proponents typically acknowledge that God does not possess contra-causal freedom. But if God is the Spirit of liberty and does not possess this type of freedom, then the burden of proof lies on proponents of libertarian liberty when it comes to man. To argue that God does possess libertarian freedom is to insist that he can lie, cheat, and steal but simply chooses not to do so. But this runs contrary to passages which state God *cannot* lie, cheat, or steal not simply that he does not *want* to do these things—although he also does not want to. If libertarian proponents are right, God must not be praised because he lacks the ability to do otherwise. Yet this is the very reason he is to be praised. Blame or praise is predicated on whether one voluntary engages in the acts in question.[88] Since this is so, man and God do not

---

[85] Edwards, *Freedom of the Will*, 305–12.

[86] Ibid., 144, 217, 22, 141, 328. Ramsay says that "the will or mind is inclined by the sway or determination of something that is not within the agent's present act" (ibid., 18).

[87] Ibid., 277–80.

[88] Ibid., 272, 326–27, 40, 42, 99–400, 14, 27–28. Edwards insists that the Arminian view of the 'freedom of indifference' obviates any notion of a virtuous or vicious quality of the mind (ibid., 325). Without determinism there is no sense to the setting forth of the

have to possess the ability of the contrary but only to act volitionally to be morally praiseworthy or blameworthy. Apart from regeneration, man lacks righteous *libido*, is not inclined towards God, is unable to please God, and is rightfully condemned. Thus the possession of virtuous love is necessary in order to bring forth acts of a virtuous choice.[89] And this possession comes via God's unprecipitated infusion of it into the soul. The effect cannot be greater than its cause.[90]

Third, according to Edwards, the will does not move itself but is moved by another. In completing the quotation of Rom 9:16, οὐ τοῦ θέλοντος οὐδὲ τοῦ τρέχοντος ἀλλὰ τοῦ ἐλεῶντος θεοῦ, Edwards locates the source of the godly inclinations, like Augustine, in the infusion of the Spirit of God.[91]

Fourth, according to Edwards, man's will is both determined and free. Edwards is one of many to recognize that causation and determinism do not imply coercion.[92] Ramsey says, "In fact, no theologian of any stature who believed in divine determinism, or in any degree of efficacy in the operation of divine grace upon the soul,

---

way of the wise or the fool (ibid., 331). Responsibility is inconsistent with the 'freedom of indifference.'

[89] Ibid., 32–33.

[90] Part of Edward's subtitle is Rom 9:16, "It is not of him that willeth...." This underlies his view that the will must be renewed before it can be necessarily (or effectually) inclined towards God. It also supports his view that a choice to believe must be caused by a virtuous love, a love which man does not have prior to its infusion into the heart by God. Thus the effect must not outdo its cause. Man does not become virtuous by choosing but chooses virtually because he is virtuous. The former is self-contradictory but is the view of Pelagians and semi-Pelagians. This is a like complaint against writers in the first chapter of this Study who argue that hardening occurs as a result of disobedience. They argue that individuals produce effects greater than its cause or have effects serving as the cause of definitionally equal effects. They who are fattened cease having the *ability* to perceive, know, and understand brought about by their *failure* to perceive, know, and understand.

[91] Jonathan Edwards, *A Treatise concerning Religious Affections, in Three Parts: Part I. Concerning the Nature of the Affections, and Their Importance in Religion. Part II. Shewing What are no Certain Signs That Religious Affections are Gracious, or That They are Not. Part III. Shewing What are Distinguishing Signs of Truly Gracious and Holy Affections* (Edinburgh: Laing & Matthews, 1746; reprint, Carlisle, PA: Banner of Truth Trust, 1997), 124–65.

[92] Edwards, *Freedom of the Will*, 37, 164, 213, 69, 77, 80, 95–97.

has ever failed to distinguish such determinism or efficacy from compulsion."[93] He goes on to say that "it is not less but more evident in systems of thought which carefully distinguish between causation and compulsion, between determinism and force, or between philosophical or moral necessity and physical necessity."[94]

Fifth, according to Edwards, to affirm God's prescience without predetermination is absurd and contradictory.[95] In this sense Edwards agrees with Aquinas and others who hold that God's knowledge is a determining factor of future events. This means that the future is fixed and therefore libertarian freedom is false. He counters the claim that God's certain knowledge has no effects or influence in making events necessary in any way. He dismisses this as beside the point.

> Whether prescience be the thing that *makes* the event necessary or no, it alters not the case. Infallible knowledge may *prove* the necessity of the event foreknown, and yet not be the thing which *causes* the necessity. If the foreknowledge be absolute, this proves the event known to be necessary, or proves that 'tis impossible but that the event should be, by some means or other, either by a decree, or some other way, if there be any other way: because, as was said before, 'tis absurd to say, that a proposition is known to be certain and infallibly true, which yet may possibly prove not true.... It is as strong arguing from the effect to the cause as from the cause to the effect. 'Tis enough, that an existence with is infallibly foreknown, cannot fail, whether that impossibility arises from the foreknowledge, or is prior to it.[96]

The Sagacity of an Atheist: A Modern Example

The problems associated with *libertarian* freedom can be best illustrated in a recent debate between William Lane Craig and atheist Antony Flew.[97] In what must be regarded as one of the most ironic role-reversals in recent philosophical exchange, an atheist clearly and cogently defends the Augustinian-Calvinistic view of freedom, sovereignty, and compatibilism as the outworking of theism, against a leading Protestant apologist who defends libertarian freedom as

---

[93] Ibid., 42.

[94] Ibid.

[95] Ibid., 262–64.

[96] Ibid., 263–64.

[97] Stan W. Wallace, ed., *Does God Exist? The Craig-Flew Debate* (Burlington, VT: Ashgate, 2003).

formulated by a Roman Catholic Jesuit (Louis De Molina). Flew's main objection is that because God is an omnipotent being that therefore "if he wanted people to behave in a certain way (as devoted and obedient children), he could perfectly well make them that way."[98] "Omnipotence could avoid all this by simply making them such that they would choose to obey Him."[99] In other words, Flew's problem is that he knows God could *determine* that all people act morally righteous without compromising their freedom and without making people robots. Because he has not, he is disturbed that God would cosign them to everlasting hell. Craig responds that God gives man 'freedom' in a libertarian sense countering Flew's objection to theism. But in doing so, Craig departs from theism (not simply Augustinian-Calvinism). And it is Flew who points this out.

Craig argues, "It is logically impossible to *make* someone *freely* do something. Libertarian freedom *entails* freedom from causal restraints. Therefore, if we are truly free and God has willed to create free creatures, then He *cannot* guarantee how free creatures will choose."[100] Elsewhere Craig writes, "But so long as people are free, there's simply no guarantee that everyone in that world would be freely saved. To be sure, God could force everyone to repent and be saved by overpowering their wills, but that would be a sort of divine rape; not a free acceptance of salvation. It is logically impossible to *make* someone do something *freely*."[101] Flew concedes that this would not be freedom but objects to the term 'coercion' as a necessary consequent of determinism. "I didn't say that God should *coerce* people—force them to do it. I said that the omnipotent God would be able to make people such that they would freely choose to do what He desired. Now you may say that this is a doctrine of predestination, and, of course, only Calvinists believe that. Not true."[102] He then

---

[98] William Lane Craig and Antony Flew, "The Craig-Flew Debate," in *Does God Exist? The Craig-Flew Debate*, ed. Stan W. Wallace (Burlington, VT: Ashgate, 2003), 27. These are some of the opening comments by Flew.

[99] Ibid.

[100] Ibid. These comments comprise a first rebuttal to Flew.

[101] Craig, "Politically Correct Salvation," 91–92.

[102] Craig and Flew, "The Craig-Flew Debate," 32.

quotes Aquinas and Luther as proof.[103] *To this Craig concedes and in conceding he destroys his own basis for rejecting the alternative to libertarian freedom.*[104] Craig also cites two oft-cited biblical texts (1 Tim 2:4; 2 Pet 3:9) supporting the notion that God's will or desire is sometimes thwarted by human will. However, he misquotes 2 Pet 3:9 and offers no exegetical defense for either passage.[105]

---

[103] Aquinas *Sum. C. Gent.* 3.2.88–89 says, "God alone can move the will as an agent without doing violence to it.... Some people, now understanding how God can cause a movement of our willingness without prejudicing the freedom of the will, have tried to explain...authoritative texts wrongly, that is, they would say that God 'works in us and to wish and to accomplish' means that He causes in us the power of willing, but not in such a way that He makes us will this or that.... These people are, of course, opposed quite plainly by authoritative texts of Holy Writ. For it says in Isaiah: 'Lord you have worked all your work in us.' Hence we received from God not only the power of willing but its employment also." Luther *Serv.* 634–35 says, "I said 'of necessity'; I did not say 'of compulsion'; I meant, by a necessity, not of *compulsion*, but of what they call *immutability*. That is to say: a man without the Spirit of God does not do evil against his will, under pressure, as though he were taken by the scruff of his neck and dragged into it, like a thief or footpad being dragged off against his will to punishment; but he does it spontaneously and voluntarily. And this willingness or volition is something which he cannot in his own strength eliminate, restrain or alter." Flew says, "I think that would be a useful thing [after citing Rom 9:18–23] to have on record in this discussion, lest we have any more of this suggestion that an omnipotent being could not cause people to freely choose Him. It's an absurd idea that He could not produce people to do freely exactly what He wanted them to do, because here you have biblical authority and the authority of three of the great doctors of the Church – Luther, Aquinas and Calvin" (ibid., 33).

[104] Craig says, "I do not agree with Thomas Aquinas on this issue. I agree with a Molinist doctrine of divine concurrence and conservation. This is a doctrine laid out by Luis Molina, who was a sixteenth-century Jesuit Counter-Reformer. Molina's view of concurrence differed from Aquinas's in the following way: Aquinas thought that God moved the will of persons to do certain effects, so that God would move my will to will to, say, lift my arm. *And, I agree, if that's the way you think of God's working, then Dr Flew is right – omnipotence could bring it about that everyone would freely do what God wants him to do*" (ibid., 32, emphasis added). This is not only the way Flew has it but the historic church.

[105] The passages cited are 2 Pet 3:9 and 1 Tim 2:4 which appear to teach that God's desire for universal salvation is thwarted by man's will. But these texts teach exactly the opposite. First Timothy 2:4 states that God "would have all men to be saved." The phrase 'all men,' however, may be understood as 'all kinds of men' (all kinds of people). Indeed, God not only desires this but accomplished it. This becomes the very reason why no stratum of mankind is to be omitted from prayer. Second Peter 3:9 is a bit more complicated. The first thing to be noted is that Craig misquotes the passage. He says, "God is not willing that *any* should perish but that *all* should reach

In an exchange echoing Edwards, Flew says, "I question how you can reconcile the Big Bang with free will. You said that every event has a cause and that nothing comes out of nothing. Well, any action has to have a cause and that cause has a cause. Thus, you can't have [libertarian] free will if everything has a cause."[106] Craig responds that only things that come to exist have a cause and actions with personal agents involve free will which fall under the rubric of *agent* causation. But does Craig actually answer the question of causation? The issue is not *who* but *how* and *why* the agent acts by accounting for *what* cause causes the agent to act in one way and not in another. William Rowe also identifies Craig's response as being evasive:

> But I suspect the questioner is still puzzled. For a free action—for example, lifting one's arm—clearly is an event that has a beginning. So, it must have a cause. What is the cause, if it is a free action? Craig's answer is that it is the agent. But then there must surely be an event which is *the agent's causing his lifting his arm*. (Or perhaps Craig would say it is 'the agent's causing his arm to rise'). But then we have the event which is *the agent's causing his lifting his arm*. And the questioner will note that this event also has a beginning and must, on Craig's principle, have a cause. What then is the cause of this event? Well, it looks like we must posit a still further event: *the agent's causing his causing his arm to rise*. And we are off to the races, an unending series of events each caused by the preceding event in the series. I suspect that it is this issue to which the questioner wanted to answer. Craig needs either to answer this question or to refine his principle so that it does not

---

repentance" (ibid., 34). But the passage actually reads, "The Lord is not negligent concerning the promise [of his return], as some consider slowness, but is long-suffering towards *you*, not willing that *any* [of you] should perish but that *all* [of you] should receive repentance." This translation maintains the identical referents of the two pronouns ὑμᾶς, τινας, and adjective πάντας (Richard J. Bauckham, *Jude, 2 Peter*, WBC, ed. Ralph P. Martin, vol. 50 [Waco, TX: Word, 1983], 313 comes close in saying the same thing). The identity of these referents are those addressed in the book of Peter, namely, 'you' the 'beloved' (2 Pet 3:1, 8) who are in the first letter described as 'elect' (1 Pet 1:1). That Peter has in mind a unified group of elect is underscored by the word for 'perish.' How can saved Christians perish? The group includes saved and unsaved (or not yet in existence) elect people. However, if the return of the Lord comes sooner than decreed (an impossible hypothetical), on God's part, then a large portion of this unified group of elect (including every Christian beyond the first century) 'perishes.' But the Lord delays the coming because he is not willing that any of you (= elect) should not find repentance but be saved.

[106] Craig and Flew, "The Craig-Flew Debate," 41.

require, or seem to require, a cause for every action and event that has a beginning.[107]

This line of questioning by Flew is designed to elicit from Craig an admission that either all things have causes (as traditional theism teaches) and in so doing leave unexplained why God did not cause his creatures to be good (problem of evil), or to get Craig to acquiesce that because he is an indeterminist when it comes to free will (agent causation is insufficient here) to be consistent in applying this to the Big Bang—therefore atheism.[108] In short, Flew wants Craig to agree there is such a thing as uncaused events so he can dismantle his cosmological argument for God's existence. Since he does this with freedom why not creation? In doing this, Flew defends a view of freedom that is simply a corollary of theism. Flew wants a debate from a consistent theist in order to discuss the problem of evil (*argumentum ad absurdum*), but Craig has departed from theism on this matter and so the problem of theism as theism is never broached. Flew, an atheist, frames the problem of causation from a traditional theistic world-view while Craig, a confessed theist, adopts a non-theistic view of causation with regard to human freedom.

As already noted, Craig concedes that God could move the will using his omnipotence to bring it about and that everyone would still act freely in doing what God caused them to do but in a later exchange he denies this. Flew questions Craig whether God is limited by man's free will and asks if free will is more powerful than God. Craig responds in libertarian fashion:

> *Craig*: In the sense that God didn't have to create free will, no. He could have created robots...God limits His control over that creature. Now, He could have controlled him in the sense of coercing him, but God chose to create moral agents who are reflections of Himself in having this kind of libertarian freedom. And then He cannot guarantee what they will do. And that's just a point of logic—you can't make someone freely do something.
>
> *Flew*: Notice that the arguments I've produced were not confined to those of Aquinas and Luther and Calvin (which I thought were pretty good to go on), but Aquinas quoted one biblical passage and I quoted another with great enthusiasm—one which Luther often repeated. It apparently didn't occur to anyone until this chap Molina, centuries later, that this was a crucial

---

[107] William Rowe, "Reflections on the Craig-Flew Debate," in *Does God Exist? The Craig-Flew Debate*, ed. Stan W. Wallace (Burlington, VT: Ashgate, 2003), 73.

[108] Ibid., 71–72.

notion which showed that God didn't really cause people freely to choose this or that. It's rather a long time afterwards. And it doesn't seem to me that there's much evidence that there is such a thing as – what do you call it?—libertarian free will, because actually freedom indicates that someone was not compelled, that they did these things of their own free will. It doesn't have anything to do with unpredictability.[109]

If an atheist can understand the true nature of freedom and the corollaries of theism why cannot a professed theist?[110] So although Craig agrees earlier that God *could* move men to act freely in making choices and they would still be free and without coercion (an anti-Molinist admission), here he caricatures this very view of freedom as coercion and puppeteering while stating his own view of freedom limits God.

One contributor to the book criticizes Flew's compatibilist 'assumption' saying that "I agree with Flew that if one is a compatibilist, then one is hard-pressed to see why God would not simply determine things so as to rule out wrong choices and their consequences" but he also agrees with Craig "that if one rejects compatibilism and holds that if persons are free in any morally significant sense then libertarianism is true, then one will take Christianity to include the claim that God created libertarianly free persons—moral agents capable of choosing wrongly and determining their own character traits."[111] He concludes by saying that Flew's

---

[109] Craig and Flew, "The Craig-Flew Debate," 44.

[110] Flew later says, "Surely to anyone who was, for the first time and without prejudice, entertaining the hypothesis that our universe is the creation of an omnipotent and omniscient God it would appear obvious that everything which occurs or does not occur within it must, by the hypothesis, be precisely and only what its creator wants, indeed causes, to occur or not to occur. What scope is there for creatures in such a universe to defy the will of their creator? What room is there even for the concept of such defiance? For a creator to punish creatures for what, by the hypothesis, that creator necessarily and as such (ultimately) causes them to do would be the most monstrous, perverse, unjust and sadistic of performances" (Antony Flew, "A Reply to my Critics," in *Does God Exist? The Craig-Flew Debate*, ed. Stan W. Wallace [Burlington, VT: Ashgate, 2003], 191; similarly Albert Einstein, *Out of My Later Years* [London: Thames & Hudson, 1950], 26–27). In stating this problem as he does, Flew not only identifies correctly the theistic world-view and its problem, but in doing so also captures precisely the interlocutor's objection in Rom 9:19.

[111] Keith Yandell, "Theism, Atheism and Cosmology," in *Does God Exist? The Craig-Flew Debate*, ed. Stan W. Wallace (Burlington, VT: Ashgate, 2003), 109. This last sentence is incoherent. How can one determine his own character traits without a

argument is powerful "against the claims *Determinism, compatibilism, and theism are all true* and *Compatibilism and theism are true.* The moral I draw is that, since theism is true, determinism and compatibilism are not true."[112] But Yandell attempts to relegate Flew's 'compatibilism' to a "controversial and powerfully criticized position."[113] Flew takes exception to this caricature insisting that "I wish he had gone on to cite some of the work of these powerful critics and to indicate what it is which he believes that I mistakenly assume to be incompatible with what."[114] He then repeats the sources (Paul, Aquinas, Calvin, Luther) and debunks the concept that non-libertarian freedom is coercive.

Flew ends his reply where Christians must begin and to which this Study has sought, by way of introduction, to broach.

> It is, finally, in the present context, high time, and perhaps overtime, to raise the question of when and how and by whom the concept of libertarian free will was first introduced. This is a question which really ought to have occurred to the Yandells after they read my quotations from Aquinas, Luther and—above all—St Paul, and before they began to accuse me of maintaining, without offering supporting argument, 'a controversial and powerfully criticized position'. Who was it by introducing the concept of libertarian free will became the first incompatibilist, and when did they do this? Presumably it was someone worried, and very understandably worried, by the appalling theological implications of compatibilism. St Paul, on the other hand, who had never heard of libertarian free will or of incompatibilism therefore has a claim to have been the first compatibilist.[115]

To this question other scholars must explore more fully and the next few years of research will certainly bear much needed fruit in this area. Although church history links this view to Pelagius, he is certainly not the original innovator of what has come to be called 'libertarian' freedom. If Flew is on the right track, as church history

---

prior inclination to do so? And does not this prior inclination act in a causative fashion thereby disproving the very freedom he espouses?

[112] Ibid., 109–10.

[113] Keith Yandell, "Some Issues in Theism and Atheism: Setting and Context," in *Does God Exist? The Craig-Flew Debate*, ed. Stan W. Wallace (Burlington, VT: Ashgate, 2003), 8.

[114] Flew, "A Reply to my Critics," 203.

[115] Ibid., 207.

and the philosophical concomitants of theism suggest, then the roots of libertarian freedom are not only non-theistic but possibly pagan.

Summary on Freedom

Both Augustine and Edwards stand in the tradition of claiming a paradox of human freedom, namely, that man is free in one sense and determined in another. Augustine emphasizes the inability of man to respond to God apart from regeneration but at the same time that man always acts freely in accordance with these inclinations. Edwards emphasizes the nature of the will as always acting in accordance with the strongest inclination at the moment of choice and against the doctrine of liberty that views the choice as one of indifference or non-causal. In this sense man is always determined but free (uncoerced). Other theologians of the past including Aquinas and Luther hold like views. These classic theologians all point to the renewing of the inclinations in regeneration as a necessary and sufficient cause for faith in Christ. Apart from this monergistic act, man remains in 'slavery' to his own evil inclinations.

Conclusion

This chapter has attempted to address issues of a philosophical nature, namely, time, causation, and freedom. Each topic is not only interrelated but intricate as made evident in several recent treatises on each topic. The evidence from both history and modern discussions point to the question of freedom as the overriding (but certainly not exclusive) concern. In many cases the desire is to make God subject to time and thus contingent in order to make room for libertarian freedom. This freedom, a doctrine popularly formulated by Pelagius (and adopted by semi-Pelagians, Arminians, Socinians, Molinists, and Openness theologians) is assumed in many (but not all) of the studies mentioned in chapter 1 but is not new. There, this view of freedom is usually unstated, seldom critically examined, yet serves as a guiding hermeneutic that dictates how Isa 6:9–10, and passages like it, can or cannot be construed. Although the issue of time is perhaps most complex and difficult to reach consensus upon, nevertheless, both issues of time and freedom are historically addressed and the church has not remained without consensus on either point. It is the issue of freedom that is most determinant in this study. The following chapters, therefore, seek to examine the biblical data on Isaianic fattening without importing this impediment.

The Wisdom Tradition

The thesis here is that Isa 6:9–10 outlines divine fattening of the heart as a prevention of perception, knowledge, and understanding.[1] Because these terms share an affinity in the wisdom tradition—along with the eyes, ears, and their functions of hearing, and seeing—the prohibition of these aspects therefore serve as a circumlocution for *the prevention of wisdom*. The 'fat-heart' is a heart without wisdom and the mode of 'fattening' involves guaranteeing this effect either by *depletion* (of misused wisdom), *deprivation* (withholding) of wisdom, or *deposition* into the heart its opposite. This act involves clarifying *how* (in terms of mode), *why* (in terms of its cause and purpose), and *what* type of act (transformation or non-transformation) Isaianic fattening embodies.

This chapter inquires into two areas and seeks to establish the thesis's point. First, is the nature of the heart in the OT naturally (congenitally) absent of *salvific* wisdom?[2] Is Isaianic fattening primarily ontological, functional, or both? Second, is the relation of wisdom and its corollaries to the possession or absence of wisdom ultimately what it means, therefore, to be fat-hearted? Is it primarily related to the cognitive, volitional, or both aspects of the human heart?[3] From this a necessary corollary follows: If the heart is naturally absent of wisdom, then one alternative of divine fattening

---

[1] This will be further validated in the next chapter on Isa 6:9–10.

[2] The use of 'congenital' describes an unusual condition present at birth while 'natural' refers to something inborn rather than acquired or having a particular character by nature. Both are synonymously used here. Ontology is the nature of a thing.

[3] Fabry says there is a fine distinction between cognition and volition as there is to theory and practice (H. J. Fabry, "לֵבָב/לֵב," *TDOT* 7:423–24).

seems to fit best, namely, God fattens (the already fat-heart) by *deprivation* of wisdom. If the heart is not naturally absent of wisdom, then the other two alternatives are legitimate options. While the end seems certain (absence of wisdom), the means (deprivation, depletion, deposition) to this end are less so. The goal here is to show that the natural condition of the heart is the key in construing 'fattening' as deprivation of the perceiving, understanding, and knowing heart. The reasoning behind this will be explained.

Congenital Condition: The Heart in Its Natural State

How might one go about establishing the notion that the heart is naturally absent of salvific wisdom? First, some texts tend to view the congenital condition of the heart as only evil and lacking in wisdom. Second, other texts show that divine wisdom is a charismatic endowment—salvific wisdom is one of these. Third, a number of passages state that man naturally lacks the fear of God, the first-fruit of wisdom. Finally, the lack of salvation is prima facie evidence of the lack of wisdom according to Isa 6:9–10. That salvific wisdom is granted does not imply that all granted wisdom is salvific. Since wisdom is part of man's psychical properties, it is necessary to glance briefly at Hebrew psychology in general.

Hebrew Psychology

Hebrew psychology is multifaceted.[4] The רוּחַ ('spirit') can refer to strong psychical excitement, the habitation of the Yahweh's רוּחַ, or man as he is empowered.[5] It can even be 'hardened' (Deut 2:30), an

---

[4] Walther Eichrodt, *Theology of the Old Testament,* trans. J. A. Baker, vol. 2, OTL, ed. G. Ernest Wright et al. (London: SCM, 1961), 131–50; Hans Walter Wolff, *Anthropology of the Old Testament,* trans. Margaret Kohl (Philadelphia: Fortress, 1974; reprint, Miffintown, PA: Sigler, 1996), 5–79.

[5] The noun רוּחַ occurs 389 times in the MT. It is translated in the LXX by approximately forty different terms or phrases. In the majority of cases it occurs as πνεῦμα 'wind; breath; spirit, Spirit' (281 times) or ἄνεμος 'wind' (fifty-one times). The other terms emphasize forces of nature, objects either of nature or man-made, emotional states, components of man, time, activities of man, or abstract concepts. Eichrodt, *Theology of the Old Testament,* 132; Wolff, *Anthropology of the Old Testament,* 32–39. See also R. Albertz and C. Westermann, "רוּחַ," *TLOT* 3:1202–20; BDB 924–26; *HALOT* 3:1197–1201; H. J. Fabry, "רוּחַ," *ThWAT* 7:385–425; M. V. Van Pelt, W. C. Kaiser Jr., and D. I. Block, "רוּחַ," *NIDOTTE* 3:1073–78.

affliction normally confined to the heart.[6] The נֶפֶשׁ ('soul') is associated with the neck, throat, or gullet and is closely allied with its effects, namely, breath (of life).[7] It is thus equated with life itself, life in the body (in contrast to רוּחַ), the individual himself, to *every type of wish, desire or vital urge,*" and "shows man primarily in his need and desire, that includes his emotional excitability and vulnerability."[8] The נְשָׁמָה ('breath') may express psychical realities or refer collectively for all life and distinguishes a living as opposed to dead person.[9] The לֵבָב/לֵב ('heart' or 'mind') is occasionally translated as 'chest' or 'conscience,' but its dominant metaphorical sense connotes the center of human psychical and spiritual life stressing the intellectual and volitional processes along with understanding in the exercise of responsibility.[10] Fabry lists its semantic range in terms of personal identity, vital center, affective center, noetic center, volitional center, and religious and ethical realm.[11]

Other parts signifying the psychic process include the כִּלְיָה ('kidneys') which can refer to the seat of emotions or the inaccessible (to all but God) conscience.[12] The מֵעֶה ('belly') and רֶחֶם ('womb' but

---

[6] The parallel phrases "hardened his spirit" (כִּי־הִקְשָׁה...אֶת־רוּחוֹ) and "made his heart strong" (וַיְאַמֵּץ אֶת־לְבָבוֹ) suggest functional obstinacy.

[7] נֶפֶשׁ occurs 757 times in the MT. The LXX translates it by ψυχή 687 times linked to breath, emotional states, persons, or acts. C. Westermann, "נֶפֶשׁ," *TLOT* 2:743–59; BDB 659–61; *HALOT* 2:711–13; H. Seebass, "נֶפֶשׁ," *ThWAT* 5:531–55; idem, "נֶפֶשׁ," *TWOT* 2:587–91; D. C. Fredericks, "נֶפֶשׁ," *NIDOTTE* 3:133–34.

[8] Eichrodt, *Theology of the Old Testament*, 138; Wolff, *Anthropology of the Old Testament*, 25, esp. 10–25.

[9] נְשָׁמָה occurs twenty-four times in the MT and associated with wind, breath, spirit, or emotions in the LXX. BDB 675; Wolff, *Anthropology of the Old Testament*, 59.

[10] לֵב occurs 602 times in the MT and לֵבָב 260 times. The LXX renderings refer to the mind, the person, or an emotion or intention. For לֵב see F. Stolz "לֵב," *TLOT* 2:638–42; BDB 524–25; *HALOT* 2:513–15; Fabry, "לֵבָב/לֵב," *TDOT* 7:399–437; Andrew Bowling, "לֵבָב," *TWOT* 1:466–67; Alex Luc, "לֵב," *NIDOTTE* 2:749–54. For לֵבָב see BDB 523–24; ibid., 40–58.

[11] Fabry, "לֵבָב/לֵב," *TDOT* 7:412–34.

[12] כִּלְיָה occurs thirty-one times in the MT. The LXX renders it νεφρός 'kidney, heart, mind,' twenty-eight times and χεῖλος 'lip, shore,' once. See A. S. Kapelrud "כִּלְיָה," *TDOT* 7:182–85; John N. Oswalt, "כלה," *TWOT* 1:440–41. The kidneys represent the seat of human joy, or grief, or one's moral character (Robert B. Chisholm, "כִּלְיָה," *NIDOTTE* 2:656–57). BDB 480; Wolff, *Anthropology of the Old Testament*, 65–66.

'compassion' in the plural) stand for the seat of the emotions.[13] The קֶרֶב ('inward parts') is a collective term for the "seat and organ of psychic process...used to denote these processes themselves...as events unfolding in Man's interior life" drawing "attention to the distinctive character and independence of the spiritual realm" from the physical.[14] The כָּבֵד ('liver')[15] is that sensual passion but more often in parallel to מֵעֶה ('belly') and נֶפֶשׁ ('soul'). The 'nose' (אַף) is associated with anger.[16] The רֹאשׁ ('head') is not a psychological phenomenon but is "the image of everything high...and dominating."[17] The 'bones' (עֶצֶם, et al.)[18] express psychic energy,

---

[13] מֵעֶה 'belly' occurs thirty-two times in the MT and refers to the inner organs of the lower abdomen, the reproductive, or digestive. It may refer to the seat of emotions especially love (Cleon L. Rogers Jr., "מֵעֶה," NIDOTTE 2:1012–13; Victor P. Hamilton, "מֵעֶה," TWOT 1:518–19). The LXX renders it κολία 'stomach, womb' (twenty-seven times). רֶחֶם occurs thirty-three times in the MT (Leonard J. Coppes, "רָחַם," TWOT 2:841–43). Usually translated by μήτρα 'womb' (sixteen times) and κοιλία 'stomach, womb' (four times) but also by φιλιάζω 'to be friendly towards,' φίλος 'beloved, friend,' οἰκτίρμων 'compassionate,' οἰκτίρω 'to have pity, compassion,' and γαστήρ 'stomach, womb,' once a piece. Eichrodt, Theology of the Old Testament, 145.

[14] The term is קֶרֶב and is translated 'midst, among' and is found in the MT 227 times. It may refer to the inward part of man (especially as a seat of thought and emotion or as the faculty of thought and emotion) (BDB 899). Eichrodt, Theology of the Old Testament, 145–46; Wolff, Anthropology of the Old Testament, 63–64.

[15] The term כָּבֵד occurs fourteen times in the MT and is translated in the LXX by three terms mostly relating to the liver, examining it, or glory. In only two cases does the 'liver' refer to humans (Prov 7:23; Lam 2:11). Most of the occurrences are in Leviticus and refer to the sacrificial animal. In Prov 7:23 it is parallel to ψυχή (נֶפֶשׁ 'soul') and Lam 2:11 it parallels καρδία (מֵעֶה 'belly'). Cf. BDB 458; John W. Oswald, "כָּבֵד," TWOT 1:426–28; P. Stenmans, "כָּבֵד," TDOT 7:21–22; Wolff, Anthropology of the Old Testament, 64.

[16] The noun אַף occurs 277 times in the MT and is translated as 'nose' or 'anger.' It is a cognate of אָנַף 'to be angry' (fourteen times in MT), and אַנַף 'face' (twice in MT). The LXX translates it mostly in terms of emotional anger. At other times depicts other body parts like the face or nose or expresses verbal notions of various sorts related to patience or even sinning. Prepositions are also used for denoting space.

[17] Wolff, Anthropology of the Old Testament, 69. The term occurs 614 times in the MT.

[18] The noun עֶצֶם occurs 126 times in the MT. Brown-Driver-Briggs list it as (1) bone that can in some cases be used as a synecdoche for the entire person including both physical and moral aspects; (2) bone of animals, and (3) substance = self (BDB 782–83).

strength, or a synecdoche for the inner man. The בָּשָׂר ('flesh')[19] stands for the whole person (or living thing), the living body controlled by the נֶפֶשׁ, and typified by powerlessness of the mortal creature and feebleness of his faithfulness and obedience to God.[20] The semantic similarity leads Wolff to say they function anthropologically under the rubric of *stereometric-synthetic* thinking.[21] But no body part rivals the heart in depicting these functional and/or ontological aspects.

The Mosaic Background

The Mosaic background presents a 'wisdom tradition,' or what would become associated with this tradition, before the wisdom genre. The depiction of the heart of wisdom, the links to wisdom, its effects (perception, understanding, and knowledge), the gratuitous impartation of the new heart with its resident wisdom, are found first in the Torah, then in the wisdom literature, and subsequently on into the prophetic materials. In the process of establishing this wisdom link, other aspects of the heart will be noted along with the categories of functional versus ontological.

The Antediluvian Heart. The first biblical reference to the heart (לֵב) in the OT occurs in Gen 6:5. It states that "every intent [or 'inclination'] of the thoughts of his heart were only evil all the time [or 'continually']." *Every, only,* and *always* evil is the "intent of the

---

[19] The noun בָּשָׂר 'flesh' is found 273 times in the MT. It can refer to the bodies of animals or man, the body itself (not a corpse however), the male organ of generation (euphemism), blood-relations, in contrast to God or spirit, or as כָּל־בָּשָׂר which occurs approximately forty-five times and refers to all living things, all animals, or all mankind (BDB 142). This term usually carries a qualitative emphasis and only rarely (Ezek 11:19 [the LXX uses the phrase καρδίαν ἑτέραν]; 36:26 [LXX reads καρδίαν καινήν]) involves a statement of status (G. Gerleman, "בָּשָׂר," TLOT 1:284–85). The LXX translates it mostly by 'flesh' and 'body' but also in terms of other body parts.

[20] See Gerleman, "בָּשָׂר," TLOT 1:283–85; HALOT 1:164; N. P. Bratsiotis, "בָּשָׂר," TDOT 2:317–32; John N. Oswalt, "בָּשָׂר," TWOT 1:135–36; Robert B. Chisholm, "בָּשָׂר," NIDOTTE 1:777–79; Wolff, Anthropology of the Old Testament, 31 (esp. 26–31).

[21] Ibid., 8, 11, 18, 23, 33, 40, 46. Stereometric refers to a *parallelism of parts to person* while synthetic is *part for function*. Together *stereometric-synthetic* thinking takes reference to the parts of the body, activities, and capacities as distinguishing marks of the whole man.

thoughts of his heart" (וְיֵצֶר מַחְשְׁבֹת לִבּוֹ).[22] This same evaluation is repeated after the flood adding that the *terminus a quo* is "from youth" (Gen 8:21).[23] That this refers to all men of all time is evident by at least three factors. First, the generation described as evil is gone so that

---

[22] Franz Delitzsch, *A New Commentary on Genesis*, trans. Sophia Taylor, vol. 1 (Edinburgh: Clark, 1888; reprint, Minneapolis: Klock & Klock, 1978), 233. He later says that this sinfulness is "the common inheritance of mankind" (ibid., 281). Leuphold states, "He discerns the inner trend of men's thoughts: they have put no restraint upon their natural inclinations…. But what a sweeping condemnation: 'only evil continually'" (H. C. Leuphold, *Exposition of Genesis*, vol. 1 [Grand Rapids: Baker, 1942], 260). There is not a great difference between 'only evil continually' (Gen 6:5) and 'from his youth' (Gen 8:21) says Leuphold (ibid., 323; cf. Philo *Deus* 20; *Conf*. 24). "Rather, man's iniquity may at one time be ample cause for destroying the earth" (ibid.). See also Claus Westermann, *Genesis 1–11: A Commentary*, trans. John J. Scullion (London: SPCK, 1984), 407–08 who rejects this statement as general about human sinfulness but rather insists it is an interpretation by J "where he is wrestling with the incomprehensibility of the decision to destroy over against the creation of humanity and trying to give reasons for it…it is something new in contrast to what has preceded" (ibid., 409). He denies it is an explanatory sentence used to "describe a general sinfulness which is concretized in individual acts" (ibid.). However, he later notes that the phrase 'from youth' implies a tendency to evil that the people grow up with (ibid., 456). On the contrary, Wenham argues that "This text asserts that every human thought from its inception is intrinsically 'evil'…a comprehensive and general term of condemnation, especially for things disapproved of by God" (Gordon J. Wenham, *Genesis 1–15*, WBC, ed. John D. W. Watts, vol. 1 [Waco, TX: Word, 1987], 144). About Gen 8:21 he says, "There can be no doubt that man's nature has not changed since before the flood" (ibid., 191). Waltke says the situation portrayed by this depravity will occur again before the second coming of Christ (Bruce K. Waltke, *Genesis* [Grand Rapids: Zondervan, 2001], 118). He also says that the flood does not fundamentally effect a change in humanity (ibid., 143). Cf. Eugene H. Merrill, *The Bible Knowledge Key Word Study: Genesis–Deuteronomy* (Colorado Springs, CO: Victor, 2003), 57–58.

[23] The phrase 'from youth' (מִן נְעוּרִים) is found nineteen times in the OT (Gen 8:21; 46:34; 1 Sam 12:2; 17:33; 2 Sam 19:8; 1 Kgs 18:12; Isa 47:12,15; Jer 3:24–25; 22:21; 48:11; Ezek 4:14; Zech. 13:5; Pss 71:5,17; 129:1–2; Job 31:18) and refers to the time of birth, the moment of moral conscious, the earliest time of remembrance, or simply a synecdoche for all of one's life. See BDB 654–55. The phrase 'from youth' expresses a state or condition (Leupold, *Exposition of Genesis*, 324). Qumran uses it on twelve occasions some of which clearly refer to infancy or being a child (1QSa 1:6; 1QHa 15:37; 17:31; 1Q18 f1 2:4; 1Q35 f1:10; 4Q223–224 f2i:49; 4Q249a f1:4; 4Q249d f1:2; 4Q249e f1i 3:4; 4Q428 f10:4; 4Q443 f1:4; 11Q5 21:13). But see Ps 58:4[3] where the wicked are estranged "from the womb" (מֵרֶחֶם). On why the righteous are such 'from the womb' see Ps 22:11[10] and 1QHa 7:15. On the wicked 'from the womb' see 1QHa 7:17, a state that is applied to all men (1QHa 12:30; 4Q507 f1:2).

Gen 8:21 must refer to the survivors (Noah and the other seven). If this refers to Noah and his family, then so does Gen 6:5. Second, it gives adequate cause for the evil effects before the flood. Otherwise, one has an effect (evil acts and retribution) without a sufficient cause (evil heart and a holy God). This text is a divine appraisal of evil in terms of its cause. This also implies that the description includes Noah and therefore dictates how 'finding grace' should be construed.[24] Noah did not earn grace or favor because he was upright but was upright because he found favor. Third, future judgment is predicated on this continuity of man's evil heart. Finally, it must refer to the nature of man not function because not all who died in the flood were functionally evil (babies and children).

Other places in the OT and extrabiblical material assume this same ontological wickedness of man in general and every person in particular.[25] No one is exempted. These passages do not merely encompass *function*, but point to the root or internal cause of that evil—the *ontology* of the heart.[26] It identifies the 'intent' or what

---

[24] The Hebrew phrase 'to find grace' (חֵן מָצָא) occurs thirty-seven times in the OT and five times in Qumran. When מָצָא is followed by חֵן in the MT, it is always in the Qal stem in the perfect tense (twenty-five times), the imperfect (nine times), the infinitive (twice), or the imperative (once). It is found only in narrative portions and thirteen times with God as the object. Cf. G. Gerleman, "מָצָא," TLOT 2:682–84. Here the passage does not state why Noah attained this favor. If Noah's heart is the same as those condemned in the flood, then he could not seek God apart from the divine initiative that is less than efficient. In this sense he *experienced* grace prior to the flood (BDB 592–93).

[25] In every case the ontology of the evil heart is explicitly mentioned as either the cause of evil in general or stubbornness in particular. The extent of the effects is varied, but the root is the same. See Gen 6:5; 8:21; Jer 3:17; 7:24; 11:8; 16:12; 18:12; Prov 26:23; Eccl. 9:3; 1QHa 15:3; 4Q299 f6ii:12; 4Q370 f1i:3; 4Q393 f3:5; 4Q436 f1a+bi:10; 4Q525 f5:6. In some passages the evil effects are emphasized rather than the nature of the heart per se (1 Sam 17:28; Zech 8:17; Pss 12:3[2]; 28:3). Ecclesiastes 9:3 begins by noting the functional evil of all mankind (like Gen 6:5) and its consequences ("This is the evil in everything that happens under the sun: The same destiny overtakes all" [9:3a]). It then points to the cause, namely, the resident evil in the heart ("The hearts of men, moreover, are full of evil and there is madness in their hearts while they live, and afterward they join the dead"). Ecclesiastes 9:1 (9:1–10) applies this original state to all men. "For the redactor of Ecclesiastes, wickedness and folly are so fundamental to the l}b ('human nature') that they are the cause of human mortality" (Fabry, "לֵבָב/לֵב," TDOT 7:423). Romans 3:9–20 indicate that everyone is 'wicked.'

[26] Each term signifies this; "the *intent* of the *thoughts* of his *heart*." The verb יָצַר can refer to both intent and act (W. H. Schmidt, "יָצַר," TLOT 2:566–68). The flood came

Augustine called the *libido*. Subsequent revelation concerns itself with *how* the heart, which is unalterably evil, can be altered to salvifically hear, see, perceive, know, and understand Yahweh. The Scriptures demonstrate that the solution is not reform but transformation into the new heart.

The Continuity of the Evil Heart. Other negative evaluations of the heart occur but not all are of an ontological sort. *Ontological* will refer to a condition of the heart that is inborn (since the fall) and true of every heart prior to or to a state that results from the divine initiative.[27] This may or may not evidence itself in generic statements or statements concerning particular individuals at particular times and places. *Functional* or *dynamic* will refer to those instances where a saying or phrase serves to highlight an activity rather than define the nature of the heart.[28] Although every activity arises from the heart, this sense seeks to identify the non-static situation of becoming (or doing) rather than being. *Ontological-functional* refers to the heart's ontology and its necessary function as identical. Finally, *functional-ontological* refers to cases where function enhances or actualizes one's ontology. Two cautions may be listed: universalizing particulars or particularizing universals and making functional statements ontological or ontological statements functional. But there may be an underlying assumption that universals may not be particularized on any occasion.

An example of each category might prove helpful. Genesis 6:5 and 8:21 are clearly *ontological* (thus universal). *Functional* or *dynamic* cases may include phrases like 'trembling heart,' 'weakness of heart,' 'hot heart,' where states, behavior, or actions do not define the heart as it

---

precisely because the evil heart of man, left unrestrained, produced a world of evil. Cf. Eichrodt, *Theology of the Old Testament*, 142–45.

[27] *Ontology* derives from the Greek for 'being' ὄντως, "pertaining to actual existence" (L&N §70.2). Pence defines it as a branch of metaphysics that is concerned with the nature of being and existence (Gregory Pence, *A Dictionary of Common Philosophical Terms* [New York: McGraw-Hill, 2000], 39). Here it will apply to the nature of the heart as it is.

[28] Pence defines *functionalism* as "a way of thinking about the mind that proposes that mental states are real but cannot, or should not, be defined by assuming a non-physical mind, but instead by their functions, particularly with respect to the behaviors they cause and produce" (ibid., 23). Here it is used to defines acts or temporary states of being.

always is. Terms like 'stubborn' or 'hard' (in some of its senses) may be *ontological-functional* because hearts are naturally stubborn and show this by varying degrees of stubbornness—the effects are used to determine the cause.[29] *Functional-ontological* involve cases that encourage the wise person to get more wisdom, be more holy, or anything having to do with quantitative/qualitative improvement or worsening. In this study, Isaianic 'fatness' will be deemed either as *ontological* or *ontological-functional* but not either *functional* or *functional-ontological*. The reason is that the heart is congenitally (and naturally) absent of salvific wisdom and evidences this noetically (absence of perception, knowledge, and understanding), volitionally (absence of repentance or the presence of rebellion), and positionally (all are unsaved in a natural state). Thus descriptions of the heart can be construed in terms of *being* (ontological), *doing* (functional), *becoming* (functional-ontological) or *being and becoming* (ontological-functional).

The only other negative uses of לֵב, besides Exod 4–14, occurs in Deut 28:65 where it mentions a 'trembling' heart and Deut 29:18 where it refers to the 'stubborn' heart.[30] The former is *functional* and the latter is *ontological-functional*. Its counterpart (לֵבָב) has several instances evidencing a negative connotation. Exodus 14:5 refers to a 'changed' heart for the worse not better and is functional.[31] Leviticus 26:36 mentions 'weakness' of heart (*functional*), the 'uncircumcised' heart (*ontological-functional*),[32] while Num 15:39 warns not to follow

---

[29] Logically it might be stated as follows: If A (new heart) then B (possesses salvific wisdom and an obedient heart). If not B (namely, is unwise and disobedient) then not A.

[30] The particular combination is לֵב + שְׁרִרוּת found ten times in the OT and twenty-seven occasions at Qumran.

[31] The phrase is לֵבָב + הָפַךְ (Exod 14:5; Isa 60:5). In Isa 60:5 it is a change for the better.

[32] This expression is *ontological-functional*. There are several phrases used for this expression: (1) 'Uncircumcised heart' [לֵבָב + עָרֵל] (Lev 26:41; cf. 1QHa 21:5 where this word for heart occurs and 'uncircumcised' is applied to the ears). This is primarily an *ontological* description. (2) 'Circumcise the heart' (= 'uncircumcised' heart) [לֵבָב + מוּל] (Deut 10:16; 30:6). In Deut 10:16 'circumcise the heart' is used in antithetical parallelism to the 'stiff-necked' (עֹרֶף + קָשָׁה) and thus here refers primarily to *rebellion*. In some contexts, to 'circumcise the heart' means to stop being rebellious. This is a *functional-ontological* usage. (3) 'Foreskinned heart' (= 'uncircumcised' heart) [לֵבָב + עָרְלָה] (Deut 10:16; Jer 4:4; 1QS 5:26). The only other

the heart at all. Deuteronomy mentions the 'melting' heart (*functional*), the 'hard' heart (*functional*), the 'exalted' heart (*functional*), 'deceived' heart (*functional*), 'grieved' heart (*functional*), 'hot' heart (*functional*), heart of 'confusion (*functional*),' and the 'dreadful' heart (*functional*).[33] It is important to note that none of these functional aspects or conditions, as limited in scope and time as they might be, can arise in an ontological vacuum. But function may describe any act from any type of being (good or bad). The neutrality of the function (not the nature) is the key issue.

Apparent Exceptions to the Evil Heart. The heart (לֵב) is also depicted in a non-negative sense. Although there are no positive occurrences in Genesis, Exodus mentions a 'glad' heart (*functional*), a 'willing' heart (*functional*), a heart 'stirred up,' (*functional*) a 'generous' heart (*functional*),[34] a 'wise' heart that is filled with the spirit/wind of wisdom (*ontological-functional*),[35] a heart stirred up in wisdom or

---

occurrence of the uncircumcised heart is with לֵב in (4) 'uncircumcised-heart' [לֵב + עָרֵל] (Jer 9:25; Ezek 44:7, 9; 4Q174 3:4; 4Q184 f2:5). Cf. 'uncircumcised-ears' (1QHa 21:5). Man has both an uncircumcised heart (ontology) and is rebellious (function). These two ideas work together. Depending on the grammatical construct and context, the various descriptions can refer to either ontology or function. All do not apply to ontology nor all to function.

[33] 'Melting heart' לֵבָב + מָסַס (Deut 1:28; 20:8; Josh 2:11; 5:1; 7:5; Isa 13:7; 19:1; 1QM 1:14; 1QHa f4:14; 10:6; 12:33; 4Q364 f21a k:18; 4Q432 f3:5; 11QT 62:4); 'Hardened heart' ('make strong') לֵבָב + אָמֵץ (Deut 2:30; 15:7; 2 Chr 36:13; used several times in DSS but always with the positive sense of 'make strong'); 'Exalted heart' לֵבָב + רוּם (Deut 8:14; 17:20; Ezek 31:10; Dan 5:20; 11:20; 1QS 4:9; 1Q22 f1ii:3; 4Q257 5:7; 4Q385a f1a bii:4; 4Q389 f8ii:6; 11QT 57:14); 'Deceived heart' לֵבָב + פָּתָה, that occurs only in Deut 11:16; 'Grieved heart' לֵבָב + רָעַע Deut 15:10; 1 Sam 1:8); Hot heart' לֵבָב + חָמַם, is found only in Deut 19:6; 'Heart of confusion' לֵבָב + תִּמָּהוֹן (Deut 28:28; 4Q385a f4:2);'Dreadful heart' לֵבָב + פַּחַד (Deut 28:67; Isa 60:5; 4Q185 f1 2i:15).

[34] 'Glad heart' לֵב + שָׂמַח (Exod 4:14; 1 Kgs 8:66; Isa 24:7; Zeph 3:14; Zech 10:7; Pss 16:9; 19:8; 33:21; 105:3; Prov 15:13, 30; 17:22; 23:15; 27:9, 11; Eccl 2:10; Esth 6:22; 1 Chr 16:10; 2 Chr 7:10; 4Q223 224 f2ii:1; 11Q5 21:12); 'Willing heart' בֵל + נָדַב (Exod 25:2; 35:21, 29; 1 Chr 29:9); 'Stirred up heart' לֵב + נָשָׂא (Exod 35:21, 26; 36:2; 2 Kgs 14:10; Lam 2:19; 2 Chr 25:19); 'Generous heart' לֵב + נָדִיב (Exod 35:22; 2 Chr 29:31).

[35] Depicted by the phrase לֵב + חָכַם (Exod 28:3; 31:6; 35:10, 25; 36:1, 2, 8; Job 37:24; 1 Kgs 3:12; Prov 10:8; 11:29; 16:21, 23; 23:15; Eccl 7:4; 8:5; 10:2; 4Q418 f81+81a:20; 4Q468a f1:2). These passages speak to the ontology of the heart in this sense: *apart from the divine impartation, wisdom is naturally absent*. This wisdom is non-salvific, but that is not the point here. The point is that this 'wisdom' is neither naturally resident nor developed but imparted. The 'wise-hearted' can be categorized as follows: (1)

simply a 'wise' heart (*ontological-functional*),[36] and includes various references to Yahweh giving or not giving wisdom and a new heart, or putting something into the heart.[37] The other term for heart (לֵבָב) is depicted as one with Yahweh's words inscribed on it,[38] that seeks God

---

Administrative wisdom that is given by God (Exod 28:3; 1 Kgs 3:13). (2) Various skills of craftsmanship that are given by God (Exod 28:3; 31:6; 35:10, 25; 36:1–2, 8). (3) General descriptions of the wise (Prov 16:21; 22:17; 23:15, 19; 27:11; Eccl 8:5; 4Q418 f81+81a:20; 4Q468a f1:2) especially in contrast to the fool (Prov 7:4; 10:8; 11:29; 15:7; Eccl 7:4; 10:2). (4) God in contrast to the wise in heart (Job 37:24). (5) Impediments to wisdom (Eccl 7:7).

[36] [לֵב + חָכְמָה] (Exod 28:3; 31:6; 35:26, 35; 36:1, 2; Pss 49:4; 17:16; Prov 2:2, 10; 14:33; Eccl 1:16, 17; 2:3; 8:16; 4Q424 f3:6). It is used in the following ways: (1) Administrative wisdom given by God (Exod 28:3; 31:6). (2) A skill in a craft given by God (Exod 35:26; 35:35; 36:1–2). (3) Wisdom of the wise in contrast to fools (Prov 14:33). (4) Experiences of the wise with wisdom (Ps 49:4[3]; Prov 2:2; Eccl 1:16–17; 2:3; 8:16). (5) The locale of wisdom as entering into the heart from without (Prov 2:10). (6) The absence of wisdom in a fool (Prov 17:16). (6) The absence of wisdom defined as a 'fat' heart as in Isaiah (4Q424 f3:6). The wisdom in each of these instances, especially the first two cases, is indeed functional but all testify to the ontological absence of wisdom. The last case of the Qumran text defines it ontologically as 'fat' but functionally as the lack of wisdom. The final cause (purpose) of wisdom is varied and indeed always functional, but its necessary impartation testifies to the ontological privation of wisdom itself (of various kinds).

[37] Exodus 35:34; 36:2; Deut 29:3[4]; 1 Kgs 3:9, 12; 10:24; Jer 24:7; 32:39; Ezek 11:19; 36:26; Ps 4:8[7]; Eccl 3:11; Lam 3:65; Ezra 7:27; Neh 2:12; 7:5; 2 Chr 9:23; 30:12. These texts can be grouped as follows: *Functional-dynamic*: (1) Gladdness (Ps 4:8[7]). (2) Anguish (Lam 3:65). He gives them 'anguish' (מְגִנַּת) of heart as a 'curse' (תַּאֲלָה) to them. This is indeed retribution but it does not involve an ontological change. (3) A desire to fulfill a plan (Ezra 7:27; Neh 2:12; 7:5). *Ontological-functional*: (1) Ability to teach (Exod 35:34). (2) Ability to perform a skill (Exod 36:2). (3) Ability of heart to know, eyes to see, or ears to hear (Deut 29:3[4]). Sometimes this has primarily in mind a skill in leadership (1 Kgs 3:9, 12; 10:24; 2 Chr 9:23), or involves salvation presented as a final cause of fearing (Jer 32:39), returning to (Jer 32:39), or obeying God (2 Chr 30:12). *Ontological*: (1) The exchange of the heart of stone with a heart of flesh (Ezek 11:19; 36:26). (2) A sense of eternity or ignorance of the future (Eccl 3:11). For various views see Fabry, "לֵב/לֵבָב," *TDOT* 7:420–21 and Gordon Johnston in the *NET BIBLE* on Eccl 3:11 fn. 13 at http://bible.org/netbible/index.htm. These *ontological-functional* and *ontological* passages relate most directly to Isa 6:9–10.

[38] [לֵבָב + דָּבַר] (Deut 11:18; 15:9; 32:46; Josh 14:7; 1 Sam 21:13; Ezek 38:10). These are all *functional-ontological* aspects referring to keeping certain thoughts in mind to effect behavior (Deut 11:18; 15:9; 32:46; Ezek 38:10), making others aware of one's inner thoughts (Josh 14:7), or keeping thoughts to oneself for future reference (1 Sam 21:12).

(Deut 4:29), has 'integrity' (in parallel with 'innocent hands),[39] is the 'undivided' heart,[40] with which one is to love God (6:5), and an 'upright' heart, that is 'soft' and 'tender,' a 'good,' 'glad,' and a 'turning' heart.[41] All of these latter usages are *functional*. Whenever an explicit cause of the positive notion of the heart is mentioned and this involves in some way an ontological aspect, it is the result of the divine activity, not a latent ability. The functional may or may not involve the divine initiative.

Yahweh's benevolence is depicted in Deut 5:29, "Oh that there were such a heart in them, to fear me and to keep all my commandments everyday so that it would be well with them and their children."[42] The expression "Oh that there were such" (מִי־יִתֵּן, 5:29; 28:67) occurs in desiderative sentences (Qal imperfect tense form) suggesting a wish for a situation that is not present.[43] However, some argue that it is an expression of divine agreement with the previous verse. Yahweh reportedly expresses a wishful desire for this present obedience to be the case now and in the future. He longs for them to always have such a heart that pledges obedience as they presently do.[44] In this view, *ontology* is set aside and the *function* is

---

[39] [לֵבָב + תָּם] (Gen 20:5, 6; 1 Kgs 9:4; Pss 78:12; 101:2).

[40] Literally, the 'whole heart' ('entire heart') [כֹּל + לֵבָב] (Deut 4:29; 6:5; 10:12; 11:13; 13:4; 26:16; 30:2, 6, 10; Josh 22:5; 23:14; 1 Sam 7:3; 12:20, 24; 1 Kgs 2:4; 8:48; 14:8; 2 Kgs 10:31; 23:25; Isa 1:5; Jer 29:13; Ezek 36:5; Joel 2:12; Pss 86:12; 111:1; 1 Chr 28:9; 2 Chr 15:12, 15; 22:9; 30:19; 31:21; 34:31; 4Q298 f1 2:100 where every man's heart is asked to 'hear'; 4Q306 f2:3; 4Q364 f28a b:8; 4Q387 f2ii:1; 4Q397 f14 21:14; 4Q398 f14 17i:7; 4Q498 f6:1; 4Q511 f22:4; 11Q5 22:12; 11QT 54:13; 11QT 59:10).

[41] 'Upright heart' לֵבָב + יָשָׁר (Deut 9:5; 1 Kgs 9:4; 2 Kgs 10:8, 15; Ps 119:7; 1 Chr 29:17; 2 Chr 29:34; CD 8:14; 19:27); 'Soft heart' [לֵבָב + רָכַךְ] (Deut 20:3; 2 Kgs 22:19; Isa 7:4; Jer 51:46; 2 Chr 34:27; 1QM 10:3; 15:8); 'tender heart' [לֵבָב + רַךְ](Deut 20:8; 2 Chr 13:7; 11QT 62:3); 'Goodness of heart' לֵבָב + טוֹב (Deut 28:47; 1 Kgs 8:18; 2 Chr 6:8); 'Heart of joy' לֵבָב + שִׂמְחָה (Deut 28:47; Isa 30:29; Jer 15:16; Ezek 36:5; 4Q185 f1 2ii:12); 'Turning heart' לֵבָב + פָּנָה (Deut 29:17; 30:17).

[42] See 4Q175 1:3–4.

[43] E. Kautzsch and A. E. Cowley, eds., *Gesenius' Hebrew Grammar*, 2d English ed. (Oxford: Clarendon, 1910), §151; Bruce K. Waltke and M. O'Connor, *An Introduction to Biblical Hebrew Syntax* (Winona Lake, IN: Eisenbrauns, 1990), §40.2.2d; C. J. Labuschagne, "נָתַן," *TLOT* 2:785–86; *HALOT* 2:575. The wish is real but the situation wished for is not present.

[44] Eugene H. Merrill, *Deuteronomy*, NAC, ed. E. Ray Clendenen and Kenneth A. Matthews, vol. 4 (Nashville: Broadman & Holman, 1994), 159; Richard D. Nelson,

emphasized. Furthermore, it is limited to a specific people at a particular time. But there is good reason to set aside this interpretation.

The following expression seems to go beyond the mere verbiage of that generation to the core of the issue. The phrase (מִי־יִתֵּן) occurs twenty-five times in the Qal imperfect tense form in the OT and in every case it conveys a *presently-contrary-to-fact* wish.[45] The sense is best expressed as, "Despite your apparent obedience, Oh I wish you *presently* had a heart that really fears me *but you do not.*" In other words, they *presently* lack a *heart* that fears him or keeps his commandments—it is a heart, therefore, that lacks wisdom.[46] This is

---

Deuteronomy: A Commentary, OTL, ed. James L. Mays, Carol A. Newsom, and David L. Petersen (Louisville, KY: Westminster, 2002), 84. However, the proper response does not necessarily reveal a proper ontology. Indeed, if A (a new heart) then B (proper and approved response) but this does not imply if B (proper and approved response) therefore A (a new heart). Thus it is quite acceptable that Yahweh, on the one hand, approves of the response while, on the other hand, wishes for them to possess the heart that generates this response in a genuine and permanent way.

[45] Exodus 16:3; Num 11:29; Deut 5:29; 28:67; Judg 9:29; 2 Sam 19:1[18:33]; Isa 27:4; Jer 8:23[9:1]; 9:1[2]; Pss 14:7; 53:7[6]; 55:7[6]; Job 6:8; 11:5; 13:5; 14:4, 13; 19:23; 23:3; 29:2; 31:31, 35; Song 8:1. In two cases it is in the Qal perfect tense from which does not convey the same sense here (Isa 42:24; Job 38:36). The phrase in the Qal imperfect almost always refers to a *contrary-to-a-past-experience* in the present but always a *presently-contrary-to-fact* wish. BDB list this under a rhetorical usage where in the imperfect it expresses a wish with "the question implying a desire that the person asked for were present" and very often represented by the phrase מִי־יִתֵּן (BDB 566f.). Thus the very thing desired is not *presently* possessed.

[46] One can check the following passages all having מִי־יִתֵּן in the Qal imperfect tense form and each expressing a *presently contrary to fact counter-factual.* Exodus 16:3 states, *"Would that* we had died by the hand of the Lord in the land of Egypt." Obviously, they had not died but were *presently* alive. Numbers 11:29 reads, *"Would that* all the Lord's people were prophets." But, all were not and are not *presently* prophets. Deuteronomy 28:67 says, "In the morning you will say, '*Would it were* even!' and at even you will say, '*Would it were* morning!'" Notice that when the utterance is made, it is *present-contrary-to-fact.* Judges 9:29 says, "And *would that* this people were under my hand! then would I remove Abimelech." But the people were not *presently* under his hand and so he did not remove Abimelech. In 2 Sam 19:1[18:33] David prays, "O my son Absalom, my son, my son Absalom! *would I had* died for thee, O Absalom, my son, my son!" But, David had not died for Absalom thus his prayer is *present-contrary-to-fact.* Isaiah 27:4 reads, "I am not angry. *If only there were* briers and thorns confronting me! I would march against them in battle; I would set them all on fire" (NIV). Again, this was a *present-contrary-to-fact* wish. Jeremiah 8:23[9:1] says, "*Oh, that my head were* a spring of waters and my eyes a fountain of tears! I would weep

an excellent case where *functional* obedience is distinguished from *ontology* and where temporary obedience is no sign of possessing the new heart. A *functional* view is resolutely refuted by this usage because their obedience is met with *presently-contrary-to-fact* statement regarding their ontology not function. But since this addresses, in retrospect, the previous wandering generation, it does not necessarily represent the current audience of Moses. Given this, who can doubt that this 'obedience' is transitory?[47] This statement cautions against inferring from functional obedience the presence of the new heart. The explanation for those wanderings is depicted in *ontological-functional* rather than *functional* categories.[48] Since they lack this type

---

day and night for the slain of my people" (NIV). But Jeremiah's head is not a spring of waters nor his eyes a fountain of tears (at least *presently*). In Jer 9:1[2] he says, "*Oh, that I had* a desert a lodging place for travelers, so that I might leave my people and go away from them" (NIV). But, alas, he does not *presently* have such a place. Both Pss 14:7 and 53:7[6] pray for a salvation from Zion, namely, that God might bring back his people from captivity. But it is not *presently* there and they are not *presently* returned. Thus although the prayer is concerned about the future, it is *present-contrary-to-fact*. The psalmist prays, "*Oh, that I had* the wings of a dove! I would fly away and be at rest" (Ps 55:7[6] NIV). But he does not have these wings *presently* and cannot fly away and rest. Job 6:8 reads, "*Oh, that I might have* my request, that God would grant what I hope for" (NIV). But, he does not *presently* have this request. Job 11:5 says, "*Oh, how I wish* that God would speak, that he would open his lips against you" (NIV). But *presently*, God had not opened his mouth to defend Job. Job castigates his friends, "*If only you would* be altogether silent" (13:5, NIV)! But they were *presently* anything but silent. Job 14:13 says, "*If only you would* hide me in the grave" (NIV). But *presently* he is not hidden in the grave. Later in 19:23*bis* Job says, "*Oh, that my words were* recorded, *oh that they were* written on a scroll." But they were not *presently* recorded or written. Job says, "*If only* I knew were to find him; if only I could go to his dwelling! I would state my case before him and fill my mouth with arguments" (NIV, Job 23:3–4; cf. 31:35). But he did not know where to find him and so *presently* he could not make his case. Job 29:2 says, "*Oh that I were* as in the months of old, As in the days when God watched over me" (ASV). But he was *presently* not in those days. In Song 8:1 it reads, "If only you were to me like a brother...." (NIV) but this was not the case. The only exceptions to these examples are rhetorical questions that demand a negative reply (Job 14:4; 31:31; 38:36). Thus when Deut 5:29 reads, "*Oh that there were* such a heart in them, that they would fear me...." (ASV), there is no evidence against but only reason for taking it as a *presently-contrary-to-fact* wish.

[47] Peter C. Craigie, *The Book of Deuteronomy*, NICOT, ed. R. K. Harrison (Grand Rapids: Eerdmans, 1976), 166.

[48] One commentator takes the expression as meaning "that with the passage of time the inclination to obey Yahweh will weaken" (A. D. H. Mayes, *Deuteronomy*, NCB, ed.

of heart apart from the divine initiative, it stands to reason that *all men of all time also lack this type of heart apart from the divine initiative* (Deut 29:3[4]). They may evidence instances of obedience, but this does not imply they have a type of heart that produces these from its ontology (or nature).[49]

Later he tells the subsequent generation to "circumcise" (*functional*) the foreskin of their heart and to stop being stiff-necked" (Deut 10:16).[50] That this command is impossible for them to complete *in some permanent way* (as illustrated above) is confirmed later when it is noted that Yahweh himself must circumcise (*ontological-functional*) their hearts else they would not (and could not *functionally*) obey him (Deut 30:6). So although the command to 'circumcise' the heart is purely *functional*, the divine activity and remedy is presented in terms of the *ontological-functional* category. Thus *a functional ought does not necessarily imply an ontological can*.[51] In the meantime ('unto this day'),

---

Ronald E. Clements [Grand Rapids: Eerdmans, 1979], 173). This is because the *ontology* behind permanent obedience is lacking.

[49] Three NT examples are the instructive and all bear evidence of wisdom influence. First, Jesus said, "If you *being evil* know how to give good gifts to your children...." (εἰ οὖν ὑμεῖς πονηροὶ ὄντες οἴδατε δόματα ἀγαθὰ διδόναι τοῖς τέκνοις ὑμῶν [Matt 7:11]). Knowing how to give good gifts (= giving gifts) does not change one from *being* evil to not *being* evil. Deeds alone do not determine goodness or badness. This indicates that Jesus points to ontology not function as the true determinant of such effects. It is not a matter of changing one's function that makes one good but the cause of any function, good or evil, which determines whether one is truly good. Second, Jesus taught in Matt 7:17–19 that a good tree brings forth good fruit and a corrupt tree brings forth evil fruit. Again, Jesus points to ontology as the root of function, or uses function as evidence of a particular ontology. He argues from cause to effect. Third, Jesus said, "Wisdom is *justified* by her children" (Matt 11:19; Luke 7:35). A wisdom principle is evident, namely, *function does not create ontology but ontology determines function and fruit.*

[50] It is quite likely that this also refers to an *ontological-functional* aspect because of circumcision's relationship to election (cf. Fabry, "לֵב/לֵבָב," *TDOT* 7:433–34). Deuteronomy 10:16, 30:6 and Jer 31:31–33, all refer to the new heart. "Just as circumcision is associated with the divine gift of the covenant as a sign of submission, so circumcision of the heart stands for this submission itself" (ibid., 434).

[51] See chapter 2 on Pelagius. Thus ought implies *natural can* but not *moral can*. The Heidelberg Catechism (1563) anticipates the objection: "Is not God unjust in requiring of man in his Law what he cannot do? No, for God so created man that he could do it. But man, upon the instigation of the devil, by deliberate disobedience, has cheated himself and all his descendants out of these gifts" (Mark A. Noll, ed., *Confessions and Catechisms of the Reformation* [Grand Rapids: Baker, 1991], 138).

Yahweh does not give them a heart to know, eyes to see, and ears to hear (Deut 29:3[4]).[52] They are *deprived* of the new heart or the heart of wisdom that produces fear of Yahweh and obedience to his law (*ontological-functional*).[53] Yahweh expresses a benevolent love in regard to the obedient heart (Deut 5:29) but he does not demonstrate beneficent love in giving it (Deut 29:3[4]) to the wandering generation.[54] They see and hear the great wonders in their deliverance from Egypt but they do not really see, hear, or understand the significance. Events that transpire before their eyes remain *noetically*

---

[52] The phrase 'unto this day' might also apply to the present generation along with the previous generation. Von Rad says it is a historical retrospect on Deut 8:2–4 (Gerhard von Rad, *Deuteronomy: A Commentary*, trans. Dorothea M. Barton, OTL, ed. G. Ernest Wright et al. [Philadelphia: Westminster, 1966], 179). Craigie includes the present generation (Craigie, *The Book of Deuteronomy*, 356). It seems that the 'you' (plural) is given in a corporate solidarity sense, i.e., the present generation is linked with the past generation. "The generations merge: all are addressed as having experienced the past from Egypt to the victories over Sihon and Og. All are challenged to obey the covenant" (Nelson, *Deuteronomy*, 340). But this does not necessarily imply that the present generation is also rebellious. Rad says, "The apocalyptic writings are the first to attribute fundamental significance to the idea that not until the hour of great crisis do the old traditions reveal themselves to the understanding" (Rad, *Deuteronomy*, 179). Thus what is hidden is a proper understanding of traditions (= 'mystery') and what is withheld is either the ability to rightly construe their traditions (wandering generation) and/or understand the explanation of that mystery by Moses (present generation). The Mosaic explanation is "in order that the audience might be brought to real *understanding* of the ways of God, real *seeing* of the acts of God, and real *hearing* of the words of God" (Craigie, *The Book of Deuteronomy*, 356). But at the present time they do not understand it but a remnant does (Merrill, *Deuteronomy*, 376). The logic of the passage seems to restrict the lack of understanding to the wilderness generation in Moab and therefore implies that this is not the case with the present generation.

[53] See also Deut 8:2; 10:12–13; 11:13, 18; 13:3; 26:16. Some view this 'deprivation' in terms of withholding spiritual insight via retribution. "Israel's perverseness...the meaning must be, has obliged Jehovah hitherto to deal with it accordingly...and to withhold from it the power of apprehending properly the duties which its relation to Jehovah had imposed upon it" (S. R. Driver, *A Critical and Exegetical Commentary on Deuteronomy*, 3d ed., ICC, ed. Samuel Rolles Driver, Alfred Plummer, and Charles Augustus Briggs [Edinburgh: Clark, 1895], 321). Although the mode of hardening is identical to what is espoused here (withholding apprehension = deprivation of wisdom), the cause lying behind this withholding is not convincing (punitive).

[54] These two chapters in Deuteronomy are deliberately linked through the verbal parallels in 5:1–5 and 28:69 29:3 [29:1–4] (Nelson, *Deuteronomy*, 340).

'mysterious' due to the lack of the divine initiative.[55] The logic of the passage seems to imply that some (at least) of the present generation, whom Moses addresses, do possess this understanding.[56]

Up to this point, the heart is shown to be depicted in terms of cognition (wisdom) and volition (rebellion), from the aspect of function or ontology, particularly or universally, and within a particular time or all times. The cognitive and volitional aspects of the heart are never entirely separate. Both can be depicted as purely functional issues (thinking foolishly or acting rebelliously) but when addressing the heart certain texts appear to identify its ontology and thus suggest an *ontological-functional* category. The key in construing hardening texts in general is identifying which psychological aspect of the heart is primarily in view, that is, the *volitional* (Pharaonic) or *noetic* (Isaianic). Pharaonic hardening focuses mostly on volition where rebellion is paramount. Isaianic fattening focuses on cognition where wisdom is predominant. Wisdom is only slightly breached in Exod 4–14 as volition is in Isaiah. However, one should not assume Pharaonic hardening and Isaianic fattening refer to the same thing.

The Wisdom Corpus

Some Statistics. It may be relevant that 20 percent (170/860) of the occurrences of לֵבָב/לֵב in the OT are found in Proverbs, Ecclesiastes, and Job—otherwise known as the OT wisdom corpus (43 percent if one adds Psalms). Among these Proverbs has the most occurrences per volume and particularly chapters 14–17, followed by Ecclesiastes then Job.[57] The ratio of לֵב to לֵבָב in the wisdom corpus is 93 percent to 7 percent as compared with the OT (omitting wisdom corpus) of 65

---

[55] Christensen argues that that God only opens up people's hearts and enables them to love him *after* they repent. He cites the Talmud (*b. Sabb.* 104a "When a person seeks to purify himself, he receives help in doing so") in support (Duane L. Christensen, *Deuteronomy 21:10–34:12*, WBC, ed. John D. W. Watts, vol. 6B [Nashville: Nelson, 2002], 711–12). But this "God helps those who help themselves by repenting" is begging the question. On the contrary, repentance *is* understanding and followed by more understanding (Herm. *Mand.* 4.30.1–2). Repentance is not the necessary condition for the new heart but the necessary consequence of it (so says Isa 6:9–10 et al.).

[56] Ibid.

[57] If Psalms were added, it would appear between Ecclesiastes and Job in regard to frequency.

percent to 36 percent.[58] This ratio may not be significant. The significance is that the heart takes on paramount importance here and is relevant in treating Isa 6:9–10 (for it employs traditions associated with wisdom).

The Book of Job. Job uses לֵב twenty times and לֵבָב nine times along these lines. First, it is the place of hidden thoughts (10:13; 17:11), intentions (34:14), firm resolve (41:24), and the origination of both unspoken (1:5; 22:22) and spoken (8:10) words. Second, it can be used for evaluating someone or something (1:8; 2:3) or beneficent love (7:17). Third, it is the moral compass (27:6) and where either uprightness resides (33:3), including the desire to get right with someone (11:13), or godlessness (36:13). Fourth, it is susceptible to deception derived through the senses, especially the eyes (15:12; 31:7, 9, 27). Fifth, it is the locus of emotions such as unhealthy fear (23:16; 37:1) or joy (29:13).

Job also embodies explicit concepts of wisdom in keeping with the Deuteronomic notions mentioned earlier. First, Yahweh is *ontologically-functionally* 'wise in heart' (9:4) whereas men are not (37:24). Second, unlike volition, the לֵב/לֵבָב by itself may substitute as a metonymy for 'wisdom' or one of its effects such as perception, knowledge, or understanding (12:3; 34:10, 34; 36:5).[59] Thus to 'take away heart' (to *deprive* one from understanding [12:24]) or 'hide' one from שֶׂכֶל 'understanding' (17:4) is the act where Yahweh refuses to grant administrative *wisdom* (but it is not limited to this function elsewhere). Third, it is God who puts wisdom (חׇכְמׇה) "in the inward parts" (בַּטֻּחוֹת)[60] and "gives perception [בִּינׇה] to the mind [לַשֶּׂכְוִי]." These latter concepts harmonize well with Deut 5:29 and 29:3[4] which defer to Yahweh's right to deprive whomsoever of wisdom, salvific or otherwise. It testifies then to the congenital absence of such.

---

[58] The nominal לֵב appears 158 times in the wisdom corpus while לֵבָב occurs twelve times, nine of which are in Job, two in Psalms, and one in Ecclesiastes. The nominal לֵב appears 444 times in the rest of the OT while לֵבָב occurs 248 times.

[59] This is a key point. The implication is that the heart is at its base a cognitive organ of perception, knowledge, and understanding more than (but not exclusive of) a volitional organ of desire.

[60] This term for 'inward parts' is used only twice in the OT (Job 38:36; Ps 51:8[6]). Both texts refer to the residence of wisdom. The term for 'mind' (שֶׂכְוִי) is a hapax.

The final cause of granting wisdom is most often a *functional* one, but the granting of wisdom itself is *ontological* and gratuitous in nature.

A few passages deserve further comment. Job 12:20 says, "He *causes* the speech of the trusty *to turn aside* [מֵסִיר 'turns aside'] he *takes away* [יִקָּח] the taste/discernment of old." The issue is whether the 'taking away' implies *depletion* of wisdom (of whatever kind) from these elders. But several non-depletive interpretations may be given. First, 'take away' may refer to the death of counselors. Thus he does not take away the discernment from *within* the elders but *from* the hearing of the people they advise by taking away the elders in death. If depletion is involved it is depletion of life (cf. 12:2).[61] Second, God may stop supplying wisdom to individual elders in the sense he holds back wisdom from reaching them (cf. 12:15; 38:36). Again, this would not necessitate depletion but deprivation. Third, the verbs 'turns aside' the lips and 'takes' understanding of the elders might be construed as *from the people* (not elders), complimentary indicating the advice given to the people is no longer issued, and focusing on the source of wisdom (God). The emphasis may fall entirely on the external.

Job 12:24 says, "He turns aside [מֵסִיר] understanding [לֵב] from the leaders of the people of the land and causes them to wander in the wilderness where there is no way. The verb for 'turn aside' may mean 'take away' in the sense of *depletion* as in Ezek 11:19 where God takes away the bad, that is, the stony heart, and replaces it with the good, that is, a heart of flesh (Ezek 36:26). But nowhere is this verb used for depleting the good from within man. An alternative rendering is based on the root of this verb 'to deviate' and may refer to God's *withholding* of further wisdom as a deviation of sorts. God 'turns aside' wisdom from reaching the destination of man's heart or from reaching the leaders through other sources. This would flow well with 17:4 where God 'hides' wisdom for it is he who imparts or refuses to impart wisdom (Job 38:36). Thus God 'turns aside' wisdom by removing the continual giving or suspending it for a time. In either case, there is no *antecedent* cause given for why God does this.

---

[61] The verb לָקַח 'to take' is sometimes used in reference to death (1 Kgs 19:10, 14; Ps 34:14; Prov 1:19; Jonah 4:3) but metaphorically of understanding (לֵב) also (Hos 4:11). The latter does not support 'depletion' but rather through harlotry and/or consumption of wine or new wine causes wisdom that is present not to function properly. It *displaces* rather than *depletes* it.

Job 17:4 says, "For you have *hidden* [צָפַנְתָּ][62] their heart from *understanding* [מִשָּׂכֶל]." Job is referring to his three friends Eliphaz, Bildad, and Zophar. The central point is not what type of wisdom is here designated but that God withholds understanding and controls whom possesses it. The divine act of hiding may be by *withholding* what has never been there or *ceasing to give* what has been given up to this point. For whatever wisdom they do possess, they still lack this wisdom—and most likely *ab initio*. There is little in Job that demands that God 'takes away,' 'turns aside,' or 'hides' wisdom by subtraction from within. It is much more likely that he does so by deprivation from without.

The Book of Proverbs. Proverbs uses לֵב ninety-seven times and לֵבָב twice and may be listed under duties, nature, and functions. Statements may be *ontological* (about its nature), *functional* (about its function), *ontological-functional* (its nature and its necessary effects), or *functional-ontological* (functions that actualize its nature). *Ontological* statements are universal whereas *functional* ones are localized in time and space. *Ontological-functional* statements are universal in the sense that the function flows from the nature necessarily. *Functional-ontological* expresses a function (good or bad) that actualizes the ontology of the heart in such a way that it creates good or bad habits. All exhortations to the good to be better or prohibitions to stop being bad are in this category and are intended to move towards authenticity. The *degrees* of goodness or badness are relative and not universal.

An important philosophical caveat may be interjected here. First, one may choose to limit statements about the heart to particular individuals at particular times and reject any claim that these describe the heart of man at all times. Certainly everyone is not functionally wicked in the same sense and wickedness itself may be limited entirely to describing behavior alone not man's nature. Indeed, man may be wicked or righteous depending on his choices. Texts that appear to be including all of humanity are merely describing horrid (or splendid) conditions at particular times and places. It is therefore illegitimate to derive a universal ontological principle from them. Those who espouse libertarian freedom generally take this position.

---

[62] This may mean, "*thou* [God] *hast treasured up* their heart *away from* understanding, kept it there from" (BDB 860).

Second, one may choose to view particular texts about particular individuals at particular times as supporting a universal ontological principle of mankind's condition that is particularized with respect to a specific context. This does not insist that all individuals are wicked in an identical functional sense or that all men are functionally as evil as they possibly can be. Rather it is affirmed that the heart of man producing these evils is equally sinful in all men of all times apart from the divine initiative.[63] This study takes the latter view and is supported by previous texts about the heart and later texts that apply limited texts to man in general.[64] Those who affirm compatibilism generally take this position.

The *duties* of the heart include the following. First, *the heart is to attend to the things of wisdom.* These include understanding (2:2), perception (8:5), knowledge (22:17), instruction (23:12), and guidance from a teacher (23:19, 26). This duty is captured by the exhortation to be wise (27:11). These duties are *functional-ontological* in the sense that accomplishing them (function) helps actualize one's ontology not by way of metaphysical metamorphosis but self-actualization. Those who possess wisdom actualize these duties. Second, *it is to obey the commandments* (3:1). This is *functional* but since it is aided by writing

---

[63] This perspective may be illustrated with a story from WWII. Yehiel Dinur, a holocaust survivor, had the opportunity to confront his archenemy Adolf Eichmann. Upon approaching him, he began to sob and collapsed to the floor but not in anger or bitterness. Later he explained to a reporter that what struck him at that moment was a terrifying realization. "I was afraid about myself," Dinur said. "I saw that I am capable to do this.... Exactly like he." The reporter was stunned. Yehiel simply responded, "Eichmann is in all of us." He realized that one of the most evil (functionally so) men in the world at that time was no different than he *on the inside*. This is what perspective two asserts.

[64] The former texts are Gen 6:5; 8:21; Deut 5:29; 29:3[4]; and passages listed in fn. 24 (above) referring to the phrase 'from youth' or 'from the womb.' The latter texts are plentiful but one passage from Paul will suffice. Romans 3:9–20 contains five OT quotations: 3:10–12 (Pss 14:1–3; 53:1–3); 3:13a (Ps 5:10); 3:13b (Ps 140:4); 3:14 (Ps 10:7); and 3:15–17 (Isa 59:7–8). The OT context of each of these quotes reveals that they are specific and apply only to the 'wicked' (however Pss 14; 53 collocate 'none' and 'wicked' together). Under the first view, Paul has no right to apply these texts to all of mankind. But he does. Since he does, he must view these particularized statements in some sense as testifying to a universal description of mankind's nature and not limited to function alone. Therefore, *OT passages dealing with the wicked that seem to point to specific individuals at particular times may not be used to deny that they describe a universal (ontological) wickedness to all of mankind all the time.*

or retaining the truth on the heart (3:3; 4:4, 21; 6:21; 7:5) and studying to give appropriate answers (15:28), it is better categorized as *functional-ontological*. Furthermore, only the wise in heart obey these commandments (10:8). It is the wise-hearted who are perceptive (16:21), served by the foolish (11:29), increase in learning (16:23), and are happy (23:15). Third, *it is to trust God rather than its own wisdom* (3:5). Fourth, *it is to abstain from evil practices* (4:23). This includes wrong emotions like jealousy (23:17), or being subject to lust (6:25), seduction (7:25), haughtiness (18:12), or rebellion (31:11).

The *nature* of the heart is also of importance. First, *the heart is naturally evil*. It contains perversity (6:14), devises evil schemes (6:18; 23:7), utters perverse things (23:33), or obfuscates its evil with deceptive words (26:23, 25). Only God knows its true nature (15:11; 21:2; 24:12; 25:3). It reflects the nature of man (27:19) and must never be trusted (28:26). It cannot be kept purified by human means (20:9) and from youth it is bound up with foolishness (22:15). Although these are *ontological-functional* statements, they may specify the fool or the wicked in *functional-ontological* statements (and degrees). The heart of the wicked or fool is of little value (10:20). It is perverse (11:20; 17:20), acts unwisely (12:8), contains deceit (12:20), studies violence (24:2), despises reproof (5:12), is proud (16:5; 21:4), will not buy wisdom because it has 'no heart' (17:16), delights not in 'understanding' (18:2), rages against Yahweh (19:3), proclaims foolishness (12:23), backslides (14:14), and does not dispense knowledge (15:7).

Second, *it naturally lacks salvific wisdom*. The absence of wisdom is termed 'no heart.' This assessment comes in the form of *evidence-inference*. The evidence is the function while the inference (though not necessarily) is a statement on ontology. This occurs in cases of adultery (6:32; 7:7; 9:4, 16), despising a neighbor (11:12), any sin or sinful pursuit (12:11; 15:21; 17:18), and is the state of the fool (10:21; 17:16). To 'gain heart' is to accept correction (15:32) or to possess wisdom (19:8) and therefore to be 'good' (22:11). Wisdom enters the heart from without (2:10). Therefore, the heart that does 'perceive' does so because it possesses 'wisdom' (10:13; 14:33), a wisdom that seeks further knowledge (15:14) and buys it (18:15).

Finally, the *functions* of the heart are significant. First, *the heart is the fulcrum of psychical activity*. It can be 'heavy' with emotion or stress (12:25; 13:12; 14:10a, 13; 15b; 17:22b; 25:20), be satisfied and content

(14:10b, 30), or be happy (15:13a, 15, 30; 17:22a; 24:17; 27:9).[65] Second, *it is the cognitive and volitional center*. The heart plans (16:1, 9; 19:21; 20:5), places trust in others (31:11), and is tested by Yahweh as to its true intentions (17:3; 21:2). The cognitive aspect is also highlighted by its translation as 'consider, know' (24:32; 27:23). All aspects of the heart are under absolute control of Yahweh (21:1).

The Book of Ecclesiastes. This book uses לֵב forty-one times and לֵבָב once. *Ontological* usages in Ecclesiastes are rare but two are definite. First, it has a longing for or sense of eternity (3:11). This is a universal but amoral attraction to transcendence that works its way out in *ontological-functional* ways by both considering temporality (7:2, 4) and discerning time and judgment (8:5). Second, the concluding words of the writer are that man's heart is full of evil and madness but the exact sense is either pertaining to his depravity or frustration that springs from inevitable death (9:3).[66] Functional implications of this are Gen 6:5 and 8:21.

Most of the usages are *functional-ontological* in nature. Qoheleth uses his God-given wisdom for seeking out wisdom of all kinds (1:13; 7:25). Indeed, he experiences the effects of gaining wisdom (1:16b) and knows both wisdom and madness (1:17; 7:25; 8:9, 16; 9:1). The

---

[65] Non-psychical references are Prov 23:34 and 30:19 where 'heart' is used to describe the midst of the sea.

[66] The phrase in question, לֵב בְּנֵי־הָאָדָם מָלֵא־רָע וְהוֹלֵלוֹת בִּלְבָבָם ("the heart of the sons of men is full of evil and madness in their heart...."), may be taken as echoing universal human depravity (Michael A. Eaton, *Ecclesiastes*, TOTC, ed. D. J. Wiseman [Downers Grove, IL: InterVarsity Press, 1983], 125–26; H. C. Leuphold, *Exposition of Ecclesiastes* [Grand Rapids: Baker, 1952], 209–10; Tremper Longman, *The Book of Ecclesiastes*, NICOT, ed. Robert L. Hubbard Jr. [Grand Rapids: Eerdmans, 1998], 227) or capitulation to evil living because of the utter despair that stems from the vanity of living righteously (George Aaron Barton, *The Book of Ecclesiastes*, ICC, ed. S. R. Driver, A. Plummer, and C. A. Briggs [Edinburgh: Clark, 1908], 159; James L. Crenshaw, *Ecclesiastes: A Commentary*, OTL, ed. Peter Ackroyd et al. [Philadelphia: Westminster, 1987], 160; Robert Gordis, *Koheleth—The Man and His World*, ed. 3d [New York: Schocken, 1968], 301). Ogilvie rejects that it is a tract on original sin (Lloyd J. Ogilvie, *Ecclesiastes, Song of Solomon*, The Communicator's Commentary, ed. Lloyd J. Ogilvie, vol. 15b [Dallas, TX: Word, 1991], 199) while others take a minimalist approach (R. N. Whybray, *Ecclesiastes*, NCB, ed. Ronald E. Clements [Grand Rapids: Eerdmans, 1989], 142; Roland Murphy, *Ecclesiastes*, WBC, ed. David A. Hubbard, Glenn W. Barker, and John D. W. Watts, vol. 23A [Dallas, TX: Word, 1992], 91). Neither approach necessarily denies the other.

heart can be guided by wisdom while using wine to cheer the flesh (2:3; 9:7). Certain behaviors can produce sinful habits while the effects are long-term (7:26). The lack of speedy justice only entices it to more evil (8:11). Extortion can make the wise man act foolishly and destroy 'heart' (= understanding [7:7]).[67] It is not his ontology that changes but the functioning pattern operating from what he is by nature that is damaged.

Many other cases depict the *function* of the heart. The heart can commune with itself (1:16a; 2:1, 15*bis*; 3:17, 18), utter before God (5:1[2]), or express emotions such as rejoicing (2:10), despairing (2:20), worrying (2:23), having joy (5:19[20]), gladness (7:3; 11:9a), or sorrow (11:10). The heart determines the nature of one's attentions in life (2:22; 7:21; 10:2, 3; 11:9b) and serves as the moral conscience (7:22).

Summary. First, there is little by way of novelty as to either differing types of heart or the relation of wisdom to the heart as seen in the Pentateuch. Second, unique concepts such as God 'takes away [lit. 'turns aside'] heart' (Job 12:24)[68] from leaders or one has 'no heart' (Prov 6:32), and other such expressions, means simply that God *deprives* it of understanding or that it *naturally* lacks understanding (as proved by acts). It does not imply that God takes away (*depletes*) what is latent in the heart. Function cannot affect ontology (Prov 20:9) but only God (Prov 22:11). It is therefore unwise to construe *functional-ontological* statements for seeking wisdom as identical to *ontological-functional statements*. Because Yahweh controls the heart completely (Prov 21:1) and the heart controls the person absolutely (Eccl 2:22; 7:21; 10:2, 3; 11:9b), he must ultimately exercise this control in affecting a change in man to redirect him towards wisdom's end. Indeed, wisdom enters the heart (Prov 2:10) and makes it wise (Prov 16:21, 23; 23:15; Eccl 7:4; 8:5; 10:2). This literature stresses using the

---

[67] The term for 'heart' is used twice alone to signify 'understanding' (Eccl 7:7; 10:3).

[68] This verb is in the Hiphil stem and is a good example of God *causing* in a *continuative* rather than in a *creative* sense man's lack of wisdom. Yahweh "causes wisdom to be continually turned from it [= deprive wisdom from the heart]." A better translation might be, "He causes understanding to deviate from...." The divine act is not a subtraction but simply a continuation of no addition of wisdom (BDB 693–94). Other examples of this sense of this verb are Exod 23:25; Deut 7:15; Josh 11:15; Isa 3:1; Amos 5:23; Zeph 3:15; Job 9:34; 33:17; 34:20; 1 Chr 17:13; 2 Chr 30:9. A noetic *depletion* (therefore transformation) only occurs in texts where evil (not good) is taken away (Ezek 11:19; 36:26).

God-given wisdom one has for assessing behavior in order to derive inferences in determining whether one genuinely possesses and exercises it rightly. Man may possess some type of wisdom naturally but all men lack salvific wisdom congenitally.

The Heart, Wisdom, and Related Terms and Concepts

This section will focus on four areas. First, possessing wisdom is the necessary and sufficient condition for having other noetic traits, namely, *understanding, perception,* and *knowledge.* Second, salvific wisdom in particular (although other types are not excluded) is imparted on the basis of the divine prerogative alone.[69] Third, wisdom is congenitally absent from the heart of man. To be *fat-hearted,* therefore, is an *ontological* statement about the *absence* of wisdom in mankind. Thus it is best to view the fat-heart as an *ontological-functional* appraisal.[70] Finally, divine fattening is best construed as the exercise of the divine prerogative to *deprive* (rather than to *deplete* or *divest*) human hearts of wisdom involving the divine decision to perpetuate the congenital state.

The discussion below is determined by Isa 6:9–10 and consults the Hebrew Bible, DSS, and other Jewish literature. Pharaonic hardening and Isaianic fattening are *ontological-functional* in nature but the former focuses primarily on volitional (rarely cognitive) effects while

---

[69] Gerhard von Rad, *Wisdom in Israel,* trans. James D. Martin (London: Abingdon, 1972), 54–57 suggests the idea that Yahweh gives wisdom as a special gift is a late development in Israel's history. But his entire supposition proceeds on questionable dating of the materials.

[70] Degrees of salvific wisdom after possessing salvation is validated in the wisdom literature and classified as *functional-ontological* above. Isaianic fattening has to do with the absence of salvific wisdom not the degree to which one is fattened. One is either 'saved' or 'unsaved' not saved by degrees or lost in degrees. Thus the fat-heart is an *ontological* state not *functional* category. However, because the fat-heart acts in ways contrary to wisdom's effects, it is said to function in a certain way, hence, *ontological-functional*. The ontology ('fatness') is the cause while the functional—including noetic (lack of perception, knowledge, and understanding) and volitional aspects (lack of repentance)—is the effects. The prophets of the OT view the fat/hard-heart as the ontological state of all mankind removed only by the gratuitous impartation of the new heart (Jer 24:7; 30:21; 31:31–33; 32:29; Ezek 11:19; 18:31; 36:26; 44:5). Isaiah 6:9–10 is merely the opposite of granting this new heart and by not granting the new heart it leaves in place the 'fat-heart.' Thus no transformation occurs, no retribution is in mind, and only deprivation adequately describes this divine act.

3333333

the latter on cognition and only by implication (repentance) the former. Failure to recognize this leads to a category-mistake. To read into one the other is to commit the fallacy of *unwarranted neglect of distinguishing peculiarities of a corpus* while to blend the two is to commit the *illegitimate totality transfer*. It is not a matter of exclusion but focus.

Noetic Ontology: A Series of Sapiential Syllogisms

The internal logic of the wisdom tradition in combination with Isaiah's version flows from the following seven lines of rationale:[71] the order of salvation, the effects of wisdom, the lack of wisdom as the fat-heart, the congenital condition of the heart, the nature of fattening as non-transformational, fattening as deprivation, and the bestowal of wisdom as gratuitous. Although these arguments are set out here in sequential and syllogistic fashion, the rest of the chapter and other chapters will proceed inductively but occasionally draw conclusions in conformity to this scheme.[72]

The Order of Isaianic Salvation (Isa 6:9–10):[73]
Exegetical Order (in reverse):[74]

---

[71] The first is not strictly a syllogism but follows the parameters of Isa 6:9–10.

[72] To avoid equivocation, it will be assumed that perception, knowledge, and understanding are to be kept in terms of Isaiah's speech throughout these syllogisms and not turned indiscriminately into a perception, knowledge, and understanding of any kind. Not all perception, knowledge, and understanding produce repentance but Isaiah's necessarily does and this makes it salvific and effectual. All that is asserted here is that all mankind naturally lacks *salvific* wisdom and this is proven *a posteriori* in that all men are not saved. This is the fat-heart according to Isaiah.

[73] Hoehner says similarly on Eph 4:17–18. "In reviewing these two verses [4:17–18] a series of causes and effects becomes apparent. The scenario could be reconstructed by reversing the direction of statements. The hardness of their hearts toward God causes their ignorance. Ignorance concerning God and his will caused them to be alienated from the life of God. Their alienation caused their minds to be darkened, and their darkened minds caused them to walk in the futility of mind" (Harold W. Hoehner, *Ephesians: An Exegetical Commentary* [Grand Rapids: Baker, 2002], 588–89). Earlier he says, "The original purpose of the mind was to be able to comprehend God's revelation, but *due to the fall* a person's mind is *unable* to accomplish this goal (μα/ταιος)" (ibid., 584 emphasis added). Behind this lies the wisdom tradition.

[74] The exegetical order is a sorites: P[1]: If fat-hearted then no wisdom. P[2]: If no wisdom then no repentance. P[3]: If no repentance then no healing/forgiveness. C: Therefore, if fat-hearted then no healing/forgiveness. This can be deconstructed as follows: (1) P[1]:

P¹: One must *repent* to be forgiven/healed—*volitional and functional*.

P²: One must *perceive* and *know* (and *understand*) with the heart to repent—*noetic and ontological-functional*.

P³: One must have a *non-fattened* heart to perceive and know (and to understand)—*ontological*.

C: For one to be forgiven/healed requires a non-fattened heart.

> *Decomposed into two syllogisms:*
> P¹: One must first *repent* to be forgiven/healed.
> P²: One must first *perceive* and *know* (and *understand*) with the heart to repent.
> C: One must first *perceive* and *know* (and *understand*) with the heart to be forgiven/healed.
>
> P¹: One must first *perceive* and *know* (and *understand*) with the heart to repent.
> P²: One must first have a *non-fattened* heart to perceive and know (and to understand).
> C: One must first have a *non-fattened* heart to be forgiven/healed.

Effects of Wisdom:

P¹: The possession/exercise of *perception, knowing* and *understanding* are evidence of the possession of wisdom—*ontological-functional*.

P²: Some hearts exercise *perception, knowing,* and *understanding*—*ontological-functional* or *functional-ontological*.

C: Therefore, some hearts possesses/exercise wisdom and its effects.

Lack of Wisdom and the Fat-heart:

P¹: Everyone who lacks perception, knowledge, and understanding does not have wisdom—*ontological-functional*.

P²: Those lacking perception, knowledge, and understanding have a fat-heart—*ontological-functional*.

C: Everyone who has a fat-heart does not have wisdom.

Fat-heart: A Congenital Condition:

P¹: The heart is naturally absent of *wisdom* or its effects—*ontological-functional*.

P²: To lack wisdom and its effects is to be fat-hearted—*ontological-functional*.

C: Man is *congenitally* fat-hearted.

Divine Fattening is Non-transformative:

P¹: Man is congenitally fat-hearted—*ontological*.

P²: God fattens man's heart.

If fat-hearted then no wisdom. P²: If no wisdom then no repentance. C: If fat-hearted then no repentance. (2) P¹: If no wisdom then no repentance. P²: If no repentance then no healing/forgiveness. C: If no wisdom then no healing/forgiveness.

C: God fattens man's heart non-transformatively.

Divine Fattening is by Deprivation:
P¹: God fattens man's heart non-transformatively
P²: Among the means of fattening (depletion, deposition, and deprivation), only one view presents fattening in a non-transformative fashion.
C: God fattens by *deprivation* (of wisdom).

Wisdom is Gratuitously Bestowed:
P¹: God fattens by depriving the heart of wisdom—*ontological*.
P²: Some hearts show evidence of having wisdom, namely, they exercise *perception, understanding,* and *knowledge—ontological-functional*.
C: God has not deprived some hearts of wisdom.

Means of Establishing the Truth of the Syllogisms

The collocation of wisdom terms is a well-recognized phenomenon. Here it will be asserted that this is not merely due to genre collocation but logical causation. There is an identifiable *causal direction of noetic qualities* as it relates to the *nature of the effects*. The validation of the syllogisms above, therefore, flows from an investigation of this collocation and logical phenomenon as set forth here and in the following chapters.

In order to avoid the *word-idea* fallacy, the following steps (or precautions) are taken in this analysis. First, each cognate of 'wisdom' (חָכְמָה, חָכָם, חָכַם)[75] is tallied for its occurrence when in collocation with 'heart' (לֵבָב/לֵב) and subsequently with certain verbs relevant to Isa 6:9–10, namely, 'to perceive,' (בִּין) 'to understand,' (שָׂכַל) and 'to

---

[75] Another term for wisdom (תּוּשִׁיָּה) occurs twelve times in the OT (Isa 28:29; Mic 6:9; Job 5:12; 6:13; 11:16; 12:16; 26:3; 30:22; Prov 2:7; 3:21; 8:14; 18:1). Two places in Job (11:6; 26:3) it occurs in collocation with 'wisdom' (חָכְמָה) and the verb 'to know' (יָדַע). In one place (Prov 8:14) it is associated with the nominal בִּינָה. See R. B. Girdlestone, *Girdlestone's Synonyms of the Old Testament,* 3d ed. (London: Nisbet, 1897; reprint, Grand Rapids: Baker, 2000), 89–90. For the general Hebrew semantic domain of 'wisdom' see Gerald H. Wilson, "חכם," *NIDOTTE* 2:130–34; J. Goetzmann and C. Brown, "Σοφία," *NIDNTT* 3:1026–33. Another term for 'understanding' is תְּבוּנָה occurring some forty-two times in the OT. It is associated with the nominal בִּינָה once (Prov 2:3), with the verbal יָדַע twice (Exod 36:1; Isa 40:14 along with the nominal דַּעַת) and with the nominal דַּעַת six times (Exod 31:3; 35:3; 1 Kgs 7:14; Isa 40:14; 44:19; Prov 2:6). See Helmer Ringgren, "בִּין," *TDOT* 2:99–107. At Qumran, Romaniuk says that "les termes HKMH, D'T et SKL sont presque synonymes" (C. Romaniuk, "Le Thème de la sagesse dans les documents de Qumran," *RevQ* 9 [1978]: 433). See also M. Saebo, "חכם," *TLOT* 1: 418–24; H. -P. Müller and M. Krause, "חָכַם," *TDOT* 4:364–85.

know' (יָדַע). This will show an order that is found also in the wisdom literature. Second, this is followed by an examination of 'heart' (לֵבָב/לֵב) when collocated with the verbs 'to perceive,' (בִּין)[76] 'to understand,' (שָׂכַל) and 'to know' (יָדַע).[77] The goal is to show the logical order in Isaiah is derived from the wisdom tradition.

There are three words of caution. First, this chapter is primarily seeking to establish the logical links of wisdom rather than provide detailed exegesis of particular passages (see chaps. 4–6). Second, not all wisdom is soteriological. So although salvific wisdom is always gratuitous, all gratuitous wisdom is not salvific. Finally, since there is a development in the prophetic materials linking salvific wisdom to the new heart that finds full bloom in the NT, one should not expect to find such exact expression in the OT.

Wisdom and the Hebrew Scriptures (MT)

The Lexical Domains. The Hebrew word for 'wisdom' occurs as a verb (חָכַם), an adjective (חָכָם), and as a noun (חָכְמָה). The goal is to establish that the lack of wisdom equals the 'fat' heart, to show man is naturally without wisdom ('fat-hearted'), and thereby prepare the way for arguing that the divine act of 'fattening' in Isaiah is best viewed as non-transformative.

The verb חָכַם occurs twenty-eight times[78] and is the cause of שָׂכַל (Prov 21:11), שָׂכַל and בִּין (Deut 32:29), or just בִּין (Job 32:9, 8–9). It occurs with לֵב four times (Prov 23:15, 19; 27:11; Eccl 2:15).[79] Indeed, the heart can be wise (Prov 23:15), wisdom can guide one's heart

---

[76] This verb is frequently associated with the terms 'to hear' and 'to see' and acknowledged to be a typical wisdom term (Ringgren, "בִּין," TDOT 2:104). The nominal form בִּינָה is "for the most part, but not exclusively, a Wisdom word" (ibid., 105). For a discussion of this term and its relationship to wisdom see Müller and Krause, "חָכַם," TDOT 4:364–85.

[77] Although the focus is on the verbal notions because Isaiah uses these forms, the nominal equivalents are not without validity: בִּינָה occurs thirty-nine times, שָׂכַל occurs sixteen times, and דַּעַת occurs seven times in the MT.

[78] In the Hiphil once (Ps 19:8); the Hithpael twice (Exod 1:10; Eccl 7:16), the Pual twice (Ps 58:6; Prov 30:24), the Piel three times (Pss 105:22; 119:98; Job 35:11), and the Qal twenty times (Deut 32:29; 1 Kgs 5:11; Zech 9:2; Job 32:9; Prov 6:6; 8:33; 9:9, 12bis; 13:20bis; 19:20; 20:1; 21:11; 23:15, 19; 27:11; Eccl 2:15, 19; 7:23).

[79] The verb חָכַם does not occur with לֵבָב nor in collocation with any of the verbs nominal cognates, שָׂכַל, בִּינָה, or דַּעַת.

(Prov 13:19), and a father desires his son to possess (or express) it (Prov 27:11). The only association with יָדַע is Prov 9:9 where a wise man (*ontological-functional*) is given instruction to become wiser (וְיֶחְכַּם־עוֹד, *functional-ontological*) and is made *to know* (הוֹדַע). The one who *ontologically* possesses wisdom seeks to acquire more wisdom to actualize his ontology—hence, *functional-ontological*.

Also instructive is that this verb only occurs in the Qal stem with the sense of 'to become wise' (ingressive) either in association with other verbs mentioned above (Deut 32:29; Job 32:9; Prov 9:9; 21:11) or with the nominal for 'heart' (Prov 23:15, 19; 27:11; Eccl 2:15).[80] This phenomenon is in contrast to other stems like the Piel 'to make wise' as in becoming skilled (Pss 105:22; 119:98; Job 35:11; cf. 2 Tim 3:15), or its passive in the Pual emphasizing the result 'having been taught/instructed' or becoming 'skilled' (Ps 58:6; Prov 30:24), the Hiphil 'cause to be made wise' (Ps 19:8), and the Hithpael 'to make oneself wise' (self-actualization) often with sardonic irony involved (Exod 1:10; Eccl 7:16).[81] Each example is *functional-ontological* where one who is wise becomes wiser (or more skilled).

The adjective חָכָם occurs 138 times and is used adjectivally, predicatively, or most often substantivally. The majority of cases refer to the noetic realm regarding wisdom in combination with synonyms or in a dialect of opposition. When found with לֵב it is linked either with God imparting wisdom into the heart for a specific skill (Exod 28:3; 31:6; 36:1, 2; 1 Kgs 3:12)[82] or just in combination with 'heart.'[83] Exodus 28:3 associates it with the 'wind [spirit] of wisdom,' רוּחַ חָכְמָה

---

[80] Müller and Krause, "חָכַם," *TDOT* 4:370 where they say that in the Qal it refers to a state of being wise. Saebo agrees and refers to it as having an "ingressive meaning, 'to become wise'" ("חָכַם," *TLOT* 1:419).

[81] But the ironic-concessive notion is also found in the Qal stem (Zech 9:2). Cf. Saebo, "חָכַם," *TLOT* 1: 419.

[82] When this is under view the heart is described as a 'wise heart' and refers either in regard to a craftsman (Exod 31:6; 35:10; 36:1, 2, 8) or craftswoman (Exod 35:25) or alone it can refer simply to a skilled craftperson (1 Chr 22:15; 2 Chr 2:7, 12, 13; Jer 10:9; Ezek 27:9). But "in other contexts...refers to an advanced state of wisdom" (Gerald H. Wilson, "חָכַם," *NIDOTTE* 2:132). This would include passages like Job 9:4; 27:24; Prov 10:8; 11:29; 16:21.

[83] Exod 35:10, 25; 36:8; Job 37:24; Prov 10:8; 11:29; 15:7; 16:21, 23; 22:17; 23:15, 19; 27:11; Eccl 7:4, 7; 8:5; 10:2.

(cf. Deut 34:9; Isa 11:2).[84] In Job 9:4 the wise hearted (חֲכַם לֵבָב), namely Yahweh, is contrasted to one who *hardens* (מִי־הִקְשָׁה) himself or acts stubbornly against him. It is often combined with בִּין in describing the wise person.[85] In three of these texts (Prov 18:15; Jer 9:11; Hos 14:10), wisdom serves as the prerequisite for 'perception.' It is collocated with בִּינָה thrice (Isa 29:14; 2 Chr 2:12, 13). Isaiah 29:14 predicts a day when Yahweh will deprive of wisdom. In 2 Chr 2:12–13, Solomon is described as a "wise [חָכָם] son who knows [יוֹדֵעַ] understanding [שֵׂכֶל][86] and perception [וּבִינָה]."

The combination with שֵׂכֶל occurs twice (Prov 16:23; 21:11). Both instances are *functional-ontological* (with the Hiphil) as the heart of the

---

[84] The Hebrew phrase רוּחַ חָכְמָה 'wind [spirit] of wisdom' occurs three times in the OT (Exod 28:3; Deut 34:9; Isa 11:2). In Isa 11:2 it parallels a more familiar expression, רוּחַ אֱלֹהִים 'wind [spirit] of God' (Gen 1:2; 41:38; Exod 31:3; 35:31; Num 24:2; 1 Sam 11:6; 16:15, 16, 23; 18:10; 19:20, 23; Ezek 11:24; 2 Chr 15:1; 24:20). See also רוּחַ־יְהוָה 'wind [spirit] of the Lord' (Judg 3:10; 6:34; 11:29; 13:25; 14:6; 15:14; 1 Sam 10:6; 16:13, 14; 19:9; 2 Sam 23:2; 1 Kgs 18:12; 19:11; 22:24; 2 Kgs 2:16; Isa 11:2; 31:3; 40:7, 13; 54:6; 59:19; 61:1; 63:14; Ezek 11:5; 37:1; Hos 13:15; Mic 2:7; 3:8; Zech 4:6; Ps 35:5; Prov 16:2; 2 Chr 18:23; 20:14). The term רוּחַ generally signifies "air in motion, a blowing, breeze, wind, nothingness, spirit, sense" (*HALOT* 3:1197). Similar notions are reflected with the Greek term πνεῦμα (E. Kamlah, J. D. G. Dunn, and C. Brown, "Πνεῦμα," *NIDNTT* 3:689–709). On the term רוּחַ "the thought implicit…is that of breathing, with the movement of air that this involves, is the outward expression of the life-force inherent in all human behavior" (ibid.). Other similar phrases occur in the OT as well: (1) רוּחַ אֵלִיָּהוּ wind/spirit of Elijah (2 Kgs 2:15); (2) רוּחַ אֱלוֹהַּ 'wind/spirit of God' (Job 27:3); (3) רוּחַ־אֵל 'wind/spirit of God' (Job 33:4); (4) רוּחַ־אֱלָהִין 'wind/spirit of gods' (Dan 4:5, 6, 15; 5:11, 14). Koehler and Baumgartner give fifteen semantic domains for רוּחַ (*HALOT* 3:1198–1201). For the sake of sensitivity to biblical theology, progressive revelation and the exploitation of its ambiguity even into the NT, the phrases involving רוּחַ will be translated neutrally as wind/spirit throughout this Study (although the writing prophets, like Isaiah, have a clearly articulate doctrine of the Spirit). For an examination of the history of the term see Van Pelt, Kaiser, and Block, "רוּחַ," *NIDOTTE* 3:1073–78.

[85] Gen 41:33, 39; Deut 1:13; 4:6; 1 Kgs 3:12; Isa 3:3; 5:21; 29:14; Jer 4:22; 9:11; Hos 14:10; Prov 1:5, 6; 14:15–16; 16:21; 17:28; 18:15; 28:11; 29:7–8; Eccl 9:11. When occurring with this verb it normally does so in the Niphal stem with its participle form fourteen times (Gen 41:33, 39; Deut 1:13; 4:6; 1 Kgs 3:12; Isa 3:3; 5:21; 29:14; Jer 4:22; Prov 1:5; 16:21; 17:28; 18:15; Eccl 9:11). Other cases involve the Qal stem in rhetorical questions (Jer 9:11; Hos 14:10), with the wicked (Prov 29:7–8), or when the prudent man is contrasted with the wicked (Prov 14:15–16). Two other usages involve the Hiphil in either a gnomic expression (Prov 1:6) or the activity of the poor man who searches out the so-called wisdom of the rich man (Prov 28:11).

[86] This is the only place where the nominal form שֵׂכֶל occurs with the adjective.

wise man is *instructed* by his own or someone else's mouth (Prov 16:23; 21:11). With יָדַע it occurs eighteen times.[87] Occasionally it is collocated with בִּין and יָדַע in the same verse (Deut 1:13; Jer 4:22; Hos 14:9) or שָׂכַל and יָדַע (2 Chr 2:12). Being wise is associated with knowing what course of action to take or what God plans to do (Isa 19:12), the interpretation of things (Eccl 8:1), or times (Esth 1:13). God calls wise men with 'knowledge' to 'hear' his words (Job 34:2, 34).[88] With דַּעַת it is found nine times.[89] God turns the wise men backwards and makes their knowledge foolish (Isa 44:25). A rhetorical question is whether a wise man answers with vain knowledge (דַעַת־רוּחַ) (Job 15:2)—a negative reply is expected. On the contrary, a wise man lays up knowledge (Prov 10:14), his tongue utters knowledge aright in contrast to fools (Prov 15:2), and his lips dispense knowledge (Prov 15:7). It is the understanding heart (lit. 'the heart that understands', לֵב נָבוֹן) that buys knowledge and the ear of the wise that seeks knowledge (Prov 18:15). When instructed the wise man not only receives knowledge (Prov 21:11) but possesses knowledge (Prov 24:5). Finally, the wise preacher teaches people knowledge (Eccl 12:9).[90]

---

[87] Deut 1:13, 15; 2 Sam 14:20; 1 Kgs 2:9; Isa 19:12; Jer 4:22; Hos 14:9; Job 34:2; Prov 9:9; Eccl 2:19; 4:13; 6:8; 8:1, 5, 17; Esth 1:13; 2 Chr 2:12, 13.

[88] Job 34:2, 34 are related passages and give meaning to isolated term לֵבָב. 34:2 says, "*Hear* my words you *wise ones*, give *ear* to me you that have *knowledge*." 34:34 reads, "Men of *heart* will say unto me, yes, every *wise one* that *hears* me." Note the collocation of terms. Wise ones 'hear' (or 'give ear') to the Lord and have 'knowledge.' The possession of wisdom, knowledge, and a hearing ear is parallel to having 'heart' (cf. Job 12:3; 34:10). Granting a 'new heart' is a circumlocution for the bestowing salvific wisdom. When Yahweh gives a new 'heart' (to know him) he gives one wisdom, perception, knowledge, and understanding that leads to repentance and therefore healing/forgiveness. The same phenomenon occurs with לֵב. To be 'without heart' is to be without understanding ([אַיִן + לֵב] Jer 5:21; Hos 7:11; 4Q381 f1:2). Yahweh takes away heart means he does not grant understanding (['deprive wisdom from the heart'] [סוּר + לֵב] 'understanding' [Job 12:24]). 'No heart' is to be without understanding ([חֲסַר־לֵב] = no understanding [trans. 'void of understanding'] Prov 6:32; 7:7; 9:4, 16; 10:13, 21; 11:12; 12:11; 15:21; 17:18; 24:30). Cf. Eichrodt, *Theology of the Old Testament*, 142–45. "When Hosea wishes to characterize the senseless political behavior of the Northern kingdom, he says that Ephraim has not heart, that is to say, no understanding" (ibid., 143).

[89] Isa 44:25; Job 15:2; Prov 10:14; 15:2, 7; 18:15; 21:11; 24:5; Eccl 12:9.

[90] Three offices in the OT reveal different *emphases*. The priest focuses on the Torah (תּוֹרָה) or 'instruction' while the wise man with 'counsel' (עֵצָה), and the prophet with 'the word' (דְּבָר). Moreover, four distinct *genres* come under the wise man's purview

These are all either *ontological-functional* or *functional-ontological* usages.

The noun חָכְמָה occurs 161 times. On twenty-one occasions it is collocated with לֵב.[91] Instances of *ontological-functional* include cases where individuals are made wise-hearted (= skilled for a craft) because God fills them with the wind [spirit] of wisdom (Exod 28:3) and puts wisdom within them (Exod 35:35; 31:6; 36:1, 2; 1 Kgs 10:24; 2 Chr 9:23).[92] On the noetic level he utilizes wisdom (*functional-ontology*) to search out things (Eccl 1:13, 17; 2:31) or explores wisdom itself (Prov 2:2; Eccl 8:16) resulting in more understanding (Prov 2:10; 10:13). The 'fool,' on the other hand, does not even see the need to buy wisdom (Prov 17:16)—thus it requires a heart of wisdom (*ontology*) to recognize the need of needing wisdom (*function*).[93] It occurs only once with לֵבָב (Ps 90:12) where dependence on Yahweh brings the right perspective on time.

It is collocated with בִּין, eleven times.[94] In every case בִּין is the outcome or outgrowth of wisdom and wisdom is the prerequisite for

---

(Prov 1:6). These include the following: the 'proverb' (מָשָׁל), 'satire' (מְלִיצָה), 'words of wisdom' (דִּבְרֵי חֲכָמִים), and the 'riddle' (חִידָה). Finally, according to Eccl 12:9, there are at least three *responsibilities* of the wise man that include teaching, researching, and writing (Müller and Krause, "חָכַם," *TDOT* 4:374).

[91] Exod 28:3; 31:6; 35:26, 35; 36:1, 2; 1 Kgs 10:24; Ps 49:4[3]; Prov 2:2, 10; 10:13; 14:33; 17:16; 28:26; 2 Chr 9:23; Eccl 1:13, 16, 17; 2:3; 8:16; Ezek 28:17.

[92] These instances are associated with a skilled craft one performs but are best understood as *ontological-functional*.

[93] Whybray says, "Wisdom…is something which can be taught, though, it should be noted, only to those who have a *natural capacity to receive it*: a number of sayings in Proverbs contrast the (naturally) 'wise son' who heeds his parents' teaching with the naturally foolish son who is incapable of profiting by it. The truest wisdom, indeed, is that of the person who continues to grow in wisdom throughout his life" (Roger N. Whybray, "Slippery Words: IV. Wisdom," *ExpTim* 89 [1977–78]: 361 emphasis added). The book of Proverbs serves as a 'testing device' like 'parables' (in the Gospels) and 'signs' (in John's Gospel) to reveal who possesses salvific wisdom. Does the fool have any capacity to receive wisdom? He has no *moral* ability to receive salvific wisdom in a *functional-ontological* sense irrespective of any other type of wisdom. There must be first an *ontological* change (from fool to wise one) in order to have the *moral* ability and *volitional* willingness to receive instruction in making one wiser (*functional-ontological*). The fool does not change himself for he lacks the ability to see a need for a change.

[94] Isa 10:13; 29:14; Jer 49:7; Prov 1:2; 10:13; 14:6, 8, 33; 17:24; Dan 1:4, 17.

בִּין. For example, Prov 14:33 says, "Wisdom resides in the heart of him that has perception; but that which is in the inward part [קֶרֶב] of fools is made known." The collocation with בִּינָה occurs seven times.[95] *Functionally*, the keeping of commandments is the embodiment of חָכְמָה and בִּינָה while Israel is reported to be a חָכָם and a וְנָבוֹן nation (Deut 4:6). *Ontologically-functionally*, "the wind [spirit] of the Lord" is the "wind [spirit] of חָכְמָה and בִּינָה...the wind [spirit] of the דַּעַת and of the fear of the Lord" that rests upon the Messiah (Isa 11:2).[96] Even the wisdom of the wise (so-called) can fail because God withholds perception from those who perceive (Isa 29:14). In Job 28:28, the fear of the Lord is wisdom and to depart from evil is perception.[97] In a *functional-ontological* usage, the listener is exhorted to get wisdom and perception (Prov 4:5) and to buy (= obtain) the truth that is wisdom, instruction, and perception (Prov 23:23). In Dan 1:20, the king evaluates Daniel and his friends as ten times better than the magicians or enchanters in Babylonian matters of wisdom and perception.

חָכְמָה is collocated with שָׂכַל thrice (Ps 111:10; Dan 1:4, 17). Daniel 1:4, 17 are replete with the terminology of the wisdom tradition:

> [4]Youths in whom is no blemish, but well-favored, and understanding [שָׂכַל] in all wisdom [חָכְמָה], and to know [יָדַע] knowledge [דַּעַת], and able to perceive [בִּין], and such as have ability to stand in the king's palace; and that he should teach them the learning [סֵפֶר] and the tongue of the Chaldeans....[17]Now as for these four youths, God gave them knowledge [מַדָּע] and understanding [שָׂכַל] in all learning [סֵפֶר] and wisdom [חָכְמָה] and have perception [בִּין] into all visions and dreams.

Daniel and these Jewish youths are educated specifically for higher civil service in Babylon. This education includes being taught Babylonian language and letters. The learning might also include mathematics, astronomy, medicine, magic arts, theology, and the art

---

[95] Deut 4:6; Isa 11:2; 29:14; Job 28:28; Prov 4:5; 23:23; Dan 1:20.

[96] For an illuminating discussion on the fear of the Lord, see Eichrodt, *Theology of the Old Testament*, 268–77.

[97] Henri Blocher, "The Fear of the Lord as the 'Principle' of Wisdom," *TB* 28 (1977): 5 regards this not as an unfortunate addition but rather a genuine goal of the poem.

of reading and writing. But in all this, God is behind their acquisition of this wisdom.[98]

There are only two examples where חׇכְמׇה occurs with יׇדַע (Job 34:2; Prov 12:15–16) but in seventeen cases it is associated with its cognate דַּעַת.[99] Two *ontological-functional* types of statements are noteworthy. In Exod 35:31, God fills Bazalel with the wind [spirit] of God in חׇכְמׇה, תְּבוּנׇה, and דַּעַת for a specific skill. Later, Isaiah predicts that the future will bring salvation accompanied by wisdom and knowledge (Isa 33:6). A *functional-ontological* example is where Isaiah denounces Babylon inferring that their cultic wisdom and knowledge perverted them in their treatment of Israel (Isa 47:10).

Other types of wisdom are also *functional-ontological* as mentioned earlier in Proverbs (2:6, 10; 8:12; 9:10; 14:6; 30:3) and Ecclesiastes (1:16, 18; 2:26) or most likely *ontological-functional* (Dan 1:4).

The Heart of the Matter. When the verb לֵב is collocated with בִּין it occurs sixteen times.[100] Solomon is the paradigmatic wise man who is given a 'hearing' and 'perceiving' heart (1 Kgs 3:9), or a 'wise' and 'perceiving' heart (1 Kgs 3:12). In Isaiah, the lack of salvific 'perception' is credited to Yahweh and linked to fattening (44:18). The heart is also parallel to 'perceiving' (Isa 57:1). In Proverbs, the one whose speech give evidence of 'perception' has wisdom (10:13) while the ability 'to perceive' is credited to a wisdom (14:33) that (*functionally-ontologically*) seeks more knowledge (Prov 15:14; 18:15). Therefore, the wise are called perceptive (16:21; Dan 10:12) in contrast to the simple (Prov 7:7) who are exhorted to 'perceive' and acquire a 'perceiving heart' (Prov 8:5). The only occurrence of בִּינׇה is Prov 3:5 where the reader is admonished to lean not towards his own perception, but trust in the Lord with all his heart. לְבׇב occurs with בִּין only twice, both in Isaiah (6:10; 32:4). Here the non-fat heart salvifically 'perceives' resulting in repentance (Isa 6:10) while in the

[98] For an excellent discussion see William McKane, *Prophets and Wise Men*, SBT, ed. C. F. D. Moule et al., vol. 44 (Naperville, IL: Allenson, 1965), 39–40, 97–98.

[99] Exod 35:31; Isa 33:6; 47:10; Prov 1:7; 2:6, 10; 8:12; 9:10; 14:6; 30:3; Eccl 1:16, 18; 2:21, 26; 7:12; 9:10; Dan 1:4.

[100] The search included within ten words on either side. Texts include the following: 1 Kgs 3:9, 12; Isa 44:18; 57:1; Jer 23:20; 30:24; Ps 33:15; Prov 7:7; 8:5; 10:13; 14:33; 15:14; 16:21; 18:15; 24:12; Dan 10:12. But four (Jer 23:20; 30:24; Ps 35:15; Prov 24:12) do not apply.

future the 'heart of the rash'[101] will be 'perceptive' in order to know the Lord (Isa 32:4).

In six cases לֵב[102] is collocated with שָׂכַל.[103] Salvific wisdom, under the classification of *ontological-functional*, occurs throughout Isaiah. Isaiah 44:18 reuses Isa 6:9–10 and reads, "They יָדַע not, neither do they בִּין for he smeared their eyes from seeing, and [smeared] their hearts from שָׂכַל." There is linguistic evidence here that שָׂכַל (Isa 44:18) is roughly synonymous to בִּין (Isa 6:10). The logical connection is made clear by the causal particle כִּי so that the divine action of smearing the eyes and heart causes the human result rather than the reverse. Proverbs 12:8 contrasts one having a heart with שֵׂכֶל to the person with a 'perverted-heart' (וְנַעֲוֵה־לֵב). God even 'hides' (deprives?) from some[104] hearts שֵׂכֶל (Job 17:4), albeit here it is most likely non-salvific. In contrast, the wise increase in understanding that arises from the heart (Prov 16:23)—a *functional-ontological* occurrence.

The heart is also used in collocation with יָדַע showing that it is God who is the architect of the heart that truly 'knows.'[105] For example, Deut 29:3[4] states about the wandering generation that "the Lord has not given you a heart to know, eyes to see, and ears to hear, unto this day."[106] Yahweh is the sole determiner of who receives a

---

[101] The verb מָהַר in the Niphal refers to being "*hurried* = anxious, disturbed; *hasty, precipitate; impetuous,* of Chaldeans" (BDB 554–55). Because of its derivation from the Aramaic, which carries the sense of being *practiced* or *skilled*, it is quite possible that this reference in Isaiah is sarcastic or derogatory of the effects gained from human or cultic wisdom.

[102] The other word for 'heart' (לְבָב) does not occur with either the verbal or nominal form of שָׂכַל.

[103] Isa 44:18; Jer 3:15; Prov 12:8; 16:23; Job 17:4; 2 Chr 30:22.

[104] 'Some' = those who do not have wisdom. Thus those who possess ontological wisdom do so because God has given it to them while others ('some') are deprived of wisdom and therefore do not have it. Thus wisdom is 'hidden' from some as opposed to all.

[105] Deut 29:3[4]; 2 Sam 14:1; Pss 36:10; 40:10; 44:21; 119:79–80; Prov 14:10, 33; 24:12; 27:23; Eccl 1:17; 7:22, 25; 8:5, 16; 11:9; Isa 6:9–10; 51:7; Jer 12:3; 17:9–10; 24:7.

[106] Prov 20:12 reads, "The hearing ear, and the seeing eye, the Lord has made even both of them." D. A. Carson, in referring to divine causality or ascribing 'ultimacy' to God says, "So thorough is the ascription of reality to God, that Moses in Deuteronomy 29:4 does not hesitate to describe Israel's slowness in terms of what Yahweh has not given them. The writer does not mean to suggest that Yahweh's gifts are niggardly, much less to ascribe sin to him; yet the Old Testament writers do not

heart that knows and who will be the recipient of salvific wisdom. Jeremiah says the heart is deceitful above all things (Jer 17:9)[107] but Yahweh is the giver of the wise heart. "And I will give them a heart to know me [*ontological*], that I am Yahweh: and they shall be my people, and I will be their God; for they shall return unto me with their whole heart [*functional*]" (Jer 24:7)—notice the order reveals the cause and effect. It is instructive to remember that Yahweh desires people to have this heart of wisdom when they do not (Deut 5:29) and also withholds it from them (Deut 29:3[4]). He promises to give it (Jer 24:7; 31:31–34; 32:39–40) and to replace the heart of *stone* (Ezek 11:19; 36:26). The divine decision to withhold this heart and to leave in place the heart of stone is Isaianic fattening (Isa 6:9–10 et al.). Fattening is non-transformational.

The nominal דַּעַת occurs six times with לֵב. Isaiah 44:19 records the condemnation of idol makers and the futility of idol-making. Isaiah 44:18 recapitulates Isa 6:9–10 and echoes both the vocabulary and strong divine causality behind the fat-heart. This *ontological-functional* statement is particularized here with idolatry. Idolatry is the functional extreme of the ontologically wicked heart. The evil *ontology* is universal but the functions vary. Together Isa 44:18–19 read as follows:

> [18]They know (יָדְעוּ) not neither do they perceive (יָבִינוּ), for he smeared their eyes from seeing and [smeared] their minds from understanding (מֵהַשְׂכִּיל). [19]No one stops to think (lit, 'no one returns to his heart' וְלֹא־יָשִׁיב אֶל־לִבּוֹ), no one has the knowledge (דַּעַת) or understanding (תְבוּנָה) to say, "Half of it I used for fuel; I even baked bread over its coals, I roasted meat and I ate. Shall I make a detestable thing from what is left? Shall I bow down to a block of wood?"

---

shy away from making Yahweh himself in some mysterious way (the mysteriousness of which safeguards him from being himself charged with evil) the 'ultimate' cause of many evils" (D. A. Carson, *Divine Sovereignty and Human Responsibility: Biblical Perspectives in Tension*, 2d ed. [Grand Rapids: Baker, 1994; reprint, Eugene, OR: Wipf & Stock, 2002], 28).

[107] This statement is an *ontological* statement of cause and effect derived by Jeremiah through *evidence-inference* and remedied only by its replacement with the new heart. The passage is occasional and explains why Judah's sins are so *functionally* prevalent, namely, because the heart of all mankind (including theirs) is *ontologically* deceitful and incurable.

This 'smearing' is neither retributional nor transformational but an explanation for their idolatry. Other cases may be cited in Job (33:3) and Proverbs (2:10; 15:14; 18:15; 22:17) alluded to earlier.

The alternate term לֵבָב is linked nineteen times with יָדַע.[108] One is particularly relevant.[109] Isaiah 32:4 mentions the future when some hearts will 'perceive to know' and represents the future gratuitous bestowal of salvific wisdom.

Summary. The OT shows that wisdom is responsible for noetic effects like perception, knowledge, and understanding. This order is logical with wisdom taking priority and the other effects as necessary consequents. Second, there are different types of wisdom including salvific and non-salvific. Although salvific wisdom is imparted, not all imparted wisdom is salvific. Third, salvific wisdom is associated with the new heart and without this no one can or will salvifically perceive, know, or understand. Absence of this wisdom is to be 'without heart,' an *ontological* state labeled 'fatness' by Isaiah. Fourth, wisdom can be viewed from various perspectives in relation to *ontology* and *function* as noted above. There are also combinations of the two including *functional-ontological* and *ontological-functional*. Depending on the perspective, these may be universally or particularly applied. Fifth, salvific wisdom is acquired gratuitously at Yahweh's discretion. The act of withholding this ontological state is termed divine 'fattening' by Isaiah. Finally, those who have salvific wisdom are duty bound to increase in wisdom.

Wisdom and the Qumran Community

The presence of wisdom phrases and terminology[110] alone has led Worrell to insist that the Qumran community is a 'wisdom

---

[108] Gen 20:6; Deut 8:2; 18:5, 21; Josh 23:14; 1 Kgs 2:44; 8:38, 39; Isa 32:4; Pss 90:12; 95:10; 139:23; Job 10:13; Dan 2:30; 2 Chr 6:30; 32:31.

[109] In most of the passages above the 'heart' is the object of the transitive notion of knowledge, i.e., the true nature of man's heart becomes known either to the subject himself or another referent (usually the Lord) altogether.

[110] See Fabry, "לֵב/לֵבָב," *TDOT* 7:436–37; Daniel J. Harrington, *Wisdom Texts from Qumran* (London: Routledge, 1996). These texts are accessed from Accordance software. Many of the translations are mine or derived from either Florentino García Martínez, ed., *The Dead Sea Scrolls Translated: The Qumran Texts in English*, trans. Wilfred G. E. Watson, 2d ed. (Grand Rapids: Eerdmans, 1996) or Michael Wise,

community.'[111] This self-understanding, says Schnabel, is evident in their use of the term עֵצָה, 'counsel/council' while those who desired to join the community are depicted as possessing דַּעַת.[112] He points out that מַשְׂכִּיל, which occurs fifty times in Qumran, is also a wisdom term and apparently identical with מְבַקֵּר, which occurs forty-two times in Qumran, the 'guardian' and teacher of the community.[113] He

Martin Abegg Jr., and Edwin Cook, eds., *The Dead Sea Scrolls: A New Translation* (San Francisco: HarperSanFrancisco, 1996). Davis also recognizes the importance of wisdom to Qumran noting the same terms suggested here (James A. Davis, *Wisdom and Spirit, An Investigation of 1 Corinthians 1.18–3:20 against Background of Jewish Sapiential Traditions in the Greco-Roman Period* [Lanham, MD: University Press of America, 1984], 32; Martin Hengel, *Judaism and Hellenism: Studies in their Encounter in Palestine in the Early Hellenistic Period*, trans. John Bowden, vol. 1 [Philadelphia: Fortress, 1974], 222). See also C. Romaniuk, "Le Thème de la sagesse dans les documents de Qumran," 429–35. Romaniuk notes that "La terminologie sapientielle des textes de Qumrân diffère sensiblement de celle de l'Ancien Testament, surtout en ce qu'elle est beaucoup plus riche" (ibid., 429). However, he notes that the terminology leans heavily on the OT.

[111] J. E. Worrell, "Concepts in the Dead Sea Scrolls" (Ph.D. diss., Claremont Graduate School, 1968), 120–54; Eckhard J. Schnabel, *Law and Wisdom from Ben Sira to Paul: A Traditional Historical Enquiry into the Relation of Law, Wisdom, and Ethics*, WUNT, ed. Martin Hengel and Otfried Hofius, vol. 16 (Tübingen: Mohr, 1985), 190–91.

[112] Schnabel, *Law and Wisdom*, 191; Romaniuk, "Le Thème de la sagesse dans les documents de Qumran," 430–31. Romaniuk states, "Dans les expression 'mystère de connaissance' et 'connaissance éternelle' le term D'T évoque la notion du plan salvifique de Dieu dans le Nouveau Testament...Seuls certains hommes sont dignes de posséder une telle sagesse; devant les autres il faut la cacher, à cause même de leur indignité (*1QS* IX, 16–17). Le mystère de la connaissance est accessible uniquement à ceux qui se soumettent à l'influence de l'Esprit et de la Vérité (*1QS* IV, 6; *1QHod.* XII, 11–12, 32–33). La sagesse que recoivent les membres de la communauté provient de l'Esprit de Conseil (*Recueil des Bénédictions* V, 25) ou de l'Esprit de Connaissance (*1QS* IV, 4). Le même Esprit est appelé ailleurs 'source de la connaissance' (*1QS* X, 12; XI, 3; *1QHod.* II, 18; XI, 29), 'Dieu de la connaissance' (*1QS* III, 15), 'connaissance éternelle' (*1QS* II, 3) et 'lumière de Dieu' (*1QS* XI, 3). Tout a été fait par cette sagesse de Dieu (*1QS* III, 15; XI, 11)" (ibid., 431).

[113] Schnabel, *Law and Wisdom*, 191. For a summary of the life and institution of the sect of Qumran see Geza Vermes and Pamela Vermes, *The Dead Sea Scrolls: Qumran in Perspective* (Philadelphia: Fortress, 1977), 87–115. Contra Lipscomb, Schnabel argues that the sapiential world-view shows that the vocabulary is not just external garb (Schnabel, *Law and Wisdom*, 192). For more discussion on the משכלים see F. F. Bruce, "The Book of Daniel and the Qumran Community," in *Neotestamentica et Semitica: Studies in Honour of Matthew Black*, ed. E. Earl Ellis and Max Wilcox (Edinburgh: Clark, 1969), 221–35 and E. Earl Ellis, "Wisdom and Knowledge in 1 Corinthians," *TB* 25 (1974): 93–95.

goes on to argue that although it is no longer valid to maintain that Qumran has no wisdom compositions,[114] it is going too far to suggest that its central concern was sapiential. The Qumran community, nevertheless, employs the terminology[115] and milieu of wisdom for expressing its system of belief and in doing so, evidences consanguinity to the OT stage of later wisdom.[116]

The Lexical Domains. A stock sapiential vocabulary derived from the study of the OT leads to examining the following occurrences and collocations at Qumran.[117] Here somewhat of the same phenomenon

---

[114] There are at least twenty-four wisdom compositions or fragments at Qumran (according to Accordance software).

[115] He notes twelve Qumran wisdom terms. The first number represents those of Schnabel while the second is that tallied by Accordance software: יָדַע (161/538), דַּעַת (18/105), חָכְמָה (9/42), חָכָם/חָכַם (37/100), בִּינָה (55/228), בִּין (21/54), דֵּעָה (62/204), תּוּשִׁיָּה (3/6), and מַחֲשָׁבָה (53/114), עׇרְמָה (10/29), מַשְׂכִּיל (11/50), שָׂכַל/שֵׂכֶל (55/168), (Schnabel, *Law and Wisdom*, 195–96). He cautions against making too fine a distinction between these terms but says that the "above-mentioned group of terms possesses the greatest weight in Essene theology" (ibid., 197). He augments this list with other important wisdom terms: עֵצָה (80/177), סוֹד (61/114), and לׇמַד (12/35). To this he attaches wisdom metaphors like 'fountain'/'spring' מַעְיָן (11/19) and מָקוֹר (32/61), 'light' רוֹא/רוּא (87/281), and 'way' דֶּרֶךְ/דָּרַךְ (134/398) (ibid., 197–98).

[116] There are several differences. First, the notion of the 'fear of the Lord' is reportedly absent (but cf. 4Q158 f6:5; 4Q175 1:3; 4Q366 f2:8; 4Q367 f2a–b:5; 4Q367 f2a–b:13; 4Q444 f1–4i+5:1; 4Q5: f35:6; 11QT 54:14). Second, the universality of wisdom is negated. Only members of the community are partakers of this wisdom. Schnabel notes *seven points of similarity* (he derives from Romaniuk, "Le Thème de la sagesse dans les documents de Qumran," 433–34): "(1) the practical character of wisdom, (2) the concept of wisdom as the principle of a morally correct life, (3) the reference to God as the one who possesses true wisdom in a unique way, (4) the thought that man's wisdom is but the participation in God's wisdom, (5) the relationship between sin and folly, (6) the conviction that wisdom not only assures the honesty of moral life but also guarantees eternal life, (7) the notion that wisdom is the highest value" (Schnabel, *Law and Wisdom*, 195). Romaniuk points out *six differences*: (1) Qumran limits the recipients of wisdom to its members only. (2) Qumran recognizes sages as a special category. (3) The OT recognizes court sages and their wisdom as a professional one. (4) The praise of God's wisdom demonstrated by his works are rare in Qumran. (5) God's wisdom is much more hypostasized in Qumran. (6) The 'fear of the Lord is the beginning of wisdom' as a concept is absent from Qumran (Romaniuk, "Le Thème de la sagesse dans les documents de Qumran," 434).

[117] חָכַם 'to be wise,' a verb, occurs six times; חָכָם 'to be wise,' an adjective, occurs thirty-six times; חָכְמָה 'wisdom,' a noun, occurs 105 times; בִּין 'to perceive,' occurs 228 times and בִּינָה 'perception,' occurs 100 times; שָׂכַל 'to understand,' occurs ninety-four

present in the OT wisdom tradition is observed in addition to further insight on the meaning of the 'fat-heart.'

The verb חָכַם occurs six times.[118] The source of wisdom is drawn from the great power of Yahweh (4Q185 f1 2i:14) who 'makes' (Hiphil) people wise in either an *ontological* or *ontological-functional* sense (4Q380 f4:3).[119] *Functional* usages include both the human and divine. Joseph is 'wise' to his brothers (4Q538 1 2:6) and God is 'wise' to the deeds of the ungodly (11Q10 25:2). It is also used in an *ontological-functional* sense of the 'wisdom' inherent in birds (11Q10 26:7).

The adjective חָכָם occurs thirty-six times. Of these instances a few are worth noting. There are two occasions where 'wise' is followed or preceded by לֵב and one case where 'wise,' לֵב, and שֵׂכַל occur together and generally fall in the category of *ontological-functional*.[120]

> 4Q418 f81+81a:20 "For God has divided the inheritance [of every living creature] and all those *wise* at *heart understand* […]."

> 4Q468a f1:2 "[– – all] *wise* of *heart* [– –]."

There are five examples where it is collocated with בִּין.[121] In a titular usage of 'wise,' most likely an *ontological-functional* example, the decisions about war are precipitated by the gathering of all the "*wise men* of the congregation, the *intelligent* and those learned in perfect behavior and the men of valor" to the community council (1Q28a 1:28).

---

times and שֵׂכַל 'understanding,' occurs seventy-four times; יָדַע 'to know,' is found 535 times and דַּעַת 'knowledge,' occurs 202 times; לֵב 'heart' appears 296 times and לֵבָב is found 172 times. In addition to these, תּוּשִׁיָּה occurs six times and תְּבוּנָה occurs five times. On the rarity of the nominal and adjectival form of 'wisdom' (חָכָם and חָכְמָה) Davis cites two reasons: (1) The 'non-use' of these terms is due to a conflict arising between the sectaries and the Hasidim on the outside. (2) The corresponding emphasis of the terms בִּינָה and שֵׂכַל are designed to emphasize 'understanding' as it relates to emphasizing a idiosyncratic strength of Qumran, viz., insight into Scripture (Davis, *Wisdom and Spirit*, 33).

[118] Two references are too fragmentary to be useful (4Q511 f3:4; 4Q570 f2:3).

[119] There are no cases found where the verbal form is used in collocation with either לֵבָב or לֵב.

[120] There are no cases where the adjectival form is used in collocation with לֵבָב.

[121] There are no cases where the adjectival form is used in collocation with בִּינָה.

4Q436 f1a+bɨ2 "...His hand ²will lift the fallen to make them receptacles of knowledge; and to give knowledge to *the wise* and increase the instruction of the upright; to *understand* ³your marvels ...."

Wisdom, when linked with 'perception' as with the OT, is sometimes associated with the wind [spirit] of God in an *ontological* or *ontological-functional* sense.[122]

4Q223 224 f2v:28 "[To find a m]an who *under[stands* and is *wise*, this is like a man where the wind [spirit] of G]od [is in him. And he appoints double in all]." (my trans.).

4Q266 f3ii:10 "And He raised up from Aaron *in]sightful* men and from Israel [CD 6:3] [w]*ise men* and He taug[ht them] what Mos[es] had said. [And they dug the well ...]."

4Q267 f2:8–9 ⁸"[From Aaron men of *knowledge* and from Israel *wise men*, [and forced them to li]sten. And they dug ⁹the well: 'A well which the princes dug, ...'" (Num 21:18).

4Q302 f2ii:2 "Please *consider* this, you who are *wise*...."

Only one example collocates it with שֶׂכֶל and most likely represents an *ontological-functional* usage.[123]

---

[122] "At Qumran, the spirit manifested its presence when a person conducted life wisely and with a view to pleasing God (1QS 5:21, 24).... This spirit was either an eschatological gift or something eternally predestinated" (Kamlah, Dunn, and Brown, "Πνεῦμα," *NIDNTT* 3:693; Davis, *Wisdom and Spirit*, 155–85). Davis recognizes the great potential of the scrolls in this area is unleashed when one recognizes the importance of רוּחַ and חָכְמָה "within the theological vocabulary of the Qumran Essenes" (ibid., 31). He notes three types of text that refer to the mode of conveying wisdom to the Qumranites. The first refers to God given revelation, a second to the influence and activity of God's Spirit, and a third set identifies an awakening or enlightenment of man's spirit that God places within them (ibid., 40–41). He suggests that the predominance of the first type of text determines how the latter two are to be understood. "Thus it is God's gracious activity in granting wisdom that is being further defined and described with reference to the divine and human spirit in the second and third type of text.... Wisdom, the gift of God, is a product of the inspiration of the divine Spirit, and the illumination of the human spirit" (ibid., 42). Thus wisdom and its impartation would fit well into an *ontological* usage.

[123] There are no cases where the adjectival form is used in collocation with the nominal שֶׂכֶל.

4Q418 f81+81a:20 "For God has divided the inheritance [of every living creature] and all those *wise* at heart *understand* [...]."

On three occasions it is collocated with יָדַע.[124] The following attacks the *functional* inabilities of the wise men in Isaiah but probably is to be taken as *ontological-functional* and is designed to question the true status of these individuals.

4Q163 f11ii:3–5 [3]"[How can you say to Pharaoh: We are sons of wise men,] [4]we are sons of [ancient ki]ngs? [Where are your *wise men*? Let them announce,] [5][if they *know*, what the God of Hosts is planning against Egypt.]" (Isa 19:9–12).

Once it is collocated with יָדַע and בִּין. Decisions about war are determined by the community council consisting of the "*wise men* of the congregation, the ones who בִּין and those who יָדַע in perfect behavior and the men of valor" (1Q28a 1:28). In addition there are three cases where it occurs with דַּעַת. Wise men are depicted as those who meditate with *knowledge* (1QHa 9:35; 4Q432 f2:2). In an instructive passage, a collocation of many of the wisdom terms is utilized.

4Q436 f1a+bi:1–4 [1]*Knowledge* ['perception' בינה] to strengthen the downcast heart, and to triumph in him over the spirit; to console those opposed in the epoch of their anguish; and his hand [2]will lift the fallen to make them receptacles of *knowledge* [דעת]; and to give *knowledge* [דעת] to the *wise* [לחכמים] and increase the instruction of the upright; to *understand* ['to perceive' להתבונן] [3]your marvels which you did in the years preceding the years, generation after generation, eternal *knowledge* ['understanding' שכל] which [4][...] before me.

The noun חָכְמָה is found 105 times. One set of examples occurs where it is collocated with לֵב.[125] There are only two places where this occurs.[126] Both cases are relevant for defining the heart by its lack of necessary requisites in understanding God's ways.

The first example (4Q424 f3:6–8) warns against sending a man with a *course* ['fat'] *heart* (שמן לב) to differentiate thoughts because

---

[124] 1Q28a 1:28; 4Q163 f11ii:4–5; 4Q411 f1ii:6–7.

[125] The only association with לֵבָב is 4Q257 6:2 where iniquity in the heart of man is contrasted with the wise man.

[126] 4Q424 f3:6–8; 4Q525 f2ii+3:3–4.

wisdom is hidden/concealed (thus absent) from his *heart* (חכמת לבו כי נסתרה)[127] and he is without *wisdom*.[128] The phraseology closely approximates the terminology (except here it is the nominal form) used in Isa 6:10 where God says to Isaiah, "Make their heart *fat*" (לֵב הַשְׁמֵן). Thus the *fat* ('fat') heart at Qumran is characterized by its alienation from and absence of wisdom. This is probably technical terminology derived from Isaiah that focuses on the inherent makeup of man and most likely an *ontological-functional* usage. If this sense is *developed* from Isaiah or showed to be instead *dependent* upon Isaiah, then Isaianic 'fattening' is likely to be *the determinative (and divine) decision to hide/conceal wisdom and its effects from the heart*. In distinction to the individual with a fat heart, the שכל submits to *instruction* (מוסר), obtains חכמה, and has pleasure in *judgment* (משפט). The *fat-heart* is defined, therefore, as a heart divinely *deprived* and *ontologically* absent of wisdom and/or its beneficial and *functional* effects.

Other aspects of this passage are instructive. First, 4Q424 is a sapiential work and therefore rooted in that tradition. Second, the 'fat-hearted' person is in a context of other characters including an unjust judge who "judges before investigating" and "believes before [examining]" (4Q424 f3:1), an inadequately qualified governor who lacks sufficient ability to judge matters of law (1:2), an emotionally prejudice person (1:3), and one with a hearing handicap who cannot hear disputes (1:4). The crescendo is the 'fat-hearted' person who lacks wisdom necessary to dig out the knowledge of the truth. Third, these characters and characteristics are contrasted to the wise, the upright, and the brave man in what appears to be a chiastic arrangement (1:7–11).[129] Fourth, the 'fat-heart' clearly carries a

---

[127] Lit., "because wisdom has been concealed/hidden from his heart." The participle is in the Niphal and modifies 'wisdom.' Thus there is a 'hidden wisdom' that is hidden because it does not reside in the fat-heart. The Niphal implies the divine agent as responsible for this deliberate hiding or concealing of wisdom.

[128] "He cannot use the skill of his hands," or lit., 'His hands do not find wisdom' (חכמת ידיו לא ימצא).

[129] There are sufficient ellipses in the passage to be less than certain but it appears there is a chiasm where the 'fat-heart' and the 'prudent man,' namely, he who has 'understanding' (שֵׂכֶל), occupy the center and thereby serve to elucidate each other. The 'fat-heart' lacks both wisdom and understanding. The 'upright' (3:8a) would probably be contrasted with the unjust judge (3:1). This suggested reconstruction, then, would place the corresponding phrase to 'brave man' (3:8b) prior to the

cognitive rather than a *volitional* emphasis as in Pharaonic hardening and therefore does not focus on *functional* stubbornness but *ontological* privation of wisdom. This distinction of cognition and volition, albeit not altogether separate, is maintained symbolically and conceptually into the NT era. Fifth, at the very least the passage is equating the 'fat-heart' with the *ontological-functional* absence of *some type of* administrative wisdom. At most it either is or includes a salvific nuance because Qumranites would not likely send a person they did not regard as on the 'inside' and contrast him with the wise person who seeks more wisdom. All outside of their community would fit that description as ontologically deprived of wisdom. Finally, it is unlikely that lack of wisdom as 'fatness' comes from anywhere other than Isaiah.[130] Therefore, it seems reasonable that the 'fat-hearted' person, for whatever else he lacks, also suffers from a deficit of *soteriological* wisdom as Isaiah describes.

The second passage (4Q525 f2ii+3:3–4) refers to the concept of searching for wisdom without a *treacherous heart* (בלב מרמה, only other occurrence of phrase is 4Q525 f5:7). This search is set in opposition to the man blessed by the possession of *wisdom*, who walks in the law of God, dedicates his *heart* to its ways, is internally driven by it, and takes pleasure in its punishments. The phrase 'treacherous heart' also occurs in Prov 12:20 where 'deceit is in the heart' of those who plan evil (מִרְמָה בְּלֶב־חֹרְשֵׁי רָע). Both Qumran passages are critical of the heart devoid of wisdom and its effects labeling it as either *course/fat* (שמן לב) or *treacherous* (בלב מרמה). The former refers primarily to the heart's sapiential ontology and noetic make-up whereas the latter primarily to its function as rebellious.

חכמה is collocated with בין eight times and often with various synonyms.[131] In an *ontological-functional* sense, it is the upright who

---

fragment and ascribe the ellipsis between 3:7 and 3:8 the correspondents to the poorly qualified governor, the overly emotional, and hard of hearing.

[130] The alternative is to suggest two independent sources. But this would require that the writer is unfamiliar with Isaiah which is most improbable. A more likely scenario is to view the writer of this wisdom text as taking a cue from Isaiah who links the lack of wisdom with Yahweh's act of 'fattening' the heart. While Isaiah stresses the divine act that leads to the state, this writer stresses the state and implies divine action (of deprivation).

[131] 1QS 4:22–23; 1QHa 18:2; 4Q381 f76 77:8; 4Q413 f1 2:1; 4Q418 f81+81a:15; 4Q418 f102a+b:3; 4Q421 f1aii b:10; 4Q428 f11:2. For an examination of Qumran's use of בִּין and its nominal form see Joachim Gnilka, *Die Verstockung Israels: Isaias 6:9–10 in der*

understand the knowledge of the Most High (1QS 4:22–23), but no one *understands* all God's *wisdom* (1QHa 18:2). Giving *wisdom* that produces *understanding* of Yahweh's great inheritance for man is a result of his grace (חסד) shown to man (4Q413 f1 2:1). Other texts speak of *understanding* that comes through *wisdom* of hands given by Yahweh (4Q418 f81+81a:15; 4Q418 f102a+b:3). As noted above (4Q421 f1aii b:10), חכמה is referred to as a yoke that brings with it שכל and בין. Several *functional-ontological* examples can be seen too. *Understanding* also utilizes *wisdom* to delve into the secret council of God's mysteries (4Q428 f11:2). In 4Q381 f76 77:8 the result of paying *attention* to (שכל) חכמה that issues from Yahweh's mouth is בין. Like above, בין is used in relation to חכמה in such a way that the former is a result of the latter, where wisdom itself is bestowed on the basis of grace, and where the one who understands does so as a result of having wisdom and subsequently utilizing wisdom to gain more understanding in matters related to God's secret mysteries.

It also occurs with בינה thrice. In 1QS 4:1–3 it occurs in the context of the spirit of light/truth and darkness/deceit and their respective rulers the Prince of Lights and the Angel of Darkness. Indeed Yahweh "created the spirits of light and of darkness and on them established all his deeds" (1QS 3:25). The path of the Prince of Lights in the world is the following:

> [2]To enlighten [להאיר] the heart [בלבב] of man, straighten out in front of him all the paths of justice and truth, establish in his heart [לבבו] respect for the precepts [3]of God; it is a spirit [ורוח] of meekness, of patience, generous compassion, eternal goodness, intelligence ['understanding' ושכל], understanding ['perception' ובינה], potent wisdom [וחכמה] which trusts in all [4]the deeds of God and depends on his abundant mercy [חסדו]; a spirit of knowledge [ורוח דעת] in all the plans of action, of enthusiasm for the decrees of justice, [5]of holy plans with a firm purpose, of generous compassion with all the sons of truth, of magnificent purity which detests all unclean idols, of unpretentious behavior [6]with moderation in everything, of prudence in respect of the truth concerning the mysteries of knowledge [רזי דעת] (1QS 4:2–6).

Another passage, reminiscent of Isa 11:2, reads elliptically as "[Lord, wind/spirit] of wisdom and perception, a wind/spirit of cou[nsel and might], wind/spirit of knowle[dge]…." (4Q161 3:16). A final elliptical

---

Theologie der Synoptiker, SANT, ed. Vinzenz Hamp and Josef Schmid, vol. 3 (Munich: Kösel, 1961), 175–76.

passage links wisdom and perception (4Q372 f3:2). It is evident that in these passages that both wisdom and its effects are brought about by an agent external to man.

It is also collocated with שכל,[132] and with other synonyms.[133] These passages tend to emphasize the *ontological-functional* aspect of wisdom. One text (1QS 4:3–4) refers to a wind [spirit] that engenders שכל, בין, and חכמה. Another (1QS 4:22–23) points to certain attributes that arise in response to the wind [spirit] of truth being poured upon a person enabling them to both בין the knowledge of the Most High, to be taught by חכמה, and to receive שכל. An additional reference (4Q381 f76 77:8) points to those who have שכל and חכמה that comes from God and results in בין. This wisdom is referred to (4Q421 f1aii b:10) as a 'yoke' of חכמה that makes one both שכל and בין. *Wisdom*, therefore, necessarily results in an increase of *knowledge* (4Q525 f1:2).

A pertinent text referred to earlier (4Q424 f3:6–7) designates the 'fat-heart' (שמן לב) as being without חכמה and חכמה is juxtaposed with the שכל man who ידע and seeks more חכמה. From these usages of חכמה in collocation with שכל, it is evident that the cause of wisdom is the wind [spirit], the evidence of wisdom is understanding, and its absence is described in terms of not only ontologically having a 'course heart' but functionally as being without understanding. In addition to this, the nominal form occurs twice (1QS 4:3, 18) with wisdom. The latter refers to God who in the mysteries of his understanding (ברזי שכלו) and in the wisdom (ובחכמת) of his glory "has determined an end to the existence of deceit."

It is also collocated with ידע.[134] In 1Q27 f1i:3 it refers to those who are evil, who do not know what the future will bring to them, and will not be saved, for "despite all their *wisdom* they do not *know* the future mystery, or בין ancient matters" (my trans.).[135] In 4Q417 f2i:6 it advises one to meditate day and night on the mystery of existence and then "you shall *know* truth and injustice, *wisdom*...."[136] A wisdom poem, probably referring to Solomon, says, that "'[...which he has

---

[132] See ibid., 179–83.

[133] 1QS 4:3–4; 4:18, 22–23; 4Q381 f76 77:8; 4Q421 f1aii b:10; 4Q424 f3:6–7; 4Q525 f1:2. Cf. ibid., 175–83.

[134] See ibid., 176–77.

[135] A parallel text is 4Q300 f3:3.

[136] A parallel text is 4Q418 f43 45i:4.

said] with the *wisdom* God gave him […] ²[…in order to *kn*]*ow wisdom* and discipline, in order ³[…] in order to increase und[erstanding {שׂכל} …]" (4Q525 f1:1–3). In a biblical text of Qumran on Ps 154, it reads "For wisdom has been granted so that the Lord's glory can be proclaimed" (11Q5 18:3). In several of these texts the emphasis falls on the divine initiative where wisdom is gratuitously *given/granted* (from the verb נתן), hence *ontological*, in order to know wisdom and increase in understanding as well as to enable the proper proclamation of God's salvation story, hence *functional* (*ontological-functional*). This 'givenness' of wisdom is also in the NT and most likely what the Synoptics have in mind rather than mere 'interpretation' or ' further explanation.'

Finally, it is collocated with דעת eight times. The *Damascus Document* 2:2–3 reads,

> ²And now, listen to me, all entering the covenant, and I will *open your ears* to the paths of ³the wicked. God loves *knowledge*; he has established *wisdom* and counsel [תושיה] before him; ⁴discernment and *knowledge* are at his service; patience is his and abundance of pardon, ⁵to atone for persons who repent from wickedness.¹³⁷

The *Rule of the Community* (*Manual of Discipline*) refers to the activity of God being responsible for taking out a spirit of deceit from the inner part of man, cleansing him with the spirit of holiness, sprinkling him with the spirit of truth, and by this "the upright will *understand knowledge* of the Most High and the *wisdom* of the sons of heaven will teach those of perfect behavior" (1QS 4:22). This is a divine act that brings *ontological* change enabling further learning, hence, *ontological-functional*. A *functional-ontological* example includes using discretion and *knowledge* to teach *wisdom* in order to *perceive* the path and deeds of the sons of men (4Q413 f1 2:1).¹³⁸ A hymnic text credits the outworking of God's deterministic counsel over all his creation to his wisdom. "And in the *wisdom* of your *knowledge* you have determined

---

¹³⁷ Phrases such as 'opening of the ear' are familiar idioms of Semitic languages that have to do with terms associated with wisdom and understanding. See Müller and Krause, "חכם," *TDOT* 4:367–68.

¹³⁸ Another text mentions that they perceive it through *wisdom* of hands he gave them dominion and to *know* (4Q418 f81+81a:15). Two other elliptical texts link wisdom and knowing together (4Q380 f6:2; 4Q525 f23:6).

their course before they came to exist" (1QHa 9:19). God loves *knowledge, wisdom* and counsel (4Q266 f2ii:3).

The Heart of the Matter. There are ten passages that collocate לב with בין.[139] Some of these passages can be cited for illustrating the relationship between the heart and 'to perceive.' The *Damascus Document* (CD 1:10), for example, describes God as *appraising* the deeds of the returnees from Babylon, in *functional* terms, because they sought him with a *perfect* ('whole') *heart* (בכלב שלם דרשוהו). Other passages point to the *ontological-functional* cases. One text (1QHa 9:37) maintains that the heart is unable to perceive certain matters, while others not only point to the ears and heart as being caused to *perceive* the truth (1QHa 15:38; 1Q35 f1:12) but credit God for enabling the ears and *heart* to *perceive* his truth (4Q428 f10:5–8). This is further explained by other references that insist that it is God who causes them to *perceive* the work because they seek him with their whole *heart*.[140] This may well refer to *functional-ontological* aspects. The application of the heart results in *perceiving* or the granting of further knowledge deep within a person (4Q525 f114ii:18). This collocation indicates that it is the heart that 'perceives' but it is the heart in its natural condition that fails to 'perceive.' Moreover, this 'perceiving' is necessarily precipitated by God's activity on the heart (*ontological*) and associated with the ears. This ability is divinely implanted within the individual in such a way that it becomes a part of him.

בינה is collocated with לב six times.[141] In each case the divine initiative in the *ontological* act is central. The *Pesher to Habakkuk* 2:8–9 refers to the eschatological times concerning traitors and the Man of Lies who is explicated by the priest. The priest is, in *ontological-functional* terms, he "whom God has given [*perception* in his heart] to interpret all ⁹the words of his servants, the prophets." One hymn reads, "⁸[I give you thanks,] Lord, for putting *perception* in the heart of your servant ⁹to know these matters, to unders[tand….]" (1QHa 6:8–9). A somewhat elliptical text that appears to stress again the divine initiative in *ontological-functional* categories reads, "[…]

---

[139] CD 1:10; 1QHa 9:37; 15:38; 1Q35f1:12; 4Q266; 4Q268; 4Q381 f1:2; 4Q418 f205:2; 4Q428 f10:5–8; 4Q525 f114ii:18.

[140] 4Q266; 4Q268.

[141] 1QpHab 2:8; 1QHa 6:8; 4Q299 f8:6; 4Q416 f2iii:13; 4Q418 f9,9a c:14; 4Q436 f1a+bi:1.

perception, he forms in our heart hunger for *understanding,* he will uncover our ears to hear [...]" (4Q299 f8:6, my trans.). This hunger can also be in terms of *functional-ontological.* Another text reads, "(If) you are poor, do not say 'I am poor and [13]cannot seek knowledge.' Bend your shoulder to all discipline and in all [...] refine your heart and in much *perception* [14]your thoughts" (4Q416 f2iii:13).[142] A final text refers to 'perception' that strengthens the downcast heart (4Q436 f1a+bi:1).

לבב is collocated with בין three times, all in elliptical texts. One text reads, "...[rebell]ion and a heart to *perceive* [his] statues [...] righteous [...]" (4Q372 f3:3, my trans.). Another text implies that it is God who "[...] causes them to *perceive* with their heart [...]" (4Q372 f8:4). Finally, a text says "[ears the mystery was - -] to [- -] to cause your hearts to *perceive*" (4Q423 f7:7). One can infer the divine initiative here but the exact sense is not certain. בינה occurs with לבב seven times.[143] *Hodayot[a]* f4:12–13 states, "[12]you have opened my heart to your *perception,* and you opened my ear [13][...] to lean on you goodness." Thus it is *ontological* change that results in *functional* allegiance. Other texts refer to the heart learning *perception* (4Q372 f3:5), God placing (נתן) within the heart דעת and *perception* (4Q426 f1i:4),[144] just *perception* (4Q511 f44 59ii:1), or causing דעת and *perception* to be in the heart (4Q511f18ii:8). As with the previous occurrences, the divine initiative, in what appears to be *ontological-functional* cases, is paramount.

There are three cases where לב is collocated with שכל.[145] Here it states that all those wise at *heart understand* (4Q418 f81+81a:20) and that this understanding in the heart is caused by God (4Q428 f18:2)—an *ontological-functional* phenomenon. There are two passages that use the nominal form שכל.[146] The *Rule of the Community* (*Manual of*

---

[142] The parallel text is 4Q418 f9,9a c:14.

[143] 1QHa f4:12; 4Q372 f3:5; 4Q426 f1i:4; 4Q510 f1:6; 4Q511 f10:3; 4Q511 f18ii:8; f44 59ii:1.

[144] 4Q510 f1:6 simply refers to the sage who speaks of God's glory to frighten away evil spirits "who strike unexpectedly to lead astray the spirit of *perception,* to make their *hearts* desolate...." This seems to imply that the empty (desolate) heart is one without perception. A parallel text is 4Q511 f10:3.

[145] 1QHa f5:11; 4Q418 f81+81a:20; 4Q428 f18:2.

[146] 1QS 2:2–3; 4Q299 f8:6.

Discipline) 2:2–3 cites the benediction priests pronounce on the members which refers to God blessing them by illuminating their *heart* "with *discernment* of life" that he might grace them with "eternal knowledge" [דדת]. Notice the order: first God granted illumination (ontological) followed by knowledge (functional). The second passage (4Q299 f8:6), referred to earlier, speaks of the hunger created in the heart for *understanding*. Both of these passages involve the divine initiative but might relate to the *functional-ontological* rather than *ontological-functional* category. לבב occurs only twice with שכל.[147] The first is a fragmentary wisdom text that reads, "[- -] the righteous ones [- -] them in the heart caused to *un[derstand]*" (4Q420 f2:9, my trans.). The second is a psalm based on Ps 154 that speaks of wisdom granted ('given') for declaring God's glory and deeds "so that his might can be made to be *understood* by those lacking heart: those found to be far from his gates" (11Q5 18:5). This is *functional-ontological* from the hearer's perspective and *ontological-functional* from the teacher's perspective. It is evident from these examples that the causal relationship is established as such that the heart is supernaturally *illumined* by God resulting in *understanding* which in turn *opens* the ear to hear. To reason backwards, the unhearing ear is that which fails to understand while the lack of understanding is a result of not being illuminated in the heart by God.

On seven occasions it is collocated with ידע.[148] The *Damascus Document* 1:10–12 (and 4Q266) shows Yahweh exercising wisdom. He בין their deeds because they sought him with their whole *heart* and he raised up the Teacher of Righteousness to direct them in the path of his *heart* and *made known* (ידע) to them what he did to the previous generation of traitors. An *ontological* issue surfaces for those who *know* righteousness as those who have the law of God in their *hearts* (4Q270 f2ii:19)—another indirect reference to the wind's [spirit's] involvement in this activity. A proleptic text (4Q381 f1:2), reminiscent of Isaianic predictions, refers to a day when the simple will בין, a group who are described as without *heart* but who will come to *know* the Lord. The phrase 'without heart' (אין לב) refers to those presently without 'understanding' that will be given such in the future and as a

---

[147] The term for 'heart' (לֵבָב) does not occur with the nominal שֵׂכֶל.

[148] CD 1:10–12; 1QHa 16:26; 4Q266; 4Q270 f2ii:19; 4Q381 f1:2; 4Q422 3:7; 4Q504 f18:2.

result will *know* God (cf. Jer 5:21; Hos 7:11).[149] A similar passage (4Q504 f18:2) depicts God as giving to the *heart* the *ontological-functional* ability to *know*.

A significant passage about Pharaoh (4Q422 3:7) maintains it is God who 'strengthened his heart to sin' (חזק 'hardened') "so that the p[eople of Israel] might know it throughout the gener[ations.] Then He changed their [water] to blood." The *he* who 'hardened' is the same *he* who turned the water into blood. Incidentally, throughout Exod 4–14 the use of this verbal form always occurs in the Piel stem as here at Qumran.[150] Of all the Qumran uses of this verb (חזק) with 'heart,' only one example has the Hiphil stem and refers to soldiers who stand with 'resolute hearts' (1QM 10:5).[151] דַּעַת occurs three times with לב and refers to removing unclean things and plotting from the *knowledge* of one's heart (1QS 10:24).[152] Significant features of the usage of 'heart' with 'to know' include the idea that the heart is that faculty that 'knows' Yahweh and his righteousness (*noetic*), the notion that this noetic ability is itself an endowment from God (*ontological*), and the theistic corollary that God controls all hearts even for sinful purposes as in the case of Pharaoh (*divine initiative*).

לבב is collocated twice with ידע. Both texts are marked by massive lacunae. The first simply says "…his heart to *know*…." (4Q385a f8:2) while the second (from Deut 18:20) reads, "[2]that prophet must be put to death. You may say to yourselves [to your heart], 'How shall we

---

[149] Similar phrases are 'no heart' (חֲסַר־לֵב), translated as 'void of understanding' (Ps 119:2, 69; Prov 3:1; 4:23; 7:10; 24:12), and 'cause to turn aside' (לֵב + סוּר) which is used to mean God 'turns aside' the heart from wisdom (Job 12:24) or he may take away a 'stony heart' (Ezek 11:19; 26:26). Thus to be 'without heart,' have 'no heart,' or to 'turn aside the heart,' is tantamount to being without 'understanding.' In addition to this, the heart is often said to be a 'hearing heart' (1 Kgs 3:9; Ezek 40:4; Ps 10:17; Prov 15:32; 22:17) while a non-hearing heart is due to hardness (Exod 7:13, 22; 8:19; 9:12; Zech 7:12; Isa 46:12). Solomon asked for a 'hearing heart' in order to govern God's people and to be able to distinguish between right and wrong (1 Kgs 3:9). This is taken by the Lord as a request for the ability 'to perceive' (בִּין) in order 'to hear' (שָׁמַע) justice and therefore grants Solomon a 'wise' (חָכָם) and 'perceiving' (בִּין) heart (1 Kgs 3:11–12). The other word for heart (לְבָב), when not modified, also carries the sense of 'understanding' (Job 12:3; 34:10, 34).

[150] Exod 4:21; 7:13, 22; 8:19[15]; 9:12, 35; 10:20, 27; 11:10; 14:4, 8, 17.

[151] 1QS 10:26; 4Q365 f2:5; f:3:3; 4Q422 f1a+bi:1; bi:4; 4Q491 f11ii:15; 4Q504 f4:12; 1QM 10:5; 1QHa 10:28.

[152] The two other texts are parallels (4Q260 5:7; 4Q427 f2:1).

recognize that ³which the Lord has not spoken" (11QT 61:2–3)? This is one of the *functions* of the heart, namely, it communes with itself. But it has a communal aspect in that this 'heart talk' amounts to a consensus of ignorance among the community. The term also occurs with דעת twice. "You placed it in his *heart* to open up the source of knowledge to all who בין. But they have changed them, through uncircumcised lips" (1QHa 10:18). Another reads, "God makes the *knowledge* of בינה shine in my heart" (4Q511 f18ii:8). Both of these latter passages point to the divine initiative in causing perception and knowing within the heart and are *ontological-functional* in orientation.

Summary. Seven basic conclusions can be stated about wisdom and Qumran. First, the similarities and dissimilarities of wisdom at Qumran and OT wisdom mentioned earlier by Romaniuk and Schnabel seem to be valid. Second, since the DSS follow in chronology the prophets, there is an employment of them in regard to wisdom that is unprecedented. Isaiah in particular is utilized to a great extent in furthering this sapiential focus. Third, wisdom involves a gratuitous act on Yahweh's part and results in an *ontological-functional* transformation of the members of the sect alone. Fourth, those outside the community are without wisdom and therefore have a 'fat-heart.' This does not imply, however, that members inherently possess this wisdom. Fifth, this wisdom is given to them through the agency of the Spirit who effects an ontological transformation, inscribes the law on the heart, and is an act often depicted in Isaianic terms. This is probably because they view themselves as the servant of Yahweh. This ontological happening is sometimes likened to a light shining in the heart. Sixth, wisdom approaches a hermeneutic construct, that is, it tends to clothe saints in sapiential terminology and motifs. This technique finds fuller expression elsewhere. Finally, the order of wisdom is the same as the OT, namely, wisdom produces perception, knowledge, and understanding.

Wisdom Tradition in the OT Apocrypha[153]

Hardening as Rebellion. The OT Apocrypha does not explicitly relate the fat-heart to the wisdom tradition. A few familiar terms and

---

[153] Translations of Apocrypha are either from the NRSV or mine.

phrases cover the topic of obduracy.[154] This plethora of phrases focuses on their rebellion that led to their historic captivities and is emphasized in the *Sitz im Leben* of Hellenistic syncretism as motivation to follow the Mosaic precepts that embody wisdom. Wisdom is used as a hermeneutic construct as it relates to the law and adherence to it.

The Sapiential Role. The idea of Isaianic 'fatness' is absent from this literature. Much of it, however, attempts to account for Israel's exile using wisdom motifs. For example, Baruch links rebellion to following the evil intentions of their heart (Bar 1:21–22; 2:8; Sir 5:2; 10:12; 11:30; 12:16; 16:20) that causes them to forsake the fountain of wisdom (Bar 3:12) and the Mosaic covenant and incur its curses (Bar 1:20–21; 2:2–29; 3:4, 8). God knows this heart thoroughly (Wis 1:6). Although disobedience is credited to being stiff-necked (Bar 2:30; 1 Esd 1:46) in captivity, the Lord promises to give them a heart that obeys and ears to hear (Bar 2:31; 2 Macc 1:3–4; Sir 17:6; 45:26). This will cause them to return to the land (Bar 2:32–35) because God puts

---

[154] First there is σκληροτράχηλος signifying 'hard-necked' or 'stubborn' and occurs twice in this literature. In Bar 2:30 they do not 'hear' because they are 'hard-necked' and deserve punishment (Sir 16:11). Second, σκληρός 'hard' occurs nine times. When used in conjunction with νῶτον 'back' (= 'hard-back'), it refers to *obstinacy in rebellion* (Bar 2:33). Used with καρδία 'heart' (= 'hard-heart') it denotes *stubbornness* (Sir 3:26, 27). Alone it carries the idea of *roughness* (1 Esd 2:22[27]), or *hardness* as in hard stone (Wis 11:4), speaking *sharply* (3 Macc 4:19; 7:6 [σκληρῶς]; Wis 4:2; Theod. Tob 3:14), planning *cruelty* (Jdt 9:13), dying an *excruciating* death (2 Macc 6:30), or being *headstrong* (Sir 30:8 as in an unbroken horse), or being *stubborn* (Bar 2:33). Third, σκληρύνω 'to make hard, stubborn' occurs four times. Used in conjunction with τράχηλος 'neck' (= 'stiff-necked') it refers to *rebellion* against God's law (1 Esd 1:46[48]; Sol 8:29). Alone it can refer to *difficulties* inflicted on individuals (1 Macc 2:30), or being *stubborn* and *disobedient* (Sir 30:12). Fourth, κατισχύω 'to overcome, strengthen' occurs eight times. It can have a sense of *overcoming an enemy* as in battle (1 Esd 5:49[50]; Jdt 11:10; Sol 2:7) or *strengthening* the hands (1 Esd 7:15), or *establishing* something in the midst of conflict (Sir 49:3). Fifth, βαρύνω 'to make heavy' occurs twelve times. This can refer literally to the *heaviness* of lead (Sir 22:14, which is likened to the heaviness of foolishness), *chains* (Sir 33:29[28]), *difficulties* imposed on others (1 Macc 8:31; Sol 2:22; 5:6), the *roughness* of war (1 Macc 9:17), an *overpowering smell* (2 Macc 9:9), *individual* (Sir 8:15), *power of the sun* (Wis 2:4), *body on the soul* (Wis 9:15), or *grief* at wrong-doing (Sir 21:24), or *suffering grief due to hard-heartedness* (Sir 3:27). Sixth, σκληροκαρδία 'hard-heartedness, stubbornness' occurs once. It refers to the *resolute heart of soldiers* prepared for battle (Sir 16:10). Seventh, σκληροτράχηλος 'hard-necked, stubborn' carries the notion of *rebellion* or *rebellious* (Sir 16:11; Bar 2:30).

the fear of himself in them (Bar 3:7; 1 Esd 8:25; Sir 1:12, 28). The captivity itself, however, is credited to God's wisdom that is inscrutable (Jdt 8:14, 27; Sir 42:18; Wis 4:17).

It is this wise heart that enables one to understand parables (Sir 3:29; 13:26). But this wisdom is predicated on election (Bar 3:27–28) and is thus not available to all even for those who seek it (Bar 3:29–4:4; Wis 8:21). Wisdom is epitomized through the book of the commandments (Bar 4:1) and further wisdom is promised upon obedience either to it (Wis 1:1; 14:30; Sir 6:37) or to wise teachers (Sir 50:28). Accolades of wisdom are also applied to the heroes like Josiah and others (1 Esd 1:31) while enemies of Israel are portrayed as fools (Sus 13:47–49). The final cause of this charismatic bestowal of wisdom, however, is obedience. It gives them ears to hear and instills the fear of the Lord that turns them from evil. This involves an *ontological-functional* happening. Fear of the Lord is also a continuing motif which accounts for the godly behavior of the saints of old (Pr Azar 3:41; Sus 13:2; Jdt 8:29; Pr Azar 3:18). This and learning wisdom are presented in *functional-ontological* terms of obeying the Mosaic Law (Bar 3:9–4:4; Sir 2:17; 26:4).

Wisdom Tradition in Philo

Hardening as Rebellion.[155] Philo mentions the hard-heart in several instances but always with the sense of rebellion in mind. He employs σκληροκαρδία once (*Spec.* 1:305). With Moses (Deut 10:16–17) he depicts the 'uncircumcised' heart as *hardened* (σκληρότης) and stubborn and advises circumcision in regard to their *hard-heartedness* (σκληροκαρδία). He admonishes his hearers not to let their *necks be stiff* (σκληρός) "that is to say, let not your mind be *unbending* nor self-willed" but "let it change so as to be come gentle, and inclined to obey the laws of nature" (*Spec.* 1:304–306). He also uses the adjective σκληρός twelve times. He likens the state of divine inspiration to being drunk (*Ebr.* 148–150) and having tasted wisdom (*Ebr.* 148). The

---

[155] Tabulations derived from Peder Borgen, Kare Fuglseth, and Roald Skarsten, *The Philo Index: A Complete Greek Word Index to the Writings of Philo of Alexandria* (Grand Rapids: Eerdmans, 2000). Critical editions consulted are Leopoldus Cohn and Paulus Wendland, eds., *Philonis Alexandrini opera quae supsrsunt. Edition Maior*, 8 vols. (Berlin: Reimeri, 1896–1930; reprint, Berlin: de Gruyter, 1962–63) and *Philo*, trans. F. H. Colson and G. H. Whitaker, 10 vols., LCL, ed. T. E. Page, E. Capps, and W. H. D. Rouse (New York: Putnam's, 1929–71).

woman who is godly and pours her soul out to the Lord and drinks no wine is described as a 'hard-day' (σκληρός) woman (*Ebr*. 149), and filled with the 'graces of God' (*Ebr*. 149). It may refer to tangible items as 'hard' (*Migr*. 50; *Abr*. 239) or hard work (*Mos*. 2:183). The soul might be *"hard* and resisting" but it may "become docile and reasonably submissive" (*Her*. 181; *Praem*. 114; *Spec*. 3:34). Esau is described as hard and stubborn (*Fug*. 42) and others as resistant (*Spec*. 2:39; *Spec*. 4:218). A final term σκληρότης is used to describe concrete things as hard (*Opif*. 62), rugged trades as opposed to the life of learning (*Sacr*. 116), or the senses (*Plant*. 133).

The Sapiential Role. Philo's wisdom vernacular is similar to the OT. He accepts a notion that not all possess wisdom and seems to oppose that it naturally resides in mankind. He says, "But the one who is filled with unalloyed *wisdom* has need only of a leathern habitation...those who are clever in such matters may make it a subject of philosophical speculation, whether it is a membrane or a *heart*." God's purpose in testing is to see what is in the heart (*Congr*. 170). He notes that the mind is sometimes without mental power and perception leaving one to see without seeing and hear without hearing (*Leg*. 2:69; 3:183). He cites Gen 6:5 several times and not only links evil acts to the evil heart (*Deus* 20; *Conf*. 24) but tends to view indolence as inherent citing Deut 29:3[4] (*Fug*. 122–23). Quoted in full it reads,

[122]For a man who is led by *innate and habitual laziness* to pay no attention to his teacher neglects what lies in front of him, which would enable him to see and hear and use his other facilities for the observation of nature's facts. Instead he twists his neck and turns his face backwards, and his thoughts are all for the dark and hidden side—of life, that is, not of the body and its parts, and so he turns into a pillar and becomes like a deaf and lifeless stone. [123]Speaking of such characters as these Moses says that they did not get 'a heart to understand, and eyes to see, and ears to hear' [Deut 29:3], but wrought out for themselves a life that was no life, blind and deaf and unintelligent and in every way maimed, setting themselves to nothing that demands their thoughts (emphasis added).

While he admonishes them (quoting Deut 4:29) to seek the Lord with their whole heart (*Fug*. 142), he also describes a change that takes place in *ontological* sounding speech and related to a compatibilism type of freedom. He says of Caleb,

[123]But in Caleb we have a total change of the man himself. For we read "there was another spirit in him" [Num 14:24], as though the ruling mind in him was changed to supreme perfection. For Caleb is by interpretation "all heart," and this is a figurative way of shewing that his was no partial change of a soul wavering and oscillating, but a change to proved excellence of the whole and entire soul which dislodged anything that was not entirely laudable by thoughts of repentance; for when it thus washed away its defilements, and made use of the lustrations and purifications of *wisdom*, it could not but be clean and fair (*Mut.* 123–24, emphasis added).

Philo never uses the fattening issue of the heart to describe this lack of wisdom.[156] However, although he views hardening in terms of stubbornness and rebellion, the concept of innate lack of wisdom is not absolutely foreign to him and the changed heart brings inevitable effects.

Wisdom Tradition in Josephus[157]

Josephus does not use παχύνω, σκληρύνω, or πωρόω. He does, however, use other terms for 'hardness' including πάχος, παχύς, παχύτης, σκληρός, and σκληρότης. Furthermore, he uses καρδία only three times. The heart is used only literally as in the case of stabbing to death (*A.J.* 5.193; 7.241; 9.118). Because of the nature of his work, in none of the cases does Josephus point either to the cognitive or volitional aspects of the heart.

Wisdom Tradition in Mishnah

There are only two cases where the wisdom terminology is used in the Mishnah. The scarcity is due to the legal nature of the corpus. Throughout the Mishnah, however, the adjective (wise) is used as a technical term for the Sages. In addition to this, those occasions that do mention wisdom indicate that the terms are still connected. In *m. Hag.* 2:1 it says that one did not expound on particular laws "unless he was a חָכָם and וּמֵבִין of his own מִדַּעְתּוֹ." The other instance is where the term for 'wisdom' occurs with 'perception' and 'knowledge.' In *m. Abot* 3:17 R. Eleazar b. Azariah says, "If there is no reverence, there is no חָכְמָה. If there is no בִּינָה, there is no דַּעַת. If there is no דַּעַת, there is

---

[156] He does use παχύνω twice in reference to Deut 32:15 (*Post.* 121; *Congr.* 160).

[157] Karl Heinrich Rengstorf, ed., *A Complete Concordance to Flavius Josephus*, 5 vols. (Leiden: Brill, 1973–83).

no בִּינָה." At the least this confirms the idea that when one aspect of wisdom is present, the others can be reasonably inferred. All are simultaneous effects of wisdom.

Conclusion

There are several lines of inferences that may be drawn from this study that impact Isa 6:9–10 and its parallels, namely, the relation of wisdom to its effects, the natural condition of the heart, the nature of hardening in general, and the role of the רוּחַ (wind/spirit). But before these issues are itemized, one area of influence must be set aside as having little to no bearing on Isaianic fattening. Pharaonic hardening bears little resemblance to wisdom, is depicted in terms of volition, and employs a different vocabulary from Isaiah. Moreover, when Pharaoh 'hardens' his heart it is in a *functional* sense only and has nothing to do with degrees of hardness or effectuating an ontological change. This is precisely due to the volition versus cognitive emphasis. What they do share alike is the mode of hardening/fattening, namely, by divine deprivation of the new heart and therefore both may be understood as assuming a non-transformational view of hardening/fattening.

This chapter has emphasized the dynamic of wisdom. Three conclusions in regard to wisdom and the exercise of its effects can rightly be inferred. First, when texts refer to the heart in the context of *understanding, perceiving,* or *knowing,* a wisdom tradition should be assumed to lie behind it because these are the effects of wisdom. Second, the wisdom tradition (MT and DSS) asserts and then assumes a particular order of operation with regard to the mental (and moral) exercises of man, namely, wisdom *produces* rather than is the *product of* understanding, perception, or knowing. These functions spring from the wise heart. Third, wisdom is acquired by a gratuitous impartation of God and is not precipitated by either external merit or internal volition. This is brought about by an *ontological* change that affects *functional* activities. Subsequent use of wisdom (*functional-ontological*) is the result of this impartation not the attainment of it. All effects of wisdom, including the seeking of more wisdom, come from the heart.

Three assertions may be made in relation to the natural condition of the heart apart from wisdom. First, the heart is congenitally void of salvific wisdom and its effects. This is to say that the heart of man lacks *understanding, perception,* and *knowledge* of God that enables him to fulfill the requirements for attaining forgiveness. Second, the heart without wisdom (and its effects) is best described as being *cognitively* fat or *volitionally* treacherous. Although the conclusion would be that man's heart is both *congenitally* lacking in both *cognition* and *volition*, this study focuses on the former as it is first in priority. Third, because man's heart is congenitally fat and it is God who gratuitously imparts wisdom that enables the exercise of these abilities, then it follows that the failure to grant or give wisdom for acquiring these qualities results in leaving man in his *ontological* state of fat-heartedness and thus is simply another way of saying that 'God fattens.' This is not in terms of degrees (fatter) but deprivation (withholding).

Three observations can be made in regard to the nature of fattening. First, since the nature of this fattening is not punitive (based on bad behavior) or transformational (from neutral to fat-hearted), it must be viewed as a *deprivational* fattening arising out of a *congenital* fat-heart. Second, God fattens the heart on the one hand, by depriving of wisdom and its benefits while on the other hand, he softens or grants a new heart by actively and gratuitously bestowing wisdom and its benefits. This results in certain inevitable effects leading to or inhibiting salvation. Third, man is *responsible* and is morally culpable for his lack of understanding, perception, and knowledge, because he is congenitally corrupt and fat-hearted. God remains the *fattener* of the heart in the sense that he holds at his discretion and will the power to either change or to leave the wicked heart of man in its natural/congenital state. Man remains responsible because he willingly despises God's wisdom and salvation.

Finally, a number of inferences can be drawn from the role of the רוּחַ (wind/spirit) as it relates to wisdom. First, wisdom necessarily derives from the heart indwelt and/or filled with the רוּחַ (wind/spirit) of wisdom and its corollaries. Second, the רוּחַ (wind/spirit) is placed gratuitously within individuals by God. Therefore, what is said of wisdom can also be said of the רוּחַ (wind/spirit), namely, both are given or withheld (sometimes referred to as 'poured out upon') on a discriminatory basis and one does not exist without the other. Where the רוּחַ (wind/spirit) inhabits, there wisdom resides. Conversely, where there is wisdom, the רוּחַ (wind/spirit) can be inferred. Third, when the רוּחַ (wind/spirit) is within, he puts into effect these virtues by writing the law on the heart whereby it becomes a new heart that perceives, understands, and knows God. The involvement of the רוּחַ will become more prominent in Isaiah and NT usage.

Isaiah 6:9–10: Its Wisdom Connection and Meaning

Introduction

The purpose of this chapter is to explore Isa 6:9–10 within a sapiential context. This will begin with the MT, broaden to its reuse in various traditions, and include the tracing of verbal notions and motifs. The goal is to discover the features, nature, and cause of the fat-heart in Isaiah. Each of these items arise from the context of Isa 6:9–10 but certainly do not include nor is it intended to include a comprehensive examination of all types of hardening. Throughout this study at least four broad issues are kept in mind including the *definition* of the fat-heart, the *act* of fattening, the *means* of acquiring wisdom, and the *basis* of fattening.

First, with the help of the wisdom tradition and Isaiah's use of that tradition, it can be established that absence of certain qualities *defines* the fat-heart. These qualities include perceiving, knowing, and understanding. To lack *salvific* wisdom is to be fat-hearted. Second, after defining the *state* the next step is seeking to understand and describe the verbal notion behind the *act* of fattening itself.[1] Since it is God who fattens, it must be asked how God ensures this absence of wisdom. Does he excise it from the heart (*depletion*), infuse its

---

[1] One moves from *describing* a state (fat) to a *defining* an action (fattening). The definition limits the possibilities to three options, namely, by *depletion*, i.e., he *subtracts* wisdom resident within the heart, by *deposition*, i.e., he *deposits* foolishness into the heart of man otherwise absent of this, or by *deprivation*, i.e. he *withholds* wisdom from the heart that is by nature absent of wisdom. The latter view demands a non-transformational view of fattening (does not go from non-fat to fat). This Study will argue that after an examination of the evidence, the latter view will be demonstrated to be the case with Isaianic fattening.

opposite into it (*deposition*), or does he withhold wisdom from it (*deprivation*)?[2] The view suggested here is the final one. If it is the latter, then the heart is congenitally fat-hearted. Indeed, the congenital view is the key to understanding the act of *divine* fattening.[3]

Third, the act of fattening cannot be divorced from the means of acquiring wisdom because its presence spells the absence of the effects of the fat-heart. Whether it is procured by human endeavor or a divine gift figures into the solution. It is significant then, that in some clear cases, these qualities come via a wisdom that is gratuitously implanted within by God so that without this infusion the heart may be understood as congenitally and therefore naturally fat-hearted.[4] The wisdom tradition may explain the variations within the traditional usage of Isa 6:9–10 that emphasize either the divine prerogative (causative) or the human condition (congenital). Both aspects are rooted in and reflect a sapiential background that supports the congenital/deprivation view.

---

[2] *Deprivation* can take several nuances in English. Webster gives the following: "1. the act of depriving. 2. the fact of being deprived. 3. dispossession; loss. 4. removal from office. 5. privation"(*Webster's Encyclopedic Unabridged Dictionary of the English Language*, [New York: Portland House, 1989], 388). The term can therefore mean either to *keep something from* someone or to *take something from* someone. For the sake of clarity, the former will be deemed *deprivation* and the latter *depletion*. Theologians define *privation* as that good thing which something or someone does not possess. An example of a *privation* in man would be physical blindness, viz., a good that is absent that ought (but is not owed) to be there. Blindness in a rock, however, is a *negation*, viz., the absence of a good thing that ought not to be there. Absence of the 'new heart' is a privation in man. It ought to be there but it is not owed to be there. To keep man in a state of privation in regard to the new heart is the continual act of deprivation (of the new heart). This latter is what Isaiah calls divine 'hardening' or better 'fattening.'

[3] If the heart, eyes, and ears are congenitally fat, blind, and deaf, then in what sense could God be said to fatten, blind, or deafen? Certainly a transformative view becomes unnecessary. The verbal idea of transitiveness, moreover, need not imply transformation but simply a *causative continuation* of that state by one who is able to change it. There is no degree in Isaianic 'fattness' anymore than there are degrees in blindness or deafness (even legal blindness is absolute). Thus to 'fatten' the already fat, to 'blind' the already blind, and to 'deafen' the already deaf *are circumlocutions for the divine decision to leave them in their fat, blind, and deaf state (as Isaiah defines).* This is divine deprivation of the new heart or Isaianic fattening.

[4] The use of 'congenital' describes an unusual condition present at birth while 'natural' refers to something inborn rather than acquired or having a particular character by nature. Both are synonymously and symbiotically employed here.

A final issue is the basis of fattening itself. The options are in terms of either *retribution* or *non-retribution*. Most studies and commentators view fattening as just retribution for past and/or present sin. Whether this is the proper understanding rests on certain assumptions and is resolved when other issues discussed above are answered. This Study challenges the retributive perspective by its appeal to Isaiah's use of wisdom, the wisdom tradition itself, and its Synoptic occurrences. The non-retributional basis of fattening, however, does not answer the question as to the basis of fattening or better, the reason for *God's role as the continuing cause of man's perpetual privation of salvific wisdom*. It only rules out one option and leaves unanswered the reason for fattening.

The goal of this chapter will be to show that the Hebrew text represents a *strong divine causality* view whereas subsequent usage may confirm this viewpoint, focus to a greater degree on *mankind's congenital fat-heartedness*, or serve to mitigate one or both of these positions. The thesis here is plainly stated: If the fat-heart is a *congenital* condition defined as lacking salvific wisdom (a privation) and thus absent of perception, understanding, and knowledge, then *divine fattening* is a perpetuating of that state and therefore necessarily neither *transformational* nor *retributional* (*lex talionis* or *quid pro quo*) but rather *deprivational*. This view represents the best appraisal of the exegetical evidence, historic traditions, and reuse of Isa 6:9–10 in the NT.

The following chapter examines the political background of Isaiah and its environment of conflict between Isaiah and the counselors as it impacts the book's literary structure and the centrality of Isa 6:9–10.[5] This is followed by a discussion of the divine council, the call structure, the wisdom influence in Isaiah, and the bifurcation of Israel. A synthetic examination reveals a wisdom metanarrative (guiding hermeneutic) where all of the parts are construed in terms of its vocabulary and motifs. Motifs from Isa 6:9–10 are employed to reinforce strong divine causality, emphasize congenital absence of wisdom, or promise salvation in terms of its reversal. Isaiah 6:9–10 is then given closer attention including its various streams of tradition.

---

[5] This is masterfully worked out in Jean Pierre Sonnet, "Le motif de l'endurcissement (Is 6,9–10) et la lecture d' «Isaïe»," *Bib* 73 (1992): 208–39.

The Essential Background of Isa 6:9–10

The Overall Context

Historical Background. Isaiah 6:1 indicates that the divine council that convenes and commissions Isaiah in the year Uzziah dies (736 B.C.).[6] However, Isa 1:1 reports that Isaiah prophesied *during* the reigns (בִּימֵי) of five kings of Judah: Uzziah/Azariah (787–736 B.C.),[7] Jotham (co-regent) (756–741 B.C.), Ahaz (co-regent) (741–736 B.C.), Ahaz (sole ruler) (736–725 B.C.), and Hezekiah (725–697 B.C.).[8] Most of Isaiah's ministry is concerned with either Ahaz in his sole rule during the Syro-Ephraimite crisis and its fallout (732–722 B.C.) or

---

[6] Uzziah is described as a godly king of Judah (2 Kgs 15:32), the father of Jonathan (1 Chr 27:25), Jotham, and grandfather of Ahaz (Isa 7:1). Uzziah began his reign at sixteen years of age and did so for fifty-two years until the age of sixty-eight (2 Chr 26:1–3). His mother's name is Jechiliah (2 Chr 26:3). During his administration the Ammonites paid him tribute (2 Chr 26:8), he fortified Jerusalem (2 Chr 26:9), and built up his military might (2 Chr 26:11–15). However, because he entered the Temple and offered incense in place of the priests, he became a leper until his dying day (2 Chr 26:16–23).

[7] This opens up the possibility (if not probability) that Isa 1–5 is during the reign of Uzziah. Milgrom argues that Isa 1:10–6:13 "stems from Uzziah's days on the basis of historical, ideological and literary evidence" (Jacob Milgrom, "Did Isaiah Prophesy during the Reign of Uzziah?" *VT* 14 [1964]: 164). The *historical* evidence includes the great peace and prosperity brought on by Uzziah's reign as well as military preparedness and agricultural abundance (ibid., 164–67). The *ideological* evidence includes reference to the temple (as opposed to Mt. Zion or Mt. Holiness), scant concern over the king or the Davidic dynasty, lack of specificity over the identity (esp. whether it is human or not) of the enemy, and sparse appeals to repentance in Isaiah (1:16–20; 2:5). The *literary* evidence of Isaiah suggests that it follows Amos in calling for repentance (Amos 5:4–6, 14–15; Isa 1:16–20), announcing an end to a time of repentance (Amos 6:7–8; Isa 5:8–23), and issuing an oracle of total doom (Amos 9:1–4; Isa 6:9–13). In light of the progression or sequence of repentance a strong argument can be made that the sequence of Isa 1:10–6:13 is indeed chronological (ibid., 172). Thus Isa 6:1–13 is not an *inaugural* call of Isaiah but rather a new phase of doom in a *sequence* of events subsequent to a period of unrepentance. This pattern of repentance (validated in Amos) along with the statement that Isaiah prophesied during the reign of Uzziah are two strong lines of evidence for arguing that Isa 1:10–5:29 precedes Isa 6 "chronologically as well as ideologically, giving us a carefully conceived, diary-precise record of the development of Isaiah's early thought" (ibid., 174).

[8] On the difficulty of determining the chronology of the kings of Israel and Judah along with a proposed solution see Gerhard Larsson, "The Chronology of the Kings of Israel and Judah as a System," *ZAW* 114 (2002): 224–35.

Hezekiah during the onslaught of the Assyrians (722–701 B.C.). The major power during this time is Assyria under Tiglath-pileser III (745/44–727 B.C.), Shalmaneser V (726–722 B.C.), Sargon II (721–705 B.C.), and Sennacherib (704–681 B.C.). The Babylonian empire is part of Assyria and is only beginning to come to power (Isa 39; Merodach-baladan 710–700 B.C.).

The first crisis is the Syro-Ephraimite incident of Isa 7–8 involving Ahaz of Judah, Tiglath-pileser III of Assyria, Rezin of Aram, Pekah of Israel, and Tabeel, a would-be replacement of Ahaz. The political intrigue involves a rebellion of Israel and Aram against Assyria. These two factions form an alliance and solicit the assistance of Judah (Ahaz). When Ahaz refuses to join the coalition, both Israel and Aram threaten to invade Judah, depose Ahaz and replace him with Tabeel. Ahaz responds with a plea to Assyria for protection for a price. This is taken as unbelief by Isaiah. Israel is subsequently sacked by Assyria but spared from complete devastation only through a tribute offered by Hoshea. A second major crisis later develops when Israel again rebels against Assyria inciting Sargon II who inflicts unrelenting devastation on Israel in 722 B.C.

Hezekiah succeeds Ahaz as king of Judah in 725 B.C., three years prior to the fall of the northern kingdom of Israel. Two skirmishes with Assyria occur during this time. In the first Judah joins a Philistine revolt (715–711 B.C.; Isa 20). Sargon II squelches it but Judah suffers only minimally. Later, perhaps sparked by the death of Sargon II (705 B.C.), Hezekiah attempts to withdraw his allegiance from Assyria with the aid of Egypt. Sennacherib responds bringing a fourth crisis to Judah (701 B.C.). He pummels the landscape and besieges Jerusalem but does not capture it (Isa 36–37; 2 Kgs 18:13–16). Judah's military strongholds are crushed by the conflagrations.[9] The subsequent devastation is catastrophic for Judah and an ignominious defeat for Hezekiah. Like Ahaz before him, Hezekiah shuns the advice of Yahweh's prophet and submits to Sennacherib. He pays tribute as an act of political common sense.[10] Like the northern tribes,

---

[9] For a description of the siege of Lachish see David Ussishkin, *The Conquest of Lachish by Sennacherib* (Tel Aviv: Tel Aviv University Publications of the Institute of Archeology, 1982). Cf. Yigael Yadin, *The Art of Warfare in Biblical Lands* (London: Weidenfield & Nicolson, 1963).

[10] Gerhard von Rad, *The Message of the Prophets*, trans. D. M. G. Stalker (New York: Harper & Row, 1965), 136.

this devastation is not total but only a typological precursor for a final blow that will occur in a hundred years.

The conflict is between Yahweh's counsel, through Isaiah, and the political advisors to the king. Each party presents their case in wisdom terms. Isaiah offers true salvation while the advisors to the king offer a purely pragmatic perspective absent of the fear of Yahweh. Politics in foreign affairs become the testing device for discovering the lack of salvific wisdom. Yahweh is behind this perpetual privation.

Literary Structure. The broader structure of Isaiah is comprised of three major sections (Isa 1–39, 40–55, 56–66) usually designated Proto-, Deutero-, and Trito-Isaiah. Some identify these sections with different prophetic figures as well as their literary unity and independence.[11] Literarily, it is divided into seven major units: three introductory collections of messages (chaps. 1–12, 13–27, 28–35), a historical narrative (chaps. 36–39), and three concluding collections of messages (chaps. 40–48, 49–54, 55–66).[12] Beyond this consensus lie a whole host of other contentious issues.[13] For the purposes of this

---

[11] Derived from Rolf Rendtorff, "The Book of Isaiah: A Complex Unity. Synchronic and Diachronic Reading," in *New visions of Isaiah,* ed. Roy F. Melugin and Marvin Sweeney, JSOTSup, ed. David J. A. Clines and Philip R. Davies, vol. 214 (Atlanta: Scholars Press, 1996), 35. On the distinctive styles in Isaiah not necessarily demanding multiple authors see J. Alec Motyer, *The Prophecy of Isaiah: An Introduction and Commentary* (Downers Grove, IL: InterVarsity, 1993), 23–25.

[12] David A. Dorsey, *The Literary Structure of the Old Testament: A Commentary on Genesis–Malachi* (Grand Rapids: Baker, 1999), 217. There may be smaller subunits as well.

[13] For various authenticity issues related to Isaiah see Ronald E. Clements, *Isaiah 1–39,* NCB, ed. Ronald E. Clements and Matthew Black (Grand Rapids: Eerdmans, 1982), 2–4, 5, 70–71. He holds that Isa 6:1–8:18 is a composition by Isaiah himself, his memoirs (*Denkschrift*), originally uttered during the Syro-Ephraimite crisis (735–733 B.C.), written sometime after 733 B.C., and subsequently placed within a larger collection of 5:1–14:17 (ibid., 4–5, 70–71). For an appraisal of Clements see Roy F. Melugin, "Introduction," in *New Visions of Isaiah,* ed. Roy F. Melugin and Marvin A. Sweeney, JSOTSup, ed. David J. A. Clines and Philip R. Davies, vol. 214 (Atlanta: Scholars Press, 1996), 16. For the views of Nehemiah Rabban on a defense of Deutero-Isaiah (as opposed to 'Third Isaiah') ascribed to a certain 'Meshullam' who is the servant of that portion of Isaiah see Risa Levitt Kohn and William H. C. Propp, "The Name of 'Second Isaiah': The Forgotten Theory of Nehemiah Rabban," in *Fortunate the Eyes that See: Essays in Honor of David Noel Freedman in Celebration of His Seventieth Birthday,* ed. Astrid B. Beck et al. (Grand Rapids: Eerdmans, 1995), 223–35.

study, these matters will be largely set aside.[14] More important than critical issues is Isaiah in its final form, as complex as that form may be.[15] On a holistic (and thus synthetic) approach, a two-part division of Isaiah may be helpful.[16]

---

[14] For a summary of critical views over the composition of Isaiah see O. Eissfeldt, *The Old Testament: An Introduction, including the Apocrypha and Pseudepigrapha, and also the Works of Similar Type from Qumran: The History of the Formation of the Old Testament*, trans. Peter R. Ackroyd (New York: Harper & Row, 1965), 303–46; Clements, *Isaiah 1–39*, 2–25; Otto Kaiser, *Isaiah 1–12*, trans. John Bowden, 2d ed., OTL, ed. Peter R. Ackroyd et al., vol. 9 (Philadelphia: Westminster, 1983), 1–10; Dorsey, *The Literary Structure of the Old Testament*, 217 n. 2; Raymond B. Dillard and Tremper Longman III, *An Introduction to the Old Testament* (Grand Rapids: Zondervan, 1994), 267–83; and H. G. M. Williamson, *The Book Called Isaiah: Deutero-Isaiah's Role in Composition and Redaction* (Oxford: Clarendon, 1994), 1–18.

[15] See Kaiser, *Isaiah 1–12*, 7. Current biblical scholarship, irrespective of source critical issues, begins by treating Isaiah 'holistically' (either diachronically or synchronically), a trend represented by the Isaiah Seminar of the Society of Biblical Literature. See Melugin, "Introduction," 13–29; Rendtorff, "The Book of Isaiah," 32–49, Christopher R. Seitz, "Isaiah 1–66: Making Sense of the Whole," in *Reading and Preaching the Book of Isaiah*, ed. Christopher R. Seitz (Philadelphia: Fortress, 1988), 108–09; Gerald T. Sheppard, "The Book of Isaiah: Competing Structures according to a Late Modern Description of Its Shape and Scope," in *Society of Biblical Literature Seminar Papers 1992*, ed. Eugene H. Lovering Jr., SBLSP, ed. Eugene H. Lovering Jr., vol. 31 (Atlanta: Scholars Press, 1992), 550 (see esp. ibid., 49 n. 1 for bibliography); Motyer, *The Prophecy of Isaiah*, 13; and Peter D. Quinn-Miscall, *Reading Isaiah: Poetry and Vision* (Louisville, KY: Westminster, 2001), 1–3. It is best to suppose that any reconstruction must follow rather than precede the redactor's final product (Rolf Knierim, "Old Testament Interpretation Reconsidered," *Int* 27 [1973]: 435–70). On the issue of creating redactional order out of apparent prophetic disorder and the lack of a sound methodology of the redactional school altogether see Yehoshua Gitay, "Prophetic Criticism—'What Are They Doing?' The Case of Isaiah—A Methodological Assessment," *JSOT* 96 (2001): 101–27. Other studies shift the focus away from the text and towards the readers of the text. One study approaches from the fictive constructs of 'implied reader' and 'implied audience' (Edgar Conrad, *Reading Isaiah* [Minneapolis: Fortress, 1991]) while another from the perspective of a fictitious fourth-century B.C. reader (Katheryn Pfisterer Darr, *Isaiah's Vision and the Family of God* [Louisville, KY: Westminster, 1994]).

[16] See William H. Brownlee, *The Meaning of the Qumran Scrolls for the Bible* (New York: Oxford University Press, 1964), 247–59; R. K. Harrison, *Introduction to the Old Testament: with a Comprehensive Review of Old Testament Studies and a Special Supplement on the Apocrypha* (Grand Rapids: Eerdmans, 1969), 764, esp. 64–800; and Craig A. Evans, "On the Unity and Parallel Structure of Isaiah," *VT* 38 (1988): 129–47. Clements has nearly the identical divisions in his commentary (Clements, *Isaiah 1–39*, 23–25).

On an immediate level there are three observations. First, 6:1–13 may be referred to as the 'memorial'/'testimony book' (*Denkschrift*) drafted most likely just after the Syro-Ephraimite crisis (736–733/732 B.C.) by Isaiah (6:1–8:18 [–9:6]). It is flanked on either side with a prologue (5:1–7, 8–24 + 10:1–3) and an epilogue (9:8–21 + 5:26–29).[17] Second, 6:1–13 is structured around three responses marked by, "and I said" (6:5, 8, 11).[18] Third, the literary structure of Isaiah 1–12 locates chapter six as central and the centrality of 6:1–13 to Isaiah's call and acceptance (6:8). This structure also highlights the contrast between Isaiah and those fattened providing the segue for the remnant motif.[19]

The Immediate Context

The more immediate context is comprised of four literary settings that are important to the immediate passage at hand.[20] These include the divine council episode, the call narrative structure, the influence of wisdom, and the identity of the remnant. Isaiah's counsel is in contrast to that of the political advisors to the king. The issue centers, as many political campaigns do, on trust. Politics and policies are used to mark allegiances and for determining the possession or absence of salvific wisdom.

The Divine Council. The immediate context is the theocentric vision of 6:1–13.[21] This text is one of three clear divine council episodes in the

---

[17] Kaiser, *Isaiah 1–12*, 4.

[18] Motyer, *The Prophecy of Isaiah*, 75.

[19] King Uzziah is probably to be compared with those fattened while Isaiah is aligned with the remnant (Gerhard F. Hasel, *The Remnant: The History and Theology of the Remnant Idea from Genesis to Isaiah*, 2d ed., AUSS, vol. 5 [Berrien Springs, MI: Andrews University Press, 1972], 299–300).

[20] See Rolf Rendtorff, "Isaiah 6 in the Framework of the Composition of the Book," in *Canon and Theology*, ed. M. Kohl, trans. M. Kohl (Minneapolis: Fortress, 1993), 170–80.

[21] Some commentators question the unity of this passage. Isaiah 6:1–11 and 6:12–13 are reportedly a combination of two prophecies where the former is the original and the latter two verses are post-Isaianic additions. For a defense of their authenticity see Mititiahu Tsevat, "The Throne Vision of Isaiah," in *The Meaning of the Book of Job and Other Biblical Studies: Essays on the Literature and Religion of the Hebrew Bible* (New York: KTAV, 1980), 162–64.

OT where five elements are prominent.[22] The three cases involve Micaiah ben Imlah (1 Kgs 22:10–28), Isaiah (6:1–13), and Ezekiel (1; 10). The five elements are the following:[23] (1) Yahweh is presented as a King, seated upon a throne.[24] (2) Heavenly creatures are in the presence of Yahweh.[25] (3) The prophet 'sees' Yahweh. (4) The oracle delivered is either what the prophet has seen or heard. (5) The time may be during the enthronement festival, although this point is speculative. Other heavenly council experiences include Amos (7; 8;

---

[22] For the Ugaritic background to the divine council see E. Theodore Mullen, *The Divine Council in Canaanite and Early Hebrew Literature*, HSM, ed. F. M. Cross Jr., vol. 24 (Chico, CA: Scholars Press, 1980) and Lowell K. Handy, *Among the Host of Heaven: The Syro-Palestinian Pantheon as Bureaucracy* (Winona Lake, IN: Eisenbrauns, 1994). See M. Saebo, "דוֹס," *TLOT* 2:793–95. For a discussion of another term for 'assembly' (דוֹר-) see Frank J. Neuberg, "An Unrecognized Meaning of Hebrew *DOR*," *JNES* 9 (1950): 215–17. His point is to show that it refers to an assembly or council. Neuberg states that the one who stands at the door and does not take part in the council is an outsider and that the term דוֹר is sometimes synonymous with סוֹד or עֵדָה (ibid., 216). Ackroyd confirms this usage (Peter R. Ackroyd, "The Meaning of דוֹר Considered," *JSS* 13 [1968]: 3–10).

[23] These elements are derived from Edwin C. Kingsbury, "The Prophets and the Council of Yahweh," *JBL* 83 (1964): 279–86; H. Wheeler Robinson, "The Council of Yahweh," *JTS* 45 (1944): 154.

[24] Yahweh as King is an expression probably coined by Isaiah (T. C. Vriezen, "Essentials of the Theology of Isaiah," in *Israel's Prophetic Heritage: Essays in Honor of James Muilenburg*, ed. Bernhard W. Anderson and Walter Harrelson [New York: Harper & Row, 1962], 132). It should also be recognized that the theme of 'holiness' is certainly prevalent here both in the refrain (6:3) and in reference to the holy stump (6:13). The adjectival form for 'holiness' (קָדוֹשׁ) occurs 117 times in the OT while thirty-eight times in Isaiah alone. Its nominal form (קֹדֶשׁ) occurs ninety-six times in the OT and only three times in Isaiah. The verbal form (קָדַשׁ) occurs three times in the OT but none in Isaiah. Holiness is the major theme of Isaiah (Motyer, *The Prophecy of Isaiah*, 76–77; J. J. M. Roberts, "Isaiah in Old Testament Theology," *Int* 36 [1982]: 131–43; Sheppard, "The Book of Isaiah," 573).

[25] On the identity and history of these beings into the NT era see Charles A. Gieschen, *Angelomorphic Christology: Antecedents and Early Evidence*, AGJU, ed. Martin Hengel et al., vol. 42 (Leiden: Brill, 1998); Larry W. Hurtado, *One God, One Lord: Early Christian Devotion and Ancient Jewish Monotheism*, 2d ed. (Edinburgh: Clark, 1998); and Richard J. Bauckham, *God Crucified: Monotheism & Christology in the New Testament* (Grand Rapids: Eerdmans, 1999). Also helpful is a study on exalted figures within Judaism in Darrell L. Bock, *Blasphemy and Exaltation in Judaism and the Final Examination of Jesus: A Philological-Historical Study of Key Jewish Themes Impacting Mark 14:61–64*, WUNT, ed. Martin Hengel and Otfried Hofius, vol. 106 (Tübingen: Mohr, 1998; reprint, Grand Rapids: Baker, 2000), 118–83.

9), Jeremiah (25; 26; 27), Isaiah (Isa 40),[26] and Job (1–2), but involve something less (or more) than the five elements.[27] The experience results in the prophet 'seeing' and 'hearing' the divine council accompanied by a message containing a negative connotation—thus a kind of counter-order prophecy.[28]

A number of inferences can be drawn on account of the divine council background. First, this incident may not commence Isaiah's ministry for occasions like this may be non-singular.[29] Second, the depiction of Yahweh on a throne may suggest some connection with his kingdom.[30] Third, the privileged encounter of Isaiah provides the basis for the establishment of insiders and outsiders.[31] Fourth, the connection of 'council' to 'counsel' and therefore 'wisdom,' may not be coincidental (Job 15:8).[32] Fifth, the structure of the divine council may support the unity of Isa 6:1–13.[33] Sixth, two divine council episodes in Isaiah (6:1–13; 40:1–8) suggest convenient markers of its

---

[26] F. M. Cross Jr., "The Council of Yahweh in Second Isaiah," *JNES* 12 (1953): 274–77. Scholars generally recognize two passages in Isaiah as divine counsel episodes (6:1–13; 40:1–8 or 40:1–11). For a discussion see Christopher R. Seitz, "The Divine Council: Temporal Transition and New Prophecy in the Book of Isaiah," *JBL* 109 (1990): 229–47.

[27] For the missing elements see Kingsbury, "The Prophets and the Council of Yahweh," 283–84.

[28] Jer 23:18, 22.

[29] For a defense of the view that this incident does not constitute Isaiah's consecration to prophecy see Tsevat, "The Throne Vision of Isaiah," 155 and Clements, *Isaiah 1–39*, 71.

[30] On the image of God as king and other images related to his kingship see J. C. L. Gibson, *Language and Imagery in the Old Testament* (Peabody, MA: Hendrickson, 1998), 121–28.

[31] E. Earle Ellis, "Perspectives on Biblical Interpretation: A Review Article," *JETS* 45 (2002): 478.

[32] Saebo, "סוֹד," *TLOT* 2:795 cites Job 15:8 and states that wisdom is gained at the divine council. The term for counsel (עֵצָה) is found nineteen times in Isaiah (5:19; 8:10; 11:2; 14:26; 16:3; 19:3, 11, 17; 25:1; 28:29; 29:15; 30:1; 36:5; 40:13; 44:26; 46:10–11; 47:13) and refers to "a decision arrived at in a council" (von Rad, *The Message of the Prophets*, 132). See William McKane, *Prophets and Wise Men*, SBT, ed. C. F. D. Moule et al., vol. 44 (Naperville, IL: Allenson, 1965), 82–83.

[33] See Tsevat, "The Throne Vision of Isaiah," 162–64 and von Rad, *The Message of the Prophets*, 118–19, 22.

division.[34] Finally, the term for 'divine council' (סוֹד) will undergo both a lexical (עֵצָה רָז)[35] and semantic change during the time of Daniel and come to be associated with secrets.[36] The Greek translation for this later term is μυστήριον 'mystery' and its association with wisdom will become marked in post-exilic prophets and on into the NT era.[37]

The Call Structure. Isaiah 6:1–13 deviates slightly from the form of the call structure.[38] Normally it has six elements including, divine confrontation, introductory word, commission, objection, reassurance, and a sign. The pattern is as follows: divine

[34] Seitz, "The Divine Council," 229–47. Seitz has set up an either-or scenario here (either it is not a divine call and therefore involves the same Isaiah, or a divine call and necessarily a different Isaiah).

[35] This term occurs nine times in OT (Dan 2:18, 19, 27, 28, 29, 30, 47; 4:6). This is the post-exilic equivalent of סוֹד and translated by μυστήριον in Daniel and equated with סוֹד in Qumran.

[36] סוֹד occurs twenty-one times in OT (Gen 49:6; Job 15:8; 19:19; 29:4; Pss 25:14; 55:15; 64:3; 83:4; 89:8; 111:1; Prov 3:32; 11:13; 15:22; 20:19; 25:9; Jer 6:11; 15:17; 23:18, 22; Ezek 13:9; Amos 3:7). This term is translated 'council' and is used to refer both to the divine council itself and the decisions it rendered. Brown says, "The fact that סוֹד is used both for the heavenly assembly and divine mystery provides an interesting clue to the development of the concept" (Raymond E. Brown, "The Pre-Christian Semitic Concept of 'Mystery'," *CBQ* 20 [1958]: 421). Earlier, H. Wheeler Robinson said similarly (Robinson, "The Council of Yahweh," 152). The LXX translation bears out this connection.

[37] Occurs thirty-one times in the LXX, eight in the canonical books (Dan 2:18–19, 27–30, 47), twelve times in the non-canonical books (Jdt 2:2; Tob 12:7,11; 2 Macc 13:21; Wis 2:22; 6:22; 14:15, 23 [cf. 7:25]; Sir 22:22; 27:16–17, 21 [cf. 3:21–22; 42:19–19; 3:19; 48:24–25; 14:20–21; 24:2; 43:32; 1:30; 47:15–17; 39:7; 1:4; 24:3ff]), and eleven times in Theodotion (Tob. 12:7,11; Dan 2:18–19, 27–30, 47; 4:9). This never translates the Hebrew סוֹד (but Symmachus and Theodotion use μυστήριον for סוֹד in Job 15:8 and the Sinaiticus suppletor has μυστήριον for סוֹד in Sir 3:19) but it does translate the Heb. רָז in Daniel. A similar term (מִסְתָּר) 'secret place' occurs six times in Qumran materials (4Q184 f1:11; 4Q201 f1i:6; f1ii:7; 4Q204 f1i:26; 4Q424 f1:4; 4Q541 f7:1). See Hellmut Brunner, "Das Herz als Sitz des Lebengeheimnisses," *AfO* 17 (1954–55): 140–41.

[38] The other call form occurs in Isa 40:1–11 where there is the introductory word (40:1–2), the commission (40:3–5, 6a), the objection (40:5–7), and the reassurance (40:8–11) (N. Habel, "The Form and Significance of the Call Narratives," *ZAW* 77 [1965]: 298, 309–17; Kaiser, *Isaiah 1–12*, 121–22, 30); Tsevat, "The Throne Vision of Isaiah," 165–66; Kaiser, *Isaiah 1–12*, 132.

confrontation (6:1–2), the introductory word (6:3–7), the commission (6:8–10),[39] the objection (6:11a),[40] and the reassurance (6:11–13).[41] The missing element is the sign feature unless chapter seven is included. Kaiser divides the passage into three scenes (6:1–4, 5–7, 8–11) followed by additions (6:12–13).[42] A significant omission to the call narrative is that it is not accompanied by "thus says Yahweh," but instead by terms reminiscent of wisdom language.[43] This observation lends weight to its intentionality and to the influence and role of wisdom in Isaiah.

The Wisdom Influence.[44] Isaiah is a prophetic book, but a number of OT scholars recognize an affinity and even a synergism of the

---

[39] Habel thinks this section is colored by the narrative of 1 Kgs 22:19–21 and is in the form of an oracle of doom (Habel, "The Form and Significance of the Call Narratives," 166).

[40] The ejaculatory form 'how long' is found twenty-nine times in the OT and always carries an indignant tone (עַד־מָתַי). (ibid.: 312 n. 33).

[41] This includes a reiteration of the oracle of doom and the mention of the remnant.

[42] Kaiser, *Isaiah 1–12*, 123.

[43] Scott points to Isa 6:9–10 as an instance of a riddle (6:9) followed by irony (6:10). "The paired imperative verbs *hear* and *understand*, *see* and *perceive* are characteristic openings of a wisdom address, as distinguished from the more usual prophetic summons, 'Hear the word of Yahweh' or 'Thus speaks Yahweh'" (R. B. Y. Scott, *The way of wisdom in the Old Testament* [New York: Macmillan, 1971], 124–25). He also notes parables in Isaiah (5:1–7 [cf. Prov 24:30–34]; 28:23–29) and points out marks of wisdom style and vocabulary (ibid., 125).

[44] The genesis for the search of sapiential influence *outside* the wisdom genre began with the monumental study by Gerhard von Rad, "The Joseph Narrative and Ancient Wisdom," in *The Problem of the Hexateuch and other Essays*, trans. E. W. Trueman Dicken (New York: McGraw Hill, 1966), 281–91. See also James L. Crenshaw, "Method in Determining Wisdom Influence upon 'Historical' Literature," *JBL* 88 (1969): 129 n. 1; idem, *Old Testament Wisdom: An Introduction* (Louisville, KY: Knox, 1998), 1–3; Gerald T. Sheppard, *Wisdom as a Hermeneutical Construct: A Study in the Sapientalizing of the Old Testament*, BZAW, ed. Georg Fohrer, vol. 151 (Berlin: de Gruyter, 1980), 1–18; Charles H. H. Scobie, "The Place of Wisdom in Biblical Theology," *BTB* 14 (1984): 43–48; R. Charles Hill, *Wisdom's Many Faces* (Collegeville, MN: Liturgical, 1996), 1–16, 37 n. 39; James D. G. Dunn, *Christology in the Making: A New Testament Inquiry into the Origins of the Doctrine of the Incarnation*, 2d ed. (Grand Rapids: Eerdmans, 1996), 163–212; For a summary of Ringgren's view of hypostasis see Ralph Marcus, "On Biblical Hypostases of Wisdom," *HUCA* 23 (1950): 158–61.

prophetic with the sapiential.[45] Although the offices of priest, wise man, and prophet continue to be distinguished after Isaiah (Jer 18:18), the intercourse opens up the possibility that Isaiah shows signs of blending the sapiential and prophetic traditions. Sonnet says, "La recherche modern a mis en valeur les contacts de l'écriture isaïenne avec le monde sapientiel."[46] The evidence of sapiential influence may be due to his conflict with statesmen whose wisdom and counsel he wishes to counter in establishing Yahweh's counsel as the only determinant in human affairs.

The sapiential-prophetic synthesis. Scott demonstrates the basic differences between the wisdom and prophetic traditions.[47] He insists on a convergence of prophecy and wisdom by the time of Isaiah as marked. Isaiah and Amos[48] bear signs of being effected by the wisdom stream of tradition. The earliest attempt to account for Isaianic influence is the 'converted-sage' hypothesis of Johannes Fichtner.[49] This view is later picked up by Scott who speculates that

---

[45] See McKane, *Prophets and Wise Men*, 65–78; Williamson, *The Book Called Isaiah*, 46–51; Katharine Delling, *'Get Wisdom, Get Insight': An Introduction to Israel's Wisdom Literature* (London: Darton, Longman & Todd, 2000), 84–86; Scott, *The way of wisdom in the Old Testament*, 101–35; Henri Blocher, "The Fear of the Lord as the 'Principle' of Wisdom," *TB* 28 (1977): 21–23. See especially the comparison Blocher makes between the motto of Proverbs and Isaiah (ibid., 22–23). See also Roger N. Whybray, "Slippery Words: IV. Wisdom," *ExpTim* 89 (1977–78): 361; E. Earle Ellis, "Wisdom and Knowledge in 1 Corinthians," *TB* 22–25 (1971–74): 88–93.

[46] Sonnet, "Le motif de l'endurcissement (Is 6,9–10) et la lecture d' «Isaïe»," 222.

[47] Wisdom to prophecy is distinct in regard to revelation versus reason, vertical versus horizontal theology, anthropocentric versus theological, historical versus ahistorical, general principles versus covenant obligations, and the vocabulary of oracles of judgment versus proverbs, riddles, parables, allegories, hortatory, debates, and soliloquies (Scott, *The way of wisdom in the Old Testament*, 113–22; Hill, *Wisdom's Many Faces*, 55 n. 7).

[48] Hans Walter Wolff, *Joel and Amos*, ed. S. Dean McBride Jr., trans. Waldemar Janzen, S. Dean McBride Jr., and Charles A. Muenchow, Hermeneia—A Critical and Historical Commentary on the Bible, ed. Frank Moore Cross Jr. et al., vol. 14 (Minneapolis: Fortress, 1977), 95–100; Kaiser, *Isaiah 1–12*, 8–9.

[49] This author is a major player in alerting other scholars to the wisdom tradition's influence on Isaiah. See Johannes Fichtner, *Die altorientalische Weisheit in ihrer israelitisch-jüdischen Ausprägung*, BZAW, vol. 62 (Giessen: Töpelmann, 1933); idem, "Jesaja unter den Weisen," in *Gottes Weisheit: Gesammelte Studien zum alten Testament*, vol. 2 (Stuttgart: Calwer, 1965), 18–26 (originally published under the same title in *TLZ* 74 [1949]: 75–80); idem, "Jahwes Plan in der Botschaft des Jesaja," in *Gottes*

Isaiah was a scribe or counselor at court before his call to prophecy.[50] This prior association reportedly accounts for his writing, wisdom vocabulary, literary forms (riddle, parable, proverbial saying),[51] and his ready access to the king and other prominent persons. As appealing as this sage-to-prophet hypothesis is, it is not supported by the evidence and most scholars accept the wisdom influence without this cumbersome hypothesis.[52] As for the exact background of Isaiah the man, it remains a matter of speculation.

William J. Whedbee and others. Whedbee offers the first comprehensive and detailed assessment of wisdom in Isaiah.[53] He argues that Isaiah is not a scribe but uses wisdom terms and genres because of his conflict with the Jerusalem scribes who dispute the wisdom of God. Jensen, along with most other scholars, questions Whedbee on the notion that the wise men disputed Yahweh's wisdom, but agrees with the majority of scholars when acknowledging that the "broader assertion of wisdom influence in Isaiah can be said to be firmly established."[54] Clements concurs saying, "That there is an important connection with the language and speech-forms of Wisdom is certainly to be conceded."[55] It is the

---

Weisheit Gesammelte Studien zum Alten Testament, 27–43 (originally published under same title in *ZAW* 63 [1951]: 16–63). See also R. T. Anderson, "Was Isaiah a Scribe?" *JBL* 79 (1960): 57–58.

[50] On constructing a composite picture of Isaiah the man see Clements, *Isaiah 1–39*, 12, 13–14; Crenshaw, *Old Testament Wisdom*, 28, cf. 29–30; Hill, *Wisdom's Many Faces*, 5; von Rad, *The Message of the Prophets*, 118–19. Isaiah uses both the vocabulary and forms of wisdom.

[51] On form-critical analyses of wisdom literature see Roland E. Murphy, "Form Criticism and Wisdom Literature," *CBQ* 31 (1969): 475–83; Crenshaw, *Old Testament Wisdom*, 27–28.

[52] See Wolff, *Joel and Amos*, 91; Whybray, "Slippery Words," 360; Shalom M. Paul, *Amos*, Hermaneia—A Critical and Historical Commentary on the Bible, ed. Frank Moore Cross Jr. et al. [Minneapolis: Fortress, 1991], 2–3). If Amos is the kernel of wisdom influence, then Isaiah is the full-grown harvest.

[53] William J. Whedbee, *Isaiah and Wisdom* (Nashville: Abingdon, 1971), 150–53.

[54] Joseph Jensen, *The Use of Tôrâ by Isaiah: His Debate with the Wisdom Tradition*, CBQMS, ed. Patrick W. Skehan et al., vol. 3 (Washington, DC: Catholic Biblical Association, 1973), 45. Cf. Sonnet, "Le motif de l'endurcissement (Is 6,9–10) et la lecture d' «Isaïe»," 212; Sheppard, *Wisdom as a Hermeneutical Construct*, 11.

[55] Clements, *Isaiah 1–39*, 14; Scobie, "The Place of Wisdom in Biblical Theology," 43, 46.

repetition of key words, according to Gibson, that serves to ease this genre-recognition.[56] Jensen directs Isaiah's speech towards a group for whom it would be particularly relevant, namely, the counselors to the king.[57] Sonnet says the use of this speech is clearly ironic.[58] Whybray refers to these antagonists as "wise men" only in the technical sense having what Saebo coins a hybrid wisdom.[59] McKane argues that these counselors are really statesmen trained as political advisors to the king who offer their own counsel in contrast to Isaiah.[60]

A significant majority of OT sapiential scholars, although differing in minor details and rejecting both the converted sage hypothesis of Fichtner and the disputation of God's wisdom of Whedbee, acknowledge a wisdom influence on Isaiah. None, however, link this directly to a definition of either the fat-heart or divine fattening although they come close.[61]

---

[56] Gibson, *Language and Imagery in the Old Testament*, 44. Interestingly, he points to wisdom vocabulary like 'know,' 'recognize,' or 'show' in the Joseph story and the book of Job. "They [Job's friends] are after all the representatives of Wisdom, the philosophy of their age – but both have to be taught hard lessons when God at last speaks for himself" (ibid., 46).

[57] Sonnet says "celui qui s'observe dans le mémorial isaïen, dans une référence aux sages et conseillers de la cour royale" (Sonnet, "Le motif de l'endurcissement (Is 6,9–10) et la lecture d' «Isaïe»," 216). It is to this group that Isa 6–8 is directed and written (ibid., 217). Cf. Jensen, *The Use of Tôrâ by Isaiah*, 51. Kaiser, *Isaiah 1–12*, 3 says that their faithlessness is reflected in their faithless form of politics and personal behavior. Milgrom notes that the first six chapters of Isaiah (1:10–6:13) identify the wicked as the leaders in Judah, viz. the elders, judges and princes who have misled the people (Milgrom, "Did Isaiah Prophesy during the Reign of Uzziah?" 171 n. 1). However, Whybray cautions that advisors are not called 'wise (men)' so it is only by inference to label these counselors as such (Roger N. Whybray, "The Sage in the Israelite Royal Court," in *The Sage in Israel and the Ancient Near East*, ed. John G. Gammie and Leo G. Perdue [Winona Lake, IN: Eisenbrauns, 1990], 133–34). But the degree of specificity required by Whybray is not necessary (von Rad, *The Message of the Prophets*, 124).

[58] Sonnet, "Le motif de l'endurcissement (Is 6,9–10) et la lecture d' «Isaïe»," 219.

[59] Whybray, "Slippery Words," 259, although he seriously doubts that there is such a class of wisdom teachers in the OT that produced a unified wisdom genre (ibid., 360; M. Saebo, "חכם," *TLOT* 1:424).

[60] McKane, *Prophets and Wise Men*.

[61] Williamson notes the wisdom terms in Isa 6:9–10 as one of those features that is programmatic for Isaiah (Williamson, *The Book Called Isaiah*, 48–49). The only missing element is the linkage of 'fattening' to this lack of salvific wisdom. He notes the

The implications to Isa 6:9–10. If wisdom is the proper background, then a few things are striking. First, few studies have exploited this and none have applied it to the fat-heart. Second, the terms and phrases in 6:9–10 are striking and may be polemically directed (ironically so) to those who are rumored to possess wisdom qualities.[62] Indeed, the words, "Hearing you will hear and not perceive" are especially stinging to sages or statesmen typically described as 'the hearing' ones.[63] Furthermore, "seeing you will see and not know" is equally devastating for those whose insights are gained through careful observation. The modus operandi of the statesmen is attacked as inadequate means for acquiring wisdom's effects. The prophecy of Isaiah may still be viewed within the genre of prophecy but the man in the mantel of the wise man utilizing and exploiting wisdom for polemic purposes.[64] It is a case where the genre form differs with its wisdom content, or what Crenshaw refers to as an occasion where "lacking such oneness, a given text participates in biblical wisdom to a greater or lesser extent."[65] By this sapiential signaling, Isaiah provides clarity to the nature of the 'fat-heart' and the background from which it is to be understood.

Other sapiential indicators. In addition to terminological and formal indicators are the thematic notions reflecting a sapiential world-view.[66] First, there is a repeated emphasis on the authority of God as creator (also parent and teacher) and thus an implied divine imperative toward creatures is assumed (1:3).[67] The emphasis on light

---

salvific issues and that texts evidence a reversal of Isa 6:9–10 in terms of this salvation.

[62] Jensen makes the link to the royal advisors and the wisdom vocabulary with a note of irony involved (Jensen, *The Use of Tôrâ by Isaiah*, 57).

[63] James L. Crenshaw, *Education in Ancient Israel: Across the Deadening Silence*, ABRL, ed. David Noel Freedman (New York: Doubleday, 1998), 126.

[64] Quinn-Miscall, *Reading Isaiah*, 3, 4; von Rad, *The Message of the Prophets*, 15; Sheppard, "The Book of Isaiah," 581.

[65] Crenshaw, *Old Testament Wisdom*, 11.

[66] Quinn-Miscall, *Reading Isaiah*, 43–67; Sonnet, "Le motif de l'endurcissement (Is 6,9–10) et la lecture d' «Isaïe»," 222.

[67] Creation is a repeated motif in Isaiah. The two verbs used are 'create' (בָּרָא) and 'make' (עָשָׂה). The former occurs twenty one times (4:5; 40:26, 28; 41:20; 42:5; 43:1, 7, 15; 45:7–8, 12, 18; 48:7; 54:16; 57:19; 65:17–18) and the latter one hundred times but

and darkness throughout also serves to highlight this act of and his sovereignty over creation.

Second, the anthropological focus (for judgment or salvation) is expanded beyond ethnic Israel to include all humanity.[68] Yahweh is the God of all humanity not just Israel. That the majority of ethnic Israel is fattened comes as a shocking (counter-order wisdom) reminder of their non-privileged status and supports a universalistic approach to humankind. Even a non-Israelite King, Cyrus, is referred to as Yahweh's shephard (רֹעִי) and anointed (לִמְשִׁיחוֹ) (Isa 44:28; 45:1). This reversal motif throughout Isaiah coincides well with a counter-order type wisdom.

Third, there is an emphasis on social justice and a demotion of cultic activities to the same (rather than higher) status. These reflect wisdom concerns.

Fourth, the absence of wisdom is echoed in catchwords (blindness and deafness) and is employed as a catchall for sin in which particular transgressions (drunkenness, arrogance, etc.) are depicted as various aspects of foolish behavior. Salvation is then framed in wisdom terms as a reversal of both condition and effects in regard to humans, animals,[69] and creation itself.[70] The reconstitution of the new heavens and earth along with the people is intent to reinstate the implicit moral order of wisdom—starting with the human heart.

Fifth, disaster and punishment are in terms of the natural and inevitable outcomes of unwise behavior (retributive justice). This particular punishment is described in the deuteronomic imagery of captivity (not fattening).

Sixth, an emphasis on righteousness and justice on both an individual and societal level directed towards those in leadership

---

only seventeen refer to creating (17:7; 27:11; 29:16; 37:16; 41:20; 43:7; 44:2, 24; 45:7, 9,12, 18; 46:10; 51:13; 54:5; 66:2, 22).

[68] See Quinn-Miscall, *Reading Isaiah*, 66; Roberts, "Isaiah in Old Testament Theology," 136.

[69] The encyclopedic reference to animals, plant life, and other natural happenings occur frequently in wisdom literature as well as Isaiah (and Amos). This probably grew out of the particularly bountiful reign of Uzziah (Quinn-Miscall, *Reading Isaiah*, 182; Wolff, *Joel and Amos*, 99; Milgrom, "Did Isaiah Prophesy during the Reign of Uzziah?" 167). Isaiah's knowledge helps him assume the mantle of a sapiential prophet.

[70] Saebo "חכם," *TLOT* 1:423–24.

reflects very much the overall concern of Proverbs. In this vein the leaders have gone the way of the fool.

Seventh, the rhetorical modus operandi of persuasion emphasizes the character of the speaker (*ethos*), emotion (*pathos*), and reason (*logos*) is a feature of wisdom throughout Isaiah and may be evidence of its influence.[71]

Eighth, the fear of Yahweh as a theme is explicitly linked to the wisdom tradition and is located in key texts throughout Isaiah.[72] It along with an emphasis on righteousness (external action) serves to highlight the religioethical outlook of wisdom.[73]

This brief survey serves to reinforce not only the presence of verbal and formal parallels to the wisdom *corpi* and nomenclature but also to illustrate the thematic links to the wisdom tradition in Isaiah.

Sapiential innovations in Isaiah. Isaiah may be seen as innovative in a few areas. First, the labeling as 'fat-hearted' one who *lacks salvific wisdom* and 'fattening' as a divine act is unique.[74] This combination is distinct from the 'hard-heart' motif of obduracy illustrated in the hardening of Pharaoh.[75] This may reflect the political environment from the perspective of illicit alliances formed in rebellion against Yahweh, alliances that are supported by their own kind of political common sense (wisdom) that rejects repentance. The second innovation is the application of the 'fat-heart' to Judah rather than

---

[71] F. Stolz, "לֵב," *TLOT* 2:640; Quinn-Miscall, *Reading Isaiah*, 118–21.

[72] Isa 11:2, 3; 33:6; 63:15–18; cf. 29:13; 50:10; 57:11; 59:19. Fattening is directly linked with the lack of the fear on the Lord in 63:15–18.

[73] Roberts, "Isaiah in Old Testament Theology," 134–36. "He may have been a critic of the professional counselors, but his criticism was in some sense an inside job. His formulation of ethical demands often takes the form of Wisdom maxims" (ibid., 135).

[74] Von Rad points out the ingenuity of Isaiah to take ideas from traditions and remodeling them in a most daring way (von Rad, *The Message of the Prophets*, 118). His message is innovative in picturing fattening as bringing about the downfall of Israel and his message of Yahweh's inclusion of other nations (ibid., 124).

[75] Not all obduracy is the same. To be 'fat-hearted,' as demonstrated below in Isaiah, refers not to *rebellion* but to *absence of salvific wisdom* and as such the phrase approaches a *terminus technicus*. Functional and therefore volitional obduracy may be expressed as being *stiff-necked, stubborn-necked, strong-necked, iron-necked,* and *hard-faced* (or *hard-forehead*). For an Arminian perspective see Roger T. Forster and V. Paul Marston, *God's Strategy in Human History* [Minneapolis: Bethany, 1973], 155–68). Stolz recognizes that the hardening of Pharaoh is in terms of intellectual and psychological deprivation (Stolz, "לֵב," *TLOT* 2: 641).

their enemies. Finally, the combination of the deuteronomic concept of the deprivation of the new heart with the sapiential tradition—as an accommodation to the polemic environment—is an innovative example in contextualization. Isaiah has thereby introduced a unique *perspective* to an old idea, a new *definition*, and an unlikely *object* of the divine act.

The Remnant. A common view of 6:11–13 is that they are additions from the sixth-century B.C. recounting the later Babylonian destruction of Jerusalem with the final clause of 6:13 added still later.[76] Isaiah 6:11–13ab points to historico-political expectations while 6:13c portends messianic expectations.[77] The same arguments used for the post-hoc view of the negative commissioning of Isaiah can also be cited here, namely, "All of the queries mentioned...appear to be raised because of an unwillingness to admit that God would ask something of such a terrible nature of his prophet."[78] In Isa 6:13c, the objection flows in the other direction, namely, that anything positive could be inferred alongside a message of judgment (6:11–13ab) is improbable.[79] The remnant motif is taken up by the important study of Gerhard F. Hasel who examines Isaiah's use of it throughout three identifiable stages of his ministry, namely, his early career (740–734 B.C.), time of Syro-Ephraimite war (734–735 B.C.), and his later career

---

[76] Clements, *Isaiah 1–39*, 72. Kaiser argues that the additions are obvious (Kaiser, *Isaiah 1–12*, 123, 33).

[77] Motyer, *The Prophecy of Isaiah*, 78. On the authenticity of the last three words "the holy seed is the stump" (זֶרַע קֹדֶשׁ מַצַּבְתָּהּ) see Samuel Iwry, "Massebah and Bamah in 1QIsaiah^a 6 13," *JBL* 76 (1957): 225–26; William H. Brownlee, "The Text of Isaiah 6:13 in the Light of DSIa," *VT* 1 (1951): 296–98; Hasel, *The Remnant*, 240–42.

[78] On the compatibility of fattening and the proclamation of salvation see Hasel, *The Remnant*, 229–33; Ivan Engnell, *The Call of Isaiah*, vol. 4, Uppsala Universitets Arsskrift (Uppsala: Lundequistska Bokhandeln, 1949), 51–52; Abraham J. Heschel, *The Prophets* (New York: Harper & Row, 1962), 90; Gerhard von Rad, *Old Testament Theology*, trans. D. M. G. Stalker, vol. 2 (New York: Harper & Row, 1962), 152–53 but contra M. M. Kaplan, "Isaiah 6:1–11," *JBL* 45 (1926): 251–59.

[79] Bernard Grosse argues that the negative part of the commission (6:9–10) is balanced out by the reference to the remnant. According to him, Isa 52:13–53:12 functions in the same way by countering the pessimism of the commission as well (Bernard Grosse, "Isaïe 52,13–53,12 et Isaïe 6," *RB* 98 [1991]: 537–43). On the salvation of the remnant see von Rad, *The Message of the Prophets*, 135–36. Of the reversal texts mentioned below, Isa 52:13–53:12 is the par excellence example.

(716/15–701 B.C.).[80] His major accomplishments include demonstrating that Isa 6:13 expresses a dual theme of judgment and salvation in light of a *historical* versus *eschatological* remnant is commensurate with Isaiah's early ministry, that the experience of Isaiah parallels the positive purpose for the remnant, and to this eschatological remnant the elective purposes of Israel are conferred.[81]

On the authenticity of 6:13, Hasel says that the only evidence against its inclusion is the final three words missing in the LXX. In favor of its authenticity is first the transcriptional probability that the Hebrew dropped off due to homoeoteleuton and second its positive inclusion in the Qumran scroll of 1QIsaᵃ. The argument for its exclusion seems to rest entirely on internal probabilities that rely on source critical assumptions that in turn are dictated by a priori notions of predictability.[82] Hasel counters redactional disparagement by pointing to internal evidence of the remnant theme in authentic passages during each stage of Isaiah's career: his early career (1:21–26 and 4:1–3), during the Syro-Ephraimite War (7:1–8:16; 'Shear-jashub 'a-remnant-shall-return'; 8:16–18),[83] and his later career (28:5–6; 30:15–17; 1:4–9[84]; 10:20–23; 37:30–32; 11:10–16[85]). Each stage, therefore,

---

[80] Hasel, *The Remnant,* 216–372.

[81] Hasel suggests that Isaiah is the prophetic representative of the future remnant who survive after judgment (ibid., 242–43, 66; Quinn-Miscall, *Reading Isaiah,* 54).

[82] Motyer says something similar but on the subject of the authorship of Isaiah and related to the skepticism of nineteenth-century rationalism that rejected predictive prophecy (Motyer, *The Prophecy of Isaiah,* 25–27).

[83] Isaiah is to take his oldest son Shear-jashub שְׁאָר יָשׁוּב (Isa 7:3), 'a remnant shall return' and visit with Ahab. For the significance of this name see Hasel, *The Remnant,* 274–86 and Gerhard F. Hasel, "Linguistic Considerations Regarding the Translation of Isaiah's 'Shear-jashub'," *AUSS* 9 (1971): 36–46. The appeal made to Ahaz, between military might verses trust in God, is really an exhortation for an unconditional *return* to Yahweh in faith (ibid., 284; cf. Vriezen, "Essentials of the Theology of Isaiah," 138 n. 16. who translates it as "a remnant will repent.").

[84] Hasel argues that the 'remnant' here is not the same referent as the 'holy seed' (6:13) or 'holy' remnant (4:3) (Hasel, *The Remnant,* 316–17).

[85] See ibid., 339–48.

reinforces the principle enunciated in 6:13c,[86] namely, that the remnant is to be saved and preserved after judgment occurs.[87]

Isaiah's Wisdom Metanarrative

Throughout Isaiah there is an emphasis on wisdom.[88] highlighted by the usage of verbal and nominal corollaries (seeing, hearing, perceiving, knowing, and understanding)[89] as well as several motifs involving the exploitation of these ideas. Each of these notions and motifs serve as a scheme or paradigm throughout Isaiah and have a reflective and refractive influence on the interpretation of Isa 6:9–10, its parallels, and the nature of fattening itself. Ultimately they are related to wisdom and therefore point to it as the key in defining the fat-heart and fattening.

Wisdom in Isaiah

Three terms begin the investigation of wisdom in Isaiah. These are the verb, חָכַם, the adjective, חָכָם, and the noun חָכְמָה.[90] Although the verb occurs nowhere in Isaiah, the adjective is found nine times. In 3:3 (and 40:20) it refers to the 'wise' political advisor in the sense of having a

---

[86] Ibid., 336–38. There is a distinction here between a purely *historical* remnant (6:13ab) with an *eschatological* remnant (6:13c) says Hasel.

[87] Ibid., 348–72. The 'remnant' of foreign nations is also taken up in Isaiah and includes Syria (17:1–6), Philistia (14:28–32), Arabia (21:13–17), and Babylon (14:22–23, part of 14:4b–21).

[88] For criteria assessing wisdom in non-wisdom literature see Crenshaw, "Method in Determining Wisdom Influence upon 'Historical' Literature," 129–42; Sheppard, *Wisdom as a Hermeneutical Construct*, 6; Murphy, "Form Criticism and Wisdom Literature," 483; John L. McKenzie, "Reflections on Wisdom," *JBL* 86 (1967): 1–9; Crenshaw, *Old Testament Wisdom*, 10; Blocher, "The Fear of the Lord as the 'Principle' of Wisdom," 12. For a charting of wisdom terms in the OT see M. Saebo, "חכם," *TLOT* 1:418.

[89] Their close association is noted by several scholars (Gerhard von Rad, *Wisdom in Israel*, trans. James D. Martin [London: Abingdon, 1972], 53, 101; Hill, *Wisdom's Many Faces*, 99–103).

[90] See Nili Shupak, *Where Can Wisdom be Found? The Sage's Language in the Bible and in Ancient Egyptian Literature*, OBO, ed. Othmar Keel, vol. 130 (Göttingen: Vandenhoeck & Ruprecht, 1993), 235–42. On the acquisition of wisdom he notes several avenues, viz., through *instruction*, *experience*, or *charismatic endowment* (ibid., 242).

skill.[91] In 5:21 it denounces the so-called wise that are 'wise' in their own eyes and בְּין in their own sight.[92] Because Isa 19:11 depicts the counsel of the 'wisest' counselors of Pharaoh as brutish, it asks, "How do you say to Pharaoh, 'I am the son of the wise man, the son of ancient kings?'" Credulity and irony is expressed by, "'Where is your *wise* men [= diviners]?...let them יֵדַע what the Lord has purposed concerning Egypt'" (19:12).[93] Like Israel, Yahweh has poured on Egypt a confused spirit resulting in a drunken stagger in their vomit (19:13–15; cf. 29:9–10). In promising judgment on Jerusalem, Yahweh will cause to perish the "חָכְמָה of the wise" and vanquish the "בִּינָה of those who perceive בְּין" (29:14).[94] In 31:2, Yahweh is 'wise' and can bring disaster in punishing evil-doers.[95] Indeed, he foils the signs of false prophets, makes fools of diviners, and "overthrows the דַּעַת of

---

[91] These skills can apply to a variety of *functional* occupations including seamanship (Ps 107:27), professional mourner (Jer 9:16), snake charmer (Ps 58:6), house builder (Prov 24:3), craftsmanship (Exod 31:3–4; 1 Kgs 71:14), magic and divination (Dan 1:20), and interpretation of dreams (Gen 41:8) (Whybray, "The Sage in The Israelite Royal Court," 133). Cf. Saebo, "חכם," *TLOT* 1:420–23. Whybray indicates that there is both a divine wisdom from God and a purely human acquired wisdom where the former is not a result of the latter (Roger N. Whybray, "Wisdom, Suffering and the Freedom of God in the Book of Job," in *In Search of True Wisdom: Essays in Old Testament Interpretation in Honour of Ronald E. Clements*, ed. Edward Ball, JSOTSup, ed. David J. A. Clines and Philip R. Davies, vol. 300 [Sheffield: Sheffield Academic Press, 1999], 233–35; Gibson, *Language and Imagery in the Old Testament*, 130).

[92] McKane, *Prophets and Wise Men*, 65–69.

[93] Ibid., 69–70. Hill reasons that these wise men come under Isaiah's condemnation because they disrespect the craft of wisdom itself. (Hill, *Wisdom's Many Faces*, 53–54). According to Hill, when the sage plays seer the prophet(s) react strongly against him. Ironically, however, Isaiah plays sage in order to undermine them.

[94] McKane, *Prophets and Wise Men*, 70–71.

[95] Ibid., 72–73. Jensen disputes the authenticity of this verse (Jensen, *The Use of Tôrâ by Isaiah*, 52). For the arguments against its authenticity see Brevard S. Childs, *Isaiah and the Assyrian Crisis*, SBT, ed. C. F. D. Moule et al. (London: SCM, 1967), 34–35 and for its authenticity see Whedbee, *Isaiah and Wisdom*, 133–35. Both Jensen and Whedbee regard Isaiah's adjectival usage of 'wise' as having a negative and polemic purpose. Whedbee thinks Childs has overlooked the crisis in court wisdom, viz., that these so-called wise men question the wisdom of the Lord in several places (5:19; 29:15; 28:23). Thus in his view the verse is entirely compatible with the rest of Isaiah. Jensen, on the other hand, disputes Whedbee's entire theory of 'crisis in court wisdom.'

the wise" (44:25).[96] These adjectival usages convey a negative connotation except 31:2.

חָכְמָה is used five times in Isaiah. In 10:13 it demonstrates the proverbial expression "the heart of the king is in the hands of the Lord as the watercourses: he turns it wherever he wishes" (Prov 21:1), and identifies the source of wisdom as Yahweh. He promises to bring judgment on the King of Assyria for such hubris in thinking that by his own 'wisdom' he had בִּין in military success. In reality, his success is all Yahweh's who uses that nation as an instrument to inflict his own wrath (10:15). In 11:2 the servant is conjoined with the רוּחַ of בִּינָה, חָכְמָה, counsel (עֵצָה), strength (גְּבוּרָה), דַּעַת, and fear (יִרְאָה) of the Lord—each wisdom term shown to be derived from the spirit/wind of the Lord. In 29:14 it is linked to בִּין and בִּינָה. In 33:6 it flourishes in a period of 'salvation' (יְשׁוּעָה) where דַּעַת and 'fear' (יִרְאָה) of Yahweh are also prevalent. In 47:10 Babylon's wisdom and דַּעַת are the product of training in spells and incantations which perverts them in heaping divine attributes to themselves.[97]

Isaiah uses the wisdom vocabulary in a number of ways. First, he employs 'wisdom' terminology in association with the spirit/wind that effects salvation and the fear of Yahweh.[98] Second, he acknowledges various types of wisdom including crafts, skills in warfare, the prophetic office, diviners, and seers, as well as a soteriological kind. Third, Isaiah assumes an order that is reflective of the wisdom tradition in other Jewish literature. Finally, Isaiah denounces a pseudo-wisdom that brings destruction.[99] Below a fuller investigation of Isaiah's terms and motifs are explored for determining how pervasive this sapiential thinking is to his world-view and as an aid for understanding his notion of divine fattening.

---

[96] McKane, *Prophets and Wise Men*, 94.

[97] Ibid.

[98] The apophthegm 'fear of Yahweh,' often referred to as the motto or keyword of wisdom writings, occurs twenty-three times in the OT. Jonah and 2 Chronicles each have one (Jonah 1:16; 2 Chr 19:9), Isaiah has three (11:2, 3; 33:6), Psalms has four (2:11; 19:10; 34:12; 111:10), and Proverbs has fourteen (1:7, 29; 2:5; 8:13; 9:10; 10:27; 14:26, 27; 15:16, 33; 16:6; 19:23; 22:4; 23:17). A variation is 'fear of Adonai' (Job 28:28) probably because Job and his friends are not Israelites. See Blocher, "The Fear of the Lord as the 'Principle' of Wisdom," 3–28; Crenshaw, *Old Testament Wisdom*, 12.

[99] Jensen, *The Use of Tôrâ by Isaiah*, 53–54.

Sapiential Notions

The Wisdom Notion of Perception.[100] The notions of 'perceiving' and 'knowing' are related to each other throughout Isaiah and linked to the heart and wisdom (Isa 6:9–10).[101] בִּין and בִּינָה, occur twenty-five times in Isaiah.[102] Early on it is pointed out that Israel neither knows nor 'perceives' the Lord (1:3).[103] Isaiah 1:1–3 may be viewed distinctively to 1:4–9 the latter of which may be descriptive of the siege of 701 B.C.[104] Thus 1:3 may be a general description of Israel's condition throughout Isaiah's ministry.[105] Twice this lack is associated

---

[100] See Shupak, *Where Can Wisdom be Found?* 243–47. "The basic meaning of *byn* is 'to become separated,' which applies to the ability to discern between alternatives and to understand perfectly through insight" (ibid., 243).

[101] Sonnet, "Le motif de l'endurcissement (Is 6,9–10) et la lecture d' «Isaïe»," 221–23.

[102] The verb occurs twenty times (1:3; 3:3; 5:21; 6:9–10; 10:13; 14:16; 28:9,19; 29:14, 16; 32:4; 40:14, 21; 43:10, 18; 44:18; 52:15; 56:11; 57:1) and the noun five times (11:2; 27:11; 29:14, 24; 33:19).

[103] The verb is a Hithpolel stem. Other uses of this stem are 14:16, 43:18, and 52:15. Wisdom texts often employ the behavior of animals to be imitated (Whybray, "Wisdom, Suffering and the Freedom of God in the Book of Job," 241–42). In Isa 1:3 the idea is that even the imparted wisdom of the animal, as deficient and sectarian as it may be, produces better results in terms of obedience than that within the members of Israel and Judah. Whybray thinks the similarity of Job 39:3–12 and Isa 1:3 suggests that the former is deliberately based on the latter (ibid., 242). Other animals used as models of behavior include the ant (Prov 6:6–9; 30:24–25), the badger, locust, and lizard (Prov 30:26–28), and the lion (30:30). Thus Isaiah is at least proceeding from the start in a like sapiential mode of reasoning.

[104] W. T. Glaassen, "Linguistic Arguments and the Dating of Isaiah 1:4–9," *JNSL* 3 (1974): 9–11 prefers to treat 1:4–9 as a unit rather than 1:2–9. He is unsure whether this marks the occasion *during* the siege of Jerusalem or *thereafter* but he favors the former (ibid., 16).

[105] Willis mentions nine different views concerning the extent of the first pericope in Isaiah. He finally settles on 1:2–20 (John T. Willis, "The First Pericope in the Book of Isaiah," *VT* 34 [1984]: 68). One view that enjoys considerable support is that 1:2–3 is the first pericope (ibid.). Even if Willis's construal is adopted, he sees 1:2–4 as an accusation against Israel (Judah) for improper response and 1:5–9 as explaining the effect of this ingratitude (ibid., 69). The time gap between these two points may be extensive. Isaiah 1:2–4 is therefore a "general description of Judah's apostasy" and "vv. 11–17 make this description specific, and v. 20 returns to the general description" (ibid., 70). He regards 1:2–20 in the form of a lawsuit (ibid., 72–74). Isaiah 1:3 may then legitimately describe the general *condition* of Israel prior to the

with not 'knowing' (יָדַע). This along with the antithetical parallelism in Isa 6:9–10 suggests they are already 'fat-hearted' *before* Isaiah is given the command to fatten their heart.[106]

Isaiah mentions the '*perceiving* charmer'[107] and parallels the verbal idea with the adjective 'wise' in the '*wise* artisan' (חָכָם). In 5:21 the phrase 'perceptive in their own sight' is clearly parallel with the phrase 'wise in their own eyes' again grouping the verb 'to perceive' with the adjective 'wise.' In 6:9 the close association of בִּין and יָדַע occurs in the phrases 'hear but not perceive' and 'see but not know.'[108] In 6:10 "*lest* they perceive with their לֵבָב" is parallel with "make their לֵב fat (שָׁמֵן)." Here the inability of the heart to 'perceive' is tantamount to having a 'fat' heart. In 10:13 the king of Assyria is condemned for saying "by my wisdom, because I perceive" that therefore he conquers nations. Here חָכְמָה and 'perceiving' are linked where the former is the cause of the latter. In 14:16 individuals 'perceive' the truth of the Assyrian king after 'seeing' (רָאָה) him fall from power.

In 28:9, Isaiah mocks the drunken priests and prophets by asking who they could possibly teach דַּעַת or cause בִּין.[109] In 28:19 it is the

---

Assyrian invasion, prior to the Syro-Ephraimite crisis, and prior to Isaiah's commission even though the actual utterance is most likely in 701 B.C.

[106] This raises the key issue, viz., how the participants of fattening can be on the one hand already fat-hearted and yet on the other hand the objects of God's further intention to fatten. This two-way causation (congenital fattening and divine fattening) goes a long way in explaining subsequent tradition and the wisdom tradition.

[107] This verb is a Niphal participle. Other occurrences of this stem are 5:21, 10:13, and 29:14.

[108] The verb here is a Qal imperative. Other occurrences in the Qal are 6:10, 32:4, 43:10, and 44:18.

[109] The verb here is Hiphil stem. Other occurrences in the Hiphil are 28:19, 29:16, 40:14, 40:21, 56:11, and 57:1. The mention of wine (יַיִן), strong drink (שֵׁכָר), drunkenness (שֵׁכָר), drunkard (שִׁכּוֹר), or drunk (שָׁכַר) occur more frequently in Isaiah (thirty times) than in any other book of the OT (Isa 5:11–12, 22; 16:10; 19:14; 22:13; 24:9, 11, 20; 28:1, 3, 7; 29:9; 49:26; 51:21; 55:1; 56:12; 63:6). Isaiah uses the *drunken-motif* to symbolize the *absence of wisdom and its effects*. Contexts where these terms occur are the following: (1) Wine and strong drink are used for constant inebriation purposes (5:11, 22; 28:1, 3). (2) Joyous occasions where God is not properly honored (5:12). (3) For times when only wine (22:13; 24:11) or strong drink (24:9) provide joy; sometimes even here Yahweh takes it away (16:10). (4) In a metaphorical sense depicting mental and spiritual dullness resulting in an incapacitation or incomprehension ultimately caused by Yahweh either towards Egypt (19:14) or the priests and prophets of Israel

perceiving of the message of destruction that will bring sheer terror to the people. In 29:14 the "חָכְמָה of their [Israel's] wise men [חֲכָם]" will perish and the "בִּינָה of those who בִּין" will be hid. Yahweh warns Jerusalem that he will withhold wisdom and perception from their wise and perceiving sages. It is clear that חָכְמָה and בִּינָה are logically associated in the same way 'wise men' and 'those who perceive' (בִּין/חָכָם) are linked. Wisdom is to perception as being wise is to exhibiting the ability to perceive. In 29:16 the misguided fancy of hiding one's secret mischievous plans from Yahweh is like saying that the wise potter does not בִּין. His salvation is promised in 32:4 to the rash in heart who will one day בִּין in order to יָדַע.

A rhetorical question is posed concerning Yahweh in 40:14. This involves inquiring if anyone has counseled him thereby 'causing him to perceive,' or 'taught (לְמַד)' him justice or דַּעַת or showed him the way of 'understanding' (תְּבוּנָה) to 'cause him to know' יָדַע.[110] In 40:21 the passage is arranged chiastically revealing a parallel of knowing/perceiving and hearing/telling:

Do you not *know* (יָדַע)?
    Have you not *heard*? (שָׁמַע)
        Has it not been *told* you from the beginning? (נָגַד)
Have you not *perceived* since the earth was founded? (בִּין)

Isaiah 43:10 reveals that Yahweh made Israel his servant to יָדַע, 'believe' (אָמַן), and בִּין that he is who he claims to be. In 43:18 they are asked if they בִּין the things of old. In 44:18 they יָדַע not neither do they בִּין because Yahweh had shut their eyes so they could not רָאָה and their לֵב so they could not שָׂכַל. This text is a reuse of Isa 6:9–10 and identifies not only the source of 'knowing' and 'perceiving' in the heart but also emphasizes the divine prerogative. It gives clarity to the nature of Isaiah's role in the fattening process as secondary at best.

In 52:15 a promise is given for the Gentiles, namely, that which has not been 'told' (סָפַר) them (i.e., have not heard) they will רָאָה, and

---

(28:7, 9; 51:21). (5) In a metaphorical sense of judgment (24:20; 49:26; 63:6). (6) Positively for referring to genuine offers of joyous occasions (55:1; 56:12). For a NT use of this motif see Howard Clark Kee, "Jesus: A Glutton and Drunkard," in *Authenticating the Words of Jesus*, ed. Bruce Chilton and Craig A. Evans (Boston: Brill, 2002), 311–32.

[110] McKane, *Prophets and Wise Men*, 81–82.

that which they have not שָׁמַע they will בִּין. Again the parallelism in "epistemological imagery" is evident where 'see' is used in the positive sense of 'perceiving.'[111] In 56:11 false teachers are referred to as 'dogs' that never יָדַע enough, shepherds who cannot יָדַע in order to בִּין. Finally, in 57:1 a parallelism is detected where the 'heart' is not only coordinate with the ability to 'perceive' but the place where perception occurs. It reads as follows:

> The righteous *perish*
> > and no one *ponders* it in his *heart*;
> Devout men are *taken away*,
> > and no one *perceives* [in his heart]
> > > that the righteous are taken away
> > > to be spared from evil.

בִּינָה occurs five times in Isaiah. The first (Isa 11:2) is most important for it describes the spirit/wind of God as a spirit/wind of wisdom that brings perception.

> The spirit/wind of the Lord will rest on him—
> the spirit/wind of wisdom (חָכְמָה) and of understanding (בִּינָה),[112]
> the spirit/wind of counsel (עֵצָה) and of power (גְּבוּרָה)
> the spirit/wind of knowledge (דַּעַת) and of the fear (יִרְאָה)[113] of the Lord—

---

[111] The phrase comes from Joel Marcus, "Mark and Isaiah," in *Fortunate the Eyes that See: Essays in Honor of David Noel Freedman in Celebration of His Seventieth Birthday*, ed. Astrid B. Beck et al. (Grand Rapids: Eerdmans, 1995), 458–59.

[112] For a discussion on the later (A.D. 180) Greek equivalent in Sirach (39:1–11) and the relationship of the Spirit of understanding to the mediation of wisdom see James A. Davis, *Wisdom and Spirit, An Investigation of 1 Corinthians 1.18–3:20 against Background of Jewish Sapiential Traditions in the Greco-Roman Period* (Lanham, MD: University Press of America, 1984), 16–26.

[113] The 'fear' of the Lord is said to be the *beginning* of wisdom probably in the sense that it is the first or primary *evidence* of it—it is not the *cause* but the *consequent* of having wisdom. In an illuminating essay, J. I. Packer says, "Neither [wisdom and *theologia*] should be seen as the fruit of intellectual acumen as such; both are effects of the divine illumination that comes to those who seek to practice 'the fear of the Lord'" (J. I. Packer, "Theology and Wisdom," in *The Way of Wisdom: Essays in Honor of Bruce K. Waltke*, ed. J. I. Packer and Sven K. Soderlund [Grand Rapids: Zondervan, 2002], 12). It seems as if he makes the condition of graced wisdom dependent on one exercising the fear of the Lord. He probably has in mind, however, those who possess the fear of the Lord based on their possession of wisdom who in turn pursue wisdom further, thus a *functional-ontological* assessment. Earlier he states, "He imparts the gift to all who sincerely seek it from him and are ready for the changes that its coming

In 27:11 it describes Israel as a people without 'perception' (cf. 29:14). In 29:24 it refers to a time after Israel's restoration from captivity when the wayward will 'gain understanding' and when those who complain will accept instruction. Isaiah 33:19 mentions the incomprehensibility of the Assyrian speech as something they neither שָׁמַע nor 'perceive.'

Several conclusions may be claimed from this brief survey. First, Isaiah's usage of בִּין is associated with wisdom and therefore Isa 6:9–10 should be construed within this tradition. Second, a logical causation similar to above is seen. Thus it is unlikely that the fat-heart that lacks the ability to בִּין (Isa 6:10) is to be understood without inferring the cause of perceiving, namely, wisdom. Third, the relationship of 'perceiving' and 'knowing' is one of necessary association. Both are effects of wisdom and being wise. Thus when the heart either lacks or possesses one, the other may be inferred. Fourth, this wisdom is associated with the spirit/wind of Yahweh so that it causes wisdom, the fear of Yahweh, and other noetic effects.

The Wisdom Notion of Knowing.[114] The second verb that is mentioned in Isa 6:9–10 is יָדַע which occurs seventy-six times in Isaiah while דַּעַת is found nine times.[115] Here they are grouped into

---

may bring" (ibid., 7). For a discussion of the term (רֵאשִׁית) and various translations ('motto,' 'chief or essential part, what comprises everything,' 'perfection,' 'beginning,' 'sum,' 'culmination') see Blocher, "The Fear of the Lord as the 'Principle' of Wisdom," 12–15. He gives four options including *first fruit, beginning, chief* or *choicest part*, and *substance* or *essence* (ibid., 14–15).

[114] Shupak, *Where Can Wisdom be Found?* 231 (see esp. 231–35) points out three senses to the verb including "to know," "to distinguish," (or "to perceive") and "to know a person carnally." Only the first two senses appear in wisdom literature. He indicates also that דַּעַת is "characteristic of the wisdom vocabulary...but also occurs frequently outside the sapiential circle (31 times)" (ibid., 233). According to him, דַּעַת is "on the one hand knowledge acquired by learning and experience and on the other *a divinely endowed gift* (Prov. 2,6–7)" (ibid., 234).

[115] 1:3; 5:5, 19; 6:9; 7:15–16; 8:4; 9:8; 12:4–5; 19:12, 21; 29:11–12, 15, 24; 32:4; 33:13; 37:20, 28; 38:19; 40:13–14, 21, 28; 41:20, 22–23, 26; 42:16, 25; 43:10, 19; 44:8–9, 18; 45:3–6, 20; 47:8, 11, 13; 48:4, 6–8; 49:23, 26; 50:4, 7; 51:7; 52:6; 53:3; 55:5; 56:10–11; 58:3; 59:8, 12; 60:16; 61:9; 63:16; 64:1; 66:14. The nominal form appears in 5:13; 11:2; 33:6; 40:14; 44:19, 25; 47:10; 58:2. Blocher refers to 'wisdom' and 'knowledge' as quasi-synonyms. "Wisdom, or דעת (if there is a nuance, it may be a greater emphasis on what lies beyond the practical), cannot be confined to morals in Proverbs 1.... We may safely conclude that Old Testament חכמה דעת also satisfied man's impulse to think and to

various subjects addressed throughout Isaiah. Seven basic relationships may be identified with some overlap occurring.

Noetic relationship of non-remnant of Israel to the Lord. Several texts point to a majority's privation of wisdom but do not include everyone and are *ontological-functional* cases. These do not 'know' (or 'perceive') him (1:3) and it is for their lack of 'knowledge' that they go into captivity (5:13). They רָאָה but do not 'know' (6:9). He indeed declares things from the beginning so that they might 'know' but no one שָׁמַע his words (41:26). They neither 'know' nor בִּין for Yahweh has shut their eyes from רָאָה and their לֵב from שָׂכַל (44:18). Jacob is Yahweh's servant, chosen, and called, but still does not 'know' the Lord (45:4). Indeed, God will gird him, but he (or they) does (do) not 'know' him (45:5). God 'knows' they are obstinate, their neck is of iron sinew, and their brow is brass (48:4). Jacob (Israel) does not שָׁמַע or 'know,' and his 'ear' is not opened because God 'knows' Jacob deals treacherously and is called a transgressor from the womb (48:8). They have not 'known' the way of peace (59:8) but 'know' their transgressions (59:12).[116]

At least two passages may be understood as *functional-ontological*. Though rebellious they fast and then question whether God has רָאָה or 'known' about their (so-called) humility (58:3). On the other hand, Yahweh has poured his anger on them but they did not 'know' nor take it to לֵב (42:25).

Others of Israel who have wisdom from Yahweh. Several passages may be classified as *ontological-functional*. God has chosen Israel as his servant to 'know,' believe, and to בִּין that he is the only Lord (43:10). The wise man (הָכָם) 'knows' what Yahweh plans to do to Egypt (19:12) and the servant of the Lord has the spirit/wind of wisdom and understanding, counsel and might, 'knowledge' and fear of the Lord upon him (11:2).[117] Two *functional-ontological* senses occur as well.

---

know—without the fateful division between θεωρία and πρᾶξις which we inherited from the Greeks" (Blocher, "The Fear of the Lord as the 'Principle' of Wisdom," 12).

[116] In-between the description is the confession of 59:9–11. They admit to waiting for light but having only darkness, for brightness but only gloom, to groping like the blind having no eyes, stumbling at noon as if it were twilight, among those of vigor as if dead, waiting for justice when there is none and salvation when it is far away from them.

[117] The phrase 'the fear of the Lord' (discussed earlier) could be "an *ironic dart flung at the ungodly*: those who lack the fear of God are ignorant of the very ABC of wisdom" (Blocher, "The Fear of the Lord as the 'Principle' of Wisdom," 15). He rejects this view

They seek the Lord and the 'knowledge' of his ways (58:2) and those who 'know' what is right, who have the law of the Lord in their לֵב, are admonished to שָׁמַע him (51:7). *Functional* usages also occur. Although they acknowledge God as their Father, they also lament that Abraham with the rest of Israel do not 'know' them (63:16). They desire Yahweh to judge and make 'known' his name (64:1). But when they 'see' the salvation of Israel their heart rejoices for it is a time when the hand of the Lord is made 'known' to his servants and his fury to his foes (64:14).

Particularly egregious acts against Yahweh are singled out. Some texts may be *ontological-functional*. They foolishly ascribe a lack of omniscience on the Lord's part by asking whether he truly שָׁמַע or 'knows' them (29:15). Israel's watchmen are described as 'blind' and lacking in 'knowledge' (56:10). Indeed, they can never 'know' enough and ironically they cannot 'know' at all (56:11). Idol makers and those associated with idols do not 'return to their לֵב neither have any 'knowledge' or תְּבוּנָה when it comes to the utter nonsense of their practices (44:19). God turns these so-called wise men back and exposes their 'knowledge' as foolishness (44:25). *Functional* cases also occur. They are summoned to שָׁמַע and draw near to 'know' the power of God (33:13). There is perhaps one case of a *functional-ontological* usage. This occurs when Babylonian wisdom and 'knowledge' are used to pervert them into sinfully ascribing to themselves divine attributes (47:10). They do not *become* bad but simply *grow* worse.

The promised future reversal of noetic privation. These cases involve a salvific and thus *ontological-functional* sense. Those who 'know' to err in spirit will come to בִּינָה the law correctly or even salvifically (29:24).[118] The לְבָב of the rash will בִּין in order 'to know' (32:4). Then

---

and shuns the 'principle' of wisdom as merely moral obedience or modesty but rather thinks it is "the renouncing of autonomy, and trusting acknowledgment of the LORD at every step of one's practical or intellectual progress. Thus understood, the saying explains the emphasis on wisdom as a gift of God, something coming from him, as in Solomon's case, and according to Proverbs 2:6" (ibid., 18). This would represent an emphasis on the *subjective* aspect with dependence on revelation functioning as the *objective* aspect.

[118] This occurs within a redemption passage (29:17–24) where the deaf will hear (29:18a), the blind will see (29:18b), the mockers will vanish (29:20a), those who do evil will be punished (29:20b), legal jurisprudence will be just (29:21), Jacob will no longer be ashamed (29:22) but will honor Yahweh appropriately (29:23), and the

there will be abundance of salvation, wisdom, and 'knowledge' (33:6). The desire of the Lord is that they might רָאָה, 'know,' and שָׂכַל that he has worked events for their good (41:20). These effects are predicated on his promise to bring the blind by a way they do not 'know' in a path they do not 'know' and by making the darkness light (42:16). He will do a new thing and they will 'know' it (43:19), 'show' (רָאָה) them things they will declare, and 'show' (רָאָה) new things, even hidden things they have not 'known' (48:6). Then Israel will 'know' that he is Lord (49:23) and 'know' his name (52:6). It is by this salvific 'knowledge' (possibly a *functional-ontological* sense) that God's righteous servant justifies many (53:11) including Gentiles (55:5). *Functional* senses also occur. Because of Yahweh's covenant and its effects, Israel will then be fulfilled ('known') among the nations and all that רָאָה them will acknowledge their status with Yahweh (61:9).

The ontological-functional wisdom of Yahweh. Isaiah often stresses, in a polemic sense, the nature (*ontology*) of Yahweh as the only wise God who is known through wisdom. Concerning the *functions* of his wisdom, it is asked whether its effects (from its *function*) are 'known' or שָׁמַע of or whether any have been told of them or if בִּין it (wisdom) from the foundation of the earth (40:21). Yahweh declares things (his wisdom) from the beginning that people may 'know' but there is none who שָׁמַע his words (41:26). He even declares beforehand and will bring about the coming messianic age so that no one can say, "Yes, I 'knew' them" (48:7). Concerning the *ontology* of God's wisdom, it is asked whether they have 'known' or שָׁמַע that there is no searching of the Lord's תְּבוּנָה (40:28). The effect of such is that Yahweh can be trusted precisely because no one has directed the spirit/wind of the Lord (אֶת־רוּחַ יְהוָה), no counselor has 'taught' him (40:13), counseled him to בִּין, taught him דַּעַת, or made 'known' the way of תְּבוּנָה (40:14). His ontology is unique in not only what he knows to be so but knows not to be so (44:8). Indeed, Israel is to 'know' this also and that he is the doer of all things, both good and bad (45:6). It is he who gives his servant a tongue that 'knows' the word that sustains

---

wayward will gain 'perception' and accept 'instruction.' Gaining 'perception' (probably through instruction) is an example of a *functional-ontological* usage. Thus they come to perceive 'salvifically' not to 'be saved' but as a result of being saved. A *functional* and non-salvific sense is where God promises Cyrus hidden riches so he will 'know' that the Lord predicted his success (45:3).

the weary (50:4, 7). He is the wise God who gives or withholds salvific wisdom at will.

The ontological inability of idols to mimic Yahweh's wisdom. Some cases are *functional* in emphasis. Those who trust in idols are challenged to declare the former things, to consider them (lay it to לֵב) and 'know' (predict) the final outcome (41:22). Isaiah sarcastically asks them to tell the future so everyone will 'know' that they are gods (41:23). Stargazers who 'know' months (make predictions) are unable to divert disaster (47:13). On an *ontological-functional* level, idol makers and their witnesses neither רָאָה nor 'know' anything (44:9) and those who worship idols simply do not 'know' in a salvific sense at all (45:20).

The knowledge of judgment or that bringing on judgment. Judgment is used for the purpose of making Yahweh known in some way. Several cases involve merely *functional* acknowledgments. When judgment falls on Israel (Assyrian invasion), all people will 'know' (recognize) that this comes from Yahweh (9:8; 37:20) or that Israel's God is the true Savior of Israel (49:26; 60:16). Other *functional* usages involve different nuances. Babylon says in its לֵבָב that it will not be either a widow or 'know' (experience) the loss of its children (47:8). Evil and desolation will come on Babylon when it does not 'know' (anticipate) it (47:11). The messianic servant 'knows' (experience the effects of) sickness because of the sins of others (53:3). One instance is *ontological-functional.* Egypt's swift judgment will lead its citizens to 'know' Yahweh in a salvific way (19:21).[119] Coming to know him, "They will turn to the Lord and he will respond to their pleas and heal them" (19:22). This is the exact pattern in Isa 6:9–10 except it applies to Egypt.

Several ideas summarize this survey. First, some in Israel do not possess the *ontological-functional* noetic quality of 'knowing' leading to bad behavior and divine punitive action (captivity).[120] Second, others

---

[119] Isaiah 19:19–22 (cf. 6:9–10). Here Egypt, Assyria, and Israel together will benefit salvifically from Yahweh (19:23–24). The order of salvation is important. It is only (1) after Yahweh makes himself *known* and (2) after they *know* Yahweh that they (3) *turn* to him and (4) he *heals* them.

[120] Tsevat argues opposite for a transformational, retributional, and therefore non-congenital view of fattening (Tsevat, "The Throne Vision of Isaiah," 163). Against this view the following points are raised: (1) It is based on an unwarranted assumption that "their guilt issues from the sinfulness of Judah (and Israel), accruing over the decades and centuries before Uzziah's death" (ibid., 163). But he offers no reason for

'know' the Lord, listen to him, and look forward to a salvation by the suffering servant who also has the spirit/wind of wisdom. Third, the particularly wicked (*functional-ontological*) do not understand because they do not 'know' Yahweh. This privation leads to idolatry and turns their sagacity into foolishness. Fourth, a salvific eschatological period is depicted in terms of granting wisdom and its effects (*ontological-functional*) on a universal scale (including non-ethnic Israel). Fifth, Yahweh and his spirit/wind are described in terms of wisdom in its fullness (*ontological-functional*) and because of this he 'knows' all things, including the future. Sixth, idols and idolatry in general cannot mimic Yahweh's wisdom and their failure is evident in the less than accurate prognostications of its prophets. Finally, the suddenness of Yahweh's justice takes those without wisdom unawares or without 'knowing' it. Everything in Isaiah is geared around the return of salvific wisdom and its effects.

The Wisdom Notion of Understanding.[121] An additional term שָׂכַל appears in a reuse of Isa 6:9–10 in 44:18. It occurs thrice while the nominal form not at all.[122] This word (along with תְּבוּנָה) is used of a future benefit of salvation, a feature deprived from lost Israel, a quality of the suffering servant, and as an attribute of the spirit/wind of the Lord. Each of these involves *ontological-functional* examples. On an eschatological note, Isa 41:20 specifies a time of blessing when the people will רָאָה, יָדַע, 'consider' (שִׂים) and שָׂכַל that the hand of the Lord has done all this. In 44:18–19 (as noted above), however, they currently יָדַע not nor בִּין because God has 'shut' ('smeared over') their eyes so they cannot רָאָה and their לֵב so they cannot שָׂכַל. No one

---

either the bad behavior arising from a non-fattened heart or for a retributive notion. (2) He concedes that his view of fattening in Isaiah *differs* from those mentioned in previous hardening episodes (Pharaoh and Sihon) but only in terms of beginning or end of a stage of judgment. He does not mention other significant differences.

[121] See Shupak, *Where Can Wisdom be Found?* 247–49. He notes five principle meanings of the term: (1) to give attention, to consider; (2) to be prudent, act prudently; (3) to prosper, have success, the result of behavior mentioned in (2); (4) to teach, give insight to someone; and (5) to understand, have comprehension (ibid., 247). "A feature common to all these applications is that the subject of *skl* is always man and not God" (ibid., 248).

[122] 41:20; 44:18; 52:13. The nominal form of 'understanding' (תְּבוּנָה), occurs three times in Isaiah (40:14; 40:28; 44:19).

returns to his לֵב neither is there דַּעַת or תְּבוּנָה. God's servant, however, will deal 'wisely' (with שָׂכַל) in his vicarious role for which he will subsequently be exalted and lifted up (52:13). Twice תְּבוּנָה is used in pointing to God's inscrutable understanding. Neither the spirit/wind of the Lord has need of instruction in 'knowledge' or 'understanding' (40:13–14) nor the Lord himself because he possesses an 'understanding' that is inscrutably boundless (40:28).

The communication of wisdom to individuals is gratuitous, results in a *removal* of the fat-heart and thus effects noetic (*ontological*) change, and produces (*functionally*) conformity to Yahweh's law and other demands.

Sapiential Motifs

Each motif below simply reinforces in various ways the sapiential notions mentioned above. The focus may be *ontological, ontological-functional, functional,* or *functional-ontological*. In addition, the subject matter may be salvific or non-salvific or involve universal or particularized situations. These motifs impact Isa 6:9–10 and its relationship to the wisdom notions.

Hearing and Seeing.[123] שָׁמַע and רָאָה occur some eighteen times in Isaiah.[124] It can generally be confined to four areas of activity or ability.

Human nature may inhibit seeing and hearing. Isaiah 30:9–10 focuses on the rebellious attitude of Israel in not trusting Yahweh but rather foreign alliances with Egypt (30:1–2). When Yahweh's advice comes from the prophet they refuse to 'hear' (listen or heed). The 'seeing' refers to the 'seers'—thus the motif here is loose. This *rebellion* is credited to hatred for Yahweh's law (30:9–10) and contempt for the prophet's instructions.[125] Human nature by *nature* is rebellious but it

---

[123] See Ronald E. Clements, "The Unity of the Book of Isaiah," *Int* 36 (1982): 117–29 who notes the motif of spiritual blindness and deafness as a prominent theme in Isa 40–66 (second Isaiah).

[124] Isa 6:9, 10; 18:3; 21:3; 30:9–10, 20–21, 30; 32:3; 33:15, 19; 37:17; 39:4–5; 42:18, 20; 52:15; 64:3; 66:8, 19.

[125] McKane, *Prophets and Wise Men*, 71–72. The law (תּוֹרָה) is mentioned twelve times in Isaiah (1:10; 2:3; 5:24; 8:16, 20; 24:5; 30:9; 42:4, 21, 24; 51:4, 7). The verbal form (יָרָה) occurs only once (2:3). Isaiah conflates the wisdom tradition with the law that reflects what is generally regarded as later developments in wisdom thinking, viz., nomistic

is flexible (diversified and iterative) by function and hence this event is an example of the *ontological-functional* category. *Functional* examples are physical failures to hear due to physical pain (21:3) or to see or hear of Yahweh's fame (18:3). Noetic failures address *moral* inability while functional only the *natural* inability (accident of geography or opportunity to hear a message).

Human nature may inhibit the benefits of seeing and hearing. The 'fat-hearted' physically see and hear but do not noetically perceive or know Yahweh (6:10–11). The former couplet 'is *functional* while the latter is *ontological-functional* and refers to noetic and moral privations. Natural physical *ability* to hear is accompanied by the moral *inability* to salvifically perceive or know. This same sense is found in Isa 42:20. Apart from the divine initiative, *this condition describes all peoples of all times*. A *functional* example occurs when they cannot hear or see (understand) the Assyrian language and refers to a natural (not moral) inability to understand it (33:19). This can be naturally overcome and therefore it may be termed *functional-ontological*. The language barrier (*functional*) can be overcome with learning whereas the former noetic barrier (*ontological-functional*) cannot apart from the divine initiative—no amount of acquired wisdom can change one's nature. When hearing and seeing depict physical features, it refers to a natural ability but when it designates a noetic issue, it refers to a moral/mental inability.

The righteous limit or enhance seeing and hearing. The righteous effect seeks to live godly (*functional-ontological*). They close their ears to (not entertaining) murder and their eyes from seeing evil (33:15; cf. 1QIsaᵃ 6:9–10).[126] A *functional* sense may apply to Yahweh 'doing' something in response to prayer. Hezekiah petitions Yahweh 'to see and hear' threats of Sennacherib (37:17). Later he prays for healing and gets it (38:5). Yahweh 'hears' (responds) to his prayers. An *ontological-functional* occurrence is in the age of salvation where the eyes will not

---

and personifying tendencies (cf. Saebo, "חמכ," *TLOT* 1:424). Sonnet says law is a wisdom term (Sonnet, "Le motif de l'endurcissement (Is 6,9–10) et la lecture d' «Isaïe»," 212).

[126] It is this passage, geared towards the righteous remnant, that provides the segue for the re-interpretation and midrash of Isa 6:9–10 in 1QIsaᵃ 6:9–10. In other words, the righteous remnant refuses to entertain the prospect of either murder or doing evil. This passage of Isaiah (33:15) is used in the DSS (1QHa 15:1–3) to assert this very notion with regard to the Qumranites. See below. Incidentally, this is the only place in Isaiah where closing the eyes and ears is portrayed in positive terms.

be dim and the ears will hear (32:3). These are noetic traits that accompany salvation.

The divine role in seeing and hearing. On a *functional* level, Yahweh's voice and judgment may be heard and seen (30:30). He is a God who man has neither seen nor heard, namely, experienced his interventions (64:3[4]). On an *ontological-functional* level, Yahweh effectually calls, through his servant, the deaf to hear, the blind to see (42:18), and causes captive Israel to see their teachers and hear his word (30:20–21)—this latter could be *functional-ontological*. Because of the Messiah, he will bless nations by enabling them to understand (52:15; cf. Rom 15:21). Isaiah thereby emphasizes the significance of wisdom and highlights the messianic servant's role in securing this ability.

Perceiving and Knowing. The second motif pair is בִּין and יָדַע. This combination is weightier than the former and occurs eight times in Isaiah.[127] If a synonym for שָׂכַל is added to the mix, it occurs once with בִּין and יָדַע (44:18) and one time with יָדַע (41:20). This motif specifies four basic aspects involving Israel's purpose for existence (43:10), its present state (1:3; 6:9; 5:21; 44:18)[128] and future hope (32:4; 43:18–19; 41:20), and its relationship to false shepherds (40:13–14; 56:11). Each of these is *ontological-functional* while one may be *functional-ontological* (56:11).

Isaiah 44:18 proves a strong divine causality behind man's inability to *perceive, know,* and *understand* God. Furthermore, this inability is linked to the 'fat-heart.' 'Blinding' and 'deafening' are either circumlocutions for fattening the heart, a figure of speech citing the effect for the cause, or both.[129] Therefore, blinding the eyes,

---

[127] Isa 1:3; 6:9; 32:4; 40:13–14; 43:10, 18–19; 44:18; 56:11.

[128] The use of animal proverbs in wisdom literature is frequent (Prov 6:6–8; 7:22; 14:4; 26:3, 11, 17; 27:8; 28:1; 30:18, 24–31). See Jensen, *The Use of Tôrâ by Isaiah*, 26–42.

[129] Oftentimes there is an interchange of actions normally associated with one organ (heart) but applied to another or *vise versa.* For example, in 1 Kgs 3:9 the heart is labeled 'a *hearing* heart' (cf. Ezek 40:4; Ps 10:17; Prov 15:32; 22:17). Although the heart is frequently referred to as 'uncircumcised,' (another obvious case of transferal!) this same phenomenon is applied to the ears (Jer 9:25; 1QHa 21:5). 'Haughtiness of heart' (Jer 48:29) is 'haughtiness of eyes' in Qumran (4Q184 f2:5; 4Q435 f2i:5; 4Q436 f1ii:3). In one Qumran text (4Q298 f1 2:100), every man's heart is admonished to 'hear.' The association and blending of such figures indicate that the 'hearing ear' and the 'seeing eyes' are essential and simultaneous functioning aspects of the heart. When the heart

making deaf the ears, and fattening the heart are designations for *depriving* the heart from understanding by leaving it its fattened state. This is relevant especially since the inability to salvifically 'know' and 'perceive' is prior to Isa 6 (1:3; 5:21), and the lack of these attributes describe the fat-heart. The conclusion is that they are already fat-hearted prior to the injunctions in Isa 6:9–10. This is supported by the exegesis of Isa 6:9–10 and subsequent tradition and favors a non-transformational if not a non-retributional basis of fattening.

Hearing and Perceiving. The third motif, שָׁמַע and בִּינָה/בִּין, occurs five times in Isaiah.[130] The movement is always *from* hearing *to* perceiving. Only one case involves a *functional* usage (33:19). However, when it involves an *ontological-functional* aspect, it always refers to a salvific issue (6:9–10; 32:33–34). Isaiah 52:15 is a reversal text, occurs in the context of the effects wrought by the suffering servant, and carries with it significant soteriological overtones. It states "that which they have not heard shall they perceive."[131] It is from Isa 52:13–53:12 that all future looking restoration passages find their genesis.[132]

In each case, mere physical and *functional* hearing is contrasted to *ontological* and noetic 'perceiving.' This condition is only to be *fully* realized, or realized to a greater extent, in the messianic age/kingdom because of the salvific work of the servant. Mankind as a whole possesses an *ontologically* fat-heart and his work reverses this condition in behalf of the many (including Jews and Gentiles) through his atonement.

---

functions properly (in a non-fattened state), it sees and hears salvifically. When one hears and sees, perceives, knows, and understands, it is because the heart is non-fat.

[130] 6:9, 10; 32:3–4; 33:19; 52:15.

[131] Isa 33:6 says, "He [Messiah] will be the sure foundation for your times, a rich store of *salvation* [יְשׁוּעָה] and *wisdom* [חָכְמָה] and *knowledge* [דַּעַת]; *the fear of the Lord* [יְהוָה יִרְאַת] is the key to this treasure" (NIV). The effects of wisdom including salvation, knowledge, and fear of the Lord, are all associated with the benefits that accrue from the Messiah. This restoration of wisdom in salvific terms (or salvation in wisdom terms) is the key in understanding Isa 52:13–53:12 as the *par excellence* reversal passage to Isa 6:9–10.

[132] For similar remarks on this reversal theme as it relates to wisdom issues see Williamson, *The Book Called Isaiah,* 48–49.

Seeing and Knowing. The fourth motif is רָאָה and דַּעַת/יָדַע which occurs ten times in Isaiah.[133] There are several *ontological-functional* usages. In 5:12–13 the people do not 'see' (consider) the work of Yahweh's hands and have no 'knowledge,' and because they have no knowledge they go into captivity (cf. 6:9). Knowledge in these texts is salvific. In Isa 44:9 the makers of idols and their witnesses are those who *never* (בַּל) 'see,' *never* (בַּל) 'know,' and will therefore be put to shame. This refers to a universal *privation* that manifests itself here in idol-making.[134] Isaiah 32:3–4 and 53:11 also fit here.[135]

A *functional-ontological* example occurs in Isa 41:20. The context refers to the Lord's commitment to Israel his servant and predicts their return to the land in its pristine form. This display demonstrates his wisdom in contrast to the false gods and pseudo-wisdom of other nations. The effect on the nations and Israel is "so that people may יִרְאוּ and וְיֵדְעוּ, may וְיָשִׂימוּ and וְיַשְׂכִּילוּ, that the hand of the Lord has done this, that the Holy One of Israel has created it."

Some cases are *functional*. In 5:19 the prophet indicts people who taunt Yahweh to hasten his work so they may 'see' and 'know' his plan. In 29:15 it refers to the wicked who think no one 'sees' or 'knows' them in the sense of finding out what they are up to. Isaiah 47:10 points to the false assurance of Babylon borne from a false wisdom. "'No one *sees* me.' Your חָכְמָה and דַּעַת mislead you when you say to yourself, 'I am, and there is none besides me.'" Finally, in Isa 58:3 the 'seeing' of the people's fasting is linked with Yahweh taking 'knowledge' of their self-affliction by doing something about it.

---

[133] 5:12–13, 19; 6:9; 29:15; 32:3–4; 44:9; 47:10; 53:11; 58:11. This search has been expanded from the normal five words differential to ten words on Accordance.

[134] The statement, "Bowlers never live forever" does not imply either that non-bowlers do live forever or even that some non-bowlers live forever. The temporality of life is particularized in the statement to bowlers but it is not confined to them. Idolaters may never 'know' in the salvific sense here, but this does not imply either that non-idolaters are excluded or that non-idolaters do 'know' salvifically. To suggest that only some people are 'evil' rather than everyone is equally untenable. See Ps 36:2 and Rom 3:18 where a particular is universalized to include everyone.

[135] The final occurrence is in Isa 53:11 where God the Father 'sees' the travail of the servant's soul and is satisfied. Then by the servant's 'knowledge' of himself he justifies many and bears their iniquities. Here 'knowledge' is pictured as a causative agent in salvation.

Two points may be noted. First, the direction of 'seeing' to 'knowing' is one-way. Second, in nearly every case the 'seeing' is *functional* whereas the 'knowing,' when concerned with salvation, is noetic and *ontological*. While the former is the gateway for the noetic, it is the latter's *ontology* that determines how that information is processed, construed, and whether it is accepted.

Missing or Rare Motifs. The motif of שָׁמַע and שֶׂכֶל/שָׂכַל occurs nowhere in Isaiah or anywhere else in the OT. The motif of בִּינָה/בִּין and שֶׂכֶל/שָׂכַל occurs nowhere in Isaiah, however, it is found outside it. The motif of יָדַע and שָׂכַל occurs twice. Isaiah 41:20 indicates a time when Judah will רָאָה, יָדַע, and שָׂכַל that he has worked events for their good (41:20). This is either an *ontological-functional* usage or a *functional-ontological* instance depending on whether it is a necessary outgrowth of salvation or a further actualization of that ontology. Isaiah 44:18 may be included as an *ontological-functional* perspective describing the deprivation of the new heart.

Seeing and Understanding. The motif of רָאָה and שֶׂכֶל/שָׂכַל occurs twice. The first is Isa 41:20 mentioned above. Isaiah 44:18 is more instructive. It uses a host of wisdom terminology, provides a helpful parallelism for understanding the relationship involved among these terms, points to the subject as Yahweh, is a reuse of Isa 6:9–10, and supports a non-punitive and non-transformational view of fattening. It says, "They יָדַע not, neither do they בִּין: for he has shut their eyes, so that they cannot רָאָה; and their לֵב so that they cannot שָׂכַל." Some aspects may be highlighted.

First, there is a double verbal parallelism with the terms 'know' and 'see' and 'perceive' and 'understand.' 'To see' is roughly equivalent with 'to know' as 'to perceive' is with 'to understand' so that to 'not see' is equivalent to 'not knowing' and 'not perceiving' is equal to 'not understanding.' Second, it is Yahweh who smears the eyes from seeing (knowing) and (smears) the heart away from understanding (perceiving). Confirmation of this point is that no Hebrew text, including Qumran, changes this verb (טָחַח) from a third person singular to a third person plural as if "they smear their own eyes" via idolatry. The LXX does change the verb to the third person but it is clearly the *divine* passive. To shift the implied agent to idols or idolatry bears the burden of proof.[136] Third, since no necessary (human) cause is mentioned, fattening must be non-punitive and an example stemming instead from *strong* divine causality. Idolatry is not the cause for smearing the eyes and heart but rather one of a plethora of *functional* effects stemming from Yahweh smearing both. Fourth, since there is no condition provided, then it is unlikely that this 'smearing' of the eyes and heart is transformative in any sense and most likely simply picturesque for divine *deprivation* of the new heart.

Seeing and Perceiving. This motif involves the combination of רָאָה and בִּין and occurs five times in Isaiah.[137] A proleptic but purely *functional* sense occurs in 14:16 where 'gaze' and 'attention' are given to the fallen Babylonian king. The rest involve an *ontological-functional* aspect of the heart and are soteriological in nature (6:9; 32:3–4; 44:18; 52:15).

Hearing and Knowing. This motif (שָׁמַע and יָדַע) occurs ten times.[138] A *functional* usage occurs in 33:13 where the people of Assyria and Judah are admonished to 'hear' what the Lord has done (with respect

---

[136] As will be shown below, the exact same phenomenon is found in the LXX translation of Isa 6:9–10 where 'fattening' is also in the passive voice. It is perhaps even more difficult to suggest here that some intermediate agency (other than personal) is responsible for the effect because the context of Isa 6 lacks anything like idolatry. But as in 44:18, the implied agent of the passive voice is Yahweh. What the Hebrew text of Isa 6:9–10 lacks by way of clear subject is made up for in 44:18. The primary reason is because the subject of the verb in the Hebrew text (*every* Hebrew text available) of 44:18 is distinct from the objects ('he' versus 'they'). To propose a Hebrew *Vorlage* behind the LXX that is based on a particular reading of these and other versions lacks evidence. Not only does the *Vorlage* not exist, but one must show that the LXX and other translations actually *demand* the third person plural תָחֹן rather than the third person singular הֵשַׁע. Granted, subsequent translations have the third person plural but in the *passive* not *active* or *middle* voice shifting the nature of the act away from the subjects. And this grammatical shift confirms rather well to the Hebrew in the MT/DSS in distinction to any supposed *Vorlage* with תחן, overthrows any notion that the MT/DSS should read as third person plural, and circumvents any reason to propose such a hypothetical *Vorlage*. *The fattener in Isaianic fattening is always Yahweh and never human or any other agent, mediate or otherwise.* This is controverted by no known facts.

[137] 6:9, 10; 14:16; 44:18; 52:15.

[138] 6:9; 32:3–4; 33:13; 40:21, 28; 41:22–23; 48:3–4, 6, 7–8; 51:7.

to punishing Judah) and 'acknowledge' his power.[139] Isaiah 40 addresses an *ontological-functional* privation. The link is made between Yahweh's promised salvation and his wisdom (40:1–11) that is contrasted with all else by a series of rhetorical questions (40:12–31). His wisdom and its effects should have been 'known,' because they 'heard' but did not 'perceive' (40:21).[140] They should have 'known' having 'heard' that the Lord is the everlasting God and his תְּבוּנָה is inscrutable (40:28). In referring to stubborn Israel (48:4) and the slouching towards idolatry (48:5–6), Isaiah begins an eschatological discourse as a polemic against false gods. He credits the divine prerogative for their past and present inability to comprehend—he has not opened their ears (48:7–8).

Isaiah 48:7–8 offer a few things worth noting. First, Isaiah uses this motif to highlight their lack of wisdom and credits this to the condition of having closed ears ("has not been opened" cf. Isa 50:5). This state is from "of old" or literally, "from then" (מֵאָז). Second, he acknowledges that they are treacherous (בָּגוֹד תִּבְגּוֹד) and rebels (וּפֹשֵׁעַ) but "from the belly" (מִבֶּטֶן). The parallel 'from then' and 'from the belly' suggests that Isaiah intends to highlight the inherent lack of *wisdom* (cognition) and *rebellion* (volition) as congenital yet divinely orchestrated. Proof is Isa 50:5 where opening the ear is a precondition for obviating rebellion and where the deuteronomistic tones are unmistakable.[141]

Finally, in contrast to the rebellious house of Israel, God's people are addressed throughout Isa 51 within the motif of 'hear/listen'

---

[139] This is spoken in the context of God punishing his people. Earlier Isaiah mentions that the promised deliverance will be a rich store of salvation, wisdom, knowledge, and where the fear of the Lord is the key to that treasure (33:6). Here in 33:13 it admonishes them to 'hear' and 'know' (acknowledge) his power, aspects of which are evidence of this salvific wisdom. Finally, it depicts the righteous who stop their ears in hearing of plots of murder and shuts their eyes in contemplating evil depicting a reversal of the effects of fattening in ironic terms (33:15b). Thus the full circle of wisdom salvation is seen in this chapter. The effects of wisdom bring a repentance that offsets punishment—the identical pattern of Isa 6:9–10. Without it, however, they are doomed to produce nothing but unrighteous deeds requiring discipline and punishment.

[140] This is thematically alluded to in Rom 10:18–21.

[141] Isaiah follows a Deuteronomic pattern of Yahweh withholding the new heart (Deut 2:30; 4:29; 5:29; 6:5; 8:2; 9:4–5, 10:12, 16; 11:13, 16, 18; 13:3; 15:7; 17:17, 20; 26:16; 28:28, 47; 29:3, 17, 18; 30:2, 6, 10, 14, 17; 32:46).

(51:1, 4, 7) and 'look/see' (51:1, 2, 5, 6) in *ontological-functional* language. These are those who pursue righteousness and seek the Lord (51:1), who will be saved and are ransomed with an everlasting salvation by God's strong arm (51:5, 6, 8, 9, 11). They indeed 'hear' the Lord, 'know' what is right, and have the law written in their hearts (51:7).[142]

Three caveats are necessary here. First, that Israel is blind and rebellious from birth only implies that each and every Israelite is congenitally absent of wisdom and an obedient heart not that each and every one is such presently. It may express one's *ontological-functional* past status rather than every particular individual's present status. Some are recipients of the new heart and do salvifically see, hear, perceive, know, and understand. Yahweh has 'opened' their ears, etc.

Second, the statements about Israel are not simply *functional* aspects but rather *ontological-functional* as 'from then' and 'from the belly' suggest. The nation is cast as a single personality that is *functionally* evil because it is *ontologically* (in the heart) evil. Ontological evil accounts for functional effects. That present inabilities are the result of bad behavior lacks support. What prompted them to act badly in the first place but an evil nature? If a nature is inclined to both good and evil then what decisively inclines the will to choose evil unless the strongest inclination at the moment of choice is itself evil to begin with? And what causes this evil inclination to be the strongest at the moment of choice as opposed to a good inclination if not another evil inclination...*ad infinitum*? The *functional* position alone neglects first causes, gives no causes, and remains, for those reasons, incoherent.

Finally, no text implies—nor can it be inferred—that prior to this indictment these individuals were at one time innocent, open eared, having seeing eyes, and possessors of salvific wisdom, but then *became* rebellious, blind and deaf, and dispossessed of wisdom because they acted badly. Were they really good people who practiced evil and therefore became evil people practicing evil who

---

[142] The association of wisdom, the Spirit, the fear of the Lord, and the law is a common collocation in later Jewish writings and on into the NT. The law becomes not only the locus of wisdom but both the standard (through obedience) by which one measures his wisdom and the goal in the pursuit of still more wisdom. See Davis, *Wisdom and Spirit*. He notes that in Sirach, for example, "the quest for wisdom is to be pursued through the understanding and interpretation of the law" (ibid., 15–16).

nevertheless become good people again by stopping the practice of evil? What are they now using in that *depleted* state to become good again? Is this absence of salvific wisdom type of wisdom better than salvific wisdom? If they are only *now* blind, deaf, and without salvific wisdom, what type of deafness, blindness, and foolishness do these individuals now possess and what kind of fanciful hope could there be that they would now or ever be wiser in this condition than before? Does not Deut 5:29 refute such a functional theory of evil?

The Text of Isa 6:9–10[143]

וַיֹּ֣אמֶר לֵ֗ךְ וְאָמַרְתָּ֙ לָעָ֣ם הַזֶּ֔ה שִׁמְע֤וּ שָׁמ֙וֹעַ֙ וְאַל־תָּבִ֔ינוּ וּרְא֥וּ רָא֖וֹ וְאַל־תֵּדָֽעוּ׃

הַשְׁמֵן֙ לֵב־הָעָ֣ם הַזֶּ֔ה וְאָזְנָ֥יו הַכְבֵּ֖ד וְעֵינָ֣יו הָשַׁ֑ע פֶּן־יִרְאֶ֨ה בְעֵינָ֜יו וּבְאָזְנָ֣יו

יִשְׁמָ֗ע וּלְבָב֥וֹ יָבִ֛ין וָשָׁ֖ב וְרָ֥פָא לֽוֹ׃

Exegesis of the Masoretic Text of Isa 6:9–10

Structure and Issues.[144] These verses do not present so much the *content* of Isaiah's message as much as both the *purpose* for it and the desired divine *effect* of it.[145] The emphases in the commands of 6:9–10 lie in the prohibition of 'perception' (6:9b, 10f) and 'knowing' (6:9c).[146] The structure of the passage in 6:10 is chiastic ABC::C'B'A' with 'shut their eyes' and 'lest they see with their eyes' occupying the C:C' positions, 'close their ears' and 'lest they hear with their ears' the B:B'

---

[143] Text used is *BHS*. For textual critical discussion see Volker A. Lehnert, *Die Provakation Israels: die paradoxe Funktion von Jes 6,9–10 bei Markus und Lukas: ein textpragmatischer Versuch im Kontext gegenwartiger Rezeptionsasthetik und Lesetheorie*, NDH, vol. 25 (Neukirchen-Vluyn: Neikirchener, 1999), 11.

[144] Franz Hesse, *Das Verstockungsproblem im alten Testament: Eine frömmigkeits geschichtliche Untersuchung*, BZAW, vol. 74 (Berlin: Töpelmann, 1955), 60–78; Joachim Gnilka, *Die Verstockung Israels: Isaias 6:9–10 in der Theologie der Synoptiker*, SANT, ed. Vinzenz Hamp and Josef Schmid, vol. 3 (Munich: Kösel, 1961), 13–16; Lehnert, *Die Provakation Israels*, 11–20, 102–27; Günter Röhser, *Prädestination und Verstockung: Untersuchungen zur frühjüdischen, paulinischen und johanneischen Theologie*, TANZ, ed. Klaus Berger, vol. 14 (Tübingen: Francke, 1994), 40, 141, 194, 243, 247.

[145] Sheppard asks "What is the message that the people in Isaiah's day are too blind to see and too deaf to hear" (Sheppard, "The Book of Isaiah," 575)? Isaiah's message is essentially, "Fear not" with the sense that they should not fear others in the face of danger but only Yahweh. This theme is consistent throughout Isaiah.

[146] Cf. Tsevat, "The Throne Vision of Isaiah," 159–61.

slot, and the 'heart' as either 'fat' or not 'perceiving' as the inclusio (A:A').[147] Each parallelism is antithetical so that 'fat' is opposite of 'perceiving' when it pertains to the heart, 'closed' is opposite of 'hearing' when applied to the ears, and 'shut' is opposite of 'seeing' when applied to the eyes.

```
A Fatten their heart
   B Close their ears
      C Shut their eyes
         D Lest
      C' See with their eyes
   B' Hear with their ears
A' Perceive with their heart
And turn
And I should heal them
```

This structure not only suggests that the 'fat' (שָׁמֵן) heart is one without בִּין, but that 'heavy ears' to 'hearing,' and 'shut' eyes to 'seeing' are also meant to be taken as antonyms. This indicates that Isaiah conceives of fattening and the fat-heart as relating to the absence of wisdom. It may affect/effect volitional issues (repenting), but the 'fattening' itself only involves the cognitive aspect of the heart.

Because 'fattening' of 6:10 is in the Hiphil imperative, the act (rather than state) arguably may be in terms of *deprivation* or *depletion* of wisdom from the heart or least likely by a *depositing* into the heart the opposite effects of wisdom.[148] The semantic relationship between 6:9 and 6:10 is one of effect to cause but the relationship within 6:10 is from cause to effect.[149] The *effects*, namely, of hearing but not perceiving, or seeing and not knowing (6:9) is *caused* by the fat-heart that lacks understanding and as such closes the ears and shuts the eyes (6:10).

---

[147] See J. L. McLaughlin, "Their Hearts Were Hardened: The Use of Isaiah 6,9–10 in the Book of Isaiah," *Bib* 75 (1994): 5. There are two terms used for heart in Isa 6:10.

[148] Although *deposition* is a viable option, no one actually adopts it.

[149] Scott points out that figures from effect to cause and cause to effect, among other things, are marks of wisdom influence (Scott, *The way of wisdom in the Old Testament*, 127; cf. Wolff, *Joel and Amos*, 93). Wolff indicates that didactic questions in free witness-speech are such that "the interrogative style, the series constructions, and the method of analogical reasoning are in accord with sapiential instruction and debate" (ibid.).

The *ultimate* (and *mediate*) cause of the fat-heart is identified by the agent of the Hiphil imperatives—'*cause* to be fat' (הַשְׁמֵן), '*cause* to be heavy' (הַכְבֵּד), and '*cause* to be shut' (הָשַׁע).[150] The nature of this cause in terms of its effect is in dispute here. Is it creative (thus transformational) or continuative (non-transformational)? Discerning the *nature* of the cause is essential in discovering the *role* of the agent in terms of how he causes fattening (by depletion, deprivation, or deposition). And these issues are informed by the nature of the heart in relation to (salvific) wisdom itself. The recipients of this act are referred to contemptuously as 'this people' (לָעָם הַזֶּה).[151] The foil to this audience is the remnant spoken of in 6:13 to whom this message is not directed—although they not only see and hear but they perceive and know it. The effects, involving the inability to perceive or know, find their source in the fat-heart. The ultimate cause of the fat-heart is Yahweh *through* his prophet (mediate cause) in either a causally *creative* (transformative) or *continuative* (non-transformative) manner. If a causally creative means is adopted then bad deeds function on a level of a contributory condition. If a causally continuative means is adopted then the heart of man is the material cause while the discretion of Yahweh is the final cause. Decisions in these matters significantly impact how one approaches NT texts.

Isaiah 6:9. Isaiah is commissioned to go to this people and say,[152] "Hear indeed but do not perceive, see indeed but do not know." The consequence or effect (without mention of the content) of his message

---

[150] Tsevat holds that Isaiah is the agent of these verbs (Tsevat, "The Throne Vision of Isaiah," 164). That Isaiah is an agent is not the issue. Two issues surface. First, what type of agency does Isaiah and his words occupy? Second, what type of causation is involved, *creative* (transformative) or *continuative* (non-transformational)?

[151] The phrase occurs ten times in Isaiah always with a derogatory tone (6:9, 10; 8:6, 11, 12; 9:15; 28:11, 14; 29:13, 14; cf. 23:13). See E. Kautzsch and A. E. Cowley, *Gesenius' Hebrew Grammar*, 2d English ed. (Oxford: Clarendon, 1910), §136b; Clements, *Isaiah 1–39*, 76; Kaiser, *Isaiah 1–12*, 131 n. 74; Milgrom, "Did Isaiah Prophesy during the Reign of Uzziah?" 172 n. 3; Vriezen, "Essentials of the Theology of Isaiah," 128, 33; Robert B. Chisholm Jr., *Handbook on the Prophets* (Grand Rapids: Baker, 2002), 26; Sonnet, "Le motif de l'endurcissement (Is 6,9–10) et la lecture d' «Isaïe»," 216.

[152] 'Go and say' is a commissioning formula used throughout the OT (Gen 41:55; Deut 5:30; Josh 9:11; 2 Sam 7:5; 1 Kgs 14:7; 18:8, 11, 14; 2 Kgs 6:3; 8:10; Isa 1:18; 6:9; 1 Chr 17:4). Kaiser notes the detached tone and the disparaging connotations here (Kaiser, *Isaiah 1–12*, 131).

(which they hear and see) to their noetic inability (perceive/know) may be understood in terms of *producing a new state, continuing a state based on a past act,* or *continuing a congenital state.*[153] These three views are set forth here.

Transformational view. A constitutional (ontological?) change occurs in the nature or state of the heart from non-fat to fat. In this sense 'fattening' is produced from what was not to what now is. The cause is due to bad behavior and is therefore brought on by divine retribution. This retribution can take the form of either *depletion* of wisdom or *deposition* of foolishness.

Transformational or *congenital view.* Either position is compatible with the idea that Isaiah's preaching makes apparent the fat-hearted condition of the hearers. The former assumes, however, that there was a time when the heart was not fat, that it produced bad effects in that non-fattened state, that the result of these deeds was divine retribution, that this retribution took the form of divine fattening, and that the fat-heart results in a constitutional change.[154] The congenital view assumes that the heart is always fat apart from the divine initiative and therefore any occasion that reveals the heart as fat is perfectly compatible with making it apparent at any time. The text suggests that they are already fat-hearted so either view is contextually supported.

Congenital view. The idea that fattening continues an on-going phenomenon. Here, fattening does not have a *terminus a quo* related to

---

[153] "In our opinion the paronomastic infinitive is always an intensifying infinitive.... The intensifying infinitive almost always occurs postpositively with *wayyqtl,* the imperative, and the participle" (Bruce K. Waltke and M. O'Connor, *An Introduction to Biblical Hebrew Syntax* [Winona Lake, IN: Eisenbrauns, 1990], §35.3.1.d). They render Isa 6:9 as "Hear indeed but do not comprehend!" and hold that it makes an affirmation in strong contrast to what follows (ibid., §35.3.1.f).

[154] Kaiser concludes that "Only from the divine commission and the prospect given in 8:11f. can we conclude that the people's sickness consists of a lack of fear of God and an inappropriate fear of men, and all the consequences which in practice arise from that .... What finds its clear fulfillment in Jer. 5.21 in the framework of a rebuke and in Deut. 29.3 in a retrospect of the history of the people, both in a natural context, here needs to be explained by a reference back, and thus opens itself to the suspicion of being parasitical on these sayings. The blindness of the people, which according to v. 10b is *already their state,* is not to be removed by the appearance of the prophet, but rather to be heightened.... If anyone hardens his heart, God will complete the hardening. Anyone whose heart is hardened has his condition made even worse by the call to repent" (Kaiser, *Isaiah 1–12,* 131–32 emphasis added).

behavior, it is not retributive, and it is not transformational. Divine fattening takes the form of *deprivation* of wisdom. The biblical texts either assume man's heart is fat or point to God's prerogative in leaving it that way.

This passage relates to the nature of fattening and how that occurs and what it entails. The first set of verbs (see/hear) uses paronomastic lexemes and a syntactical construction (Qal imperative + Qal infinitive absolute) in which the protasis may serve either to *emphasize* continual action or to *intensify* the verbal notion. Although the latter is preferred, either sense is acceptable. Together these initial verbs (hear/see) function rhetorically either as a straightforward command or an ironical challenge or both.[155] It is unlikely that the imperatives function *solely* in a rhetorical[156] or descriptive fashion but may be viewed, in addition to these, as prescriptive.[157] They are not only commanded to 'hear' and 'see' the message of Isaiah but indeed they will hear and see it.

---

[155] The grammatical form (Qal imper. + Qal infin. abs.) has identical verbal stems. This pattern occurs eight times in the OT (Judg 5:23; Isa 6:9*bis*; 55:2; Jer 22:10; Job 13:17; 21:2; 37:2) and serves to magnify either the *certainty of* or *intensify* the verbal idea. See Kautzsch and Cowley, *Gesenius' Hebrew Grammar*, §113r; Waltke and O'Connor, *An Introduction to Biblical Hebrew Syntax*, §§34.1d, 35.3.1. Gitay indicates that 6:9 is "a verse designed to manipulate the audience" whereas in 6:10 the "alteration provides a feeling of movement" and "the utilization of the infinitive absolute intensifies the idea of the verb and expresses as well 'the long continuance of an action'" (Gitay, "Prophetic Criticism," 114–15).

[156] The 'sarcastic' (ironic) usage of the imperative is demonstrated in 1 Kgs 2:22 where David is speaking to Bathsheba about Adonijah in his request for one of his father's (David's) virgin harem girls (Abishag the Shunammite). This request is possibly an underhanded attempt by Adonijah to usurp the kingdom away from Solomon. Solomon responds sarcastically to Bathsheba: "Request the kingdom for him—after all, he is my older brother!" Amos 4:4 is another example within a context rife with sarcasm over the pampered women ('cows of Bashan') who oppress others. The desired outcome is judgment. Therefore the Lord says, "Go to Bethel and sin; go to Gilgal and sin yet more." See Waltke and O'Connor, *An Introduction to Biblical Hebrew Syntax*, §34.4b.

[157] This is the position of Hans Wildberger, *Jesaja 28–39: Das Buch der Prophet und seine Botschaft*, BKAT, ed. M. Noth and H. W. Wolff, vol. 10 (Neukirchen-Vluyn: Neukirchener, 1982), 255 as brought out by Craig A. Evans, *To See and Not Perceive: Isaiah 6:9–10 in Early Jewish and Christian Interpretation*, JSOTSup, ed. David J. A. Clines and Philip R. Davies, vol. 64 (Sheffield: JSOT, 1989), 171 n. 9. Chisholm holds that the imperatival forms in 6:9–10 are employed rhetorically "and anticipate the response Isaiah would receive" (Chisholm, *Handbook on the Prophets*, 26).

The two positive commands in the protasis are merely physical phenomena involving hearing and seeing. The following two concessive or prohibitory verbs of the couplets are in the apodosis and are noetic phenomena of perceiving and knowing. These latter verbs are stated in the Qal imperfect tense form, preceded by אַל, "but you will *not* perceive" (וְאַל־תָּבִינוּ) and "but you will *not* know" (וְאַל־תֵּדָעוּ),[158] and best rendered with a jussive meaning, "but do not perceive...but do not know."[159] In favor of the jussive is the frequency of the form following an imperative along with the regularly occurring pattern in Isaiah.[160] Because of this likelihood, therefore, they should be construed as semantically imperatival. The commands follow a pattern of *concession* (hear/see) to *prohibition* (perceive/know). The impression is that the directives are rhetorical because they include both what they *can* do (hear, see) and *cannot* do (perceive, know). They can and will exhibit acoustic and ocular abilities but they will not and cannot exercise appropriate noetic abilities towards a salvific end. Isaiah's message is a sarcastic challenge given to those who assume they can perceive and know in a salvific fashion. It both mocks and exposes the limits of non-salvific wisdom and human abilities.

The 'you' implied in these verbs is anaphoric to the opprobrious phrase 'this people' (לְעָם הַזֶּה) which appears limited to the non-remnant of Israel. The negated effects are בִּין and יָדַע which serve in

---

[158] This is a possible rendering by itself, i.e., it can be taken as an imperfect rather than a jussive (Kautzsch and Cowley, *Gesenius' Hebrew Grammar*, §109k).

[159] Evans, *To See and Not Perceive*, 171 n. 3. He notes earlier that the imperfects are imperatival in function and serve to convey sarcasm here (ibid., 18); Kautzsch and Cowley, *Gesenius' Hebrew Grammar*, §109 indicate that it may be a negative wish or imprecation. Used with the אַל it expresses "the conviction that something cannot or should not happen"(ibid.). The jussive overlaps with the imperative especially when a negative imperatival role is intended (Waltke and O'Connor, *An Introduction to Biblical Hebrew Syntax*, §34.1b, 2b). "The second volitional form signifies purpose or result, in contrast to the sequence *imperative + imperative*" (ibid., §34.6a).

[160] There are eighteen passages where the imperfect is in the Qal stem and carries the Jussive meaning (6:9; 7:4; 13:2; 16:3–4; 29:1; 34:1; 35:3–4; 37:20; 40:9; 41:1; 43:6; 45:8; 49:13; 52:11; 54:2; 55:6–7; 58:1; 65:5). Other stems of the imperfect are the Hiphil (21:6; 22:4; 41:21–22; 54:2), the Piel (16:3; 36:11), and the Hithpael (55:2). Several of these instances are preceded by אַל (6:9; 7:4; 16:3; 22:4; 35:3–4; 36:11; 40:9; 43:6; 52:11; 54:2; 58:1; 65:5). Whenever an imperfect is joined with אַל and preceded by an imperative, it is always jussive in meaning.

6:10 as prerequisites for 'turning' and receiving 'healing.' The essential thrust of the commission is to guarantee judgment by the prevention of salvific perception and knowledge.[161] But the prevention of perception and knowledge are not the judgment itself but only the means to this end. The continuation of noetic inability (or privation) demonstrates *strong* divine causality in fattening whereas the effect of sin works in synergism with *weak* divine causality in exile. The former is a refusal to be gracious in overturning their ontology whereas the latter is an act of retributive justice because of their functions.

Isaiah 6:10. The commands to Isaiah include causing the heart to be 'fat' / 'hard' (הַשְׁמֵן), causing their ears to be 'dense' (הַכְבֵּד), and causing their eyes to be 'smeared' (הָשַׁע).[162] The irony involved is that the states are already in effect at the time of the commission. If not, they would be saved because salvific wisdom *inevitably* leads to repentance as the following clause will show. The *purpose* of these commands is 'lest' (or 'otherwise') they will see with their eyes, hear with their ears, understand (יָבִין) with their heart, and return and be healed.[163] While the tone of the passage is reflective of the genre of a judgment oracle, two other points are critical. The first involves the precise nature of the verbs related to wisdom and each other, while the second entails the semantic nuance of the פֶּן clause with the imperfect. The former issue is aided by solving the latter. But prior to examining the verbs of the פֶּן clause, it is necessary to focus immediately on the Hiphil imperatives of the main clause.

---

[161] Motyer, in espousing the psychological view of fattening, suggests that subsequent rejection of Isaiah's preaching might prove "to be the point at which the heart is hardened beyond recovery" a "psychological process" where "their response would reach the point of no return" (Motyer, *The Prophecy of Isaiah*, 79). Motyer seems to assume that only further rejection renders incapable the heart to unfatten itself. But how can a fat-heart that is defined as without 'understanding' ever recover of its own power?

[162] E. Jenni and D. Vetter, "עֵין," *TLOT* 2:877 translate this phrase as "to plaster over."

[163] The terms for 'heart' are different. The first is לֵב and the second is לְבָב. Stolz says, "the chronological sequence of the two terms may not be determined" (Stolz, "לֵב," *TLOT* 3:638). See also Hellmut Brunner, "Das hörende Herz," *TLZ* 79 (1954): 697–700 and ibid., "Das Herz als Sitz des Lebengeheimnisses," 140–41.

The verbal semantics of the main clause. All three verbs are Hiphil imperatives conveying a *causative* force. In contrast to the Piel stem, the Hiphil may be understood in the sense of *continuing* rather than *creating* a state or condition.[164] The idea is that Isaiah is to *cause* their hearts to be (remain) hard ('fat'), to *cause* their ears to be (remain) dense, and to *cause* their eyes to be (remain) smeared.[165] In contrast to the Hithpael, it is non-reciprocal or non-reflexive and does not bring

---

[164] Waltke and O'Connor, *An Introduction to Biblical Hebrew Syntax*, §27.1d. They say that with the Piel "the object is transposed passively into a new state or condition" where the act is philosophically referred to as 'accidental' "because the object makes no contribution to the verbal notion" whereas with the Hiphil "the object participates in the event expressed by the verbal root" (ibid.). Thus to depict a transformative view of hardening, the Piel would be better a representative than the Hiphil. A sample sense of the Piel would read, "He makes the heart *fattened*" (accidentally) while the Hiphil "He (direct participant as first subject) *causes* the heart *to be fat* (indirect participant as second subject)." "In E. A. Speiser's view the Hiphil originally signified: 'X (the subject) caused that Y (the second subject) *be* or *do* something'" (ibid., emphasis added). The basic difference between the Piel and the Hiphil in terms of causation is that the former is *factitive* and focuses on the resultant state (He caused him to be *dead*) whereas the Hiphil is *causative* and focuses on the act (He caused him *to die*). Whether the Hiphils are *delocutive-causative* or *simple causative* is difficult to tell at this point. The *permissive* Hiphil, as noted by Waltke and O'Connor, occurs with Hiphils of Qal verbs used transitively in three-place (sometimes two-place) predicates as in Exod 33:12 (ibid., §27.3b–c). It carries the sense that represents the action as agreeable to the object (ibid., §27.5). The rarity of the usage (only one example is provided with non-personal objects [Ezek 32:14]) makes the sense applied to Isa 6:9–10 only possible but very unlikely. However, if this is the sense, "*Let* their hearts be fat, *let* their ears be dense, and *let* their eyes be besmeared," then the appeal is to Isaiah and impacts little on *how* fattening actually occurs. In this case a better label might be the *toleration* Hiphil where "the caused activity is welcome to the undersubject [Isaiah] but unacceptable or disagreeable to a third party [those who are fattened]" (ibid., §27.5c).

[165] The exact role Isaiah plays in this process is unclear. One issue revolves around the causal chain in fattening as well as the causal role assigned to each cause. But central to this discussion is the nature of fattening, i.e., transformational versus non-transformational. Until this is solved, Isaiah's role will remain a mute point. The non-transformative view adopted here is that Isaiah's speech constitutes some type of performative utterance that does not create but rather provides the occasion for a continuation of an on-going phenomenon. See Tsevat, "The Throne Vision of Isaiah," 164 who argues that Isaiah is to bring about the effects of the imperatives and von Rad, *The Message of the Prophets*, 124–25. It seems heuristically prudent, as well as in line with Ockham's razor, to position Yahweh as the *ultimate* cause, Isaiah and his words as a *contributory* cause, and the heart of the people as the *material* cause of fattening.

about a state. Unlike the Piel, the Hiphil focuses on the *act* rather than the *state*. This is a critical point because שָׁמֵן is stative and therefore the *act* is directed towards the *agent's role in causation* rather than the object. The Hiphil is ideally suited to capture a scenario where *a determinative act of the agent, which involves both a non-transformative causative continuance and a non-conditioned aspect of continuance (strong divine causation), may be emphasized.* The verbs are therefore best rendered as *constative* rather than *ingressive* or *telic.*[166]

Following this reading, neither Isaiah nor his words are either *efficient* or *instrumental* causes but most likely *contributory* causes. He and his speech are contributory causes to Yahweh's efficient causal continuation of fattening. The verbal dynamics of the each causative verb focuses then on the *continuing* rather than *creative* aspect of causation. The alternatives are that Yahweh is implicated in either *depositing* foolishness into the heart or taking away wisdom by *depletion* rather than *deprivation.*[167] But these alternatives are unlikely

---

[166] Waltke defines constative as "referring to the remaining or persisting in a state" (Waltke and O'Connor, *An Introduction to Biblical Hebrew Syntax*, 690). On Isa 6:10 Ross questions the ingressive notion of this verb (Allen P. Ross, *Introducing Biblical Hebrew* [Grand Rapids: Baker, 2001], §30.3). In a personal correspondence, Waltke says, "I do not think the grammar can decide the issue of whether it is ingressive or constative. Stative verbs tend to go either way" (Bruce K. Waltke, *Re: "Fatten" in Isa 6:10: A Question on the Hiphil* [AOL Correspondence] [America Online, June 29 2004, accessed]).

[167] In other words, the causative aspect of the Hiphil is not *creative* (transformational) but *continuative*. God does not actually manufacture a fat-heart from a non-fat-heart. Instead he both causes these fat-hearts to continue in that state by determining to leave them as such and by doing so purposes a negative reaction to the message of his prophet. Isaiah is commissioned to effectuate the *furtherance* of Yahweh's causative *continuance* of fattening in the context of his preached message. This is slightly different than the view espoused by Key (A. F. Key, "The Magical Background of Isaiah 6:9–13," *JBL* 86 [1967]: 198–204) who understands the language as performative to the extent that Isaiah is alleged to actually *create* the fat-heart by his speech. Two books on performative speech that continue to influence exegetical works are J. L. Austin, *How to Do Things with Words*, ed. J. O. Urmson and Marina Sbisà, 2d ed. (Cambridge, MA: Harvard University Press, 1975) and J. R. Searle, *Speech Acts: An Essay in the Philosophy of Language* (Cambridge: Cambridge University Press, 1969). In an introduction to wisdom, Crenshaw refers to the early association of wisdom in Mesopotamia and Egypt with magic (Crenshaw, *Old Testament Wisdom*, 5). The least that can be derived from this is that the wisdom tradition shows a penchant and therefore provides a precedent for citing performative speech as part of that genre.

with the Hiphil stem, condemn man not for what he is by nature but for what Yahweh transforms him into being, and fail to account for like effects prior to this.

Isaianic fattening of the heart. 'Make fat' (הַשְׁמֵן) may convey the idea of 'making heavy.'[168] This is the only place in the MT where the verb occurs in a Hiphil imperative form; the only other Hiphil is Neh 9:25. As a verb it appears five times[169] while as an adjective ten times.[170] Three observations favor rendering the phrase '*cause* their heart to *remain* fat.' First, as previously indicated, Isaiah earlier mentions their general condition (in *dramatic* or *lyrical speech*)[171] as neither *knowing* nor *perceiving* their master, both componential noetic deficiencies of the fat-heart (1:3). Second, the OT elsewhere insists that man without the new heart is hard/fat-hearted, a state remedied only by the gratuitous bestowal of the new heart by Yahweh.[172] Third, if the fat-

---

[168] BDB 1081–82. They indicate that the causative notion can be to "*shew fatness* (inner causat.); *make fat* (dull, unreceptive)" (ibid.). The former applies to Neh 9:25 while the latter to Isa 6:10. The sense of Isa 6:10 would be, "they are unreceptive and I will guarantee they will remain so." Although one may focus on volitional ends ('unreceptive'), Isaiah is concerned with the absence of wisdom ('dull') as the means to this end.

[169] Deut 32:15*bis*; Isa 6:10; Jer 5:28; Neh 9:25.

[170] Gen 49:20; Num 13:20; Judg 3:29; Isa 30:23; Ezek 24:14, 16; Hab 1:16; Neh 9:25, 35; 1 Chr 4:40. It also occurs as a noun ('oil') fifty-nine times in the MT.

[171] Quinn-Miscall, *Reading Isaiah*, 15. He thinks this noetic state is "a story of past actions (raising and rebelling) with present consequences (not knowing)" (ibid., 17). Thus although he views the heart as already fat, he clearly understands it as retributional and transformational with the *terminus a quo* pushed back to an earlier time. The reverse situation seems more likely, viz., past, present, and future behavior as well as the present and future consequences (esp. going into captivity) are the result of not 'knowing' or 'perceiving.'

[172] This is supported by several lines of evidence: First, a non-hearing ear is explicitly credited to the hard-heart (Exod 7:13, 22; 8:19; 9:12; Zech 7:12; Isa 46:12; 4Q365 f2:5). It is irrelevant that these texts are primarily volitional in distinction to cognitive because *both* aspects are dealt with in the new heart and a non-hearing ear applies to both. Second, various texts testify to God 'giving' or not 'giving' wisdom, or putting something into the heart or giving a new or causing a fat/hard-heart (Exod 35:34; 36:2; Deut 29:3; 1 Kgs 3:9, 12; 10:24; Jer 24:7; 32:39; Ezek 11:19; 36:26; Ps 4:7; Eccl 3:11; Lam 3:65; Ezra 7:27; Neh 2:12; 7:5; 2 Chr 9:23; 30:12). Third, Ezekiel states that when God gives 'one heart' (Jer 32:39; Ezek 11:19; 1 Chr 12:39; 2 Chr 30:12; 4Q183 f1ii:4) along with the indwelling Spirit, he replaces the heart of stone with a heart of flesh (Ezek 11:19; 36:26; Job 41:16; 1QHa 21:11; 4Q427 f10:2, 3; 4Q436 f1a+bi:10). *This is the primary sense in which Isaiah speaks of fattening and in this sense everyone without*

heart is defined as absence of salvific wisdom, and man's heart is innately absent of this wisdom, then the act of fattening must necessarily be deprivational (rather than depletion/divesting or depositing). Thus Isaiah's commission does not *commence* a new noetic reality by subtraction or addition as much as it *continues* and *confirms* the divine intention towards a present human condition, namely, to abandon it to its fat-hearted state by *depriving* it of the addition of salvific wisdom.

Some theories about these verbs may be dismissed. It is possible, because of the rarity of the verbal stem שָׁמֵן, to label it (along with the following verbs) as an adjective and thereby render it (and subsequent phrases) as a predicate construction. This construal would place 'heart' as the subject and read, "The heart of this people is/will be fat/hard." The command and causative force is replaced by one of present or future reality—their hearts are already/will be fat/hard. Although either rendering is possible, neither is very probable, even though the present tense agrees in principle to the above reason for sustaining they are currently in a fat-hearted condition.[173] An alternate theory, arising out of the translation of the verbs in the passive by the LXX, renders the verbal stem as Hophal rather than

---

exception has a fat-heart. In addition, it is clearly God who gives or withholds 'hearing ears' and 'seeing eyes' (Deut 29:4; Prov 20:12). The retributive notion suffers several critical flaws: (1) It assumes that the fat-heart always refers to stubbornness and therefore omits all references to the fat-heart that is replaced by the new covenant heart of flesh that sees, hears, perceives, knows, and understands—and these are *cognitive* not *volitional* elements. (2) It ignores new covenant language which presupposes that all people are (conceived and) born with a fat-heart. The retributional view does not adequately account for why anyone at anytime would ever fail to have a congenitally fat-heart. Given this interpretation, fattening cannot be understood as retributional, transformational, or confined to volition (stubbornness).

[173] To sustain the parallelism of syntax, the other verbals must be turned into adjectives as well. But there are several impediments. (1) Although שָׁמֵן can take an adjectival form, it is rare (only ten times) and only three have the article preceding it (Num 13:20; Ezek 34:16; Neh 9:35). (2) Although כָּבֵד can take an adjectival form (forty-one times), it rarely occurs with the article before it (1 Kgs 3:9; 12:4; 2 Chr 10:4). (3) The stem שָׁעַע never occurs as an adjective and only three times as a verb (Isa 6:10; 29:9*bis*). So although it is possible to take the first two as adjectives it is not so for the last. (4) No other text (1QIsaᵃ, LXX, Targum, NT) renders these terms in any other form than the verb. For these reasons and for preventing disruption to the verbal parallelism, it is best to regard these as verbs not adjectives.

Hiphil.[174] But neither the transformation of this verb into an adjective or a Hophal stem carry much weight especially when the motivation behind such exegesis seems not to be so much the harshness of the causative aspect of the Hiphil as it is with the *role* of agency involved.[175] The object of this first verbal action, then, is the heart—'*cause* the heart to *continue* to be fat/hard.' The recipients of this fattened heart are 'this people' (הָעָם הַזֶּה), a phrase that carries a pejorative connotation in distinguishing them from both Isaiah and the remnant.

Dense ears and besmeared eyes. The second verbal notion addresses the ears. 'Cause their ears to be (remain) *dense*.' The word for 'dense' (כָּבֵד), as discussed earlier, conveys the general sense of being heavy, weighty, burdensome, or honored. In the Hiphil it refers to making ears heavy, dull or unresponsive.[176] Because this is dealing with an *ontological-functional* effect of the heart in this context, this act perpetuates an inability in the cognitive realm. A similar expression refers to 'opening the ears' effecting functional responsiveness.[177] But

---

[174] There are only two cases of the Hophal imperative in the OT (Jer 49:8; Ezek 32:19).

[175] The Hophal is the passive form of the Hiphil. In this stem, the causative element is not done away with but shifts in terms of the nature of the cause as necessarily solicited by external contingencies. The nature of causation is best coined as *reactionary* or what this dissertation refers to as *weak* divine causality. Here the object in some way causes the subject to perform the action. The implication to the passage at hand is that since the objects of fattening have in some way caused God to perform this action, then they must have done something to bring it about. The sense is, "Cause them to be fat-hearted *because they asked for it*." This construal squares with the retributional (and thus transformational) position of fattening. The Hiphil, on the other hand, simply insists that the subject *causes* the action either directly or mediated through another without mention of any contingent basis for that action. "Cause them to be fat-hearted." The voice is normally active in such cases. The characteristics of the Hiphil stem allow for the congenital non-retributional and non-transformational view of fattening as well as for a mediatorial role assigned to Isaiah in this process.

[176] BDB 457.

[177] Isa 35:5; 42:20. The usual expression is "to stretch out" or "incline" (נָטָה) the ear to hear with the notion of heeding what is spoken. Whenever this verb is used in connection with ears it always takes the Hiphil stem (except 4Q434 f1i:2; 4Q437 f1:2). First, it occurs in contexts where Israel cries out to Yahweh for his help and intervention (2 Kgs 19:16; Isa 37:17; Pss 17:6; 31:3; 71:2; 86:1, 3; 102:3; Dan 9:18; 11Q5 24:4) or recounts his faithfulness in doing so (Ps 116:2; 4Q428 f21:3; 4Q434 f1i:2). Second, it occurs where Yahweh calls for Israel to respond to their God (Isa 55:3; Ps 78:1). Third, it describes Israel's perpetual unfaithfulness either in the past (Jer 7:24,

this latter expression appears more volitionally rather than cognitively oriented. The act of causing the ears to remain dense (rather than unresponsive) circumvents the appropriate cognitive response (= understanding) to what is heard.

The third verbal form focuses on the eyes. 'Cause their eyes to be (remain) *smeared over*.' The verb is שׁעע and pictures a smearing of the eyes to the point of blindness. In the Hiphil it refers to causing the eyes to be smeared over to be (remain) blind.[178] As with the ears, a similar phrase is 'opening the eyes,' a cognitive idiom[179] that occurs seventeen times in the OT with the sense that it brings a new awareness whether the subject is divine or human. Both of these verbal ideas refer to the lack of noetic response-*ability* and are the result of the act of causal continuation of the 'fat'/'hard' heart. Like the heart, these effects are not a result of a transformation but conditions brought about as the inevitable effects of the fat-heart. The effect rather than the cause of the fat-heart is non-hearing ears and non-seeing eyes.

The final פן *clause.* The פן clause commences with this negative adverb (conjunction) normally used in dependent verbal clauses for a

---

26; 11:8; 17:23; 25:4; 34:14; 44:5) or present time (Jer 35:15). Fourth, it is used to call others unto a new obedience away from past allegiances (Ps 45:11), to obey the teachings of one's father (Prov 2:2; 4:20; 5:1, 13; 22:17), or to meet the needs of the poor (4Q434 f1i:2). Finally, it is used for the act of paying close attention to parables and dark sayings (Ps 49:5). Thus to "incline the ear" to something is to take heed or pay special attention to what is spoken, taught, or requested by another. But in order to incline the ear (volitionally), it must be opened (ontologically). This command ensures that the latter will continue and thus the former will not happen.

[178] BDB 1044.

[179] In the Niphil פקח depicts an epiphany due to some event (salvation) that takes place (Gen 3:5, 7; Isa 35:5). In the Qal God opens the eyes of Hagar to see a well she had not previously been aware of (Gen 21:19) or the eyes and ears of the poor (4Q434 f1i:3). It may refer to a child opening its eyes (2 Kgs 4:35), to a rich man who opens his eyes and realizes he has lost everything (Job 27:19), or to a man who arises from sleep (Prov 20:13). Humans pay attention to (= help) the plight of the poor (4Q434 f1i:2) and petition God to open his (God's) eyes to their situation to which he responds with deliverance (2 Kgs 6:17*bis*; 6:20*bis*). The phrase is sometimes combined with the similar idiom "open your ears" in a human request for God to come to the rescue (2 Kgs 19:16; Job 14:3; Isa 37:17; Dan 9:18). For Yahweh to "open his eyes," means he protects Israel (Zech 12:4) or it points to his omniscience (Jer 32:19). Yahweh can also use Israel to open the eyes of Gentiles to salvation (Isa 42:7) or simply those in need (4Q437 f1:2). In every case it refers to a new state of awareness or knowledge.

finite purpose: "Seal their eyes *lest* they see with their eyes, hear with their ears, and perceive with their heart."[180] This negative final connotation is the *prima facie* reading. It refers to a contingency contained in the main clause represented as either an explicit prohibition, command, or action that *necessarily prevents* subsequent action contained in the פֶּן clause from occurring— *A otherwise B* or *not B if A*.[181] This is supported through the use of פֶּן in cases where it is followed by the imperfect verb tense (122 times in MT). In Isaiah alone, it occurs six times in this form (6:10; 27:3; 28:22; 36:18; 48:5, 7). A brief examination of these verses in Isaiah indicates how the clause may be construed from a semantic point of view.

Referring to the future of Israel and depicting them as a vineyard, Yahweh says he will water it continually, guard it day and night, *lest* anyone harm it (Isa 27:3). A semantic equivalent would be, no one will harm it *if* he waters and guards it continually. Israel is later told to *stop* mocking Isaiah's message of judgment *lest* their chains in captivity will become heavier (28:22). Their chains would become heavier *if* they did not stop mocking. The messenger from Sennacherib warns the men of Israel *not* to listen to Hezekiah, "*lest* he incite you" to war against Syria (36:18). The sense is that Hezekiah will incite you *if* you do listen to him. Yahweh declares things beforehand *lest* they say their idol has made it come to pass (48:5). This may be transformed to say idolaters will not insist an idol made it come to pass *if* Yahweh declared things beforehand. Finally, Isa 48:7 declares that Yahweh reveals things anew *lest* they say they already had heard of them. Transformed it reads they do not say they have already heard them *if* Yahweh reveals things anew. The translation 'lest' or 'otherwise' reflects a prohibition of an effect by taking away the cause.

These usages reveal five clear cases of a *negative* purpose 'so that not,' 'lest,' or 'otherwise' (27:3; 28:22; 36:18; 48:5, 7). The semantic equivalent of the negative purpose is by negating the apodosis (it becomes the new protasis) and by changing the protasis into a conditional statement (it becomes the new apodosis). Under this construal the *negative* purpose reads, "*lest* [or 'otherwise'] they see with their eyes, hear with their ears, perceive with their heart, and

---

[180] Waltke and O'Connor, *An Introduction to Biblical Hebrew Syntax*, 661.

[181] BDB 814–15. The conjunction occurs only with the imperfect and perfect verb tenses.

turn and be healed."[182] The transformation reads, "They do *not* see
with their eyes, hear with their ears, perceive with their heart, and
turn and be healed *if* he causes the heart of this people to be [remain]
fat/hard and ears to be [remain] heavy and eyes to be [remain]
smeared." This negative telic clause states that the fattening of the
heart is the necessary and sufficient cause behind the inability of
individuals to exercise the necessary requirements for securing
healing, namely, repentance.[183] This final clause, then, is "une
dénonciation ironique" precisely because they are unable to repent
prior to the divine initiative.[184]

Two important corollaries follow from this examination and
relates to the logical necessity of the effects when the cause is present.
The argument is in the form of a disjunction: A (fattened) *or* B
(wisdom leading to repentance) implies that *if* not B (wisdom leading
to repentance) *then* A (fattened) and *if* not A (fattened) *then* B (wisdom
leading to repentance). First, this means that if one does not
salvifically perceive, know, and understand, then he is fat-hearted
and fattened (continually deprived of wisdom). Second, it rules out a
third alternative else a contradiction occurs (A *and* B or not A *and* not
B)—either the person is simultaneously fat-hearted *and* possesses
salvific wisdom leading to repentance or a person is simultaneously

---

[182] 'Healing' is also linked to the Isaianic description in 1:5–6 where their rebellion is
associated with their sickly state. "Why should you be beaten anymore? Why do you
persist in rebellion? Your whole head is injured, your whole heart (לֵבָב) afflicted.
From the sole of your foot to the top of your head there is no soundness—only
wounds and welts and open sores, not cleansed or bandaged or soothed with oil"
(NIV). An obvious connotation in Isaiah's use of the image of 'healing' is certainly
'forgiveness' not only as indicated by the term 'repentance' but because other
translations of this text use the term for 'forgiveness' rather than 'healing.' Healing
occurs six times in Isaiah (6:10; 19:22; 30:26; 53:5; 57:18, 19; cf. Matt 8:17) and accrues
towards its recipients (the 'many') due to the work of the suffering servant on their
behalf (Isa 53:5; Grosse, "Isaïe 52,13–53,12 et Isaïe 6," 538; cf. Quinn-Miscall, *Reading
Isaiah*, 90–91).

[183] Repentance (שׁוּב) is a key idea throughout Isaiah occurring fifty-one times and is
used in conjunction with the remnant (שְׁאָר) theme (1:25–27; 5:25; 6:10, 13; 9:11–12, 16,
20; 10:4, 21–22; 12:1; 14:27; 19:22; 21:12; 23:17; 28:6; 29:17; 31:6; 35:10; 36:9; 37:7–8, 29,
34, 37; 38:8; 41:28; 42:22; 43:13; 44:19, 22, 25; 45:23; 46:8; 47:10; 49:5–6; 51:11; 52:8; 55:7,
10–11; 58:12–13; 59:20; 63:17; 66:15). See Quinn-Miscall, *Reading Isaiah*, 56–57;
Milgrom, "Did Isaiah Prophesy during the Reign of Uzziah?" 170). In Isaiah
hardening is used to guarantee non-repentance and therefore justify the captivity.

[184] Sonnet, "Le motif de l'endurcissement (Is 6,9–10) et la lecture d' «Isaïe»," 221.

not fat-hearted *and* does not possess salvific wisdom leading to repentance. However, the semantic situation of the פֶּן clause as it relates to the main clause does not warrant either sense. There is no middle ground or third alternative.[185] This supports a congenital fat-hearted view and non-transformation understanding of divine fattening.

Divergent Streams of Isa 6:9–10

Qumran.[186] There is only one biblical text (1QIsaᵃ)[187] and possibly one non-biblical reference (4Q162 f1 3:1–9) that touches on Isa 6:9–10. The latter can be set aside as it has little bearing on the modification or meaning assigned to the passage.[188] When one compares the Hebrew text of 1QIsaᵃ with the MT, however, several variations emerge.[189] The

---

[185] Of the 122 cases of פֶּן followed (within five words) an imperfect verb, there are no clear cases where the subject is non-distributive. Two cases are dissuasive and do not apply (Jer 51:46; Job 36:18). Thus there is no room for a third alternative. A third alternative would read as follows: "Otherwise they (some not all) will see with their eyes, (some not all) hear with their ears, and (some not all) understand with their heart and (some not all) turn again, and (some not all) be healed." Problems: (1) This creates the category of the non-fattened heart that does not perceive. But the very definition of the fat-heart is the inability to perceive. So in creating a third category it merely makes a distinction without a difference. (2) It assumes depletion, namely, some hearts would perceive and thus to prevent perception they are fattened. But this does not account for why they presently do not perceive if fattening is a depletion of this ability.

[186] I am sometimes aided by the translation of Martin Abegg Jr., Peter Flint, and Eugene Ulrich, eds., *The Dead Sea Scrolls Bible: The Oldest Known Bible Translated for the First Time into English* (New York: HarperCollins, 1999).

[187] The Hebrew text of 1QIsaᵃ and 1QIsaᵇ are used for Isa 6:9–10, 29:9–10, 32:3–4, 42:6–7, 18–20, 43:7–8, 44:18, 63:17. Access to the text comes from Miller Burrows, John C. Trever, and William H. Brownlee, eds., *The Isaiah Manuscript and the Habakkuk Commentary*, The Dead Sea Scrolls of St. Mark's Monastary, vol. 1 (New Haven: American Schools of Oriental Research, 1950) and Eleazar Lipa Sukenik, ed., *The Dead Sea Scrolls of the Hebrew University* (Jerusalem: Magnes, 1955).

[188] The text (4Q162 3:7–9) is marked by lucanae: It reads as follows: [– –] אמר "And say [– –]" [– – תדעו ואל אור] ר ראו "Indeed seeing [you will see but not know – –]" [– –] תבי "You will come [– –].'"

[189] These differences and the significance of these differences are discussed in Evans, *To See and Not Perceive*, 60.

significant[190] differences include the following. First, the double substitution of a causal עַל for the negative particle אַל, both of which precede verbs for בִּין and יָדַע.[191] The sense is therefore altered from "hear but *do not* perceive, see but *do not* know" to "hear *because* you may perceive, see *because* you may know."[192]

Second, the final *nûn* is missing from the first verb of 6:10 (הַשְׁמֵן/השם) involving a root substitution from a Hiphil imperative 'to make fat' (שָׁמֵן) to a Hiphil imperative 'to make appalled' (שָׁמֵם).[193] This alteration signals several changes. First, the speaker is no longer Isaiah the prophet and the audience no longer disobedient Israel but the community of sectarians (or sectaries as some call them).[194] Second, because of the audience change, the obduracy motif is missing. Third, the assumed response elicited is based on their

---

[190] There are insignificant differences including the addition of ו four times either within or at the end of a word (ובאזניו/ובאזוניו · ואזניו/ואוזניו · ויאמר/ויואמר · ישמע/ישמעו); the omission of ו at the beginning of a word (וראו/ראו), or the addition of ה at the end of a word (ואמרת/ואמרתה). "The plural form ישמעו instead of the singular is grammatically correct here" (Paulson Pulikottil, *Transmission of Biblical Texts in Qumran: The Case of the Large Isaiah Scroll 1QIsaᵃ*, JSPSup, ed. Lester L. Grabbe and James H. Charlesworth, vol. 34 [Sheffield: Sheffield Academic Press, 2001], 140).

[191] This change is consistent and deliberate throughout the scroll. See ibid., 139–40 and his chart comparing the interchange of these two prepositions in 1QIsaᵃ and *BHS* on 217.

[192] Brownlee, *The Meaning of the Qumran Scrolls for the Bible*, 186 translates the passage as follows (the brackets indicate the translation taken in this dissertation):

Keep on listening, because you may *understand*; [בִּין 'to perceive,'] Keep on looking, because you may *perceive*! [יָדַע 'to know,'] Make the heart of this people appalled: Stop its ears and turn away its eyes—lest it see with its eyes and hear with its ears. Let it *understand* in its heart [בִּין 'to perceive,'] and return and be healed (emphasis added).

[193] This verb occurs, in various forms, ten times in Isaiah (33:8; 49:8, 19; 52:14; 54:1, 3; 59:16; 64:4*bis*; 63:5) with Isa 52:14 bearing the closest semantic parallel. See Pulikottil, *Transmission of Biblical Texts in Qumran*, 139–40.

[194] It is going too far to say with van der Kooij that the speaker is a teacher who emphasizes insight and knowledge and then is converted (A. van der Kooij, *Die alten Textzeugen des Jesajabuches: Ein Beitrag zur Textgeschichte des Alten Testaments*, OBO, ed. Othmar Keel, Bernard Trémel, and Erich Zenger, vol. 35 [Fribourg: Universitätsverlag, 1981], 85). On the sociological definition and components of a 'sect' and whether and under what definition Qumran should be referred to as a 'sect' see Jutta M. Jokiranta, "'Sectarianism' of the Qumran 'Sect': Sociological Notes," *RevQ* 78 (2001): 223–39.

reaction to the awfulness of sin rather than an inevitable judgment because of sin, previous or congenital (cf. Isa 33:15).[195]

Third, a substitution of בְ for וֹ (ולבבו/בלבבו) serves essentially to break the chain of verbal ideas in the פֶּן clause as they relate to the heart. The phrase evolves from "*and* בְּיָן [with] its [their] heart" to the bare "בְּיָן *with* its [their] heart."

In general the Qumran text changes to Isa 6:9–10 are what Paulson Pulikottil refers to as a piece of theological exegesis designed to distinguish Qumran from the rest of Israel. This is accomplished through the means of *textual harmonization*, that is, alterations to Isa 6:9–10 that conform to another text within the same book, namely, Isa 33:15.[196] Altered is the prohibition of perception and knowing in 6:9 to being appalled at sin so that they might come to perceive and know. The MT in 6:10 commands the heart to be fattened ('make fat') which keeps them deaf, blind, and unable to turn and be healed. The Qumran text, however, commands the Qumranites to be appalled at sin and to stop their own ears and eyes at the sound and sight of it in the hope that the heart will understand and turn to God and they will

---

[195] The intention of the text is encapsulated in the following passage. 1QHa 15:1–3 reads, "¹[…] I remain silent […] ²[…] my arm is broken at the elbow, my feet sink in the mud, my eyes are blind from having seen evil, ³my ears, through hearing the shedding of blood, my heart is horrified at wicked schemes, for Belial is present when the inclination of their being becomes apparent" (Florentino García Martínez, ed., *The Dead Sea Scrolls Translated: The Qumran Texts in English*, trans. Wilfred G. E. Watson, 2d ed. [Grand Rapids: Eerdmans, 1996], 342–43).

[196] Pulikottil, *Transmission of Biblical Texts in Qumran*, 44–129. He points out four general categories of changes made by 1QIsaᵃ in light of the MT: (1) *Harmonization*: this involves aligning elements of one text to another. It is subdivided into *contextual* (influenced by immediate context), *textual* (influenced by other passage[s] in same book), or *intertextual* (influenced by passages in other books). (2) *Explication*: depicts the filling of conceptual voids in the text by explanations and interpretations. This refers either to clarifying the meaning of the *Vorlage* (explanations) or importing foreign meanings into the text (interpretations). (3) *Modernization*: linguistic changes that update the text. (4) *Contextual*: cleaning up of grammatical and syntactical irregularities. Pulikottil puts Isa 6:9, specifically the intentional change of עַל for אַל, as an interpretative explication (ibid., 81). He insists that this is intentional change, and that it "has the effect of reversing the meaning of the passage—a pessimistic statement that the people will not repent is turned to one of hope and expectation" (ibid.). However, he does not note the textual harmonization to Isa 33:15 (as shown by comparing 1QHa 15:1–3; 21:5; 4Q510 f1:6; 4Q511 f10:3)—a change designed to identify Qumran with the righteous remnant and to emphasize their duty to eschew sin.

be healed. In the Hebrew text שָׁעַ is parallel with the heart's *inability* to בִּין, whereas the Qumran text 'be appalled' (שָׁמֵם) parallels the idea of the non-fattened heart's *ability* to 'perceive.' While the MT sounds a *judgment oracle* in 6:9 followed by the divine *means* it is accomplished and the *result* it ensures (6:10), the Qumran text holds out a hopeful prophetic commission in the form of a *repentance text* involving a *condition* in 6:9 followed by the human *means* which if fulfilled will bring an *accomplishment,* namely, healing (6:10). Thus the role of the prophet is altered from perpetuating 'fatness' to inspiring repentance and the text is changed from an *ontological-functional* emphasis to a *functional-ontological* one.[197]

As noted in chapter 1, Craig Evans treats changes like these in his *To See and Not Perceive* as attempts by later traditions to mitigate passages where the implications of monotheism appear too blatant. The Qumran text here is, in his words, "a most remarkable effort at circumventing the original meaning."[198] However, Evans may have missed the intent here. The changes do not mitigate either *theistic* implications or the *theological* notions of the wisdom tradition. Nor does his claim *sufficiently* take into account the distinctive audience, the harmonizing to Isa 33:15, or subsequent non-mitigating reuse of Isa 6:9–10 in the Qumran scrolls. Although it is difficult to be certain, the Qumran text appears designed for a group equated with the 'remnant' (the covenanters of the sect) or prospective converts while the MT addresses the non-remnant of Israel. If it is granted that Isaiah's commission did not include the remnant as the object of his fattening motif, then Qumran is in agreement with Isaiah's bifurcation of ethnic Israel. Therefore, by altering the text in its particulars and genre, based on Isa 33:15, it becomes necessary to shift the audience as well. More likely, however, shifting the audience made necessary the adjusting of the text. The intent is to emphasize the righteous behavior of those who see and hear. There is therefore

---

[197] The change of the oracle of judgment into a repentance text is due to the sectarian notion that judgment is reserved only for those outside the group while they (Qumran) are the recipients of God mercy and grace. See James A. Sanders, "From Isaiah 61 to Luke 4," in *Christianity, Judaism and Other Greco-Roman Cults: Studies for Morton Smith at Sixty,* ed. Jacob Neusner, vol. 1 (Leiden: Brill, 1975), 93–97; Craig A. Evans, "1QIsaiah^a and the Absence of Prophetic Critique at Qumran," *RevQ* 11 (1984): 537–42; idem, "The Text of Isaiah 6:9–10," *ZAW* 94 (1982): 415–18.

[198] Evans, *To See and Not Perceive,* 60.

no compelling evidence that suggests this harmonization denies divine fattening, threatens monotheism, mitigates God's sovereignty, or implies the Qumranites do not view the heart as congenitally fat. Rather, it focuses on the remnant's ability to perceive, understand, and to turn to God.

The Greek Versions and Texts.[199] Meaningful alterations to the MT are noted in order to demonstrate the perspective of the LXX and other Greek versions.[200] The LXX reads as follows with an English translation accompanying it:[201]

⁹καὶ εἶπεν πορεύθητι καὶ εἰπὸν τῷ λαῷ τούτῳ ἀκοῇ ἀκούσετε καὶ οὐ μὴ συνῆτε καὶ βλέποντες βλέψετε καὶ οὐ μὴ ἴδητε ¹⁰ἐπαχύνθη γὰρ ἡ καρδία τοῦ λαοῦ τούτου καὶ τοῖς ὠσὶν αὐτῶν βαρέως ἤκουσαν καὶ τοὺς

---

[199] The critical edition used for the LXX is Joseph Ziegler, ed., *Isaias*, Septuaginta, Vetus Testamentum Graecum Auctoritate Academiae Scientiarum Gottingensis editum, vol. 14 (Göttingen: Vandenhoeck & Ruprecht, 1983).

[200] On the differences here, see Hesse, *Das Verstockungsproblem*, 62–63; Gnilka, *Die Verstockung Israels*, 13–16.

[201] Several variants of the Greek text are worth noting. 6:9: (1) the phrase πρὸς τὸν λαὸν τοῦτον is placed after πορεύθητι in several late MSS (393 [8ᵗʰ] 534 [9ᵗʰ] Athanasius II 1001), the form of which is found exactly in Acts 28:26. This is no doubt a case where the LXX variants have arisen due to NT influence rather than the reverse. MS 534 replaces τῷ λαῷ τούτῳ with αὐτοῖς while Athanasius with αὐτῷ in the attempt to reduce the redundancy. (2) The pattern of a concessive notion (either noun or ptcp.) followed by the future indicative and then the emphatic negation in the subjunctive is slightly interrupted by some variants. The tendency is to replace the future indicatives (ἀκούσετε/βλέψετε) with a subjunctive mood but the pattern is not consistent. 6:10: (1) One variant (MS 93 [13ᵗʰ]) omits the phrase τοῦ λαοῦ τούτου and replaces it simply with ἡμῶν which amounts to including Isaiah within the group having a thick/dull heart. (2) A few MSS omit the first pronoun αὐτῶν including א* [4ᵗʰ] (along with 538 [12ᵗʰ], Athanasius II 1001, Basil, Theodoret von Cyrus [who has the second pronoun], Tertullian III 384) which the NT also does. (3) A few MSS (377 [11ᵗʰ] 407 [9ᵗʰ] 534 [11ᵗʰ]) omit the final phrase καὶ τῇ καρδίᾳ συνῶσι probably due to *homoeoteleuton* (similar ending with ἀκούσωσι). (4) ἐπιστρέψωσι (aor. act. subj.) is replaced by the future active indicative ἐπιστρέψουσι in א 26 et al. This variant is mirrored in the NT MSS as well. This is done presumably in keeping with the following future tense ἰάσομαι. Other MSS (36 [11ᵗʰ] 46 [13ᵗʰ]) simply replace the final verb with the subjunctive ἰάσωμαι. (5) Symmachus replaces ἐπαχύνθη ('it has grown thick/dull') with ἐλιπάνθη ('it has become fat') in an uncharacteristically literal rendering of the Hebrew. (6) Symmachus also replaces the adverb βαρέως with the more idiomatic verbal form (imperf. act. ind.) ἐβάρυνε (along with 710 [10ᵗʰ]).

ὀφθαλμοὺς αὐτῶν ἐκάμμυσαν μήποτε ἴδωσιν τοῖς ὀφθαλμοῖς καὶ τοῖς ὠσὶν ἀκούσωσιν καὶ τῇ καρδίᾳ συνῶσιν καὶ ἐπιστρέψωσιν καὶ ἰάσομαι αὐτούς

[9]And he said, "Go and speak to this people, 'In hearing you will hear but not understand and although seeing you will see but not perceive.' [10]For the heart of this people has been made thick ('dull') and their ears are hard of hearing and their eyes they have closed lest they should see with their eyes and hear with their ears and understand with their heart and turn and I will heal them.

Significant distinctions include the following. First, there is an altering of the idiomatic imperatival phrases (שִׁמְעוּ שָׁמוֹעַ and וּרְאוּ רָאוֹ) with intensifying force ('certainly'/'indeed' hear/see') into both a noun in the dative (ἀκοῇ) or a concessive participle (βλέποντες), each governed by a future tense verb (ἀκούσετε/βλέψετε) denoting a prediction[202] of a state of being ('in hearing/seeing you will hear/see').[203] The MT emphasizes the command to hear/see while the Greek version simply predicts or concedes that they will hear/see. It

_____

[202] The future is probably best represented as *ingressive*. However, the time of the ingressive idea of the main verbs is governed by the time of the verbal noun or concessive participle so that *whenever hearing* and *whenever seeing* really points back to an indefinite period, viz., when they first begin to physically hear/see. In that vein the expression is tantamount to saying that they never either perceived or understood when they physically began to see and to hear. If the *terminus a quo* is conception and this is the point of fattening, then this view is necessary. However, if the *terminus a quo* is during one's lifetime then one has to wonder why they did not believe the message prior to this fat-hearted state, *how* they could have produced effects of which would bring on the fat-heart, and *what* advantage there is to being non-fat-hearted in the first place.

[203] This Hebrew construction (Qal imper. + Qal infin. abs.) is rendered in seven ways by the Greek version. (1) καταράσει καταράσασθε, cognate dative + aorist middle imperative (Judg 5:23); (2) ἀκουῇ ἀκούσετε, cognate dative + future active indicative (Isa 6:9a); (3) βλέποντες βλέψετε, concessive participle + future active indicative (Isa 6:9b); (4) ἀκούσατε, aorist active imperative (Isa 55:2); (5) κλαύσατε κλαυθμῷ, aorist active imperative + cognate dative (Jer 22:10); (6) ἀκούσατε ἀκούσατε, aorist active imperative + aorist active imperative (Job 13:17; 21:2); and (7) ἄκουε ἀκοήν, present active imperative + cognate accusative noun (Job 37:2). That only Isa 6:9 renders it without the imperative (*bis!*) suggests a deliberate aversion to it in favor of a future state of hearing/seeing. This points to the conclusion that the changes in Isa 6:9 are *intentional alterations* of the Hebrew sense in order to avoid the imperatival nuance. The consistent rendering of this construction elsewhere argues that the original Hebrew rendering is indeed *imperatival* in its connotation.

is also possible that the Greek translators see irony lying behind the commands to hear and see. The stress in the former lies in the divine authority underlying the verbal commands whereas the latter assumes either a concession or matter-of-factness in its occurrence and occasion.

The second change involves the altering of the Hiphil imperative (הַשְׁמֵן), to 'make fat' with 'heart' as the object, into an aorist passive indicative verb (ἐπαχύνθη), to 'grow thick' (=fat) with the 'heart' as subject, to indicate fattening as a forgone state.[204] For an exact equivalent of the Hebrew sense one would expect an imperative form of the verb rather than a passive indicative.[205] The significance of this is the following. First, the people are viewed as already in a state of fat-heartedness and stress is placed here (*consummative* aorist). The shift is not simply one of *agency* of cause, from God to the people (for

---

[204] In Classical Greek the verb παχύνω refers to 'fattening' as a result of feeding a city (Aeschylus *Suppl.* 618), a 'cat' (Aristophanes *Ach.* 791), cattle (Plato *Resp.* 1.343b), or a horse (Xenophon *Eq.* 12.20). It can be used to characterize humans that are 'fat' and out of shape (Plato *Georg.* 518c; Plutarch *Sol.* 20.5) or to 'growing a fortune,' (Aeschylus *Sept.* 771). It can also refer to something fat like the legs of a horse (Xenophon *Eq.* 1.5), making something 'thick' like bones (Herodotus *Hist.* 3.12.2), or well developed like muscles (Xenophon *Symp.* 2.17). Its corresponding nominal form πάχος simply refers to being 'thick' (Hesiod *Op.* 497) as in a 'thick pine' (Hesiod *Op.* 509) or a 'thick neck' (Homer *Od.* 9.372). The verb occurs in the LXX six times (Deut 32:15; 2 Sam 22:12; Ode 2:15; Eccl 12:5; Isa 6:10; 34:6) and translates four Hebrew verbs (עָבָה, 'to be thick,' סָבַל, 'to bear a load,' שָׁמֵן, 'to grow fat,' דָּשֵׁן, 'to be fat'). The Greek verb occurs only twice in the NT, both a quotation of Isa 6:9–10 (Matt 13:15; Acts 28:27; *1 Clem.* 3:1). Classical Greek uses a word for 'hard-hearted' (τλησικάρδιος) that appears only once and refers to the *insensitivity* of the gods (Aeschylus *Prom.* 160). Other terms connected with the heart are 'patient of heart,' or 'stouthearted' (ταλακάρδιος, Aeschines 3.184; Hesiod *[Scut.]* 424; Plutarch *Cim.* 7.4; Sophocles *Oed. col.* 540), 'black-hearted' (μελανοκάρδιος, Aristophanes *Ran.* 470), and 'bold of heart' (θρασυκάρδιος, Bacchylides 20.5; 13.106; Hesiod *[Scut.]* 448; Homer *Il.* 10.41; 13.343). The LXX, therefore, renders the MT quite accurately here and suggests that a *cognitive* rather than *volitional* issue is in mind.

[205] Since שָׁמֵן only occurs once in the Hiphil imperative in the OT (Isa 6:9), a clue to how Hiphil imperatives are rendered by the LXX have been sought within Isaiah. The Hiphil imperative occurs seventy-one times. All but nine cases are rendered with the imperative mood (6:10bis; 7:4; 10:30; 26:19; 41:21, 22; 43:8; 45:21). Of these four have the future middle indicative (10:30; 26:19; 41:22; 45:21), one is an aorist active infinitive (7:4), three are aorist active indicative (6:10b; 41:21; 43:8) and only one is an aorist passive (6:9a). Thus it is unlikely that the passive rendering in Isa 6:9a is meant to reflect the Hiphil imperative form. Rather it appears it is designed to make a semantic, albeit complimentary, distinction.

the agent is the same), but to *type* of cause, from ultimate to material.[206] There is no shift of agents but only focus. Second, the agent of this fattening is other than the recipients as denoted by the *simple* passive voice. It is not likely a *permissive* passive and the sense of reciprocity in fattening would be much better expressed by the middle voice.[207] Therefore, the voice most likely reflects the divine passive and is contingent (*weak* divine causality), retributive, and therefore transformational, or non-contingent (*strong* divine causality) and therefore either arbitrary or congenital and thus an instance of deprivation. In sum, their hearts have *become* or have been *allowed to remain* fattened at the discretion of God. Since there is no detectable retributive element, fattening is best understood as stemming from strong not weak divine causality.

The third change is the addition of an *explanatory* or *causal* subordinate conjunction, γάρ. This conjunction replaces a directive to the prophet through the use of imperatives with a subordinating clause explaining the cause behind the lack of perception and knowledge. It modifies the verbs συνῆτε and ἴδητε explaining the reason why they do not either 'perceive' or 'know.' Instead of causing their heart to be 'fat,' their ears to be 'heavy,' and their eyes to be 'shut,' this clause points to a present reality that then becomes the very grounds for the alleged failure.

The fourth change is from Hiphil imperatives to aorist indicatives where the ears are already 'deaf' and eyes are already 'closed.' The final clause is essentially unaltered but the referent is different in conformity to the respective text. The MT represents Yahweh's

---

[206] Robert M. Arida, "Hearing, Receiving and Entering ΤΟ ΜΥΣΤΗΡΙΟΝ ΤΑ ΜΥΣΤΗΡΙΑ: Patristic Insights Unveiling the *Crux Interpretum* (Isaiah 6:9–10) of the Sower Parable," *SVTQ* 38 (1994): 216 recognizes the change in tenses from the MT to the LXX as a shifting of responsibility in terms of cause, but not in the nature of the cause itself. He does point out that "the causative element, whether it be God or the 'dull' (unfeeling) disposition of the audience, plays a pivotal role in the Isaiah prophecy" (ibid., 216). He regards the commonality of the LXX and the MT (with Mark 4) to be the shared eschatological perspective worked into the salvation history scheme (ibid., 218). The eschatological scheme worked out in *Heisgeschichte* is no doubt at work here but the reciprocity that Arida argues for (in receiving the mysteries) relies too heavily on anthropological assumptions of later patristic writers (Irenaeus of Lyons, John Chrysostom, Cyril of Alexander, and Victor of Antioch).

[207] The *permissive* passive is a rare semantic tag and usually occurs in imperatival constructions. Thus there must be strong evidence to accept this rendering.

purpose in determining their condition whereas the LXX presents the people's *condition* brought about by Yahweh's purpose. Both assume a *strong* divine causative role.

The fifth change is an insignificant variation involving the use of negation clauses. Whereas the Hebrew commands them not (אַל) to 'perceive' or to 'know' and modifies jussive verbs, the Greek uses the *emphatic negation* (οὐ μή) and modifies subjunctive verbs. In keeping with the perspective of each rendering, the Hebrew negation emphasizes the divine causative aspect while the Greek highlights the latent inability on the part of the recipients stemming from a fat-heart. In this respect, the LXX may be viewed as a 'harder' text than the MT.[208] Even though the divine factor is in the background and the present state of the heart is the foreground, the passive voice still points toward the divine prerogative. The Greek rendering may presuppose the wisdom tradition underlying the Hebrew text of Isa 1:3 and 5:13. These show that the non-remnant lack 'knowledge' and are therefore already fat-hearted.

Along with determining the cause of fattening is the related issue of discovering the *terminus a quo*. If it is congenital then it points to conception onwards and is a continual state of being interrupted only by the gratuitous infusion of saving wisdom. If its occurrence is during the lifetime of a person, then it is an occasion that not only brings on a condition but also is a result of particular occurrences that have elicited the condition (either self-imposed or by another). The text does not state *when* this state occurs or what conditions bring about this state, only that it is at the present time their condition. The assumption usually attached to the verbs is that there was a time when the heart was not fat, now it is fat, therefore these individuals *did* something to bring on the state of fatness—a divine *quid pro quo*. This assumption finds little support in Isaiah where fatness of heart appears as an already on-going phenomenon.

In addition, the understanding heart is *never* referred to in terms of 'taking away' but only in terms of 'giving' or 'not giving.' If fattening occurs during one's lifetime (transformational view), is a result of bad behavior (retributive), and thus done by God (form of divine causation), yet the fat-heart is defined primarily by its inability to salvifically perceive, know, and understand, then it is required to

---

[208] Symmachus and א use a synonym ἐλιπάνθη ('has become fat') for ἐπαχύνθη ('has become thick'). Cf. Deut 32:15; Neh 9:25; *Odes Sol.* 2:15; Sir 35:6; 38:11.

view that form of fattening the heart as *taking away* a heart that does perceive, know, and understand. Little support is offered for that interpretation based on the evidence. This alone does not prove the congenital fat-hearted point of view but rather casts doubt on the assumption that the fat-hearted state finds its *terminus a quo* during the lifetime of an individual elicited by bad behavior as a necessary cause (behavior that brings God's retribution in the form of fattening).

This is where the crux of the issue lies, not so much in acquiescing to divine causation, but rather identifying *what* causes or motivates God to fatten (human acts or the divine inscrutable will?), *how* does he fatten (transformation or deprivation?) and *who* does he fatten (non-fat hearts or congenitally fat-hearts?). In addition, the criticism of the transformational/retributive view offered here reveals several assumptions at work on an a priori level that influence how the evidence is construed. The transformational and retributive view is rarely articulated (if so only the retributional aspect) and validation of the transformational notion is never given.

The Targum.

ואמר איזיל ותימר לעמא הדין דשמעין משמע ולא מסתכלין וחזן מחזא ולא ⁹
ידעין: ¹⁰טפיש לביה דעמא הדין ואודנוהי יקר ועינוהי תמטים דלמא יחזון
בעיניהון ובאודנהון ישמען ובליבהון יסתכלון ויתובון וישתביק להון:

⁹And he said, "Go and speak to this people who indeed hear but do not perceive and indeed see but do not know." ¹⁰Make the heart of this people stupid and make their ears heavy and shut their eyes lest they see with their eyes and hear with their ears and perceive with their hearts and repent and it be forgiven them.[209]

---

[209] The Aramaic text relied on is that of Alexander B. Sperber, ed., *The Latter Prophets according to Targum Jonathan*, vol. 3, The Bible in Aramaic, ed. Alexander B. Sperber (Leiden: Brill, 1962) aided by the English translation of Bruce D. Chilton, Michael Maher, and Martin McNamara, *The Isaiah Targum*, trans. Bruce D. Chilton, The Aramaic Bible: The Targums, vol. 11 (Wilmington, DE: Glazier, 1987). It is notoriously difficult to date the Targums. They are generally assumed later than the first century and can date up to the middle ages. The earliest evidence of Targums at Qumran includes Leviticus (4Q156) and Job (4Q157; 11Q10) but none on Isaiah. Although the Targums on the prophets are more or less distinctive and may contain later redactions up into the Islamic period, the Isaiah Targum is reported to contain early traditions dating to the first two centuries after Christ. One value of any Targum is the possibility of unique readings that may be early. For an excellent introduction see Craig A. Evans, *Noncanonical Writings and New Testament Interpretation* (Peabody, MA: Hendrickson, 1992), 97–113.

The text has two noteworthy differences with the MT.[210] First it prefaces the verb for 'hear' with a relative pronoun -ד ('who') transforming the following into a relative clause modifying 'people' (לְעַמָּא).[211] Isaiah is sent to people described as those *who* "hear indeed, but do not perceive, and see indeed, but do not know." The remaining clause is *noetically* redundant as Isaiah is commissioned to "make the heart of this people stupid, and their ears heavy and shut their eyes; lest they see with their eyes and hear with their ears, and perceive with their hearts, and repent and it be forgiven them." This redundancy supports a *continuative* rather than *creative* causative view of fattening. The sapiential tradition provides the ready-made solution by recognizing mankind as already (and thus congenitally) fat-hearted (without wisdom and its effects) and further divine action as necessarily deprivational in nature.

Second, the final clause changes the first person singular in the Hebrew phrase וְרָפָא לוֹ "and I will heal them" to the third person singular וישתביק להון "and it be forgiven them." The reference to forgiveness in place of healing is normally depicted as substituting a literal sense for the metaphorical picture given in the Hebrew and Greek versions. Chilton says "comparison with 19:22 demonstrates that there was no necessity to decipher the healing phrase with a reference to forgiveness, so that this feature of the agreement of this passage with Jesus' teaching is all the more striking."[212] However, the reference to Isa 19:22 shows that there is no consistent pattern of replacing healing for forgiveness in the Targum. Despite the intrigue, little semantic difference appears between healing and forgiveness.

Three important points of the Targum text are emphasized. First, the people are described as *already* unperceptive and unknowing, two

---

[210] See Hesse, *Das Verstockungsproblem*, 64; Gnilka, *Die Verstockung Israels*, 16.

[211] Gnilka, *Die Verstockung Israels*, 16. BDB 1087–88 list three usages of this particle די: (1) As a *relative pronoun*, "part. of relation, who, which, that." (2) As the *mark of the genitive* denoting possession. (3) As a *conjunction*, "that, because." The usage here is the relative pronoun. The significance of these other usages will be apparent when Mark 4:12 is discussed, especially when some scholars propose that Mark misunderstood the Aramaic particle as conveying the conjunctive sense when he writes ἵνα instead of the relative pronoun sense as ὅς.

[212] Chilton, Maher, and McNamara, *The Isaiah Targum*, 15. Chilton is referring to the last phrase of Mark 4:12 where it reads καὶ ἀφεθῇ αὐτοῖς ("and it will be forgiven them") in agreement with the Targum and Peshitta but against the MT, Qumran texts, and Greek versions. This will be taken up in chapter 5.

constituents of fattening and proof of the absence of salvific wisdom; and this is presumably *prior* to divine fattening which brings about these same effects. A *continuing* causative sense to 'fattening' construed in terms of non-transformation and *deprivation* seems the best appraisal of this text because it combines an already (6:9) and not-yet (6:10) aspect to fattening. Second, the translation still suggests *strong divine causality* with the phrase "make the heart of this people stupid." This action is redundant if fattening, that brings the same effects, is not deprivational and non-transformational in nature. To lack any one effect of wisdom (in 6:9 it is two, namely, perceiving and knowing) is to lack all the effects of wisdom. Therefore, to fatten ('make stupid') the already fat-heart in order to ensure it does not 'perceive' (6:10), must entail a divine decision to leave them in their fat-hearted condition.[213] Finally, the reference to forgiveness over healing does not alter the text in its essential meaning. The best model of fattening for handling this translation is the non-transformative view.

The Peshitta.

⁹ܘܐܡܪ ܠܝ. ܙܠ ܐܡܪ ܠܥܡܐ ܗܢܐ. ܫܡܥܘ ܡܫܡܥ ܘܠܐ
ܬܣܬܟܠܘܢ. ܘܚܙܘ ܡܚܙܐ ܘܠܐ ܬܕܥܘܢ. ¹⁰ܐܥܒܝ ܠܗ ܠܒܗ
ܕܥܡܐ ܗܢܐ ܘܐܕܢܘܗܝ ܐܘܩܪ ܘܥܝ̈ܢܘܗܝ ܥܡܨ. ܕܠܐ ܢܚܙܐ
ܒܥܝ̈ܢܘܗܝ. ܘܢܫܡܥ ܒܐܕܢܘܗܝ. ܘܢܣܬܟܠ ܒܠܒܗ ܘܢܬܘܒ
ܘܐܫܒܘܩ ܠܗ.

⁹And he said to me, "Go, say to this people, 'Hear indeed but do not perceive and indeed see but do not know." ¹⁰For the heart of this people is obscure ('blackened') and make their ears heavy and shut their eyes lest they see with their eyes and hear with their ears and perceive with their heart and turn and I will forgive them.[214]

---

[213] The 'hearing' and 'seeing' in 6:9 are purely physical features and it is unlikely that 6:10 means that they will suffer physical blindness and deafness. Furthermore, the statements referring to the eyes and ears in 6:10 undergo equivocation in 6:10 because of 'perceive' and 'know' in 6:9. The flexibility of the semantic domains of these verbs may permit such an equivocation. To make them non-equivocal is not to argue for progression but for physical deafness and blindness. Therefore, to infer that hearing/seeing in 6:9 advances to deafness/blindness in 6:10 as though it is incremental or progressive is not supported.

[214] S. P. Brock, ed., *Isaiah*, The Old Testament in Syriac according to the Peshitta Version, ed. The Peshitta Institute (Leiden: Brill, 1987). For aid in assessing the lexical sense of the Syriac, dependence is made to J. P. Margoliouth, ed., *Supplements to the*

The translation agrees with the MT with only a few minor variations.[215] First, for "Make fat/hard the heart of this people," the version reads, *"For/because* the heart of this people is obscure" (ܟܐܡ ܟܢܝܢ ܡܠ ܠܝܟ ܡܠ, ܪܢ ܐܟ) referring to a present condition of the heart. Second, the negative clause is made explicit with ܟܠܐ "in order that they should *not* see" in keeping with the particle's sense in the MT and other versions. Third, the version ends the final phrase in agreement with the Targum, "and I will *forgive* them" (ܡܠ ܘܐܫܪܘܩ ܟܘܢ). This version pictures Isaiah being sent to a people already incapable of perceiving and knowing the significance of his message. This incapacity is credited to the obscured heart or literally, the heart *blackened with smoke*. Effects accompanying this include that the ears are heavy and the eyes are shut. It is this condition of the blackened heart, defined as the inability to perceive, that accounts for their inability to see and hear or repent and thus receive forgiveness.

The Jerusalem Talmud. This corpus discusses Isa 6:10 only once in *y. Ber.* 2:3.[216] The passage in the Mishnah (*m. Ber.* 2:3), upon which it

---

Thesaurus Syriacus of R. Payne Smith (Oxford: Clarendon, 1927; reprint, Hildesheim and New York: Olms, 1981). For aid in understanding the grammar reference is made to Takamitzu Muraoka, *Classical Syriac: A Basic Grammar with a Chrestomathy*, Porta Linguarum Orientalium, ed. Werner Diem and Franz Rosenthal, vol. 19 (Wiesbaden: Harrassowitz, 1997). Cf. Harold K. Moulton, "Ancient Translations," *BT* 29 (1978): 307–11.

[215] There are also a number of variants as well (Brock, ed., *Isaiah*, 11). Isa 6:9: (1) For ܐܢܙܪ a ninth century MS and a lectionary read ܙܪ. (2) For ܟܠܐ a lectionary omits it entirely while an eleventh century MS omits only the *waw*. Isa 6:10: (1) For ܙܪ several witnesses including a sixth, eighth, ninth, tenth, and two eleventh century MSS, have ܝܪ ('to depart'). (2) For ܡܠ one eleventh century MS omits it entirely.

[216] For the Hebrew of the Jerusalem Talmud I am dependent on Heinrich W. Guggenheimer, ed., *The Jerusalem Talmud [Talmud Yerushalmi] First Order: Zeraïm Tractate Berakhot*, trans. Heinrich W. Guggenheimer, SJFWJ, ed. E. L. Ehrlich, vol. 18 (Berlin: de Gruyter; New York, 2000), 207–08. See also Tzvee Zahavy, ed., *The Talmud of the Land of Israel: A Preliminary Translation and Explanation*, trans. Tzvee Zahavy, CSJH, ed. William Scott Green and Calvin Goldscheider, vol. 1 (Chicago: University of Chicago Press, 1989), 85–87. For the English, deference is given to Jacob Neusner, ed., *The Mishnah: A New Translation*, trans. Jacob Neusner (New Haven: Yale University Press, 1988), 5. For the Hebrew text of the Mishnah reference is made to the Six Divisions of the Mishnah (Shisha Sidrei Mishnah). Eshkol Edition. Electronic text used by permission of D.B.S., Jerusalem, Israel. Morphological separators added by OakTree Software, Inc. Copyright © 2000 by OakTree Software, Inc. Version 1.7.

comments, provides a conceptual link to Isa 6:10 because it refers to the *Shema* which is not only a *spoken* prayer involving the ear, but begins with *"Hear*, O Israel" (שְׁמַע יִשְׂרָאֵל).[217] The Mishnah addresses the participant in the context of meeting or not the specific requirements associated with uttering this prayer. The criteria include that the prayer must be audible to his ears, recited properly without error (without mispronunciation or slurring), and in its proper order. The Talmud then quotes a prayer of Rebbi Aha (the week-day eighteen benedictions of the *Amidah*). What is particularly striking is the order in the part of the prayer that pertains to human needs: knowledge, repentance, forgiveness, salvation, healing. This order is exactly the same as Isa 6:9–10.

> Rebbi Aha in the name of Rebbi Joshua ben Levi: Also he who composed this prayer composed it in good order. The first three and the last three are the praise of the Omnipresent, the middle ones are the needs of the creatures. Give us knowledge. You gave us knowledge, accept our repentance. You accepted our repentance, forgive us. You forgave us, save us.[218]

The next part of the Talmud comments upon the third benediction of this prayer and the source of this knowledge that brings insight that is followed by repentance.

> Rebbi Jeremiah said: 120 elders, among them more than 80 prophets, instituted this prayer. Why did they follow "the holy God" by "He Who favors with knowledge [הדעת]?" Because (*Is.* 29:23–24) "they sanctify the Holy One of Jacob" is followed by "and those of erring spirit will know [וידעו] insight [בינה]." "Knowledge" [דיעה] followed by "Repentance," [לתשובה] (*Is.* 6:10) "Make fat the heart of this people, make it hard of hearing and its eyes sticky, that it should not see with its eyes, nor hear with its ears, nor understand with its heart, because if it would repent then it would be healed."[219]

---

[217] The Jerusalem (better, Palestinian) Talmud is usually dated around A.D. 400–425 and made up of the Mishnah (A.D. 200–220) that represents oral traditions of the tannaic period (50 B.C.–A.D. 200) and Tosepta (A.D. 220–230) with interpretative additions called Gemara. Although the documents date later than the NT era, traditions may go back earlier. For details see Evans, *Noncanonical Writings and New Testament Interpretation*, 114–48.

[218] *y. Ber.* 2:3.

[219] Ibid.

Several observations about the text are noteworthy. First, the parallelism between "the holy God" and "they sanctify the Holy One of Jacob" seems to provide the condition for a second parallelism "He Who favors with knowledge" and "those of erring spirit will know insight." Although it is not altogether clear, it seems that Yahweh only fattens the heart *so long as* they do not sanctify the Holy One of Jacob. Second, once the condition is met, Yahweh grants insight and knowledge that is then accompanied by repentance, forgiveness, and redemption. Third, the quotation of Isa 6:10 follows the MT until the פֶּן clause. הַשְׁמֵן לֵב־הָעָם הַזֶּה וְאָזְנָיו הַכְבֵּד וְעֵינָיו הָשַׁע, "Make fat the heart of this people, their ears heavy, and shut their eyes..." is followed by, עַד וּלְבָבוֹ יָבִין וָשָׁב וְרָפָא לוֹ, "*until* they perceive with their heart, return ['repent'], and I will heal them." The עַד clause clearly transforms intentional fattening that prevents understanding, turning, and healing, into a temporal condition.[220]

Fourth, the passage is informed as to its intent and causal operations by the conditionality of the prayer itself. Whereas the passage divorced from the prayer seems to suggest that God will fatten until they are given insight and knowledge, the actual requirement for removing the fat-heart is proper worship. Proper worship becomes the condition for understanding and perceiving while repentance the condition for forgiveness. They will remain fattened until they properly glorify Yahweh (in prayer). Having met this condition, Yahweh gives them perception that results in their repentance. The human participants, therefore, become the all-determining factor for the initiation, continuation, and cessation of the fat-hearted state. This is the first clear instance of *weak* as opposed to *strong* divine causality.

The use of this text is different from that presented in the MT and early versions. Yahweh continues to fatten but only on a contingent basis. The people can reverse the fattening effects themselves by properly worshipping him. Since the condition can be fulfilled by those not healed, forgiven, or redeemed, this suggests that they are in a state of fat-heartedness at the time of accomplishing this condition. The rabbis place individuals in a fat-hearted condition without accounting for how individuals become fattened in the first place, the natural state of the heart, or how a fat-heart could effectuate a

---

[220] When עַד 'until' is a conjunction and used with the imperfect, it may refer to future time (BDB 724–25).

condition that precipitates Yahweh's reversal of the hardening effect. The effect (properly worshipping God in prayer) seems to assume the very things (knowledge, perception) that are granted as a result of the condition being met. Although the logical sequencing after meeting the condition is identical to the MT and other translations, the conditions of fattening itself are clearly at variance. This interpretation espouses a retributional and transformational view of fattening as well as introduces a contingency for its reversal.

The Babylonian Talmud. Isaiah 6:10 is mentioned three times in the Babylonian Talmud (*b. Ros Has.* 17b; *b. Meg.* 17b; *b. Sabb.* 33b). The first (*b. Ros Has.* 17b) has to do with the order of repentance and its relation to sin and Yahweh's mercy and grace. It reads:

> R. Johanan said: Great is the power of repentance that it rescinds a man's final sentence, as it says, *Make the heart of this people fat and make their ears heavy and shut their eyes, lest they seeing with their eyes and hearing with their ears and understanding with their heart return and be healed.* Said R. Papa to Abaye: Perhaps this was before the final sentence?—He replied: It is written, 'and he be healed.' What is that which requires healing? You must say, the final sentence.

The Hebrew is identical to the MT but stresses what repentance brings, namely, a healing that rescinds man's final sentence. Above, the Jerusalem Talmud slightly alters the text of Isaiah; but here its Babylonian counterpart does not follow suit. Although the focus is on final judgment and repentance, the text as it stands defines the fat-heart as the absence of wisdom's benefits, namely, seeing, hearing, and understanding. But wisdom is tangential. The focus is on repentance and a healing that takes place *after* the prayer is completely recited. Like the Jerusalem Talmud healing occurs by following two mandates, namely, repenting and uttering the final sentence. Unlike the Jerusalem Talmud, man does not seem to provide the condition for reversing the fattening effects, at least it is not mentioned (but it may be implied).

The second text (*b. Meg.* 17b) occurs in the context of *hearing* and like the Jerusalem Talmud it mentions the eighteen benedictions of the *Amidah* prayer and how to utter it correctly. On the specifics of the prayer, the Talmud argues the following:

What reason had they for mentioning understanding after holiness? Because it says, *They shall sanctify the Holy One of Jacob and shall stand in awe of the God of Israel* [Isa 29:23], and next to this, *They also that err in spirit shall come to understanding*. What reason had they for mentioning repentance after understanding? Because it is written, Lest they, *understanding with their heart, return and be healed* [Isa 6:10]. If that is the reason, healing should be mentioned next to repentance?—Do not imagine such a thing, since it is written, *And let him return to the Lord and he will have compassion upon him, and to our God, for he will abundantly pardon* [Isa 55:7]. But why should you rely upon this verse? Rely rather on the other!—There is written another verse, *Who forgiveth all thine iniquity, who healeth all thy diseases, who redeemeth thy life from the pit* [Ps 103:3], which implies that redemption and healing come after forgiveness. But it is written, 'Lest they return and be healed'? That refers not to the healing of sickness but to the healing [power] of forgiveness.

A few observations can be made based on this passage. First, in explicating the purpose of the prayer the attention is turned to the *ordo salutis*. Holiness comes first, followed by understanding, repentance, forgiveness, and finally healing. This holiness is brought on by the presence of the Lord who brings understanding. Like the Jerusalem Talmud, holiness is the condition for the benefits of wisdom. Second, the interlocutor focuses on the issue of repentance following the bestowal of wisdom. He asks, "If that is the reason, healing should be mentioned next to repentance?" But the following comments make it clear that healing is reserved especially *after* (and because of) forgiveness not *before*—at least sequentially speaking. Finally, noteworthy is the relationship between healing and forgiveness—they are treated as synonymous. Healing is really the healing power of forgiveness and forgiveness is nothing more than spiritual healing. Although distinguished, they appear as dual aspects of the same phenomenon.

The final passage (*b. Sabb.* 33b) is a response by rabbi Judah to the question, "Why does this affliction [croup] commence in the bowels and end in the throat?" He says, "Through the kidneys counsel, the heart gives understanding, and the tongue gives form, yet the mouth completes it." The sense is that the disease begins and ends in the same manner as the noetic process occurs. It starts in the kidneys, proceeds to the heart, then to the tongue, and finally the mouth. The reference to "the heart gives understanding" alludes to Isa 6:10, a passage that is a major proof-text for postulating that understanding arises from the heart. That seems to be the only reason it is used here.

Summary

Isaiah receives a commission from the divine council that involves the fates of men. This fate is spoken of in terms of fattening the heart, deafening the ears, and blinding the eyes of the majority of ethnic Israel to prevent their turning to the Lord and healing. The *fat-heart* and *fattened* heart is depicted as a lack of 'knowledge' (6:9), 'perception' (6:10), or 'understanding' (44:18), terms and effects of which link it to wisdom. *Fattening* is therefore a guarantee of this lack by *depletion, deposition,* or more likely *deprivation*. If so then it is not the result of retributive justice but has as its purpose retributive justice in terms of captivity. Integral to the commission are the terms and the motifs utilized by Isaiah that point the reader back to the wisdom tradition as both the source of these notions and the key in discovering the definition of both the fat-heart and fattening. Only after this is understood does Yahweh's role clearly emerge. Isaiah is commissioned to go to a people that are *already* fat-hearted and to preach a message that provides the further occasion for causally continuing the state and effects of that fattening. But this commission is presented in terms of *strong* divine causality. His message emphasizes, therefore, the divine prerogative, namely, that *God chooses to actively deprive some of wisdom and its benefits* of knowing, perceiving, and understanding. By this deprivation, he causally perpetuates the fat-heart and guarantees the effects of which will only then bring on his retributive justice.

Conclusion

The textual stream of Isa 6:9–10 along with its traditional renderings demonstrates two complementary ideas with regard to the fat-heart—the third represented by the Jerusalem Talmud is an exception.[221] First, it is God who causes the heart to be fat. Second, man is congenitally fat-hearted and therefore responsible for the effects and consequences of this fattening. These two divergent traditions exists as complimentary truths when coupled with the wisdom tradition. With the aid of the sapiential background from the OT, Qumran, and other Jewish literature, it has been shown that man

---

[221] There is a reuse of Isa 6:9–10 throughout Isaiah (29:9–10; 42:18–20; 43:7–8; 44:18; 63:17; 32:3–4; 42:6–7) and subsequent rendering of these texts by other traditions (translations).

is *naturally* without perception, understanding, and knowledge of God, the very requisites necessary for forgiveness/healing. If one combines these two ideas together, namely, that man is naturally fat-hearted and that it is God who fattens, it is reasonable to conclude that the nature of this fattening *must be viewed as primarily deprivational rather than transformational and punitive in nature*. The commission of Isaiah to preach a message of judgment included foremost of all the deprivation of the רוּחַ (wind/spirit) and its effects (wisdom and its effects) along with repentance and its effects (forgiveness/healing). The cause of this deprivation is not Isaiah but God.

Isaiah 6:9–10: The Markan Usage

Mark 4:10–12: The Purpose of Parables

[10]And when he was alone, the ones with him associated with the Twelve began to ask him about the parables. [11]And he said to them: "To you [on the inside] the mystery of the Kingdom of God has been given [by means of imparted wisdom], but to those, the ones who are on the outside [to whom wisdom has not been imparted], everything [teachings and deeds of Jesus] remains in riddles [12]*in order that* although indeed seeing they should not perceive and although indeed hearing they should not understand *otherwise* they should turn [or 'repent] and it should be forgiven them."

The Immediate Context

Mark 4:1–34 and 13:1–37 represent the two major blocks of teaching in this Gospel. In Mark 4 the emphasis falls on hearing, while Mark 13 on seeing (13:1–37).[1] The conceptual design moves in a direction emphasizing the motifs of hearing/seeing. Mark 4:1–34 is a collection of parables dealing with the growth of the kingdom. First, there is the parable of the sower, its purpose, and explanation for Jesus' success and failure (4:1–20).[2] Second, Jesus gives several seed parables addressing the inevitable growth of the kingdom and emphasizing the responsibility of man

---

[1] Ben Witherington, *The Gospel of Mark: A Socio-Rhetorical Commentary* (Grand Rapids: Eerdmans, 2001), 160 n. 54; Robert H. Stein, "Is Our Reading the Bible the Same as the Original Audience's Hearing It? A Case Study in the Gospel of Mark," *JETS* 46 (2003): 63–78; Étienne Trocmé, "Why Parables? A Study of Mark IV," *BJRL* 59 (1976–77): 458.

[2] It includes the parable (4:1–9), the purpose of parables (4:10–12), and an interpretation (4:13–20). For a structural (via chiasm) appraisal of Mark 4 see Greg Fay, "Introduction to Incomprehension: The Literary Structure of Mark 4:1–34," *CBQ* 51 (1989): 65–81. He places 4:10–12 in parallel with 4:21–25.

(4:21–34). The light under the bushel highlights the responsibility to what is heard and offers significant parallels to 4:10–12 (4:21–25).[3] The parable of the mysterious growth of the seed (4:26–29) and the minuscule nature of the mustard seed (4:30–32) testify to the supernatural element and extensive growth of the kingdom. The series of parables is capped by the explanation for the parabolic nature of Jesus' teaching (4:33–34).

The Exegesis of 4:10–12

The Problems. The first problem is the harshness of the saying. The difficulty of this *crux interpretum* is well known.[4] The primary issue centers on the ramifications of the ἵνα clause as *purpose*.[5] Various solutions are proposed. Sometimes source and redaction criticism are used to disprove these words represent either Jesus or the evangelist.[6] A detection of literary seams is apparent but that this proves inauthenticity or intrusiveness by the evangelist is less convincing. Others link the ending of the Isaian quote to the Targum and conjecture a mistranslation or simply interpret it in conformity to the spirit of the Aramaic. But textual amendation is unlikely and the Targum is not much help since it assumes they are already fat-hearted. The major solution is grammatical and involves alternative nuances to ἵνα and μήποτε as well as the syntactic relationship between the two—coordinate or hypotactic. The solution below will argue that ἵνα is purposive, μήποτε is hypotactic rather than

---

[3] Ibid., 68–73.

[4] See Charles Allen Woodward, "The Place of Mark 4:10–12 in the Second Gospel" (Th.D. diss., New Orleans Baptist Theological Seminary, 1979), 1–2; William Robert Myers, "Disciples, Outsiders, and the Secret of the Kingdom: Interpreting Mark 4:10–13" (Th.M. thesis, McGill University, 1960), introduction, 2; F. F. Bruce, *Hard Sayings of Jesus*, The Jesus Library, ed. Michael Green, vol. 1 (Downers Grove, IL: InterVarsity, 1983), 100, 102; C. H. Dodd, *The Parables of the Kingdom*, 2d rev. ed. (New York: Scribner's, 1972), 13–18; Joachim Jeremias, *The Parables of Jesus*, trans. S. H. Hooke, 3d ed. (New York: Scribner's, 1972), 13–18.

[5] Not infrequently an appeal to Hebrew psychology is used to overturn notions of teleology or purpose. Woodward believes the solution is found in recognizing the concept of secondary causality (Woodward, "The Place of Mark 4:10–12 in the Second Gospel," 26).

[6] C. G. Montefiore, *The Synoptic Gospels*, vol. 1 (London: Allen & Unwin, 1909), 123, 134.

coordinate with ἵνα, and therefore μήποτε is best translated as 'in order that...not' or 'otherwise.'

The second problem is the source of the saying. The primary focus here is not to discover the *ipsissima verba* or *vox* of Jesus through source and redaction criticism, but rather to get to the issues surrounding the use of Isa 6:9–10 in relation to 'fattening.'[7] This includes the multifauceted subject matter that naturally surfaces in these verses and impacts this subject. Each topic will be used to support the overall thesis that fattening (here in the NT called 'hardening') is divinely purposed, caused, and yet congenital.[8]

The third problem is the form of the saying. On the form of 4:10–12, Taylor suggests it is a pronouncement story, Hurtado a prophetic irony, a piece of *post hoc* rhetoric, and Witherington a piece of 'counterorder wisdom.'[9] Pesch insists "es ist ein paränetisches Predigtwort apokalyptisch-esoterischer Provenienz."[10] Kelber argues that Mark 4:10–34 "constitutes a sayings gospel or revelation discourse of the kind that has come to light near Nag Hammadi" where esoteric secrecy serves an important socio-linguistic function.[11]

---

[7] Robert W. Funk, Roy W. Hoover, and The Jesus Seminar, *The Five Gospels: The Search for the Authentic Words of Jesus* (New York: Macmillan, 1993), 55. Cf. Philip Sellew, "Oral and Written Sources in Mark 4.1–34," *NTS* 36 (1990): 234–67; Mary Ford, "Seeing, But Not Perceiving: Crisis and Context in Biblical Studies," *SVTQ* 35 (1991): 107–15.

[8] Witherington, *The Gospel of Mark*, 160. After looking at Greco-Roman rhetoric and parables he holds it is persuasively oriented, deals with the discouragement of the sower, directed to a like *Sitz im Leben*, and that the determinant is the nature of the soil (ibid., 162).

[9] Vincent Taylor, *The Gospel according to St. Mark: The Greek Text with Introduction, Notes, and Indexes*, 2d ed. (London: Macmillan, 1966), 254; Larry W. Hurtado, *Mark*, rev. ed., NIBC, ed. W. Ward Gasque, vol. 2 (Peabody, MA: Hendrickson, 1989), 73–74 where he calls it such because it is presented as giving the result as though it was intended when it was not. See also Witherington, *The Gospel of Mark*, 163–64; C. Cohen, "Wisdom/Wisdom Literature," in *The Oxford Dictionary of the Jewish Religion,* ed. R. J. Zwi Werblowsky and Geoffrey Wigoder (New York: Oxford University Press, 1997), 723.

[10] "It is a parenthetical preached-word of apocalyptic-esoteric origin" (Rudolf Pesch, *Das Markusevangelium*, vol. 1, HKNT, ed. Alfred Wilkenhauser, Anton Vögtle, and Rudolf Bultmann, vol. 2 [Freiburg: Herder, 1984], 237).

[11] Werner H. Kelber, "Narrative and Disclosure: Mechanisms of Concealing, Revealing, and Reveling," *Semeia* 43 (1988): 4.

Taylor seems correct in form and Pesch rightly captures the eschatological overtones and origins but Hurtado relies on an interpretive scheme that rejects divine purpose without recourse to a purpose determined by result and Kelber is in danger of anachronism but nevertheless insightful.[12] Witherington's 'counterorder wisdom' suggestion captures the unsettling, disturbing, and ominous tones of the passage that are meant to disrupt the status quo.

The Setting. The meanderings of Jesus. "And when he was[13] alone...." The *setting* is a transitional scene[14] and an idyllic environment of isolation apart from the crowds where the disciples could question him privately.[15] This isolation appears difficult to harmonize with the

---

[12] His essay frequently refers to the esoteric secrecy in Mark 4 in terms of wisdom and parabolic wisdom (ibid., 10–11). Via holds the necessary precondition for understanding is endowment (Dan O. Via, "Irony as Hope in Mark's Gospel: A Reply to Werner Kelber," *Semeia* 43 [1988]: 24). He asks why the word in Mark is only effective for some and not all. Ultimately he holds, "It is Mark's belief that the revealer of the seed-word himself cannot say exactly how human pre-understanding and revealing word interact, which makes it possible—or necessary—to say that everything comes from God, but some things come from the human person" (ibid., 24).

[13] Moule takes "*As soon* as he was..." in combination with the two imperfects ἠρώτων and ἔλεγεν to arrive at the sense of "*Whenever* he was..." indicating a repeated process throughout Jesus ministry (C. F. D. Moule, "Mark v, 1–20 Yet Once More," in *Neotestamentica et Semitica: Studies in Honour of Matthew Black*, ed. E. Earl Ellis and Max Wilcox [Edinburg: Clark, 1969], 101).

[14] For a minor textual issue see Ezra P. Gould, *Critical and Exegetical Commentary on the Gospel according to Mark* (Edinburg: Clark, 1896; reprint, New York: Scribner's, 1913), 71. The phrase καὶ ὅτε occurs twenty-six times in the NT and is confined to the Gospels (Matt 21:1; 27:31; Mark 4:6, 10; 7:17; 11:1, 15:20; Luke 2:21, 22, 42; 6:13; 22:14; 23:33), Acts (1:13; 22:20), and Revelation (1:17; 5:8; 6:3, 5, 7, 9; 10:3, 4, 10; 12:13; 22:8) and is used either to highlight a new scene or identify a fundamental shift within the narrative.

[15] κατὰ μόνας is used adverbially of *place*, serves to isolate or separate *by* (BDAG 511–12), and modifies ἐγένετο. The phrase appears ten times in the LXX (Gen 32:17; Judg 7:5; 17:3; 1 Macc 12:36; 2 Macc 15:36, 39; Pss 4:8; 33:15; 141:10; Jer 15:17; Lam 3:28). The exact phrase only occurs here and Luke 9:18. See A. T. Robertson, *A Grammar of the Greek New Testament in the Light of Historical Research*, 4th ed. (Nashville: Broadman, 1934), 244, 550, 653; Gould, *Gospel according to Mark*, 71 n. 1; MHT 3:18, 21. The uniqueness of the phrase is evidence that Mark took this over from his source. Elsewhere he uses κατ᾽ ἰδίαν seven times (4:34; 6:31, 32; 7:33; 9:2, 28; 13:3)

locales and audience.[16] But the difficulty arises from assuming that Jesus remains in the boat. In 4:1 Jesus is in a boat teaching while the crowd is on the shores listening to his parables. In 4:10–12 he is alone either because he has exited the boat or crossed the lake where his followers could approach him. Here he explains the incomprehension of outsiders in Isaian language while interpreting the parable of the sower (4:13–20) and giving additional parables (4:21–32). The summary in 4:33–34 is oriented towards explaining unbelief.[17] Later in the evening Jesus crosses to the other side of the lake (4:35). This scenario requires a bit of imagination but it is not far-fetched even if one recognizes the composite nature of the passage.[18]

The motif of isolation. Mark uses the motif of isolation or privacy to highlight the distinction between insiders and outsiders. This privacy motif may be linked to the secrecy motif where the former arises because of the latter.[19] This is its first occurrence in Mark. Private instruction occurs in 4:14–20, 33–34 (explanation of parable), 7:18–22 ('catalogue' of sins defiling community), 9:28–29 (the disciples activity as exorcists), 10:10–12 (about divorce/remarriage), and 13:1–37 (apocalyptic discourse to four disciples). In the latter scene, two

---

which otherwise occurs eleven times in the NT (Matt 14:13, 23; 17:1, 19; 20:17; 24:3; Luke 9:10; 10:23; Acts 23:19; Gal 2:2; 2 Tim 1:9).

[16] This creates two major problems, namely, being approached while 'alone' and large crowds to a private setting. See Robert A. Guelich, *Mark 1–8:26*, WBC, ed. Ralph P. Martin, vol. 34A (Dallas: Word, 1989), 203–05. Guelich explains that "this shift then provided an occasion later for the insertion of the more esoteric theme of 4:11–12 between 4:3–8 and 14–20 and for adding the appropriate conclusion in 4:34" (ibid., 203). See also Hugh Anderson, *The Gospel of Mark*, NCB, ed. Ronald E. Clements and Matthew Black (London: Marshall, Morgan, and Scott, 1976), 129.

[17] After a revelation or teaching Jesus would be alone with his disciples (Woodward, "The Place of Mark 4:10–12 in the Second Gospel," 41; Witherington, *The Gospel of Mark*, 166; Joachim Gnilka, *Theologie des neuen Testaments*, HKNT, ed. Joachim Gnilka and Lorenz Oberlinner, vol. 5 [Freiburg: Herder, 1994], 156–59).

[18] See Fred D. Gealy, "The Composition of Mark 4," *ExpTim* 48 (1936–37): 41. He explains the inconsistency in terms of Mark leaving "the world of space-time for the world of ideas."

[19] See William Wrede, *The Messianic Secret*, trans. J. C. G. Greig (Cambridge: Clarke, 1971). See also Albert Schweitzer, *The Mystery of the Kingdom of God: The Secret of Jesus' Messiahship and Passion*, trans. Walter Lowrie (New York: Dodd, 1914). For an examination of Wrede, especially on 4:10–12, see Peter H. Igarashi, "The Mystery of the Kingdom (Mark 4:10–12)," *JBR* 24 (1955–56): 83–89.

private parables are given (13:28, 34) and the discourse is followed by an explanation with no passing in scene.[20] *Public* parables in Mark have three categories: polemical (12:1–11), kingdom oriented, especially in regard to its hiddenness (3:22), and didactic (4:11–12).[21] The commonality of public parables (except 13:28, 34) is that they come in response to either hostility or culpable incomprehension of the hearers in respect to the person and work of Jesus. Isolation is not limited to explanation but rather intimacy.

The Occasion. This involves a question or several questions over the nature of parabolic teaching. "They began to question[22] him about the parables." There are a number of issues that bear on the discussion of wisdom. First, the issue concerns parables not merely a parable. This may suggest Mark changes it to the plural, derives it from a collection

---

[20] Culled from Schuyler Brown, "The Secret of the Kingdom of God (Mark 4, 11)," *JBL* 92 (1973): 69–70. He says the secrecy motif covers two contents, one *kerygmatic* ('Jesus is the Christ') and the other *didactic* (community catechesis, various instructions and exhortations) (ibid., 72).

[21] Ibid., 73; Joachim Gnilka, *Die Verstockung Israels: Isaias 6:9–10 in der Theologie der Synoptiker*, SANT, ed. Vinzenz Hamp and Josef Schmid, vol. 3 (Munich: Kösel, 1961), 71. Each private instruction is marked with wisdom elements: (1) 4:10–12 deals with parables, mysteries, insiders and outsiders, seeing, hearing, understanding, and forgiveness. (2) 4:14–20 addresses the inability of the heart to produce fruit without imparted wisdom or the inevitability of doing so with it. (3) 7:18–22 mentions they are without understanding and perception and this is because the heart is congenitally evil. (4) 9:28–29 is a rebuke to the disciples who cannot cast out a "dumb and deaf" spirit. (5) 10:10–12 comes after the reason for Moses permitting divorce, viz., because they have *hard*-hearts ([σκληροκαρδία = rebellious] 10:5). (6) 13:1–37 has to do with the future and seeing into it, not being led astray, having the Spirit inspire them in their utterances, a statement admonishing the reader to 'understand' the prophetic text (if the reader read aloud then this involves the ears also), the elect, learning a lesson from the fig tree in order to know the nearness of prophesied events, and not knowing the exact hour. Each is *an attempt of Jesus to explain human failure* on the part of either outsiders or the disciples.

[22] C. E. B. Cranfield, *The Gospel according to Saint Mark*, CGTC, ed. C. F. D. Moule (Cambridge: Cambridge University Press, 1972), 152. The imperfect may be intended to highlight the tentative or hesitant nature of the request rather than the forceful nature of the aorist (MHT 3:64–65, as noted by Buist M. Fanning, *Verbal Aspect in New Testament Greek*, OTM, ed. J. Barton et al. [Oxford: Clarendon, 1990], 289). Moule takes ἠρώτων as true *ingressive* imperfect (Moule, "Mark v, 1–20 Yet Once More," 102; Woodward, "The Place of Mark 4:10–12 in the Second Gospel," 46).

of parables in the plural, or something deeper.[23] Since this is the third parable recorded in Mark (3:23–26, 27; 4:3–8), the disciples may have in mind parabolic teaching in general. *Why are you teaching this way?* A theory of parables can then be given. But since the exact question about the parables is not stated it might have to do with the 'mystery'—but even *which* aspect of the mystery (presumably of the kingdom) must be inferred. The question, therefore, could involve the mystery over the constituents of the kingdom (noted by the soils) that ultimately turn on the nature of מָשָׁל/παραβολή as both teachings and acts. *Why do some understand and other do not?*[24] Finally, since the parable is interpreted (4:13–20) the question could be about the meaning of the specific parable given. Second, Jesus' response should be seen as having a didactic purpose concerning the mystery of

---

[23] This noun functions as an accusative of *direct object*, or better, *object double-accusative of person thing* (αὐτὸν...τὰς παραβολάς) modifying ἠρώτων. The article is a *generalizing* or *categorical plural* (see Max Zerwick, *Biblical Greek Illustrated by Examples*, trans. Joseph Smith, Scripta Pontificii, vol. 114 [Rome: Editrice Pontificio Istituto Biblico, 1963], §7; cf. MHT 3:25–26). For τὰς παραβολάς some MSS A *f*[1] 𝔐 vg[cl] sy[p.h] bo[ms] read τὴν παραβολήν (along with von Soden, Lachmann, and MT). Ambrozic dismisses von Soden's reading as unwarranted (Aloysius M. Ambrozic, *The Hidden Kingdom—A Redaction-critical Study of the References to the Kingdom of God in Mark*, CBQMS, ed. Joseph A. Fitzmyer et al., vol. 2 [Washington DC: Catholic Biblical Association, 1972], 46–47). Other MSS read τὶς ἡ παραβολὴ αὕτη ('What does this parable mean') D W Θ *f*[13] 28. 565. 2542 it; Or[lat]. Text: ℵ B C L Δ 892. 2427 *pc* vg[st] sy[s] co and reflect τὴν παραβολὴν ταύτην in 4:13. Internal evidence is divided where the plural is original and the singular is a later correction (Philip Bailey, *The Blindness of the Jews in Matthew 13:13–15, Mark 4:12 and Luke 8:10* [Rome: Typis Scholae Tipographicae Missionariae Dominicanae, 1956], 9) or the singular is original and the plural is a correction (Guelich, *Mark 1–8:26*, 205; Ambrozic, *The Hidden Kingdom*, 52; Craig A. Evans, *To See and Not Perceive: Isaiah 6:9–10 in Early Jewish and Christian Interpretation*, JSOTSup, ed. David J. A. Clines and Philip R. Davies, vol. 64 [Sheffield: JSOT, 1989], 204 n. 46). Kirkland (J. R. Kirkland, "The Earliest Understanding of Jesus' Use of Parables: Mark IV 10–12 in Context," *NovT* 19 [1977]: 4–5) says the view that Mark pluralized the singular from his source is based on questionable assumptions. "The plural suggests that 10–12 is a separate unit" (Taylor, *The Gospel according to St. Mark*, 255).

[24] The first explanation goes with 4:11, the second explanation with 4:12 (Isa 6:9–13), and the third with 4:13–20. On the second explanation see John W. Bowker, "Mystery and Parable: Mark iv. 1–20," *JTS* 25 (1974): 312; Trocmé, "Why Parables?" 461–63; Fay, "Introduction to Incomprehension," 75–76.

providence.[25] His answer takes unexpected turns, goes beyond the contours of the questioners or question, and suggests another question may have been more appropriate.

The Audience. *'Those with him' and 'the Twelve.'* Who is asking the question? This seems to include two groups: the Twelve and those with them. The phrase οἱ περὶ αὐτὸν σὺν τοῖς δώδεκα is unique to Mark.[26] Ambiguity lies with the identity of 'those with' the Twelve, not the Twelve. One issue is whether this is a chance gathering or a closed group. Moule suggests the former but Bowker and others show that the phrase is technical referring to partisan followers beyond the apostolic band.[27] This group can only be some disciples (cf. 4:33–34).[28]

---

[25] Eckhard J. Schnabel, "The Silence of Jesus: The Galilean Rabbi Who was More Than a Prophet," in *Authenticating the Words of Jesus*, ed. Bruce Chilton and Craig A. Evans (Boston: Brill, 2002), 205.

[26] Gnilka, *Die Verstockung Israels*, 24. The phrase (article + περὶ αὐτός) 'the ones with him' yields six instances in the NT (Mark 3:34; 4:10; Luke 22:49; Acts 13:29; 23:15; Jude 1:7) while the phrase 'with the Twelve' is a *hapax*. On this phrase see MHT 3:16, 270; BDF §228; Woodward, "The Place of Mark 4:10–12 in the Second Gospel," 44 who wrongly cites James A. Brooks and Carlton L. Winbery, *Syntax of New Testament Greek* (Washington, DC: University Press of America, 1979), 61–62; Ernest Best, "Mark's Use of the Twelve," *ZNW* 69 (1978): 18.

[27] Based on Josephus (*A.J.* 6.319; 7.307; 16.238; 17.283; 18.260; *J.W.* 1.515), Bowker argues that the phrase includes an "intentional allegiance to Jesus" (Bowker, "Mystery and Parable," 309; Thomas Walter Manson, *The Teaching of Jesus: Studies of Its Form and Content* [Cambridge: Cambridge University Press, 1963], 75 n. 3; Woodward, "The Place of Mark 4:10–12 in the Second Gospel," 44, 46; Myers, "Disciples, Outsiders, and the Secret of the Kingdom," 146–47; C. H. Turner, "'The Disciples' and 'the Twelve'," *JTS* 28 [1927]: 22–30; K. H. Rengstorf, "μανθάνω," *TDNT* 4:415–61). Manson points to the same expression in 2 Maccabees for the sense of 'followers,' 'partisans,' or a 'retinue' of someone (cf. LXX Gen 37:23; 2 Sam 15:18; 2 Macc 1:13; 2:2; 8:16; 12:5,20; 13:15; 14:30; 15:13; 3 Macc 1:27; 6:1; 4 Macc 1:12; 4:5; Sir 19:30; Ezek 38:6). This evidence argues against Moule's chance gathering (Moule, "Mark v, 1–20 Yet Once More," 98).

[28] The term 'disciple,' although not mentioned here, is used forty-six times in Mark (2:15–16, 18, 23; 3:7, 9; 4:34; 5:31; 6:1, 29, 35, 41, 45; 7:2, 5, 17; 8:1, 4, 6, 10, 27, 33–34; 9:14, 18, 28, 31; 10:10, 13, 23–24, 46; 11:1, 14; 12:43; 13:1; 14:12–14, 16, 32; 16:7). The Markan emphasis on disciples as both privileged (private explanation) but fearful, incomprehensive, and objects of rebuke is lessened in Matthew and Luke (Ernest Best, "The Role of the Disciples in Mark," *NTS* 23 [1976–77]: 390, 84–401; Best, "Mark's Use of the Twelve," 18).

Another issue is the relationship of the two groups to each other and whether redaction plays a part and how this impacts the insider/outsider constituency. Gould identifies the former as the disciples, Meye argues for a subset group of the Twelve, while Ambrozic holds it a circumlocution for the Twelve but having the readers primarily in mind.[29] Others attribute the confusion to a Markan redaction.[30] This may take four forms.[31] First, the entire phrase is a Markan creation. Its clumsy syntax argues against this. Second, the phrase 'those with him' come from tradition while 'the Twelve' is a Markan addition.[32] Third, 'the Twelve' comes from the tradition and Mark adds 'those with him.' Fourth, both phrases are combined from divergent traditions. Taylor maintains that the phrase points to a distinction between the disciples and the Twelve.[33] Best argues that the role of the disciples in Mark is in contrast with the Twelve accounting for the Markan addition (of the Twelve) here. How Mark uses the disciples and the Twelve may yield more tangible solutions.[34]

The disciples. Best distinguishes between disciples and the Twelve among whom are the three and Peter—thus four groups in all.[35] The disciples could occupy a purely historical position, signify others who claim apostolicity, other groups within the church, or serve a purely

---

[29] The disciples are distinguished from the crowds and the Twelve (Gould, *Gospel according to Mark*, 71). Meye sees the disciples as a subgroup of the Twelve but Ambrozic thinks this is unnecessary. The disciples are a wider group but include the Twelve (Ambrozic, *The Hidden Kingdom*, 70–72; Robert P. Meye, "The Messianic Secret and Messianic Didache in Mark's Gospel," in *Oikonomia: Heilsgeschichte als Thema der Theologie*, ed. Felix Christ [Hamburg-Bergstedt: Reich, 1967], 61–66; idem, "Those about Him with the Twelve," *SE* 2 [1964]: 211–18; idem, *Jesus and the Twelve: Discipleship and Revelation in Mark's Gospel* [Grand Rapids: Eerdmans, 1968], 152–56).

[30] Anderson, *The Gospel of Mark*, 130.

[31] Best, "The Role of the Disciples in Mark," 377–401; Best, "Mark's Use of the Twelve," 16–18.

[32] Kirkland, "The Earliest Understanding of Jesus' Use of Parables," 4; Best, "The Role of the Disciples in Mark," 383–87, 433–34.

[33] Taylor, *The Gospel according to St. Mark*, 255.

[34] See Jack Dean Kingsbury, *Conflict in Mark: Jesus, Authorities, Disciples* (Minneapolis: Fortress, 1989) and Ernest Best, *Disciples and Discipleship: Studies in the Gospel according to Mark* (Edinburgh: T&T Clark, 1986).

[35] Best, "The Role of the Disciples in Mark," 377.

informational role. He argues that most occurrences of 'the disciples' come from the tradition while references to 'the Twelve' from the redaction. Best rejects the idea that Mark is attacking the Twelve, Peter, or John but he does assign roles for the disciples, the Twelve, the Three, the Four, John, and Peter. Three points of a negative light come from comparing the traditional versus redaction material. These are the fear of the disciples, the failure of the disciples to understand, and Jesus' rebukes to them.[36] A recent study by Danove using neutral, sophisticating, and deconstructive rhetorical strategies arrives at similar results. The negative emphases include lack of understanding, lack of faith, fear, and amazement towards all outsiders and also towards the disciples.[37] The tradition is heightened by Mark and subsequently de-emphasized in Matthew and Luke.[38] The positive evaluation of the disciples increases only in the second portion of Mark. The disciples may also represent the church as evidenced by the eucharistic symbolism, the call of the twelve, and the secret instructions.[39] This may explain the emphasis on private instruction in a 'house.'[40]

The Twelve.[41] From a redactional point of view, the Twelve are probably representative of the missionaries of the world or the

---

[36] These ideas are as follows: (1) Fear of the disciples (Tradition: 6:49; Redaction: 4:41; 6:45, 50; 9:32; 10:32). (2) The failure of the disciples to understand (Tradition: 5:31; 6:37; 8:4; 9:18–19; Redaction: 6:52; 7:17; 8:17–21; 9:32; 14:31). (3) Jesus' rebuke of them (Tradition: 10:13–14; 14:27; Redaction: 8:15–21, 33; 9:33–37). See ibid., 387. He says that in order for Mark to explain the true meaning of the cross he has to present the disciples as those who misunderstand its power (ibid., 388).

[37] Paul Danove, "The Narrative Rhetoric of Mark's Ambiguous Characterization of the Disciples," *JSNT* 70 (1998): 21–38.

[38] Best, "The Role of the Disciples in Mark," 389–90.

[39] Ibid., 396–97.

[40] The house is a place of intimacy in Mark. Two terms are used: οἰκία occurs eighteen times and οἶκος thirteen times. See ibid., 400; Best, "Mark's Use of the Twelve," 19.

[41] In Mark 'the Twelve' occurs eleven times (Mark 3:14, 16; 4:10; 6:7; 9:35; 10:32; 11:11; 14:10, 17, 20, 43), the eleven once (16:14 [long ending]), and ten once (10:41). Mark 3:14 is the only anarthrous 'the Twelve' and 1 Cor 15:5 treats it as technical post-resurrection (add to this Q). Best thinks 'the Twelve' comes from the tradition and Mark's *use* rather than *preponderance* of the expression makes it exceptional (Best, "Mark's Use of the Twelve," 12). The representatives of Jesus are referred to as disciples (forty-six times), the Twelve (eleven times), and apostles (once or twice;

ministers of the church.[42] Jesus appoints them to preach (3:14), sets Peter as the head (if genuine 3:16), distinguishes them from others (4:10), sends them forth two by two (6:7), teaches them about servanthood (9:35), warns them what will happen in Jerusalem (10:32), accompanies them to Bethany (11:11), is betrayed by one of them, Judas (14:10, 20, 43), and is with them (14:17). Use of the number elsewhere suggests a literary penchant designed to reinforce the importance of the Twelve (5:25, 42; 6:43; 8:19). Compared with the disciples this term is generally connected to notions of being sent, a functional mode, and not intended to be sharply distinguished with 'disciples.'[43]

The crowd. The term almost always appears in the singular and suggests the crowd is viewed as a "unified sociological entity."[44] Best subjects this group to traditional and redactional changes in Mark.[45] He concludes that they never act as a foil to Jesus, are not the recipients of private instruction, do not journey with Jesus, are not afraid of what Jesus says or does, are not represented as failing to understand what Jesus says (though they do), are not prohibited from disclosing information (individuals are when it comes to healing), are not given positions after the resurrection, are not pictured as failing in action (but are not given duties either), are not defended by Jesus from criticism, do not mediate between Jesus and others, do not act in behalf of Jesus, and when called by Jesus either respond and become disciples or reject the call.[46] On the whole this group is not given any unitary or positive role and are not to be confused with the disciples. It is the object of evangelism and from this group the disciples are

---

3:14; 6:30). For the phrase περὶ αὐτὸν σὺν τοῖς δώδεκα some MSS D W Θ *f*[13] 28. 565. 2542 it sy[s]; (Or[lat]) read simply μαθηταὶ αὐτοῦ, "his disciples." This is a harmonization to Matthew and Luke.

[42] Best, "The Role of the Disciples in Mark," 399–400.

[43] Best, "Mark's Use of the Twelve," 32–35.

[44] Best, "The Role of the Disciples in Mark," 390. The term for 'crowds' occurs thirty-eight times in this Gospel (Mark 2:4, 13; 3:9, 20, 32; 4:1, 36; 5:21, 24, 27, 30–31; 6:34, 45; 7:14, 17, 33; 8:1–2, 6:34; 9:14–15, 17, 25; 10:46; 11:18, 32; 12:12, 37, 41; 14:43; 15:8, 11, 15) and only once is in the plural (10:1). One include 'many' (πολύς) and the indefinite plural. The religious ὁ λαός is avoided for this group (Mark 7:6; 14:2).

[45] Ibid., 391.

[46] Ibid., 392.

called. They are friendly but not good. They are taught in parables but not given the interpretations.[47] But Best is incorrect here. They are at times given explanations concerning parables, teachings, and deeds.[48] But it is still unlikely that they are those with the Twelve.

The enemies. The enemies are depicted in the persons of the Pharisees, scribes, chief priests, Herodians, Sadducees, and rulers.[49] This group commits the more serious offense than merely misunderstanding the person and role of Jesus because they determinately bring about his death. Within this group can be placed such characters as Herod, Pilate, and Judas. They certainly are not those with the Twelve but they are at times given explanations regarding the parables, teachings, and acts of Jesus.[50]

Summary. A limited spectrum of groups may be classified as 'insiders.' These include 'the disciples and the Twelve rather than a subgroup. This insider status is marked by *intimacy* rather than *absence of parabolic teaching* or being *recipients of explanations*. Outsiders include the ambivalent crowd, outspoken enemies, or inside traitors (Judas)—Judas requires further nuancing of insiders.

The Παραβολάς *and* Πάντα *(part 1). Linguistic background of the parable.* Gnilka says, "Es ist einhellige Auffassung daß Mark durch das Stichwort παραβολή veranlaßt wurde, das Logion Vers 11f in das Gleichniskapitel zu stellen."[51] The παραβολή, however, occurs fifty times in the NT, all but two (Heb 9:9; 11:19) in the Synoptics: twenty-one times it has the article preceding it, seventeen of which are

---

[47] Best also notes they are invited to become disciples, instructed about discipleship, forgiveness of sins, about divorce, and told of the identity of Jesus in veiled form (ibid., 398).

[48] They receive (1) explanations of parables in 3:26–27, 35 and 4:22, (2) an explanation of a teaching in 2:10–11, and (3) an explanation of an act in 2:19–22.

[49] This group is represented by various smaller groups (ἀρχιερεύς, βασιλεύς, γραμματεύς, ἡγεμών, Ἡρῳδιανοί, πρεσβύτερος, συνέδριον, ανδ Φαρισαῖος).

[50] Explanations to this group include the following: (1) Teachings of Jesus (2:10–11; 14:61a, 62; 15:2b, 5), (2) Acts of Jesus (2:19–22, 25–28), and (3) Parables of Jesus (3:26–27, 35; 12:10).

[51] Gnilka, *Die Verstockung Israels*, 24; John Drury, "The Sower, The Vineyard, and the Place of Allegory in the Intepretation of Mark's Parables," *JTS* 24 (1973): 375–77.

singular and four are plural (Matt 13:53; 21:45; Mark 4:10, 13b).[52] It occurs in the LXX forty-six times of which twelve are in the apocrypha and thirty-four in the canonical books.[53] In all but one case (Eccl 1:17, הוֹלֵלוּת 'madness') it translates the Hebrew term מָשָׁל 'proverb.' However, מָשָׁל is translated by several Greek terms and this seems to suggest a broader sense to παραβολή.[54] Snodgrass suggests it can refer to a taunt, byword, lament, oracle, discourse, or riddle. The NT employs it as a proverb, riddle, comparison, an example story, a story with two levels of meaning, allegory, a symbol, or to convey an idea 'figuratively.' Its rarity in Josephus, Philo, Plato, and Aristotle suggests an obscurity that the translators of the LXX brought to prominence and "the evangelists would catapult to notoriety."[55] Confining it to parabolic speech apart from symbolic acts may be overly reductionistic.

    The OT non-linguistic background. The concept of מָשָׁל/παραβολή in the OT is a form of analogical thinking, rarely in legal texts (mostly in

---

[52] Matt 13:3, 10, 13, 18, 24, 31, 33–36, 53; 15:15; 21:33, 45; 22:1; 24:32; Mark 3:23; 4:2, 10–11, 13, 30, 33–34; 7:17; 12:1, 12; 13:28; Luke 4:23; 5:36; 6:39; 8:4, 9–11; 12:16, 41; 13:6; 14:7; 15:3; 18:1, 9; 19:11; 20:9, 19; 21:29; Heb. 9:9; 11:19. See Manson, *The Teaching of Jesus*, 59 n. 1, 66–74; Witherington, *The Gospel of Mark*, 161–63 for a discussion on Greco-Roman rhetoric and the parable; BDAG 759–60; Bailey, *The Blindness of the Jews in Matthew 13:13–15, Mark 4:12 and Luke 8:10*, 43; Anderson, *The Gospel of Mark*, 130 who rejects 4:11–12 as the words of Jesus. See Myers, "Disciples, Outsiders, and the Secret of the Kingdom," 152–61.

[53] Canonical: Num 23:7,18; 24:3,15, 20–21, 23; Deut 28:37; 1 Sam 10:12; 24:14; 2 Sam 23:3; 1 Kgs 5:12; 2 Chr 7:20; Pss 43:15; 48:5; 68:12; 77:2; Prov 1:6; Eccl 1:17; 12:9; Mic 2:4; Hab 2:6; Jer 24:9; Ezek 12:22–23; 16:44; 17:2; 18:2–3; 19:14; 21:5; 24:3; Dan 12:8. Non-canonical: Tob 3:4; Wis 5:4; Sir 1:25; 3:29; 13:26; 20:20; 38:34; 39:2–3; 47:15, 17; Theod. Tob 3:4.

[54] Besides παραβολή it is translated by ἀφανιτμός 'disappearing, destruction, extermination, vanishing' twice (1 Kgs 9:7; Ezek 14:8), θρῆνος 'lament, lamentation' once (Isa 14:4), προοίμιον 'parable, poem' twice (Job 27:1; 29:1), παιδεία 'instruction, discipline' once (Prov 25:1), and παροιμία 'proverb, parable' twice (Prov 1:1; 26:7). A few other cases involve graphic confusion where מָשָׁל 'rule' is assumed and thus the verb κατάρχω 'to rule, begin' (Joel 2:17; Zech 9:10) and δουλεία 'slavery' (Prov 26:9) results.

[55] Klyne Snodgrass, "Parables and the Hebrew Scriptures," in *To Hear and Obey: Essays in Honor of Fredrick Carlson Holmgren*, ed. Bradley J. Bergfalk and Paul E. Koptak (Chicago: Covenant Publications, 1997), 168. As a byword or taunt-song it is absent in the NT (Myers, "Disciples, Outsiders, and the Secret of the Kingdom," 157). See Josephus *A.J.* 8.44*bis*; Philo *Conf.* 99; *QG* 1.2.54; *QE* 2.3.

prophetic literature, psalms, and proverbs), occurs in the context of judgment and indictment, and designed to confront (in OT) more than exegete (rabbis).[56] OT examples that have parallels in the NT include juridical parables, fables, story types, acted parables, and symbolic visions and dreams.[57] Evans says the relationship is either with the Hebrew genre חִידָה, (oracle, riddle, or proverb)[58] or מָשָׁל.[59] He takes it as a word of judgment that identifies the good seed (Bowker) and positively judges by promoting obduracy.[60] He points to a tradition that links parables with Isa 6 (*Ascen. Isa.* 4:20–21) and concludes that the prepositional phrase 'in parables' (4:12) suggests a similar parabolic word of judgment as in Isaiah.[61]

Brown identifies a wisdom theme. He notes that in post-exilic books, like Sirach, wisdom is used as an agent of God in revealing mysteries and this includes *through* studying ancient traditions and parables.[62] The mysteries and aspects of them are revealed to those

---

[56] Snodgrass, "Parables and the Hebrew Scriptures," 168–69.

[57] *Juridical parables* (2 Sam 12:1–14; 14:1–20; 1 Kgs 20:35–42; Isa 5:1–7), *fables* (Jdg 9:7–15; 2 Kgs 14:9–10), *story types* as narratives or allegories (Ezek 16:1–54; 17:2–24; 19:2–9, 10–14; 23:1–49; 24:3–14), *acted parables* (footwashing, miracles, entry into Jerusalem, cleansing of temple, etc.), and *symbolic visions and dreams*. These require interpretation (Jer 24:1–10; Amos 7:1–9; 8:1–3; Zech 1:7–8:1–3; Dan 2; 7 (ibid., 170–71; G. K. Falusi, "Jesus' Use of Parables in Mark with Special Reference to Mark 4:10–12," *IJT* 31 [1982]: 35–46).

[58] It occurs seventeen times in the canonical books but translated by five Greek terms: (1) αἴνιγμα 'obscurity' (Num 12:8; 1 Kgs 10:1; Prov 1:6; Dan 8:23; 2 Chr 9:1). (2) πρόβλημα 'riddle' (Judg A 14:12, 13, 14, 15, 16, 18, 19; Judg B 14:13, 14, 15, 16, 18, 19; Pss 49:5[48:5]; 78:2[77:2]; Theod. Dan 8:23). (3) προβάλλω 'to put forth' (Judg B 14:12). (4) διήγμα 'story, tale' (Ezek 17:2). (5) διήγησις 'tale, declaration' (Hab 2:6; cf. Luke 1:1). See Trocmé, "Why Parables?" 461–62.

[59] Craig A. Evans, "A Note on the Function of Isaiah vi, 9–10 in Mark iv," *RB* 88 (1981): 235.

[60] See Bowker, "Mystery and Parable," 300–17.

[61] Evans, "A Note on the Function of Isaiah vi, 9–10 in Mark iv," 235 n. 9 (although he refers to it as 6:20); Evans, *To See and Not Perceive*, 105–06. Ambrozic, *The Hidden Kingdom*, 82 says the term מָשָׁל in *1 Enoch* applies to visions and its interpretation. Cf. F. Hauck, "παραβολή," *TDNT* 5:744–61; Matt 13:35 *v.l.*

[62] Raymond E. Brown, "The Pre-Christian Semitic Concept of 'Mystery'," *CBQ* 20 (1958): 417–43. He lists Sir 47:15–17 and 39:7. Cf. Richard J. Clifford, *The Wisdom Literature*, Interpreting Biblical Texts, ed. Gene M. Tucker (Nashville: Abingdon, 1998), 166; Craig A. Evans, "On the Isaianic Background of the Sower Parable," *CBQ*

with imparted wisdom through the use of מָשָׁל/παραβολή.[63] The necessary condition for understanding a parable is the καρδία συνετοῦ and οὖς ἀκροατοῦ that are the desires of a 'wise' (σοφοῦ) man (Sir 3:29). The Apostolic Fathers agree with this assessement.[64] Given this wisdom background, parables *become* riddles only to those without imparted wisdom, or those without an understanding heart or hearing ear. *They are not enigmatic of themselves.* Recognizing this helps identify the true purpose of parables.

Summary of Mark 4:10. Mark 4:10 shows a *setting* of isolation focusing on intimacy. The *occasion* is the question for parabolic teaching and its relationship to the constituency's ability to hear and accept Jesus' teaching. The *audience* is comprised of partisan followers. Parables have several functions but are confined mostly to sapiential and prophetic materials with the *public* purpose of indicting, judging, or making an eschatological separation in addition to teaching. Its *private* use is primarily pedagogic. Wisdom is linked to parables as the prerequisite for understanding them. In Isaianic terms, only those without a fat-heart can see through them to the mysteries. In the parable of the sower, the good soil (non-fat/new heart), or one with imparted wisdom, receives the seed (message of the kingdom) and bears fruit. Verse 10 pictures the setting, occasion, and audience from which the question arises while verses 11–12 give a twofold answer explaining the cause of insider belief and outsider unbelief.

The Sapiential Affinity. On a redaction level, Mark 4:11 contains elements that may reflect Pauline or Jewish-Christian and Aramaic influence—elements then credited to church formulations.[65] Gealy

---

47 (1985): 464–68. Evans links the parable to the efficacy of God's word to bear fruit in identifying 'insiders' and 'outsiders.'

[63] Bowker limits the knowledge to *mishnah* defining insiders as having more information (Bowker, "Mystery and Parable," 304).

[64] *Barn.* 6:10 indicates the endowment of wisdom is the prerequisite for understanding secrets and parables. Explanation is required because parables are obscure to some (*Barn.* 17:2; Herm. *Vis.* 1.11:2; 5.25:5). The foolish (Herm. *Mand.* 10.40:3–4), the sluggish, or arrogant person cannot understand them (Herm. *Sim.* 5.56:1, 57:1–5, 58:1, 5; 59:8; 9.82:5, 106:4). Explanations come voluntarily from an angel after edification by the Spirit (Herm. *Sim.* 9.78:1).

[65] Anderson, *The Gospel of Mark*, 130–31. He cites four points of fact: (1) 'mystery,' (2) 'those outside,' (3) 'everything in parables,' and (4) 'so that' and 'lest.' The first two are related to Pauline and Revelation, whereas the third and fourth to Aramaic-

suggests that Mark 4 is strung together entirely on the theory of parables.[66] Taylor does not credit the words to Jesus but relates the entire arrangement to "that which we find repeatedly in Proverbs, Ecclesiastes, and the Wisdom of Sirach."[67] Barton says that Mark is preoccupied with obstacles to wisdom here and throughout the Gospel where a conflict is between two types of wisdom.[68] The *Sitz im Leben*, sapiential terms, and themes probably trigger a wisdom arrangement only enhanced if Mark is patterned after Isa 52:13–53:12.[69]

Jesus begins his response with a characteristic didactic formula, "and he said to them"[70] usually deemed a Markan 'link-phrase.'[71] Essame says this phrase in the imperfect gives the effect of continuity in narration and translates it as "another saying of his was this." He points to a similar phrase in rabbinic literature where Rabbis are introduced by הוּא הָיָה אֹמֵר "he used to say" and concludes that not

---

speaking Palestine. Cf. Michael D. Goulder, "Those Outside (MK. 4:10–12)," *NovT* 33 (1991): 294–95; Falusi, "Jesus' Use of Parables in Mark," 42.

[66] Gealy, "The Composition of Mark 4," 40. He says 'and he said to them' is too stereotypical, the ineptitude of 4:11–12 suggests Mark used it to unite it with 4:3–9, and the interpretation (4:14–20) and sayings of 4:21–25 are unrelated to parables (Vincent Taylor, *The Formation of the Gospel Tradition* [London: Macmillan, 1935], 90–91). On the source/redaction issue see Gealy, "The Composition of Mark 4," 41. However, he regards 4:11–12 as central and determinative of the entire section (ibid., Guelich, *Mark 1–8:26*, 205).

[67] Taylor, *The Formation of the Gospel Tradition*, 92.

[68] Stephen C. Barton, "Gospel Wisdom," in *Where Shall Wisdom Be Found? Wisdom in the Bible, the Church, and the Contemporary World*, ed. Stephen C. Barton (Edinburgh: T&T Clark, 1999), 98–101.

[69] John D. Grassmick, "Mark," in *The Bible Knowledge Commentary: An Exposition of the Scriptures by Dallas Seminary Faculty*, ed. John F. Walvoord and Roy B. Zuck, vol. 2 (Wheaton, IL: Victor, 1983), 100; Igarashi, "The Mystery of the Kingdom (Mark 4:10–12)," 86–87. See *1 Clem.* 16:3–17.

[70] See Moule, "Mark v, 1–20 Yet Once More," 102. καὶ ἔλεγεν is normally used to introduce a new saying *within a discourse* already begun while καὶ λέγει αὐτοῖς is used with a change of speaker to introduce a saying *within a dialogue* (Sellew, "Oral and Written Sources in Mark 4.1–34," 254–55). Since it is opposite in 4:11, 13, Sellew thinks 4:11–12 is an insertion.

[71] Myers, "Disciples, Outsiders, and the Secret of the Kingdom," 170; Kirkland, "The Earliest Understanding of Jesus' Use of Parables," 5; Sellew, "Oral and Written Sources in Mark 4.1–34," 254.

only are these the words of Jesus but that Jesus intends his sayings, like the Rabbis, to be memorized.[72] If so, then this captures the importance of the following statements, conveys the self-understanding of Jesus (if the arrangement is due to maintaining the *Geist* of Jesus) as a wisdom teacher, and reaffirms the reliability (or authenticity) of the saying itself.

The Disclosure. The exclusiveness of the mystery. The response is in terms of explaining why they do understand (partially)[73] the parables (4:11) while to others they (and his acts) remain riddles (4:12). "To you [on the inside] the mystery of the Kingdom of God has been given [by means of imparted wisdom], but to those who are on the outside [to whom wisdom has not been given], everything [teachings and deeds of Jesus] remains in riddles." Several observations about the text validate this translation. First, the position of the pronoun 'to you' marks it as emphatic and places a premium status on them as 'understanders' as opposed to outsiders.[74] The contrast to 'those on the outside' implies the translation, "To you *on the inside*." Second, the position of μυστήριον is equally emphatic.[75] Mark stresses *to whom*

---

[72] W. G. Essame, "Καί ἔλεγεν in Mark iv. 21, 24, 26, 30," *ExpTim* 77 (1965–66): 121; Darrell L. Bock, "The Words of Jesus in the Gospels: Live, Jive, or Memorex?" in *Jesus under Fire*, ed. Michael J. Wilkins and J. P. Moreland (Grand Rapids: Zondervan, 1995), 73–99.

[73] Partial understanding is literarily related to the two-fold miracle of the blind man. The story in 8:22–26 is sandwiched between 8:17–21 (rebuke of disciples for incomprehensiveness) and 8:27–30 (Peter's confession). The first half of Mark describes the first stage of healing from *blindness* while the second part describes the second half of their healing from *post-blind syndrome*. Post-blind syndrome is the ability to see but inability to put things together or synthesize them correctly (Oliver W. Sacks, *An Anthropologist on Mars: Seven Paradoxical Tales* [Berkeley, CA: University of California Press, 1996], 108–52).

[74] Gnilka, *Theologie des neuen Testaments*, 156; cf. George Eldon Ladd, *A Theology of the New Testament*, ed. Donald A. Hagner, rev. ed. (Grand Rapids: Eerdmans, 1993), 235. Légasse says, "Essentiellement, il s'agit d'une déclaration de Jésus concernant les privilégiés exclusifs de la connaissancedes mystères du royaume, déclaration appuyée d' une référence à Is., vi.9–10" (S. Légasse, "La Revelation aux νήπιοι," *RB* 67 [1960]: 327–28; Best, "Mark's Use of the Twelve," 18).

[75] Gnilka gives some variants not listed in NA[27]. (1) Some MSS (A K W Δ) simply read δέδοται τὸ μυστήριον. Here the emphatic position of μυστήριον is altered. (2) Other MSS (G Σ ca. 10 minuscule) follow Matt 13:11 and Luke 8:10 read δέδοται γνῶναι τὰ μυστήρια. The addition of the phrase 'to know' and the pluralization of μυστήριον is

and *what* is given more than *how* it is given.[76] The nature of the 'giving,' however, is determinate. A derivative of μυστήριον is καμμύω,'I close the eyes' or 'I shut the eyes' (cf. Matt 13:15) and is suggestive of insider illumination as much as the noetic opacity of those on the outside.[77] μυστήριον occurs twenty-eight times in the NT; six are anarthrous mostly confined to Paul while twenty have the article where seventeen are singular and three are plural.[78] There is little to suggest that the mystery given is the *explanation* (interpretation) of the parable for that comes later.[79] Fay rightly says

---

a product of assimilation to the other Synoptics. (3) A large number of minuscules (sy^P it vg arm) read δέδοται γνῶναι τὸ μυστήριον. This is only a partial assimilation leaving μυστήριον as singular. (4) Some MSS (א D K W Θ) read τά (Gnilka, *Die Verstockung Israels*, 23).

[76] Woodward, "The Place of Mark 4:10–12 in the Second Gospel," 47 who places the stress on 'givennness' rather than the mystery or the recipients of the mystery.

[77] Robert M. Arida, "Hearing, Receiving and Entering TO ΜΥΣΤΗΡΙΟΝ/ΤΑ ΜΥΣΤΗΡΙΑ: Patristic Insights Unveiling the *Crux Interpretum* (Isaiah 6:9–10) of the Sower Parable," *SVTQ* 38 (1994): 213 n. 3; Otto A. Piper, "The Mystery of the Kingdom of God: Critical Scholarship and Christian Doctrine," *Int* 1 (1947): 186.

[78] This noun is anarthrous six times in the NT mostly confined to Paul (Rom 16:25; 1 Cor 2:7; 4:1; 14:2; 15:51; Rev 17:5). It occurs twenty times with the article where seventeen are singular (Mark 4:11; Rom 11:25; 1 Cor 2:1; Eph 1:9; 3:3, 4, 9; 5:32; 6:19; Col 1:26, 27; 2:2; 4:3; 1 Tim 3:9; Rev 1:20; 10:7; 17:7) and three are plural (Matt 13:11; Luke 8:10; 1 Cor 13:2). The singular may signify Pauline influence (Woodward, "The Place of Mark 4:10–12 in the Second Gospel," 50). The predominance of the singular argues against the infernce of the Greek mystery-metaphor of the Graeco-Roman cults (*NewDocs* 6:202). Both the singular and plural forms occur at Qumran ([רז and סוד] see Ambrozic, *The Hidden Kingdom*, 87, 87–90) and occur in apocalyptic Judaism (Günther Bornkamm, "μυστήριον," *TDNT* 4:802–28). It occurs twenty-eight times in the LXX, eight times in Daniel (2:18, 19, 27, 28, 29, 30, 47*bis*) and always translating the noun רז either in the singular (Dan 2:18, 19, 27, 30, 47b; Theod. Dan 2:18, 19, 27, 30, 47b) or plural (Dan 2:28, 29, 47a; Theod. Dan 2:28, 29, 47a). Apocryphal texts have the singular (Jdt 2:2; Tob 12:7, 11) but in sapiential passages mostly the plural (2 Macc 13:21; Wis 2:22; 6:22; 14:15, 23; Sir 22:22; 27:16, 17, 21). These include a secret council (Jdt 2:2), secrets of a king (Tob 12:7, 11), told to an enemy (2 Macc 13:21), mysteries of God (Wis 2:22), wisdom and its mysteries (Wis 6:22), cultic (pagan) ceremonies (Wis 14:15, 23), and secrets of a friend (Sir 22:22; 27:16, 17, 21). The background is the Hebrew סוד (Cranfield, *The Gospel according to Saint Mark*, 152–53) but μυστήριον does not normally translate סוד with few exceptions (cf. Sir 3:19, Í suppletor; Job 15:8, Symmachus and Theod.).

[79] Brown, "The Secret of the Kingdom of God (Mark 4, 11)," 62. On the other hand, it is not simply the secret of Jesus' identity (Gnilka, *Die Verstockung Israels*, 36).

the contrast is not between methods (parables versus explanation) but why one method (parables) produces two responses.[80]

The complexity of the mystery. The singular number of the noun sparks various views. Brown suggests that the mystery relates specifically to the disciples' question, conforms to the emphatic nature of the pronoun, and relates to the mystery of election. In commenting on Qumran he says that in apocalyptic books mysteries are visions offered to a few (2 *Bar.* 48.2–3) who are the wise (*4 Ezra* 12.36–37). Here the community's special mystery must not be given to outsiders (1QS 4:6; 8:11–12; 9:17, 21–22; CD 15:10–11; Josephus *B.J.* 2.8.7) who are not interested in them anyway (*1 En.* 80:7; 1QS 5:11).[81] This retiscence "touches on the question of God's predilection, a mystery that has not been revealed to men."[82] Ladd believes that "Mark's wording suggests a single truth, the others a truth embodied in *several aspects.*"[83] Manson says it encompasses the total religious revelation made in Jesus.[84] Piper holds "It is God's decree that those who are open-minded to the approach of the 'kingdom' shall perceive its secret, but that it shall be withheld from the rest. Thus interpreted, the open-mindedness is the prerequisite but not the cause of perceiving the secret."[85] He says the mystery is the indwelling Christ which enables him to view the inner dynamic as the key to this open-mindedness and that "the secret must be imparted by God."[86] Marcus says the mystery here has to do with why people do not *recognize* who Jesus is.[87] Thus the parabolic form "is commonly used to test the

---

[80] Fay, "Introduction to Incomprehension," 71 n. 27.

[81] Joel Marcus, "Mark 4:10–12 and Marcan Epistemology," *JBL* 103/4 (1984): 559–61 and 63–64. He says the theme of revelation to a few is "the motif of 'higher wisdom through revelation'" (ibid., 560). Cf 1QHa 13:36; 1QS 3:23; CD 3:18.

[82] Raymond E. Brown, "The Semitic Background of the New Testament musthrion (I)," *Bib* 39 (1958): 431. He says in the denial to outsiders is the reality of the positive side of election emphasized (ibid., 431 n. 2).

[83] Ladd, *A Theology of the New Testament*, 91 n. 4.

[84] William Manson, *Jesus the Messiah* (London: Hodder & Stoughton, 1943), 36, 45, 55.

[85] Piper, "The Mystery of the Kingdom of God," 189.

[86] Ibid., 192.

[87] Marcus, "Mark 4:10–12 and Marcan Epistemology," 567 n. 36.

sagacity of the hearer. It conceals and reveals at the same time."[88] Fay recognizes that parables may only be understood by those described as 'good ground.'[89] Parables test and reveal who has wisdom—the *noetic* feature of an insider. Insiders also inquire for deeper understanding and receive it.

The Access to the 'Mystery.' Ambrozic says the terms used for mystery are applied to various hidden realities including evil, cosmic issues, man's actions, and divine providence. Qumran literature and the pseudepigrapha (*1 En., 2–3 Bar., 4 Ezra*) specify a number of mysteries relating to evil, cosmic occurrences, God's will and human action, and those of the last times.[90] Brown says that although it is associated for a time in Daniel with eschatological mystery, this simply represents "a development of the more ancient concept of the prophet's introduction into the heavenly assembly and hearing there what God planned to do."[91] Brown recognizes that the concept of the heavenly 'council' has its roots in Babylonian and Ugaritic sources but that it undergoes further development in pre-exilic and post-exilic Judaism.[92] In the OT this heavenly council gives access to and marks the true prophet of Yahweh (Amos 3:7) while Qumran's secrets include their interpretation of the law entrusted to initiates but kept from outsiders.[93] The vehicle in post-exilic literature is no longer the

---

[88] Piper, "The Mystery of the Kingdom of God," 195. "A secret...requires illumination as to its details. But this illumination remains incomprehensible to those who do not know the secret. To them, the parables are code language" (ibid.). "This understanding must be *given* to men" (ibid., 199). Cf. Sellew, "Oral and Written Sources in Mark 4.1–34," 266.

[89] Fay, "Introduction to Incomprehension," 73.

[90] Ambrozic, *The Hidden Kingdom*, 92–94.

[91] Brown, "The Pre-Christian Semitic Concept of 'Mystery'," 423. Cf. Madeleine I. Boucher, *The Mysterious Parable: A Literary Study*, CBQMS, ed. Bruce Vawter et al., vol. 6 (Washington DC: Catholic Biblical Association, 1977), 56–60; Woodward, "The Place of Mark 4:10–12 in the Second Gospel," 47–49. Ladd, *A Theology of the New Testament*, 91–92.

[92] See E. Theodore Mullen, *The Divine Council in Canaanite and Early Hebrew Literature*, HSM, ed. F. M. Cross Jr., vol. 24 (Chico, CA: Scholars Press, 1980) and Lowell K. Handy, *Among the Host of Heaven: The Syro-Palestinian Pantheon as Bureaucracy* (Winona Lake, IN: Eisenbrauns, 1994).

[93] CD 3:18–20; 1QS 4:6; 9:17, 22; CD 15:10–11; Josephus *B.J.* 2.8.7. The consequence of revealing the mysteries to outsiders is that God seals them up (1QHa 5:25–26; 2:9–10;

vision or divine council but the use of imparted wisdom in studying the traditions and/or parables (Sir 47:15–17). The vehicle through which the mystery comes is *demoted* but the recipients of the mysteries are nevertheless *expanded*.[94]

The 'Givenness' of the Mystery. *The nature and means of 'givenness.* 'The *nature* and *means* of this givenness are two essential features in recognizing that explanations are not primarily in mind but rather imparted wisdom. Mark 4:33 says Jesus speaks to them as they were 'able to hear.' The primary issue focuses on ability that is marked by the presence or absence of wisdom. What is the nature of this givenness? How is this wisdom acquired? δέδοται is an *extensive* perfect with the *simple* passive voice (no agency expressed) in the indicative mood.[95] The voice most likely reflects the divine passive. God acts in such a way that the mystery has been *given* to them.

The verb occurs 415 times in the NT of which eighty-five are in the passive voice.[96] Mark 6:2 refers to the divine bestowal of wisdom as evident in Jesus—it is something supernaturally resident. This

---

5:8–9; cf. 1:26–27; 10:4–5; 11:4). Paradoxically, outsiders are really not interested in them anyway (1QHa 5:11 and Frag 6:5). On the cognizance of at least five modes of secrecy or secret knowledge available to Mark see C. L. Mearns, "Parables, Secrecy and Exchatology in Mark's Gospel," *SJT* 44 (1991): 424–26. These include the use of Isa 6:9–10, the *raz-pesher* tradition of hermeneutics, the hidden Messiah texts, the connotations of μυστήριον, and the linguistic ambiguity of מָשָׁל.

[94] Several scholars hold a purely functional appraisal of insider/outsider (Arida, "Hearing, Receiving and Entering ΤΟ ΜΥΣΤΗΡΙΟΝ/ΤΑ ΜΥΣΤΗΡΙΑ," 213–15). Arida holds that any idea of exclusivity smacks of Gnosticism and downplays 'free-will' (ibid., 231). See also Kelber, "Narrative and Disclosure," 1–20; Via, "Irony as Hope in Mark's Gospel," 21–27.

[95] There is some variation in the phrase δέδοται γνῶναι τὸ μυστήριον in MSS 341 ℵ B C*[vid] (Zane C. Hodges and Arthur L. Farstad, *The Greek New Testament according to the Majority Text*, 2d ed. [Nashville: Nelson, 1985], 117). Marcus notes that "God stands behind the eye-opening and blinding described in Mark" (Marcus, "Mark 4:10–12 and Marcan Epistemology," 561). Jeremias says δέδοται, γίνεται, and ἀφεθῇ are circumlocutions for the divine activity (Jeremias, *The Parables of Jesus*, 15–16).

[96] Matt 7:7; 10:19; 12:39; 13:11–12; 14:9, 11; 16:4; 19:11; 21:43; 25:29; 26:9; 28:18; Mark 4:11, 25; 5:43; 6:2; 8:12; 13:11; 14:5; Luke 6:38; 8:10, 18, 55; 11:9, 29; 12:48; 19:26; 22:19; John 1:17; 3:27; 6:65; 12:5; 19:11; Acts 4:12; 8:18; 24:26; Rom 5:5; 12:3, 6; 15:15; 1 Cor 1:4; 3:10; 11:15; 12:7–8; 2 Cor 8:1; 12:7; Gal 2:9; 3:21–22; Eph 3:2, 7–8; 4:7; 6:19; Col 1:25; 1 Tim 4:14; 2 Tim 1:9; Jas 1:5; 2 Pet 3:15; Rev 6:2, 4, 8, 11; 7:2; 8:2–3; 9:1, 3, 5; 11:1–2; 12:14; 13:5, 7, 14–15; 16:8; 19:8; 20:4.

same passive form is used in each parallel passage (Mark 4:11 = Matt 13:11*bis* = Luke 8:10) and a few other texts (Matt 19:11; 1 Cor 11:15). Matthew and Luke add (or modify) "given *to know* the mysteries" thereby making explicit an implicit wisdom motif. In Matt 19:11 the saying is 'given' only to those destined for marriage while in 1 Cor 11:15 a woman's hair is 'given' as a covering—surely these instances can *not* involve *active* reception. In each case the 'giving' is by *fiat* and does not infer an active reception to complete it. Other instances of the passive show that the *nature* of the givenness (related to the kingdom) is *strong* divine causality while it is by *means* of imparted (unprecipitated by human activity) wisdom.[97] This identifies an *ontological-functional* phenomenon.

The relation of 'givenness' to wisdom. Myers examines whether there is any precedence for the expression 'giving a mystery' and if its uniqueness argues it is an idiom. The phrase 'given *to know* the

---

[97] The *perfect passive participle* appears only in the sense requiring *no human contingency* (John 3:27; 6:65; 19:11; Acts 4:12; 2 Cor 8:1). The *future passive indicative*: (1) Future is *contingent* upon human condition (Matt 7:7; Luke 6:38; 11:9; Jas 1:5 [more wisdom]). (2) Future is *not contingent* on human condition (Matt 10:19; 12:39; 6:4; Mark 8:12; Luke 11:29; 19:26). (4) Future is *contingent* on human *state* of having wisdom (Matt 13:12; 25:29; Mark 4:25; Luke 8:18). (4) Could be *contingent* or *non-contingent* based on human activity (Matt 21:43; Acts 24:26). The *aorist passive indicative*: (1) Act assumes human *condition* (Matt 14:11; Rev 6:11; 8:2; 9:1; 11:1; 19:8) or *state* (John 12:5) to complete the giving. (2) Act is by *fiat* (Matt 28:18; John 1:17; 2 Cor 12:7; Gal 3:21; Eph 3:8; 4:7; Rev 6:2; 4, 8; 7:2; 8:3; 9:3, 5; 11:2; 12:14; 13:5, 7, 14, 15; 16:8; 20:4) and sometimes refers to wisdom (Luke 12:48). (3) It requires a *condition* to be met but *not* on the part of the one receiving it (1 Tim 4:14; all *aorist passive infinitives* are here [Matt 14:9; 26:9; Mark 5:43; 14:5; Luke 8:55]). The *aorist passive participle* is used only in the sense requiring *no human contingency* (Rom 5:5; 12:3, 6; 15:15; 1 Cor 1:4; 3:10; Gal 2:9; Eph 3:2, 7; Col 1:25; 2 Tim 1:9) where wisdom is sometimes the object given (Mark 6:2; 2 Pet 3:15). The *present passive indicative*: (1) It requires a *condition* to be met but *not* on the part of the one receiving it (Acts 8:18). (2) *No human contingency* needed (1 Cor 12:7; also *present passive participle* [Luke 22:19]) and can involve the gift of wisdom (1 Cor 12:8). The *aorist passive subjunctive*: (1) *No human contingency* needed (Mark 13:11). (2) *Human contingency* required (Gal 3:22). (3) Could be *contingent* or *non-contingent* (Eph 6:19). Every use of the perfect passive of this verb requires one to understand the act of 'giving' as via fiat and unconditioned on the one receiving it. Most other grammatical forms require this same sense. It is unlikely, statistically speaking, for this 'giving' in Mark 4:11 to be based on the objects *actively* receiving. This requires one to view the 'giving' in terms of a passive reception of something by divine fiat (divine passive) based on divine selection.

mysteries' is indeed a Semitic idiom and is found in the DSS.[98] Even the concept of knowledge and mysteries are connected but not with the sense of 'giving.'[99] The problem is that nowhere in the rest of the NT or outside of it is 'mystery' referred to as 'given.' Instead mystery is in terms of revealing and revelation. He concludes that since the Hebrew terms יָדַע and דַּעַת are connected with this expression, that therefore 'to reveal a mystery' and 'to give to know a mystery' are equivalent in meaning.[100] The former is shorthand for the latter.

A fuller explanation is that what is 'given' may not simply be the mystery but what is required in order to 'know' the mystery. Because 'know' is present in several expressions of the phrase and a constituent of wisdom, it provides a good basis (in light of sapiential thinking) that what is elliptical in the Markan phrase is the granting of wisdom which enables one to gain access to the mystery(ies) of the kingdom.[101] Jesus says, "To you on the inside (who have wisdom) the mystery of the kingdom of God is given while those on the outside (who do not have wisdom) the mystery is not given and this explains why some believe and others do not."[102] Although the 'mystery' is audibly spoken or visually witnessed to all who physically hear and see, without the possession of wisdom enabling deeper (salvific) aspects of perception, knowledge, and understanding, the mystery is not divinely 'given.' Explanations may be 'given' but if

---

[98] Myers, "Disciples, Outsiders, and the Secret of the Kingdom," 172. He cites 1QHa 4:27; 7:26; 11:10; 1QS 9:10 but none of these apply. Cf. 1QS 9:18; 1QHa 9:21; 12:27; 13:26; 18:4; 19:4, 9, 16; 20:13, 20; 4Q418 f123ii:4; 4Q427 f8ii:18; 4Q428 f9:1 [1QHa 15:26–27]; 4Q511 f28 29:3.

[99] Ibid. He cites 1QHa 2:13; 12:13; 1QS 4:6; 1QpHab 7:5 (cf. Wis 2:22). Cf. 1QHa 5:3, 6, 20; 10:13; 16:11; 26:1; 1Q27 f1i:3; 4Q257 5:3; 4Q259 3:17; 4Q300 f3:2–3; 4Q301 f1:2 (riddles & parables); 4Q405 f3ii:9; f13:3; 4Q417 f1i:13, 18, 25; 4Q511 f28 29:3.

[100] Ibid., 123–24, 35, 74.

[101] The Hebrew equivalent for the passive δίδωμι is נָתַן and in several instances it refers to wisdom that is given by God to his people (Exod 36:1; Dan 7:4; cf. Wis 3:14; 7:7; Sir 6:37; 37:21).

[102] Although the term μυστήριον can be construed as a subject or direct object, the passive voice of the verb and the resulting clumsy syntax make the later unlikely. Thus the 'mystery' is the subject that is given to them *by means of imparted wisdom.* This elliptical preposition ('by means of wisdom') identifies those 'on the inside' ('to you'). Matthew and Luke change this to the object and replace the subject with the implied wisdom.

incomprehension follows, then the 'wisdom' required is either not given (*ontological-functional*) or 'given' but undeveloped (*functional-ontological*). The former is the condition of outsiders while the latter insiders.

The relation of 'givenness' to wisdom not further explanation. The imparted wisdom perspective counters claims that the mystery is concerned merely with an accepting though not unquestioning response to Jesus,[103] or simply more light given in the explanation,[104] and therefore renders misguided the endeavor to show that parables are meant to be understood by everyone as opposed to being opaque to some.[105] Indeed, both multiple senses of the lexeme (parable and riddle) and dual effects of the form can be more fully appreciated when wisdom's presence or absence is the assumed vehicle behind the phenomenon, namely, the explanation for the paradoxical noetic perpiscuity and obscurity of parables, teachings, and deeds. Proving that the external form is perspicuitous does not address the problem of internal *noetic* obscurity due to lack of wisdom. Luther says,

> What is this [Isa 6:9–10] but to say that 'free-will' (or, the human heart) is so bound by the power of Satan that, *unless it be wondrously quickened* by the Spirit of God, it cannot of itself see or hear things which strike upon ear and eye so manifestly that they could not almost be touched by hand? So great is the misery and blindness of mankind! Thus, too, the very evangelists, when they wondered how it could be that the Jews were not won by the works and words of Christ, incontrovertible and undeniable as they were, answered from themselves that self-same passage of Scripture, which teaches that man, *left to himself,* seeing sees not and hearing hears not. What is more fantastic? 'The light shineth in darkness, and the darkness comprehendeth it not' (John 1.5). Who would believe it? Who ever heard of such a thing?—that light should shine in darkness, yet the darkness remain darkness, and not receive illumination![106]

---

[103] Guelich, *Mark 1–8:26*, 207; Moule, "Mark v, 1–20 Yet Once More," 99–104; Légasse, "La Revelation aux νήπιοι," 321–48.

[104] Moule, "Mark v, 1–20 Yet Once More," 104–06; Kirkland, "The Earliest Understanding of Jesus' Use of Parables," 5–6.

[105] Moule, "Mark v, 1–20 Yet Once More," 106; Kirkland, "The Earliest Understanding of Jesus' Use of Parables," 13.

[106] Luther *Serv.* 3.5 (under 'The blindness of man does not disprove the clarity of Scripture'). See also Roland H. Bainton, *Here I Stand: A Life of Martin Luther* (New York: Abingdon-Cokesbury, 1950), 220–24.

Summary. To hear or see מָשָׁל/παραβολή without possessing salvific wisdom amounts to noetic riddle, whereas to hear or see מָשָׁל/παραβολη precipitated by imparted wisdom means knowing the secrets of the kingdom. To one group on the 'inside' parables make sense or at least begin to make sense while to those on the 'outside' these same parables about the realities of the kingdom, as well as the deeds of Jesus that exercise and implement those truths, remain in riddles. Leaving some in the dark is not only the purpose of parables but also a consequence of not having wisdom. The divine intent to keep it so, in Isaianic terms, is fattening. The divine *intent* to maintain the fat-heart that prevents illumination in the form of imparted wisdom accounts for the division among men and defines the divine *act*.

The Referent of the Mystery. The 'mystery of the kingdom of God' delimits in some respect the referent of the mysteries to the kingdom although it does not explicate its content.[107] The phrase 'of the kingdom' functions as a *partitive* genitive (mystery is a subset of multiple aspects of the kingdom) or a genitive of *reference* (mystery is about the nature of the kingdom) modifying τὸ μυστήρov. The further modifying phrase 'of God' identifies the possessor of the kingdom. Insiders, or those with wisdom, have at their disposal the means of acquiring information about the inbreaking of God's reign.

The 'Outsiders' to the Mystery. *The contrasting groups.* "But to those, the ones on the outside, all things come in riddles." The remote demonstrative pronoun ἐκείνοις is contrasted to the personal pronoun ὑμῖν above.[108] Both are datives of *indirect object* to their respective verbs, δίδωμι or γίνομαι.[109] Gealy places the contrast between 'mystery' and 'parables' so that parables are not mysteries,

---

[107] The content of the mystery may be "the presence of God's eschatological rule now, though in a limited, vulnerable way" (Guelich, *Mark 1–8:26*, 206; Woodward, "The Place of Mark 4:10–12 in the Second Gospel," 53; Myers, "Disciples, Outsiders, and the Secret of the Kingdom," 114–36).

[108] δέ introduces an independent clause functioning as *contrastive*. The phrase ἐκείνοις δέ occurs eleven times in the NT with a negative (Matt 13:11; Mark 4:11; 12:7; Luke 12:47; John 10:6; 11:13; Rom 11:3) or positive contrast (Mark 16:20; John 2:21; 11:29; Acts 21:6).

[109] See MHT 3:45.

mysteries are not to be found in the parables, and parables are to outsiders while mysteries (in direct form) are for those on the inside.[110] Contrary to Gealy it might be noted that although parables come to and are designed for both groups, they have a dual purpose. To one it is a teaching tool (parables) that in combination with imparted wisdom leads to the mysteries of the kingdom while to the other it (as well as all things) remains 'in riddles.' The parable is a teaching tool designed to foster understanding for those possessing wisdom. To suggest that parables are only to outsiders because mysteries are only to insiders is going too far.[111]

Jewish precedent of 'outsiders.' There is evidence that 'outsiders' should be construed in *ontological-functional* as opposed to merely *functional* terms. The phrase τοῖς ἔξω functions as a dative in simple apposition to ἐκείνοις so that ἐκείνοις contrasted with ὑμῖν are 'those on the outside' (ἔξω/ἔξωθεν) implying that the ὑμῖν are those on the inside (ἔσω/ἔσωθεν).[112] The phrase is somewhat technical and designates unbelievers in Paul or those who do not belong to the circle of disciples or those outside of salvation.[113]

---

[110] Gealy, "The Composition of Mark 4," 41.

[111] Nor does it account for the parable of the fig tree (13:28–31) that is given only to the Four.

[112] The formula (art. + ἔξω) occurs six times in the NT (Mark 4:11; Acts 26:11; 1 Cor 5:12; 2 Cor 4:16; Col 4:5; 1 Thess 4:12) where four are *substantival* (Mark 4:11; 1 Cor 5:12; Col 4:5; 1 Thess 4:12) and two are *adjectival* (Acts 26:11; 2 Cor 4:16). A similar expression (art. + ἔξωθεν) occurs seven times (Matt 23:25; Mark 7:18; Luke 11:39, 40; 1 Tim 3:7; 1 Pet 3:3; Rev 11:2) where three are *substantival* (Mark 7:18; Luke 11:40; 1 Tim 3:7). An opposite expression (art. + ἔσω) is found four times (Rom 7:22; 1 Cor 5:12; 2 Cor 4:16; Eph 3:16) but only once as a *substantive* in contrast to outsiders (1 Cor 5:12). A similar phrase (art. + ἔσωθεν) is found only once (Luke 11:40) and replaces ἔξω here in Mark 4:11 in MSS B Z 1424. 2427 *pc*. WH have this variant in their margin. The phrase (art. + ἔξω) also occurs eight times in the LXX (2 Kgs 16:18; 1 Chr 26:29; Esth 9:19; 2 Macc 1:16; Job 1:10; including Theod. Dan 4:15, 23) and translates twice the adjective חִיצוֹן 'outside' (2 Kgs 16:28; 1 Chr 26:29). There is a similarity to Judaism's use of the nominal חוּץ (Woodward, "The Place of Mark 4:10–12 in the Second Gospel," 54–55).

[113] Goulder, "Those Outside (MK. 4:10–12)," 289–302. Outsiders include the devil (MM §1854), non-disciples, non-Christians, and non-Pythagoreans (BDAG 354). Johannes Behm, "ἔξω," *TDNT* 2:575–76 adds Herodotus *Hist.* 9.5; Thucydides *Hist.* 5.14.3; 4.66.2; and Josephus *A.J.* 15.314. It may imply dependence on Paul (Dodd, *The Parables of the Kingdom*, 14) or Jesus (A. T. Cadoux, *The Theology of Jesus* [London: Nicholson & Watson, 1940], 49) but similarity may be credited to a common

The concept of outsider-insider is not strange to Jewish ears and tends to focus on the *ontology* of things or people.[114] Strack and Billerbeck note that the phrase for 'external books' (בספרים החיצנים) used in *Sanh.* 10:1 designates non-canonical texts (*Qoh.* 12:12) and heretics.[115] However, חיצון and חוץ occur in the MT, the DSS, and the Mishnah but without significance. But the expression 'man of the land' אִישׁ אֶרֶץ and [116] the similar 'people of the land' עַם הָאָרֶץ appear in the MT and DSS and refer to unbelievers. For similar reasons, Ambrozic intimates that it is not necessary to propose mystery cults as the background for semantically similar expressions.[117] The distinguishing feature of these phrases is that they point to things or groups that are *ontologically* distinct from God's people. In Mark it refers directly to the enemies of Jesus as well as the crowds.[118] Goulder, following Trocmé, says τοῖς ἔξω includes Jesus' family (3:31–35) and the scribes so that when they depart only those around him (3:34) and the Twelve (3:20) are left.[119] More likely this phrase designates those who are *ontologically* unlike the disciples.

---

environment (Myers, "Disciples, Outsiders, and the Secret of the Kingdom," 137). For a dichotomy based on ontology see 1QS 3:20–22.

[114] Some apply it to those outside of Israel (Gnilka, *Die Verstockung Israels*, 83–84; Boucher, *The Mysterious Parable*, 44, 82) or unbelieving ethnic Jews (Str-B 2:7; Guelich, *Mark 1–8:26*, 207; E. Sjöberg, *Der verborgene Menschensohn in den Evangelien* [Lund: Gleerup, 1955], 224; Ambrozic, *The Hidden Kingdom*, 79). Context argues against an ethnic criterion (Mark 3:31–32) and probably to a unified social group with a common belief (Günther Bornkamm, "μυστήριον," *TDNT* 4:804; Myers, "Disciples, Outsiders, and the Secret of the Kingdom," 136–46; Ambrozic, *The Hidden Kingdom*, 71–72). Less convincingly is that the crowd is in-between insiders and outsiders (Marie-Joseph Lagrange, "Le but des paraboles d'après l'évangile selon saint Marc," *RB* 7 [1910]: 26; Edward F. Siegman, "Teaching in Parables (Mk iv. 10–12; Lk viii. 9–10; Mt xiii. 10–15)," *CBQ* 23 [1961]: 173) or that insider-outsider is a functional designation (Moule, "Mark v, 1–20 Yet Once More," 99; Arida, "Hearing, Receiving and Entering ΤΟ ΜΥΣΤΗΡΙΟΝ/ΤΑ ΜΥΣΤΗΡΙΑ," 215).

[115] Str-B 2:7; Ambrozic, *The Hidden Kingdom*, 53, 105.

[116] Only one passage in the MT meets the criterion (Lev 18:27; 4Q365 f22a b:3).

[117] Cranfield, *The Gospel according to Saint Mark*, 154; Igarashi, "The Mystery of the Kingdom (Mark 4:10–12)," 84.

[118] Ambrozic, *The Hidden Kingdom*, 62–72.

[119] Goulder, "Those Outside (MK. 4:10–12)," 298; Trocmé, "Why Parables?" 463–66.

Other terms for 'outsiders.' Myers gives more detail on the use of this motif.[120] First, the Lukan parallel uses τοῖς δὲ λοιποῖς instead of τοῖς ἔξω (Luke 8:10). The Lukan phrase, in terms of the NT, usually designates Christians (1 Thess 4:13; 5:6; Eph 2:3) but can also refer to non-Christians (Rom 11:7).[121] His association with Paul may suggest a predestinarian aspect to this phrase. Second, there is the terminology designating Pharisaic brotherhoods that may originate prior to the time of Jesus.[122] Here members are called הברים and outsiders 'people of the land' (עַם הָאָרֶץ).[123] Third, there are other more functionally oriented terms in the NT standing for outsiders. The noun ἰδιώτης is used five times in the NT and refers to those who are 'untrained' or 'uneducated.'[124] Another term is ἀλλογενής ('stranger, foreigner, alien') which occurs only in Luke 17:18 and applies to the Samaritan leper, an outsider *par excellent* (John 4:9). Myers points out a usage in Sir 45:13 where it may include non-Jews "but its more specific reference seems to be to those who are not the sons of Aaron, that is, anyone who is outside the priestly tribe."[125] Finally, Qumran material uses picturesque descriptions of non-members like 'sons of darkness'

---

[120] Myers, "Disciples, Outsiders, and the Secret of the Kingdom," 138–46.

[121] The phrase occurs ninety-eight times in the NT mostly in Luke-Acts. Myers says the parallel variant in Matt 6:7 has ἐθνικοί instead of οἱ λοιποί. It may have an alliteration background linked to the Aramaic that underlies Luke's οἱ λοιποί in 5:47; 6:7, 32 (Matthew Black, *An Aramaic Approach to the Gospels and Acts*, 3d ed. [Oxford: Oxford University Press, 1967], 133; Myers, "Disciples, Outsiders, and the Secret of the Kingdom," 139). It also refers to unbelievers in 2 *Clem.* 13:1.

[122] Jacob Neusner, "The Fellowship (חבורה) in the Second Jewish Commonwealth," *HTR* 53 (1960): 125–42 argues that these fellowships originate prior to the time of Hillel and Shammai. See Saul Lieberman, "The Discipline in the So-Called Dead Sea Manual of Discipline," *JBL* 71 (1952): 199–206; Myers, "Disciples, Outsiders, and the Secret of the Kingdom," 140.

[123] See Neh 10:28–31 where it describes heathen people living in the land (*m. Demai* 2:2, 3; *t. Demai* 2:2; *Pesah.* 49b). See James H. Charlesworth, *The Old Testament Pseudepigrapha & The New Testament: Prolegomena for the Study of Christian Origins* (Harrisburg, PA: Trinity Press International, 1998), 20–22.

[124] Acts 4:13; 1 Cor 14:16, 23–24; 2 Cor 11:6. It may be used by Paul to designate adherents who were neither unbelievers nor full members (BDAG 468; Myers, "Disciples, Outsiders, and the Secret of the Kingdom," 143).

[125] Ibid., 144.

(בְּנֵי חוֹשֶׁךְ)[126] as well as עַם הָאָרֶץ.[127] Also employed is a phrase used to designate members only, namely, the 'sons of light'[128] or 'the many.' Although some of these designations may be functional, most are *ontological-functional* designations. It is to these 'followers' that status is assumed and privileges accrue.

The Παραβολάς *and* Πάντα *(part 2). The parable as noetic 'riddle.'* To those on the outside "all things become [or 'are'] in riddles."[129] γίνομαι probably has the sense of ἐστίν here and emphasizes the obscurity of both the teachings and deeds of Jesus.[130] Cranfield treats the entire phrase ἐν παραβολαῖς τὰ πάντα γίνεται as independent where παραβολή is understood as 'riddle' (מָשָׁל is equivalent with חִידָה = 'riddle', 'dark saying'),[131] and γίνομαι is equivalent to ἐστίν ('all things are obscure'). This encompasses a broader application than just parables. It includes the entire ministry of Jesus and the parallelism fits best, he says, with the two halves of 4:11.[132] The prepositional phrase 'in riddles' is so understood by several leading scholars.[133] However, others assign the dative to the *instrumental* sense

---

[126] 1QS 1:10; 1QM 1:1, 7, 10, 16; 3:6, 9; 13:16; 14:17; 16:11; 4Q256 1:9; 4Q491 f8 10i:14; f11ii:9; 4Q496 f3:7.

[127] 1QM 10:9; 1QHa 5:15; 12:26; 4Q160 f3 5ii:5; 4Q247 f1:5; 4Q381 f69:1; 4Q495 f1:1. See E. E. Urbach, *The Sages: Their Concepts and Beliefs*, 2 vols. (Jerusalem: Magnes, 1975); Charlesworth, *The Old Testament Pseudepigrapha & The New Testament*, 101 n. 29–31.

[128] 1QS 1:9; 2:16; 3:13, 24–25; 1QM 1:1, 3, 9, 11, 13–14; 13:16; 4Q177 f12 13i:7, 11; 4Q266 f1a b:1; 4Q510 f1:7; 4Q511 f10:4; 11Q13 2:8.

[129] Cf. Aristotle *Rhet*. 2.20.2–4; Plato *Pol*. 2.5. Manson treats the parable from מָשָׁל perspective instead of the classical Greek meaning (Manson, *The Teaching of Jesus*, 65). See also Evans, *To See and Not Perceive*, 92).

[130] The verb is λέγεται in D Θ 28. 565. 1424. 2542 *pc* it vg[ms] (sa). Gnilka adds Σ to this list (Gnilka, *Die Verstockung Israels*, 23; Ambrozic, *The Hidden Kingdom*, 91). This change limits the 'all things' to Jesus' speech or parabolic teaching rather than to his whole ministry, viz., deeds and words (see note below on πάντα). See also Igarashi, "The Mystery of the Kingdom (Mark 4:10–12)," 84–85.

[131] Various parallelisms argue for synonymy (Hab 2:6; Pss 49:5[4]; 78:2; Prov 1:6; Ezek 17:2; 1QpHab 8:6; 4Q300 f1aii b:1; 4Q301 f1:2).

[132] Cranfield, *The Gospel according to Saint Mark*, 154–55; Ambrozic, *The Hidden Kingdom*, 78–79, 90–91; Ford, "Seeing, But Not Perceiving," 117.

[133] Gnilka notes that Jeremias understands 'parable' not as *Gleichnis* (parable) but *Rätselwort* (riddle) based on the Hebrew מָשָׁל (Gnilka, *Die Verstockung Israels*, 25;

and translate 'by riddles' (deliberate obscurity) or 'by parables' (as if it is a teaching method reserved for outsiders and private instruction to insiders) but the better sense is a dative of *space* or *sphere*.[134] Support is sometimes taken from John 16:25 where speaking 'plainly' (παρρησία) is contrasted with the 'proverb/parable' (παροιμία). But this may be more a *noetic* than a *linguistic* appraisal of the disciples.[135] Thus parables and deeds designed to illuminate those on the inside confuse those without supernaturally imparted wisdom. The phrase 'in parables' is not 'in parables *without interpretation*' as Moule suggests but rather the teaching and ministry activity of Jesus comes 'in riddles *to those without wisdom.*'[136] The issue is *ontological* privation of salvific wisdom not absence of *linguistic* clarity.

Taylor, *The Gospel according to St. Mark*, 156). "The transition from parable to secret was a natural one to make linguistically" (Mearns, "Parables, Secrecy and Exchatology," 425).

[134] It may be *instrumental* (C. F. D. Moule, *An Idiom Book of New Testament Greek*, 2d ed. [Cambridge: Cambridge University Press, 1959], 77) or *instrumental* having a *sociative* function (Zerwick, *Biblical Greek Illustrated by Examples*, §§116–19). Against the *instrumental* sense are the following points. First, when γίνομαι is preceded or followed by ἐν where the prepositional phrase modifies the verb, it is always non-*instrumental* in sense (Matt 11:21, 23; 20:26; Mark 4:11, 35; 9:33; Luke 10:13; 16:12; 19:17; 20:33; 22:26; 23:31; John 1:28; 1 Cor 2:3; 16:14; 2 Cor 1:19; 3:7; Phil 1:13; 2:7; 3:6; 1 Tim 2:14; 1 Pet 1:15; Rev 1:9; 11:13). The only possible exception is 1 Thess 2:5. Second, when παραβολή is in the *instrumental* sense it is either naked (Mark 4:33) or ἐν + παραβολή and the main verb is verbs of speaking (λαλέω, εἶπον, ἀνοίγω, διδάσκω) or τίθημι (Matt 13:3, 10, 13, 34, 35; 22:1; Mark 3:23; 4:2, 30, 33; 12:1). Third, the parallel but elliptical passage (Luke 8:10) is most likely a dative of *space/sphere* as well and the elliptical verb is most likely γίνομαι (cf. Heb 11:19). Fourth, the use of τὰ πάντα lessens the restriction to spoken parables and includes both deeds and speech. In conclusion, although the prespositional phrase ἐν + παραβολή is almost always *instrumental* when connected with verbs of speaking, it is not so when linked to γίνομαι.

[135] παροιμία, largely a Johannine term and contrasted to παρρησία (John 10:6; 16:25, 29; 2 Pet 2:22), occurs seven times in the OT including twice in canonical books translating מָשָׁל (Prov 1:1; 26:7) and five times in Sirach (6:35; 8:8; 18:29; 39:3; 47:17). The wisdom context of these texts indicates *noetic obtuseness* rather than *linguistic obscurity*. Certainly the Book of Proverbs is not enigmatic. Parable to 'text' and 'plain speaking' to 'interpretation' is a Gnostic development also in the *Shepherd of Hermes* (Mearns, "Parables, Secrecy and Exchatology," 426–28).

[136] Moule, "Mark v, 1–20 Yet Once More," 104; Gealy, "The Composition of Mark 4," 43; Woodward, "The Place of Mark 4:10–12 in the Second Gospel," 34. Cf. *Diogn.* 11:2, 5.

The parallelism to μυστήριον. The exact sense of the prepositional phrase is further confirmed by the parallelism of the passage. Two major views are given. The first view argues that μυστήριον and παραβολαῖς are parallel so that the latter refers to the entire ministry of Jesus and is translated 'riddles.'[137] A second major view espoused by Baird suggests that the parallelism is not with παραβολή/μυστήριον but with τὰ πάντα/μυστήριον so that explanations to the disciples are contrasted with parables to outsiders.[138] Parables are riddles in an external sense baffling to all including the disciples and unraveled only by further explanation or interpretation. His parallelism (similar to Moule) runs as follows:

1. τὸ μυστήριον τῆς βασιλείας τοῦ θεοῦ   τὰ πάντα
2. δέδοται   γίνεται
3. ὑμῖν   ἐκείνοις δὲ τοῖς ἔξω
4. (with explanations)   ἐν παραβολαῖς[139]

But the inferences drawn from the parallelism are not necessary. First, if the contrast is antithetical, then ἐν παραβολαῖς is opposite of 'with explanations' and restricted to linguistic ambiguity of parables but does not account for τὰ πάντα. Here τὰ πάντα excludes explanations in the same way τὸ μυστήριον excludes parables. In Mark both deeds and words are matters of incomprehension underscored by the switch in '*seeing*/hearing.' Second, it does not explain instances where the disciples are given parables without explanations unless solicited by the disciples (4:10–12; 7:14–15, 17–23), why unbelievers are given explanations (3:22–26; 4:21–22; 7:14–15 [a parable]; 12:10–11), how they understood parables (12:12), and why when only the disciples are present he gives parables with

---

[137] Woodward, "The Place of Mark 4:10–12 in the Second Gospel," 39–40. This view is also taken by Jeremias, Josef Schmid, Rudolf Schnackenburg, Mauser, Lane, and Gnilka (Gnilka, *Die Verstockung Israels*, 25). See also Mearns, "Parables, Secrecy and Exchatology," 431 who says, "They [parables] were transparent for those with faith, though they would remain opaque to the unbelieving."

[138] J. Arthur Baird, "A Pragmatic Approach to Parable Exegesis: Some New Evidence on Mark 4:11, 33–34," *JBL* 76 (1957): 202. Others holding to his view include T. Alec Burkill, William Manson, and Günther Bornkamm.

[139] Ibid., Marcus, "Mark 4:10–12 and Marcan Epistemology," 565 n. 33.

explanations (13:28–31).[140] Third, it does not explain why non-parables are accompanied by explanations.[141] Is Jesus' non-parabolic teaching also linguistically obscure? Fourth, since Godbey has demonstrated that a parable can be an acted מָשָׁל, it is more likely that both the spoken and acted ministry of Jesus are what is in mind by τὰ πάντα.[142] If τὰ πάντα are broader than parables, then ambiguity goes beyond *linguistics* to a *noetic* phenomenon and what is given goes deeper than *explanations* to *imparted wisdom*.

The referent of τὰ πάντα. What is the proper referent of τὰ πάντα?[143] There are three major views represented by various scholars. First, some apply it to parables only (Manson and Moule).[144] But this seems overly restrictive. Second, others apply it to both parables and the teaching of Jesus (Jeremias, Hauck, and Ambrozic).[145] But this limits it to the spoken word. Third, a majority

---

[140] Baird, "A Pragmatic Approach to Parable Exegesis," 206; Ford, "Seeing, But Not Perceiving," 117–19.

[141] A saying about forgiveness (2:5) is explained (2:8–12), a discussion on marriage (10:2–9) requires explanation (10:10–12), rising from the dead (9:9–10) gets no explanation, the statement about the death, burial, and resurrection (9:31) needs but gets no explanation (9:32), the destruction of the temple (13:2) gets fuller explanation (13:5–37), the betrayal (14:18) gets an explanation (14:19–21), the rebuilding of the temple (14:56–60) gets no answer (14:61), his identity as the Christ (14:61) gets an answer (14:62), whether he is King of the Jews (15:2a) gets an answer (15:2b), and when he is accused (15:3) is not (15:4–5). This may be expanded to acts as well. Eating with sinners (2:15–17) requires explanation (2:17), non-fasting (2:18) requires explanation (2:19–22), grain plucking (2:23–24) requires explanation (2:25–28), healing on the Sabbath (3:1–6) requires explanation, and both bread miracles (6:30–44; 8:1–10) require explanation (6:52; 8:14–21).

[142] Allen Howard Godbey, "The Hebrew *māšāl*," *AJSL* 39 (1922–24): 89–95. This probably accounts for why the same quotation of Isaiah can apply to non-verbal 'signs' in John 12:38–41. See Mearns, "Parables, Secrecy and Exchatology," 427, 33.

[143] The article τά is omitted in ‭א‬ D K W Θ 28. 565. 1424. 2542 *al*, but retained in A B C L *f*[1.13] 33. 2427 𝔐 bo. This omission is followed by both Tischendorf[8] and Bover in their editions.

[144] William Manson, "The Purpose of Parables: A Re-Examination of St. Mark iv.10–12," *ExpTim* 68 (1956–57): 133; Moule, "Mark v, 1–20 Yet Once More," 103.

[145] Bastiaan van Elderen, "The Purpose of the Parables according to Matthew," in *New Dimensions in New Testament Study*, ed. Richard N. Longenecker and Merrell C. Tenney (Grand Rapids: Zondervan, 1974), 180.

of scholars apply it to parables, public teaching, and deeds of Jesus (Gnilka, Woodward, Robinson, Mauser, Cranfield, Lane, Evans).[146]

In support of this final view is that misunderstandings in Mark are explicitly tied to three areas: parables, teachings, and actions of Jesus.[147] "People saw (feedings and other miracles) and heard (parables and other teachings), but they did not perceive who Jesus was (1:27; 4:41)."[148] Thus 'seeing' and 'hearing' are implicitly the faculties that expose the inability to understand. If only parables (or explanations) are in mind then one would expect 'seeing' to be omitted entirely or placed second in the following Isaian quote. This order suggests that much more is included than merely hearing parables or public teaching.[149] Further, *seen* probably reflects an acted מָשָׁל and accounts for its inclusion. The expansion to 'all things,' then, suggest either that the disciples' question is more profound than originally conceived or that Jesus takes the initiative in expanding the answer in conscious awareness of both the spoken and acted מָשָׁל/παραβολή. The spoken and acted מָשָׁל/παραβολη is to outsiders *noetic riddle*. They lack the *ontological-functional* capacities of salvific wisdom.

Isaiah 6:9–10: Observations and Evaluation. Some general observations about Mark 4:12 and Isa 6:9–10 are in order. First, Mark 4:12 is a digest rather than a quotation of Isa 6:9–10.[150] "Nur der

---

[146] James M. Robinson, *The Problem of History in Mark*, SBT, vol. 21 (London: SCM, 1957), 76; Cranfield, *The Gospel according to Saint Mark*, 154–55; William L. Lane, *The Gospel according to Mark*, NICNT, ed. F. F. Bruce (Grand Rapids: Eerdmans, 1974), 158; Woodward, "The Place of Mark 4:10–12 in the Second Gospel," 57; Thomas W. Leahy, "review of *Verstuckung Israels, Isaias 6, 9–10 in der Theologie der Synoptiker*, by Joachim Gnilka," *JBL* 81 (1962): 87–89; Gnilka, *Die Verstockung Israels*, 26. "Wie das 'Geheimnis des Gottesreiches' nicht nur aus den Gleichnissen, sondern auch aus dem übrigen Tun Jesu…." (ibid.). Cf. Brown, "The Secret of the Kingdom of God (Mark 4, 11)," 63 n. 20.

[147] Mark 6:52; 8:17, 21; 4:12; 7:14–17.

[148] Woodward, "The Place of Mark 4:10–12 in the Second Gospel," 57.

[149] Evans, *To See and Not Perceive*, 104.

[150] Franz Hesse, *Das Verstockungsproblem im alten Testament: eine frömmigkeits geschichtliche Untersuchung*, BZAW, vol. 74 (Berlin: Töpelmann, 1955), 64. Longenecker views the various statements (Mark 4:12, Matt 13:13, and Luke 8:10) as allusions to Isa 6:9–10 rather than quotations of Isaiah because of the exact quotation

zweite Teil von Vers 9 and fünf Wörter von Vers 10 werden geboten."[151] Second, the ἵνα-clause replaces the imperative of Isa 6:9. Third, the order of hearing/seeing in the MT, LXX, DSS, Targum, and Peshitta is reversed to seeing/hearing.[152] Fourth, after μήποτε the following clause of Isa 6:10 is omitted: ἴδωσιν τοῖς ὀφθαλμοῖς καὶ τοῖς ὠσὶν ἀκούσωσιν καὶ τῇ καρδίᾳ συνῶσιν καί. Fifth, the last line in the Hebrew לוֹ אֶרְפָּא, or the LXX καὶ ἰάσομαι αὐτούς is altered to read καὶ ἀφεθῇ αὐτοῖς against the MT, DSS, and LXX but with the Targum and Peshitta.[153]

Several grammatical variations show an affinity with the Targum.[154] These include the following: (1) The third person plural for second person plural in Isa 6:9 (contra MT and LXX) and non-imperative forms (contra LXX). The shift to the third person is "in order to accommodate the syntactical alteration from direct speech (as v. 9 is in the Masoretic Text) to a relative clause."[155] (2) The verb

---

in Matt 13:14–15 (Richard N. Longenecker, *Biblical Exegesis in the Apostolic Period*, 2d ed. [Grand Rapids: Eerdmans, 1999], 44).

[151] Gnilka, *Die Verstockung Israels*, 16. Jesus performs a task similar to the Teacher of Righteousness at Qumran according to 1QpHab 7:1–5 (Marcus, "Mark 4:10–12 and Marcan Epistemology," 563 n. 22).

[152] On a macrolevel (as noted earlier) Mark 4 emphasizes 'hearing' and Mark 13 'seeing.' But on a microlevel (Mark 4:12), 'seeing' is placed before 'hearing' to emphasize the ambiguous nature of the מָשָׁל/παραβολή.

[153] Some MSS replace ἀφεθῇ with ἀφεθήσομαι as in D* or ἄφησω in D² it. See Hesse, *Das Verstockungsproblem*, 64; Gnilka, *Die Verstockung Israels*, 23; Manson, "The Purpose of Parables," 133; Bruce, *Hard Sayings of Jesus*, 101; Woodward, "The Place of Mark 4:10–12 in the Second Gospel," 62, 70. Some MSS add to the pronoun an explicit object (or subject) of the verb, viz., τὰ ἁμαρτήματα ("the sins") A D Θ *f*¹³ 33 𝔐 lat sy. Text: ℵ B C L W *f*¹ 28*. 892*. 2427. 2542 *pc* b co (Bailey, *The Blindness of the Jews in Matthew 13:13–15, Mark 4:12 and Luke 8:10*, 9; Hodges and Farstad, *The Greek New Testament according to the Majority Text*, 117).

[154] Cranfield, *The Gospel according to Saint Mark*, 155. For a comparative layout of the MT, LXX, Targum, Matt 13:14–15, Acts, Mark 4:12, Matt 13:13 and Luke 8:10 see Gnilka, *Die Verstockung Israels*, 14–15. For differences with LXX and similarities with Targum see Craig A. Evans, "The Function of Isaiah 6:9–10 in Mark and John," *NovT* 24 (1982): 124–28; idem, *To See and Not Perceive*, 91–99.

[155] Evans, "The Function of Isaiah 6:9–10 in Mark and John," 127. Goulder says the third person is required by the ἵνα and therefore this and other similarities are insignificant. Instead he links 4:10–12 to 3:20–35 via three terms ἔξω, περὶ αὐτόν, and ἀφίημι (Goulder, "Those Outside (MK. 4:10–12)," 297).

'forgive' for 'heal' in Isa 6:10. (3) The passive voice 'forgiven' reads with the Targum (καὶ ἀφεθῇ αὐτοῖς = ולהון לשתביק) instead of the active (Qal) in the MT and LXX. Bock points out Mark's affinity to the Targum, including its causative connotation (with the MT, DSS), the parallel of the Targum's limiting relative pronoun to Mark's outsiders, and the similar ending on 'forgiveness,' and agrees with Jeremias that these factors most likely point to a Palestinian setting but not necessarily to its original form.[156] Aside from these similarities the vocabulary is Septuagintal.

The Ἵνα *Clause and Isa 6:9–10.* The ἵνα is a subordinating conjunction that modifies γίνομαι above. It gives the divine purpose, reason, or result for why the parables, teaching, and deeds of Jesus are riddles to those on the outside, or it simply defines them more particularly. No less than seven usages for this conjunction are offered by scholars including, *purpose (final, telic), causal, result (consecutive, ecbatic), relative clause, epexegetical,* equivalent to ἵνα πληρωθῇ, and *imperatival.*[157] Below these views are examined more closely starting with what is largely regarded as the least probable alternative and ending with the most likely.

*The imperatival-*ἵνα. The imperatival sense is an independent usage of the clause and rendered, "Let them see." Cadoux holds this view and Turner says it may derive from Semitic influence.[158]

---

[156] Darrell L. Bock, *Luke 1:1–9:50,* BECNT, ed. Moisés Silva, vol. 3A (Grand Rapids: Baker, 1994), 740.

[157] Wallace lists this as either *result* or *purpose-result* ἵνα-clause (Daniel B. Wallace, *Greek Grammar beyond the Basics: An Exegetical Syntax of the New Testament* [Grand Rapids: Zondervan, 1996], 473–74). BDF §369(2) argue that ἵνα is *final* "(theory that some are incapable of repentance), softened by Mt 13:13 to causal ὅτι (διὰ τοῦτο in answer to διὰ τί 10)." BDAG also prefer the *final* sense (BDAG 477). Incidentally, Smyth indicates that ἵνα-*result* never occurs in classical Greek (Herbert Weir Smyth, *Greek Grammar,* ed. Gordon M. Messing, rev. ed. [Cambridge, MA: Harvard University Press, 1956], §2193). This does not argue that *result* is not an option here (guilty of semantic obsoletism) but that it is a relatively new semantic tag in the Hellenistic era. Cf. Gnilka, *Die Verstockung Israels,* 45–48; Elderen, "The Purpose of the Parables according to Matthew," 188; Myers, "Disciples, Outsiders, and the Secret of the Kingdom," 162–70; Witherington, *The Gospel of Mark,* 166–67.

[158] C. J. Cadoux, "The Imperatival Use of ἵνα in the New Testament," *JTS* 42 (1941–42): 165–73 where he simply proposes the possibility of this sense to Mark 4:12 without supporting it (ibid., 173); Taylor, *The Gospel according to St. Mark,* 257. For Turner see MHT 3:94–95; 4:23.

However, the prevalence of the imperatival-ἵνα in Hellenistic Greek invalidates the claim of an exclusive Semitic influence or Semitism.[159] In addition it should be rejected for the following reasons. First, it is unlikely that ἵνα is independent from γίνομαι. Second, it does not fit the semantic situation of the ἵνα-imperative, namely, it does not follow a verb of saying, praying, or exhortation. Third, it is an attempt to harmonize with the imperatival phrase of the MT. Finally, it makes little sense in context where one expects a subordinate and thus dependent clause with the ἵνα.

Epexegetical-ἵνα. This is a dependent substantival usage when modifying a noun, adjective, or verb. Here it modifies 4:11b and is rendered, "that is...." Suhl, Lampe, and Pesch subscribe to this view.[160] Several arguments are used in support of this construal. First, Mark 9:12 allegedly employs the ἵνα clause in this manner. But this usage does not parallel Mark 4:12 where an articular substantival participle might be expected rather than an anarthrous participle. Furthermore, this may work both ways. Second, since the functional use of Isa 6:9–10 is applied to the disciples in Mark 8:18 (Jer 5:21), this argues for a utilitarian rather than purposive sense here. But Mark 8:18 is an interrogative designed pragmatically to rebuke the disciples. Although several scholars see a distinction between Mark 4 and Mark 8, the failure to recognize the precise distinction leads to equating the disciples' *partial* lack of comprehension from post-blind

---

[159] Horsley cites Pernot, Mandilaras, and Connolly showing that this is perfectly normal Greek (*NewDocs* 5:57). Brooks-Winbery (Brooks and Winbery, *Syntax of New Testament Greek*, 124) describe it as an idiom in Hellenistic Greek for when the subjunctive is in place of the imperative mood and is preceded by verbs of saying, praying, or exhortation (none of these indicators are present here in Mark 4:12). Wallace (Wallace, *Greek Grammar Beyond the Basics*, 476–77) says it is an independent usage, i.e., not dependent on a previous verb (and thus not subordinate), and cites clear examples including Mark 5:23; Eph 5:33; Matt 20:33; Mark 10:51; 1 Cor 7:29; 2 Cor 8:7; Gal 2:10; and Rev 14:13.

[160] Alfred Suhl, *Die Funktion der alttestamentlichen Zitaten und Anspielungen im Markusevangelium* (Gütersloh: Mohn, 1965), 66, 94, 149–51 (a qualifying consecutive relative clause); Peter Lampe, "Die markinische Deutung des Gleichnisses vom Sämann, Markus 4, 10–12," *ZNW* 65 (1974): 140–50; Pesch, *Das Markusevangelium*, 239; Guelich, *Mark 1–8:26*, 211. Exactly what it modifies is unclear. First, it may modify 'parables' or 'riddles.' The following phrase would then expand on the riddle-like response to Jesus' teaching or deeds. Second, it may expand on the meaning or connotation of γίνομαι. It would focus on what is meant by becoming.

syndrome (8:17–21), a *functional-ontological* issue, with *total* incomprehension due to blindness, an *ontological-functional* issue.

Equivalent το ἵνα πληρωθῇ. The elliptical part of the fulfillment formula is represented by ἵνα. This fulfillment formula may be an extension of either purpose or result.[161] Lagrange is the first to propose such a view but is followed by Bailey, Piper, and Jeremias.[162] Neither Lagrange nor Jeremias provide any examples of this usage in Mark. Myers writes, "The closest existing New Testament analogy in which ἵνα is without a finite verb that can be supplied from the context is 1 Cor. 1:31.... But here the phrase on which the interpretation depends is clearly stated—γεγραπται."[163] Gnilka (who argues opposite) provides the best argument for it as both purpose and preemptory.[164] He says, "Das ἵνα in Mk 4, 12 ist Überleitungspartikel, selber noch nicht zum Zitt gehörig. Weil das Schriftwort unmittelbar folgt, kann man es gut als Abbreviatur für ἵνα πληρωθῇ verstehen. Spätere ἵνα πληρωθῇ Aussagen konnten sich auf diese ältesten Überlegungen stützen."[165] Moreover, fulfillment formulas in Mark are overwhelmingly from Isaiah.[166] This would coalesce well with Matthew's formula if Mark in any way depends on that Gospel.

Several shortcomings may be cited. First, ἵνα seems not to be preempting a fulfillment formula but rather the first part of the Isaian interpretation. Otherwise, this would be the only case in Mark where he omits the fulfillment formula for Isaiah (or any other text). Second,

[161] Kirkland takes it as consecutive-fufillment (Kirkland, "The Earliest Understanding of Jesus' Use of Parables," 7).

[162] Marie-Joseph Lagrange, *Évangile selon Saint Marc,* Etudes biblique (Paris: Lecoffre, 1966), 99; Lagrange, "Le but des paraboles d'après l'évangile selon saint Marc," 28; Bailey, *The Blindness of the Jews in Matthew 13:13–15, Mark 4:12 and Luke 8:10,* 65–66; Piper, "The Mystery of the Kingdom of God," 183–200; Jeremias, *The Parables of Jesus,* 17.

[163] Myers, "Disciples, Outsiders, and the Secret of the Kingdom," 162. See also Evans, *To See and Not Perceive,* 93; Gnilka, *Die Verstockung Israels,* 45–48; Siegman, "Teaching in Parables," 176; Minette de Tillesse, *Le secret messianique dans L'Evangile de Marc,* LD, vol. 47 (Paris: Cerf, 1968), 159.

[164] Gnilka, *Die Verstockung Israels,* 47.

[165] Ibid., 48.

[166] Mark 1:2; 7:6; 9:12–13; 10:4–5; 11:17; 12:19; 14:21, 27; cf. 7:6; 12:10; 14:49.

ἵνα never functions this way in Mark nor fulfillment in the mode of a promise-fulfillment pattern as that found in Matthew.[167] Instead ἵνα has more of a "qualifying or interpretive function."[168] Hauck insists that "the softer reading of ἵνα in the sense of ἵνα πληρωθῇ...is an illegitimate alleviation of the difficulty."[169] Evans points out that if this view is correct it does not necessarily obviate a purposive sense but it does break the coordinating syntax of the ἵνα/μήποτε construction and therefore another solution must be sought.[170]

Myers captures it well when he says, "As Matthew Black has pointed out, Mark wrote and intended not only the ἵνα but also the μήποτε. To 'remove' the former and not deal adequately with the latter allows the difficulty to remain. What was true of attempts to retain the ἵνα but to make it less offensive is also true of the μήποτε; to suggest that it means 'perhaps' or 'unless' may be comforting but it does not appear convincing either."[171] Comforting because this construal places the μήποτε clause as the condition for the effects of the ἵνα clause, namely, if one repents he will see, perceive, hear, and understand. This view treats the ἵνα without dealing adequately with μήποτε and suffers the same critique under either a coordinate or hypotactic syntax. It is evident that the ἵνα/μήποτε constructions stand or fall together.

Relative pronoun from Aramaic. The chief point of contention is that Mark has mistranslated the Aramaic relative particle -ד into ἵνα instead of ὅς.[172] Because the underlying Aramaic particle is ambiguous, it can be rendered as a relative pronoun (ὅς), a genitive

---

[167] Suhl, *Die Funktion*, 66, 94, 149–51; J. Dupont, "Le chapitre des paraboles," *NRTh* 89 (1967): 806; Guelich, *Mark 1–8:26*, 211.

[168] Ambrozic, *The Hidden Kingdom*, 67.

[169] Friedrich Hauck, "παραβολή," *TDNT* 5:758 n. 102.

[170] Evans, *To See and Not Perceive*, 94. But Evans relies too heavily on a coordinate syntax for his view. If the syntax between ἵνα and μήποτε is hypotactic rather than coordinate, then his argument carries less weight.

[171] Myers, "Disciples, Outsiders, and the Secret of the Kingdom," 162.

[172] There are many supposed mistranslations in the NT proposed by Aramaic experts. See Joseph A. Fitzmyer, *Essays on the Semitic Background of the New Testament* (London: Scholars Press, 1974), 93–217 and idem, *A Wandering Aramean: Collected Aramaic Essays* (Missoula, MT: Scholars Press, 1979), 14–15. Cf. Taylor, *The Formation of the Gospel Tradition*, 110–13.

marker, or as a conjunction (ὅτι, ἵνα).[173] The Targum translation would require ὅς (or οἵτινες) and for this reason it is suspected that Mark (or redactor) goofed. The leading proponent of this view is Thomas Walter Manson.[174] Fueling this is Mark's final phrase that follows the Targum. Taking the ἵνα as reflecting either 'so that' or 'who' requires one to treat the μήποτε as 'perhaps' or 'unless' rather than 'lest' (still assuming a coordinate syntax). "The meaning of Jesus' saying would then be: 'For those outside everything is in parables, (for those, namely) *who* see indeed but do not perceive, *who* hear indeed but do not understand; perhaps (unless) they may turn again and be forgiven.'"[175] This view may be set aside for the following reasons. First, it is highly speculative and concedes that the Greek text *prima facie* teaches the opposite view. Second, it suggests that the Targumic ending supports the emphasis of the Targum for the entire passage—but this is not necessary. Third, it requires a coordinate relationship between ἵνα and μήποτε where the μήποτε clause becomes the condition for the fulfillment of the ἵνα clause. Finally, it does not adequately explain why Luke either retains the ἵνα clause or why both Matthew and Luke omit the μήποτε clause.

Causal-ἵνα. This is a disputed semantic tag for this early Koine Greek but if legitimate is a dependent rendering of the clause. Three lines of reasoning are used to support the causal sense of the ἵνα-clause: First, the presence of the causal sense in later patristic literature. Second, the parallel of ἵνα to Matthew's ὅτι may suggest that the former be understood by the latter. Third, the supposed presence of NT cases where ἵνα is plausibly rendered makes it a viable option here. Various scholars taking this view include Jannaris, Burkill, Lohmeyer, La Cava, and others.[176]

[173] MHT 2:469–70; Zerwick, *Biblical Greek Illustrated by Examples*, §§425–26.

[174] Manson, *The Teaching of Jesus*, 57–81.

[175] Bruce, *Hard Sayings of Jesus*, 102. For a refutation of Manson see Black, *An Aramaic Approach to the Gospels and Acts*, 211–16; Taylor, *The Gospel according to St. Mark*, 257.

[176] Antonius N. Jannaris, *An Historical Greek Grammar Chiefly of the Attic Dialect* (Reinheim: Lokay, 1968; reprint, Hildesheim: Olms, 1968), §1741; T. Alec Burkill, *Mysterious Revelation: An Examination of the Philosophy of St. Mark's Gospel* (Ithica, NY: Cornell University Press, 1963), 112; Ernst Lohmeyer, *Das Evangelium des Markus: Erganzungsheft, Kritisch-exegetischer Kommentar über das Neue Testament*, ed. Heinrich von August and Wilhelm Meyer, vol. 2 (Göttingen: Vandenhoeck & Ruprecht, 1957), 84; F. La Cava, "L' ἵνα causal nel Nuovo Testamento," *ScC* 65 (1937): 301–04. Cf. Urban Holzmeister, review of *Ut videntes non videant*, by Francesco La Cava, *Bib* 17

The relation to Apollonius Dyscolus. First, Apollonius Dyscolus is cited in support of the causal-ἵνα for NT literature in general and this passage in particular. Most grammarians, however, regard the causal-ἵνα as a later development in Koine Greek. [177] Recently, Ineke Sluiter has shown that the passages in Apollonius are made-up examples and not literary citations.[178] However, he then goes on to cite eleven clear and unambiguous literary cases (from nine texts) where the causal sense occurs thereby justifying the ancient grammarian's thesis that "that conjunction is always followed by an aorist subjunctive, the main sentence has a past tense, and, finally, in all examples the ἵνα-clause precedes the main clause."[179] The patristic (not NT) literature demonstrates that the causal sense occurs in cases where the teleological (final) innuendo is an impossible option. "The Apollonian conditions for a causal interpretation of ἵνα seem, therefore, to be generally valid."[180] Sluiter shows that Apollonius' conditions include past tense constructions for the ἵνα clause, namely, an aorist in the subjunctive mood where *cause* (represented by the ἵνα-clause), precedes *effect* (represented by the main clause) in the past tense. The causal-ἵνα is a legitimate category found in sub-literary colloquial

---

(1936): 512–14. For a strong refutation of this view see Gnilka, *Die Verstockung Israels*, 45–46 who says, "Die Argumente für ein kausales ἵνα in Mk 4,12 sind von der Grammatik her gesehen zu schwach" (ibid., 46). See also Hans Windisch, "Die Verstockungsidee in Mk 4:12 und das Kausale-ἵνα in der späteren Koine," *ZNW* 26 (1927): 203–09. "A causal view of ἵνα is possible acc. to later *koine* usage, and in this case the ὅτι of Mt. would be an intentional clarification, but one can hardly adopt this interpretation here" (Friedrich Hauck, "παραβολή," *TDNT* 5:757 n. 95).

[177] See Zerwick, *Biblical Greek Illustrated by Examples*, §413; Hesse, *Das Verstockungsproblem*, 64. Cf. Apollonius Dyscolus *Synt.* 381–82; *Coni*. 243–44.

[178] Ineke Sluiter, "Causal ἵνα, Sound Greek," *Glotta* 70 (1992): 39–53.

[179] Ibid., 40. Texts include the following: (1) *Anth. Pal.* 9:169; (2) John Chrysostomus *Sac.* 1. 4.33 (*SC* 272); (3) Basilius of Caesarea *Regulae brevious tractatae*, 1237–40: Question 233 (*PG* 31); (4) Pseudo-Johannes Chrysostomus *Oratio catechetica in dictum evangelii: simile est regnum caelorum homini patrifamilias, qui exiit primo mane conducere operarios in vineam suam* [*Matth.* 20:1], (*PG* 59, 582); (5) Pseudo-Johannes Chrysostomus *Sac.* 1. 7 (*PG* 48, 1069); (6) John Chrysostomus, *Paenit.* 8 (*PG* 49, 339); (7) John Chrysostomus *Virginit.* 22, 1 (*SC* 125); (8) John Chrysostomus *Hom. Act.* 3 (*PG* 60, 40); (9) Severianus of Gabala *homil. In qua potestate* (*PG* 56, 419). The *syntactial* and *grammatical* pattern is as follows: ἵνα-clause (aorist subjunctive) + main clause (main verb is past tense [usually] of indicative mood).

[180] Sluiter, "Causal ἵνα, Sound Greek," 49.

language of the educated Greek.[181] No clear instances, however, are found in the NT.

The relation to Matt 13:13. Second, the parallel passage in Matt 13:13 suggests that the ὅτι-causal clause may disambiguate the Markan ἵνα clause. This is certainly possible but it presupposes Matthew is interpreting Mark and that the causal-ἵνα is a legitimate NT category. Zerwick cites several NT passages in support of this sense (John 8:56, Rom 5:20, 6:1, 1 Cor 7:34, 3 John 8, 2 Cor 4:7, 12:9, Rev 14:13, 22:14 and some papyri).[182] This argument is invalid because the patristic and papyri evidence do not support the semantic situation for any of these examples.[183] Turner includes 1 Pet 4:6. He cautions that "the ἵνα of Mk 4[12] = Lk 8[10] is transformed into causal ὅτι in the Mt-parallel, but this would not prove identity of meaning...the consecutive [result] of NEB is not so good as final [purpose] (OT background) or causal (good precedent and excellent sense)."[184] But there is no precedent for the causal-ἵνα and the semantic situation established for this usage does not fit any of these passages. Second, even if it did fit, the causal tag would still have to avoid the fallacy of semantic anachronism.[185] Third, that Matthew uses a causal-ὅτι instead of Mark's ἵνα does not demand an *interpretation* of Mark's ἵνα-clause but rather either an *alteration* (or *redaction*) of Mark for his own purposes or a *different perspective* of the same basic truth.[186]

Summary against causal view. Four fundamental reasons are contrary to the causal usage. First, of the nine NT examples, all may

---

[181] This could be given more impetus given the recent article of Stein (Stein, "Is Our Reading the Bible the Same as the Original Audience's Hearing It?" 63–78).

[182] Zerwick, *Biblical Greek Illustrated by Examples*, §§413–14.

[183] All of the examples given may be given alterntive grammatical tags.

[184] MHT 3:102. See also A. T. Robertson and W. Hersey Davis, *A New Short Grammar of the Greek Testament* (Grand Rapids: Baker, 1958), §426(c) and A. T. Robertson, "The Causal Use of ὅτι," in *Studies in Early Christianity: Presented to Chamberlin Porter and Benjamin Wisner Bacon by Friends and Fellow-Teachers in America and Europe*, ed. Shirley Jackson Case (New York: Century, 1928), 49–57. He rejects the causal use of ἵνα in the NT.

[185] See D. A. Carson, *Exegetical Fallacies*, 2d ed. (Grand Rapids: Baker, 1996), 32–34 and Moisés Silva, *Biblical Words and their Meaning: An Introduction to Lexical Semantics*, rev. and exp. ed. (Grand Rapids: Zondervan, 1994), 17–51.

[186] This study tries to avoid the Synoptic problem. See David Alan Black and David R. Beck, eds., *Rethinking the Synoptic Problem* (Grand Rapids: Baker, 2001).

be alternatively interpreted and no example is clear and unambiguous. Second, clear examples of the causal ἵνα in patristic literature occur where other alternative senses *are necessarily* ruled out. Third, none of the NT examples fit the semantic pattern where the condition (contained in the ἵνα clause) is already fulfilled and the consequent (contained in the main clause) is recently fulfilled. Fourth, none of the examples cited follow the 'regular' grammatical pattern for the causal ἵνα established by Sluiter, namely, *ἵνα-clause (aor. subj.) + main clause (MV is past tense [usually] of indicative mood).* Rather, in every NT case the ἵνα-clause *follows* rather than *precedes* the main clause thereby failing the semantic situation test structurally and semantically. In conclusion the ἵνα-clause in Mark 4:12 does not fit the established pattern and makes the words of van Elderen obsolete: "Recent studies of the use of ἵνα in Koine Greek has shown that the rigid categories of earlier grammarians cannot be maintained. Hence, there is no compelling reason to impose the classical interpretation of purpose upon this ἵνα clause. The attestation of causal ἵνα both in and outside of the NT and the present context [Matt 13] are in favor of such an interpretation."[187]

*Result (consecutive, ecbatic)-*ἵνα. This is a dependent usage of ἵνα. Scholars taking this view include Moule, Blakeney, Sutcliffe, Peisker, Anderson, Chilton, Woodward, Charue, Meinertz, and Feuillet.[188] Moule says that "The Semitic mind was notoriously unwilling to draw a sharp dividing-line between purpose and consequence" and that ἵνα with the Subjunctive expresses a consecutive (result) sense while ὥστε with the infinitive a final (purposive) nuance. He states, "It is far more reasonable to take both ἵνα and μήποτε as instances of the Semitic blurring of purpose and result, so that Matthew's change

---

[187] Elderen, "The Purpose of the Parables according to Matthew," 188. He cites BDF §369(2) and Zerwick, *Biblical Greek Illustrated by Examples*, §§412–13 in support but the sources and appeals to them are circular.

[188] Moule, "Mark v, 1–20 Yet Once More," 95–113; E. H. Blakeney, "The 'Ecbatic' use of ἵνα in N. T.," *ExpTim* 53 (1941–42): 377–78; Edmund F. Sutcliffe, "Effect as Purpose: A Study in Hebrew Thought Patterns," *Bib* 35 (1954): 320–27; Carl Heinz Peisker, "Konsekutives ἵνα in Markus IV, 12," *ZNW* 59 (1968): 126–27; Anderson, *The Gospel of Mark*, 131; Bruce D. Chilton, *A Galilean Rabbi and his Bible*, GNS, ed. Robert J. Karris, vol. 8 (Wilmington, DE: Glazier, 1984), 95; Woodward, "The Place of Mark 4:10–12 in the Second Gospel," 64, 77. For more scholars holding this view see Gnilka, *Die Verstockung Israels*, 46–47 (he lists A. Charue, M. Meinertz, and A. Feuillet on 46 n. 12) who himself refutes this view.

of ἵνα to ὅτι is essentially true to the sense while his illogical retention of the μήποτε is true to the Semitic idiom."[189]

Lagrange criticizes this view noting that the conjunction has such a meaning only with verbs that express request while with other verbs only purpose.[190] Porter says that Moule's interpretation belies theological presuppositions and rejects his view as driven by theology not grammar.[191] Gnilka reasons that because Jesus explains why outsiders are judged and answers a question regarding the preceding parable then only a causal or final sense can apply but that the former is to be rejected.[192] The view is rejected for three reasons. First, the result sense may not fit the verbal indicators. Second, the question of the disciples and context argue against it. Third, theological and philosophical a priori against the purposive sense is not positive reason for a consecutive view. But those who take the result view often see parables as 'riddles' in external form and 'interpretation' in private as giving of the mystery. If 'in riddles' is primarily an anthropological rather than a linguistic phenomenon, then result ἵνα becomes logically consistent, grammatically feasible (although less so that purpose), and contextually viable.

Purpose (final, telic)-ἵνα. Various purposes of the purposive view. This is a dependent syntactical arrangement. The majority of grammarians and commentators hold to this view.[193] The purposive

[189] Moule, *An Idiom Book of New Testament Greek*, 142; idem, "Mark v, 1–20 Yet Once More," 105. Evans regards Moule as holding to the causal view (Evans, *To See and Not Perceive*, 94).

[190] Lagrange, "Le but des paraboles d'après l'évangile selon saint Marc," 28. Cf. Wallace, *Greek Grammar Beyond the Basics*, 473 where two clear examples are given and both are interrogatives.

[191] Stanley E. Porter, *Idioms of the Greek New Testament*, 2d ed., Biblical Languages, vol. 2 (Sheffield: Sheffield Academic Press, 1994), 236 and idem, *Verbal Aspect in the Greek of the New Testament, with Reference to Tense and Mood*, Studies in Biblical Greek, ed. D. A. Carson, vol. 1 (New York: Lang, 1989), 325 (and esp. n. 4).

[192] See Gnilka, *Die Verstockung Israels*, 47.

[193] BDF §369(2); Porter, *Verbal Aspect in the Greek of the New Testament*, 325; idem, *Idioms of the Greek New Testament*, 236; Wallace, *Greek Grammar Beyond the Basics*, 473–74; Richard A. Young, *Intermediate New Testament Greek: A Linguistic and Exegetical Approach* (Nashville: Broadman & Holman, 1994), 186–87; Hesse, *Das Verstockungsproblem*, 64; Victor B. Curry, "The Nature and Use of the ἵνα Clause in the New Testament" (Th.D. diss., Southern Baptist Theological Seminary, 1949); W. Marxsen, "Redaktionsgeschichtliche Erklärung der sogenannten Parabeltheorie des

statement may imply a variety of nuances.[194] Manson maintains that parables are primarily for unbelievers to convert them which seems to run counter to his claim that ἵνα is purposely designed to compound obduracy. Key promotes a magical or causative (purposive) notion of judgment but over emphasizes the performative nature of the words and their opacity that prevents understanding and repentance. He likens Isaiah's words to babbling in an ecstatic state. Eakin links it to

---

Markus," ZTK 52 (1955): 269; Bailey, The Blindness of the Jews in Matthew 13:13–15, Mark 4:12 and Luke 8:10, 61; Jeremias, The Parables of Jesus, 10–11; Black, An Aramaic Approach to the Gospels and Acts, 211–16; David Daube, "Public Pronouncement and Private Explanation in the Gospels," ExpTim 57 (1945–46): 175–77; idem, The New Testament and Rabbinic Judaism (London: Athlone, 1965; reprint, Peabody, MA: Hendrickson, 1998), 149; Eduard Schweizer, The Good News according to St. Mark (Richmond, VA: Knox, 1970), 93; Walter Grundmann, Das Evangelium nach Markus, THKNT, ed. Erich Fascher, Joachim Rohde, and Christian Wolff, vol. 2 (Berlin: Evangelishe Verlagsanstalt, 1984), 92; Sjöberg, Der verborgene Menschensohn in den Evangelien, 124; Taylor, The Gospel according to St. Mark, 256–57; Cranfield, The Gospel according to Saint Mark, 155–56; Manson, "The Purpose of Parables," 132–35; Dupont, "Le chapitre des paraboles," 806; Burkill, Mysterious Revelation, 99, 110–11; M. Hermaniuk, La parabole évangélique: Enquête exégétique et critique (Bruges: Desclée, 1947), 304, 310, 314; Lagrange, "Le but des paraboles d'après l'évangile selon saint Marc," 28; idem, Évangile selon Saint Marc, 98–99; Gnilka, Die Verstockung Israels, 47–48; Johannes Horst, "οὖς," TDNT 5:554; Andrew F. Key, "The Magical Background of Isaiah 6:9–13," JBL 86 (1967): 198–204; Frank E. Eakin, "Spiritual Obduracy and Parable Purpose," in The Use of the Old Testament in the New and Other Essays: Studies in Honor of William Franklin Stinespring, ed. James M. Efird (Durham, NC: Duke University Press, 1972), 87–107; Pesch, Das Markusevangelium, 237; Evans, "A Note on the Function of Isaiah vi, 9–10 in Mark iv," 234–35; idem, "The Function of Isaiah 6:9–10 in Mark and John," 124–28; idem, To See and Not Perceive, 95–99; Hurtado, Mark, 73–74; Bruce M. Metzger, "The Formulas Introducing Quotations of Scripture in the NT and the Mishnah," JBL 70 (1951): 306; Boucher, The Mysterious Parable, 42–63; Ethelbert Stauffer, "ἵνα," TDNT 3:327; Howard Clark Kee, Community of the New Age. Studies in Mark's Gospel, rev. ed. (Macon, GA: Mercer University Press, 1983), 58; G. R. Beasley-Murray, Jesus and the Kingdom of God (Grand Rapids: Eerdmans, 1986), 106; Eugene E. Lemcio, "External Evidence for the Structure and Function of Mark iv. 1–20, vii. 14–23 and viii. 14–21," JTS 29 (1978): 323–38; Joel Marcus, The Mystery of the Kingdom of God, SBLDS, ed. Charles Talbert, vol. 90 (Atlanta: Scholars Press, 1986), 119–21; idem, "Mark and Isaiah," in Fortunate the Eyes that See: Essays in Honor of David Noel Freedman in Celebration of His Seventieth Birthday, ed. Astrid B. Beck et al. (Grand Rapids: Eerdmans, 1995), 457; Aloysius M. Ambrozic, "Mark's Concept of the Parable," CBQ 29 (1967): 220–27; idem, The Hidden Kingdom, 67–68.

[194] See Woodward, "The Place of Mark 4:10–12 in the Second Gospel," 17–23 for a plethora of purposes proposed by others.

the post hoc rejection of the Gospel by the Jews under the influence of Paul. Daube, Taylor, and Brown hold that the purpose is to conceal the truth from outsiders in line with Rabbinic patterns. Others (Via, Nineham, Schweitzer, Lenski) relate this to their particular view of predestination. Lemcio reasons that it is purposive only after the unpardonable sin and Lenski after man's unbelief. Hurtado translates it non-literally as 'prophetic irony.' Gould argues that Mark's statement applies to Jesus' teaching as ironic but not if applied to parables. Cranfield maintains that Jesus' entire ministry is riddle to outsiders but that parables are veiled revelation taught to the crowds while insiders are given the whole scoop. Jeremias thinks the purpose to conceal is the Father's not Jesus'. Schweizer and Martin emphasize the miraculous nature of hearing and propose that the purpose is to divide between those with this gift and those without it. This latter view is nearest to the point here and resonates well with the wisdom tradition and context.

Additional arguments from Evans. Evans offers five additional arguments (after going through alternative views) for the purposive interpretation. First, the OT establishes a precedent for that idea—the Exodus tradition, the confounding of human wisdom (2 Sam 17:4; 1 Kgs 12:15), deceiving (1 Kgs 22:13–23) and God as source and cause of the condition of dumbness, deafness, and blindness (Exod 4:11).[195] God deceives and hardens Israel's enemies (Deut 2:30), Israel's foolish leaders, and Israel herself (Isa 6:9–10; 29:9–10; 63:17). Second, the saying of Mark 4:24–25 comports well with the final interpretation of 4:11–12. The threat of obduracy in 4:24a along with the two principles in 4:24b–25 "('more will be given' and 'what he has shall be taken away') imply that it is God who gives and takes away divine insight. (The passive verbs are surely instances of the 'divine passive')."[196] The saying "If any man has ears to hear" (4:9, 23) reasserts the same idea that it is God who gives ears to hear. "Those who do not 'hear', do not because God has not given them 'ears.'"[197] It is wrong, he says, to view the lack of comprehension as removal "as the result of willful

---

[195] See also Robert B. Chisholm, "Does God 'Change His Mind'?" *BSac* 152 (1995): 377–99; idem, "Does God Deceive?" *BSac* 155 (1998): 11–28.

[196] Evans, *To See and Not Perceive*, 97. This would imply depletion rather than deprivation but he later explains in such a way as to rule out depletion. The 'taking away' is not divine insight but whatever falls short of it.

[197] Ibid.; Marcus, "Mark 4:10–12 and Marcan Epistemology," 562. Cf. 1QHa 9:21.

ignorance...as an act of divine judgment or of divine mercy."[198] It should rather be viewed, although he does not explicitly assert this, as a deprivation of wisdom that secures incomprehension.

Fourth, the Gospel of John collaborates this interpretation of the obduracy theme in non-Synoptic circles (John 12:38–40). This suggests Mark's idea is not an aberration. Further, if John depends on Mark, then at least one biblical interpreter took Mark's ἵνα/μήποτε unambiguously this way.[199] The conjunctions are coordinate (both give purpose for speaking in parables)[200] and semantically purposive.[201] Fifth, although Isa 6:9–10 is not quoted in Paul, other texts like it are (Isa 29:10; Deut 29:3–4) as seen in Rom 9:6–29 and 11:8. His view shows that an early understanding of hardening could have existed for Mark as well. Evans insists that ultimately Mark uses the text to explain Jewish rejection of the gospel. He concludes that the purpose of parables is to prevent 'outsiders' from understanding, repenting, receiving forgiveness, that parables are thus 'riddles' in

---

[198] Bruce Hollenbach, "Lest They Should Turn and Be Forgiven: Irony," *BT* 34 (1983): 318.

[199] James D. Dvorak, "The Relationship between John and the Synoptic Gospels," *JETS* 41 (1998): 201–13.

[200] They are semantically parallel but below the view is taken that the conjunctions are not coordinate to each other but rather μήποτε is subordinate or hypotactic to ἵνα.

[201] There are various phrases and terms for 'unless' in Greek. If Mark intended the μήποτε clause to be exceptive 'unless,' other phrases may have been employed to convey this point. (1) ἐκτὸς εἰ μή occurs three times in the NT (1 Cor 14:5; 15:2; 1 Tim 5:19) and is unambiguously exceptive. (2) παρεκτός occurs three times in the NT (Matt 5:32; Acts 26:29; 2 Cor 11:28) and is unambiguously exceptive. (3) πλὴν ὅτι (or πλήν) occurs twice in the NT (Acts 20:23; Phil 1:18) and is unambiguously exceptive. (4) ἐὰν μή (εἰ μή) is used many times (48 + 86 = 134) in the NT and almost always exceptive. (5) μή is used many times, but only rarely exceptive. (6) εἰ μήτι (ἄν) occurs three times in the NT (Luke 9:13; 1 Cor 7:5; 2 Cor 13:5) and is unambiguously exceptive. (7) ὅτι ἐὰν μή occurs three times in the NT (Matt 5:20; Acts 15:1; 2 Thess 2:3) and is unambiguously exceptive. Evans lists only the first three instances. The point is this. If Mark intended to use μήποτε with an exceptive sense ("unless")—thus making this clause logically prior to the ἵνα clause—he probably would have substituted a less ambiguous term or phrase for that sense. If μήποτε did carry an exceptive sense, then there is no reason Matthew would exclude it. Because he does not include it, this raises suspicions as to its unambiguous nature in conveying an exceptive sense. To say it is ambiguous ("lest" or "unless") concedes the point, viz., it probably did mean "lest." This is the crux of Evans' argument.

contrast to the unfolding 'secret' (μυστήριον), and that the disciples as 'insiders' are given the secret of the kingdom (4:24–25).[202]

Summary of views. Reasons for rejecting alternative views. In summary, alternative views of the ἵνα-clause other than purpose are viewed as less probable. Attempts are made to reproduce the original commission (imperatival), propose a functional model of fattening (epexegetical), do away with translating ἵνα (fulfillment formula), suggest a mistranslation from the Aramaic (relative pronoun), read later usage into the NT (causal), or require a linguistic (or possibly wisdom) issue of obscurity (result). The latter view is closest and may be blended with the purposive view.

Reasons for accepting purpose (or purpose-result) view. The *purpose* view of ἵνα is most probable and carries with it the idea that the riddle phenomenon is manifest through parabolic teaching and ministry feats of Jesus for the purpose of revealing human nature for what it truly is, namely, either productive or unproductive soil. The text, with these considerations in mind, assumes that man's heart left to its own (without imparted wisdom) is without exception fat/hard and therefore unwise, impotent, and unrepentant. It is not the purpose of parables to be deliberately or linguistically obscure (= in riddles) or to keep all information from the hearers (with the exception of private explanation). It is the purpose of God to withhold the knowledge of the kingdom to some by not imparting wisdom, which enables perception, knowledge, and understanding to occur, and thereby guarantee that what is spoken or done in relation to that kingdom comes off *noetically* (not linguistically) as riddle or mystery.

The divine withholding of wisdom guarantees the continuance of the noetic phenomenon ('in riddles'). The purpose is 'in order that' (or 'with the result that' or most likely *purpose-result*) they should not perceive, understand, repent, and be forgiven.[203] Since the latter presupposes that no one without wisdom would or will perceive, understand, repent, and be forgiven, it is suggested that those who do are beneficiaries of imparted wisdom. In this scheme Jesus uses the question about 'parables' wherein equivocation on the multiple senses of that term is utilized and expanded to 'all things' and segues

---

[202] Evans, "The Function of Isaiah 6:9–10 in Mark and John," 130.

[203] *Purpose-*ἵνα focuses on *intention, result-*ἵνα on *unintended* result, and *purpose-result-* ἵνα on the *intention and sure accomplishment* of the verbal action (Wallace, *Greek Grammar Beyond the Basics*, 472–73).

into the explicit congenital condition of the heart and the implicit gratuitous nature of the gift of God.[204]

Seeing But Not Perceiving. *The emphasis on seeing over hearing.* Beyond the observation that the grammatical construction argues for a purpose sense as primary,[205] this phrase shows where the immediate if not remote priority lies in regard to the previous discussion. The phrase βλέποντες βλέπωσιν is represented grammatically as an adverbial participle of *concession, progressive* present, and *simple* active modifying the main verb which is either *iterative* or *gnomic* present, *simple* active, and *purpose, result,* or *purpose-result* subjunctive in a ἵνα clause.[206] Answering four questions is essential in confirming its emphasis and grammatical tags. First, what is the difference between 'see' and 'perceive?' Second, what did they see and not perceive? Third, how is it possible to see and not perceive? Fourth, why do some perceive while others do not?

The lexical link of 'seeing' to wisdom. Because of the ordering of the clauses, emphasis falls on 'seeing' the deeds and ministry feats of Jesus rather than 'hearing' his teachings.[207] βλέπω occurs 133 times in the NT and fifteen times in Mark.[208] Here it refers to the act of

---

[204] Some commentators think Mark 4:12 is the 'parable' referred to in 4:13 (Trocmé, "Why Parables?" 463). Kirkland, Boobyer, Bowker, and Wrede also hold this view (Kirkland, "The Earliest Understanding of Jesus' Use of Parables," 1–21).

[205] Structurally, ἵνα + participle occurs seventeen times in the NT. When limited to the present participle it is found on six occasions (Mark 4:12; Luke 8:10; John 20:31; Acts 5:15; 1 Cor 9:18; 2 Cor 13:10)—all of these are clearly within *purpose* clauses except 1 Cor 9:18 (which is *epexegetical* most likely). There are only five cases where this construction (ἵνα + ptcp. [pres.] + verb [subj.]) occurs in the NT and that includes all the above *except* 1 Cor 9:18. So in every case where that formula occurs, it is clearly *purpose* ἵνα.

[206] BDF §422.

[207] Evans, *To See and Not Perceive,* 104; Wilhelm Michaelis, "ὁράω," *TDNT* 5:315–67. On the couplets see Taylor, *The Gospel according to St. Mark,* 256; Gould, *Gospel according to Mark,* 72; Manson, "The Purpose of Parables," 134. On the underlying Hebrew construction see Bailey, *The Blindness of the Jews in Matthew 13:13–15, Mark 4:12 and Luke 8:10,* 29.

[208] Mark 4:12, 24; 5:31; 8:15, 18, 23, 24; 12:14, 38; 13:2, 5, 9, 23, 33.

physically seeing or observing.[209] It is used in the LXX to translate eight different Hebrew verbs or expressions in the MT but none implying more than physical sight.[210] Forty-nine times it translates רָאָה 'to see,' fifteen times פָּנָּ 'to turn,' seven times the noun פָּנֶה 'before' or 'face', and once a piece the adjective פִּקֵּחַ 'seeing', שָׁקַף 'to look,' חָזָה 'to see,' פְּנִימִי 'inner' and נָבַט 'to look.' So although they physically see, this ocular phenomenon is not accompanied by a noetic aftermath of 'perceiving.' The reason seems to be that they lack something, namely, the ontological ability to salvifically perceive the ministry feats of Jesus.

The verb εἶδον occurs 341 times in the NT and forty-three times in Mark.[211] It has a *noetic* connotation. It refers to the noetic exercise of 'perceiving'[212] and oftentimes to a 'seeing' accompanied (in context) by a perception of some sort.[213] In context it refers to the act of perceiving "by sight of the eye, *see, perceive*."[214] The point is that although the *necessary* condition for perceiving is physically seeing, the latter is not *sufficient* to bring about the former. This verb is not found in the LXX but ὁράω (a close synonym) is.[215] It occurs 1,503

---

[209] Mark 4:12, 24; 5:31; 8:15, 18, 23–24; 12:14,38; 13:2, 5, 9, 23, 33 Cf. BDAG 178–79; *DELG* 1:179–80. For various nuances see L&N §§ 13.134; 24.7; 24.41; 27.58; 30,1, 120; 32.11; 68.6; 82.10.

[210] The verb βλέπω occurs 133 times in the LXX. It translates the following Hebrew verbs or terms: (1) The verb רָאָה 'to see' forty-nine times. (2) The verb פָּנֶה 'to turn' fifteen times. (3) The noun פָּנֶה 'before' or 'face' seven times. (4) The adjective פִּקֵּחַ 'seeing' once. (5) The verb שָׁקַף'to look' once. (6) The verb חָזָה 'to see' once. (7) The adjective פְּנִימִי 'inner' once. (8) The verb נָבַט 'to look' once.

[211] Mark 1:10, 16, 19; 2:5, 12, 14, 16; 4:12; 5:6, 14, 16, 22, 32; 6:33–34, 38, 48–50; 7:2; 8:33; 9:1, 8–9, 14–15, 20, 25, 38; 10:14; 11:13, 20; 12:15, 28, 34; 13:14, 29; 14:67, 69; 15:32, 36, 39; 16:5.

[212] Mark 2:5; 4:12; 9:1; 12:28, 34.

[213] Mark 2:12, 16; 6:33, 38, 49, 50; 7:2; 8:33; 9:25, 38; 10:14; 11:13; 12:15, 34; 13:14, 29; 14:67, 69; 15:32, 39.

[214] BDAG 279; cf. L&N §32.11; MM §3708 indicate that in wall-scratchings it occurs without an object as here.

[215] Two lexical issues surface here. First, εἶδον appears as a second aorist form of ὁράω but also as a separate lexeme in the NT (BDAG 279–80, 719–20). The former does not appear in the LXX but the latter occurs 1,503 times. Second, ὁράω also appears in the NT 113 times. Their semantic domains overlap with rare exceptions albeit εἶδον is always transitive and directed more to noetic or emotional issues while ὁράω may be transitive or intransitive and may be broader or more restrictive.

times mostly translating the verb רָאָה 'to see' 1,037 times and חָזָה 'to see, behold' sixty-seven times.[216] Interestingly, it translates יָדַע in Isa 6:9 and רָאָה in Isa 6:10. The link to the wisdom tradition of both verbs, especially the former, is overwhelming. In contrast to Woodward, the miracle of comprehension is not promised to all.[217] The net impression is that without the ability to perceive, the deeds (including the miraculous) of Jesus remain meaningless. They indeed physically *see* them but do not noetically *perceive* of their significance.[218]

Hearing But Not Understanding. *The lexical link of 'hearing' to wisdom.* This phrase is identical to the above in grammatical construction.[219] In both clauses (see/perceive and hear/understand) the first verb contains within its semantic domain the noetic sense captured in the second.[220] Like above, the 'hearing' is an *external* (and in this case, acoustic) phenomenon. ἀκούω occurs 428 times in the NT and forty-three times in Mark.[221] It is accompanied (in context) by understanding (genuine or artificial),[222] is equated with understanding,[223] or is followed by συνίημι.[224] The major lexicon on

---

[216] It also translates חָלַם 'to dream' ten times, יָדַע 'to know' eight times, עַיִן 'eye' six times, הִנֵּה 'behold' five times, and twenty-two other terms once or twice a piece.

[217] Woodward, "The Place of Mark 4:10–12 in the Second Gospel," 63. Myers locates the cause of failure to either lack of perception or stubbornness but favors the former (Myers, "Disciples, Outsiders, and the Secret of the Kingdom," 197).

[218] Prov 20:12 says, "The hearing ear and the seeing eye, the Lord has made them both." Cf. Myers, "Disciples, Outsiders, and the Secret of the Kingdom," 186–200. The divine initiative is here reflected in the 'blessedness' of those who have ears to hear (4:9, 23, 24–25).

[219] See MHT 2:444; BDF §422.

[220] Both βλέπω and ἀκούω in the LXX are future tense while in the NT they are subjunctive. Porter says this is aspectually more significant than even the exact nuance of the ἵνα clause above (Porter, *Verbal Aspect in the Greek of the New Testament*, 325).

[221] Mark 2:1,17; 3:8, 21; 4:3, 9, 12, 15–16, 18,20, 23–24, 33; 5:27; 6:2, 11, 14, 16, 20, 29, 55; 7:14, 25, 37; 8:18; 9:7; 10:41, 47; 11:14, 18; 12:28–29, 37; 13:7; 14:11, 58, 64; 15:35 (16:11).

[222] Mark 2:17; 3:8, 21; 4:12, 15, 16, 18, 20, 24; 5:27; 6:2, 11, 16, 20, 29; 7:25; 10:47; 11:14, 18; 12:28, 37; 13:7; 14:11, 58, 64; 15:35; 16:11.

[223] All occurring in Mark 4 (4:3, 9, 23, 33).

[224] Mark 4:12; 7:14.

the NT gives seven semantic domains for ἀκούω ranging from the faculty of hearing to the noetic concept of understanding.[225] The verb occurs 1022 times in the LXX and translates שָׁמַע in the majority of cases.[226] It is thus primarily focused on the phenomenon of hearing but in Mark 4 it is exploited to include 'understanding' also (4:33).

The lexical link of 'understanding' to wisdom. The verb συνίημι occurs twenty-six times in the NT and five times in Mark.[227] In the LXX it occurs 118 times and translates the Hebrew verb בִּין forty-eight times,[228] שָׂכַל twenty-six times,[229] יָדַע twice,[230] רָאָה twice,[231] and a few other verbs.[232] This sapientially rich vocabulary and the Isaianic fattening background add significance to the Markan usages. Mark 4:12 refers to 'understanding' associated with wisdom (or lack thereof). In 6:52 the disciples fail to 'understand' the significance of the loaves miracle because "their heart was hardened" (ἀλλ᾽ ἦν

---

[225] BDAG 37–8. Cf. L&N §§24.52, 58, 63, 67; 31.56; 21.1, 46; 33.212; 36.14; 56.13; MM §191; Gerhard Kittel, "ἀκούω," *TDNT* 1:216–25; *DELG* 1:50–51. BDAG 38 list ἀκούω in Mark 4:33 under the sense "to hear and understand a message, *understand*."

[226] Other terms include the following: (1) אֹזֶן 'ear' (Gen 23:10; Ezek 9:5; 10:13; Job 13:17). (2) הָיָה 'to be' (Gen 39:18). (3) שָׁמַר 'to keep watch, preserve' (Josh 22:2). (4) קָשַׁב 'to attend, listen' (Isa 32:3; 48:18; 51:4; Jer 6:10, 17*bis*; 18:18; 2 Chr 20:15). (5) יָדַע 'to know' (Isa 32:4). (6) אָזַן 'to hear' (Isa 32:9; Job 32:11; 2 Chr 24:19). (7) פָּתַח 'to open' (Isa 35:5). (8) רָאָה 'to see' (Jer 2:31). (9) נָגִיד 'leader, ruler' (Job 29:10). (10) בּוֹא 'to come' (Job 42:11). (11) לֶקַח 'instruction' (Prov 16:21). (12) נָפַל 'to fall' (Dan 4:28). (13) יָצָא 'to go out' (2 Chr 26:15).

[227] Matt 13:13–15, 19, 23, 51; 15:10; 16:12; 17:13; Mark 4:12; 6:52; 7:14; 8:17, 21; Luke 2:50; 8:10; 18:34; 24:45; Acts 7:25; 28:26–27; Rom 3:11; 15:21; 2 Cor 10:12; Eph 5:17.

[228] Deut 32:7; 1 Kgs 3:9; Isa 1:3; 6:9, 10; 43:10; 52:15; Jer 9:11; Hos 4:14; 14:10; Mic 4:12; Pss 5:2; 19:13[18:13]; 28:5[27:5]; 33:15[32:15]; 49:21[48:21]; 50:22[49:22]; 58:10[57:10]; 73:17[72:17]; 82:5[81:5]; 92:7[91:7]; 94:7[93:7]; 94:8[93:8]; 107:43[106:43]; 119:95[118:95]; 119:100[118:100]; 119:104[118:104]; 139:2[138:2]; Job 15:9; 31:1; 32:12; Prov 2:5, 9; 8:9; 21:29; 28:5; 29:7; Dan 11:33; Theod. Dan 11:33; Ezra 8:5, 16; Neh 8:2, 3, 8, 12; 13:7; 1 Chr 25:7; 2 Chr 34:12.

[229] Deut 29:8; 32:29; Josh 1:8; 1 Sam 18:14, 15; 1 Kgs 2:3; 2 Kgs 18:7; Isa 52:13; Jer 9:23; 23:5; Amos 5:13; Pss 2:10; 14:2[13:2]; 36:4[35:4]; 41:2[40:2]; 53:5[52:3]; 64:10[63:10]; 101:2[100:2]; 106:7[105:7]; 119:99[118:99]; Prov 21:11, 12; Dan 11:35; 12:3; Theod. Dan 11:35; 12:3.

[230] Exod 36:1; Job 36:4.

[231] 2 Sam 12:19; Jer 20:12.

[232] About a half-dozen instances occur of other verbs that are not significant here.

αὐτῶν ἡ καρδία πεπωρωμένη). This lack of understanding spells hardness of heart. In 7:14 Jesus asks them to 'hear' and 'understand' which provides another example of the verbs paired together when a parable is in mind (7:17). In 8:17–18 Jesus 'knows' (γνούς) when the disciples reason about the bread, what they are discussing, and asks both why they neither νοεῖτε nor συνίετε and then directly, "Have your hearts been hardened" (πεπωρωμένην ἔχετε τὴν καρδίαν ὑμῶν)? He then cites Isa 6:10, "Having eyes you do not see, and having ears you do not hear, and you do not remember."[233] Understanding of this sort is congenitally absent from the heart of man and so man is congenitally hard-hearted.[234] But since this passage refers to the disciples, it is most likely rhetorical and therefore *functional-ontological*.[235]

The NT context of the lexeme for 'to understand.' Throughout the NT συνίημι is used in the following contexts.[236] First, it is a *prerequisite for appreciating Jesus' teachings* (Matt 15:10; Mark 7:14). Second, it sometimes *accompanies explanations as a rhetorical devise*. This is done either to acknowledge (Matt 16:12; 17:13) or to inquire (Mark 8:17; 8:21) whether the disciples possess it. Third, in private it is often *used to explain unbelief or define the hard-heart* (Matt 13:13, 14, 15, 19, 23; Mark 4:12; Luke 8:10; Acts 28:26, 27). Fourth, it occurs *in connection with ambiguous sayings*. Jesus' parents misunderstand his saying, 'I must be about my Father's business' (Luke 2:50) or above parables. Fifth, it occurs in regard to *the nature of actions and linked to the hard-heart*. Israel misunderstands the purpose of Moses in killing an Egyptian (Acts 7:25) while the disciples of Jesus' misunderstand the miracle of the loaves (Mark 6:52; 8:17). Sixth, it occurs *in explanations of the divine prerogative in concealing/revealing*. Here it is in reference to the 'hiding' theme (Luke 18:34) or the 'opening' theme (Luke 24:45). Seventh, it is a *congenital defect of mankind* (Rom 3:11). To lack it in

---

[233] This text conflates Isa 6:10 with Jer 5:21 and Ezek 12:2. Jeremiah 5:21 reads literally, 'without heart,' a phrase that occurs twice in the MT (Jer 5:21; Hos 7:11) and is usually translated 'without understanding.'

[234] Witherington concedes that listening is equated with understanding and that this knowledge is not latent to man (Witherington, *The Gospel of Mark*, 167).

[235] Goulder, "Those Outside (MK. 4:10–12)," 302.

[236] See BDAG 972; L&N §§32.5, 26; MM §4920 note that συνίημι takes the place of ἐπίσταμαι. But see Mark 14:68 (Marcus, "Mark 4:10–12 and Marcan Epistemology," 569–70).

regard to God's will is to be 'foolish' or 'unwise' (Eph 5:17); and to use one's own subjectivism to measure oneself is evidence of its absence (2 Cor 10:12). Finally, it is *promised to Gentiles* (Rom 15:21) based on a reversal of the Isaian fattening motif (Isa 6:9–10) brought through the suffering servant (Isa 52:15). In harmony with Isaiah, the term points to a sapiential affiliation while usage reveals its necessary possession for acquiring knowledge of the mysterious and the divine.

Summary on the cause of perception and understanding. What or who is the cause of *perception* and *understanding*? As discussed in chapter three, these noetic aspects are necessary effects of wisdom, a wisdom that is non-congenital and gratuitously imparted to some. The quotation of the Isaian passage is designed to highlight the divine prerogative regarding the continuance of its absence and to reveal the congenital condition of man.[237] To be without this wisdom is to be fat/hard-hearted. Mark simply adopts Isaiah's sapiential world-view (chapter four) in his thematic correspondence to the reversal theme of Isa 52:13–53:12. It is the work of the suffering Servant in redemption that undoes the effects of fattening. The OT use of wisdom terms, Isaiah's linkage to the fat-heart, extrabiblical references, and NT occurrences each support the position that divine Isaianic fattening is *deprivational* in nature and involves a withholding of wisdom. To be *fattened* is a statement of the divine intention to deprive of wisdom, on the one hand, but to be a recipient of imparted wisdom, on the other hand, is a result of divine *transformation* (in regeneration). These are asymmetrical but non-contingent aspects of the dual divine act of regeneration and preterition.

Repentance and Forgiveness.[238] *The semantic domains of* μήποτε. The final clause of the Isaian allusion begins with μήποτε which reflects the unambiguous Hebrew פֶּן 'so that...not' or 'otherwise' and the more ambiguous Aramaic דִלְמָא 'perhaps' or 'maybe.' On the Greek side, Louw and Nida give three senses for the conjunction including *an indefinite negated point of time* ('never, not ever, at no time'), pertaining to *not being certain* ('can be, might be, whether perhaps'), and a *marker of negative purpose with apprehension* ('in order that...not,

---

[237] See 1QHa 9:19–20; 5:9–10; CD 2:13; 1QS 3:18–21; 4:11.

[238] The stress in 4:12 falls into a chiastic order: seeing and hearing (stressed), perceiving and understanding (unstressed), turning (unstressed) and forgiveness (stressed). See Ambrozic, *The Hidden Kingdom*, 68–69.

so that…not, lest' or 'otherwise').[239] Gnilka lays out two primary options for the Greek taken by scholars in light of the Hebrew and Aramaic. First, *ob nicht vielleicht* ('if not perhaps'), a view advanced by Lohmeyer, (William) Manson, Cranfield, and Horst.[240] He says this is "grammatikalisch durchaus möglich" and cites NT and extra-biblical examples.[241] Second, using the Targum the unambiguous Hebrew פֶּן becomes subject to the ambiguous Aramaic דלמא and yields the sense of either *vieleicht* ('perhaps' or 'maybe') or *es sei denn daß* ('it should be because that').[242] Gnilka says that Mark clearly understands μήποτε as final and (following Schnackenburg) holds that the clause is *coordinate* rather than *subordinate* to ἵνα.[243] A coordinate relationship demands treating it in the same sense as ἵνα so that both ἵνα and μήποτε give the purpose of parabolic speech (and acts).[244] However, a hypotactic structure is also a possibility and the lexeme alone is sufficient to view it as final as well.

---

[239] L&N §§67.10; 71.18; 89.62; BDAG 648–49. The negative purpose may be translated as either 'so that…not' or 'otherwise.' The logic of the negative purpose is *if A then not B* or *A otherwise B*. μήποτε occurs twenty-five times in the NT and twenty-one clearly take this nuance (Matt 4:6; 5:25; 7:6; 13:15, 29; 15:32; 25:9; 27:64; Mark 4:12; 14:2; Luke 4:11; 12:58; 14:8, 12, 29; 21:34; Acts 5:39; 28:27; Heb 2:1; 3:12; 4:1. Only three take the uncertain nuance (Luke 3:15; John 7:26; 2 Tim 2:25) while only one an indefinite point of time (Heb 9:17).

[240] Gnilka, *Die Verstockung Israels*, 48–49.

[241] Ibid., 49 n. 26.

[242] Cf. Str-B 1:662 list seven rabbinic cases where they neither understand Isa 6:9–10 as a message of hardening nor in the Targumic sense of 'perhaps.' Gnilka, however, notes later Rabbinic usages which pick up on the last three words of Isa 6:10 וְרָפָא לֹו וָשָׁב ("and turns and I will heal him"): *Mek. Exod.* 19,2 (69b) reads, "and scantily turns, so I will heal him." *S. Eli. Rab.* 16 (82) insists that Isaiah simply misunderstood God. Cf. Guelich, *Mark 1–8:26*, 210 and Cranfield, *The Gospel according to Saint Mark*, 156–57 for a listing of views and supporters. Cf. Falusi, "Jesus' Use of Parables in Mark," 40–41.

[243] Gnilka, *Die Verstockung Israels*, 49; Guelich, *Mark 1–8:26*, 210. The passage need not have gone through a sectarian stage prior to Mark in order for it to exclude unbelieving Jews as well as unbelieving Gentiles.

[244] Whether μήποτε is syntactically *coordinate* or *subordinate* to ἵνα depends on whether it modifies only γίνομαι (coordinate) or any or all of the other verbs. On μήποτε see Robertson, *A Grammar of the Greek New Testament*, 1415; idem, *Word Pictures in the New Testament*, vol. 1, *Matthew and Mark* (Nashville, TN: Broadman, 1930), 286.

Four primary lexical construals of μήποτε. There are essentially four construals of this conjunction as represented by various scholars: (1) *negative purpose* ('in order that...not' or 'otherwise'), (2) *uncertainty* ('can be, might be, whether perhaps'), (3) *temporal indefiniteness* ('never, not ever, at no time'), or (4) *contingency* ('unless').[245] μήποτε occurs twenty-five times in the NT and twenty-one are the negative purpose. Uncertainty occurs three times and the indefinite only once.[246] The contingency usage does not occur in the NT. Added to this are two reasons for taking the Aramaic into consideration. First, the Markan text apparently cites or alludes to the *Targum of Isaiah*. Second, rabbinic exegesis (Talmuds) interprets the final clause of the Isaian quotation as promising forgiveness in the sense of 'unless' or 'perhaps' (favoring coordinate syntax). In either case, repentance becomes the condition for wisdom's effects as well as forgiveness (healing). The only other option for this view is to treat the text as saying that repentance is a condition solely for forgiveness, a supposition of which few (of any view) would disagree. But there are no clear instances of a contingent nuance to this conjunction in the NT.

One construal of μήποτε involves a coordinate structure. The key in this discussion is the precise syntactical relationship of ἵνα and μήποτε. The latter is either *coordinate* or *subordinate* to ἵνα. In a *coordinate* sense both clauses modify γίνομαι and give the reason for all things being in parables to outsiders. This ordering tilts towards treating both clauses as purpose although some attempt to make the μήποτε clause the condition for the fulfillment of the ἵνα clause. Contrary to the coordinate syntax are several points. First, although there is strong precedent for the *semantic* nuance of both conjunctions,

---

[245] Ambrozic notes that the non-purposive usages of μήποτε in the NT are in passages introducing a question clause (Luke 3:15; John 7:26; 2 Tim 2:25) (Ambrozic, *The Hidden Kingdom*, 68). Guelich takes Mark 4:12 as a question and construes the passage functionally as holding out the possibility of change because the disciples are elsewhere described in the same language (8:14–21) (Guelich, *Mark 1–8:26*, 212). See also Manson, "The Purpose of Parables," 132–35; Bailey, *The Blindness of the Jews in Matthew 13:13–15, Mark 4:12 and Luke 8:10*, 10–13; Hollenbach, "Lest They Should Turn and Be Forgiven: Irony," 312.

[246] Negative purpose (Matt 4:6; 5:25; 7:6; 13:15; 13:29; 15:32; 25:9; 27:64; Mark 4:12; 14:2; Luke 4:11; 12:58; 14:8, 12, 29; 21:34; Acts 5:39; 28:27; Heb 2:1; 3:12; 4:1), uncertainty (Luke 3:15; John 7:26; 2 Tim 2:25), and temporal indefiniteness (Heb 9:17). The logical function of the negative purpose is *if A then not B* or *A otherwise B*.

the *syntactic* arrangement is not required by the final sense. Second, it produces a redundancy that leaves unaccounted for the difference in subject matter addressed. Third, it requires a distance between the main verb and the latter subordinating conjunction to the neglect of other more immediate verbs in context. Fourth, it does not adequately address the wisdom terms and their relation to repentance in 4:12c but rather leaves them dangling and without either a logical relationship or cohesion. Finally, it violates the usage of the μήποτε clause. This conjunction rarely occurs in a coordinate way when following a subordinate conjunction within twenty-five words.[247] For these reasons the coordinate as opposed to subordinate syntactical relationship should be set aside.

Another construal of μήποτε involves a hypotactic structure. The *subordinate* rendering, on the other hand, indicates that all things spoken and performed by Jesus become 'in riddles' to those on the outside for the purpose/result of not perceiving or understanding. In turn, these latter deficiencies of perception and understanding are the result of divine deprivation of wisdom that is purposed and if possessed would inevitably produce repentance and forgiveness. Here the clear link between repentance and forgiveness is maintained but more importantly the logical connection and necessary causation between perception/understanding and repentance is made explicit. Repentance does not secure wisdom, nor does repentance and forgiveness together secure wisdom, but rather wisdom secures repentance that provides the necessary and sufficient condition for forgiveness to occur. Only the subordinate syntactic arrangement recognizes and places emphasis on the necessity and sufficiency of

---

[247] In nearly every NT case it involves a *hypotactic* not *coordinate* syntax as it relates to the previous conjunction: (1) ὅτι/μήποτε (Matt 4:6; 15:32; Luke 4:11). (2) ἵνα/μήποτε (Mark 4:12). (3) ὡς/μήποτε (Luke 12:58). (4) ὅταν/μήποτε (Luke 14:8, 12). (5) εἰ/μήποτε (Acts 5:39). The only exceptions are Luke 14:29 (ἵνα/μήποτε) and Heb 9:17 (ἐπεί/μήποτε) where the two conjunctions occur consecutively. In the LXX a similar phenomenon occurs. *Coordinate* instances are the following: (1) μήποτε/μήποτε (2 Sam 1:20; 1 Kgs 18:27; 1 Macc 12:40; Sir 42:9, 10). (2) ὡς/μήποτε (Gen 3:22; Exod 13:17; Sir 30:12). (3) ἕως/μήποτε (Gen 38:11). (4) καίπερ/μήποτε (4 Macc 4:13). The rest are unambiguously *subordinate* usages: (1) ὅτι/μήποτε (Gen 20:2; 26:7, 9; 32:12; 1 Macc 13:17; TobB 2:13). Several cases involve direct discourse and therefore unrelated either coordinately or hypotactically (Gen 50:5; Exod 13:17; Num 16:34). (2) εἰ/μήποτε (Jdt 5:21; Sir 19:13). ὅπως/μήποτε (Exod 5:3). (3) ὥστε/μήποτε (JudgA 7:2; JudgB 7:2). There are no cases in either the NT or the LXX where ἵνα/μήποτε involves an unambiguous coordinate syntax.

wisdom for repentance to occur. Both conjunctions are still purposive, one positive and the other negative. μήποτε is best translated as 'in order that...not' or 'otherwise' as in "otherwise [they do perceive and understand and] they should turn and it should be forgiven them." This implies that those who do repent and find forgiveness do so because they possess wisdom and that these are necessary effects of possessing such wisdom.

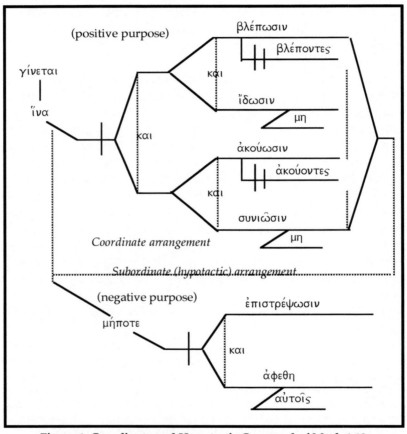

Figure 1: Coordinate and Hypotactic Construal of Mark 4:12

Parables are not spoken to be linguistically obscure so that this obscurity serves a dual purpose, namely, to ensure that incomprehension occurs and to prevent repentance. Instead parables and deeds are spoken and performed in such a way that those without imparted wisdom are unable to noetically filter them in a meaningful and salvific fashion. Because they lack perception and understanding, both the teachings and deeds of Jesus remain mysteries or become riddles. This riddle phenomenon is secured by the *deprivation* of wisdom (hardening) that has as its divine purpose-result the guarantee of the absence of perception and understanding. This congenital absence and further divine deprivation is in turn related syntactically in a hypotactic form and logically as cause to the effect of repentance and forgiveness. Without the former the latter do not occur but with the former the latter invariably ('otherwise') takes place. The human heart left alone is sufficient to secure unrepentance while imparted wisdom is the necessary and sufficient condition for repentance to occur.

Mark 4:33–34: A Recapitulation

Relation to 4:10–12

These verses function as a conclusion to the immediate statements of 4:30–34 and to the parable section as a whole.[248] Gealy says that here in 4:33–34 Mark gives his own interpretation of the logion of 4:10–12.[249] The chiastic ordering of the chapter confirms this notion: Parable (4:3–9), logion (4:10–12), transition to interpretation of parable (4:13), interpretation of parable (4:14–20), transition to interpretation of logion (4:21–25, 26–29, 30–32), and interpretation of logion (4:33–34).[250] Source and redaction issues abound. Best says 4:34b is Markan because it accords well with 4:11 but not with 4:33. Here the writer defines the group as 'disciples' and thus distinguishes them from the Twelve or the crowd.[251] Anderson recalls that 4:33 is thought traditional while 4:34 is deemed redactional. Mark 4:33 reportedly portrays the original intent of parables to be in figurative language accommodating to the capacity of listeners to understand while 4:34 corresponds to the esoteric aspect.[252] Here the identical pattern is seen

---

[248] Witherington, *The Gospel of Mark*, 172.

[249] Gealy, "The Composition of Mark 4," 41–43. He argues that 4:13 is an artificial literary product of Mark designed to give reason for the interpretation of the parable.

[250] This chiasm does not support the argument made by Kirkland (with Boobyer, Bowker, and Wrede) that 'parable' in 4:13 refers to 4:11–12. See Kirkland, "The Earliest Understanding of Jesus' Use of Parables," 1–21.

[251] Best, "Mark's Use of the Twelve," 18.

[252] Anderson, *The Gospel of Mark*, 140.

in relation to 4:10–12, namely, public teaching in accordance with their ability to 'hear,' followed by private instruction where Jesus would elucidate on all matters.

Parables and Wisdom

Mark continues by saying, "And with many such parables he customarily[253] spoke to them the word as they were able to hear." Context seems to suggest that although the mode is *speaking* in parables about the word of the kingdom, the end of the saying includes the all-inclusive πάντα. This may mean 'all things about them [parables] that pertain to his activity,' 'his activity,' or both. The audience is 'them' and while Taylor points to the earlier crowds of 4:1, it certainly includes insiders as well.[254] Hurtado regards the reference to their 'ability to hear' as proof that 4:10–12 is ironic.[255] Anderson likewise says that this "indicates that this parabolic mode of language is accommodated to the limits of human understanding."[256] Similarly, Witherington says this clause "stresses that the response to Jesus' teaching was limited by the audience's willingness or readiness to hear and understand what he was saying."[257] Either view is harmonious with the wisdom background of 4:10–12. The text refers, therefore, to the *ability* to hear and therefore includes a deeper sense than merely the physical. Rephrased in this light, Jesus speaks just as they are able to perceive and understand. This suggests that although his speech is wide in scope, it is limited in intent to those possessing wisdom and an accommodation for

---

[253] Fanning lists this under customary or iterative imperfect (Fanning, *Verbal Aspect*, 247; Wallace, *Greek Grammar Beyond the Basics*, 548). Robertson notes that Moulton (MHT 1:128) represents the iterative imperfect by the graph (. . . . .) then cites Mark 4:33 (Robertson, *A Grammar of the Greek New Testament*, 884). Since the *customary* is really a subset or specialized form of the *iterative*, it is best to regard it as a better tag (cf. Witherington, *The Gospel of Mark*, 172). See Fanning, *Verbal Aspect*, 287.

[254] Taylor, *The Gospel according to St. Mark*, 271.

[255] Hurtado, *Mark*, 78.

[256] Anderson, *The Gospel of Mark*, 141.

[257] Witherington, *The Gospel of Mark*, 172. He also observes that Jesus speaks parables only in Galilee not Judea (Ben Witherington, *Jesus the Seer: The Progress of Prophecy* [Peabody, MA: Hendrickson, 1999], 246–92).

development in wisdom. Its pedagogical purpose is less linked to outsiders who do not possess the ability to perceive or understand.[258]

Private Teaching and Πάντα

"But without a parable he did not speak to them but privately to his own disciples he explained all things." The focus is on the teaching aspect of parables, the private instruction[259] to his disciples,[260] and the further explanation given to them. Two things can be noted in this regard. First, the verb ἐπιλύω 'explain' occurs only twice in the NT (Acts 19:39), not at all in the LXX, and its nominal form ἐπίλυσις is a NT hapax (2 Pet 1:20). The verb carries the idea of explaining while the noun refers to the act of explanation or interpretation.[261] Second, this explaining pertains to 'all things.'[262] The neuter gender points beyond parables to include the explanation of the acts of Jesus as well. Thus in harmony with 4:10–12, Jesus speaks parables of which those possessing wisdom inquire more insight from him in private and to whom Jesus expounds not just the meaning of parables but the deeper significance of his own deeds as they relate to the inbreaking of the kingdom.

Mark 8:17b–18a, 21: Wisdom and the Hard-heart

Similarities to Mark 4:10–12

This passage is another example of a Markan text under the influence of Isa 6:9–10.[263] Jesus utilizes Isaianic terms and sapiential word-view

---

[258] Gould, *Gospel according to Mark*, 83.

[259] The phrase κατ ἰδίαν occurs eighteen times in the NT (Matt 14:13, 23; 17:1, 19; 20:17; 24:3; Mark 4:34; 6:31, 32; 7:33; 9:2, 28; 13:3; Luke 9:10; 10:23; 23:19; Gal 2:2; 2 Tim 1:9) and is common in the κοινή inscriptions and papyri (Robertson, *A Grammar of The Greek New Testament*, 224; BDAG 511; Baird, "A Pragmatic Approach to Parable Exegesis," 201–7).

[260] The phrase τοῖς ἰδίοις in 'to his own disciples' implies a loyalty or partisan following reflected earlier in 4:10–12. See Taylor, *The Gospel according to St. Mark*, 271; MHT 3:18.

[261] For the verb see BDAG 375; L&N §§30.81; 33.141. On the noun see BDAG 375; L&N §§133, 141.

[262] Some MSS limit this to parables by replacing πάντα with αὐτάς (from ἑαυτοῦ) in D W it.

[263] Hesse, *Das Verstockungsproblem*, 66.

and applies it to his own disciples.[264] Several scholars note dissimilarities with Mark 4. Boucher says Mark 4:10–12 does not have hardness of heart but rather its effects.[265] Ambrozic notes that compared with Mark 4:12 it is missing a key element, namely, the last line of 4:12 in reference to repentance and forgiveness.[266] He concludes that this means the disciples are assured of their conversion; but a literary evaluation may be that they are already converted (on the inside) and what is anticipated is part two of their two-stage healing miracle. The mention of hard-hearted has a rhetorical purpose (rebuke) while the absence of the latter clause favors their possession of salvific wisdom. This is a *functional-ontological* passage.

Schuler Brown recognizes the similarity of Mark 4:10–12 and 8:17–18 but also that the object of "the incomprehension cannot be concerned with the same thing in each case."[267] He argues that Mark 4 centers on the 'mystery' whereas here it concerns Jesus' identity. Further, mysteries are revealed by parables and explanations of parables while here through the healing of the blind man.[268] However the response of the disciples in both passages is very similar. In Mark 4 the disciples understand in part and seek more understanding while here they are unclear but are subsequently illumined by Jesus (through Peter's confession).[269] The negative evaluation does not make them 'outsiders' any more than 4:13 does. If being on the 'outside' is merely a functional category as Moule and others argue, then Jesus not only fails to label them as such, but he violates his own modus operandi towards outsiders in giving more information.[270] Apocalyptic literature indicates that epistemological fullness will only

---

[264] Moule, "Mark v, 1–20 Yet Once More," 99; Jeremias, *The Parables of Jesus*, 15.

[265] Boucher, *The Mysterious Parable*, 60. He says, "Hardness of heart, blindness, and deafness are three equivalent terms for obduracy; their opposites are faith and repentance." Kirkland thinks incomprehension is the cause of hardness rather than the reverse (Kirkland, "The Earliest Understanding of Jesus' Use of Parables," 9).

[266] Ambrozic, *The Hidden Kingdom*, 69.

[267] Brown, "The Secret of the Kingdom of God (Mark 4, 11)," 62.

[268] Gnilka, *Die Verstockung Israels*, 37–38.

[269] Sir 24:21; Augustine *Trin.* 15.2.

[270] Bowker, "Mystery and Parable," 313.

be fully realized in the eschaton. Until then, those chosen will continue to be epistemologically imperfect.[271]

The Context

The passage arises from a misunderstanding of a saying of Jesus. They neglect to bring bread and Jesus warns them to beware of the leaven of the Pharisees and Herod (8:14–15). This saying fosters more disputes among the disciples and summons a series of rebukes from Jesus in the form and flurry of seven interrogatives with an explanation of the miracle of the loaves (8:16–18). He expects them to derive a lesson from the aftermath based on the number of baskets taken up in the two feeding miracles (8:19–21; 6:30–44; 8:1–10). Their incomprehension sparks the interrogatives pointing out their noetic deficiency using the Isaian quotation (8:18) and in light of it (8:21). The subsequent miracle of the two-stage healing of the blind man is designed to illustrate the motifs of 'seeing they see but do not perceive *clearly*' more than 'hearing they hear and do not understand *clearly*.' Although a sharp dichotomy is not warranted, the emphasis here falls on the former. They fail to draw the right conclusions from the things they see. The disciples are like the first-stage healing, that is, "I see men as trees walking" (8:25). They are not blind, but they do not see clearly. The second stage is required which is actualized through correction and clarification. Only after Jesus lays his hands on the man's eyes does he look intently, is restored, and sees all *things* clearly. After this miracle comes Peter's confession (who represents the disciples) on Jesus' identity (8:27–30). The supernatural nature of noetic revelation implicit in Peter's confession is made more explicit in Matthew (16:18) but still incomplete (8:33; cf. 9:10, 32; 14:68, 71; 15:32, 39). Thus the literary connection is noted, the nature of their incomprehension is defined, the object of their confusion is settled, and the cause of the revelation is strongly implied.

Wisdom and Hardening

Jesus and Wisdom. How does the Isaian quotation help in understanding divine hardening and its relationship to wisdom? The

---

[271] Marcus, "Mark 4:10–12 and Marcan Epistemology," 560–61, 567–70. Qumran teaches a dualism of insider/outsider and a continuing incomprehension within the community (1QS 3:20–22; 5:24–26; 6:19–22).

feature that distinguishes this passage from Mark 4:10–12 is its explicit mention of the hard-heart. Here wisdom terminology and Isaianic fattening converge within a sapiential world-view. Jesus 'knew' what they were discussing and arguing and then addresses them.[272] The implied object of their discussion is best rendered, "after knowing *the nature of their discussion about the bread*."[273] It is not coincidental that the term for 'know' is used here.[274] The verb γινώσκω occurs 222 times in the NT and 754 times in the LXX.[275] It is found mostly in Isaiah and translates in the majority of cases יָדַע and דַּעַת but also includes בִּין, רָאָה, חָזָה, יָעַץ, נָגַד, שָׁמַע, and תָּכַן. As the consummate wise teacher, Jesus can see actions of his disciples and perceive their significance. The disciples, on the other hand, cannot yet adequately reciprocate.

The Interrogatives of Jesus and the Lexical Links to Wisdom. The questions come in sharply rhetorical flurries. First, he asks them why they are arguing over the issue of not having bread.[276] The second question is based on an inference from this discussion. "Do you not yet *perceive* nor *understand*?" The conjunction οὔπω functions adverbially for time, modifies νοέω, and serves to reinforce

---

[272] The text reads simply καὶ γνούς leaving the object of that knowing to be inferred.

[273] After this verb is added ὁ Ἰησοῦς in א A C D (L) W Θ $f^{1.13}$ 33 𝔐 lat sy sa^{mss} to make the subject of the verb λέγει explicit. Variant is added after αὐτοῖς in L. Text: א^1 B Δ 892*. 2427 aur i sa^{mss} bo; Various critical editions retain this variant including von Soden, Vogels, and Merk.

[274] It may mean supernatural knowledge (Ladd, *A Theology of the New Testament*, 231) or arise because of the dispute (Taylor, *The Gospel according to St. Mark*, 366).

[275] See BDAG 200 where they list this usage in Mark under the title "to be aware of someth., *perceive, notice, realize*." Cf. L&N §§27.2; 32.16; MM §1097; Rudolf Bultmann, "γινώσκω," *TDNT* 1:689–719.

[276] The verb διαλογίζομαι is followed by indirect discourse (rather than causal ὅτι). Various MSS add to this ἐν ἑαυτοῖς, ὀλιγόπιστοι = "among yourselves, you of little faith" in Δ^{45} W f^{13} *pc* (sa^{mss}). Other MSS add ἐν ταῖς καρδίαις ὑμῶν, ὀλιγόπιστοι = "in your hearts, you of little faith" in (D ἐν ταῖς καρδίαις) Θ 28. 565. 700 *pc* (it) sy^{h**}. The former makes explicit that the disciples' conversation sparks Jesus attention while the latter it is the secret ponderings of their hearts. Both are additions to modify and harmonize (ὀλιγόπιστοι) with Matthew (Matt 6:30; 8:26; 14:31; 16:8; cf. Luke 12:28). Taylor regards it as authentic (Taylor, *The Gospel according to St. Mark*, 367).

exasperation on Jesus' part while expecting an affirmative answer.[277] νοέω occurs fourteen times in the NT[278] and thirty-one times in the LXX.[279] It mostly translates בִּין ten times,[280] שָׂכַל five times,[281] and a half dozen other terms.[282] Here it addresses the inability of their minds to grasp or comprehend something due to lack of careful thought.[283] In literary terms, they still see men as trees walking. συνίημι is discussed earlier and its wisdom connection is apparent. Together both terms support the wisdom elements that lack full bloom in the disciples. The third question (really rebuke)[284] follows logically, "Do you have hardened hearts?" The grammar is unusual here but it should not be rendered as the ASV ("have ye your heart hardened?") as if the participle is middle reflexive. Here is evidence that the Isaianic fattening motif is conceptualized from the perspective of the sapiential world-view.

The Hard-Heart and Lack of Wisdom. The text reads, πεπωρωμένην ἔχετε τὴν καρδίαν ὑμῶν?[285] πωρόω 'I harden' literally refers to a

---

[277] BDAG 737. οὐ intends to solicit an affirmative answer here. There are only two cases in the NT where οὔπω follows a question (Mark 4:41; 8:17) and is itself interrogative (Zerwick, *Biblical Greek Illustrated by Examples*, §447). The answer expected is rather odd: "Yes we do not yet either perceive or understand."

[278] Matt 15:17; 16:9, 11; 24:15; Mark 7:18; 8:17; 13:14; John 12:40; Rom 1:20; Eph 3:4, 20; 1 Tim 1:7; 2 Tim 2:7; Heb 11:3.

[279] 1 Sam 4:20; 2 Sam 12:19; 20:15; 2 Macc 14:30; Prov 1:2–3, 6; 8:5; 16:23; 19:25; 20:24; 23:1; 30:18; 28:5; 29:19; Job 33:3, 23; Wis 4:14, 17; 13:4; Sir 11:7; 31:15; Isa 32:6; 44:18; 47:7; Jer 2:10; 10:21; 20:11; 23:20; Bar 6:41.

[280] 2 Sam 12:19; Jer 2:10; Prov 1:2, 6; 8:5; 19:25; 20:24; 23:1; 28:5; 29:29.

[281] Isa 44:18; Jer 10:21; 20:11b; Prov 1:3; 16:23.

[282] שִׂית 'to put, set' (1 Sam 4:20), שָׁחַת 'to destroy, corrupt' (2 Sam 20:15), עָשָׂה 'to do, make' (Isa 32:6bis), שִׂים 'to put, set' (Isa 47:7), כָּשַׁל 'to stumble' (Jer 20:11a), and מָלַל 'to say' (Job 33:3). None of these are related to the discussion.

[283] BDAG 674–75. It is used in wills with the sense of being sane or in one's right mind (MM §3539); J. Behm, "νοέω," *TDNT* 4:948–51. From Homer onward it derives from νοῦς and designates a thought that may be mixed with feeling (*TLNT* 2:123).

[284] This is a "stern rebuke" (Anderson, *The Gospel of Mark*, 202). See Richard A. Young, "A Classification of Conditional Sentences Based on Speech Act Theory," *GTJ* 10 (1989): 29–50.

[285] On the article see MHT 3:23, §2; Robertson, *A Grammar of the Greek New Testament*, 409, 789. There are various textual variants with regard to the phrase πεπωρωμένην

callus developed on the extremities or a stone formed in the bladder (and is discussed earlier in chapter 4).[286] The etymology of the term, however, is not relevant. In each case the term is used in the NT to refer directly or indirectly with the Isaian passage and always in the context of wisdom.[287] Applied to the heart it signifies *the absence of perception and understanding*, or better, *the hard-heart is a heart absent of salvific wisdom and its effects*. Here the verb is a *predicate* participle in the first predicate position modifying καρδίαν. Robertson notes that out of ἔχω and the perfect participle came the periphrastic participle so common in modern Greek.[288] It most likely represents an *intensive* use of the perfect, a *simple passive* voice without agency expressed, or less likely a *causative* or *permissive* passive.[289]

Woodward argues that the hardening of the disciples in 6:52 and 8:17 "means lack of perception rather than a rebellious attitude."[290]

ἔχετε τὴν καρδίαν ὑμῶν. It is replaced by (1) ἔτι (ὅτι 047. 1424 *pc*) πεπωρωμένην ἔχετε τὴν καρδίαν ὑμῶν ("are your hearts *still* hard" or "*because* your hearts are hard") in A 𝔐 f 1 vg sy[(s.p).h] and by (2) πεπωρωμένη ὑμῶν ἐστιν ἡ καρδία ("your hearts are hard") in (D πεπωρωμένη ἐστιν ἡ καρδία ὑμῶν) Θ (0143[vid] πεπωρωμένη ἐστιν ὑμῶν ἡ καρδία). 565 (it) co. As text but ἔχοντες (replacing ἔχετε) in 28. The text: Δ[45vid] ℵ B C L N W Δ f[1.13] (28). 33. 579. 892*. 1241. 2427. 2542 *pc*. The presence of ἔτι probably came from the ending of the verb συνίετε (dittography to graphic confusion caused by homoeoteleuton) along with the sense that seems to justify its presence. The reading ἔχετε over ἐστίν is overwhelming and in all MSS except D and Θ (Bruce M. Metzger, *A Textual Commentary on the Greek New Testament*, 2d ed. [Stuttgart: Deutsche Bibelgesellschaft, 1994], 98).

[286] Mark uses σκληροκαρδία in 10:5 and 16:14 to refer to the hard-heart in the sense of *rebellion* (cf. Deut 10:16; Sir 16:11; Jer 4:4). The English translation of 'hard-heart' hides the distinction the Greek terms make.

[287] Whether this is the verb πωρόω (Mark 6:52; 8:17; John 12:40; Rom 11:7; 2 Cor 3:14; Herm. *Mand.* 4.30.1–2 [although the interlocutor conveys a Rabbinic understanding]; 12.47.1–4) or the noun πώρωσις (Mark 3:5; Rom 11:25; Eph 4:18).

[288] Robertson, *A Grammar of the Greek New Testament*, 902.

[289] Ibid., 656–57. MS D reads πεπηρωμένη ('incapacitated,' 'blinded') ἐστιν ἡ καρδία ὑμῶν (Taylor, *The Gospel according to St. Mark*, 366). For a discussion of the possible confusion in the MSS tradition of πωρόω/πηρόω and πώρωσις/πήρωσις see Karl Ludwig Schmidt, "Die Verstockung des Menschen durch Gott," *TZ* 1 (1945): 13–14. See variants to Mark 3:5.

[290] Woodward, "The Place of Mark 4:10–12 in the Second Gospel," 95–96. He notes that the Pharisees and disciples are 'hardened' in different ways (ibid., 107) and that there are two conceptions of 'hardness' (ibid., 115).

Zemek also observes that the disciples "experienced a mental malfunction (they still had not put the pieces together about the stupendous miracle that they had witnessed hours earlier)."[291] In this passage, therefore, Jesus does not assert they are ontologically hard-hearted but links their incomprehension to Isaianic fattening that does in a functional sense. Only here in 6:52 does Mark directly state that the disciples have a hard-heart. But this is a similar context as the miracle of bread where the latter (Mark 8:17–18) serves to explain the first instance as a *functional-ontological* rather than an *ontological-functional* issue.[292]

The Heart in Mark

The Congenital Nature of the Heart. Another Markan text (7:14–23) is important for establishing that Mark views hardness of heart (= absence of wisdom) as a congenital condition. First, 7:17–18 uses the familiar phrase, 'Are you also without understanding' as both a signal (anaphoric) to Isa 6:9–10 (and Mark 4:13) and the hardening motif, and as a rhetorical device recapitulating the disciples' incomprehension theme. Jesus asks, "'Do you not see that whatever goes into a man from the outside cannot defile him, since it enters, not his heart but his stomach, and so passes on.... What comes out of a man is what defiles a man. For from within, out of the heart of man comes.... All these evil things come from within, and they defile the man'" (7:18b–23). This is part of the private instructions to the disciples.[293] The rebuke is ironic because the disciples lack the very understanding that reportedly resides in and is the character of the new heart that in turn makes evident the sinful condition of the hard-heart.

---

[291] George J. Zemek, *Doing God's Business God's Way: A Biblical Theology of Ministry* (Mango, FL: Doing God's Business God's Way, n.d.), 40; Hesse, *Das Verstockungsproblem*, 5. Later he says, "Jesus muß auch seinen Jüngern ein verstocktes Herz vorwerfen, weil sie den eigentlichen Sinn seiner Worte nicht verstehen" (ibid., 66).

[292] The disciples are functionally (not ontologically) hard-hearted and functionally (not ontologically) outsiders.

[293] Brown, "The Secret of the Kingdom of God (Mark 4, 11)," 68–69.

The Inferences Drawn from the Congenital Nature of the Heart. This passage is instructive for ascertaining Mark's view of the hard-heart. Things from the outside (foods here) entering in are unable to make the heart evil. The heart is viewed as more than ontologically sufficient of itself for the functional evil thereof. This Markan assessment favors a congenitally hard-hearted view and at the same time contrasts the notion that something (or someone) from *without* (God, parables, sermons, etc.) affects the heart *changing* it from one state (non-hard) to another (hard). That external stimuli can be used to *reveal* the nature of the heart hardly argues that it materially alters the heart from neutral to hard (not to mention a neutral heart changing itself into such). God's actions to the heart, involving a *change of state,* are decidedly one-directional—from hard-hearted to the new heart, never from the new or 'neutral' heart to hard-hearted. This passage instructs the view that when God hardens from an Isaianic perspective (fattens), involving wisdom and its possession, it is *deprivational* rather than *transformational* (via *depletion* or *deposition*) in nature. For God to *materially* harden an already hard-heart is superfluous, a view that violates Mark's own statements on the heart, namely, that it is incorruptible from without, but inherently corrupt within and produces nothing but that which corrupts without.

The Isaian Passage

Because the lack of perception and understanding is defined as the hard-heart, Jesus links it directly to the Isaian quotation of Isa 6:10 but conflates it with Jer 5:21 and Ezek 12:2 which are echoes of Isa 6:9–10. Here the terms take on a noetic nuance. "Having eyes you do not *see* and having ears you do not *hear* and you do not *remember*." The verb see, hear, and remember are all noetic (not ocular or acoustic) functions. The final phrase, "and you do not remember" is added in light of the context regarding the bread miracle.[294] The climax is reached in 8:21, "And he says to them, 'Do you not yet understand?'"[295] This question, as with the rest, is designed

---

[294] Some MSS attempt to keep the sapiential vocabulary intact in concert with the parallel passage above. See Taylor, *The Gospel according to St. Mark,* 367.

[295] The adverb οὔπω is replaced by several variants in the MSS tradition. (1) πῶς οὐ ("Why do you not understand?") in B G 28. 579. 700. 2427[vid]. 2542 *pm* b d q or by (2)

rhetorically (and thus pragmatically) as an emphatic declaration, evaluation, command, or something else. Here it is probably an *evaluation of the situation* that is a negative one designed to express disappointment and belittlement.[296]

Myers reasons that "If the 'leaven of the Pharisees' means their desire for a sign, and the disciples failed to get the significance of Jesus' warning about asking for signs, it is possible that Mark 8:17–18 was spoken to them as a rebuke."[297] Anderson states that the disciples' misunderstanding here is apparently ineradicable and the following miracle story illustrates that nothing short of a miracle of God's grace "can bestow believing-understanding on those who have eyes yet do not see."[298] There are indeed *degrees* in the possession of wisdom but no degrees in hardness/fattness when it comes to lack of salvific wisdom.

Conclusion

The Gospel of Mark is influenced significantly by the suffering servant passage of Isaiah (Isa 52:13–53:12). This may be due to Christian suffrage in the Roman environment where the message has become unfruitful. Due to the *Sitz im Leben* and the deliberate patterning in accordance to the quintessential reversal theme of Isa 6:9–10, the wisdom influence is strongly felt, seen, and heard throughout the Gospel. The Isaian metanarrative is likewise discernible in the hardening motif. While Isaiah defines the *fat-heart* as absence of wisdom and divine *fattening* as a deprivation of this benefit, the same ideas are evident. Hardening as a theme is utilized in reference to outsiders and insiders but with different senses. Outsiders are *ontologically-functionally* fat/hard-hearted while insiders (believers) may be *functionally-ontologically* fat/hard-hearted.

πῶς οὔπω ("Why do you not yet understand?") in A D N W Θ (*f*[13] πῶς οὖν οὔπω ["How is it, therefore, that you do not yet understand?"]) 33. 565 *pm* lat sy[p.h]. Text: ℵ C K L Δ *f*[1] 892. 1241. 1424. *al* k sy[s].

[296] Young, *Intermediate New Testament Greek*, 222; Robertson, *Word Pictures in the New Testament*, 332.

[297] Myers, "Disciples, Outsiders, and the Secret of the Kingdom," 196 n. 4.

[298] Anderson, *The Gospel of Mark*, 202. See similar statements of Best, "The Role of the Disciples in Mark," 384–85; Marcus, "Mark 4:10–12 and Marcan Epistemology," 569; Mearns, "Parables, Secrecy and Exchatology," 431–35.

The parabolic passage of 4:10–12 accounts for the rejection and acceptance of the message of Jesus. The riddle phenomenon is purely noetic rather than linguistic and comes about through the teachings and deeds of Jesus. It reveals the good soil as fruitful while exposing the bad soil as hard and unfruitful. Insider and outsider status is revealed through response to Jesus' teachings and deeds. Private instruction is to those seeking further clarification. The riddle phenomenon is due to a divinely purposed deprivation of wisdom that in turn prevents repentance and forgiveness. Because Mark focuses on the disciples' incomprehension and in light of the two-fold miracle of the healing of the blind man, it is understandable that the disciples are simultaneously cured of blindness but not post-blind syndrome. They are insiders who function at times as those with hard-hearts. Their lack of perception and understanding regarding the person and work of Jesus is, therefore, rhetorically linked to the fat-heart of Isaiah. This hardness is purely functional rather than ontological and does not threaten their status as insiders. As insiders they continue to get private instruction and continue to incrementally advance in wisdom.

Isaiah 6:9–10: Matthew and Luke

Matthew 13:10–17: The Reason for Parables

[10]Then the disciples came and said, "Why do you keep on speaking to them in parables?" [11]So he answered and said to them: "To you it [wisdom] has been given to know the mysteries of the Kingdom of heaven, but to them it [wisdom] is not been given [to know the mysteries]. [12]For whosoever has [wisdom], it [wisdom] will be given to him and it will abound, but whosoever does not have [wisdom] even that [wisdom] which he has will be taken away from him. [13]*For this reason* I speak to them in parables *because* although seeing they do not see, and although hearing, they neither hear nor understand. [14]And the prophecy of Isaiah is fulfilled among them which says, 'In hearing you will certainly hear but will not understand, and although seeing you will certainly see but will not perceive.' [15]*For* the heart of this people has become fat and their ears hard of hearing, and their eyes they have closed *otherwise* they should see with their eyes and hear with their ears and understand with their heart and they should turn and I will heal them.' [16]But your eyes are blessed because they see and your ears [are blessed] because they hear. [17]For I solemnly tell you, that many prophets and righteous (ones) desired to see the things which you see and did not see, and to hear the things which you hear and did not hear."

The matter Matthew poses is simply a question of *why*. Luke's question is geared to the *meaning* of a specific parable. Mark focuses on *purpose* and Matthew on the *reason* and *cause*.

The Question and Expected Form of Answer

Matthew's διὰ τί 'why' expects a *causal* response, a *reason* for rather than the *purpose* or *meaning* of parables.[1] The phrase διὰ τί occurs

---

[1] "The focus of Jesus' reply (vv. 11–17) is not so much on the disciples' understanding as on the fact that the revelation is given to some and not to others and why" (D. A. Carson, "Matthew," in *The Expositor's Bible Commentary*, ed. Frank E. Gaebelein, vol. 2 [Grand Rapids: Zondervan, 1995], 307).

twenty-six times in the NT.[2] Six patterns emerge: (1) A *real question* followed by a *causal conjunction* ὅτι or διά with the accusative.[3] (2) A *real question* followed by an *explanation*.[4] (3) A *real question* followed by a *rhetorical question*.[5] (4) A *rhetorical question* followed by an *explanation*.[6] (5) A *real question* followed by a *rhetorical question* then *explanation*.[7] (6) A *real question* left unanswered.[8] The first and second options are most likely but priority lies on the first.

The first view demands either ὅτι or διά with the accusative. The ὅτι[a] is *recitative* while the following διά τοῦτο gives the *logical inference* (for the interlude) while the subsequent ὅτι[b] gives the *cause* and answer to the original question. Given this construal, there is an aside between the question *why* and the answer given in the form of an *interlude* (recitative ὅτι) and *inference* (διά τοῦτο).

The First Interlude on Privilege

The Divine Discrimination and Wisdom. *The clause and the audience.* The preface to Jesus' reply (ὁ δὲ ἀποκριθεὶς εἶπεν) favors construing the following ὅτι clause as *recitative* rather than *causal*. He answers 'them,' namely, the disciples not the crowd.[9]

Two views of the ὅτι[a] *clause.* The following ὅτι clause either reads as a *causal* 'because' or a *recitative* and left untranslated.[10] If the

---

[2] Matt 9:11, 14; 13:10; 15:2, 3; 17:19; 21:25; Mark 2:18; 7:5; 11:31; Luke 5:30; 19:23, 31; 20:5; 24:38; John 7:45; 8:43, 46; 12:5; 13:37; Acts 5:3; Rom 9:32; 1 Cor 6:7*bis*; 2 Cor 11:11; Rev 17:7.

[3] Matt 13:10; 17:19; Luke 19:31; 24:38; John 8:43; 12:5; Rom 9:32; 1 Cor 6:7*bis*; 2 Cor 11:11.

[4] Matt 9:11; Mark 7:5; Luke 5:30; John 7:45; 13:37.

[5] Matt 15:2–3; Mark 2:18.

[6] Mark 11:31; Luke 19:23; 20:5; John 8:46; Acts 5:3; Rev 17:7.

[7] Matt 9:14.

[8] Matt 21:25.

[9] Some MSS omit this pronoun (א C Z 892 pc ff[1] k bo). Text: B D L W Θ *f*1.13. 33 𝔐 lat sy sa mae. Tischendorf[8], WH, von Soden, and NA[25] omit this pronoun as well.

[10] Evans is right when he says that Jesus does not really answer the question here but does so in 13:13 (Craig A. Evans, *To See and Not Perceive: Isaiah 6:9–10 in Early Jewish and Christian Interpretation*, JSOTSup, ed. David J. A. Clines and Philip R. Davies, vol. 64 [Sheffield: JSOT, 1989], 108; Bastiaan van Elderen, "The Purpose of the Parables according to Matthew," in *New Dimensions in New Testament Study*, ed. Richard N.

former, then it offers an immediate answer to the διὰ τί in 13:10 whereas if the latter it affords something of an interlude before the explicit *reason* is given in the διὰ τοῦτο clause of 13:13a and *cause* (ὅτι) in 13:13b. Carson argues that the recitative ὅτι never follows the phrase ὁ δὲ ἀποκριθεὶς εἶπεν. But given these strictures, neither does the causal ὅτι.[11] There is good reason to take this first ὅτι as direct discourse.

Against the causal sense of ὅτι[a] are the following factors. First, the other Synoptics are either *indirect* (Luke) or *direct* (Mark) discourse. Second, there are twelve examples where the pattern involving ἀποκρίνομαι followed by ὅτι (within five words) is found and in every case but three the ὅτι-clause is *direct discourse*.[12] The three exceptions are a *causal* (John 1:50) and two *indirect discourse* and translated 'that' (John 18:37; Acts 25:16). Thus the ὅτι[a]-clause is most likely *direct discourse*, followed by the logical *inference* (διὰ τοῦτο) of the wisdom interlude, and then a *causal* sense (ὅτι[b]) that the original question solicits. The διὰ τοῦτο is both anaphoric of the original question and anticipatory of the subsequent causal ὅτι clause for the answer.

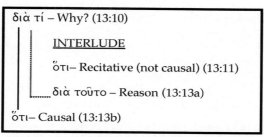

Figure 2: Structural Justification for Interlude

Longenecker and Merrell C. Tenney [Grand Rapids: Zondervan, 1974], 182). Alexander also takes it as causal (Joseph A. Alexander, *The Gospel according to Matthew Explained* [London: Nisbet, 1861; reprint, Lynchburg, VA: James, 1979], 356).

[11] Only two passages fit the pattern Carson advances, viz., Matt 13:11 and Matt 19:4. Since the former is disputed, this does not furnish ample evidence for his case. Moreover, the latter ὅτι is indirect discourse not causal. This leaves Carson without clear examples (Carson, "Matthew," 307).

[12] Matt 19:4; Mark 8:4; 12:29; Luke 4:12; 7:43; 13:2; 13:14 (second ὅτι); John 18:8. The three exceptions are John 1:50; 18:37; Acts 25:16.

Giving, withholding, and the congenital condition. Three other elements may be briefly noted. First, there is a positive side to 'giving' that reflects the divine initiative, recalls the wisdom tradition, and reinforces the *strong* divine causality implicit in the text. δίδωμι likely reflects the divine passive.[13] Since no contingency is listed for this action, it is best to view it as non-contingent.[14] What is given is not bestowed in response to what the disciples do.[15] The subject of the verb may be either implied or be the following infinitive phrase.[16] In the latter the knowledge of the mysteries of the kingdom is given to them while in the first instance the subject is wisdom and the infinitive phrase following is the purpose for wisdom being given in order to know. Thus knowing is a noetic consequence of imparted wisdom not simply more information. Conversely, it is not the kingdom that is withheld from outsiders but rather wisdom itself.[17] If

---

[13] The verb (δέδοται) is a circumlocution for divine activity and thus emphasizes the gift of God (Elderen, "The Purpose of the Parables according to Matthew," 182–83). The form implies "an authoritative predetermination.... *Given*, not conceded as a right, but granted as a favor" (Alexander, *The Gospel according to Matthew Explained*, 356).

[14] See comments on Mark 4:11 above. The expression 'given to you' (irrespective of voice) occurs thirty-three times in the NT either six times in the form ὑμεῖς δίδωμι (Matt 13:11; Luke 8:10; 12:32; 16:12; 22:19; John 6:27) or twenty-seven times as δίδωμι ὑμεῖς (Matt 7:7; 20:4; Mark 13:11; Luke 6:38; 10:19; 11:9; 12:32; 21:15; John 6:32*bis*; 7:19, 22; 13:15, 34; 14:16, 27; 15:16; 16:23; Acts 13:34; Rom 15:5; 1 Cor 1:4; 2 Cor 5:12; Eph 1:7; 3:16; 1 Thess 4:2; 2 Thess 3:9, 16; Rev 2:23). There are basically two types of giving: contingent and non-contingent as related to human behavior.

[15] The phrase 'given to know' occurs only here and Luke 8:10. The entire phrase ὑμῖν δέδοται γνῶναι τὰ μυστήρια τῆς βασιλείας is identical in Matt 13:11 and Luke 8:10, with Matthew rounding it off with τῶν οὐρανῶν and Luke with τοῦ θεοῦ (sometimes termed Q). The phrase 'to know the mysteries' (ידע רזים) is in Qumran literature (1QpHab 7:4–5; 1QHa 1:21; 2:13; 4:27). Alexander says this knowing is "directly, by explicit statement, either without the veil of parable, or with the aid of an infallible interpretation" (Alexander, *The Gospel according to Matthew Explained*, 356). But he seems to overlook that 'givenness' is prior to the interpretation.

[16] The infinitive can be a substantival use as *subject* (of passive verb) or most likely it is an adverbial infinitive of *purpose* or *result* modifying the controlling verb δέδοται. Under the first view it would read, "To know the mysteries of the kingdom of heaven has been given to you." The second view would read, "*Wisdom* has been given to you in order that you might know the mysteries of the kingdom of heaven."

[17] See Matt 11:25–27 = Luke 10:21–22. See William Robert Myers, "Disciples, Outsiders, and the Secret of the Kingdom: Interpreting Mark 4:10–13" (Th.M. thesis,

wisdom is divinely withheld, then man is *congenitally* fat/hard-hearted. This sentiment seems to provide the reason for his allusion and then the explicit citation of Isa 6:9–10.

Second, there is a negative side to giving that reflects the divine initiative and highlights the congenital condition. There are thirty examples (twenty-nine verses) in the NT of the negative side to 'giving.'[18] In four of these passages the voice is passive (Matt 12:39; 13:11; 16:4; Luke 11:29). Several texts may provide a key to understanding these sayings. "But he said unto them, 'Not all men can receive this saying, but they to whom it is given'" (Matt 19:11). The second, "A man can receive nothing except it be given him from heaven" (John 3:27). Both texts presuppose an inability apart from some heavenly intervention to accept certain sayings or things. The 'givenness' is monergistic not synergistic or contingent upon an active receiving but is the same thing as having it (1 Cor 4:7). The statement, "I received my eyes from my mother" does not imply an active but rather a passive reception. Therefore, it is not merely 'explanation' that is given that makes the saying acceptable, but something about the nature of the 'giving' that makes the saying (whatever it may be) that follows understandable. The 'giving' is a charismatic endowment of salvific wisdom and is received, in terms of voice, in the same sense that human characteristics are 'received' from parents.

Finally, there is the phenomenon of 'riddle.' The final phrase of 13:11, in light of the wisdom context, now comes to full force. "But to those it [wisdom] is not given." The sense is, "To those who do not know the mysteries of the kingdom do not know so because wisdom's prerequisite is not given to them by God." The remote demonstrative pronoun ἐκείνοις reads for Mark's 'to those on the outside' (τοῖς ἔξω) and Luke's 'to the rest' (τοῖς λοιποῖς). Whereas Mark positively states, "all things come in riddles," and Luke "in

---

McGill University, 1960), 179; M. Jack Suggs, *Wisdom, Christology, and Law in Matthew's Gospel* (Cambridge: Harvard University Press, 1970), 71–97; Myers, "Disciples, Outsiders, and the Secret of the Kingdom," 181. Myers links it to poetic speech and argues that it is non-literal (ibid.). This makes little sense out of the divine initiative of giving and not giving and the recourse to 'poetic' seems raised only to alleviate a difficult concept.

[18] Matt 7:6; 12:39; 13:11; 16:4; 24:29; 25:42; Mark 4:7; 12:14; 13:24; Luke 7:44–45; 11:8, 29; 19:23; John 3:27; 6:32, 65; 7:19; 19:9, 11; Acts 7:5; 12:23; 13:35; 19:31; 1 Cor 14:7; 2 Cor 12:7; 2 Tim 1:7; Jas 2:16; Rev 16:9. Ten of these do not apply (Matt 7:6; John 3:27; 6:32, 65; 7:19; 19:11; Acts 19:31; 1 Cor 14:7; 2 Cor 12:7; Rev 16:9).

parables (or riddles)," Matthew stresses the negative aspect of the divine prerogative "not given" in relation to parables.[19] The remote demonstrative pronoun serves to contrast the referents of the personal pronoun ὑμῖν.[20] To the disciples wisdom is given which enables them to understand the mysteries of the kingdom whereas to the others wisdom is withheld (*deprived*) rather than *depleted* or its opposite (foolishness) *deposited*. Wisdom is simply "not given in order to not know." Thus parables are not linguistically obscure but are instead instruments to reveal the hidden things from the foundation of the world to a designated group (Matt 13:35; Ps 78:2).[21]

The Divine Initiative and Wisdom. The positive bestowal of wisdom. The focus on wisdom is preserved in 13:12 in a short saying consisting of two parts. There is an assumed elliptical reference to wisdom in each couplet. The Synoptic parallels are essentially the same. The sense would read as follows. "For the one who has [wisdom] it [namely, the effects of wisdom] will be given to him and it [wisdom] will abound. But the one who does not have [wisdom] even that which he has [namely, the effects of wisdom] will be taken from him."[22] It is grammatically equivalent to reading this sentence hypothetically as, "*If* one has wisdom, *then....*" The supplying of 'wisdom' to the

---

[19] "These mysteries of the kingdom both reveal and conceal truths of the kingdom of heaven, so that it is appropriate that these parables followed immediately after the Jewish leaders rejected Jesus" (Mark L. Bailey, "The Parable of the Sower and the Soils," *BSac* 155 [1998]: 175).

[20] See A. T. Robertson, *A Grammar of the Greek New Testament in the Light of Historical Research*, 4th ed. (Nashville: Broadman, 1934), 707; MHT 3:45; Myers, "Disciples, Outsiders, and the Secret of the Kingdom," 164.

[21] Fred B. Craddock, *Luke*, IBC, ed. James Luther Mays and Paul J. Achtemeier (Louisville, KY: Knox, 1990), 107. The Hebrew term behind the quotation of Ps 78:2 is חִידָה 'riddle, enigmatic, perplexing saying, or question.'

[22] In the explanation of the parable, the central concern of the seed sown on the wayside is the lack of 'understanding' (συνίημι [13:4, 19]). This lack precedes the snatching of the word by the evil one from the heart and guarantees that even that which they had (the message of the kingdom) is taken away. This situation is in distinction to the fruitful ground (heart) that hears the word, 'understands' it, (συνίημι [13:8–9, 23]), and bears fruit. The contrast is between two types of hearts, why one heart is fruitful and the other is not, and thus the presence or absence of wisdom.

translation is supported by the odd grammar of the relative clauses.[23] The first relative pronoun (ὅστις) is *independent* in that it is not the subject of the main verb in the following main clause (δοθήσεται). Rather, the implied object of the main verb in the relative clause (ἔχω), "He who has *wisdom*," becomes the subject of the verb in the main clause, "*wisdom* will be given." However, in the latter main clause 'wisdom' becomes a synecdoche for the effects rather than the cause. In this way the referent of the relative pronoun (ὅστις) is the same as the personal pronoun (αὐτῷ) and part one of the saying is chiastic. The end is that this same wisdom will abound still more.

The negative withholding of wisdom. Part two consists of two relative clauses followed by a main clause. The first relative pronoun (ὅστις) is independent because the subject (like above) is not the same subject of the following relative clause (καὶ ὅ ἔχει) but rather the final prepositional phrase (ἀπ᾿ αὐτοῦ). The sense of part two is that the one who does not have wisdom even the effects of it gained will be lost.[24] Part one is the explanation for knowing mysteries while part two is in contrast to part one explaining why others do not comprehend the mysteries.

The Answer Part 1: Paraphrase of Isa 6:9–10

The Reason for Parables. The phrase διὰ τοῦτο occurs sixty-four times in the NT in real and supposed answers and inferences and translated as *therefore* or *for this reason, (namely) that.*[25] Grammatically it can refer to what precedes or follows.[26] However, in every case in

---

[23] See Stanley E. Porter, *Idioms of the Greek New Testament*, 2d ed., Biblical Languages, vol. 2 (Sheffield: Sheffield Academic Press, 1994), 246.

[24] The verb for 'take away' is αἴρω. Here it functions as a *gnomic* future, *simple* passive without agency expressed, a *declarative* indicative, and modifies ὅ ἔχει (James A. Brooks and Carlton L. Winbery, *Syntax of New Testament Greek* [Washington, DC: University Press of America, 1979], 170; Porter, *Idioms of the Greek New Testament*, 246). For a similar principle in rabbinic Judaism see *b. Ber.* 40a; *b. Sukkah* 46a; *Qoh. Rab.* 1:7; *Gen. Rab.* 20:5; *t. Sotah* 4.17–19; *b. Sotah* 9b. Alexander understands this in a retributional sense (Alexander, *The Gospel according to Matthew Explained*, 357) while Luz thinks what is taken away is the kingdom (Ulrich Luz, *The Theology of the Gospel of Matthew*, trans. J. Bradford Robinson, New Testament Theology, ed. James D. G. Dunn [Cambridge: Cambridge University Press, 1995], 86 n. 3).

[25] BDAG 224.

[26] Alexander, *The Gospel according to Matthew Explained*, 358.

Matthew this phrase is used to *draw a logical inference derived from a previous argument*.[27] Here it is also resumptive. If, as argued above, the point of the interlude pertains to the possession or lack of wisdom, then Jesus is reflecting a theory of parables which views their utility in primarily revealing the sagacity of the hearers. Jesus points to the distinguishing feature of disciples, namely, their gratuitous possession of wisdom (13:11), and the benefits that accrue more and more to its possessors (13:12). If this is the reason that he speaks in parables, then it is misleading to construe parables as a *punishment* based on bad behavior instead of a *testing device* to reveal the internal character of the hearers, namely, to expose those with and without wisdom.[28]

Mitigation Versus Grammatical Necessity. Many scholars note the 'softening' effect of Matthew's ὅτι compared to Mark's ἵνα but others testify to Matthew's harsh predestinarian tones.[29] To suppose mitigation requires several steps: a source theory where Matthew depends on Mark, that the change in Matthew is deliberate, that Matthew disagrees with Mark, that ὅτι in Matthew is less offensive than ἵνα, and that no grammatical reason can be made for Matthew's rendition of ὅτι but redaction. But if the construal of the ὅτι clause above is correct (recitative) and yet the διὰ τί demands a causal ὅτι clause in response, then grammatical reasons alone require Matthew to have it here. The alternatives are either redaction and redundancy or neither.

According to Matthew, Jesus speaks in parables *because* they do not see, hear, or understand (βλέποντες οὐ βλέπουσιν καὶ ἀκούοντες οὐκ ἀκούουσιν οὐδὲ συνίουσιν). This inability to see, hear, and understand is Isaiah's (and Mark's) definition of the fat/hard-heart. That God *purposes* man to be fat/hard-hearted (in

---

[27] Matt 6:25; 12:27, 31; 13:13, 52; 14:2; 18:23; 21:43; 23:34; 24:44.

[28] Scannell argues for a retributional use of Isa 6:9–10 in Matthew (Timothy J. Scannell, "Fulfillment of Johannine Signs: A Study of John 12:37–50" [Ph.D. diss., Fordham University, 1998], 80). This seems unlikely.

[29] Donald A. Hagner, *Matthew 1–13*, WBC, ed. Ralph P. Martin, vol. 33A (Dallas: Word, 1993), 371; Evans, *To See and Not Perceive*, 108; Frank E. Eakin, "Spiritual Obduracy and Parable Purpose," in *The Use of the Old Testament in the New and Other Essays: Studies in Honor of William Franklin Stinespring*, ed. James M. Efird (Durham, NC: Duke University Press, 1972), 107.

Mark) in no way counters the claim that man *is* congenitally fat/hard-hearted (in Matthew). Matthew's putative use of Mark may only accentuate this. God both *purposes* to fatten (via deprivation) in Mark and man *is* fat-hearted (congenitally) in Matthew.

The Answer Part 2: Quotation of Isa 6:9–10

The Reliance on the LXX. The above indirect allusion to Isa 6:9–10, which highlights the congenital condition of man is demonstrated by the verbatim citation of the LXX which emphasizes the congenital condition.[30] Some have argued that the passage is an unnecessary amplification and inauthentic,[31] others the very words of Jesus, the *ipsissima verba*,[32] or a particular comment from the OT as it relates to Jesus' ministry.[33] Hermeneutically it is a form of typological (or double) fulfillment.[34] If this is correct, then like Mark, Matthew weds a *purposive* sense of hardening within a *congenitally* fat/hard-hearted matrix.

The Lexical Connections to Wisdom. The wisdom motifs predominate. "In hearing you will hear and not[35] understand

---

[30] Evans, *To See and Not Perceive*, 107; Myers, "Disciples, Outsiders, and the Secret of the Kingdom," 177.

[31] See the three reasons of Torrey as given by Philip Bailey, *The Blindness of the Jews in Matthew 13:13–15, Mark 4:12 and Luke 8:10* (Rome: Typis Scholae Tipographicae Missionariae Dominicanae, 1956), 16–19. For a contra argument see Carson, "Matthew," 310.

[32] Bailey, *The Blindness of the Jews in Matthew 13:13–15, Mark 4:12 and Luke 8:10*, 17; Hagner, *Matthew 1–13*, 373.

[33] George Eldon Ladd, *A Theology of the New Testament*, ed. Donald A. Hagner, rev. ed. (Grand Rapids: Eerdmans, 1993), 219.

[34] Craig L. Blomberg, "Interpreting Old Testament Prophetic Literature in Matthew: Double Fulfillment," *TJ* 23 (2002): 19, 27; Moises Mayordomo, review of *The Fulfillment Quotations in Matthew: When God is Present in Full Humanity*, by Jean Miller, *RevTL* 2 (2000): 54–57.

[35] The presence of οὐ μή is usually confined to OT quotes and most likely *prohibitory* rather than *emphatic negation* (E. D. W. Burton, *Syntax of the Moods and Tenses in New Testament Greek*, 3d ed. [Chicago: University of Chicago Press, 1900; reprint, Grand Rapids: Kregel, 1994], §167; MHT 3:96, 95–98).

(συνίημι)."[36] This is followed by, "And although seeing you will see and not perceive (from εἶδον)." The parallel suggests both phrases are concessive highlighting the acoustic and ocular phenomenon in contrast with the noetic deficiency as inadequate means of acquiring the wisdom necessary for salvation. In order for these avenues to be effective, it must be met by indwelling wisdom.[37]

Why do they neither understand nor perceive? "*For the heart of this people is fat.*" This is the *explanation*. παχύνω, 'to grow thick, dull'[38] occurs only here and Acts 28:27, six times in the LXX, and translates four Hebrew verbs, עָבָה 'to be thick' (Deut 32:15), שָׁמֵן 'to grow fat' (Isa 6:10), דָּשֵׁן 'to be fat' (Isa 34:6), and סָבַל 'to bear a load' (Eccl 12:5; cf. Ode 2:15). In its metaphorical sense the Greek verb means *to become impervious* (to water), *insensitive*, or *dull*.[39] The passive voice is *simple* without agency expressed (the divine passive may be inferred). Only if fattening is deprivational does the divine passive make sense.

The Final Clause. The final μήποτε is most likely rendered as *purpose-result* (in order that…not/lest/otherwise) but not in a coordinate but in a hypotactic syntax (lest/otherwise) not to ἵνα but γάρ.[40] It *modifies*

---

[36] For comments on the unusual construction ἀκοῇ ἀκούσετε see Robertson, *A Grammar of the Greek New Testament*, 530–31; Max Zerwick, *Biblical Greek Illustrated by Examples*, trans. Joseph Smith, Scripta Pontificii, vol. 114 (Rome: Editrice Pontificio Istituto Biblico, 1963), §369; MHT §1:75–6; Bailey, *The Blindness of the Jews in Matthew 13:13–15, Mark 4:12 and Luke 8:10*, 28; *NewDocs* 3:61.

[37] Calvin notes that "all were not endued with true understanding to comprehend what he said" and that "it is the Lord who pierces the ears" citing Ps 60:7 (John Calvin, *Commentary on a Harmony of the Evangelists Matthew, Mark, and Luke*, trans. William Pringle [Edinburgh: Calvin Translation Society, 1845–46; reprint, Grand Rapids: Baker, 1999], 101).

[38] For a discussion see earlier note in chapter 3.

[39] BDAG 790; MM §3975; K. L. Schmidt and M. A. Schmidt, "παχύνω," *TDNT* 5:1025. L&N §32.45 say it (παχύνομαι) means "to become unable to understand or comprehend as the result of being mentally dull or spiritually insensitive — 'to be unable to understand, to be mentally dull.'…'for the heart of this people has become unable to understand' or '…incapable of understanding.'" "*Waxed gross*, grown fat, here a figure for inveterate insensibility" (Alexander, *The Gospel according to Matthew Explained*, 359).

[40] It reflects the Hebrew פֶּן or Aramaic דלמא. Cf. C. F. D. Moule, *An Idiom Book of New Testament Greek*, 2d ed. (Cambridge: Cambridge University Press, 1959), 155; MHT

at least two of the preceding verbs (ἀκούω, and καμμύω), *governs* at least three verbs following (εἶδον, ἀκούω, and συνίημι), and possibly others (ἐπιστρέφω and ἰάομαι).[41] The 'turning' is the effect not the cause of hearing, seeing, and understanding while 'healing' is the outcome of 'turning.'[42]

The Second Interlude on Privilege

The Divine Initiative in Relation to 'Eyes' and 'Ears.' "The beatitude in Matt 13:16–17 par. has a structure built on synonymous and antithetical parallelism."[43] The divine initiative is highlighted. Both Matthew and Luke refer to the blessedness of the eyes of the disciples but Matthew *because* they see and hear (13:16) while Luke simply notes the blessedness of eyes *that* see the things they do without the reference to the causal idea or ears at all (10:23).[44] Matthew preempts his next reference to the prophets and righteous ones with ἀμήν (13:17)[45] while Luke omits this and exchanges δίκαιοι for βασιλεῖς

2:420; Robertson, *A Grammar of the Greek New Testament*, 988; Alexander, *The Gospel according to Matthew Explained*, 359.

[41] So Hagner, *Matthew 1–13*, 374 and MHT 3:100.

[42] On the future tense of ἰάομαι see Burton, *Syntax of the Moods and Tenses in New Testament Greek*, §199; MHT 2:74; Robertson, *A Grammar of the Greek New Testament*, 200–01; B. F. Westcott and F. J. A. Hort, *Introduction to the New Testament in the Original Greek: With Notes on Selected Readings* (New York: Harper and Brothers, 1882; reprint, Peabody, MA: Hendrickson, 1988), 309.

[43] John P. Meier, "'Happy the Eyes That See': The Tradition, Message, and Authenticity of Luke 10:23–24," in *Fortunate the Eyes that See: Essays in Honor of David Noel Freedman in Celebration of His Seventieth Birthday*, ed. Astrid B. Beck et al. (Grand Rapids: Eerdmans, 1995), 476.

[44] Zerwick notes that here in Matthew is the causal ὅτι whereas the like saying in Luke 10:23 has a relative pronoun, *blessed are the eyes which see* (Zerwick, *Biblical Greek Illustrated by Examples*, §424; G. R. Beasley-Murray, *Jesus and the Kingdom of God* [Grand Rapids: Eerdmans, 1986], 358 n. 67; Meier, "Fortunate the Eyes that See," 475).

[45] This *assertive* particle comes from the Hebrew אָמֵן and always begins a solemn declaration but used by Jesus to strengthen the previous statement (BDAG 53). Justin (*Apol.* 65) testifies to its usage of the church as uttered corporately after prayers and thanksgiving. See H. Schlier, "ἀμήν," TDNT 1:336–38 and Ralph P. Martin, *Worship in the Early Church* (Westwood, NJ: Revell, 1964), 36–37. While Meier says the authenticity for this saying is difficult to determine (Meier, "Fortunate the Eyes that See," 476), Fitzmyer thinks it is original to Q (Joseph A. Fitzmyer, *The Gospel according*

(10:24). This 'blessedness' is the effect of the divine initiative not further explanation.[46] Spicq recognizes that discernment is a gift and cites Matt 16:17 in support.[47] This accounts for the supernatural 'understanding' in the parable and for productive versus unproductive soils (= hearts).

The Relation to the Prophets and Righteous Saints of the OT. It is important to recognize what is and is not asserted concerning these prophets and righteous ones of the OT.[48] They *desired* to see and hear what the apostles now see and hear but did not,[49] did not hear and did not either perceive or understand because they did not hear or see these things at all, but did not first hear and see and then not perceive, know, or understand. They are not outsiders. A negative evaluation can only be perpetuated when 'insiders' are defined exclusively as those who know the mysteries via further explanation.

Summary

Matthew's emphasis on wisdom, including its themes and vocabulary, probably arises both from the nature of his audience of Christian scribes as well as those from whom they are recently separated (Jewish scribes). This portion of Matthew is designed to show why there is opposition to Jesus. It focuses on the *reason* of and *cause* for parables rather than the *purpose* or *meaning* of them. An interlude on wisdom follows and is shown to be the necessary ingredient for understanding parables and the kingdom and is the product of the divine initiative. In a cryptic wisdom saying, Matthew explains why some know mysteries while others do not. Again, the divine initiative is key and wisdom is gratuitously bestowed or justly withheld. The difference to Mark (on Isa 6:9–10) is not proof of 'mitigation,' which is a highly subjective evaluation, but is demanded

---

to *Luke*, AB, ed. William Foxwell Albright and David Noel Freedman, vol. 2 [Garden City, NY: Doubleday, 1985], 875).

[46] *Pss. Sol.* 18:6; 17:44. See Elderen, "The Purpose of the Parables according to Matthew," 188 and Carson, "Matthew," 311.

[47] *TLNT* 2:439–40. See also Matt 11:25–27.

[48] See *TLNT* 1:324 n. 23.

[49] The textual reading of D for εἶδαν (ἠδυνήθησαν ἰδεῖν) "they were unable to see," is open to ambiguity (cf. 1 Pet 1:10–12).

by the grammar. The *reason* (διὰ τοῦτο) for parables is to divide those with wisdom from those without it. The parable is a *sifting device* to test the sagacity of the hearers rather than as exclusively an *instrument of punishment* or a *pedagogical accommodation* to outsiders designed to foster understanding. The allusion to Isa 6:9–10 gives the *cause* (ὅτι) behind speaking in parables, namely, because they lack wisdom, or, they have fat/hard-hearts. The formal citation adds divine *purpose* to congenital fat/hard-heartedness. A second interlude focuses then on those who do have wisdom based on the divine initiative. In no wise do those with wisdom have a basis for boasting or those without it for complaining.

Luke 8:9–10: The Meaning of This Parable[50]

⁹And his disciples were asking what this parable might be [mean?]. ¹⁰And he said, "It [wisdom] has been given to you in order to know the mysteries of the Kingdom of God, but to the rest in parables, in order that although seeing they should not perceive, and although hearing they should not understand."

The Exegesis of 8:9–10

The Occasion. The question about the parable. In fostering universalism, Luke omits the Markan opening clause, "And when he was alone" as well as "those about him with the disciples."[51] Luke presents the question in indirect discourse and the optative mood[52] and so creates an almost philosophical atmosphere.

---

[50] Parallels include *Gos. Thom.* 34:2–13; *Cop. Gos. Thom.* 5, 9, 17, 20, 24, 28, 38–39, 49, 62, 83, 108; 2 *Esd* (= 4 *Ezra*) 8:41–44; 1 *Clem.* 24:5; Herm. *Sim.* 9.78.5–10; *Ps.-Clem.* 3.14; Justin *Dial.* 125.1.

[51] John Nolland, *Luke 1–9:20*, WBC, ed. Ralph P. Martin, vol. 35A (Dallas: Word, 1989), 379.

[52] Some MSS change this to direct discourse in conformity to the other Synoptics. After αὐτοῦ is added λέγοντες in A Θ Ψ *f*¹³ 𝔐 f l q syʰ. Text: 𝔓⁷⁵ B 579 bo. See Zane C. Hodges and Arthur L. Farstad, eds., *The Greek New Testament according to the Majority Text*, 2d ed. (Nashville: Nelson, 1985), 212; Nolland, *Luke 1–9:20*, 377; François Bovon, *Luke 1: A Commentary on the Gospel of Luke 1:1–9:50*, ed. Helmut Koester, trans. Christine M. Thomas, Hermeneia—A Critical and Historical Commentary on the Bible, ed. Helmut Koester et al. (Minneapolis: Fortress, 2002), 311. On the Optative see James Allen Hewitt, *New Testament Greek: A Beginning and Intermediate Grammar* (Peabody, MA: Hendrickson, 1986), 195; BDF §386; MHT 3:122–23, 130–31; 4:62; Stanley E. Porter, *Verbal Aspect in the Greek of the New*

Specifically, the question concerns the meaning of *this* parable (of the sower)[53] or its sense.[54] The implication of this question is that the disciples did not *fully* understand (rather than *completely misunderstood*) the parable of the sower and this solicits both the interlude and an interpretation. They simply seek more understanding.[55]

The parable of the sower. The question concerns a parable not parables. Jesus interposes a general remark (or interlude) before directly answering the question. The parable seems simple enough to understand apart from the interpretation given but the explanation suggests a deeper meaning.[56] The plural may suggest awareness and regard of the issues raised in the other Gospels (a source matter)[57] or, like Mark, Jesus may have in mind the noetic deficiency (absence of wisdom) of the listeners rather than either the genre of parable or its linguistic obscurity. Jesus' reply suggests the latter.

The focus is the miraculous production of and from the honest and good heart. The seed represents the word while the soil the disposition (ontology) of the person.[58] Accordingly, it is the 'honest' and 'good' heart that bears fruit (ἐν καρδίᾳ καλῇ καὶ ἀγαθῇ).[59] The

---

Testament, with Reference to Tense and Mood, Studies in Biblical Greek, ed. D. A. Carson, vol. 1 (New York: Lang, 1989), 170, 76.

[53] I. Howard Marshall, *The Gospel of Luke: A Commentary on the Greek Text,* NIGTC, ed. I. Howard Marshall (Grand Rapids: Eerdmans, 1978), 321.

[54] Darrell L. Bock, *Luke 1:1–9:50,* BECNT, ed. Moisés Silva, vol. 3A (Grand Rapids: Baker, 1994), 727; Luke Timothy Johnson, *The Gospel of Luke,* SP, ed. Daniel J. Harrington, vol. 3 (Collegeville, MN: Liturgical, 1991), 132.

[55] Fred B. Craddock, *Luke,* IBC, ed. James Luther Mays and Paul J. Achtemeier (Louisville, KY: Knox, 1990), 111.

[56] Ibid., 108.

[57] Bock, *Luke 1:1–9:50,* 727; Alfred Plummer, *A Critical and Exegetical Commentary on the Gospel according to St. Luke,* 5th ed., ICC, ed. S. R. Driver and C. A. Briggs (Edinburgh: T&T Clark, 1964), 219.

[58] Bovon, *Luke 1,* 308. "The soil [= predisposition] must be good, the farmer [= teacher] skillful, and the seed [= lesson of the teacher] viable" (Ps.-Plutarch [*Lib. ed.*] 4 [2b]; cf. Plato *Phaedr.* 276B–277A).

[59] Ibid. Cf. *4 Ezra* 9:31; 8:41.

parable depicts the sower not as foolish but tragic,[60] focuses on the irregular condition of the unfruitful soil rather than the behavior of the sower,[61] and emphases the miraculous production of a hundredfold.[62] Thus here in Luke two hearts are in contrast, the miraculously productive verses the naturally unproductive, the unnaturally good verses the naturally bad.

The Interlude. The addressees. The purpose of the interlude is for Jesus to explain *why* there are good (productive) hearts and bad (unproductive) hearts. The former is miraculous. It is not necessary to be too detailed on the passage for much is similar to Matthew and Mark. Jesus answers in a context where there is no doubt of referent.[63] But although the referent to direct speech might be clear, the audience may be wider than the disciples. This wider audience is thus privy to a wisdom interlude and an interpretation following. He follows with a direct discourse without ὅτι (like Mark but unlike Matthew) and maintains some type of dichotomy between the hearers as indicated by 'to you' (ὑμῖν) and 'to the rest' (τοῖς λοιποῖς).[64] This distinction is determined by presence or absence of understanding[65] although Green rejects any such dichotomy.[66]

---

[60] Ibid., 308 n. 27. "Luke localizes the event in the heart, which is visited first by God and then the devil" (ibid., 309). "This is not far from the two 'drives' of rabbinic literature" (ibid., 309; he refers to 2 Esd 4:28–32). It may not be far but it is not exact either. Both potentialities are not in the same soils. The heart is either good or bad not both good and bad.

[61] The blame is laid on the irregular condition of the soil not the sower (ibid., 309). The lack of 'moisture' (Luke 8:6, ἰκμάς) brings to mind the springs near Jericho mentioned by Josephus (*B.J.* 4.8.3 §471). Even this feature is reminiscent of wisdom's use of springs (see chapter 3 above and comments on wisdom). On the good heart Bovon says, "This field is good earth and thus stands for people who not only hear but also persevere in the word and bring forth fruit" (ibid., 311).

[62] Ibid., 311.

[63] See Luke 8:10, 30, 52; 9:13, 59; 10:37; 11:46; 16:6, 7, 30; 18:21, 27, 41; 19:34; 20:24; 21:8; 22:34, 35, 38, 71.

[64] Bock, *Luke 1:1–9:50*, 728 n. 23; Marshall, *The Gospel of Luke*, 322.

[65] Johnson, *The Gospel of Luke*, 134.

[66] Joel B. Green, *The Gospel of Luke*, NICNT, ed. Gordon D. Fee (Grand Rapids: Eerdmans, 1997), 326.

The audience may indeed be mixed but Green goes too far. He intimates that the Isaian quote is merely descriptive rather than ontological and "not God's doing or the outworking of his predetermination."[67]   Points of contention with Green include assuming that insiders are defined by further explanation, downplaying the explicit antecedent of ὑμῖν ('disciples'), making light of the distinction between 'you' and 'others,'[68] disregarding the Synoptic parallels, viewing the dichotomy of hearers in terms of further explanation rather than noetic privation, and not accounting for the different nature of the soils (hearts). "'Good soil,' after all, is recognized as good only when its fruitfulness has become evident."[69] Indeed, but the issue is *why* one soil is good and another bad. He is restricted to the effects of the heart rather than the miraculous cause of the heart's production. He rules out God's predetermination but this predetermination seems to be the best explanation.

In Luke-Acts the status of the disciples as those who are privileged is highlighted but nuanced.[70] Privilege may apply to Yahweh giving the law (Deut 4:7–8; Ps 147:20), developing the oral Mishnah (*Pesiq. Rab.* 5:11), or showing mysteries (Dan 2:28, 44). But these privileges are all connected with external revelation alone. The wisdom tradition indicates that revelation, interpretation, and secrets are *given* to those already with wisdom who *fear* him.[71] It is the impartation of wisdom that most likely identifies the nature of the division between 'you' and the 'rest' especially when (or under the assumption that) both groups are privy to further explanation. Bovon recognizes a link between the 'insider-outsider' contrast and the *Sitz im Leben*[72] of Gentile isolation; but sociological isolation may only be the fruit of a more fundamental and ontological diversity.

---

[67] Ibid.

[68] If Green is correct here and the audience is comprised of both 'to you' and 'the rest' it leaves in limbo the nature of the distinction. The distinction might still be between those with wisdom and those without it since (as with most parables) outsiders are indeed exposed to the interpretation of the parable.

[69] Green, *The Gospel of Luke*, 326.

[70] Luke 10:21, 23–24; 12:32; 22:29; Acts 13:48.

[71] See similar comments by Cyril of Alexandria *Comm. Luke* 41.

[72] Bovon, *Luke 1*, 312.

The contrasted parallelism and ellipsis. It is well recognized that there is a 'contrasted parallelism' and 'significant ellipsis' in regard to the stated subject as well as the fleshed out couplet, but this is often linked to additional revelation (without mentioning wisdom),[73] the secrecy motif vestigial in Luke,[74] and private explanation.[75] This becomes the enablement required by the passage.[76] But this view supposes that parables are linguistically obscure, that explanations are only to the disciples, and that 'enabling' is external not noetic. There is an inability theme running throughout this text (and others) but it is ontological and noetic rather than functional and linguistic.

The 'further explanation' view. The appeal of this view is that it identifies immediately what is 'given' and how one comes to know *more* in contrast to others. But it does not adequately explain *how* one comes to know at all, *why* one seeks out to know more in *contrast* to others, or why when given the explanation some (crowd) remain uncomprehending. The view itself remains agnostic concerning the initial cause of knowing, how one knows anything from parables, why some seek to know more, or how some fail to understand after an explanation. It does not explain why some hearts are congenitally unreceptive to the message of the kingdom while others are miraculously receptive. Nascent fruitfulness is left without a cause.

The 'further explanation' view limits the seed or its fruitfulness only to the explanation apart from the parable. But this seems to locate the problem in the seed not the soils. But the 'seed' is the word of God in any form not just explanations. If this 'seed' is limited to the explanation, then why do only *some* understand? How can there be any fruitful soil at all, even among the disciples, if parables are incomprehensible to everyone? If explanations come to the crowds too then why do they persist in their incomprehension? The fundamental problem is that it does not fully appreciate the link of

---

[73] The two phrases come from Bock, *Luke 1:1–9:50*, 728. Presumably what is 'given' is the explanation. See also Marshall, *The Gospel of Luke*, 322; Bovon, *Luke 1*, 312; Evans, *To See and Not Perceive*, 117.

[74] Johnson, *The Gospel of Luke*, 132.

[75] "If some know the mysteries of the kingdom of God, others are not so favored" (Nolland, *Luke 1–9:20*, 379). But this leaves open how they are favored. If by private explanation, one is left to explain how private versus open explanation differ.

[76] Green, *The Gospel of Luke*, 326 emphasis added.

knowledge and its sapiential roots. The miraculous (supernatural) element attached to this antecedent wisdom is omitted. It is for these reasons that a different subject should be considered, namely, wisdom itself is that which is 'given.'

Postulating the right subject with the appropriate syntax. The phrase can be construed in two ways relative to δίδωμι and γνῶναι. First, the infinitive following may be substantival and thus the explicit *subject* of the verb. This would leave the matter of *how* these mysteries are known in question. Thus one may supply (in the appropriate place) either 'further explanation' or 'wisdom.' Second, the infinitive may be adverbial of *purpose* (or *result*), modifying δίδωμι but leaving the subject to be inferred. Although the majority of commentators favor this latter syntax, supplying the subject becomes the key crux. Most favor 'interpretation' rather than 'wisdom.' The sense of the former, "To you *further explanation* [= it] is given *upon request* in order that you might know the mysteries of the kingdom. But to the rest in parables *without explanations.*"

Problematic is its adoption of the rare *permissive/causative* passive,[77] implying that the parable is linguistically incomprehensible, insistence that interpretations given to mixed audiences imply no sort of dichotomy, inability to account for the disappointment of Jesus, assuming that explanations (the part) are the total (the whole) of 'giving,' and substituting for the 'miraculous' (or supernatural) a purely non-miraculous interchange.

Explanations in Luke. Only disciples are audience. The 'further explanation' view seems to run counter to the use of 'parables' in Luke itself.[78] Sometimes only the disciples are the audience. In 12:25–40 Peter asks if the 'parable' is intended for a limited group or everyone (12:41). Jesus' response is still another parable (12:42–48) suggesting that parables may be used as explanations. In 19:11–27 Jesus speaks a parable to his disciples without an explanation. These two facts suggest that parables are not linguistically obscure but rather the phrase 'in parables' refers to a noetic obscurity limited to those without wisdom. And this obscurity persists even in the face of further explanation.

---

[77] In this case it is rare and usually found with imperatives not indicatives.

[78] Luke 4:23; 5:36; 6:39; 8:4,9–11; 12:16, 41; 13:6; 14:7; 15:3; 18:1, 9; 19:11; 20:9, 19; 21:29.

Only the enemies are the audience. In 4:23 Jesus puts words into the mouths of his enemies who will utter a mocking parable to him concerning his earlier miraculous deeds. So here it is not technically Jesus giving a parable but rather those on the outside giving him one. But Jesus apparently understands the parable and needs no accompanying explanation. In 5:36 Jesus first gives an explanation followed by a parable (5:33–39). This seems to be opposite of the further explanation view.

An individual is the audience. Jesus explains the dangers of desiring wealth with selfish motives by means of a parable (12:13–21). But this parable comes with its own explanation (12:21).

A mixed group is the audience. Most parables fall into this category. In 6:39–42 both the disciples and multitude are addressed (6:17). In 8:4–8 he speaks to the crowds but only later asked by his disciples the meaning (8:9). It is possible to infer the crowds as part of the audience although they do not ask the question. Jesus then contrasts the disciples' knowledge of the kingdom to 'in parables (riddles)' of the rest (8:10). An interpretation is then provided (8:11–15). In 13:6–9 a parable is given without explanation. Luke 14:7–11 records a parable with an explanation (14:11). Luke 15:3–7 is a parable with a series of parables following (15:8–10; 11–32) each with their own interpretation (15:10, 31–32). Luke 18:1–8 is a parable with its own interpretation (18:1, 8). Another parable follows (18:9–14) with an interpretation (18:14). In 20:9–18 Jesus' enemies 'know' he speaks the parable against them (20:19). Jesus tells his disciples about the signs of the time by the parable of the fig tree (21:29–33) with its own explanation (21:31–33). If the 'givenness' refers to explanations, then there is no distinction between the disciples and the crowds accounting for why one understands and another does not.

The effect of 'in parables.' As with Mark, the pertinent phrase is "to the rest *in parables*." Most commentators designate this phrase as referring to those in contrast to the disciples, a subgroup of the disciples, or the elect.[79] Bovon says, "the parables stand before them like unsolved riddles."[80] And this 'riddle phenomenon' points not to a linguistic obscurity nor an omitted explanation but rather a noetic

---

[79] Plummer, *Gospel according to St. Luke*, 219; Marshall, *The Gospel of Luke*, 322.

[80] Bovon, *Luke 1*, 312; Joachim Gnilka, *Die Verstockung Israels: Isaias 6:9–10 in der Theologie der Synoptiker*, SANT, ed. Vinzenz Hamp and Josef Schmid, vol. 3 (Munich: Kosel, 1961), 126–27; Nolland, *Luke 1–9:20*, 380.

deficiency despite the presence of one or both.[81] A rendering based on this might read as follows: "But to the rest *to whom wisdom has not been given in order to know the mysteries of the kingdom of God, they [mysteries] remain* in riddles." *The segue from linguistic genre to the noetic obscurity is predicated on first the equivocation of 'parables' to 'riddles,' then linguistics to psychology, and therefore the plural is deliberate to this end.* This interpretation further justifies the allusion to Isa 6:9–10 below.

The Paraphrase of Isa 6:9–10. *The* ἵνα *clause.* Virtually the same range of views posed for Mark's ἵνα apply here and[82] is best understood as a *purpose-result* ἵνα.[83] Some matters might be clarified. First, the conjunction modifies either the implied οὐ δέδοται γνῶναι "it is not given to know" or the implied εἰμί (or γίνομαι) in "is/remains/becomes in riddles." The latter seems more likely but both conform to Mark 4:11 and the wisdom tradition. In either case, the focus is either on the *cause* or *effect* of privation. Second, it may be noted that the 'seeing' does not appear limited and so 'hearing' should not be limited either. The problem is not lack of information but absence of the good and honest heart.

The missing μήποτε *clause.* Although Luke mimics Mark, it nevertheless appears 'softer' in tone because it lacks the μήποτε clause.[84] But its absence here does not demand this[85] nor does its absence in Matthew's paraphrase indicate mitigation is underway. Plummer is insightful here:

---

[81] Wolff says, "The authorized person is incomprehensible without the energy of the divine *r*. [רוּחַ]" (Hans Walter Wolff, *Anthropology of the Old Testament*, trans. Margaret Kohl [Philadelphia: Fortress, 1974; reprint, Miffintown, PA: Sigler, 1996], 35). Thus the pellucidy of the words themselves are not in question but rather the obtuseness in the uncomprehending heart of the listeners.

[82] See previous chapter and footnotes. In addition see Marshall, *The Gospel of Luke*, 323; and Joseph A. Fitzmyer, "The Use of the Old Testament in Luke-Acts," in *Society of Biblical Literature Seminar Papers 1992*, ed. Eugene H. Lovering Jr., vol. 31 (Atlanta: Scholars Press, 1992), 527.

[83] Bovon, *Luke 1*, 312; Craddock, *Luke*, 112.

[84] Bock, *Luke 1:1–9:50*, 727.

[85] Craig A. Evans, *Luke*, NIBCNT, ed. W. Ward Gasque, vol. 3 (Peabody, MA: Hendrickson, 1990), 126.

At first sight it might seem as if the ἵνα of Lk. and Mk. was very different from the ὅτι of Mt. But the principle that he who hath shall receive more, while he who hath not shall be deprived of what he seemeth to have, explains both the ἵνα and the ὅτι. Jesus speaks in parables, *because* the multitude see without seeing and hear without hearing. But He also speaks in parables in order that they may see without seeing and hear without hearing. They 'have not' a mind to welcome instruction, and therefore they are taught in a way which deprives them of instruction, although it is full of meaning to those who desire to understand and do understand. But what the unsympathetic 'hear without understanding' they remember, because of its impressive form; and whenever their minds become fitted for it, its meaning will become manifest to them.[86]

This is a sapiential rendition without explicitly making that connection. The 'givenness' of this mind (of wisdom) is precisely the difference between the honest and good heart that bears fruit (understands) and the heart that does not. The giving is supernatural, gratuitous, and makes one 'fitted' to understand while the withholding is Isaianic fattening.

The cause of God giving to one the honest and good heart may be explained within a sapiential world-view of causation that is apart from human conditions. Job suffers for nothing he has done in this life. It is not punitive, judicial, or a result of his evil acts. Similarly, in John a man is born blind but quite apart from either his or his parents' evil acts (cf. John 9:1–3).[87] This passage is then linked by the author to Isaianic hardening in John 12:40. In the latter it then suggests that John also views hardening in terms of deprivation of sight rather than as a punishment for past indiscretions. God causally hardens and blinds only in a *continuative* rather than a *creative* sense.

The omission of the μήποτε clause, even if dependent on Mark, is not evidence of any type of mitigation. Rather the best explanation is

---

[86] Plummer, *Gospel according to St. Luke*, 219–20.

[87] John 9 is literarily connected to John 12:40 which quotes Isa 6:9–10. Thus while John 9 teaches that the man is born *congenitally* blind, John 12:40 teaches that everyone is born spiritually blind. Like John 9, John 12 does not teach that man *becomes* 'hard-hearted' or 'blind' but that man is congenitally blind and hard-hearted. The continuance of that state is 'hardening' while its reversal (in Johannine language) is the new birth. For a similar argument see D. A. Carson, *Divine Sovereignty and Human Responsibility: Biblical Perspectives in Tension,* 2d ed. (Grand Rapids: Baker, 1994; reprint, Eugene, OR: Wipf & Stock, 2002), 127–28.

that the effect of the possession of wisdom would be rightly inferred rather than blatantly stated.

Seeing and hearing. Luke has the same order of Mark in seeing and hearing but it is shorter and in summary form.[88] Johnson takes both phrases as purely linguistic and informational: "seeing they will not see (because they lack the interpretation) and hearing they will not understand (because they lack the interpretation)."[89] Contrary to this Meier writes that there is an eschatological reversal underway in connection with the blessedness regarding the noetic ability to see and hear with and without interpretation (Luke 10:23–24; 24:16, 31, 45).[90] He says that Luke 10:23 represents a reversal in future eschatology whereas Luke 10:24 is a reversal in present or realized eschatology.[91] This is especially relevant in terms of Isaianic statements on this reversal.

If this is an eschatological and noetic reversal, then it is not merely a matter of getting the inside scoop on the meaning of a particular parable. 'Hearing' occurs eight times alone in Luke 8:4–21 and implies something more than simply physical ears or further interpretation.[92] Hearing harks back to the wisdom motif confirmed by the phrase, "the one who has ears, let him hear." This does not imply being privy to further explanation but rather *possessing imparted wisdom*. Indeed, if parables are incomprehensible apart from explanation, then why issue the challenge "he that has ears to hear let him hear?" Bovon suggests that it "indicates that 'hearing' is not an outer, acoustic activity, but an inner, consensual attitude"[93] while Nolland holds that

---

[88] Marshall, *The Gospel of Luke*, 322; Bovon, *Luke 1*, 316; Nolland, *Luke 1–9:20*, 380; Bock, *Luke 1:1–9:50*, 728 n. 24. Bock argues, "The concept of judgment because of hardness of heart is found often in the NT (John 3:17–19; 9:39–41; Rom. 1:18–32; 9:17–18; Acts 28:26–27). The parables' purpose for the rest of humanity is to prevent their comprehension of God's plan" (ibid., 729). Part one of his statement rings true but the latter part may allow for modification provided here.

[89] Johnson, *The Gospel of Luke*, 132.

[90] Meier, "'Happy the Eyes That See'," 466–77.

[91] Ibid., 469.

[92] Bovon says 'hear' here implies acceptance and obedience (Bovon, *Luke 1*, 306). Incomprehension on the part of the disciples, even in regard to non-parabolic speech, is also divinely orchestrated (9:44–45; cf. 10:21–22).

[93] Ibid., 314. He is close but speaking in terms of volition not cognition.

it "is viewed in terms of a supernatural inward illumination which comes by God's grace as privilege and gift."[94] Along with the sapiential view, then, man congenitally lacks the ability to 'see,' 'hear,' and 'understand.' It is not mere explanation that man lacks, but infused wisdom, and this lack produces the effect of 'in riddles' in regard to the mysteries.

Summary

Luke is written within a sapiential *Sitz im Leben*, from a sapiential *modus operandi*, and (most likely) in a genre that has strong affinity to wisdom literature. These aspects complement the Isaianic usage of Isa 6:9–10. Luke, in distinction to Mark or Matthew, emphasizes the universality of the message in both parabolic and explanatory formats as well as the miraculous production of the 'honest and good heart' that bears fruit. The interlude of Jesus is designed to account for both nascent and continual fruitfulness by linking it to the prerogative of God to give or withhold salvific wisdom. Parables are not obscure but the effect of the teachings of the kingdom are nevertheless met with a noetic obtuseness termed 'in parables' or better 'in riddles.' This is not a linguistic but a noetic and salvific appraisal. Although Luke does not mention 'fattening/hardening,' the concept is present. Thus Luke alludes to Isa 6:9–10 to describe this state of continued mental dullness. The divine intention is to *perpetuate* rather than *create* this mental and spiritual state.

Like other usages, it accounts for why one understands (cognitive) and accepts (volitional) the mysteries of the kingdom while another does not. It emphasizes the sovereign activity of God in both aspects while effectively undercutting any type of merit-based theology. A situation may be that one has wisdom without interpretation (OT prophets) or interpretation without wisdom (crowds) but the ideal is to possess wisdom and have a proper construal of things (disciples). Parables function, then, both as a sifting device and as a convenient catch-word that permits an exploitation of its semantic nuances in order to describe a mental (heart) condition—the absence of wisdom. Some hearts are supernaturally transformed into the 'honest and good' heart while others are left to themselves to remain in this condition of foolishness. While this transformation occurs on the basis

---

[94] Nolland, *Luke 1–9:20*, 381; cf. Johnson, *The Gospel of Luke*, 134.

of grace in terms of strong divine causality, the nature of divine fattening is the opposite. It is non-transformational but divinely perpetuated. Thus God fattens by depriving of wisdom (the new heart) and perpetuating a congenital state.

Conclusion

Both Matthew and Luke function towards Mark analogous to the way the traditions and versions of Isa 6:9–10 do in the OT for the Hebrew text. In both situations a larger paradigm is assumed where a stream of strong divine causality in perpetuating a condition is compatible with the view that this condition is congenital. The vortex from which these views find their compatibilism is the sapiential tradition. There is a consistent theme where man finds himself not only in an unfortunate noetic state of privation that prevents salvation but at the discretion of God's mercy in reversing this fortune or perpetuating it through deprivation. Nothing man does either solicits this mercy or conversely incurs fattening (or hardening). A major emphasis is therefore placed on the divine intent and prerogative. The Synoptics see together from the same hermeneutical construct and in no wise mitigate the other.

Accomplishments of Inquiry

The purpose of this Study was threefold: to show man is naturally absent of wisdom, to demonstrate the divergent emphases or streams arising from Isa 6:9–10 are compatible and linked to the wisdom tradition, and to show that divine (Isaianic) fattening is best understood as deprivation rather than some form of transformation. Divine fattening, therefore, is non-punitive, non-transformational, and therefore congenital.

Chapter 1 aided this by surveying both general works on hardening/fattening and specific treatments of Isa 6:9–10. Although some see through the punitive notion of hardening/fattening, few studies entertain a non-transformational view and fewer distinguished divine fattening or hardening. The natural privation of the heart is barely if at all related to fat-heartedness. Many hold a view of man that makes it impossible.

Chapter 2 examined philosophical issues of God, time, causality, and freedom as the outgrowth of chapter 1. Of these views, liberty is crucial and interferes with exegesis when libertarian freedom is the construct. This dissertation kept to traditional theism and a form of compatibilism in regard to freedom. Therefore, making God bound to time and thereby subject to change (via human causation) in order to preserve libertarian freedom is set aside so the text may be approached without these assumptions.

Chapter 3 examined the wisdom tradition in the OT, DSS, and other literature in order to search for a connection between Isa 6:9–10 and sapiential thinking. Part of this included showing that human nature is congenitally absent of wisdom and in need of divine activity to salvifically exercise wisdom. This sets the stage for viewing 'fattening' as congenital and fattening as non-transformational (deprivation).

Chapter 4 examined Isa 6:9–10, its wisdom notions and motifs and attempted to show that its sapiential orientation generates the connection of fatness to lack of wisdom. Little evidence exists that fattening is a punitive act. Rather it is a divine activity that has punishment as its final cause. Subsequent tradition presents man as already 'fat-hearted' as well as divinely caused to be 'fat-hearted.' The solution sought a way to maintain these features by arguing that 'fattening' is not a transformation but a divine decision to perpetuate this congenital state.

Chapter 5 examined Mark in general and parables in particular and how Isa 6:9–10 shows up in a sapiential passage. Parables were shown not to be linguistically opaque but rather instruments to expose the noetic state of man that is obscure. The latter is coined as the phenomenon of 'in riddles.' The wisdom that overcomes this state is divinely and gratuitously imparted to some. But the effect of leaving others in this state of non-salvific confusion is equivalent to Isaianic fattening.

Chapter 6 rounded out the Synoptic question by looking briefly at Matthew and Luke. Matthew preserves a tradition similar to the LXX and insists that man is already (congenitally) fat/hard-hearted. Instead of proposing mitigation as the solution, attention turned to the interludes that focus on the impartation of salvific wisdom. The internal grammar of Matthew provides its own explanation without recourse to source theories. Luke engages in interludes and like Mark makes much out of the phrase 'in riddles' as a noetic rather than linguistic issue. His emphasis on the universality of the Gospel aids in doing away with insider/outsider in terms of private explanation. Furthermore, the use of parables and explanations to a wider audience suggests a noetic basis for division.

This study shows that there is an overriding metanarrative at work in the use of Isa 6:9–10 that begins in Deuteronomy. It is contexualized by Isaiah as 'fattening' and emphasizes both man's congenital privation and God's right to deprivation. This dominant theme is carried on into John and Paul with even more intensity and clarity. Unfortunately, space, time, and freedom forbid such an excursion.

Bibliography

Primary Sources

Abegg, Martin, Jr., Peter Flint, and Eugene Ulrich. *The Dead Sea Scrolls Bible: The Oldest Known Bible Translated for the First Time into English.* New York: HarperCollins, 1999.

Aeschylus. Translated by Herbert Weir Smyth. 2 vols. Loeb Classical Library, ed. T. E. Page, E. Capps, W. H. D. Rouse, L. A. Post, and E. H. Warmington. New York: Putnam's; London: Heinemann, 1922–26.

Aicher, Georg. *Das Alte Testament in der Mischna.* Edited by Otto Bardenhewer. Biblische Studien, vol. 11. St. Louis: Herder, 1906.

Aland, Kurt, et al., eds. *The Greek New Testament.* 4th rev. ed. Stuttgart and New York: United Bible Societies, 1993.

———, ed. *Synopsis of the Four Gospels: Greek-English Edition of the Synopsis Quattuor Evangeliorum.* 10th ed. Stuttgart: Biblia-Druck, 1993.

Ames, William. *The Marrow of Theology.* Translated by John D. Eusden. Grand Rapids: Baker, 1968.

Anselm of Canterbury. Edited by Jasper Hopkins and Herbert Richardson. 2d ed. 4 vols. New York: Mellen, 1975–76.

Aquinas. *On the Eternity of the World.* Translated by Cyril Vollert, Lottie H. Kendzierski, and Paul M. Byrne. 2d ed. Mediaeval Philosophical Texts in Translation, ed. Richard C. Taylor, vol. 16. Milwaukee, WI: Marquette University Press, 1984.

———. *On the Truth of the Catholic Faith. Summa contra Gentiles.* Translated by Anton C. Pegis. 4 vols. Garden City, NY: Imagine, 1955–57.

———. *Summa theologiae. Latin Text and English Translation, Introductions, Notes, Appendices, and Glossaries.* 56 vols. Cambridge, England: Blackfriars; New York: McGraw-Hill, 1964–.

———. *Summa theologica.* Translated by Fathers of the English Dominican Province. 5 vols. Westminster, MD: Christian Classics, 1981. Reprint, New York: Bezinger, 1947–48.

Aristophanes. Translated by Jeffrey Henderson. 4 vols. Loeb Classical Library, ed. T. E. Page, E. Capps, W. H. D. Rouse, L. A. Post, and E. H. Warmington. Cambridge, MA: Harvard University Press; London: Heinemann, 1998.

Aristotle. *The "Art" of Rhetoric.* Translated by John Henry Freese. Loeb Classical Library, ed. G. P. Goold. Cambridge, MA: Harvard University Press; London: Heinemann, 1926.

———. *The Categories, On Interpretation.* Translated by Harold P. Cooke and Hugh Tredennick. Loeb Classical Library, ed. T. E. Page, E. Capps, W. H. D. Rouse, L. A. Post, and E. H. Warmington. Cambridge, MA: Harvard University Press; London: Heinemann, 1938.

———. *The Metaphysics.* Translated by Hugh Tredennick. 2 vols. Loeb Classical Library, ed. G. P. Goold. Cambridge, MA: Harvard University Press; London, Heinemann, 1956–58.

———. *The Physics.* Translated by Philip H. Wicksteed and Francis M. Comford. Rev. ed. 2 vols. Loeb Classical Library, ed. T. E. Page, E. Capps, W. H. D. Rouse, L. A. Post, and E. H. Warmington. Cambridge, MA: Harvard University Press; London: Heinemann, 1957–60.

St. Augustine's Confessions. Translated by William Watts. 2 vols. Loeb Classical Library, ed. G. P. Goold, vol. 26–27. Cambridge, MA: Harvard University Press, 1977–79.

The Works of Saint Augustine: A Translation for the 21st Century. Edited by John E. Rotelle. Translated by Edmund Hill. 28 vols. Brooklyn, NY: New City, 1990–.

Augustine. *Christian Instruction, Admonition and Grace, The Christian Combat, and Hope and Charity.* Translated by John J. Gavigan, John Courtney Murray, Ropert P. Russell, and Bernard M. Peebles. Fathers of the Church, ed. Rudolph Arbesmann, Roy Joseph Deferrari, Stephan Kuttner, Martin R. P. McGuire, Wilfrid Parsons, Bernard M. Peebles, Robert P. Russell, Anselm Strittmatter, and Gerald G. Walsh, vol. 2. New York: Cima, 1947.

———. *The City of God against the Pagans.* Translated by George E. McCracken, William M. Green, David S. Wiesen, Philip Levine, Eva Matthews Sanford, William McAllen Green, and William Chase Greene. 7 vols. Loeb Classical Library, ed. T. E. Page, E. Capps, W. H. D. Rouse, L. A. Post, and E. H. Warmington. London: Heinemann, 1957–66.

———. *On the Freedom of the Will.* Translated by Carroll Mason Sparrow. University of Virginia Studies, vol. 4. Charlottesville, VA: University of Virginia Press, 1947.

———. *Four Anti-Pelagian Writings.* Translated by John A. Mourant and William J. Collinge. Fathers of the Church, ed. Rudolph Arbesmann, Roy Joseph Deferrari, Stephan Kuttner, Martin R. P. McGuire, Wilfrid Parsons, Bernard M. Peebles, Robert P. Russell, Anselm Strittmatter, and Gerald G. Walsh, vol. 86. Washington, D.C.: Catholic University Press, 1992.

———. *On Christian Doctrine; The Enchiridion.* Translated by J. F. Shaw and S. D. Salmond. 2d ed. Edinburgh: Clark, 1877.

———. *Select Letters.* Translated by James Houston Baxter. Loeb Classical Library, ed. G. P. Goold. Cambridge, MA: Harvard University Press, 1980.

———. *The Teacher. The Free Choice of the Will. Grace and Free Will.* Translated by Ropert P. Russell. Fathers of the Church, ed. Rudolph Arbesmann, Roy Joseph Deferrari, Stephan Kuttner, Martin R. P. McGuire, Wilfrid Parsons, Bernard M. Peebles, Robert P. Russell, Anselm Strittmatter, and Gerald G. Walsh, vol. 59. Washington, D.C.: Catholic University of America Press, 1968.

———. *Tractates on the Gospel of John.* Translated by John W. Rettig. Vol. 78, 79, 88, 90, 92. Fathers of the Church, ed. Rudolph Arbesmann, Roy Joseph Deferrari,

Stephan Kuttner, Martin R. P. McGuire, Wilfrid Parsons, Bernard M. Peebles, Robert P. Russell, Anselm Strittmatter, and Gerald G. Walsh. Washington, D.C.: Catholic University of America Press, 1988.

Beer, Georg, and O. Holtzmann. *Die Mischna; Text, Übersetzung und ausführliche Erklärung*. Giessen: Töpelmann; parts issued after 1970– published by Berlin: de Gruyter, 1912–69.

Berkowitz, Luci, and Karl A. Squitier. *Thesaurus Linguae Graecae: Canon of Greek Authors and Works*. 3d ed. New York: Oxford University Press, 1990.

Boethius. *The Theological Tractates, with An English Translation*. Translated by H. F. Stewart, E. K. Rand, and S. J. Tester. Loeb Classical Library, ed. E. H. Warmington, vol. 74. Cambridge, MA: Harvard University Press, 1973.

Borgen, Peder, Karl Fuglseth, and Roald Skarsten. *The Philo Index: A Complete Greek Word Index to the Writings of Philo of Alexandria*. Grand Rapids: Eerdmans; Leiden: Brill, 2000.

Brock, S. P., ed. *Isaiah*. The Old Testament in Syriac according to the Peshitta Version, ed. The Peshitta Institute. Leiden: Brill, 1987.

Burrows, Miller, John C. Trever, and William H. Brownlee, eds. *The Isaiah Manuscript and the Habakkuk Commentary*. The Dead Sea Scrolls of St. Mark's Monastery, vol. 1. New Haven: American Schools of Oriental Research, 1950.

Calvin, John. *The Institutes of Christian Religion*. Translated by Tony Lane and Hilary Osborne. Grand Rapids: Baker, 1986.

Charles, R. H., ed. *Apocrypha and Pseudepigrapha of the Old Testament*. 2 vols. Oxford: Clarendon Press, 1913.

Charlesworth, James H. *Graphic Concordance to the Dead Sea Scrolls*. Princeton Theological Seminary Dead Sea Scrolls Project. Tübingen: Mohr; Louisville, KY: Westminster and Knox, 1991.

———, ed. *The Old Testament Pseudepigrapha*. 2 vols. Garden City, NY: Doubleday, 1983–85.

———, F. M. Cross, et al., eds. *The Dead Sea Scrolls: Hebrew, Aramaic, and Greek Texts with English Translations*. Princeton Theological Seminary Dead Sea Scrolls Project, ed. James H. Charlesworth, 5 vols. Tübingen: Mohr, 1994–.

Chilton, Bruce D., Michael Maher, and Martin McNamara. *The Isaiah Targum*. Translated by Bruce D. Chilton. The Aramaic Bible: The Targums, vol. 11. Wilmington, DE: Glazier, 1987.

Christian and Pagan in the Roman Empire: The witness of Tertullian. Edited by Robert D. Sider. Fathers of the Church, ed. Rudolph Arbesmann, Roy Joseph Deferrari, Stephan Kuttner, Martin R. P. McGuire, Wilfrid Parsons, Bernard M. Peebles, Robert P. Russell, Anselm Strittmatter, James Edward Tobin, and Gerald G. Walsh, vol. 2. Washington, D.C.: Catholic University of America Press, 2001.

Clement of Alexandria. Translated by G. W. Butterworth. Loeb Classical Library, ed. T. E. Page, E. Capps, and W. H. D. Rouse. Cambridge, MA: Harvard University Press, 1939.

The Complete Dead Sea Scrolls in English. Translated by Geza Vermes. New York: Allen Lane and Penguin, 1997.

Cohn, Leopoldus, and Paulus Wendland., eds. *Philonis Alexandrini opera quae supersunt. Edition Maior*, 8 vols. Berlin: Reimeri, 1896–1930. Reprint, Berlin: de Gruyter, 1962–63.

Cowley, Arthur E., ed. *Aramaic Papyri of the Fifth Century BC.* Oxford: Clarendon Press, 1923.

Cyril, of Alexander. *Commentary on the Gospel of Saint Luke.* Translated by R. Payne Smith: USA: Studion, 1983.

The Dead Sea Scriptures, in English Translation. 3d rev. ed. Translated by Theodor H. Gaster. Garden City, NY: Anchor, 1976.

Denis, Albert-Marie, and Y. Janssens, ed. *Concordance Grecque des Pseudépigraphes D'Ancien Testament: Concordance Corpus des textes Indices.* Louvain: Université Catholique de Louvain, 1987.

Elliger, Karl, and W. Rudolph, eds. *Biblia Hebraica Stuttgartensia.* Stuttgart: Deutsche Bibelgesellschaft, 1977.

Collected Works of Erasmus. Edited by R. J. Schoeck and B. M. Corrigan. 86 vols. Buffalo, NY: University of Toronto Press, 1974.

Erasmus, Desiderius. *Controversies.* Edited by Charles Trinkaus. Translated by Peter Macardle and Clarence H. Miller. Collected Works of Erasmus, vol. 76. Toronto: University of Toronto Press, 1999.

————. *Controversies.* Edited by Charles Trinkaus. Translated by Clarence H. Miller. Collected Works of Erasmus, vol. 77. Toronto: University of Toronto Press, 2000.

Epstein, I., ed. *Hebrew-English Edition of the Babylonian Talmud.* Translated by I. Epstein et al., 38 vols. London: Soncino, 1960–.

Fitzmyer, Joseph A. *The Dead Sea Scrolls: Major Publications and Tools for Study.* Society of Biblical Literature Resources for Biblical Study, ed. W. Lee Humphreys, vol. 20. Atlanta: Scholars Press, 1990.

Freedman, H., and M. Simon, eds. *Midrashim.* 5 vols. London: Soncino, 1977.

García Martínez, Florentino, ed. *The Dead Sea Scrolls Translated: The Qumran Texts in English.* Translated by Wilfred G. E. Watson, 2d ed. Grand Rapids: Eerdmans, 1996.

Gianotti, Charles R. *The New Testament and the Mishnah: A Cross-Reference Index.* Grand Rapids: Baker, 1983.

Grenfell, Benard P., and Arthur S. Hunt, eds. *The Oxyrhynchus Papyri.* 67 vols. London: Egyptian Exploration Fund, 1898–1999.

Guggenheimer, Heinrich W., ed. *The Jerusalem Talmud [Talmud Yerushalmi] First Order: Zeraïm Tractate Berakhot.* Translated by Heinrich W. Guggenheimer. Studia Judaica: Forschungen zur Wissenschaft des Judentums, ed. E. L. Ehrlich, vol. 18. Berlin: de Gruyter; New York, 2000.

Herodotus. Translated by A. D. Godley. 4 vols. Loeb Classical Library, ed. T. E. Page, E. Capps, W. H. D. Rouse, L. A. Post, and E. H. Warmington. Cambridge, MA: Harvard University Press, 1957–61.

Hesiod. *Hesiodi Theogonia: Opera et dies; Scutum.* Edited by Friedrich Solmsen, R. Merkelbach, and M. L. West. Oxford: Clarendon, 1970.

Homer. *The Iliad.* Translated by A. T. Murray. 2 vols. Loeb Classical Library, ed. T. E. Page, E. Capps, W. H. D. Rouse, L. A. Post, and E. H. Warmington. Cambridge, MA: Harvard University Press; London: Heinemann, 1954–57.

————. *The Odyssey.* Translated by A. T. Murray. 2 vols. The Loeb Classical Library, ed. T. E. Page, E. Capps, W. H. D. Rouse, L. A. Post, and E. H. Warmington. Cambridge, MA: Harvard University Press; London: Heinemann, 1946.

Horsley, G. H. R., and S. R. Llewelyn, eds. *New Documents Illustrating Early Christianity.* 8 vols. Sydney: Macquarie University Press, 1981–98.

Irenaeus. *Against the Heresies*. Translated by Dominic J. Unger. Ancient Christian Writers, ed. Walter J. Burghardt, Thomas Comerford Lawler, and John J. Dillon, vol. 55. New York: Paulist, 1992–.

Jerome. *Dialogus adversus Pelagianos*. Translated by C. Moreschini. Corpus Christianorum. Series Latina, vol. 80. Turnholti, Belgium: Brepols, 1990.

———. *The Letters of St. Jerome*. Translated by Charles Christopher Mierow. Ancient Christian Writers, ed. Johannes Quasten and Walter J. Burghardt, vol. 33. New York: Newman; London: Longmans, 1963–.

———. *Select Letters of St. Jerome*. Translated by F. A. Wright. Loeb Classical Library, ed. G. P. Goold. Cambridge, MA: Harvard University Press; London: Heinemann, 1980.

Josephus. Translated by H. St. J. Thackeray, Ralph Marcus, and Louis H. Feldman. 10 vols. Loeb Classical Library, ed. G. P. Goold, T. E. Page, E. Capps, W. H. D. Rouse, and E. H. Warmington. Cambridge, MA: Harvard University Press; London: Heinemann, 1926–65.

Kuhn, Karl Georg. *Konkordanz zu den Qumrantexten*. Göttingen: Vandenhoeck and Ruprecht, 1960.

Lust, J., E. Eynikel, and K. Hauspie, eds. *A Greek-English Lexicon of the Septuagint*. 2 vols. Stuttgart: Deutsche Bibelgesellschaft, 1992–97.

Luther and Erasmus: Free Will and Salvation. Translated by E. Gordon Rupp, A. N. Marlow, Philip S. Watson, and B. Drewery. Library of Christian Classics, ed. John Baillie, John T. McNeill, and Henry P. van Dusen, vol. 17. Philadelphia: Westminster, 1969.

Luther, Martin. *The Bondage of the Will: The Masterwork of the Great Reformer*. Translated by J. I. Packer and O. R. Johnston. Old Tappan, NJ: Revell, 1957.

———. *Commentary on Romans*. Translated by J. Theodore Mueller. Grand Rapids: Zondervan, 1954. Reprint, Grand Rapids: Kregel Publications, 1976.

———. *Works*. Edited by Jaroslav J. Pelikan. 55 vols. St. Louis, MO: Concordia, 1955–.

Margoliouth, J. P., ed. *Supplements to the Thesaurus Syriacus of R. Payne Smith*. Oxford: Clarendon, 1927. Reprint, Hildesheim and New York: Olms, 1981.

Mayer, Günter. *Index Philoneus*. Berlin and New York: de Gruyter, 1974.

Six Divisions of the Mishna (Shisha Sidrei Mishna). Eshkol Edition Electronic text used by permission of D.B.S., Jerusalem, Israel Morphological separators added by OakTree Software. Copyright © 2000 by OakTree Software,Version 1.8.

Molina on Divine Foreknowledge : Part IV of the Concordia. Translated by Alfred J. Freddoso. Ithica, NY: Cornell University Press, 1988.

Neusner, Jacob, ed. *The Mishnah: A New Translation*. Translated by Jacob Neusner. New Haven: Yale University Press, 1988.

Origen. *Contra Celsum*. Translated by Henry Chadwick. 2d ed. New York: Cambridge University Press, 1980.

———. *Der Kommentar zum Evangelium nach Mattäus*. Translated by Hermann J. Vogt. Bibliothek der griechischen Literatur, vol. 18. Stuttgart: Hiersemann, 1983–90.

———. *On First Principles: Being Koetschau's Text of the De Principiis*. Translated by G. W. Butterworth. Gloucester, MA: Smith, 1966.

———. *Treatise on the Passover; and, Dialogue of Origen with Heraclides and His Fellow Bishops on the Father, the Son, and the Soul*. Translated by Robert J. Daly. New York: Paulist, 1992.

The Letters of Pelagius and His followers. Translated by B. R. Rees. Rochester, NY: Boydell, 1991.

Pelagius: Life and Letters. Translated by B. R. Rees. Rochester, NY: Boydell, 1998.

Philo. Translated by F. H. Colson and G. H. Whitaker. 10 vols. Loeb Classical Library, ed. T. E. Page, E. Capps, and W. H. D. Rouse. New York: Putnam's; London: Heinemann, 1929–71.

Philo. *Opera Quae Supersunt.* Edited by Leopoldus Cohn and Paulus Wendland, 8 vols. Berlin: Reimer, 1896–1930. Reprint, Berlin: de Gruyter, 1962–63.

Plato. *Euthyphro; Apology; Crito; Phaedo; Phaedrus.* Translated by Harold North Fowler. Loeb Classical Library, ed. T. E. Page, E. Capps, W. H. D. Rouse, L. A. Post, and E. H. Warmington. Cambridge, MA: Harvard University Press, 1914.

———. *Lysis, Symposium, Gorgias.* Translated by W. R. M. Lamb. Loeb Classical Library, ed. T. E. Page, E. Capps, W. H. D. Rouse, L. A. Post, and E. H. Warmington. Cambridge, MA: Harvard University Press; London: Heinemann, 1932.

———. *The Republic.* Translated by Paul Shorey. 2 vols. Loeb Classical Library, ed. T. E. Page, E. Capps, W. H. D. Rouse, L. A. Post, and E. H. Warmington. Cambridge, MA: Harvard University Press, 1943.

———. *The Statesman; Philebus.* Translated by Harold N. Fowler and W. R. M. Lamb. The Loeb Classical Library, ed. T. E. Page, E. Capps, W. H. D. Rouse, L. A. Post, and E. H. Warmington. Cambridge, MA: Harvard University Press, 1925.

Plutarch's Lives. Translated by Perrin Bernadotte. 11 vols. Loeb Classical Library, ed. T. E. Page, E. Capps, W. H. D. Rouse, L. A. Post, and E. H. Warmington. Cambridge, MA, 1949–59.

Rengstorf, Karl Heinrich. *A Complete Concordance to Flavius Josephus.* 5 vols. Leiden: Brill, 1973–83.

Duns Scotus, John. *Philosophical Writings: A Selection.* Translated by Allan Wolter. Edinburgh: Nelson, 1962.

Septuaginta, Vetus Testamentum Graecum Auctoritate Academiae Scientiarum Gottingensis Editum. 24 vols. Göttingen: Vandenhoeck and Ruprecht, 1931–present.

Sophocles. Translated by F. Storr. 2 vols. Loeb Classical Library, ed. T. E. Page, E. Capps, W. H. D. Rouse, L. A. Post, and E. H. Warmington. Cambridge, MA: Harvard University Press; London: Heinemann, 1962.

Sperber, Alexander B., ed. *The Latter Prophets according to Targum Jonathan,* vol. 3. The Bible in Aramaic, ed. Alexander B. Sperber. Leiden: Brill, 1962.

Stenning, John F., ed. *The Targum of Isaiah.* Oxford: Clarendon Press, 1949.

Strack, Hermann L., and Paul Billerbeck. *Kommentar zum Neuen Testament aus Talmud und Midrasch.* 6 vols. Munich: Beck, 1922–61.

Sukenik, Eleazar Lipa, ed. *The Dead Sea Scrolls of the Hebrew University.* Jerusalem: Magnes, 1955.

Taylor, Bernard A. *The Analytical Lexicon to the Septuagint: A Complete Parsing Guide.* Grand Rapids: Zondervan, 1994.

Tertullian: Adversus Marcionem. Translated by Ernest Evans. 2 vols. Oxford Early Christian Texts. Oxford: Clarendon, 1972.

Tertullian: Apologetical works, and Minucius Felix: Octavius. Translated by Rudolph Arbesmann, Emily Joseph Daly, and Edwin A Quain. Fathers of the Church, ed. Rudolph Arbesmann, Roy Joseph Deferrari, Stephan Kuttner, Martin R. P.

McGuire, Wilfrid Parsons, Bernard M. Peebles, Robert P. Russell, Anselm Strittmatter, James Edward Tobin, and Gerald G. Walsh, vol. 10, 1950.

Tertullian. *Traité de la prescription contre les hérétiques*. Translated by P. de Labriolle. Sources chrétiennes, ed. H. de Lubac, J. Daniélou, and C. Mondésert, vol. 46. Paris: Cerf, 1957.

Theophilus, Saint. *Trois livres à Autolycus*. Translated by Jean Sender. Sources chrétiennes, ed. H. de Lubac and J. Daniélou, vol. 20. Paris: Cerf, 1948.

The Tosefta: Translated from the Hebrew. Translated by Jacob Neusner. South Florida Studies in the History of Judaism, ed. Jacob Neusner, William Scott Green, and James F. Strange, vol. 10. New York: Ktav, 1977. Reprint, Atlanta: Scholars Press, 1990.

Thucydides. Translated by Charles Forster Smith. 4 vols. Loeb Classical Library, ed. T. E. Page, E. Capps, W. H. D. Rouse, L. A. Post, and E. H. Warmington. New York: Putnam's; London: Heinemann, 1919–23.

Turrettini, François. *Institutes of Elenctic Theology*. Edited by James T. Dennison Jr. Translated by George M. Giger. 3 vols. Phillipsburg, NJ: Presbyterian & Reformed, 1992–.

Webster's Encyclopedic Unabridged Dictionary of the English Language. New York: Portland, 1989.

Whitelocke, Lester T., ed. *An Analytical Concordance of the Books of the Apocrypha*. Washington, DC: University Press of America, 1978.

Wise, Michael, Martin Abegg Jr., and Edwin Cook. *The Dead Sea Scrolls: A New Translation*. San Francisco: HarperSanFrancisco, 1996.

Xenophon. Translated by Carleton L. Brownson and E. C. Marchant. 4 vols. Loeb Classical Library, ed. T. E. Page, E. Capps, W. H. D. Rouse, L. A. Post, and E. H. Warmington. Cambridge, MA: Harvard University Press; London: Heinemann, 1918–23.

Zahavy, Tzvee, ed. *The Talmud of the Land of Israel: A Preliminary Translation and Explanation*. Translated by Tzvee Zahavy. Chicago Studies in the History of Judaism, ed. William Scott Green and Calvin Goldscheider, vol. 1. Chicago: University of Chicago Press, 1989.

Ziegler, Joseph, ed. *Isaias*. In *Septuaginta, Vetus Testamentum Graecum Auctoritate Academiae Scientiarum Gottingensis*, vol. 14. Göttingen: Vandenhoeck & Ruprecht, 1967.

Books

Abbott, T. K. *The Epistles to the Ephesians and to the Colossians*. International Critical Commentary, ed. Samuel Rolles Driver, Alfred Plummer, and Charles Augustus Briggs. Edinburgh: Clark, 1897.

Adler, Mortimer J. *Aristotle for Everybody: Difficult Thought Made Easy*. New York: Simon & Schuster, 1978.

———. *How to Think about the Great Ideas: From the Great Books of Western Civilization*. Edited by M. Weismann. Chicago: Open Court; La Salle, 2000.

———. *The Idea of Freedom: A Dialectical Examination of the Conceptions of Freedom*. Garden City, NY: Doubleday, 1958.

Alexander, Joseph A. *The Gospel according to Matthew Explained*. London: Nisbet, 1861. Reprint, Lynchburg, VA: James Family Christian Publishing, 1979.

Allo, Ernest B. *Première Épître aux Corinthiens*. 2d ed. Paris: Gabalda, 1956.

Ambrozic, Aloysius M. *The Hidden Kingdom—a Redaction-Critical Study of the References to the Kingdom of God in Mark*. Catholic Biblical Quarterly Monograph Series, ed. Joseph A. Fitzmyer, Raymond E. Brown, Jr. Frank M. Cross, J. Louis Martyn, Dennis J. McCarthy, Roland E. Murphy, and Bruce Vawter, vol. 2. Washington, DC: Catholic Biblical Association, 1972.

Ames, William. *The Marrow of Sacred Divinity, Drawn out of the Holy Scrpitures, and the Interpreters thereof, and Brought into Method*. Translated by John Dykstra Eusden. Boston: Pilgrim, 1968. Reprint, Grand Rapids: Baker, 1997.

Anderson, Hugh. *The Gospel of Mark*. New Century Bible, ed. Ronald E. Clements and Matthew Black. London: Marshall, Morgan, and Scott, 1976.

Archer, Gleason L., and G. C. Chirichigno. *Old Testament Quotations in the New Testament: A Complete Survey*. Chicago: Moody, 1983.

Augustijn, Cornelis. *Erasmus: His Life, Works, and Influence*. Translated by J. C. Grayson. Toronto: University of Toronto Press, 1995.

Austin, J. L. *How to Do Things with Words*. Edited by J. O. Urmson & Marina Sbisà. 2d. ed. Cambridge, MA: Harvard University Press, 1975.

Bailey, Kenneth E. *Poet and Peasant and through Peasant Eyes. A Literary-Cultural Approach to the Parables in Luke*. 2 vols. Grand Rapids: Eerdmans, 1983.

Bailey, Philip. *The Blindness of the Jews in Matthew 13:13–15, Mark 4:12 and Luke 8:10*. Rome: Typis Scholae Tipographicae Missionariae Dominicanae, 1956.

Bainton, Roland H. *Here I Stand: A Life of Martin Luther*. New York: Abingdon-Cokesbury; Nashville, 1950.

Ball, Edward, ed. *In Search of True Wisdom: Essays in Old Testament Interpretation in Honour of Ronald E. Clements*. Journal for the Study of the Old Testament: Supplement Series, ed. David J. A. Clines and Philip R. Davies, vol. 300. Sheffield: Sheffield Academic Press, 1999.

Barnett, Paul. *The Second Epistle to the Corinthians*. New International Commentary on the New Testament, ed. Gordon D. Fee. Grand Rapids: Eerdmans, 1997.

Barr, James. *Semantics of Biblical Language*. Oxford: Oxford University Press, 1961.

Barrow, John and Frank Tipler. *The Anthropic Cosmological Principle*. Oxford: Clarendon, 1986.

Barton, George Aaron. *The Book of Ecclesiastes*. The International Critical Commentary on the Old Testament, ed. S. R. Driver, A. Plummer, and C. A. Briggs. Edinburgh: Clark, 1908.

Basinger, David and Randall Basinger., ed. *Predestination and Free Will: Four views of Divine Sovereignty & Human Freedom*. Downers Grove, IL: InterVarsity, 1987.

Bauckham, Richard J. *God Crucified: Monotheism & Christology in the New Testament*. Grand Rapids: Eerdmans, 1999.

———. *Jude, 2 Peter*. Word Biblical Commentary, ed. Ralph P. Martin, vol. 50. Waco, TX: Word, 1983.

Beasley-Murray, G. R. *Jesus and the Kingdom of God*. Grand Rapids: Eerdmans, 1986.

Beavis, Mary Ann. *Mark's Audience. The Literary and Social Setting of Mark 4, 11–12*. Journal for the Study of the New Testament: Supplement Series, ed. David Hill and David E. Orton, vol. 33. Sheffield: JSOT, 1989.

Beck, Astrid B., Andrew H. Bartelt, Paul R. Raabe, and Chris A. Franke, eds. *Fortunate the Eyes that See: Essays in Honor of David Noel Freedman in Celebration of His Seventieth Birthday*. Grand Rapids: Eerdmans, 1995.

Beilby, James K. and Paul R. Eddy, eds. *Divine Foreknowledge: Four Views*. Downers Grove, IL: InterVarsity, 2001.

Belleville, Linda L. *2 Corinthians*. The IVP New Testament Commentary Series, ed. Grand R. Osborne. Downers Grove, IL: InterVarsity, 1996.

Best, Ernest. *Disciples and Discipleship: Studies in the Gospel according to Mark*. Edinburgh: Clark, 1986.

Betz, Otto. *Offenbarung und Schriftforschung in der Qumransekte.* Wissenschaftliche Untersuchungen zum Neuen Testament, ed. Joachim Jeremias and D. Otto Michel, vol. 6. Tübingen: Mohr, 1960.

Black, David Alan and David R. Beck, eds. *Rethinking the Synoptic Problem*. Grand Rapids: Baker, 2001.

Black, Matthew. *An Aramaic Approach to the Gospels and Acts*. 3d ed. Oxford: Oxford University Press; 1967.

Blaising, Craig A. and Darrell L. Bock. *Progressive Dispensationalism: An Up-to-Date Handbook of Contemporary Dispensational Thought*. Wheaton, IL: Victor, 1993.

Blank, Sheldon H. *Prophetic Faith in Israel*. New York: Harper, 1958.

Blomberg, Craig L. *Interpreting the Parables*. Downers Grove, IL: InterVarsity, 1990.

Bock, Darrell L. *Blasphemy and Exaltation in Judaism and the Final Examination of Jesus: A Philological-Historical Study of Key Jewish Themes Impacting Mark 14:61–64*. Wissenschaftliche Untersuchungen zum Neuen Testament, ed. Martin Hengel and Otfried Hofius, vol. 106. Tübingen: Mohr, 1998. Reprint, Grand Rapids: Baker, 2000.

———. *Luke 1:1–9:50*. Baker Exegetical Commentary on the New Testament, ed. Moisés Silva, vol. 3A. Grand Rapids: Baker, 1994.

———. *Proclamation from Prophecy and Pattern: Lucan Old Testament Christology*. Journal for the Study of the New Testament Supplement Series, ed. David Hill and David E. Orton, vol. 12. Sheffield: Sheffield Academic Press, 1987.

Boman, Thorleif. *Hebrew Thought Compared with Greek*. Translated by Jules L. Moreau. New York: SCM, 1960.

Borchert, Gerald L. *John 12–21*. New American Commentary, ed. David S. Dockery, Richard R. Melick Jr., Paige Patterson, Curtis Vaughan, and Linda L. Scott. Nashville: Broadman & Holman, 2002.

Boucher, Madeleine I. *The Mysterious Parable: A Literary Study*. Catholic Biblical Quarterly Monograph Series, ed. Bruce Vawter, Schuyler Brown, Frank M. Cross Jr., John H. Elliott, J. Louis Martyn, Dennis J. McCarthy, John L. McKenzie, Roland E. Murphy, and Patrick W. Skehan, vol. 6. Washington, DC: Catholic Biblical Association, 1977.

Bovon, François. *Luke 1: A Commentary on the Gospel of Luke 1:1–9:50*. Edited by Helmut Koester. Translated by Christine M. Thomas. Hermeneia—A Critical and Historical Commentary on the Bible, ed. Helmut Koester, Harold W. Attridge, Adela Yarbro Collins, Eldon Jay Epp, and James M. Robinson. Minneapolis: Fortress, 2002.

Boyd, Gregory A. *The God of the Possible: A Biblical Introduction to the Open View of God*. Grand Rapids: Baker, 2000.

Bray, Gerald., ed. *1–2 Corinthians*. Ancient Christian Commentary on Scripture, ed. Thomas C. Oden, vol. 7. Downers Grove, IL: InterVarsity, 1999.

Brooks, James A. and Carlton L. Winbery. *Syntax of New Testament Greek*. Washington, DC: University Press of America, 1979.

Brown, Raymond E. *The Semitic Background of the Term "Mystery" in the New Testament.* Facet Books: Biblical Series, ed. John Reumann, vol. 21. Philadelphia: Fortress, 1968.

Brownlee, William H. *The Meaning of the Qumran Scrolls for the Bible.* New York: Oxford University Press, 1964.

Bruce, F. F. *Biblical Exegesis in the Qumran Texts.* Grand Rapids: Eerdmans, 1959.

————. *1 and 2 Corinthians.* New Century Bible, ed. Matthew Black. Grand Rapids: Eerdmans, 1971.

————. *Hard Sayings of Jesus.* The Jesus Library, ed. Michael Green, vol. 1. Downers Grove, IL: InterVarsity, 1983.

Bryan, Christopher. *A Preface to Romans: Notes on the Epistle in Its Literary and Cultural Setting.* Oxford: Oxford University Press, 2000.

Bultmann, Rudolf. *The History of the Synoptic Tradition.* Translated by John Marsh. San Francisco: Harper & Row, 1963.

————. *The Second Letter to the Corinthians.* Translated by Roy A. Harrisville. Minneapolis: Augsburg, 1985.

————. *Theology of the New Testament.* Translated by Kendrick Grobel, 2 vols. New York: Scribner's, 1951–55.

Burkill, T. Alec. *Mysterious Revelation: An Examination of the Philosophy of St. Mark's Gospel.* Ithica, NY: Cornell University Press, 1963.

Burney, C. F. *The Aramaic Origin of the Fourth Gospel.* Oxford: Oxford University Press, 1922.

————. *The Poetry of Our Lord.* Oxford: Clarendon Press, 1925.

Burns, J. Patout., ed. *Theological Anthropology.* Translated by J. Patout Burns. Sources of Early Christian Thought, ed. William G. Rusch. Philadelphia: Fortress, 1981.

Burton, E. D. W. *Syntax of the Moods and Tenses in New Testament Greek.* 3d ed. Chicago: University of Chicago Press, 1900. Reprint, Grand Rapids: Kregel, 1994.

Bush, George. *Notes, Critical and Practical, on the Book of Exodus; Designed as a General Help to Biblical Reading and Instruction.* New York: Newman & Ivison, 1852. Reprint, Minneapolis, MN, Klock & Klock, 1981.

Buttrick, George Arthur. *The Parables of Jesus.* New York: Harper and Brothers, 1928.

Byrne, Brendan. *Romans.* Sacra pagina, ed. Daniel J. Harrington, vol. 6. Collegeville, MN: Liturgical, 1996.

Cadoux, A. T. *The Theology of Jesus.* London: Nicholson & Watson, 1940.

Calvin, John. *Commentary on a Harmony of the Evangelists Matthew, Mark, and Luke.* Translated by William Pringle. Edinburgh: Calvin Translation Society, 1845–46. Reprint, Grand Rapids: Baker, 1999.

Carson, D. A. *Divine Sovereignty and Human Responsibility: Biblical Perspectives in Tension.* 2d ed. Grand Rapids: Baker, 1994. Reprint, Eugene, OR: Wipf & Stock, 2002.

————. *Exegetical Fallacies.* 2d ed. Grand Rapids: Baker, 1996.

————. *The Gospel according to John.* Grand Rapids: Eerdmans, 1991.

Cassuto, Umberto. *A Commentary on the Book of Exodus.* Translated by Israel Abrahams. Jerusalem: Magnes, 1967.

Charlesworth, James H. *The Old Testament Pseudepigrapha & The New Testament: Prolegomena for the Study of Christian Origins.* Harrisburg, PA: Trinity Press International, 1998.

Childs, Brevard S. *The Book of Exodus: A Critical, Theological Commentary*. Old Testament Library, ed. Peter Ackroyd, James Barr, Bernhard W. Anderson, James L. Mays, and John Bright, vol. 2. Philadelphia: Westminster, 1974.

————. *Isaiah and the Assyrian Crisis*. Studies in Biblical Theology, ed. C. F. D. Moule, J. Barr, Peter Ackroyd, Floyd V. Filson, and G. Ernest Wright. London: SCM, 1967.

Chilton, Bruce D. *A Galilean Rabbi and His Bible*. Good News Studies, ed. Robert J. Karris, vol. 8. Wilmington, DE: Glazier, 1984.

Chisholm Jr., Robert B. *Handbook on the Prophets*. Grand Rapids: Baker, 2002.

Christensen, Duane L. *Deuteronomy 21:10–34:12*. Word Biblical Commentary, ed. John D. W. Watts, vol. 6B. Nashville: Nelson, 2002.

Clements, Ronald E. *Exodus*. Cambridge Bible Commentary, ed. P. R. Ackroyd, A. R. C. Leaney, and J. W. Packer. Cambridge: Cambridge University Press, 1972.

Clements, Ronald E. *Isaiah 1–39*. New Century Bible, ed. Ronald E. Clements and Matthew Black. Grand Rapids: Eerdmans, 1982.

Clifford, Richard J. *The Wisdom Literature*. Interpreting Biblical Texts, ed. Gene M. Tucker. Nashville: Abingdon, 1998.

Cole, R. Alan. *Exodus: An Introduction and Commentary*. Tyndale Old Testament Commentaries, ed. D. J. Wiseman. Downers Grove, IL: InterVarsity, 1973.

Conrad, Edgar. *Reading Isaiah*. Minneapolis: Fortress, 1991.

Copan, Paul. *"True for You, But Not for Me": Deflating the Slogans that Leave Christians Speechless*. Minneapolis: Bethany, 1998.

Cosgrove, Charles H. *Elusive Israel: The Puzzle of Election in Romans*. Louisville, KY: Westminster and Knox, 1997.

Craddock, Fred B. *Luke*. Interpretation: A Bible Commentary for Teaching and Preaching, ed. James Luther Mays and Paul J. Achtemeier. Louisville, KY: Knox, 1990.

Craig, William Lane. *The Existence of God and the Beginning of the Universe*. San Bernardino, CA: Here's Life Publishers, 1979.

————. *God, Time, and Eternity: The Coherence of Theism II: Eternity*. Boston: Kluwer, 2001.

————. *Time and Eternity: Exploring God's Relationship to Time*. Wheaton, IL: Crossway, 2001.

————. *The Tensed Theory of Time: A Critical Examination*. Synthese Library: Studies in Epistemology, Logic, Methodology, and Philosophy of Science, ed. Jaakko Hintikka, Dirk van Dalen, Donald Davidson, Theo A. F. Kuipers, Patrick Suppes, and Jan Wolenski, vol. 293. Boston: Kluwer, 2000.

————. *The Tenseless Theory of Time: A Critical Examination*. Synthese Library: Studies in Epistemology, Logic, Methodology, and Philosophy of Science, ed. Jaakko Hintikka, Dirk van Dalen, Donald Davidson, Theo A. F. Kuipers, Patrick Suppes, and Jan Wolenski, vol. 294. Boston: Kluwer, 2000.

————, and Quentin Smith. *Theism, Atheism, and Big Bang Cosmology*. Oxford: Clarendon, 1993.

————, and Walter Sinnott-Armstrong. *God? A Debate between a Christian and an Atheist*. Point/Counterpoint Series, ed. James P. Sterba, vol. 2. Oxford: Oxford University Press, 2004.

Craigie, Peter C. *The Book of Deuteronomy*. New International Commentary on the Old Testament, ed. R. K. Harrison. Grand Rapids: Eerdmans, 1976.

Cranfield, C. E. B. *The Epistle to the Romans*. 2 vols. The International Critical Commentary, ed. J. A. Emerton and C. E. B. Cranfield. Edinburgh: Clark, 1975–79.

————. *The Gospel according to Saint Mark*. Cambridge Greek Testament Commentary, ed. C. F. D. Moule. Cambridge: Cambridge University Press, 1972.

Crenshaw, James L. *Ecclesiastes: A Commentary*. The Old Testament Library, ed. Peter Ackroyd, James Barr, Bernhard W. Anderson, James L. Mays, and John Bright. Philadelphia: Westminster, 1987.

————. *Education in Ancient Israel: Across the Deadening Silence*. Anchor Bible Reference Library, ed. David Noel Freedman. New York: Doubleday, 1998.

————. *Old Testament Wisdom: An Introduction*. Louisville, KY: Knox, 1998.

Darr, Katheryn Pfisterer. *Isaiah's Vision and the Family of God*. Louisville, KY: Westminster and Knox, 1994.

Daube, David. *The New Testament and Rabbinic Judaism*. London: Athlone, 1965. Reprint, Peabody, MA: Hendrickson, 1998.

Davies, Paul. *God and the New Physics*. New York: Simon & Schuster, 1983.

————, and John Gribbin. *The Matter Myth: Dramatic Discoveries That Challenge Our Understanding of Physical Reality*. New York: Simon & Schuster, 1992.

Davis, James A. *Wisdom and Spirit, An Investigation of 1 Corinthians 1.18–3:20 against the Background of Jewish Sapiential Traditions in the Greco-Roman Period*. Lanham, MD: University Press of America, 1984.

Delitzsch, Franz. *A New Commentary on Genesis*. Translated by Sophia Taylor, vol. 1. Edinburgh: Clark, 1888. Reprint, Minneapolis, MN: Klock & Klock, 1978.

Delling, Katharine. *'Get Wisdom, Get Insight': An Introduction to Israel's Wisdom Literature*. London: Darton, Longman & Todd, 2000.

Dillard, Raymond B., and Tremper Longman III. *An Introduction to the Old Testament*. Grand Rapids: Zondervan, 1994.

Dillmann, August. *Die Bücher Exodus und Leviticus*. Leipzig: Hirzel, 1880.

Dodd, C. H. *The Parables of the Kingdom*. 2d rev. ed. New York: Scribner's, 1972.

Dorsey, David A. *The Literary Structure of the Old Testament: A Commentary on Genesis–Malachi*. Grand Rapids: Baker, 1999.

Driver, S. R. *A Critical and Exegetical Commentary on Deuteronomy*, 3d ed. International Critical Commentary, ed. Samuel Rolles Driver, Alfred Plummer, and Charles Augustus Briggs. Edinburgh: Clark, 1895.

Dunn, James D. G. *Christology in the Making: A New Testament Inquiry into the Origins of the Doctrine of the Incarnation*. 2d ed. Grand Rapids: Eerdmans, 1996.

Dunnam, Maxie D. *Exodus*. The Communicator's Commentary, ed. Lloyd J. Ogilvie, vol. 2. Waco, TX: Word, 1987.

Eaton, Michael A. *Ecclesiastes*. Tyndale Old Testament Commentaries, ed. D. J. Wiseman. Downers Grove, IL: InterVarsity Press, 1983.

Edwards, James R. *Romans*. New International Commentary on the New Testament, ed. W. Ward Gasque. Peabody, MA: Hendrickson, 1992.

Edwards, Jonathan. *Freedom of the Will*. Edited by Paul Ramsey. The Works of Jonathan Edwards, ed. Perry Miller, vol. 1. New Haven, CT: Yale University Press, 1957.

————. *A Treatise concerning Religious Affections, in Three Parts: Part I. Concerning the Nature of the Affections, and Their Importance in Religion. Part II. Shewing What are no Certain Signs That Religious Affections are Gracious, or That They are Not. Part III.*

Shewing What are Distinguishing Signs of Truly Gracious and Holy Affections. Edinburgh: Laing & Matthews, 1746. Reprint, Carlisle, PA: Banner of Truth Trust, 1997.

Eichrodt, Walther. *Theology of the Old Testament.* Translated by J. A. Baker. Vol. 2. Old Testament Library, ed. G. Ernest Wright, John Bright, James Barr, and Peter Ackroyd. London: SCM, 1961.

Einstein, Albert. *Out of My Later Years.* London: Thames & Hudson, 1950.

Eissfeldt, O. *The Old Testament: An Introduction, Including the Apocrypha and Pseudepigrapha, and Also the Works of Similar Type from Qumran: The History of the Formation of the Old Testament.* Translated by Peter R. Ackroyd. New York: Harper & Row, 1965.

Engnell, Ivan. *The Call of Isaiah.* Vol. 4. Uppsala Universitets Arsskrift. Uppsala: Lundequistska Bokhandeln, 1949.

Erb, M. *Porosis und Ate. Begriffsgeschichtliche Untersuchungen zur neutestamentlichen Verstockungstheologie und ihren Beziehungen zur hellenischen Religiosität.* Tübingen: Huth, 1964.

Evans, Craig A. *Luke.* New International Biblical Commentary on the New Testament, ed. W. Ward Gasque, vol. 3. Peabody, MA: Hendrickson, 1990.

————. *Noncanonical Writings and New Testament Interpretation.* Peabody, MA: Hendrickson, 1992.

————. *To See and Not Perceive: Isaiah 6:9–10 in Early Jewish and Christian Interpretation.* Journal for the Study of the Old Testament: Supplement Series, ed. David J. A. Clines and Philip R. Davies, vol. 64. Sheffield: JSOT, 1989.

Fanning, Buist M. *Verbal Aspect in New Testament Greek.* Oxford Theological Monographs, ed. J. Barton, R. C. Morgan, B. R. White, J. MacQuarrie, K. Ware, and R. D. Williams. Oxford: Clarendon, 1990.

Fee, Gordon D. *The First Epistle to The Corinthians.* New International Commentary on the New Testament, ed. Gordon D. Fee. Grand Rapids: Eerdmans, 1987.

Fichtner, Johannes. *Die altorientalische Weisheit in ihrer israelitisch-jüdischen Ausprägung.* Beihefte zur Zeitschrift für die alttestamentliche Wissenschaft, vol. 62. Giessen: Töpelmann, 1933.

Fischer, John Martin. *The Metaphysics of Free Will: An Essay on Control.* Aristotelian Society Series, ed. Martin Davies, vol. 14. Cambridge, MA: Blackwell, 1994.

Fitzmyer, Joseph A. *Essays on the Semitic Background of the New Testament.* London: Scholars Press, 1974.

————. *The Gospel according to Luke.* Anchor Bible, ed. William Foxwell Albright and David Noel Freedman, vol. 2. Garden City, NY: Doubleday, 1985.

————. *The Semitic Background of the New Testament: Volume Ii: A Wandering Aramean: Collected Aramaic Essays.* The Biblical Resource Series. Grand Rapids: Eerdmans, 1997.

————. *A Wandering Aramean: Collected Aramaic Essays.* Missoula, MT: Scholars Press, 1979.

Frame, John M. *No Other God: A Response to Open Theism.* Philipsburg, NJ: Presbyterian and Reformed, 2001.

Franzmann, Martin H. *Romans: A Commentary.* Concordia Commentary Series. St. Louis: Concordia, 1968.

Fretheim, Terence E. *Exodus*. Interpretation: A Bible Commentary for Teaching and Preaching, ed. James Luther Mays and Patrick D. Miller. Louisville, KY: Knox, 1991.

————. *The Suffering of God: An Old Testament Perspective*. Overtures to Biblical Theology, ed. Walter Brueggemann, John R. Donahue, Sharyn Dowd, and Christopher R. Seitz. Philadelphia: Fortress, 1984.

Funk, Robert W., Roy W. Hoover, and The Jesus Seminar. *The Five Gospels: The Search for the Authentic Words of Jesus*. New York: Macmillan, 1993.

Ganssle, Gregory E., ed. *God & Time: Four Views*. Downers Grove, IL: InterVarsity, 2001.

Garland, David E. *2 Corinthians*. New American Commentary, ed. David S. Dockery, vol. 29. Nashville: Broadman & Holman, 1999.

Gaston, Lloyd. *Paul and the Torah*. Vancouver, BC: University of British Columbia Press, 1987.

Geisler, Norman L. *Thomas Aquinas: An Evangelical Appraisal*. Grand Rapids: Baker, 1991.

————, and Paul D. Feinberg. *Introduction to Philosophy: A Christian Perspective*. Grand Rapids: Baker, 1980.

Gerstner, John H. *Primitive Theology: The Collected Primers of John H. Gerstner*. Morgan, PA: Soli Deo Gloria Publications, 1996.

Gesenius, William. *A Hebrew and English Lexicon of the Old Testament*. Translated by Edward Robinson, ed. Francis Brown, S. R. Driver and Charles A. Briggs. Oxford: Clarendon, 1906, 1951.

Gibson, J. C. L. *Language and Imagery in the Old Testament*. Peabody, MA: Hendrickson, 1998.

Gieschen, Charles A. *Angelomorphic Christology: Antecedents and Early Evidence*. Arbeiten zur Geschichte des antiken Judentums und des Urchristentums, ed. Martin Hengel, Peter Schäfer, Pieter W. van der Horst, Martin Goodman, Daniel R. Schwartz, and Cilliers Breytenbach, vol. 42. Leiden: Brill, 1998.

Gilbert, Maurice, ed. *La Sagasse de l'Ancien Testament*. 2d ed.. Bibliotheca ephemeridum theologicarum lovaniensium, vol. 51. Louvain: Université Catholique de Louvain, 1990.

Girdlestone, R. B. *Girdlestone's Synonyms of the Old Testament*. 3d ed. London: Nisbet, 1897. Reprint, Grand Rapids: Baker, 2000.

Gitay, Yehoshua. *Isaiah and His Audience: The Structure and Meaning of Isaiah 1–12*. Studia semitica neerlandica, ed. W. A. M. Beukens et al. Assen: Van Gorcum, 1991.

Gnilka, Joachim. *Theologie des neuen Testaments*. Handkommentar zum neuen Testament, ed. Joachim Gnilka and Lorenz Oberlinner, vol. 5. Freiburg: Herder, 1994.

————. *Die Verstockung Israels: Isaias 6:9–10 in der Theologie der Synoptiker*. Studien zum alten und neuen Testaments, ed. Vinzenz Hamp and Josef Schmid, vol. 3. Munich: Kösel, 1961.

Godet, Frederic Louis. *Commentary of St. Paul's Epistle to the Romans*. Translated by A. Cusin. Edinburgh: Clark, 1883. Reprint, Grand Rapids: Zondervan Publishing House, 1956.

Gordis, Robert. *Koheleth—The Man and His World*. 3d. New York: Schocken, 1968.

Gould, Ezra P. *Critical and Exegetical Commentary on the Gospel according to Mark*. Edinburgh: Clark, 1896. Reprint, New York: Scribner's, 1913.

Grant, Frederick C. *The Earliest Gospel*. New York: Abingdon-Cokesbury, 1943.

Green, Joel B. *The Gospel of Luke*. New International Commentary on the New Testament, ed. Gordon D. Fee. Grand Rapids: Eerdmans, 1997.

Grundmann, Walter. *Das Evangelium nach Markus*. Theologischer Handkommentar zum Neuen Testament, ed. Erich Fascher, Joachim Rohde, and Christian Wolff, vol. 2. Berlin: Evangelishe Verlagsanstalt, 1984.

Guelich, Robert A. *Mark 1–8:26*. Word Biblical Commentary, ed. Ralph P. Martin, vol. 34A. Dallas: Word, 1989.

Haenchen, Ernst. *A Commentary on the Gospel of John: Chapters 7–21*. Translated by Robert W. Funk. Edited by Robert W. Funk and Ulrich Busse. Hermeneia—A Critical and Historical Commentary on the Bible, ed. Helmut Koester, Eldon Jay Epp, Robert W. Funk, George W. MacRae, and James M. Robinson, vol. 2. Philadelphia: Fortress, 1980.

Hagner, Donald A. *Matthew 1–13*. Word Biblical Commentary, ed. Ralph P. Martin, vol. 33A. Dallas: Word, 1993.

Handy, Lowell K. *Among the Host of Heaven: The Syro-Palestinian Pantheon as Bureaucracy*. Winona Lake, IN: Eisenbrauns, 1994.

Harrington, Daniel J. *Wisdom Texts from Qumran*. London: Routledge, 1996.

Harrison, R. K. *Introduction to the Old Testament: with a Comprehensive Review of Old Testament Studies and a Special Supplement on the Apocrypha*. Grand Rapids: Eerdmans, 1969.

Heschel, Abraham J. *The Prophets*. New York: Harper & Row, 1962.

Hasel, Gerhard F. *The Remnant: The History and Theology of the Remnant Idea from Genesis to Isaiah*. 2d ed. Andrews University Seminary Studies, vol. 5. Berrien Springs, MI: Andrews University Press, 1972.

Hauser, Hermann J. *Strukturen der Abschlusserzählund der Apostelgeschichte (Apg 28, 16–31)*. Analecta Orientalia, ed. Dionisio Minguez and Albert Vanhoye, vol. 86. Rome: Biblical Institute, 1979.

Hawking, Stephen W. *A Brief History of Time: From the Big Bang to Black Holes*. New York: Bantam, 1988.

Hays, Richard B. *The Faith of Jesus Christ: An Investigation of the Narrative Substructure of Galatians 3:1–4:11*. The Biblical Resource Series, ed. Astrid B. Beck and David Noel Freedman. Grand Rapids: Eerdmans, 2002.

Hengel, Martin. *Judaism and Hellenism: Studies in Their Encounter in Palestine in the Early Hellenistic Period*. Translated by John Bowden. Vol. 1. Philadelphia: Fortress; London: SCM, 1974.

———, and Roland Deines. *The Pre-Christian Paul*. Translated by John Bowden. Philadelphia: Trinity Press International, 1991.

Hermaniuk, M. *La parabole évangélique: Enquête exégétique et critique*. Bruges: Desclée, 1947.

Hesse, Franz. *Das Verstockungsproblem im alten Testament: eine frömmigkeits geschichtliche Untersuchung*. Beihefte zur Zeitschrift für die alttestamentliche Wissenschaft, vol. 74. Berlin: Töpelmann, 1955.

Hewitt, James Allen. *New Testament Greek: A Beginning and Intermediate Grammar*. Peabody, MA: Hendrickson, 1986.

Hill, R. Charles. *Wisdom's Many Faces*. Collegeville, MN: Liturgical, 1996.

Hodges, Zane C., and Arthur L. Farstad. *The Greek New Testament according to the Majority Text,* 2d ed. Nashville: Nelson, 1985.

Hoehner, Harold W. *Ephesians: An Exegetical Commentary.* Grand Rapids: Baker, 2002.

Hoglund, Kenneth G., Elizabeth F. Huwiler, Jonathan T. Glass, and Roger W. Lee, eds. *The Listening Heart: Essays in Wisdom and the Psalms in Honor of Roland E. Murphy.* Journal for the Study of the Old Testament, ed. David J. A. Clines and Philip R. Davies, vol. 58. Sheffield: JSOT, 1987.

Holwerda, David E. *Jesus and Israel: One Covenant or Two?* Grand Rapids: Eerdmans, 1995.

Hooker, Morna D. *From Adam to Christ: Essays on Paul.* Cambridge: Cambridge University Press, 1990.

Hughes, Philip Edgcumbe. *Paul's Second Epistle to the Corinthians: The English Text with Introduction, Exposition and Notes.* New International Commentary on the New Testament, ed. Ned B. Stonehous. Grand Rapids: Eerdmans, 1962.

Hunter, A. M. *Interpreting the Parables.* Philadelphia: Westminster, 1960.

Hurtado, Larry W. *Mark.* Rev. ed. New International Biblical Commentary, ed. W. Ward Gasque, vol. 2. Peabody, MA: Hendrickson, 1989.

———. *One God, One Lord: Early Christian Devotion and Ancient Jewish Monotheism.* 2d ed. Edinburgh: Clark, 1998.

Hyatt, J. Philip. *Exodus.* New Century Bible, ed. Ronald E. Clements, vol. 1. Grand Rapids: Eerdmans, 1971.

Jannaris, Antonius N. *An Historical Greek Grammar Chiefly of the Attic Dialect.* Reinheim: Lokay, 1968. Reprint, Hildesheim: Olms, 1968.

Jastrow, Robert. *God and the Astronomers.* New York: Norton, 1978.

Jensen, Joseph. *The Use of Tôrâ by Isaiah: His Debate with the Wisdom Tradition.* Catholic Biblical Quarterly Monograph Series, ed. Patrick W. Skehan, Thomas O. Barrosse, Schuyler Brown, Frank M. Cross Jr., J. Louis Martyn, Dennis J. McCarthy, Roland E. Murphy, and Bruce Vawter, vol. 3. Washington, DC: Catholic Biblical Association, 1973.

Jeremias, Joachim. *Jerusalem in the Time of Jesus: An Investigation into Economic & Social Conditions during the New Testament Period.* Translated by F. H. Cave and C. H. Cave. Philadelphia: Fortress, 1969.

———. *The Parables of Jesus.* Translated by S. H. Hooke. 3d ed. New York: Scribner's, 1972.

Johnson, Luke Timothy. *The Gospel of Luke.* Sacra pagina, ed. Daniel J. Harrington, vol. 3. Collegeville, MN: Liturgical, 1991.

Kaiser, Otto. *Isaiah 1–12.* Translated by John Bowden. 2d ed. Old Testament Library, ed. Peter R. Ackroyd, James Barr, Bernhard W. Anderson, John Bright, and James L. Mays, vol. 9. Philadelphia: Westminster, 1983.

Kaiser, Walter C., Jr. *Toward an Old Testament Theology.* Grand Rapids: Zondervan, 1978.

Käsemann, Ernst. *Commentary on Romans.* Edited and translated by G. W. Bromiley. 4th ed. Grand Rapids: Eerdmans, 1980.

Kautzsch, E. and A. E. Cowley, eds. *Gesenius' Hebrew Grammar.* 2d English ed. Oxford: Clarendon, 1910.

Kee, Howard Clark. *Community of the New Age. Studies in Mark's Gospel.* Rev. ed. Macon, GA: Mercer University Press, 1983.

Kenny, Anthony. *The Five Ways: Saint Thomas Aquinas' Proofs of God's Existence*. Notre Dame, IN: University of Notre Dame, 1969.

Kingsbury, Jack Dean. *Conflict in Mark: Jesus, Authorities, Disciples*. Minneapolis: Fortress, 1989.

Kissinger, Warren S. *The Parables of Jesus: A History of Interpretation and Bibliography*. ATLA Bibliography Series, ed. Kenneth E. Rowe, vol. 4. Metuchen, NJ: Scarecrow, 1979.

Klauck, Hans-Josef. *Allegorie und Allegorese in synoptischen Gleichnistexten*. Neutestamentliche Abhandlungen, ed. Augustinus Bladau, Max Meinertz, and Joachim Gnilka, vol. 13. Munster: Aschendorf, 1978.

Kooij, A. van der. *Die alten Textzeugen des Jesajabuches: Ein Beitrag zur Textgeschichte des Alten Testaments*. Orbis biblicus et orientalis, ed. Othmar Keel, Bernard Trémel, and Erich Zenger, vol. 35. Fribourg: Universitätsverlag, 1981.

Kreeft, Peter, ed. *A Summa of the* Summa: *The Essential Philosophical Passages of St. Thomas Aquinas'* Summa Theologica *Edited and Explained for Beginners*. San Francisco: Ignatius, 1990.

Kruse, Colin G. *Paul, The Law, and Justification*. Peabody, MA: Hendrickson, 1996.

Kühschelm, Roman. *Verstockung, Gericht und Heil: exegetische und bibeltheologische Untersuchung zum sogenannten Dualismus und Determinismus in Joh 12, 35–50*. Frankfurt am Main: Hain, 1990.

Ladd, George Eldon. *The Presence of the Future: The Eschatology of Biblical Realism*. Grand Rapids: Eerdmans, 1974.

———. *A Theology of the New Testament*. Edited by Donald A. Hagner. Rev. ed. Grand Rapids: Eerdmans, 1993.

Lagrange, Marie-Joseph. *Évangile selon Saint Marc*. Etudes biblique. Paris: Lecoffre, 1966.

Lane, William L. *The Gospel according to Mark*. New International Commentary on the New Testament, ed. F. F. Bruce. Grand Rapids: Eerdmans, 1974.

Lehnert, Volker A. *Die Provakation Israels: die paradoxe Funktion von Jes 6,9–10 bei Markus und Lukas: ein textpragmatischer Versuch im Kontext gegenwartiger Rezeptionsasthetik und Lesetheorie*. Neukirchener theologische Dissertationen und Habilitationen, vol. 25. Neukirchen-Vluyn: Neukirchener, 1999.

Leenhardt, Franz J. *The Epistle to the Romans: A Commentary*. Translated by Harold Knight. London: Lutterworth, 1961.

Leuphold, H. C. *Exposition of Ecclesiastes*. Grand Rapids: Baker, 1952.

———. *Exposition of Genesis*. Vol. 1. Grand Rapids: Baker, 1942.

Lincoln, Andrew T. *Ephesians*. Word Biblical Commentary, ed. Ralph P. Martin, vol. 42. Dallas: Word, 1990.

Lindars, Barnabas. *The Gospel of John*. New Century Bible, ed. Matthew Black. London: Oliphants, 1972.

Lohmeyer, Ernst. *Das Evangelium des Markus: Erganzungsheft, Kritisch-exegetischer Kommentar über das Neue Testament*. Edited by Heinrich von August and Wilhelm Meyer. Vol. 2. Göttingen: Vandenhoeck & Ruprecht, 1957.

Longman, Tremper. *The Book of Ecclesiastes*. The New International Commentary on the Old Testament, ed. Robert L. Hubbard Jr. Grand Rapids: Eerdmans, 1998.

Louw, J. P., and E. A. Nida. *Greek-English Lexicon of the New Testament Based on Semantic Domains*. New York: United Bible Societies, 1988.

Luz, Ulrich. *The Theology of the Gospel of Matthew*. Translated by J. Bradford Robinson. New Testament Theology, ed. James D. G. Dunn. Cambridge: Cambridge University Press, 1995.

Manson, Thomas Walter. *The Teaching of Jesus: Studies of Its Form and Content*. Cambridge: Cambridge University Press, 1963.

Manson, William. *Jesus the Messiah*. London: Hodder & Stoughton, 1943.

Marcus, Joel. *The Mystery of the Kingdom of God*. Society of Biblical Literature Dissertation Series, ed. Charles Talbert, vol. 90. Atlanta: Scholars Press, 1986.

Marshall, I. Howard. *Kept by the Power of God: A Study of Perseverance and Falling Away*. Minneapolis: Bethany, 1969.

————. *The Gospel of Luke: A Commentary on the Greek Text*. New International Greek Testament Commentary, ed. I. Howard Marshall and W. Ward Grasque. Grand Rapids: Eerdmans, 1978.

————. *Luke: Historian and Theologian*. Grand Rapids: Zondervan, 1970.

Martin, Ralph P. *2 Corinthians*. Word Biblical Commentary, ed. Ralph P. Martin, vol. 40. Waco, TX: Word, 1986.

————. *Worship in the Early Church*. Westwood, NJ: Revell, 1964.

Mastricht, Peter van. *A Treatise on Regeneration*. Edited by Brandon Withrow. Morgan, PA: Soli Deo Gloria, 2002.

Mayes, A. D. H. *Deuteronomy*. New Century Bible, ed. Ronald E. Clements. Grand Rapids: Eerdmans, 1979.

McCartney, Dan, and Charles Clayton. *Let the Reader Understand: A Guide to Interpreting and Applying the Bible*, 2d ed. Philipsburg, NJ: Presbyterian & Reformed, 2002.

McKane, William. *Prophets and Wise Men*. Studies in Biblical Theology, ed. C. F. D. Moule, J. Barr, Peter Ackroyd, Floyd V. Filson, and G. Ernest Wright, vol. 44. Naperville, IL: Allenson, 1965.

McTaggart, John McTaggart Ellis. *The Nature of Existence*. Cambridge Paperback Library, ed. C. D. Broad, vol. 2. Cambridge: Cambridge University Press, 1927.

Melugin, Roy F., and Marvin A. Sweeney, eds. *New Visions of Isaiah*. Journal for the Study of the Old Testament: Supplement Series, ed. David J. A. Clines and Philip R. Davies, vol. 214. Sheffield: Sheffield Academic Press, 1996.

Merrill, Eugene H., ed. *The Bible Knowledge Key Word Study: Genesis—Deuteronomy*. Colorado Springs, CO: Victor, 2003.

————. *Deuteronomy*. New American Commentary, ed. E. Ray Clendenen and Kenneth A. Matthews, vol. 4. Nashville: Broadman & Holman, 1994.

Metzger, Bruce M. *A Textual Commentary on the Greek New Testament*. 2d ed. Stuttgart: Deutsche Biblegesellschaft; New York: United Bible Societies, 1994.

Meye, Robert P. *Jesus and the Twelve: Discipleship and Revelation in Mark's Gospel*. Grand Rapids: Eerdmans, 1968.

Meyenfeldt, Frederik Henrik von. *Het hard (leb, lebab) in het Oude Testament*. Academic proefchrift. Leiden: Brill, 1950.

Michaels, J. Ramsey. *John*. New International Biblical Commentary, ed. W. Ward Gasque. Peabody, MA: Hendrickson, 1989.

Michel, Otto. *Der Brief an die Römer*. 5th ed. Kritisch-exegetischer Kommentar über das neu Testament, ed. Ferdinand Hahn, vol. 4. Göttingen: Vandenhoeck & Ruprecht, 1978.

Minette de Tillesse, G. *Le secret messianique dans L'Evangile de Marc.* Lectio divina, vol. 47. Paris: Cerf, 1968.

Montefiore, C. G. *The Synoptic Gospels.* Vol. 1. London: Allen & Unwin, 1909.

Moo, Douglas J. *The Epistle to the Romans.* New International Commentary on the New Testament, ed. Gordon D. Fee. Grand Rapids: Eerdmans, 1996.

Morris, Leon. *The Gospel according to John: The English Text with Introduction, Exposition and Notes.* Grand Rapids: Eerdmans, 1971.

————. *The Gospel according to Matthew.* Grand Rapids: Eerdmans, 1992.

Motyer, J. Alec. *The Prophecy of Isaiah: An Introduction and Commentary.* Downers Grove, IL: InterVarsity, 1993.

Moule, C. F. D. *An Idiom Book of New Testament Greek.* 2d ed. Cambridge: Cambridge University Press, 1959.

Mount, Christopher. *Pauline Christianity: Luke-Acts and the Legacy of Paul.* Novum Testamentum Supplements, ed. C. K. Barrett, J. K. Elliott, A. J. Malherbe, M. J. J. Menken, M.M. Mitchell, and D. P. Moessner, vol. 104. Leiden: Brill, 2002.

Mullen, E. Theodore. *The Divine Council in Canaanite and Early Hebrew Literature.* Harvard Semitic Monographs, ed. F. M. Cross Jr., vol. 24. Chico, CA: Scholars Press, 1980.

Muraoka, Takamitzu. *Classical Syriac: A Basic Grammar with a Chrestomathy.* Porta Linguarum Orientalium, ed. Werner Diem and Franz Rosenthal, vol. 19. Wiesbaden: Harrassowitz, 1997.

Murphy, Roland. *Ecclesiastes.* Word Biblical Commentary, ed. David A. Hubbard, Glenn W. Barker, and John D. W. Watts, vol. 23A. Dallas, TX: Word, 1992.

Murray, Iain H. *Spurgeon and Hyper-Calvinism: The Battle for Gospel Preaching.* Edinburgh: Banner of Truth Trust, 1995.

Murray, John. *Redemption: Accomplished and Applied.* Grand Rapids: Eerdmans, 1955.

Nelson, Richard D. *Deuteronomy: A Commentary.* Old Testament Library, ed. James L. Mays, Carol A. Newsom, and David L. Petersen. Louisville, KY: Westminster; Knox, 2002.

Noll, Mark A., ed. *Confessions and Catechisms of the Reformation.* Grand Rapids: Baker, 1991.

Nolland, John. *Luke 1–9:20.* Word Biblical Commentary, ed. Ralph P. Martin, vol. 35A. Dallas: Word, 1989.

Oesterley, W. O. E. *The Gospel Parables in the Light of their Jewish Background.* London: SPCK, 1936.

Ogilvie, Lloyd J. *Ecclesiastes, Song of Solomon.* The Communicator's Commentary, ed. Lloyd J. Ogilvie, vol. 15b. Dallas, TX: Word, 1991.

Packer, J. I., and Sven K. Soderlund, eds. *The Way of Wisdom: Essays in Honor of Bruce W. Waltke.* Grand Rapids: Zondervan, 2000.

Paul, Shalom M. *Amos.* Hermeneia—A Critical and Historical Commentary on the Bible, ed. Frank Moore Cross Jr., Klaus Baltzer, Paul D. Hanson Jr., S. Dean McBride, Peter Machinist, and Roland E. Murphy. Minneapolis: Fortress, 1991.

Pence, Gregory. *A Dictionary of Common Philosophical Terms.* New York: McGraw-Hill, 2000.

Pentecost, J. Dwight. *Thy Kingdom Come.* Wheaton, IL: Victor, 1990.

Pesch, Rudolf. *Das Markusevangelium.* Vol. 1. Handkommentar zum Neuen Testament, ed. Alfred Wilkenhauser, Anton Vögtle, and Rudolf Bultmann, vol. 2. Freiburg: Herder, 1984.

Pinnock, Clark H., ed. *The Grace of God and the Will of Man: A Case for Arminianism*. Minneapolis: Bethany, 1995.

———. *The Most Moved Mover: A Theology of God's Openness*. Grand Rapids: Baker, 2001.

Piper, John. *The Justification of God: An Exegetical & Theological Study of Romans 9:1–23*. 2d ed. Grand Rapids: Baker, 1993.

———, Justin Taylor, and Paul Kjoss Helseth., eds. *Beyond the Bounds: Open Theism and the Undermining of Biblical Christianity*. Wheaton, IL: Crossway, 2003.

Placher, William C. *The Domestication of Transcendence: How Modern Thinking about God Went Wrong*. Louisville, KY: Westminster; Knox, 1996.

Plummer, Alfred. *A Critical and Exegetical Commentary on the Gospel according to St. Luke*. 5th ed. International Critical Commentary, ed. S. R. Driver and C. A. Briggs. Edinburgh: Clark, 1964.

Porter, Stanley E. *Verbal Aspect in the Greek of the New Testament, with Reference to Tense and Mood*. Studies in Biblical Greek, ed. D. A. Carson, vol. 1. New York: Lang, 1989.

———. *Idioms of the Greek New Testament*. 2d ed. Biblical Languages, vol. 2. Sheffield: Sheffield Academic Press, 1994.

Prior, Authur. *Papers on Time and Tense*. Oxford: Clarendon, 1968.

———. *Past, Present and Future*. Oxford: Clarendon, 1968.

Pulikottil, Paulson. *Transmission of Biblical Texts in Qumran: The Case of the Large Isaiah Scroll 1QIsaᵃ*. Journal for the Study of the Pseudepigrapha: Supplement Series, ed. Lester L. Grabbe and James H. Charlesworth, vol. 34. Sheffield: Sheffield Academic Press, 2001.

Quinn-Miscall, Peter D. *A Nightmare/A Dream*. Journal for the Study of the Old Testament: Supplement Series, ed. David J. A. Clines and Philip R. Davies, vol. 281. Sheffield: Sheffield Academic Press, 1999.

———. *Reading Isaiah: Poetry and Vision*. Louisville, KY: Westminster; Knox, 2001.

Rad, Gerhard von. *Deuteronomy: A Commentary*. Translated by Dorothea M. Barton. Old Testament Library, ed. G. Ernest Wright, John Bright, James Barr, and Peter Ackroyd. Philadelphia: Westminster, 1966.

———. *Message of the Prophets*. Translated by D. M. G. Stalker. New York: Harper & Row, 1965.

———. *Old Testament Theology*. Translated by D. M. G. Stalker. Vol. 2. New York: Harper & Row, 1962.

———. *Wisdom in Israel*. Translated by James D. Martin. London: Abingdon; SCM, 1972.

Räisänen, Heikki. *The Idea of Divine Hardening: A Comparative Study of the Notion of Divine Hardening, Leading Astray and Inciting to Evil in the Bible and the Qur'an*. Publications of the Finnish Exegetical Society, vol. 25. Helsinki: Finnish Exegetical Society, 1976.

———. *Die Parabeltheorie im Markusevangelium*. Schriften der finnischen exegetischen Gesellschaft, vol. 25. Helsinki: Finnish Exegetical Society, 1973.

Rauscher, Johann. *Vom Messiasgeheimnis zur Lehre der Kirche: die Entwicklung der sogenannten Parabeltheorie in der synoptischen Tradition (Mk 4, 10–12 par Mt 13, 10–17 par Lk 8, 9–10)*. Desselbrunn, Austria: Rauscher, 1990.

Ridderbos, Herman N. *Paul: An Outline of His Theology*. Translated by John Richard de Witt. Grand Rapids: Eerdmans, 1975.

Robertson, A. T. *A Grammar of the Greek New Testament in the Light of Historical Research*. 4th ed. Nashville: Broadman, 1934.

———. *Word Pictures in the New Testament*. Vol. 1, *Matthew and Mark*. Nashville, TN: Broadman, 1930.

———, and W. Hersey Davis. *A New Short Grammar of the Greek Testament*. Grand Rapids: Baker, 1958.

Robertson, O. Palmer. *The Israel of God: Yesterday, Today, and Tomorrow*. Philipsburg, NJ: P & R Publishers, 2000.

Robinson, James M. *The Problem of History in Mark*. Studies in Biblical Theology, vol. 21. London: SCM, 1957.

Röhser, Günter. *Prädestination und Verstockung: Untersuchungen zur frühjüdischen, paulinischen und johanneischen Theologie*. Texte und Arbeiten zum neutestamentlichen Zeitlalter, ed. Klaus Berger, François Vouga, Michael Wolter, and Dieter Zeller, vol. 14. Tübingen: Francke, 1994.

Ross, Allen P. *Introducing Biblical Hebrew*. Grand Rapids: Baker, 2001.

Sacks, Oliver W. *An Anthropologist on Mars: Seven Paradoxical Tales*. Berkley, CA: University of California Press, 1996.

Sanders, John. *The God Who Risks: A Theology of Providence*. Downers Grove, IL: InterVarsity, 1998.

Sanders, E. P. *Paul and Palestinian Judaism: A Comparison of Patterns of Religion*. London: SCM, 1977.

Sarna, Nahum M. *Exodus: The Traditional Hebrew Text with the New JPS Translation*. The JPS Torah Commentary, ed. Nahum M. Sarna and Chaim Potok. Philadelphia: Jewish Publication Society, 1991.

Schaff, Philip. *History of the Christian Church*. Vol. 3. New York: Scribner, 1867. Reprint, Grand Rapids: Eerdmans, 1952–53.

Schlatter, Adolf. *Romans: The Rightousness of God*. Translated by Siegfried S. Schatzmann. Peabody, MA: Hendrickson, 1995.

Schnabel, Eckhard J. *Law and Wisdom from Ben Sira to Paul: A Traditional Historical Enquiry into the Relation of Law, Wisdom, and Ethics*. Wissenschaftliche Untersuchungen zum Alten und Neuen Testament, ed. Martin Hengel and Otfried Hofius, vol. 16. Tübingen: Mohr, 1985.

Schnackenburg, Rudolf. *The Gospel according to St. John. Volume Three: Commentary on Chapters 13–21*. Translated by David Smith and Richard Foley. Handcommentar zum Neuen Testament, ed. Sarafin de Ausejo et al. New York: Crossroad, 1982.

Schökel, Luis Alonso. *A Manual of Hebrew Poetics*. Translated by Luis Alonso Schökel and Adrian Gaffy. Subsidia biblica, vol. 11. Rome: Editrice Pontificio Istituto Biblico, 1988.

Schreiner, Thomas R., and Bruce A. Ware, eds. *Still Sovereign: Contemporary Perspectives on Election, Foreknowledge, and Grace*. Grand Rapids: Baker, 2000.

Schweitzer, Albert. *The Mystery of the Kingdom of God: The Secret of Jesus' Messiahship and Passion*. Translated by Walter Lowrie. New York: Dodd; Mead, 1914.

———. *The Quest of the Historical Jesus*. Translated by W. Montgomery. 2d. ed. London: Black, 1911.

Schweizer, Eduard. *The Good News according to St. Mark*. Richmond, VA: Knox, 1970.

Scott, James M. *2 Corinthians*. New International Biblical Commentary on the New Testament. Peabody, MA: Hendrickson, 1998.

Scott, R. B. Y. *The Way of Wisdom in the Old Testament*. New York: Macmillan, 1971.

Searle, J. R. *Speech Acts: An Essay in the Philosophy of Language*. Cambridge: Cambridge University Press, 1969.

Sheppard, Gerald T. *Wisdom as a Hermeneutical Construct: A Study in the Sapientalizing of the Old Testament*. Beihefte zur Zeitschrift für die alttestamentliche Wissenschaft, ed. Georg Fohrer, vol. 151. Berlin: de Gruyter; New York, 1980.

Shires, Henry M. *Finding the Old Testament in the New*. Philadelphia: Westminster, 1974.

Shupak, Nili. *Where Can Wisdom be Found? The Sage's Language in the Bible and in Ancient Egyptian Literature*. Orbis biblicus et orientalis, ed. Othmar Keel, vol. 130. Göttingen: Vandenhoeck & Ruprecht, 1993.

Sider, John W. *Interpreting the Parables*. Grand Rapids: Zondervan, 1995.

Silva, Moisés. *Biblical Words and their Meaning: An Introduction to Lexical Semantics*. Rev. and exp. ed. Grand Rapids: Zondervan, 1994.

Sjöberg, E. *Der verborgene Menschensohn in den Evangelien*. Lund: Gleerup, 1955.

Smyth, Herbert Weir. *Greek Grammar*. Edited by Gordon M. Messing. Rev. ed. Cambridge, MA: Harvard University Press, 1956.

Sproul, R. C. *Not a Chance: The Myth of Chance in Modern Science & Cosmology*. Grand Rapids: Baker, 2000.

———. *Willing to Believe: The Controversy over Free Will*. Grand Rapids: Baker, 1997.

Stuhlmacher, Peter. *Paul's Letter to the Romans: A Commentary*. Translated by Scott J. Hafemann. Louisville, KY: Westminster, 1994.

Suhl, Alfred. *Die Funktion der alttestamentlichen Zitaten und Anspielungen im Markusevangelium*. Gütersloh: Mohn, 1965.

Taylor, Richard. *Metaphysics*. 3d ed. Foundation of Philosophy Series, ed. Elizabeth Beardsley, Monroe Beardsley, and Tom L. Beauchamp, vol. 18. Englewood Cliffs, NJ: Prentice-Hall, 1983.

Taylor, Vincent. *The Formation of the Gospel Tradition*. London: Macmillan, 1935.

———. *The Gospel according to St. Mark: The Greek Text with Introduction, Notes, and Indexes*. 2d ed. London: Macmillan, 1966.

Tillesse, Minette de. *Le Secret Messianique dans L'evangile de Marc*. Lectio divina, vol. 47. Paris: Cerf, 1968.

Urbach, E. E. *The Sages: Their Concepts and Beliefs*. 2 vols. Jerusalem: Magnes, 1975.

Ussishkin, David. *The Conquest of Lachish by Sennacherib*. Tel Aviv: Tel Aviv University Publications of the Institute of Archeology, 1982.

Varvis, Stephen. *The "Consolation" of Boethius: An Analytical Inquiry into His Intellectual Processes and Goals*. Vol. 16. Distinguished Dissertation Series. San Francisco: Mellen, 1991.

Vermes, Geza, and Pamela Vermes. *The Dead Sea Scrolls: Qumran in Perspective*. Philadelphia: Fortress, 1977.

Wallace, Daniel B. *Greek Grammar beyond The Basics: An Exegetical Syntax of the New Testament*. Grand Rapids: Zondervan, 1996.

Wallace, Stan W., ed. *Does God Exist? The Craig-Flew Debate*. Burlington, VT: Ashgate, 2003.

Waltke, Bruce K. *Genesis*. Grand Rapids: Zondervan, 2001.

———, and M. O'Connor. *An Introduction to Biblical Hebrew Syntax*. Winona Lake, IN: Eisenbrauns, 1990.

Ware, Bruce A. *God's Lesser Glory: The Diminished God of Open Theism*. Wheaton, IL: Crossway, 2000.

Wenham, Gordon J. *Genesis 1–15*. Word Biblical Commentary, ed. John D. W. Watts, vol. 1. Waco, TX: Word, 1987.

Westermann, Claus. *Genesis 1–11: A Commentary*. Translated by John J. Scullion. London: SPCK, 1984.

Whedbee, William J. *Isaiah and Wisdom*. Nashville: Abingdon, 1971.

White, James R. *The Potter's Freedom: A Defense of the Reformation and a Rebuttal of Norman Geisler's Chosen But Free*. Amityville, NY: Calvary, 2000.

Whybray, R. N. *Ecclesiastes*. New Century Bible Commentary, ed. Ronald E. Clements. Grand Rapids: Eerdmans, 1989.

Wildberger, Hans. *Isaiah 1–12*. Translated by Thomas H. Trapp. Continental Commentaries. Minneapolis: Fortress, 1991.

————. *Jesaja 28–39: Das Buch der Prophet un seine Botschaft*. Biblischer Kommentar altes Testament, ed. M. Noth and H. W. Wolff, vol. 10. Nuekirchen-Vluyn: Neukirchener, 1982.

Wilkinson, David. *God, The Big Bang and Stephen Hawking*. Grand Rapids: Monarch, 1993.

————. *God, Time and Stephen Hawking*. Grand Rapids: Monarch, 2001.

Williams, Ronald J. *Hebrew Syntax: An Outline*. 2d ed. Toronto: University of Toronto Press, 1976.

Williamson, H. G. M. *The Book Called Isaiah: Deutero-Isaiah's Role in Composition and Redaction*. Oxford: Clarendon, 1994.

Wilson, Douglas, ed. *Bound Only Once: The Failure of Open Theism*. Moscow, ID: Canon, 2001.

Wise, Michael, Martin Abegg, Jr., and Edwin Cook. *The Dead Sea Scrolls: A New Translation*. San Francisco: HarperSanFrancisco, 1996.

Witherington, Ben III. *The Gospel of Mark: A Socio-Rhetorical Commentary*. Grand Rapids: Eerdmans, 2001.

————. *Jesus the Seer: The Progress of Prophecy*. Peabody, MA: Hendrickson, 1999.

————. *Paul's Narrative Thought World: The Tapestry of Tragedy and Triumph*. Louisville, KY: Westminster and Knox, 1994.

Wolff, Hans Walter. *Anthropology of the Old Testament*. Translated by Margaret Kohl. Philadelphia: Fortress, 1974. Reprint, Miffintown, PA: Sigler, 1996.

————. *Joel and Amos*. Edited by S. Dean McBride Jr. Translated by Waldemar Janzen, S. Dean McBride Jr., and Charles A. Muenchow. Hermeneia—A Critical and Historical Commentary on the Bible, ed. Frank Moore Cross Jr., Klaus Baltzer, Paul D. Hanson, S. Dean McBride Jr., and Roland E. Murphy, vol. 14. Minneapolis: Fortress, 1977.

Wrede, William. *The Messianic Secret*. Translated by J. C. G. Greig. Cambridge: Clarke, 1971.

Wuest, Kenneth S. *Romans in the Greek New Testament*. Wuest's Word Studies. Grand Rapids: Eerdmans, 1955.

Yadin, Yigael. *The Art of Warfare in Biblical Lands*. London: Weidenfield & Nicolson, 1963.

Young, Richard A. *Intermediate New Testament Greek: A Linguistic and Exegetical Approach*. Nashville: Broadman & Holman, 1994.

Zemek, George J. *Doing God's Business God's Way: A Biblical Theology of Ministry*. Mango, FL: Doing God's Business God's Way, n.d.

Zerwick, Max. *Biblical Greek Illustrated by Examples*. Translated by Joseph Smith. Scripta Pontificii, vol. 114. Rome: Editrice Pontificio Istituto Biblico, 1963.

Essays

Barton, Stephen C. "Gospel Wisdom." In *Where Shall Wisdom Be Found? Wisdom in the Bible, the Church, and the Contemporary World*, ed. Stephen C. Barton, 93–110. Edinburgh: Clark, 1999.

Beare, Francis W. "Romans, Letter to the." In *The Interpreter's Dictionary of the Bible: An Illustrated Encyclopedia*, ed. George Authur Buttrick, vol. 4, 112–22. New York: Abingdon, 1962.

Behm, Johannes. "ἔξω." In *Theological Dictionary of the New Testament*, ed. Gerhard Kittel, trans. Geoffrey W. Bromiley, vol. 2, 575–76. Grand Rapids: Eerdmans, 1964.

Bornkamm, Günther. "μυστήριον." In *Theological Dictionary of the New Testament*, ed. Gerhard Kittel, trans. Geoffrey W. Bromiley, vol. 4, 813–17. Grand Rapids: Eerdmans, 1967.

Bock, Darrell L. "The Words of Jesus in the Gospels: Live, Jive, or Memorex?" In *Jesus under Fire*, ed. Michael J. Wilkins and J. P. Moreland, 73–99. Grand Rapids: Zondervan, 1995.

Boyd, Gregory A. "The Open-Theism View." In *Divine Foreknowledge: Four Views*, ed. James K. Beilby and Paul R. Eddy, 13–47. Downers Grove, IL: InterVarsity, 2001.

———. "An Open-Theism Response (to Simple-Foreknowledge)." In *Divine Foreknowledge: Four Views*, ed. James K. Beilby and Paul R. Eddy, 104–108. Downers Grove, IL: InterVarsity, 2001.

———. "An Open-Theism Response (to Middle-Knowledge)." In *Divine Foreknowledge: Four Views*, ed. James K. Beilby and Paul R. Eddy, 144–48. Downers Grove, IL: InterVarsity, 2001.

———. "An Open-Theism Response (to Augustinian-Calvinist)." In *Divine Foreknowledge: Four Views*, ed. James K. Beilby and Paul R. Eddy, 190–94. Downers Grove, IL: InterVarsity, 2001.

Bruce, F. F. "The Book of Daniel and the Qumran Community." In *Neotestamentica et Semitica: Studies in Honour of Matthew Black*, ed. E. Earl Ellis and Max Wilcox, 221–35. Edinburgh: Clark, 1969.

Bultmann, Rudolf. "γινώσκω." In *Theological Dictionary of the New Testament*, ed. Gerhard Kittel, trans. Geoffrey W. Bromiley, vol. 1, 689–719. Grand Rapids: Eerdmans, 1964.

Childs, Brevard S. "Midrash and the Old Testament." In *Understanding the Sacred Text: Essays in Honor of Morton S. Enslin on the Hebrew Bible and Christian Beginnings*, ed. John Beumann, F. W. Beare, Sheldon H. Blank, and John L. McKenzie, 47–59. Valley Forge, PA: Judson, 1972.

Cohen, C. "Wisdom/Wisdom Literature." In *The Oxford Dictionary of the Jewish Religion*, ed. R. J. Zwi Werblowsky and Geoffrey Wigoder, 722–23. New York: Oxford University Press, 1997.

Collins, C. John. "כָּבֵד." In *New International Dictionary of Old Testament Theology & Exegesis*, ed. Willem A. VanGemeren, vol. 1, 557–87. Grand Rapids: Zondervan, 1992.

Coppes, Leonard J. "קָשָׁה." In *Theological Wordbook of the Old Testament*, ed. R. Laird Harris, Gleason L. Archer Jr., and Bruce K. Waltke, vol. 2, 818. Chicago: Moody, 1980.

Craig, William Lane. "A Middle-Knowledge Response (to Open-Theism)." In *Divine Foreknowledge: Four Views*, ed. James K. Beilby and Paul R. Eddy, 55–60. Downers Grove, IL: InterVarsity, 2001.

———. "A Middle-Knowledge Response (to Simple-Foreknowledge)." In *Divine Foreknowledge: Four Views*, ed. James K. Beilby and Paul R. Eddy, 109–13. Downers Grove, IL: InterVarsity, 2001.

———. "The Middle-Knowledge View." In *Divine Foreknowledge: Four Views*, ed. James K. Beilby and Paul R. Eddy, 119–43. Downers Grove, IL: InterVarsity, 2001.

———. "A Middle-Knowledge Response (to Augustinian-Calvinist)." In *Divine Foreknowledge: Four Views*, ed. James K. Beilby and Paul R. Eddy, 202–206. Downers Grove, IL: InterVarsity, 2001.

———. "Politically Correct Salvation." In *Christian Apologetics in the Postmodern World*, ed. Timothy R. Phillips and Dennis L. Ockholm, 75–97. Downers Grove, IL: InterVarsity, 1995.

Craig, William Lane., and Antony Flew. "The Craig-Flew Debate." In *Does God Exist? The Craig-Flew Debate*, ed. Stan W. Wallace, 17–47. Burlington, VT: Ashgate, 2003.

Daube, David. "Public Retort and Private Explanation." In *The New Testament and Rabbinic Judaism*, 141–50. London: Athlone, 1956.

Eakin, Frank E. "Spiritual Obduracy and Parable Purpose." In *The Use of the Old Testament in the New and Other Essays: Studies in Honor of William Franklin Stinespring*, ed. James M. Efird, 87–107. Durham, NC: Duke University Press, 1972.

Elderen, Bastiaan van. "The Purpose of the Parables according to Matthew 13:10–17." In *New Dimensions in New Testament Study*, ed. Richard N. Longenecker and Merrell C. Tenney, 180–90. Grand Rapids: Zondervan, 1974.

Evans, Craig A. "Hardness of Heart." In *Dictionary of Jesus and the Gospels*, ed. Joel B. Green, Scot McKnight and I. Howard Marshall, 298–99. Downers Grove, IL: InterVarsity, 1992.

———. "Obduracy and the Lord's Servant: Some Observations on the Use of the Old Testament in the Fourth Gospel." In *Early Jewish and Christian Exegesis: Studies in Memory of William Hugh Brownlee*, ed. Craig A. Evans and William F. Stinespring, vol. 10, 221–36. Atlanta: Scholars Press, 1987.

Fabry, H. -J. "לֵבָב/לֵב." In *Theological Dictionary of the Old Testament*, ed. G. Johannes Botterweck and Helmer Ringgren, vol. 7, 427–28. Grand Rapids: Eerdmans, 1995.

Fichtner, Johannes. "Jesaja unter den Weisen." In *Gottes Weisheit: Gesammelte Studien zum alten Testament*, vol. 2, 18–26. Stuttgart: Calwer, 1965.

Fitzmyer, Joseph A. "The Use of the Old Testament in Luke-Acts." In *Society of Biblical Literature Seminar Papers 1992*, ed. Eugene H. Lovering Jr., vol. 31, 524–38. Atlanta: Scholars Press, 1992.

Flew, Antony. "A Reply to my Critics." In *Does God Exist? The Craig-Flew Debate*, ed. Stan W. Wallace, 189–220. Burlington, VT: Ashgate, 2003.

Flint, Thomas P. "Two Accounts of Providence." In *Divine and Human Action: Essays in the Metaphysics of Theism*, ed. Thomas V. Morris, 147–81. Ithica, NY: Cornell University Press, 1988.

Geisler, Norman L. "God Knows All Things." In *Predestination & Free Will: Four Views of Divine Sovereignty & Human Freedom,* ed. David Basinger and Randall Basinger, 63–84. Downers Grove, IL: InterVarsity, 1986.

Goetzmann, J., and C. Brown. "Σοφία." In *The New International Dictionary of New Testament Theology,* ed. Colin Brown, trans. G. H. Boobyer et al., vol. 3, 1026–33. Grand Rapids: Zondervan, 1986.

Grassmick, John D. "Mark." In *The Bible Knowledge Commentary: An Exposition of the Scriptures by Dallas Seminary Faculty,* ed. John F. Walvoord and Roy B. Zuck, vol. 2, 95–197. Wheaton, IL: Victor, 1983.

Gunn, David M. "The 'Hardening of Pharaoh's Heart': Plot, Character and Theology in Exodus 1–14." In *Art and Meaning: Rhetoric in Biblical Literature,* ed. David J. A. Clines, David M. Gunn, and Alan J. Hauser. Journal for the Study of the Old Testament: Supplement Series, ed. David J. A. Clines and Philip R. Davies, vol. 19, 72–96. Sheffield: JSOT, 1982.

Hauck, F. "παραβολή." In *Theological Dictionary of the New Testament,* ed. Gerhard Friedrich, trans. Geoffrey W. Bromiley, vol. 5, 744–61. Grand Rapids: Eerdmans, 1967.

Hays, Richard B. "PISTIS and Pauline Christology: What Is at Stake?" In *Society of Biblical Literature Seminar Papers 1991,* ed. David J. Lull. Atlanta: Scholars Press, 1991, 714–29.

Helm, Paul. "An Augustinian-Calvinist Response (to Open-Theism)." In *Divine Foreknowledge: Four Views,* ed. James K. Beilby and Paul R. Eddy, 61–4. Downers Grove, IL: InterVarsity, 2001.

————. "An Augustinian-Calvinist Response (to Simple-Foreknowledge)." In *Divine Foreknowledge: Four Views,* ed. James K. Beilby and Paul R. Eddy, 114–18. Downers Grove, IL: InterVarsity, 2001.

————. "An Augustinian-Calvinist Response (to Middle-Knowledge)." In *Divine Foreknowledge: Four Views,* ed. James K. Beilby and Paul R. Eddy, 155–59. Downers Grove, IL: InterVarsity, 2001.

————. "The Augustinian-Calvinist View." In *Divine Foreknowledge: Four Views,* ed. James K. Beilby and Paul R. Eddy, 161–89. Downers Grove, IL: InterVarsity, 2001.

————. "Response to Alan G. Padgett." In *God and Time: Four Views,* ed. Gregory E. Ganssle, 111–14. Downers Grove, IL: InterVarsity, 2001.

————. "Response to Nicholas Wolterstorff." In *God & Time: Four Views,* ed. Gregory E. Ganssle, 214–18. Downers Grove, IL: InterVarsity, 2001.

————. "Response to William Lane Craig." In *God & Time: Four Views,* ed. Gregory E. Ganssle, 161–64. Downers Grove, IL: InterVarsity, 2001.

Hesse, F. "חזק." In *Theological Dictionary of the Old Testament,* ed. G. Johannes Botterweck and Helmer Ringgren, trans. David E. Green, vol. 4, 301–8. Grand Rapids: Eerdmans, 1980.

Horst, Johannes. "οὖς." In *Theological Dictionary of the New Testament,* ed. Gerhard Kittel, trans. Geoffrey W. Bromiley, vol. 5, 543–58. Grand Rapids: Eerdmans, 1967.

Hunt, David P. "A Simple-Foreknowledge Response (to Open-Theism)." In *Divine Foreknowledge: Four Views,* ed. James K. Beilby and Paul R. Eddy, 48–54. Downers Grove, IL: InterVarsity, 2001.

————. "The Simple-Foreknowledge View." In *Divine Foreknowledge: Four Views*, ed. James K. Beilby and Paul R. Eddy, 65–103. Downers Grove, IL: InterVarsity, 2001.

————. "A Simple-Foreknowledge Response (to Middle-Knowledge)." In *Divine Foreknowledge: Four Views*, ed. James K. Beilby and Paul R. Eddy, 149–54. Downers Grove, IL: InterVarsity, 2001.

————. "A Simple-Foreknowledge Response (to Augustinian-Calvinist)." In *Divine Foreknowledge: Four Views*, ed. James K. Beilby and Paul R. Eddy, 195–201. Downers Grove, IL: InterVarsity, 2001.

Kamlah, E., J. D. G. Dunn, and C. Brown. "Πνεῦμα," In The New International Dictionary of New Testament Theology, ed. Colin Brown, trans. G. H. Boobyer et al., vol. 3, 689–709. Grand Rapids: Zondervan, 1986.

Kee, Howard Clark. "Jesus: A Glutton and Drunkard." In *Authenticating The Words of Jesus*, ed. Bruce Chilton and Craig A. Evans, 311–32. Boston: Brill, 2002.

Kittel, Gerhard. "ἀκούω." In *Theological Dictionary of the New Testament*, ed. Gerhard Kittel, trans. Geoffrey W. Bromiley, vol. 1. Grand Rapids: Eerdmans, 1964.

Koehler, Ludwig, and Walter Baumgartner. "רוּחַ." In *The Hebrew and Aramaic Lexicon of the Old Testament*, rev. by Walter Baumgartner and Johann Jakob Stamm, trans. M. E. J. Richardson. Leiden: Brill, 1996, 1197–1201.

Kohn, Risa Levitt, and William H. C. Propp. "The Name of 'Second Isaiah': The Forgotten Theory of Nehemiah Rabban." In *Fortunate the Eyes That See: Essays in Honor of David Noel Freedman in Celebration of His Seventieth Birthday*, ed. Astrid B. Beck, Andrew H. Bartelt, Paul R. Raabe, and Chris A. Franke, 223–35. Grand Rapids: Eerdmans, 1995.

Locke, John. "An Essay Concerning Human Understanding." In *Lock, Berkeley, Hume*. Great Books of the Western World, ed. Robert Maynard Hutchins, Mortimer J. Adler, and Wallace Brockway, vol. 35, 83–395. Chicago: Encyclopedia Britannica, 1952.

Marcus, Joel. "Mark and Isaiah." In *Fortunate the Eyes That See: Essays in Honor of David Noel Freedman in Celebration of His Seventieth Birthday*, ed. Astrid B. Beck, Andrew H. Bartelt, Paul R. Raabe, and Chris A. Franke, 449–66. Grand Rapids: Eerdmans, 1995.

Meier, John P. "'Happy the Eyes That See': The Tradition, Message, and Authenticity of Luke 10:23–24." In *Fortunate the Eyes that See: Essays in Honor of David Noel Freedman in Celebration of His Seventieth Birthday*, ed. Astrid B. Beck, Andrew H. Bartelt, Paul R. Raabe, and Chris A. Franke, 467–77. Grand Rapids: Eerdmans, 1995.

Melugin, Roy F. "Introduction." In *New Visions of Isaiah*, ed. Roy F. Melugin and Marvin A. Sweeney. Journal for the Study of the Old Testament: Supplement Series, ed. David J. A. Clines and Philip R. Davies, vol. 214, 13–29. Atlanta: Scholars Press, 1996.

Meye, Robert P. "The Messianic Secret and Messianic Didache in Mark's Gospel." In *Oikonomia: Heilsgeschichte als Thema der Theologie*, ed. Felix Christ, 61–66. Hamburg-Bergstedt: Reich, 1967.

Michaelis, Wilhelm. "ὁράω." In *Theological Dictionary of the New Testament*, ed. Gerhard Kittel, trans. Geoffrey W. Bromiley, vol. 5, 315–67. Grand Rapids: Eerdmans, 1967.

Moule, C. F. D. "Mark v, 1–20 Yet Once More." In *Neotestamentica et Semitica: Studies in Honour of Matthew Black*, ed. E. Earl Ellis and Max Wilcox, 95–113. Edinburgh: Clark, 1969.

Oswalt, John N. "כָּבֵד." In *Theological Wordbook of the Old Testament*, ed. R. Laird Harris, Gleason L. Archer Jr., and Bruce K. Waltke, vol.1, 426–28. Chicago: Moody, 1980.

Packer, J. I. "Theology and Wisdom." In *The Way of Wisdom: Essays in Honor of Bruce K. Waltke*, ed. J. I. Packer and Sven K. Soderlund, 1–14. Grand Rapids: Zondervan, 2002.

Padgett, Alan G. "Eternity as Relative Timelessness." In *God & Time: Four Views*, ed. Gregory E. Ganssle, 92–110. Downers Grove, IL: InterVarsity, 2001.

Patzia, A. G. "Wisdom." In *Dictionary of the Later New Testament & Its Developments*, ed. Ralph P. Martin and Peter H. Davids, 1200–04. Downers Grove, IL: InterVarsity, 1997.

Rad, Gerhard von. "The Joseph Narrative and Ancient Wisdom." In *The Problem of the Hexateuch and other Essays*, trans. E. W. Trueman Dicken. New York: McGraw Hill, 1966, 281–91.

Rendtorff, Rolf. "The Book of Isaiah: A Complex Unity. Synchronic and Diachronic Reading." In *New Visions of Isaiah*, ed. Roy F. Melugin and Marvin A. Sweeney. Journal for the Study of the Old Testament: Supplement Series, ed. David J. A. Clines and Philip R. Davies, vol. 214, 32–49. Atlanta: Scholars Press, 1996.

———. "Isaiah 6 in the Framework of the Composition of the Book." In *Canon and Theology*, ed. M. Kohl, trans. M. Kohl, 170–80. Minneapolis: Fortress, 1993.

Ringgren, Helmer. "בִּין." In *Theological Dictionary of the Old Testament*, ed. G. Johannes Botterweck and Helmer Ringgren, trans. John T. Willis, vol. 2, 99–107. Grand Rapids: Eerdmans, 1975.

Robertson, A. T. "The Causal Use of ὅτι." In *Studies in Early Christianity: Presented to Chamberlin Porter and Benjamin Wisner Bacon by Friends and Fellow-Teachers in America and Europe*, ed. Shirley Jackson Case, 49–57. New York: Century, 1928.

Rowe, William. "Reflections on the Craig-Flew Debate." In *Does God Exist? The Craig-Flew Debate*, ed. Stan W. Wallace, 65–73. Burlington, VT: Ashgate, 2003.

Saebo, M. "חכם." In *Theological Lexicon of the Old Testament*, ed. Ernst Jenni and Claus Westermann, vol. 1, 418–24. Peabody, MA: Hendrickson, 1997.

Sanders, James A. "From Isaiah 61 to Luke 4." In *Christianity, Judaism and Other Greco-Roman Cults: Studies for Morton Smith at Sixty*, ed. Jacob Neusner, vol. 1, 75–106. Leiden: Brill, 1975.

Schlier, H. "ἀμήν." In *Theological Dictionary of the New Testament*, ed. Gerhard Kittel, trans. Geoffrey W. Bromiley, vol. 1, 335–38. Grand Rapids: Eerdmans, 1964.

Schmidt, K. L., and M. A. Schmidt. "παχύνω," In *Theological Dictionary of the New Testament*, ed. Gerhard Kittel, trans. Geoffrey W. Bromiley, vol. 5, 1022–31. Grand Rapids: Eerdmans, 1967.

Schnabel, Eckhard J. "The Silence of Jesus: The Galilean Rabbi Who Was More Than a Prophet." In *Authenticating the Words of Jesus*, ed. Bruce Chilton and Craig A. Evans, 203–57. Boston: Brill, 2002.

———. "Wisdom." In *Dictionary of Paul and His Letters*, ed. G. F. Hawthorne, R. P. Martin and D. G. Reid, 967–73. Downers Grove, IL: InterVarsity, 1993.

Seitz, Christopher R. "Isaiah 1–66: Making Sense of the Whole." In *Reading and Preaching the Book of Isaiah*, ed. Christopher R. Seitz, 108–9. Philadelphia: Fortress, 1988.

Sheppard, Gerald T. "The Book of Isaiah: Competing Structures according to a Late Modern Description of Its Shape and Scope." In *Society of Biblical Literature Seminar Papers 1992*, ed. Eugene H. Lovering Jr., vol. 31, 549–82. Atlanta: Scholars Press, 1992.

———. "Wisdom." In *The International Standard Bible Encyclopedia*, rev. ed., ed. G. Bromiley, vol. 4, 1074–82. Grand Rapids: Eerdmans, 1988.

Snodgrass, Klyne. "Parable." In *Dictionary of Jesus and the Gospels*, ed. Joel B. Green, Scot McKnight and I. Howard Marshall, 591–601. Downers Grove, IL: InterVarsity, 1992.

———. "Parables and the Hebrew Scriptures." In *To Hear and Obey: Essays in Honor of Fredrick Carlson Holmgren*, ed. Bradley J. Bergfalk and Paul E. Koptak, 164–77. Chicago: Covenant Publications, 1997.

Stauffer, Ethelbert. "ἵνα." In *Theological Dictionary of the New Testament*, ed. Gerhard Kittel, trans. Geoffrey W. Bromiley, vol. 3, 323–33. Grand Rapids: Eerdmans, 1965.

Stendahl, Krister. "The Called and the Chosen. An Essay on Election." In *The Root of the Vine: Essays in Biblical Theology*, ed. Anton Fridrichson, 63–80. New York: Philosophical Library, 1953.

Stenmans, P. "כָּבֵד." In *Theological Dictionary of the Old Testament*, ed. G. Johannes Botterweck and Helmer Ringgren, trans. David E. Green, vol. 7, 13–22. Grand Rapids: Eerdmans, 1995.

Stolz, F. "לֵב." In *Theological Lexicon of the Old Testament*, ed. Ernst Jenni and Claus Westermann, vol. 2, 641. Peabody, MA: Hendrickson, 1997.

Tsevat, Matitiahu. "The Throne Vision of Isaiah." In *The Meaning of the Book of Job and Other Biblical Studies: Essays on the Literature and Religion of the Hebrew Bible*, 155–76. New York: Ktav, 1980.

Vriezen, T. C. "Essentials of the Theology of Isaiah." In *Israel's Prophetic Heritage: Essays in Honor of James Muilenburg*, ed. Bernhard W. Anderson and Walter Harrelson, 128–46. New York: Harper & Row, 1962.

Wakely, Robin. "חָזַק." In *New International Dictionary of Old Testament Theology & Exegesis*, ed. Willem A. VanGemeren, vol. 2, 63–87. Grand Rapids: Zondervan, 1992.

Walker, Larry and I. Swart. "קָשָׁה." In *New International Dictionary of Old Testament Theology & Exegesis*, ed. Willem A. VanGemeren, vol. 3, 997–99. Grand Rapids: Zondervan, 1997.

Weber, Carl Philip. "חָזַק." In *Theological Wordbook of the Old Testament*, ed. R. Laird Harris, Gleason L. Archer Jr., and Bruce K. Waltke, vol. 1, 276–77. Chicago: Moody, 1980.

Westermann, C. "כָּבֵד." In *Theological Lexicon of the Old Testament*, ed. Ernst Jenni and Claus Westermann, vol. 2, 590–602. Peabody, MA: Hendrickson, 1997.

Whybray, Roger N. "The Sage in The Israelite Royal Court." In *The Sage in Israel and the Ancient Near East*, ed. John G. Gammie and Leo G. Perdue, 133–39. Winona Lake, IN: Eisenbrauns, 1990.

———. "Wisdom, Suffering and the Freedom of God in the Book of Job." In *In Search of True Wisdom: Essays in Old Testament Interpretation in Honour of Ronald E.*

Clements, ed. Edward Ball. Journal for the Study of the Old Testament: Supplement Series, ed. David J. A. Clines and Philip R. Davies, vol. 300, 231–45. Sheffield: Sheffield Academic Press, 1999.

Wilckens, Ulrich. "σοφία." In *Theological Dictionary of the New Testament*, ed. Gerhard Kittel, trans. Geoffrey W. Bromiley, vol. 7, 465–528. Grand Rapids: Eerdmans, 1976.

Wilson, Gerald H. "חכם." In *New International Dictionary of Old Testament Theology & Exegesis*, ed. Willem A. VanGemeren, vol. 2, 130–34. Grand Rapids: Zondervan, 1992.

Wolterstorff, Nicholas. "Response to Alan G. Padgett." In *God & Time: Four Views*, ed. Gregory E. Ganssle, 120–23. Downers Grove, IL: InterVarsity, 2001.

———. "Unqualified Divine Temporality." In *God & Time: Four Views*, ed. Gregory E. Ganssle, 187–213. Downers Grove, IL: InterVarsity, 2001.

Woude, A. S. van der. "חָזַק." In *Theological Lexicon of the Old Testament*, ed. Ernst Jenni and Claus Westermann, vol. 1, 403–6. Peabody, MA: Hendrickson, 1997.

———. "קָשָׁה." In *Theological Lexicon of the Old Testament*, ed. Ernst Jenni and Claus Westermann, vol. 3, 1175–76. Peabody, MA: Hendrickson, 1997.

Yandell, Keith. "Some Issues in Theism and Atheism: Setting the Context." In *Does God Exist? The Craig-Flew Debate*, ed. Stan W. Wallace, 1–16. Burlington, VT: Ashgate, 2003.

———. "Theism, Atheism and Cosmology." In *Does God Exist? The Craig-Flew Debate*, ed. Stan W. Wallace, 95–114. Burlington, VT: Ashgate, 2003.

Zipor, H. "קָשָׁה." In *Theologisches Wöterbuch zum Alten Testament*, ed. G. Johannes Botterweck and Helmer Ringgren, vol. 7, 205–11. Stuttgart: Kohlhammer, 1993.

Periodicals

Aageson, James W. "Scripture and Structure in the Development of the Argument in Romans 9–11." *Catholic Biblical Quarterly* 48 (1986): 265–89.

Ackroyd, Peter R. "The Meaning of Hebrew דּוֹר Considered." *Journal of Semitic Studies* 13 (1968): 5–8.

Ambrozic, Aloysius M. "Mark's Concept of the Parable." *Catholic Biblical Quarterly* 29 (1967): 220–27.

Anderson, Hugh. Review of *Mark's Audience: The Literary and Social Setting of Mark 4.11–12*, by Mary Ann Beavis. *Journal of Theological Studies* 42 (1991): 657–58.

Anderson, R. T. "Was Isaiah a Scribe?" *Journal of Biblical Literature* 79 (1960): 57–58.

Arida, Robert M. "Hearing, Receiving and Entering ΤΟ ΜΥΣΤΗΡΙΟΝΤΑ ΜΥΣΤΗΡΙΑ: Patristic Insights Unveiling the *Crux Interpretum* (Isaiah 6:9–10) of the Sower Parable." *St. Vladimir's Theological Quarterly* 38 (1994): 211–34.

Atkinson, James. Review of *Bondage of the Will*, by Martin Luther. *Church Quarterly Review* 159 (1958): 450–51.

Bailey, Mark L. "The Parable of the Sower and the Soils." *Bibliotheca Sacra* 155 (1998): 172–88.

Baird, J. Arthur. "A Pragmatic Approach to Parable Exegesis: Some New Evidence on Mark 4:11, 33–34." *Journal of Biblical Literature* 76 (1957): 201–07.

Beale, G. K. "An Exegetical and Theological Consideration of the Hardening of Pharaoh's Heart in Exodus 4–14 and Romans 9." *Trinity Journal* 5 (1984): 129–54.

Beavis, Mary Ann. Review of *To See and Not Perceive: Isaiah 6.9–10 in Early Jewish and Christian Interpretation*, by Craig A. Evans. *Journal of Theological Studies* 42 (1991): 264–66.

Best, Ernest. "Mark's Use of the Twelve." *Zeitschrift für die neutestamentliche Wissenschaft* 69 (1978): 11–35.

———. "The Role of the Disciples in Mark." *New Testament Studies* 23 (1976–77): 377–401.

Blackman, E. C. "Divine Sovereignty and Missionary Strategy in Romans 9–11." *Canadian Journal of Theology* 11 (1965): 124–34.

Blakeney, E. H. "The 'Ecbatic' Use of ἵνα in N. T." *Expository Times* 53 (1941–42): 377–78.

Blocher, Henri. "The Fear of the Lord as the 'Principle' of Wisdom." *Tyndale Bulletin* 28 (1977): 3–28.

Blomberg, Craig L. "Interpreting Old Testament Prophetic Literature in Matthew: Double Fulfillment." *Trinity Journal* 23 (2002): 17–33.

Boers, Harry R. "The Doctrine of Reprobation and the Preaching of the Gospel." *The Reformed Journal* 15 (1965): 13–17.

———. "Reprobation: Does the Bible Teach It?" *The Reformed Journal* 25 (1975): 7–10.

Boyd, Gregory A. "Christian Love and Academic Dialogue: A Reply to Bruce Ware." *Journal of the Evangelical Theological Society* 45 (2002): 233–43.

Bowker, John W. "Mystery and Parable: Mark iv. 1–20." *Journal of Theological Studies* 25 (1974): 300–17.

Bröker, Günther. Review of *The Idea of Divine Hardening*, by Heikki Räisänen. *Theologische Literaturzeitung* 99 (1974): 338–42.

Brower, K. E. Review of *To See and Not Perceive: Isaiah 6.9–10 in Early Jewish and Christian Interpretation*, by Craig A. Evans. *Evangelical Quarterly* 63 (1991): 264–65.

Brown, Schuyler. "The Secret of the Kingdom of God (Mark 4, 11)." *Journal of Biblical Literature* 92 (1973): 60–74.

Brown, Raymond E. "The Pre-Christian Semitic Concept of 'Mystery'." *Catholic Biblical Quarterly* 20 (1958): 417–43.

———. "The Semitic Background of the NT *mustērion* (I)." *Biblica* 39 (1958): 426–48.

———. "The Semitic Background of the NT *mustērion* (II)." *Biblica* 40 (1959): 70–87.

Brownlee, William H. "The Text of Isaiah 6:13 in the Light of DSIa." *Vetus Testamentum* 1 (1951): 296–98.

Brunner, Hellmut. "Das Herz als Sitz des Lebengeheimnisses." *Archiv für Orientforschung* 17 (1954–55): 140–41.

———. "Das hörende Herz." *Theologische Literaturzeitung* 79 (1954): 697–700.

Cadbury, Henry J. "Lexical Notes on Luke-Acts; III, Luke's Interest in Lodging." *Journal of Biblical Literature* 45 (1926): 305–22.

Cadoux, C. J. "The Imperatival Use of ἵνα in the New Testament." *Journal of Theological Studies* 42 (1941–42): 165–73.

Caird, G. B. "Predestination—Romans 9–11." *Expository Times* 68 (1956–57): 324–27.

Campbell, D. A. "False Presuppositions in the ΠΙΣΤΙΣ ΧΡΙΣΤΟΥ Debate: A Response to Brian Dodd." *Journal of Biblical Literature* 116 (1997): 713–19.

———. "Romans 1:17—A Crux Interpretum for the ΠΙΣΤΙΣ ΧΡΙΣΤΟΥ Debate." *Journal of Biblical Literature* 113 (1994): 265–85.

Carmignac, Jean. Review of *Verstockung Israels, Isaias 6, 9–10 in der Theologie der Synoptiker*, by Joachim Gnilka. *Revue de Qumran* 3 (1962): 585–87.

Cerfaux, Lucien. "'L'aveuglement d'esprit' dans l'Évangile de Saint Marc." *Le Muséon* 59 (1946): 267–79.

———. "La connaissance des secrets du Royaume d'après Mt., 13, 11 et parallèles." *New Testament Studies* 2 (1955–56): 238–49.

Chilton, Bruce. Review of *To See and Not Perceive: Isaiah 6.9–10 in Early Jewish and Christian Interpretation*, by Craig A. Evans. *Critical Review of Books in Religion* (1991): 80–83.

Chisholm, Robert B. "Divine Hardening in The Old Testament." *Bibliotheca Sacra* 153 (1996): 410–34.

———. "Does God 'Change His Mind'?" *Bibliotheca Sacra* 152 (1995): 387–99.

———. "Does God Deceive?" *Bibliotheca Sacra* 155 (1998): 11–28.

Claassen, W. T. "Linguistic Arguments and the Dating of Isaiah 1:4–9." *Journal of Northwest Semitic Languages* 3 (1974): 1–18.

Clements, Ronald E. "The Unity of the Book of Isaiah." *Interpretation* 36 (1982): 117–29.

Cohen, Abraham. "חשע, הכבר, השמן." *Bet Mikra* 50 (1972): 360–61.

Coppens, J. Review of *Verstockung Israels, Isaias 6, 9–10 in der Theologie der Synoptiker*, by Joachim Gnilka. *Ephemerides theologicae lovanienses* 38 (1962): 117–19.

Crenshaw, J. L. "Method in Determining Wisdom Influence upon 'Historical' Literature." *Journal of Biblical Literature* 88 (1969): 129–42.

Cross, F. M. Jr. "The Council of Yahweh in Second Isaiah." *Journal of Near Eastern Studies* 12 (1953): 274–77.

———, and D. N. Freedman. "The Blessing of Moses." *Journal of Biblical Literature* 67 (1948): 191–210.

Danove, Paul. "The Narrative Rhetoric of Mark's Ambiguous Characterization of the Disciples." *Journal for the Study of the New Testament* 70 (1998): 21–38.

Daube, David. "Public Pronouncement and Private Explanation in the Gospels." *Expository Times* 57 (1945–46): 175–77.

Dodd, B. "Romans 1:17—A Crux Interpretum for the ΠΙΣΤΙΣ ΧΡΙΣΤΟΥ Debate?" *Journal of Biblical Literature* 114 (1995): 470–73.

Dodd, C. H. "The Dialogue Form in the Gospels." *Bulletin of the John Rylands University Library of Manchester* 37 (1954): 54–67.

Dupont, J. "Le chapitre des paraboles." *La nouvelle revue théologique* 89 (1967): 803–06.

Dvorak, James D. "The Relationship between John and the Synoptic Gospels." *Journal of the Evangelical Theological Society* 41 (1998): 201–13.

Ellis, E. Earle. "Perspectives on Biblical Interpretation: A Review Article." *Journal of the Evangelical Theological Society* 45 (2002): 473–95.

———. "Wisdom and Knowledge in 1 Corinthians." *Tyndale Bulletin* 25 (1974): 82–98.

Essame, W. G. "Καὶ ἔλεγεν in Mark iv. 21, 24, 26, 30." *Expository Times* 77 (1965–66): 121.

Evans, Craig A. "The Function of Isaiah 6:9–10 in Mark and John." *Novum Testamentum* 24 (1982): 124–28.

———. "An Interpretation of Isa. 8.11–15 Unemended." *Zeitschrift für die alttestamentliche Wissenschaft* 97 (1985): 112–13.

———. "On Isaiah's Use of Israel's Sacred Tradition." *Biblische Zeitschrift* 30 (1986): 92–99.

———. "On the Isaianic Background of the Sower Parable." *Catholic Biblical Quarterly* 47 (1985): 464–68.

————. "A Note on the Function of Isaiah VI, 9–10 in Mark, IV." *Revue biblique* 88 (1981): 234–35.

————. "1QIsaiah³ and the Absence of Prophetic Critique at Qumran." *Revue de Qumran* 11 (1984): 537–42.

————. "The Text of Isaiah 6.9–10." *Zeitschrift für die alttestamentliche Wissenschaft* 94 (1982): 415–18.

————. "On the Unity and Parallel Structure of Isaiah." *Vetus Testamentum* 38 (1988): 129–47.

Fay, Greg. "Introduction to Incomprehension: The Literary Structure of Mark 4:1–34." *Catholic Biblical Quarterly* 51 (1989): 65–81.

Feinberg, John. "Divine Causality and Evil: Is There Anything Which God Does Not Do?" *Christian Scholar's Review* 16 (1987): 394–402.

Fichtner, Johannes. "Jahwes Plan in der Botschaft des Jesaja." *Zeitschrift für die alttestamentliche Wissenschaft* 63 (1951): 16–33.

————. "Jesaja unter dem Weisen." *Theologische Literaturzeitung* 74 (1949): 75–80.

Flusser, David. Review of *Prädestination und Verstockung*, by Günter Röhser. *Journal for the Study of Judaism in the Persian, Hellenistic, and Roman Periods* 26 (1995): 372–73.

Ford, Mary. "Seeing, But Not Perceiving: Crisis and Context in Biblical Studies." *St. Vladimir's Theological Quarterly* 35 (1991): 107–25.

Gallagher, Eugene V. Review of *Mark's Audience: The Literary and Social Setting of Mark 4.11–12*, by Mary Ann Beavis. *Catholic Biblical Quarterly* 53 (1991): 692–93.

Garland, David E. Review of *To See and Not Perceive: Isaiah 6.9–10 in Early Jewish and Christian Interpretation*, by Craig A. Evans. *Review and Expositor* 89 (1992): 413–14.

Garrett, James L. Review of *Bondage of the Will*, by Martin Luther. *Southwest Journal of Theology* 4 (1961): 118–19.

Gealy, Fred D. "The Composition of Mark 4." *Expository Times* 48 (1936–37): 40–43.

Gerhardsson, Birger. "The Parable of the Sower and its Interpretation." *New Testament Studies* 14 (1967–68): 165–93.

Gitay, Yehoshua. "Prophetic Criticism—'What Are They Doing?' The Case of Isaiah—A Methodological Assessment." *Journal for the Study of the Old Testament* 96 (2001): 101–27.

Glaassen, W. T. "Linguistic Arguments and the Dating of Isaiah 1:4–9." *Journal of Northwest Semitic Languages* 3 (1974): 1–18.

Godbey, Allen Howard. "The Hebrew *māšāl*." *American Journal of Semitic Languages and Literature* 39 (1922–24): 89–108.

Goulder, Michael D. "Those Outside (MK. 4:10–12)." *Novum Testamentum* 33 (1991): 289–302.

Grappe, Charles. Review of *Prädestination und Verstockung*, by Günter Röhser. *Revue d'histoire ecclésiastique* 77 (1997): 206.

Grenz, Stanley J. "*Die begrentzte Gemeinschaft* ('The Boundaried People') and the Character of Evangelical Theology." *Journal of the Evangelical Theological Society* 45 (2002): 301–16.

Grosse, Bernard. "Isaïe 52,13–53,12 et Isaïe 6." *Revue biblique* 98 (1991): 537–43.

Habel, N. "The Form and Significance of the Call Narratives." *Zeitschrift für die alttestamentliche Wissenschaft* 77 (1965): 297–323.

Hanges, James C. Review of *Prädestination und Verstockung*, by Günter Röhser. *Critical Review of Books in Religion* 9 (1996): 262–64.

Hanson, Anthony. "The Oracle in Romans 11:4." *New Testament Studies* 19 (1972–73): 300–302.

———. Review of *To See and Not Perceive: Isaiah 6.9–10 in Early Jewish and Christian Interpretation,* by Craig A. Evans. *Expository Times* 101 (1989–90): 212.

Hasel, Gerhard F. "Linguistic Considerations Regarding the Translation of Isaiah's 'Shear-jashub'." *Andrews University Seminary Studies* 9 (1971): 36–46.

Heflin, Boo. Review of *To See and Not Perceive: Isaiah 6.9–10 in Early Jewish and Christian Interpretation,* by Craig A. Evans. *Scottish Journal of Theology* 34 (1992): 37–38.

Highfield, Ron. "The Function of Divine Self-Limitation in Open Theism: Great Wall or Picket Fence?" *Journal of the Evangelical Theological Society* 45 (2002): 279–99.

Hollenbach, Bruce. "Lest They Should Turn and Be Forgiven: Irony." *The Bible Translator* 34 (1983): 312–21.

Holzmeister, Urban. Review of *Ut videntes non videant,* by Francesco La Cava. *Biblica* 17 (1936): 512–14.

Horton, Michael S. "Hellenistic or Hebrew? Open Theism and Reformed Theological Method." *Journal of the Evangelical Society* 45 (2002): 317–41.

Houlden, Leslie. Review of *Mark's Audience: The Literary and Social Setting of Mark 4.11–12,* by Mary Ann Beavis. *Theology* 93 (1990): 481–82.

Hunt, David P. "Divine Providence and Simple Foreknowledge." *Faith and Philosophy* 10 (1993): 394–414.

Iwry, Samuel. "Massebah and Bamah in 1QIsaiah^a 6, 13." *Journal of Biblical Literature* 76 (1957): 225–32.

Johnson, Dan G. Review of *To See and Not Perceive: Isaiah 6.9–10 in Early Jewish and Christian Interpretation,* by Craig A. Evans. *Catholic Biblical Quarterly* 53 (1991): 666–67.

———. "The Structure and Meaning of Romans 11." *Catholic Biblical Quarterly* 46 (1984): 91–103.

Jokiranta, Jutta M. "'Sectarianism' of the Qumran 'Sect': Sociological Notes." *Revue de Qumran* 78 (2001): 223–39.

Kaplan, M. M. "Isaiah 6:1–11." *Journal of Biblical Literature* 45 (1926): 251–59.

Kelber, Werner H. "Narrative and Disclosure: Mechanisms of Concealing, Revealing, and Reveiling." *Semeia* 43 (1988): 1–20.

Key, Andrew F. "The Magical Background of Isaiah 6:9–13." *Journal of Biblical Literature* 86 (1967): 198–204.

Kingsbury, Edwin C. "The Prophets and the Council of Yahweh." *Journal of Biblical Literature* 83 (1964): 279–86.

Kingsbury, Jack Dean. Review of *Die Parabeltheorie im Markusevangelium,* by Heikki Räisänen. *Theologische Zeitschrift* 32 (1976): 108–109.

Kirkland, J. R. "The Earliest Understanding of Jesus' Use of Parables: Mark IV 10–12 in Context." *Novum Testamentum* 19 (1977): 1–21.

Knierim, Rolf. "Old Testament Interpretation Reconsidered." *Interpretation* 27 (1973): 435–70.

Kuhn, Hans-Wolfgang. Review of *Die Parabeltheorie im Markusevangelium,* by Heikki Räisänen. *Theologische Literaturzeitung* 101 (1976): 121–23.

La Cava, F. "L' ἵνα Causal Nel Nuovo Testamento." *La scuola cattolica* 65 (1937): 301–04.

Lagrange, Marie-Joseph. "Le but des paraboles d'après l'évangile selon saint Marc." *Revue biblique* 7 (1910): 5–35.

Lampe, Peter. "Die markinische Deutung des Gleichnisses vom Sämann, Markus 4, 10–12." *Zeitschrift für die neutestamentliche Wissenschaft* 65 (1974): 140–50.

Larsson, Gerhard. "The Chronology of the Kings of Israel and Judah as a System." *Zeitschrift für die alttestamentliche Wissenschaft* 114 (2002): 224–35.

Leahy, Thomas W. Review of *Verstockung Israels, Isaias 6, 9–10 in der Theologie der Synoptiker*, by Joachim Gnilka. *Journal of Biblical Literature* 81 (1962): 87–89.

Légasse, S. "La Révélation aux νήπιοι." *Revue biblique* 67 (1960): 321–48.

Lemcio, Eugene E. "External Evidence for the Structure and Function of Mark iv. 1–20, vii. 14–23 and viii. 14–21." *Journal of Theological Studies* 29 (1978): 323–38.

Lieberman, Saul. "The Discipline in the So-Called Dead Sea Manual of Discipline." *Journal of Biblical Literature* 71 (1952): 199–206.

Longacre, Robert E, and Wilber B. Wallis. "Soteriology and Eschatology in Romans." *Journal of the Evangelical Theological Society* 41 (1998): 367–82.

Mangum, R. Todd. "Is There a Reformed Way to Get the Benefits of the Atonement to 'Those Who Have Never Heard?'" *Journal of the Evangelical Society* 47 (2004): 121–36.

Malina, Bruce J. Review of *The Idea of Divine Hardening*, by Heikki Räisänen. *Catholic Biblical Quarterly* 36 (1974): 135–36.

Manson, William. "The Purpose of Parables: A Re-Examination of St. Mark iv. 10–12." *Expository Times* 68 (1956–57): 132–35.

Marcus, Ralph. "On Biblical Hypostases of Wisdom." *Hebrew Union College Annual* 23 (1950): 157–71.

Marcus, Joel. "Mark 4:10–12 and Marcan Epistemology." *Journal of Biblical Literature* 103/4 (1984): 557–74.

Marxsen, W. "Redaktionsgeschichtliche Erklärung der Sogenannten Parabeltheorie des Markus." *Zeitschrift für Theologie und Kirche* 52 (1955): 255–71.

Mavrodes, George. "A Reply to Professors Feinberg and Pinnock." *Christian Scholar's Review* 16 (1987): 403–4.

———. "Is There Anything Which God Does Not Do?" *Christian Scholar's Review* 16 (1987): 384–91.

Mayordomo, Moises. Review of *The Fulfillment Quotations in Matthew: When God is Present in Full Humanity*, by Jean Miller. *Review of Theological Literature* 2 (2000): 54–57.

McKay, K. L. "Time and Aspect in New Testament Greek." *Novum Testamentum* 34 (1992): 209–28.

McKenzie, John L. "Reflections on Wisdom." *Journal of Biblical Literature* 86 (1967): 1–9.

———. Review of *Verstockung Israels, Isaias 6, 9–10 in der Theologie der Synoptiker*, by Joachim Gnilka. *Theological Studies* 23 (1962): 459–61.

McLaughlin, John L. "Their Hearts Were Hardened: The Use of Isaiah 6,9–10 in the Book of Isaiah." *Biblica* 75 (1994): 1–25.

Mearns, C. L. "Parables, Secrecy and Eschatology in Mark's Gospel." *Scottish Journal of Theology* 44 (1991): 423–42.

Metzger, Bruce M. "The Formulas Introducing Quotations of Scripture in the NT and the Mishnah." *Journal of Biblical Literature* 70 (1951): 297–307.

Meye, Robert P. "Those about Him with the Twelve." *Studia evangelica* 2 (1964): 211–18.

Milgrom, Jacob. "Did Isaiah Prophesy during the Reign of Uzziah?" *Vetus Testamentum* 14 (1964): 164–82.

Mosley, A. W. "Historical Reporting in the Ancient World." *New Testament Studies* 12 (October 1965): 10–26.

Moulton, Harold K. "Ancient Translations." *The Bible Translator* 29 (1978): 307–11.

Muddiman, John. Review of *Mark's Audience: The Literary and Social Setting of Mark 4.11–12*, by Mary Ann Beavis. *Expository Times* 102 (1990–91): 278–79.

Murphy, Roland E. "Form Criticism and Wisdom Literature." *Catholic Biblical Quarterly* 31 (1969): 475–83.

Neuberg, Frank J. "An Unrecognized Meaning of Hebrew *DOR*." *Journal of Near Eastern Studies* 9 (1950): 215–17.

Neusner, Jacob. "The Fellowship (חבירה) in The Second Jewish Commonwealth." *Harvard Theological Review* 53 (1960): 125–42.

Peisker, Carl Heinz. "Konsekutives ἵνα in Markus IV, 12." *Zeitschrift für die neutestamentliche Wissenschaft* 59 (1968): 126–27.

Pinnock, Clark H. "A Comment on 'Is There Anything Which God Does Not Do?' By George Mavrodes." *Christian Scholar's Review* 16 (1987): 392–93.

———. "There is Room for Us: A Reply to Bruce Ware." *Journal of the Evangelical Theological Society* 45 (2002): 213–19.

Piper, Otto A. "The Mystery of the Kingdom of God: Critical Scholarship and Christian Doctrine." *Interpretation* 1 (1947): 183–200.

Roberts, J. J. M. "Isaiah in Old Testament Theology." *Interpretation* 36 (1982): 130–43.

Robinson, D. W. B. "The Salvation of Israel in Romans 9–11." *Reformed Theological Review* 26 (1967): 81–96.

Robinson, H. Wheeler. "The Council of Yahweh." *Journal of Theological Studies* 45 (1944): 151–57.

Robinson, J. Armitage. "Πωρωσις and πηρωσις." *Journal of Theological Studies* 3 (1901): 81–93.

Robinson Jr., William C. "The Quest for Wrede's Secret Messiah." *Interpretation* 27 (1973): 10–30.

Romaniuk, C. "Le Thème de la Sagesse dans les Documents de Qumran." *Revue de Qumran* 9 (1978): 429–35.

Sanders, John. "Be Wary of Ware: A Reply to Bruce Ware." *Journal of the Evangelical Theological Society* 45 (2002): 221–31.

Schmidt, Karl Ludwig. "Die Verstockung des Menschen durch Gott." *Theologische Zeitschrift* 1 (1945): 1–17.

Schnackenburg, Rudolf. Review of *Verstockung, Gereicht und Heil. Exegetische und bibeltheologische Untersuchungen zum sogenannten «Dualismus» und «Determinismus» in Joh 12,35–50*, by Roman Kühschelm. *Biblische Zeitschrift* 35 (1991): 272–74.

Schweizer, Edward. "Miszellen 1. Petrus 4, 6." *Theologische Zeitschrift* 8 (1952): 152–54.

Scobie, Charles H. H. "The Place of Wisdom in Biblical Theology." *Biblical Theology Bulletin* 14 (1984): 43–48.

Seitz, Christopher R. "The Divine Council: Temporal Transition and New Prophecy in the Book of Isaiah." *Journal of Biblical Literature* 109 (1990): 229–47.

Sellew, Philip. "Oral and Written Sources in Mark 4.1–34." *New Testament Studies* 36 (1990): 234–67.

Siegman, Edward F. "Teaching in Parables (Mk iv. 10–12; Lk viii. 9–10; Mt xiii. 10–15)." *Catholic Biblical Quarterly* 23 (1961): 161–81.

Sluiter, Ineke. "Causal ἵνα, Sound Greek." *Glotta* 70 (1992): 39–53.

Sonnet, Jean-Pierre. "Le motif de l'endurcissement (Is 6,9–10) et la lecture d' «Isaïe»." *Biblica* 73 (1992): 208–39.

Stein, Robert H. "Is Our Reading the Bible the Same as the Original Audience's Hearing It? A Case Study in the Gospel of Mark." *Journal of the Evangelical Theological Society* 46 (2003): 63–78.

Sutcliffe, Edmund F. "Effect as Purpose: A Study in Hebrew Thought Patterns." *Biblica* 35 (1954): 320–27.

Taeger, Jens-W. Review of *Mark's Audience: The Literary and Social Setting of Mark 4.11–12*, by Mary Ann Beavis. *Theologische Literaturzeitung* 116 (1991): 352–54.

Turner, C. H. "'The Disciples' and 'the Twelve'." *Journal of Theological Studies* 28 (1927): 22–30.

Tworuschka, Udo. Review of *The Idea of Divine Hardening*, by Heikki Räisänen. *Zeitschrift für Religions- und Gestesgeschichte* 26 (1974): 174–75.

Via, Dan O. "Irony as Hope in Mark's Gospel: A Reply to Werner Kelber." *Semeia* 43 (1988): 21–27.

———. "Matthew on the Understanding of the Parables." *Journal of Biblical Literature* 84 (1965): 430–32.

Ware, Bruce A. "Defining Evangelicalism's Boundaries Theologically: Is Open Theism Evangelical?" *Journal of the Evangelical Theological Society* 45 (2002): 193–212.

———. "Rejoinder to Replies by Clark H. Pinnock, John Sanders, and Gregory A. Boyd." *Journal of the Evangelical Theological Society* 45 (2002): 245–56.

Watson, Philip S. Review of *Bondage of the Will*, by Martin Luther. *Expository Times* 69 (1958–59): 267.

Wellum, Stephen J. "Divine Sovereignty-Omniscience, Inerrancy, and Open Theism: An Evaluation." *Journal of the Evangelical Theological Society* 45 (2002): 257–77.

Whybray, Roger N. "Slippery Words: IV. Wisdom." *Expository Times* 89 (1977–78): 359–62.

Williamson, H. G. M. Review of *To See and Not Perceive: Isaiah 6.9–10 in Early Jewish and Christian Interpretation*, by Craig A. Evans. *Vetus Testamentum* 40 (1990): 509.

Willis, John T. "The First Pericope in the Book of Isaiah." *Vetus Testamentum* 34 (1984): 63–77.

Wilson, Robert R. "The Hardening of Pharaoh's Heart." *Catholic Biblical Quarterly* 41 (1979): 18–36.

Windisch, Hans. "Die Verstockungsidee in Mk 4:12 und das Kausale ἵνα in der späteren Koine." *Zeitschrift für die neutestamentliche Wissenschaft* 26 (1927): 203–09.

Young, Richard A. "A Classification of Conditional Sentences Based on Speech Act Theory." *Grace Theological Journal* 10 (1989): 29–50.

Unpublished Materials

Curry, Victor B. "The Nature and Use of the ἵνα Clause in the New Testament." Th.D. diss., Southern Baptist Theological Seminary, 1949.

Evans, Craig A. "Isaiah 6:9–10 in Early Jewish and Christian Interpretation." Ph.D. diss., Claremont Graduate School, 1983.

Foster, Barry M. "The Contribution of the Conclusion of Acts to the Understanding of Lucan Theology and the Determination of Lucan Purpose." Ph.D. diss., Trinity International University, 1997.

Myers, William R. "Disciples, Outsiders, and the Secret of the Kingdom: Interpreting Mark 4:10–13." Th.M. thesis, McGill University, 1960.

Puskas, Charles B. "The Conclusion of Luke-Acts: An Investigation of the Literary Function and Theological Significance of Acts 28:16–31." Ph.D. diss., Saint Louis University, 1980.

Scannell, Timothy J. "Fulfillment of Johannine Signs: A Study of John 12:37–50." Ph.D. diss., Fordham University, 1998.

Stanford, Leo P. "Interpretation, Motive and Procedure in the Ante-Nicene Use of Isaiah 6:9–10: A Comparative Study." Ph.D. diss., Marquette University, 1975.

Waltke, Bruce K. Re: "Fatten" in Isa 6:10: A Question on the Hiphil. America Online, June 29 2004. Accessed AOL Correspondance.

Woodward, Charles Alan. "The Place of Mark 4:10–12 in the Second Gospel." Th.D. diss., New Orleans Baptist Theological Seminary, 1979.

Worrell, J. E. "Concepts of Wisdom in the Dead Sea Scrolls." Ph.D. diss., Claremont Graduate School, 1968.

Computer Software

Accordance Bible Software Scholar's Collection 6.9. OakTree Software, Altamonte Springs, FL. 2005.

Author Index

Cyril of Jerusalem, 15

D

Danove, Paul, 243
Darr, Katheryn Pfisterer, 164
Daube, David, 47, 277, 278
Davies, Paul, 57, 58, 60, 61, 82, 304
Davis, James A., 136, 138, 139, 184, 199
Davis, W. Hersey, 274
Delitzsch, Franz, 103
Delling, Katharine, 170
Dillard, Raymond B., 164
Dinur, Yehiel, 118
Dodd, C. H., 15, 48, 51, 235, 259
Dorsey, David A., 163, 164
Drury, John, 47, 245
Dunn, James D. G., 128, 139, 169, 309
Dupont, J., 271, 277
Dvorak, James D., 279
Dyscolus, Apollonius, 273

E

Eakin, Frank E., 49, 52, 277, 310
Eaton, Michael A., 120
Eddy, Paul R., 32, 67
Edwards, Jonathan, 56, 58, 71, 78, 83, 84, 85, 86, 87, 88, 89, 92, 96
Eichmann, Adolf, 118
Eichrodt, Walther, 49, 53, 55, 99, 100, 101, 105, 129, 131
Einstein, Albert, 58, 61, 94
Eissfeldt, O., 164
Elderen, Bastiaan van, 44, 265, 268, 275, 304, 306, 314
Ellis, E. Earle, 22, 136, 167, 170, 237
Engnell, Ivan, 176
Erasmus, Desiderius, 3, 15, 42, 83
Erb, M., 2
Erskine, John, 85
Essame, W. G., 249, 250
Evans, Craig A., 2, 21, 23, 24, 25, 30, 32, 37, 38, 164, 183, 204, 205, 215, 218, 224, 228, 240, 241, 247, 248, 262, 266, 267, 270, 271, 276, 277, 278, 279, 280, 281, 304, 310, 311, 319, 322

F

Fabry, H. J., 98, 99, 100, 104, 108, 112, 135
Falusi, G. K., 247, 249, 287
Fanning, Buist M., 239, 292
Farrer, Austin, 15
Farstad, Arthur L., 254, 267, 315
Fay, Greg, 234, 240, 251, 252, 253
Feinberg, John, 72, 74, 75, 76, 77, 78, 79, 80
Feuillet, A., 275
Fichtner, Johannes, 170, 172
Fischer, John Martin, 42
Fitzmyer, Joseph A., 46, 51, 240, 271, 313, 322
Flew, Antony, 89, 90, 91, 92, 93, 94, 95
Flint, Peter, 215
Flint, Thomas P., 42
Flusser, David, 27
Ford, Mary, 236, 262, 265
Forster, Roger T., 175
Foster, Barry M., 3, 24, 28, 29, 30, 31, 32, 33, 37, 44, 51
Frame, John M., 43, 57
Fredericks, D. C., 100
Fretheim, Terence E., 42, 43
Fuglseth, Kare, 152
Funk, Robert W., 236

G

Gallagher, Eugene V., 26
Ganssle, Gregory E., 57, 61, 65, 66, 69
Garrett, James L., 3
Gealy, Fred D., 50, 238, 248, 249, 258, 259, 263, 291
Geisler, Norman L., 45, 76, 78
Gerhardsson, Birger, 48
Gerleman, G., 102, 104
Gerstner, John H., 81
Gibson, J. C. L., 5, 167, 172, 179
Gieschen, Charles A., 166
Girdlestone, R. B., 125
Gitay, Yehoshua, 164, 204
Glaassen, W. T., 181
Gnilka, Joachim, 2, 19, 20, 37, 38, 45, 142, 200, 219, 225, 238, 239, 241, 245, 250, 251, 260, 262, 264, 266,

Scripture Index

Job 7:17, 115
Job 8–9, 126
Job 8:10, 115
Job 9:4, 115, 127, 128
Job 9:34, 121
Job 10:13, 115, 135
Job 11:5, 110, 111
Job 11:6, 125
Job 11:13, 115
Job 11:16, 125
Job 12:2, 116
Job 12:3, 115, 129, 149
Job 12:15, 116
Job 12:16, 125
Job 12:20, 116
Job 12:24, 115, 116, 121, 129, 149
Job 13:5, 110, 111
Job 13:17, 204, 220, 284
Job 14:3, 212
Job 14:4, 110, 111
Job 14:13, 110, 111
Job 15:2, 129
Job 15:8, 167, 168, 251
Job 15:9, 284
Job 15:12, 115
Job 17:4, 115, 116, 117, 133
Job 17:11, 115
Job 19:19, 168
Job 19:23, 110, 111
Job 21:2, 204, 220
Job 22:22, 115
Job 23:3, 110
Job 23:3–4, 111
Job 23:16, 115
Job 26:3, 125
Job 27:1, 246
Job 27:3, 128
Job 27:6, 115
Job 27:19, 212
Job 27:24, 127
Job 28:28, 131, 180
Job 29:1, 246
Job 29:2, 110, 111
Job 29:4, 168
Job 29:10, 284
Job 29:13, 115
Job 30:22, 125
Job 31:1, 284
Job 31:9, 115
Job 31:18, 103
Job 31:27, 115
Job 31:31, 110, 111
Job 31:35, 110, 111

Job 32:9, 126, 127
Job 32:11–12, 284
Job 33:3, 115, 135, 297
Job 33:4, 128
Job 33:17, 121
Job 33:23, 297
Job 34:2, 129, 132
Job 34:10, 115, 129, 149
Job 34:14, 115
Job 34:20, 121
Job 34:34, 115, 129, 149
Job 35:11, 126, 127
Job 36:4, 284
Job 36:5, 115
Job 36:13, 115
Job 36:18, 215
Job 37:1, 115
Job 37:2, 204, 220
Job 37:24, 107, 108, 115, 127
Job 38:36, 110, 111, 115, 116
Job 39:3–12, 181
Job 41:16, 209
Job 41:24, 115
Job 42:11, 284

Psalms
Ps 1–2, 59
Ps 2:10, 284
Ps 2:11, 180
Ps 3:13–17, 118
Ps 4:7, 209
Ps 4:8, 108, 237
Ps 5:2, 284
Ps 10:17, 149
Ps 12:3, 104
Ps 14:1–3, 118
Ps 14:2, 284
Ps 14:7, 110, 111
Ps 16:9, 107
Ps 17:6, 211
Ps 17:16, 108
Ps 19:8, 107, 126
Ps 19:10, 180
Ps 19:13, 284
Ps 25:14, 168
Ps 26, 59
Ps 27, 59
Ps 28:5, 284
Ps 31:3, 211
Ps 33:10–11, 45
Ps 33:15, 132, 237, 284
Ps 33:16–17, 45

Studies in Biblical Literature

This series invites manuscripts from scholars in any area of biblical literature. Both established and innovative methodologies, covering general and particular areas in biblical study, are welcome. The series seeks to make available studies that will make a significant contribution to the ongoing biblical discourse. Scholars who have interests in gender and sociocultural hermeneutics are particularly encouraged to consider this series.

For further information about the series and for the submission of manuscripts, contact:

Hemchand Gossai
Department of Religion
Muhlenberg College
2400 Chew Street
Allentown, PA 18104-5586

To order other books in this series, please contact our Customer Service Department:

(800) 770-LANG (within the U.S.)
(212) 647-7706 (outside the U.S.)
(212) 647-7707 FAX

or browse online by series at:

WWW.PETERLANG.COM